POLITICAL
HELL-RAISER

POLITICAL HELL-RAISER

THE LIFE AND TIMES OF SENATOR
BURTON K. WHEELER
OF MONTANA

MARC C. JOHNSON

UNIVERSITY OF OKLAHOMA PRESS : NORMAN

This book is published with the generous assistance of the
Burton K. Wheeler Center at Montana State University–Bozeman.

Library of Congress Cataloging-in-Publication Data

Names: Johnson, Marc C., 1953– author.
Title: Political hell-raiser : the life and times of Senator Burton K. Wheeler of Montana / Marc C.
Johnson.
-Description: First edition. | Norman, Oklahoma : University of Oklahoma Press, [2019] |
    Includes bibliographical references and index.
Identifiers: LCCN 2018025837 | ISBN 978-0-8061-4085-8 (hardback)
ISBN 978-0-8061-9486-8 (paper)
Subjects: LCSH: Wheeler, Burton K. (Burton Kendall), 1882–1975. | Legislators—United
    States—Biography. | United States. Congress. Senate—Biography. | United States—Politics
    and government—1901–1953. | Montana—Politics and government—20th century. |
    Montana—Biography. | BISAC: BIOGRAPHY & AUTOBIOGRAPHY / Political. |
    HISTORY / United States / State & Local / West (AK, CA, CO, HI, ID, MT, NV, UT, WY). |
    HISTORY / Modern / 20th Century.
Classification: LCC E748.W5 J64 2019 | DDC 328.73/092 [B] —dc23
LC record available at https://lccn.loc.gov/2018025837

The paper in this book meets the guidelines for permanence and durability of the Committee on
Production Guidelines for Book Longevity of the Council on Library Resources, Inc. ∞

For Trish—with all my love and with enduring gratitude

CONTENTS

ILLUSTRATIONS

PREFACE

If I seem to have done everything the hard way,
I have no regrets—I would do it the same way again.
—SENATOR BURTON K. WHEELER

This book has its roots in a question. How was it that 1920s Montana, a remote western state with little more than a half million people, produced two U.S. senators, each a progressive Democrat, who almost simultaneously conducted two of the most sensational investigations of political corruption in American history while each was a member of the Senate minority?

Burton K. Wheeler, an outspoken, rumpled, engaging lawyer from Butte, probed corruption in the U.S. Justice Department during the Harding administration, resulting in the resignation of Attorney General Harry Daugherty. At about the same time, Wheeler's mentor, Thomas J. Walsh, a reserved, understated, dignified attorney from Helena, investigated the Teapot Dome oil leasing scandal, ultimately sending Interior Secretary Albert Bacon Fall to prison. Walsh's career has been the subject of scholarly biographies, and the Teapot Dome hearings have been well chronicled, but Wheeler's more colorful and controversial career, spanning the turbulent and enduringly fascinating years between World War I and the end of World War II, has only been assessed sporadically and incompletely. This book is the first attempt to analyze Wheeler's entire career, including his many accomplishments and contradictions, as well as the enormous political storms that he both fostered and endured. I have researched Wheeler's story for more than a decade, and with this book I hope to illustrate why he deserves a more prominent place in U.S. history.

Wheeler—B. K. to friends—was the most powerful politician Montana ever produced, which is saying something. The state's voters elected the first woman to Congress, Jeannette Rankin in 1916. Mike Mansfield served five House terms and then four Senate terms and is the longest-serving majority leader in Senate history. Pat Williams served nine terms in the House of Representatives as a champion of wilderness, Native Americans, and the arts and humanities. And Max Baucus served six Senate terms from 1978 to 2014 and chaired the Senate Finance Committee for seven years. Of course Montana has also spawned political hacks and more than a few scoundrels.

Throughout his career Wheeler exhibited political independence and bipartisanship that has in recent times become exceedingly rare, if in fact those qualities still exist. While he could be a fiercely partisan Democrat, he also routinely endorsed and campaigned for Republicans who shared his progressive thinking. Wheeler's bipartisan "machine," including a political partnership with a Republican governor, dominated Montana's politics for several years, even as he openly quarreled with fellow Democrats, particularly U.S. senator James Murray. Had the world situation not made a third Franklin Roosevelt term possible in 1940, Wheeler might have inherited and even expanded Roosevelt's New Deal coalition and ridden that support to the White House. He fell short but still came closer to the presidency than any Montanan ever has.

Wheeler's personal and political independence—he easily wore the label of maverick—places him in the company of some of the Senate's giants, including Robert M. La Follette Sr., who Wheeler joined as the vice presidential running mate on the Progressive Party ticket in 1924, and Wheeler's progressive Republican friends William E. Borah, George Norris, and Hiram Johnson. Wheeler's aversion to party loyalty echoes the political career of Oregon's Wayne Morse. He could be as crusty as Arizona's Barry Goldwater, as eloquent—and wordy—as Daniel Patrick Moynihan, and as down to earth as his friend Harry Truman. Huey Long, the Louisiana populist, considered the Montanan his best friend in the Senate and believed Wheeler should have been president. Long called Wheeler the most courageous politician he had ever known.

Over the course of his career Wheeler was called both a Bolshevik and a reactionary conservative. He was neither but rather a member of a group of twentieth-century politicians like William Jennings Bryan, La Follette, and Borah, who were neither traditional liberals or conventional conservatives but rather skeptics who distrusted Wall Street, detested concentrated power, and rejected centralization and regimentation. Historian David A. Horowitz has called them "insurgent progressives." The terms "progressive" and "liberal" are frequently used interchangeably in our day, and Wheeler described himself using both words, but labels are difficult to attach to his kind of independence. Perhaps the best term to describe Wheeler is "western progressive"—describing a particular kind of independent that helped define the politics of the western United States in the early twentieth century. Wheeler considered his life in politics to be a running battle against concentrated power, and he fought against it whether it occurred on Wall Street or in the White House.[1]

"Controversy has sparked my public life from start to finish," Wheeler wrote sixteen years after he lost a primary election while seeking a fifth Senate term. "I have been accused of almost everything but timidity. My opponents taught me self-reliance—and that the best defense is a good offense." Wheeler displayed a ready smile—though he was rarely photographed grinning—and a sense of humor but also a temper. He suffered neither fools nor political opponents gladly. His son Edward, who practiced law with his father in the fifties and sixties, remembered walking down a street in Butte with his father and encountering an acquaintance who lavished praise on the politician. "Great to see you, B. K.! I'm such a great admirer of yours. I've always been a supporter," the man gushed. Wheeler listened and then snorted, "What a line of guff. You have never been a supporter of mine and have always worked against me. I know it and you know it. Who are you trying to fool?" Edward said his father could look any man in the eye, call him an SOB, and never let the smile leave his face.[2]

I was attracted to Wheeler for the same reasons people gravitate to authentic, colorful, and candid public figures. Independence, a willingness to buck the status quo, a passion for civil liberties, defense of free speech, and championing the cause of the common person are enduring values in any age, and Wheeler exemplified all of those. Additionally, Wheeler was passionately antiwar, not a pacifist but a politician profoundly reluctant to use military force and deeply concerned about the creation of an American empire. "Intervention in foreign wars, civil or otherwise, is fraught with grave danger" and stationing U.S. military forces around the globe is almost always a serious mistake, he said. "We try to 'buy' with foreign aid the friendship of nations we seek as allies, and like all friendships that are bought they are ephemeral. I think most of the money we spend in vain pursuit of friends is wasted . . . it goes into the pockets of the dictators, princes, ruling families, or generals that control the countries we seek to aid." Wheeler wrote that in 1962. His brand of non-interventionism—historian Robert David Johnson has placed Wheeler in the group he calls "peace progressives"—was widely discredited after World War II, and the Montanan's epic battles with Franklin Roosevelt over foreign policy now largely define his legacy in a negative way. Yet the foreign policy perspective of Wheeler and other noninterventionists, as historian Justus Doenecke writes, "still has contemporary significance. Their warnings against presidential duplicity remain timely, as does their critique of messianic policy pronouncements." Wheeler never regretted his fight against war because, as Doenecke asserts, for the prewar noninterventionists "the crusade was always one of highest patriotism—and wisdom as well."[3]

Wheeler did not make it easy for a biographer. This very public man was not a keeper of diaries, and, while always candid about his views, he rarely disclosed his motivations. Unfortunately he seems to have destroyed many files on leaving the

Senate in January 1947, and what Wheeler letters remain generally deal with the final years of his career. Many of his contemporaries, however, left a robust written record that allows his career and personality to come into focus. This book is therefore an effort to provide a critical assessment and to understand the contemporary significance of a consequential American politician who had substantial impact on some of the most important events of the twentieth century. Wheeler's story also helps illuminate the extent to which the nation's politics, and the politics of the Senate, changed in the postwar period. Wheeler would have abhorred most of the changes—the hyper-partisanship, the vast expansion of interest group influence, the growth of presidential power at the expense of the Congress, the rise of the national security state, and the endless deployment of the U.S. military in every corner of the world.

Long after his tumultuous career came to an end, Wheeler remarked that his "zest for making full use of a senator's powers," coupled with his penchant for political independence, had placed him in the middle of many of the major issues of his time. In writing his political biography I have attempted to place Burton Kendall Wheeler in the context of his times and also explain how a political hell-raiser from sparsely populated Montana became one of the most important U.S. senators in the first half of the twentieth century.

The story begins in the town that locals call Butte, America.

POLITICAL
HELL-RAISER

1   THE BLACK HEART OF MONTANA

Butte is the black heart of Montana, feared and distrusted.
— JOSEPH KINSEY HOWARD

Not every politician is able to identify an event, a singular moment, that has defined one's entire career and shaped a political philosophy. Burton K. Wheeler experienced such an event in the summer of 1917 when he was thirty-five and the U.S. attorney in Butte, Montana. The event was the sadistic, politically motivated murder of a labor organizer in Butte.

The labor organizer was Frank Little, the executive chairman of the radical Industrial Workers of the World. The IWW (or Wobblies, as they were known) advocated class struggle spurred by "One Big Union" that was intended, in the words of one historian, to "transform American workers into a revolutionary vanguard."[1]

Little had come to Butte, the rough, often violent copper-mining town high in the Rocky Mountains, to agitate against what he considered a capitalist-inspired European war fought by the working class for the benefit of kings and tycoons. His fiery speeches, condemning President Woodrow Wilson, capitalism, imperialism, the draft, and U.S. involvement in World War I, prompted intense, sustained demands for Little's arrest for sedition. B. K. Wheeler stood against the public frenzy and refused to arrest a man for opposing a war.

A group of vigilantes kidnapped and executed Little, touching off a sustained period of hysteria in the state—"Montana's Agony," historian Arnon Gutfeld has called it— that was virtually unprecedented in American history. Protections for free speech virtually disappeared. Books were banned and the German language outlawed. Hundreds were arrested and many imprisoned. The entire state fell into an orgy of patriotic excess and political unrest. Many politicians not only accepted the chaos but even encouraged the assault on civil liberties, seeing an opportunity to consolidate personal power and punish enemies real and imagined. Wheeler was one of the few who stood against the excesses and kept his head amid months of violence, fear, and political reprisals. Rejecting the prevailing sentiment and defending dissenters eventually cost Wheeler his job as U.S. attorney, and it appeared that a promising political career had been ruined. Yet Wheeler doggedly fought back and improbably prevailed, eventually winning four terms in the U.S. Senate.[2]

Having seen in 1917 how war-induced hysteria and patriotic excess can overwhelm free speech and common sense, Wheeler fiercely opposed all forms of concentrated power and for the remainder of his life stood against war. He came to value independence more than political party, and he embraced, even welcomed, controversy, which became a fixture of his career. That career began when the young New Englander arrived in Montana, a place resident author Joseph Kinsey Howard called "a state of few people, entirely surrounded by space."[3]

———

It is a long way—geographically, culturally, industrially, and politically—from Hudson, Massachusetts, to Butte, Montana. Wheeler made that long journey in 1905 at the age of twenty-three. Both sides of Wheeler's family traced their New England roots to the mid-seventeenth century, with some of Wheeler's Quaker ancestors settling in Massachusetts to avoid religious persecution in England. One of Wheeler's earliest known ancestors, Obadiah Wheeler, was a founder of Concord, Massachusetts. The youngest of ten children, Burton Kendall was born on February 27, 1882, in Hudson, an industrial town fifteen miles southwest of Concord. By his latter recollection, his early years "passed in a pleasant if somewhat austere atmosphere." His father, Asa Leonard Wheeler, from the Quaker side of the family, was a cobbler, an easygoing and tolerant head of his large family. Wheeler's mother, Mary Elizabeth, who died while Wheeler was still in high school, was reserved and very religious; she was clearly the stronger parent, encouraging her youngest to get as much education as possible. His mother may have been the first to suggest that B. K. study law.[4]

Wheeler family politics leaned Republican, although Wheeler would later often repeat a story of how, as a high school debater, he had defended the free silver, low-tariff policies of Democratic presidential candidate William Jennings Bryan. That experience may have influenced Wheeler's eventual decision to identify with, if not always embrace, the Democratic Party. Following graduation from high school, Wheeler headed west, convinced that he could work his way through law school at the University of Michigan. The 130-pound six-footer, by this time afflicted with the asthma that would plague him all his life, landed a job working in the Dean's Office and further

A young Burton K. Wheeler at about the time he
attended the University of Michigan law school. (*Photo
in possession of author*)

supplemented meager savings by waiting tables in a student boardinghouse. Wheeler's
academic career was workmanlike, his course work rated on a pass-fail scale. All that
can be known from the surviving records is that he successfully completed the work
to obtain a law degree.[5]

Wheeler met his future wife in Illinois during a summer away from law school and
while selling *Dr. Chase's Recipe Book,* a volume containing recipes, tips for midwives,
and advice for treating almost every known ailment—and many imaginary ones. "I
can't honestly say that it was love at first sight, [but] it was clearly the loveliest sight
Illinois had displayed thus far," Wheeler would recall. Lulu White, a prim, religiously
devout, no-nonsense midwesterner, would become her husband's chief political supporter and advisor and play a significant role in his career. The couple agreed there
would be no wedding until the young attorney was established and able to provide for
them both. Rejecting advice from his law school dean that he seek work with a large
eastern law firm, Wheeler instead went west, looking for adventure, opportunity, and
a climate to ease his asthma. The Yankee found what he was looking for in Butte, one

of the west's most colorful and politically raucous mining towns. After two years of work in a small law office handling real estate matters, criminal defense, the claims of injured workers, and even a bit of legislative lobbying, B. K. married Lulu. The couple bought a modest brick home in a working-class, ethnically diverse neighborhood on Second Street.[6]

"Like the frontier itself," historian Mike Malone writes, "Butte was rich, unabashedly exploited, turbulent—and endlessly fascinating," a place that promised spectacular wealth for some and reasonably good jobs for thousands. Butte also featured a political culture poisoned by labor-management controversy, involving frequent shocking violence and stunning levels of corruption. "Butte was born of violence, bred in it, and lives it," Joseph Kinsey Howard wrote in his classic *Montana: High, Wide and Handsome*. Howard quoted a onetime Butte police chief as saying his town was "an island of easy money surrounded by whisky." The novelist Dashiell Hammett worked for a time as a Pinkerton detective in Butte during an early twentieth-century strike and drew upon his experience for his first novel—*Red Harvest*. Hammett called his imaginary town Poisonville, but his inspiration was Butte. "The city wasn't pretty," Hammett wrote. "Most of its builders had gone in for gaudiness. Maybe they had been successful at first. Since then the smelters whose brick stacks stuck up tall against a gloomy mountain to the south had yellowed-smoked everything into uniform dinginess. The result was an ugly city of forty thousand people, set in an ugly notch between two ugly mountains that had been all dirtied up by mining. Spread over this was a grimy sky that looked as if it had come out of the smelters' stacks."[7]

Butte's mines were the world's greatest producers of copper, responsible for a third of all the red metal produced in the United States. Butte's multicultural workforce consisted of first-generation Irish, Cornish, Italian, German, Polish, Swedish, Slovak, and Finnish immigrants. The miners were tough, abused, sentimental, and fearless, their work brutally hard. "You could never understand how hot, how really hot and humid, it would be in some of those places," one miner recalled. "You work in your yard and the sweat might roll down your face. Well, down in the mine, it was nothing to take off your mine undershirt and ring it out . . . or you took off your boots and dumped the water out." Butte's mines were also exceedingly dangerous. In the four years before 1913, 162 local miners died in mine accidents, and more than 5,200 sustained injuries serious enough to require medical attention.[8]

The physical toll and daily danger were offset, at least some of the time, by reasonably good wages. The monthly payroll in Butte often topped $1.5 million, but job security was nonexistent, and the town was a difficult place to raise a family. "Sometimes I think that the women had it tougher than the men," one miner recalled. "The men just did the work, and that was it. But the women, they had to take care of the kids, do the wash and the cooking, see their husbands off to work." Frequently those husbands came home late or occasionally not at all. There were many distractions, principally drink and female companionship at places named the Bucket of Blood and the Cesspool. Only New Orleans and perhaps San Francisco boasted more "ladies of the line." One miner remembered, "You could get a shot and a beer for a dime. You'd have 50 cents, and you wouldn't even get out of Finntown [a neighborhood on the east side of Butte and home to many miners]. Hell, by the time you got down to Park Street, you were smashed." The hatchet-waving, anti-alcohol crusader Carry Nation came to Butte in 1910, determined to deal with the taverns and the prostitutes. She showed up one evening at the ABC Dance Hall on South Wyoming Street to deliver one of her famous sermons. After listening for a few moments, the bartender simply said, "For God's sake, woman, get out of here." She did, and Butte carried on.[9]

Yet Butte had another side: a cultured, even sophisticated city of music, drama, and art. Enrico Caruso and Sarah Bernhardt performed there. Teddy Roosevelt dined at the luxurious Silver Bow Club, and the mayor once gave the key to the city to Éamon de Valera, the president of the Provisional Irish Republic, who left town with $12,000 to support the Irish Freedom Fund.[10]

Butte's politics bent toward the radical. Eugene V. Debs, Socialist Party candidate for president, garnered nearly 30 percent of the vote in Butte in 1912, when the city had a Socialist mayor in office. The best election campaign venue for a politician was a saloon, and there were 275 of them in which to buy a drink and often a vote.

The elegant Hennessey Building at the corner of Granite and Main Street was home to a first-class department store where miners and their families could shop for the latest fashions on the first five floors. Montana politicians got their orders and the state's political strings were pulled on the sixth floor, where the Anaconda Copper Mining Company had its headquarters.[11]

By the time Wheeler arrived in Butte in 1905, Anaconda was very much in its ascendancy and "the company," as Montanans called it, would only grow bigger and more influential over the next half century. By one estimate, three-quarters of all wage earners in Montana directly or indirectly owed their livelihood to Anaconda. The company owned most of the mines in Butte as well as copper and zinc concentrators, a leaching plant, a sulfuric acid plant, smelters in Great Falls, Butte, and the town of Anaconda, refineries and zinc works in Utah and Arizona, and various facilities in New Jersey and Chicago. By the beginning of the twentieth century, the company's mining properties, water rights, and real estate had an estimated value of $75 million (nearly $2 billion today). The company's timberlands were worth another $5 million, and by the beginning of World War I the value of the metal Anaconda had on hand was $37 million.[12]

In 1912, the Great Falls Power Company and a number of smaller electric utilities consolidated, and the resulting Montana Power Company became, as locals said, a "twin" of Anaconda, owned by those who owned the mining company. By the early 1920s, after completing the largest merger deal in the history of Wall Street, Anaconda became the fourth-largest company in the world and controlled the world's greatest copper reserves. The *New York Evening Post* noted, "Anaconda Copper is rapidly assuming a position in the American industrial kingdom second only to the gigantic United States Steel." Montana became in many ways a corporate colony, with local workers extracting the state's abundant natural resources, while the resulting wealth flowed to absentee shareholders of a vast multinational corporation. Anaconda, in turn, assured its dominance in Montana by extending its economic and political tentacles to every corner of the state and every level of government.[13]

Two Irishmen, John D. Ryan and Cornelius F. "Con" Kelley, guided the rise of Anaconda, and both climbed from the bottom to the top of the corporate ladder. Ryan expanded the Anaconda empire by creating Montana Power. Kelley, Ryan's protégé, began his career working in the mines but eventually became company president and then chairman of the board. After Kelley died in 1957 his *New York Times* obituary required two long paragraphs just to list his corporate directorships.[14]

Anaconda exerted influence in Montana in a variety of ways, not least through a stable of newspapers owned or somehow controlled by the company. For most of the first half of the twentieth century, Anaconda owned the *Anaconda Standard*, the *Butte Daily Post*, the *Missoula Sentinel*, the *Billings Gazette*, the *Helena Independent*, the *Livingston Enterprise*, and the paper that Wheeler is reported to have said he did not need to read because he could smell it, the *Missoulian*. From time to time other papers—daily and weekly—were owned or controlled by the company, their editorial positions influenced from the sixth floor of the Hennessey Building in Butte. Montana had many small independent newspapers, but it was a rare small-town editor who did not find it expedient to simply go along with Montana's prevailing economic and political sentiment, more often than not dictated by Anaconda. Historian Bradley Snow writes that the "chief hallmarks of the Company's seemingly timeless political orientation include: defense of 'its prerogatives' in the state, the maintenance of low corporate and individual taxation rates, keeping government regulation of business to a minimum, the protection of private property rights, and a general opposition to 'liberal' or 'progressive' or overly 'independent' political candidates."[15]

Long after his elective political career was over, B. K. Wheeler would say, "If you wanted to be nominated for dog catcher in Butte, Montana in those days, you had to go up to the sixth floor of the Hennessey Building where Anaconda Copper offices were located and take off your hat and say, 'Please can I run for dog catcher?'" In

1910 Wheeler received support from the company and was elected as a Democrat to the Montana legislature. He was twenty-eight, the youngest man in the House of Representatives. Ruggedly good looking, usually with a smile on his face, and "with his omnipresent cigar and his dented Stetson," as one observer noted, "he looked the part of a politician."[16]

"It sounds incredible now," Wheeler wrote in his memoirs, "but when I went to Helena for the opening of the Legislature in January 1911, I was naïve enough to believe I would be allowed to act as a free agent." Democrats controlled the Montana House of Representatives, while Republicans held a majority in the senate, but in reality the Anaconda ran the legislature. Wheeler's first major clash with Anaconda came when he bucked the company on the major issue facing the legislature—the election of a U.S. senator.[17]

Before adoption of the Seventeenth Amendment, it was state legislatures that elected U.S. senators by majority vote of all the members. With Democrats holding fifty-six of the legislature's 101 seats in 1911, it was a foregone conclusion that Montana lawmakers would select a Democrat for the Senate, but the party was nearly evenly split over which Democrat that would be. The company's preferred candidate was W. G. Conrad, a banker from Great Falls, while Wheeler and more progressive legislators favored Helena attorney Thomas J. Walsh. Wheeler did not know Walsh well, but he considered the reserved, dignified attorney the "much better man" for the office. Wheeler may also have been motivated to support Walsh because of Anaconda's dislike of Walsh. "He had tried and won mining and personal injury suits against" Anaconda, Wheeler said, and Walsh "had defended labor leaders, another unforgivable sin in the eyes of the Company."[18]

Without a consensus candidate the selection process gridlocked. Legislators voted more than fifty times to try and break the impasse. Lawmakers, under increasing pressure with each new ballot, were promised lucrative rewards to change a vote or threatened with ruin for not changing. "The political future of each [legislator] depends almost absolutely upon the degree in which they acquiesce in any demand which may be made of them by the forces so powerful in the country," Tom Walsh wrote to William Jennings Bryan as the standoff continued. "To no small extent their business interests are clearly subject to destruction" if they thwarted the will of Anaconda, he said. Wheeler, a young and barely established lawyer, stubbornly held out, supporting Walsh even when company emissaries promised sizeable retainers—as much a $9,000—if he would change his allegiance.[19]

Finally, on March 2, 1911, the last day of the Montana legislative session, the stale-mate broke. A compromise candidate, Democrat Henry L. Myers of Hamilton, a judge and former legislator, secured a majority and was elected to the Senate. Wheeler ultimately did change his vote and support Myers, but only on the fifty-fifth and final ballot and only after Walsh had given up the race. The unrelenting pressure and the flagrant efforts to bribe legislators outraged Wheeler, who was convinced that company-sponsored corruption had kept Walsh from a Senate seat he deserved. The distasteful process helped forge Wheeler's first important political alliance, and his loyalty and courage impressed Walsh, who became a mentor to the young legislator.[20]

Loyalty to Walsh came with a price. Not a single supporter of his Senate candidacy made the list of legislative candidates from Butte's Silver Bow County in 1912. Wheeler failed to win even election as a delegate to the county Democratic convention. "A studied effort has been made," Walsh later wrote to Wheeler, "to eliminate from the delegation every man of whose amenability there might be the slightest doubt."[21]

But Wheeler refused to be intimidated or to quit, a refusal that marked his politics. With encouragement from friends, Walsh included, Wheeler announced a bid for the 1912 Democratic nomination for Montana attorney general. While admitting that he was still forming a political philosophy, Wheeler was clear about his opposition to Montana's entrenched, concentrated economic and political power, and he would champion the working class. He campaigned hard, enjoying his first statewide political exposure, but lost the Democratic nomination at the state party convention by three votes. Walsh lamented his young protégé's defeat, which he later attributed to "relentless opposition of a great corporation that was powerful in our political lives." As if to confirm Walsh's analysis of the power of the corporation in Montana politics, the man who defeated Wheeler, Dan Kelly, was elected attorney general in 1912 but then resigned midterm to join the Anaconda Company's legal department.[22]

Walsh also refused to quit in 1912, with Montana's other Senate seat now his objective. His likelihood of going to Washington improved substantially when voters approved a measure requiring the state legislature to select the candidate who garnered the greatest popular vote in an advisory ballot. The scheme was still a step removed from direct election of senators, but it did allow Walsh to appeal directly to Montana voters rather than having to confront the company's influence in the legislature. Walsh won the Senate endorsement in a three-way race that included incumbent Republican senator Joseph M. Dixon, the most progressive candidate in the contest and also a frequent adversary of Anaconda. When confronted with an uncomfortable choice between the openly antagonistic Dixon and the more restrained Walsh, the state's corporate forces—the same ones that had fought bitterly to deny Walsh a Senate seat just months earlier—now quietly backed the Democrat. Having realized his Senate aspirations, Walsh quickly adapted to the rule for survival in Montana politics. One could be elected as a progressive, but long-term survival required avoiding open battles with Montana's economic interests. During his twenty year Senate career Walsh would thrive by observing that rule.[23]

Walsh's election to the Senate facilitated the unlikely resurrection of Wheeler's political career when Walsh bestowed upon his young friend the most important patronage position at his disposal, the job of U.S. attorney. The position paid the princely sum of $4,000 a year (nearly $100,000 today), and the fortunate attorney blessed with the federal appointment could supplement that salary by maintaining a private practice on the side. Walsh, with Senator Myers's concurrence, persuaded U.S. Attorney General James C. McReynolds to nominate Wheeler for the post, and he was formally appointed in October 1913. "All ambitious Democrats looking for a stool at the pie counter please take notice and govern [yourselves] accordingly," taunted the *Billings Gazette*, which saw the appointment as payback for Wheeler's loyalty to Walsh. The *Anaconda Standard* said it directly. Wheeler had "finally received his reward for his loyalty to T. J. Walsh."[24]

Walsh counseled the inexperienced U.S. attorney to build a record as a diligent, industrious worker and to avoid using his new position to settle old political scores. "I admonish you to be cautious and not allow the strenuous political contests through which we have passed to bias your judgment in connection with the duties of the office," Walsh wrote to Wheeler. It was good advice, and for many months Wheeler followed the counsel while giving his office a bipartisan flavor by retaining a prominent Republican, Sam Ford, as his chief assistant. Keeping Ford in his office brought criticism from some partisan Democrats, but Wheeler, the youngest U.S. attorney in the country and anxious to prove himself, said he wanted all the help he could find. The Wheeler-Ford relationship, personal, political, and bipartisan, would endure for years and eventually produce, at least for a short time in the early 1940s, a genuine political machine in Montana.[25]

The U.S. attorney's work was often routine, with typical cases involving the sale of liquor on a Montana Indian reservation or a civil case where violations of federal law were at issue. The workload was heavy, but Wheeler still had time to maintain a robust and lucrative private practice. His office in uptown Butte's Hirbour Building was but a half block away from the corporate offices of Anaconda.

In June 1916, Wheeler's legal workload and political profile rose dramatically thanks to a sensational case of apparent corruption involving members of Montana's political and economic elite. Wheeler secured fraud indictments against eleven prominent defendants, all politically well connected and all involved with the Northwestern Trustee Company, ostensibly created to build homes and apartments in Montana. The Northwestern case was Wheeler's first significant prosecution and demonstrated his eagerness to root out corruption without regard to political consequences.

Two of the men indicted—State Treasurer William C. Rae and Secretary of State Adelbert M. Alderson—were prominent Democrats, both elected in the 1912

Democratic sweep. All the defendants were charged with using the mail to defraud Montana farmers and other investors who had been promised handsome dividends from their investments. As Wheeler's prosecution seemed to prove, much of the money generated by Northwestern stock sales funded various "promotional" activities, including, apparently, enriching the company's officers and board members.[26]

Still, many Montana Democrats were incensed that Wheeler's indictments targeted Democratic officeholders. The case also briefly implicated the conservative Democratic governor, Samuel V. Stewart, who, while not indicted, became a bitter Wheeler adversary. Stewart managed to win reelection in 1916, but many other Democrats were thrown out of office by voters disgusted by what appeared to be widespread Democratic corruption. Many party loyalists felt Wheeler was responsible for stoking the controversy. When the trial of Northwestern defendants finally began in January 1917, the aggressive but untried prosecutor faced off against some of the top legal talent in Montana—"the cream" of the state bar, the *Helena Independent* said. Dan Kelly, the former attorney general who had defeated Wheeler in 1912, now worked for the Anaconda Company and was one of several attorneys with ties to the company sitting at the defense table. Even Tom Walsh's law partner, another former Montana attorney general, C. B. Nolan, was retained to assist the defense. Wheeler believed, probably correctly, that the company paid the legal retainers of the defense attorneys.[27]

Wheeler, his prosecutorial inexperience on full display, laid out the complicated case but also swamped the jury with documents, including more than two hundred exhibits in the first week of the trial alone. His slipshod preparation drew a sharp rebuke from federal judge George Bourquin, a crusty Republican appointee known for his fidelity to the Constitution and his dictatorial demeanor in the courtroom. At one point Bourquin, later to play key roles in Wheeler's political career, told the U.S. attorney: "If you have not shown enough letters already to show that the company used the mails, why you never will."[28]

Fearing jury tampering, a legitimate concern borne out by subsequent events, Wheeler asked Bourquin to sequester the jury, claiming he had seen defense lawyers "entertaining" jurors in various Helena establishments. Bourquin refused the request, and after ten days of testimony the jury returned guilty verdicts against just two minor defendants. The most prominent figures, including the two former Democratic office holders, were acquitted. Wheeler was stunned by the verdicts and refused to accept the outcome, complaining again to the judge that jury tampering had taken place. This time Bourquin agreed and essentially instructed Wheeler to file contempt charges against two of the defense attorneys, Kelly and a prominent Republican, Albert J. Galen, who was yet another former Montana attorney general.[29]

Rather than merely defend the two attorneys, Anaconda Company lawyers attacked Wheeler's integrity and accused him of pursuing a personal vendetta. After considering the evidence, Judge Bourquin, as independent and incorruptible as Wheeler, found Kelly and Galen guilty of improperly influencing the jury, and each was fined $500, a penalty upheld on appeal.[30]

The Northwestern case was a tipping point in Wheeler's development as a prosecutor and politician. By fearlessly confronting a significant segment of Montana's political establishment, including prominent members of his own party, Wheeler displayed real independence, integrity, and courage, and he seemed to thrive on the experience. By securing two minor but not insignificant convictions and exposing jury tampering, Wheeler went from being an irritant to the Montana power structure to a dangerous adversary. And Judge Bourquin's unwillingness to be cowed provided Wheeler with an early lesson about the importance of judicial independence. The Northwestern case set the scene for what came next for Wheeler, the sensational murder of Frank Little.[31]

———

Just before midnight on June 28, 1917, less than two months before Little was murdered in Butte, fire broke out at the 2,400-foot level of one of North Butte Mining Company's underground mines, the Speculator. Over one hundred years later the Speculator Mine Disaster remains the single worst hard-rock mining calamity in U.S. history. One hundred sixty-three miners died, and the mine sustained millions of dollars' worth of damage. The enormous loss of life stunned Butte, but the agony for survivors was compounded when word spread that many miners had perished while clawing to escape the flames, trapped against a concrete bulkhead a half-mile underground. Montana law required iron doors that could swing open in such circumstances, but the grisly death toll made clear that the law had not observed. Seeking better wages and working conditions in the wake of the disaster, workers—not only miners but also electricians, machinists, and others—walked off the job. By the end of June, 15,000 of Butte's 16,500 mineworkers were striking. The labor turmoil generated national headlines, and, with the United States four months into a war in Europe, the strike held major implications for American preparedness. Mine operators, the Woodrow Wilson administration, and Montana's powerful economic interests were desperate to end the strike and regain access to a major source of copper, a metal used for everything from electrical wire to shell casings.[32]

Amid this turmoil labor organizer Frank Little arrived in Butte determined to rally striking miners to the cause of the IWW, but as historian Michael Punke has written, Little "was the last thing Butte needed. He was, without apology, gasoline on a fire." Addressing six thousand people at a baseball field on July 19, Little advocated a "worldwide revolution" and condemned American involvement in the war. The message resonated with many of his listeners, including members of Butte's sizeable Irish-American population. For many of Butte's Irish, U.S. participation in the war amounted to a thoughtless sacrifice of working-class soldiers forced to fight to preserve a British Empire that denied Irish independence. Little spoke at second large rally on July 27 and referred to President Wilson as a "lying tyrant" and the Constitution as "a mere scrap of paper which can be torn up." American soldiers fighting in France, he said, were "uniformed scabs." Little's rhetoric was obviously provocative, and many Montana newspapers termed it treasonous. Editorialists wondered how long the good people of Butte would put up with "seditious talk" from a dangerous radical.[33]

At 3:00 A.M. on August 1—less than three weeks after Little's arrival in Butte—a handful of masked and armed men scrambled out of a large black car in front of a boardinghouse on the mostly deserted North Wyoming Street. The house was next door to Finlander Hall, a popular gathering spot for Butte's striking miners. The car was left idling, with one man acting as lookout while five other men broke down a door, waking the terrified boardinghouse proprietor, Nora Byrne. Pointing a flashlight in her face, the men demanded that Byrne tell them where Frank Little was sleeping, and soon another door was kicked open. Little was heard to mutter, "Wait till I get my hat." No need for that, one of the men responded, "Where you're going, you won't need a hat." Wearing only long underwear and hobbled by a broken leg suffered before arriving in Montana, Little was hauled into the street and stuffed into the car. Before traveling far, the car stopped, and Little was tied to the rear bumper and dragged for some distance, far enough to tear away his kneecaps. He might have been unconscious and perhaps was already dead when a rope was slipped around his neck and his body tossed from a railroad trestle on the outskirts of town.[34]

Robert W. Brown was on his way to work at daybreak when he spotted the battered corpse and informed authorities. Only after Little's body was cut down did the coroner and Butte's police chief notice the placard pinned to his underwear. "Others take notice," the sign read, "first and last warning, 3-7-77." Across the bottom of the placard, in red ink, were written the letters "L-D-C-S-S-W-T." The L was circled. The number 3-7-77 was an old symbol of vigilante justice dating from Montana's violent territorial days. Later it would become clear to the leaders of the strike that the letters on that placard were the first letters of their last names. The circled L apparently stood for Little.[35]

A coroner's jury concluded that "unknown persons" had murdered Frank Little. The responsible parties have never been identified. Little's funeral was one of the largest ever in Butte. The crowd sang the "Marseillaise," and more than three thousand people walked with the casket and thousands more lined the streets as it passed. Little's

The casket of IWW organizer Frank Little is carried from Duggan's Mortuary in Butte.
(*Butte-Silver Bow Public Archives, PH366.005*)

headstone in Butte's Mountain View Cemetery reads: "Slain by Capitalist Interests for Organizing and Inspiring His Fellow Men."[36]

While Montana newspapers advanced many theories about the murder—that it was the spontaneous act of a mob, the work of soldiers angry at being called "scabs," and even that Little was killed by rival labor leaders—Wheeler immediately condemned what he called "a damnable outrage, a blot on the state and the city." He also pledged assistance to state and local authorities investigating the murder and explicitly rejected the notion that Little's speech, while clearly inflammatory, constituted grounds for his arrest, let alone his murder. Many striking miners had their own theory about the execution: the Anaconda Company, with means, motive, and opportunity, had killed Frank Little simply because he was causing trouble for mine operators. Wheeler agreed, telling a Justice Department colleague, "I think the Company had him hung."[37]

Astoundingly, some blamed Wheeler for the murder, saying that his failure to arrest Little had led to the organizer's death. "The federal authorities, not only in Montana but throughout the West," the *Butte Miner* contended, "seem to be very lax in their duty when they allow such treasonable and incendiary agitators to travel at will around the country spreading the doctrine of hatred of this nation and its institutions." Will Campbell, the editor of the *Helena Independent* and a patriotic zealot with minimal regard for civil liberties, editorialized that there was but one sentiment in Helena: "Good work: let them continue to hang every IWW in the state." Montanans found it "beyond comprehension," Campbell wrote, that the "war department has not ordered certain leaders arrested and shot" for what they were saying. Campbell suggested that more "IWW tongues [would] wag" unless the courts and military authorities did more to stop the "treason" of agitators like Frank Little. The *Miner* simply declared that Little's "death is no loss to the world."[38]

———

A week before Little's murder, and under mounting public pressure fueled by the alarm spread across the pages of Anaconda Company–controlled newspapers, Wheeler had investigated the labor organizer's alleged seditious language and concluded that Little had violated no law. He presented the results of his investigation directly to the legal counsel of the Anaconda Company and demanded that attorney Lewis O. Evans show him specific language in the Espionage Act of 1917 that permitted Little's arrest solely on the basis of what he had said at a public meeting. Evans replied that other U.S. attorneys had found ways to initiate prosecutions of seditious speech and that Wheeler ought to work harder to make an arrest.[39]

Wheeler remained convinced that the Butte strike, the action that had drawn Little to Montana in the first place, had less to do with antiwar sentiment or radical politics than with the legitimate grievances of miners concerned about wages and working conditions. The deadly mine fire, Wheeler believed, was the true catalyst for the massive walkout, even as company-controlled newspapers asserted that labor union "radicals" were exploiting the event to fuel antiwar, pro-German sentiment. Wheeler, increasingly the recipient of editorial venom, became incensed by the one-sided coverage in company newspapers and even complained to U.S. attorney general Thomas Gregory about what he called the "unfounded" reports of the cause of Butte's labor unrest. It seemed as though a kind of patriotic neurosis was engulfing Montana—editor Campbell actually claimed that Arizona Apaches, influenced by the IWW, had taken to the warpath—and the hysteria, Wheeler knew, would undercut his reappointment to another four-year term as U.S. attorney.[40]

Even after the strike ended in the fall of 1917, Wheeler continued to face an avalanche of criticism about his performance, including complaints to the Justice Department that he was not merely an IWW sympathizer but a member of the radical union. Wheeler was not an IWW member and not entirely sympathetic with the union's aims, but the allegation proved toxic, and Tom Walsh, who effectively controlled the decision about

Wheeler's reappointment as U.S. attorney, came under growing pressure to dump Wheeler. Governor Stewart, among others, made no secret of his desire to see Wheeler ousted. "We are today either loyal citizens . . . or else we are traitors," the governor said in a comment that was widely seen as directed at Wheeler. Wheeler determinedly made the case for keeping his job. "If any of my enemies can produce anything to show that I have not faithfully discharged the duties of the office, you may rest assured that I would not attempt to be reappointed," he wrote to Walsh. Besides, Wheeler said, he did "not like the idea of quitting under fire." Faced with conflicting advice about his controversial protégé—Wheeler and a few supporters urging reappointment but many of Walsh's best friends counseling that continuing support for the embattled U.S attorney might imperil his own reelection in 1918—the senator equivocated.[41]

While waiting for definitive word about his reappointment, Wheeler was drawn into yet another controversy, this time growing from a sensational espionage case brought against a Montana rancher. The case involved Ves Hall, a Rosebud County stockman who, it was reported to Wheeler's office late in 1917, had been heard speaking disparagingly of the president and the war effort. Hall reportedly told neighbors that he would flee the country to avoid being drafted and that he hoped Germany would win the war. It was also claimed that Hall had said the sinking of the British passenger liner *Lusitania* by a German submarine in 1915 had been justified because the ship was carrying munitions. Under intense pressure to prosecute Hall, Wheeler finally, with considerable reluctance, brought charges against the rancher under the Espionage Act, which essentially made it a crime to interfere with the nation's armed forces. It was the first case brought in Montana under the law, and Judge Bourquin, whom Wheeler knew from the Northwestern case, presided at Hall's trial.[42]

Wheeler may truly have believed that Hall's outspoken antiwar rhetoric constituted a crime under the Espionage Act—authorities across the country were using the law to suppress speech critical of the war—but it seems more likely that he was confident that a life-tenured federal judge with a demonstrated commitment to civil liberties would not permit a miscarriage of justice in what must have looked to him like a straightforward First Amendment case. Wheeler may also have rationalized that prosecuting Hall would ease the pressure on Walsh over his reappointment and temper the criticism he was receiving for not pursuing other alleged Espionage Act violations. Montana newspaper coverage of the Hall case was intense and sensational, with editorials demanding a conviction. Bourquin, calm and imposing while the hysteria grew ever more frantic, admitted that he found the rancher's words "unthinkable" but nevertheless ordered Hall's acquittal without allowing the case to go to the jury. Wheeler received the outcome he desired but was immediately attacked for mishandling the case and for not appealing Bourquin's directed verdict, a move Wheeler contended correctly was procedurally impossible.[43]

A few days after Bourquin's controversial ruling, Governor Stewart announced that an extraordinary session of the Montana legislature would convene in February 1918. The purpose of the special session, Stewart would soon make clear, was to demonstrate how little tolerance existed in Montana for talk or action that was deemed anti-American or antiwar. If federal officials and laws were ineffective in silencing the speech and curtailing the actions of men like Frank Little and Ves Hall, then the state legislature would act.

During the special legislative session the Montana Council of Defense—like other state councils modeled on the Council of National Defense and encouraged by President Wilson to coordinate state-by-state war efforts—was authorized "to do all acts and things not inconsistent with the Constitution or laws of the State of Montana, or the United States, which are necessary . . . for public safety." In practice the council operated with scant regard for the Constitution or laws and served as a super court, legislature, investigative body, and public enforcer, empowered to protect the citizens of Montana from whatever members of the council—all appointed by Governor Stewart—decided they needed protection from. The council's subsequent actions, in the words of historian Michael Punke, amounted to "harassment, inquisition, and some of the most dramatic nationwide restrictions on constitutional freedom in modern American history."[44]

In the name of "public safety," the council further aroused the hysteria that was touching every corner of Montana. The *Roundup (Mont.) Record* reported, for example, that a "crowd went into the high school, secured all the German textbooks, carried them to the business center, and burned them amid cheers and the singing of patriotic songs. Following this, then more suspected pro-Germans were required to kiss the flag and take an oath of allegiance." Neighbors accused each other of being German spies, German airships were reported over the Bitterroot Valley, and the council banned public meetings, held mysterious secret sessions, and condemned anyone who questioned its actions. Hundreds of Montanans were arrested and dozens ultimately went to prison with sentences of up to twenty years and fines of up to $20,000.[45]

The 1918 special legislative session also passed a gun registration law and considered but failed to approve a resolution demanding Judge Bourquin's resignation. A second bipartisan resolution sought to censure Wheeler—accused of failing to prosecute unpatriotic speech and by extension helping bring about Frank Little's murder—but it failed by two votes. More Republicans than Democrats opposed the anti-Wheeler measure, a sign of how badly his support among Democrats had deteriorated.[46]

In early April, Wheeler wrote again to Walsh pleading for a show of support from his mentor and benefactor. "If I am reappointed," he told Walsh, "you will lose some friends, but if I am not reappointed you will lose a great many. . . . I am not saying this in the spirit of boastfulness, or for the purpose of clubbing you as the *Butte Miner* suggests, but . . . so that you will really understand somewhat the conditions in Montana." Everyone knows, Wheeler wrote, "that these attacks upon me have been made because . . . I prosecuted the Northwestern Trustee case and because . . . I incurred the ill will of the Company at the time I was in the legislature six years ago."[47]

Wheeler's heartfelt if increasingly desperate plea had the desired effect, at least temporarily. A week later Walsh, still harboring profound concern about what Wheeler's reappointment meant to his own political fortunes but unwilling to abandon a friend, formally requested that the Wilson administration reappoint his protégé. Wheeler's conduct, Walsh informed the Justice Department, had been thoroughly reviewed, and to not reappoint him would give credence to the suggestions that Wheeler was disloyal or in sympathy with those who were. The Anaconda Company–controlled press reacted predictably. "The people want action. They want results. Let Wheeler go," the *Helena Independent* demanded. It was time to have a U.S attorney who was "a patriotic citizen."[48]

Walsh's support failed to blunt what had become near unanimous opposition to Wheeler among Montana's conservative Democratic establishment. The governor and many Democrat legislators had supported the effort to censure Wheeler, and Democratic Senator Henry Myers, never a fan of Wheeler, let it be known that he wanted a new U.S. attorney appointed. Will Campbell's *Helena Independent*, a reliable Anaconda Company mouthpiece, demanded Wheeler's head on a near-daily basis. The intense criticism crested on June 1, 1918, when the Montana Council of Defense summoned Wheeler to appear at an investigative hearing.[49]

The hearing amounted to a show trial presided over by some of Wheeler's most ardent and powerful critics. Governor Stewart chaired the session. Campbell, the newspaper editor and Wheeler critic, was a council member, and the Anaconda Company dispatched lawyer Lewis O. Evans to serve as a legal advisor during Wheeler's hearing. "I am perfectly willing that the Board should investigate me as far as they like," Wheeler told the council. "I state to you, just the same as I stated to the [U.S.] Attorney General, that if this Board can point to some act where I have been derelict in my office, I am perfectly willing to send in my resignation."[50]

Wheeler faced unrelentingly hostile and occasionally bizarre questioning, with council members homing in on his response to Little's public speeches before his death. One member contended that, had Wheeler and the courts done their duty, "it would not have been necessary for the citizens of Butte to hang Mr. Little." Wheeler objected sharply to the characterization. Little had been murdered, he said, and the murder had been sensationalized in order to "create . . . sentiment against our office."[51]

The Hall case was revisited, as was IWW involvement in the Butte strike the preceding summer. Wheeler was accused of being a socialist, to which he replied, "I am not a

Socialist, never have been a Socialist, and never expect to be a Socialist." He objected to characterizations of IWW strength in Montana as well as the union's responsibility for labor unrest. Both had been vastly overstated, he said, reminding the council that the 1917 strike involved thousands of miners, most of whom "were substantial citizens, workmen of Butte . . . and the vast majority of them were not IWW's." In fact, Wheeler said, the actual number of IWW members in Butte was more likely in the neighborhood of five hundred to seven hundred men, and, while some of them were "low down trash of the earth" for whom he had no sympathy, it was incorrect to label all Montana union men as radicals. Wheeler again contended that the strike had occurred not because of the actions of a handful of radical agitators but because a walkout was the only way to highlight the miners' legitimate grievances following the horrific mine disaster.[52]

The council's questioning went on: Why had Wheeler failed to prosecute "aliens," and why was the U.S. attorney not more patriotic? At one point Campbell said, "You haven't made any address on behalf of the Liberty Loan, or the war saving stamp, or the Red Cross. Just state whether you have, or not." Wheeler said he had not but was not opposed to doing so. During one particularly intrusive line of inquiry Wheeler was asked, "What is your approximate worth? Just in round numbers?"

"I don't care to go into my private worth for publication over the state," Wheeler replied, but his questioner persisted. "Just in round numbers. Fifty thousand, or twenty thousand dollars?" Wheeler finally said his federal salary was $4,000 a year, but he had a large indebtedness because he had borrowed money to buy a building in Butte and still owed a substantial amount to the bank. Wheeler generally held up well under the intense questioning, employing at various times sarcasm, wit, anger, and barely undisguised contempt, and he consistently maintained he would not give in to the hysteria brought about by the war.[53]

It was clear that Wheeler's grilling by the members of the Council of Defense would up the pressure on Walsh to pull back his support for the embattled U.S. attorney. After the hearing, Campbell and J. Bruce Kremer, a Democrat openly antagonistic to Wheeler and employed by the Anaconda Company, drafted a council memorial and sent it to Walsh. The times demanded, the council said, public officials who "not only possess honesty and ability but [also] must be vigorous and enthusiastic in the suppression of internal disorders."[54]

Meanwhile, Walsh continued to struggle with an uncomfortable political choice, a choice Wheeler well understood. "I regret exceedingly that I should have been the apparent cause of so much trouble to you," Wheeler wrote to Walsh in early July, "but do not see how it could be avoided very well." And finally he offered to step aside. "If you feel that my remaining in office is going to be a loadstone [burden] to you in the

Montana U.S. senator Thomas J. Walsh, Wheeler's
early political mentor. (*Library of Congress Prints and
Photographs Division, Washington, D.C.*)

coming election, I am willing to sacrifice all my pride and send in my resignation to
the Attorney General." Walsh must have been tempted to accept the offer, but he again
hesitated, telling a leading Montana Democrat that Wheeler had "been guilty of a lot
of political indiscretions" but that his "official record is without a blemish." Walsh also
remembered how Wheeler had stood by him at considerable peril to Wheeler's own
ambitions. "I felt myself deeply indebted to him for the steadfastness with which he
adhered to me at the legislative session of 1911."[55]

Walsh was trying to balance two competing political factions. To be reelected he
needed the support of liberal and progressive Montanans, many of whom continued
to support Wheeler, but at the same time the senator dared not alienate moderates
and conservatives, including Democrats like Governor Stewart and Senator Myers.
Walsh's political calculation was further complicated by the fact that two opponents
stood in his reelection path, a conservative Republican, Oscar M. Landstrum, and a
third-party candidate, Montana's incumbent progressive Republican congresswoman
Jeannette Rankin. Rankin enjoyed a solid following across Montana, particularly from

members of the increasingly influential Nonpartisan League. Rankin was admired by some and loathed by others for having voted against the U.S. declaration of war with Germany. In the small world of Montana politics, Wheeler enjoyed a personal friendship with Rankin's brother, Wellington, also a progressive Republican and a former law partner of Walsh.[56]

With Wheeler and Walsh in almost constant communication about the former's reappointment and the latter's reelection, Walsh implored Wheeler to try to placate some of his critics, particularly the bombastic Will Campbell. Wheeler could not bring himself to go that far. "My frank opinion about Campbell is that he is as dirty and low down a cur as I know. . . . He is just a cheap political grafter who is willing to sell his manhood and his brains for a few dollars." A few days later Walsh tried a different tack, begging Wheeler to engage in "a little diplomacy" because, Walsh said, he was convinced his Republican opponent would use the Wheeler controversy against him and that Jeannette Rankin would be the beneficiary. Walsh also suggested that Wheeler might try to convince Rankin to abandon her candidacy, a suggestion Wheeler ignored.[57]

Meanwhile another labor crisis erupted. On August 17, 1918, several national IWW leaders were convicted in Chicago of violating the Espionage Act, a general strike call was issued, and authorities in Butte moved to round up many of the city's labor leaders. As historian Jerry Calvert describes: "Military intelligence agents, local policemen, and private detectives raided the offices of the [pro-miner] *Butte Bulletin*, the independent Metal Mine Workers Union, and the IWW. Without search warrants, these enthusiastic enforcers of law arrested dozens of men and held them without charge for the Montana Council of Defense. Additional sweeps uncovered 'slackers' who were arrested without the authority of warrants."[58]

The massive roundup disgusted Wheeler, and, as usual, he was aggressive in responding, reporting to the Justice Department that the raids were not only unnecessary but also counterproductive. He was correct. Two thousand miners immediately walked off the job to protest the arrests. Wheeler moved quickly and deftly to deal with the crisis, enlisting the National War Labor Board to encourage a peaceful end to the walkout. Wheeler also told strikers that copper was critical to the war effort and that if they went back to work underground he would do everything he could to force an investigation into working conditions. This helped ease tensions.[59]

Wheeler was also determined to expose the Anaconda Company's deceitful tactics that he knew were contributing to the constant labor-management turmoil. Wheeler suspected that company undercover detectives had infiltrated the IWW leadership, and, summoning two of the leaders to his office, he told them he believed that a number of top union officials were paid informers for Anaconda. One of the men finally admitted that Wheeler was right and that the company had actually helped prompt the most recent walkout to make the miners look bad, thus further eroding union solidarity. Wheeler went public with this information in an open letter to Anaconda's legal counsel Dan Kelly. "The IWW organization did herald or call the strike in Butte. That much is true," Wheeler wrote to Kelly. But "they were encouraged to do so by paid agents of your company. These agents are high in the counsel of the IWW local union." The letter created a sensation. Once miners realized that the company was using the strike to discredit and even destroy the union, the walkout ended quickly. "Not only was the company spying on unions," historian K. Ross Toole wrote in his 1954 doctoral dissertation. "Unions were spying on each other, and (and the alliteration is necessary) spies spied on spies." Wheeler exposed the subterfuge.[60]

In early October 1918, a month before Walsh faced voters, Wheeler made a final plea to keep his job. "The so called radicals of Butte," he told the senator, "will do all in their power for you, and we can line them up almost to a man if you can get that appointment through."[61]

At precisely this time, Anaconda's legal counsel was preparing a response to Wheeler's "open letter" accusing the company of helping create Butte's labor unrest. Kelly's response to Wheeler appeared in the *Helena Independent* on October 3, just as Wheeler left for meetings in Washington, D.C. The Anaconda attorney blasted Wheeler as "either an official slacker or a liar" and concluded, "I believe you to be both."[62]

Three days later in Washington, in the company of two Montana Democratic Party leaders, Wheeler and Walsh sat down for what must have been an awkward meeting. It was finally time for Wheeler to step aside, Walsh said. If Wheeler refused, Walsh's Senate seat would be lost simply for supporting Wheeler's reappointment. Despite his earlier offer to step aside, Wheeler was in no way happy with the demand, as he recounted years later to Walsh's biographer: "Walsh came to see me at the Raleigh Hotel. He said he was afraid they were going to beat him. I told him, 'I made my enemies in the first place by supporting you.' I told him I would resign though if he thought he was going to get beat." And true to his word, Wheeler immediately resigned.[63]

Walsh offered consolation prizes, including the prospect of a federal judgeship in the Panama Canal Zone or commission as a colonel in the army. Wheeler declined and ended the discussion, saying simply, "I'm going back to Montana." Wheeler was replaced as U.S. attorney by E. C. Day, a leader of the conservative faction in the Montana Democratic Party and a man acceptable to the company. And Wheeler did return to Montana—ill-tempered, disillusioned, and unwilling to make a public statement of support of Walsh, which might have been helpful to the senator's efforts to keep Wheeler's "radical" supporters in his camp. Instead Wheeler issued a statement about his resignation that was printed in the *Butte Miner* on October 10, 1918:

> By way of explanation for this action I desire to say that the Anaconda Copper Mining Company . . . through its press, through those who owe their political existence to that concern, and their representatives, [has] carried on a campaign of misrepresentation and vilification against me . . . and unfortunately by reason of the same, many honest, patriotic citizens of Montana have become imbued with the idea that I have been faithless to the trust imposed in me . . . [T]he friends and political advisers of the Honorable Thomas J. Walsh feel that my remaining in office may mean his defeat.

Wheeler concluded, "I have tendered my resignation rather than sacrifice my friend."[64]

With Wheeler no longer a campaign issue, Walsh's reelection effort finally gained momentum. Governor Stewart began campaigning for him, coverage of Walsh's speeches in Anaconda-controlled papers improved, and the Wilson administration provided support, including a warm personal endorsement from the president. Walsh won reelection but by fewer than six thousand votes, gathering barely 41 percent of the votes in the three-way race. In Silver Bow County, home to Wheeler and the most intense labor unrest, Walsh bested Jeannette Rankin by fewer than one hundred votes.[65]

Walsh went on to serve with great distinction for fourteen more years in the Senate, exposing the Teapot Dome scandal, and would have served as attorney general in the Roosevelt administration had he not died on the eve of taking office. Did he sacrifice Wheeler in order to appease the Anaconda Company and save his political career? Walsh's biographer concludes what seems hardly debatable: Walsh "wanted to return to the Senate and was willing to make the necessary moves regarding Wheeler in order to win re-election."[66]

Walsh's chief political advisor—his Helena law partner, C. B. Nolan—was more candid. A month after Walsh had been safely returned to the Senate, Nolan told the senator he had won reelection only because of the help received from the Anaconda Company and that the help had materialized once Wheeler had resigned. "Good riddance to bad rubbish," Nolan said of Wheeler. "The election returns show most conclusively that the Company did all that it possibly could to bring about your election and without the financial assistance that was given by Con Kelley [Anaconda's president], our situation would be critical in meeting the expense account that was contracted."[67]

Wheeler had yet to learn the hard lesson of Montana politics: long-term political survival demanded some accommodation with the economic powers that dominated the state. Walsh's reelection in 1918 proved he had mastered the lesson. Wheeler finally wrote the senator in December 1918 telling him that although he was "really glad" to see Walsh reelected, he was "disappointed" that Walsh had caved in to the pressure that demanded Wheeler's job as the price of victory. Wheeler then offered a comment that, given all the vilification he had suffered, could not possibly have reflected his true feelings. "I feel better off out of the office and politics than in, and only hope that I may be endowed with good judgment enough to remain out of politics for the future, but have no doubt my enemies will take care of that."[68]

The political and personal adversity Wheeler suffered during World War I did not defeat him but rather toughened him. Instead of being driven out of public life, his experiences made him even more determined to win political office, and soon he was plotting a comeback.

There is an enduring and larger lesson in Wheeler's story during this period. His support for civil liberties, so controversial in 1918, has stood the test of time, while those who helped create Montana's Agony have long stood condemned. "To read the record of Wheeler's inquisition today," historian K. Ross Toole has written, "is at once depressing and encouraging—depressing because here was a governmental body (the Council of Defense) at the service of corporate interests coldly and viciously accusing Wheeler of disloyalty to his own country and wrapping its own views in the flag of patriotism; encouraging, because under this barrage of bigotry and hypocrisy, Wheeler stood up to them."[69]

2   BOXCAR BURT BECOMES SENATOR WHEELER

The chief plank in Mr. B. K. Wheeler's program is to drive the
Anaconda Copper Mining Company out of the state.

—*GREAT FALLS TRIBUNE*, 1920

Driven from office, his fledging political career in tatters, and with reputation sullied, B. K. Wheeler almost immediately launched a political comeback, setting his sights on winning the Montana governorship in 1920. Wanting to advance progressive ideas, wield political power, and settle old scores, Wheeler and his wife—she was as upset as he was about his treatment by Democrats and the Anaconda Company—discussed whether he should run as a Republican, a Democrat, or an independent. He settled on staying in the Democratic Party, but he also openly championed the ideas of, and was endorsed by, the Nonpartisan League (NPL), an underfinanced, fragile coalition of radical farmers, labor leaders, socialists, and perhaps even a few Bolsheviks. The NPL effectively hijacked the Montana Democratic Party in 1920 and installed Wheeler as the movement's gubernatorial candidate.[1]

Montana has a long history of nasty, bitter campaigns, but the 1920 race for governor remains in a category all its own. Wheeler was accused of endorsing "free love" and labeled a closet "Bolshevik" intent on establishing a Soviet-style government in Montana. Huge billboards appeared across the state featuring, as Wheeler later remembered, a "huge red hand dripping blood." Wheeler called the election "one of the bitterest and roughest political campaigns in American history." "I was very nearly lynched," and not just once, he said.[2]

———

The 1920s have become in American memory a decade of prosperity, fueled by free spending and unregulated financial speculation; a decade defined by flappers, bathtub gin, and enormous optimism about the future. But there was another side to the decade. The Russian Revolution was still in its infancy and radical political movements seemed to be gaining strength around the globe. Labor unrest, not unlike the kind experienced in Butte during the war, was widespread across the United States. An IWW-led strike crippled Seattle for several weeks in 1919, American Legionnaires and Wobblies clashed in Centralia, Washington, that November, leaving five dead, and strikes shut down much of the steel and coal industries. By one estimate there were more than three thousand strikes involving four million American workers during 1919 and 1920, as a "red scare" swept the country. Thousands of alleged radicals, many of them immigrants, were arrested and hundreds deported.[3]

A postwar economic depression crippled the Montana farm economy, adding to a discernable sense of upheaval and despair. Even a plague of insects and drought visited the state. Enterprising farmers imported more than a hundred thousand turkeys to help battle a grasshopper infestation, but the birds did little good, and roast turkey became a fixture on the menu of many small-town restaurants. During May and June 1917 barely a third of an inch of rain fell in Havre, a farm and railroad town about thirty-five miles south of the Canadian border. Then the real drought hit. Seed became difficult to find, mortgages were called, and farm prices, in the few places where a crop could be harvested, were frightfully low. The effects of farm depression on Montana and its politics were dramatic. An exodus of families from failed farms began, as K. Ross Toole has written, "in the fall of 1917; by the summer of 1918 it was well under-way; by the summer of 1919 it was a flood." In-migration essentially ended, and during the 1920s Montana was the only state in the nation to lose population.[4]

The bitterness engendered by these hard facts was palpable in farm country. The depression in farm prices, drought, the influx and then retreat of the "honyockers," the often ill-prepared, novice farmers who fell victim first to real estate speculators and then to the destruction of their dreams, created a fertile breeding ground for radical political solutions, particularly those advocated by the insurgent Nonpartisan League.[5]

The political influence of the NPL had begun seeping into the plains of northeastern Montana in 1916. Across the border in North Dakota that year the league elected a full slate of statewide candidates and began to implement a program of sweeping economic reform. Led by Arthur C. Townley, a failed farmer, former socialist, and organizational genius from Beach, North Dakota, league leaders believed farmers' problems could only be addressed by more effective political action. The leaders were determined to attract the disaffected, particularly farmers, from both major parties—hence the "nonpartisan" label—and mobilize them, creating a grassroots movement.[6]

However, where Townley and his followers saw political and economic reform, others visualized the makings of communist revolution. In North Dakota, the league advocated state ownership of grain elevators, flour mills, and packinghouses. The league demanded creation of rural credit banks operated at cost and a program of state-supported hail insurance. Townley established a newspaper—the *Nonpartisan Leader*—and developed a dues-paying membership. To be a "Leaguer" meant paying annual dues to support the organization, and recruiters fanned out across North Dakota to sign up every farmer. "Find out the damn fool's hobby," one league organizer advised, "and then talk it. If he likes religion, talk Jesus Christ; if he's against the government, damn the Democrats; if he's afraid of whiskey, preach prohibition; if he wants to talk hogs, talk hogs—talk anything he'll listen to, but talk, talk, until you get his God-damned John Hancock to a check for six dollars." Critics said it amounted to rank socialism or worse. "While it would be untrue to say that every socialist is a free lover," the *Grand Forks Herald* concluded, "we know of no advocate of free love who is not an avowed socialist. Most of the men who are of the inner circle in the management of the Nonpartisan League are men who appear to have drifted into socialism through failure in every other line of activity . . . among them are men who are advocates of almost every wild vagary ever put forth under the name of socialism." League leaders fought back against the wildest allegations directed at the movement and succeeded, at least temporarily, in tapping a deep vein of economic grievance in farm country. Townley became one of the great farm organizers in American history, and he was determined to expand beyond his base in North Dakota.[7]

By 1920 the league boasted twenty thousand dues-paying members in Montana, many living in the northeastern corner of the state, an area described by some as Montana's "red corner." The *Producers News*, published at Plentywood in Sheridan County, served as mouthpiece for the radical farm movement in general and the Nonpartisan League in particular. One early edition of the paper featured a front-page photo of Wheeler under the headline, "Will Farmers Allow Sinister Influence to Get Their Friend," a reference to Wheeler's battles with the Anaconda Company. The paper's editorials were later often influenced by what appeared in the Communist Party USA's *Daily Worker*.[8]

As the league expanded its influence in Montana, its organizers and representatives became the focus of fierce opposition. NPL organizers and supporters were not allowed to speak in many communities, and some were assaulted. League organizer J. A. "Mickey" McGlynn, a young Sydney, Montana, farmer, for example, tried to speak in Miles City, but a mob, reportedly including prominent local businessmen and lawyers, forced him into the basement of the Elks Lodge and laid on a savage beating. Local authorities refused to investigate the assault but did question McGlynn about his loyalty.[9]

Intellectual "radicalism" was also under assault in Montana. In 1919, a University of Montana economics professor, Louis Levine, lost his teaching and research post for producing a small, scholarly book, *The Taxation of Mines in Montana*. Levine arrived at the hardly astounding conclusion that the Anaconda Company had been paying little or no taxes for years. The company retaliated by first applying pressure to stop publication of Levine's study and then successfully demanding that the professor be fired. Montana legislators called for investigations of the university, and legislation was introduced to eliminate the position of chancellor since, it was alleged, the incumbent was obviously "too socialist" for the job. The *Great Falls Tribune* said it was clear that Missoula, home to the university, had "always been a hot bed of scholastic intrigue and insubordination."[10]

Fearing the potential political power of an increasingly angry and restive collection of radicalized Montana farmers, a special session of the state legislature in 1919 voted to suspend the state's new open primary law. Conservative business and political interests could scarcely contain their apprehension at the prospect that an open primary might become an effective political tool in the hands of "radicals," particularly if the league succeeded in using the wide-open nominating process to gain control of one or both of Montana's major political parties. Since the open primary law had been put on the books by the citizen initiative process, suspending it also required voter approval. The resulting political brawl absorbed the attention of both parties and contributed to the general turmoil. Wheeler defended the open primary, ensuring that he would have the support of the league and its followers in the gubernatorial election, but that support also guaranteed that his opponents would continue to define him as a dangerous radical.[11]

"We issued a statement urging every citizen to meet this attack on popular government," Wheeler later recalled, and he assumed a leadership role in a statewide organization formed to save the open primary. "I was a member of the organization's executive committee, which numbered both Republicans and Democrats. The group was set up independently of the Nonpartisan League because the League was being stigmatized in the press as 'red socialist.'" Wheeler's adversaries, not surprisingly, ignored that careful distinction.[12]

Adequate signatures were eventually gathered to guarantee a delay in the repeal vote until after the 1920 primary election, and leaders of the Nonpartisan League became increasingly confident that candidates worthy of league support, particularly in the governor's race, could be nominated in both major parties. It was an ambitious but not completely realistic goal. The league's political power, if it could be realized, rested in uniting the substantial yet fractious forces of the Montana farm and mine. Put another way, the state's farmers tended to hate mining companies, believing that mine owners never shouldered a fair share of the state's tax burden. Miners, often treated shabbily by mine owners, came by their hatred naturally. Disdain of big economic interests was therefore a common feature of both groups of voters, although their specific political and economic interests often diverged. Still, in a way rarely seen before in Montana, farmers and their wary allies in the mines began to coalesce into a potent political force in 1919 and 1920. Wheeler emerged as their champion.[13]

———

The Anaconda Company–aligned press, fearing the prospect of a Wheeler political resurrection so soon after having contributed to the end of his tenure as U.S. attorney, promulgated the notion that Wheeler was indeed radicalized and had joined forces with "the disturbing and troublemaking elements of the Non-Partisan League." He had indeed joined forces.[14]

In advance of the primary election, league members held a joint convention with the Montana Labor League. Both groups planned to endorse gubernatorial candidates, and Wheeler sought their endorsement. His only serious opposition for league backing came from his close friend and former assistant, the Republican attorney general Sam Ford. When Ford's support withered, convention delegates embraced Wheeler as their standard bearer. Accepting the endorsement, Wheeler cautioned supporters against overoptimism, and he predicted that defeat at the polls would destroy the nonpartisan movement. After some debate, the convention opted to attempt to run its slate of Nonpartisan League–endorsed candidates, Wheeler most prominently, on the Democratic ticket, although Wheeler made it clear that he had no objection to running as a Republican if the League was determined to make its play in that party's primary.[15]

Wheeler told his wife to expect "a mean and dirty campaign," certain that Montana business interests and their newspaper allies would fight bitterly to deny him election. The assault began almost immediately. The *Anaconda Standard* said Wheeler was at the head of a pack of "red radicals" and "professional agitators" determined to wreck the state's economy. The *Butte Miner* began to refer dismissively to Wheeler as "Butte's leading farmer," and the paper ominously editorialized that "no man can sit quietly by and see his state virtually made an annex of Bolshevik Russia." Wheeler's first campaign stop after the league convention was in Dillon, a rugged mining and cattle town high in the Beaverhead Valley in southwestern Montana. In Dillon, Wheeler received a preview of what he would face if he succeeded in capturing the Democratic nomination for governor.[16]

———

Dillon leaders were determined to keep political riff-raff under control in their town. An ordinance was passed banning political speeches from the steps of City Hall, at least speeches not endorsed by the local Republican or Democratic Party chairmen. Local

Thirty-eight-year-old B. K. Wheeler in 1920
when he embraced the Nonpartisan League
movement, ran for governor of Montana, and
lost in a landslide. Two years later he won the
first of four terms in the U.S. Senate. (*Library
of Congress Prints and Photographs Division,
Washington, D.C.*)

police made it clear that an unapproved speaker, even one talking on a street corner,
could be arrested. Not wanting to spend the night in jail, Wheeler scheduled his rally
and speech at a ranch just outside of town. Accounts of precisely what happened at the
rally vary greatly, but apparently, even before Wheeler got to his feet to speak, a crowd
of angry men threatened him. A scuffle broke out, a knife was produced, someone
was stabbed, and in the confusion Wheeler and an escort managed a hasty getaway.
"Quickly there were cries of 'Get a rope,'" Wheeler wrote years later, and, in what
for him was a rare understatement, he recalled, "I began to feel uncomfortable." The
candidate and a supporter made their way to the railroad siding at the tiny hamlet of
Bond, north of Dillon, where they sought refuge in the station, which turned out to be
simply a boxcar on a siding. Wheeler waited out a tense night in the sealed boxcar, with
a friendly farmer standing guard outside with a rifle. The farmer had taken up sentry
duty, he told Wheeler, because several automobiles full of men had come to his place

looking for the disappeared candidate. Eventually the candidate's pursuers arrived at the boxcar, but the gun-toting farmer held them off with a promise to "shoot anyone full of lead who opens that door." By dawn the Silver Bow County sheriff arrived from Butte—legally Dillon was out of his jurisdiction—and Wheeler was escorted back to Butte. Anti-Wheeler newspapers had a grand time with the story, christening the Democratic candidate "Boxcar Burt."[17]

"Boxcar Is a Refuge for Politician," said the *Anaconda Standard.* The paper's report dismissed what happened in Dillon, calling it a "tale . . . purely imaginary." The *Butte Bulletin,* partial to Wheeler's candidacy and a voice of the radical left in Montana, portrayed the escapade much differently. "Seek Murder of Wheeler at Dillon," the *Bulletin's* headline read. "The lawless element in Beaverhead County has been urged by corrupt politicians of the Beaverhead County seat [Dillon], presumably acting on orders from the Anaconda Company's headquarters in Butte, to 'get Mr. Wheeler.'" The *Bulletin's* socialist editor, Bill Dunne, called the Dillon mob "a gang of pug uglies."[18]

Fearing that a candidate with Nonpartisan League endorsement was tantamount to a Democratic Party defeat in the general election, an increasingly worried collection of anti-Wheeler Democrats set about keeping the party from being hijacked by Wheeler and his friends, the "socialistic radicals." Conservative Democrats coalesced around Montana's incumbent lieutenant governor, William W. McDowell, a champion of the Irish independence movement, among other things. The struggle to win the Democratic primary, McDowell's supporters asserted, was "a straight fight between the reds and the Americans." Democratic National Committee member and Anaconda lobbyist J. Bruce Kremer, the Butte lawyer who helped engineer the Council of Defense opposition to Wheeler, and Governor Sam Stewart joined the McDowell forces and worked hard to stop Wheeler. This conservative Democratic challenge further complicated Wheeler's political task. He needed to find a way to appeal to the party rank and file, many of whom were more conservative than him, while not alienating radical league supporters who expected Wheeler to push the NPL agenda, even to the point of repudiating the Democratic Party's presidential ticket. Senator Walsh, again caught in the uncomfortable middle, attempted peacemaking by insisting that the league and regular Democrats find a way to work together in the interest of electing all Democrats, including Wheeler.[19]

Wheeler tiptoed through this balancing act and on the strength of a unified, proleague majority won the Democratic primary in late August, beating McDowell by more than fourteen thousand votes. League-endorsed candidates won every important race, but the bruising primary left Montana Democrats badly divided, with the Nonpartisan League endorsement driving conservative Democrats and some moderates away from

Wheeler's candidacy. Montana Republicans, meanwhile, guaranteed that the general election would be a battle between two progressives. Former senator Joseph Dixon held off five Republican challengers (Attorney General Ford entered the Republican race late and finished third) to secure his party's gubernatorial nomination. For the first time in its history, as historian Bradley Snow has noted, "the company [Anaconda] was without a gubernatorial candidate to its genuine liking."[20]

In a play for some semblance of Democratic Party unity, Wheeler began to refer to himself as a "Jeffersonian Democrat" in touch with the needs and aspirations of working people on farms and in the mines. He removed any doubt about his support for the national ticket when he met with Democratic presidential candidate James M. Cox, the Ohio governor, in Great Falls. Cox offered his own glowing endorsement, saying of the gubernatorial candidate: "You Montana Democrats have in this young man Wheeler a splendid and courageous man." Walsh also endorsed the ticket that Wheeler was heading, although with limited enthusiasm.[21]

Wheeler articulated a progressive economic message during the campaign, often highlighting the league's call for public ownership of agricultural processing facilities. "Public ownership of grain elevators and flourmills is no more socialistic than public ownership of the public schools," Wheeler said in one speech. His crowds were often large, and he regularly reminded voters that he was "born in the shadow of Bunker Hill" and knew "no form of government other than the American system—and want to know no other." Wheeler's real concern, however, remained the Anaconda Company and his belief that it dominated Montana politics. In a speech in Hamilton, Wheeler said he would see to it that the state capitol was moved from the Hennessey Building, Anaconda's headquarters in Butte, back to Helena where it belonged.[22]

The *Great Falls Tribune*, among others, denounced Wheeler's attacks on Montana business and suggested that his election would destroy the state's economy. "The blunt question is pertinent," the *Tribune* said. "Do we wish to turn the governmental machinery of the state into the hands of a candidate who openly declares that he intends to use it as an endeavor to bring about this type of destruction?"[23]

The "destroy the economy" charge, particularly in light of the generally depressed Montana economy, seriously damaged Wheeler's chances. During a speech late in the campaign he attempted to answer the charge in personal terms. "All the money I have is invested in Butte," he said, "and I am not going to put the Anaconda Company out of business. If I did, the difference would be that I would have to walk out (of Butte) and they would ride out in Pullmans." Then he added, in case anyone missed his true intent, "I will put them out of politics."[24]

Despite the intensity of the attacks on Wheeler, the Anaconda Company had no remotely attractive options in the 1920 gubernatorial campaign. Wheeler, the

Democrat, was a well-established foe supported, in the company view, by a radical mob of socialist farmers, occasionally violent miners, and various reformers and anti-corporate do-gooders. The Republican candidate, Joe Dixon, nearly as much a political radical as Wheeler, also had a history of hostility to Montana business interests. It was indeed, as journalist Joseph Kinsey Howard would note, "an unhappy company which confronted the 1920 state election."[25]

Joseph Dixon, the Republican candidate, was one of the most impressive and important figures in Montana's colorful political history. Like Wheeler, Dixon was born to a Quaker family. After growing up in North Carolina, he attended Quaker colleges and after studying law relocated to Missoula in 1891. There Dixon participated in local politics, was elected to Congress, and in 1907 was chosen by the state legislature for a U.S. Senate seat. At every step of Dixon's political development he displayed a progressive, independent streak that frequently placed him at odds with the more conservative rank and file of the Montana Republican Party. Dixon eventually neglected his own political career and further alienated party leaders when he managed his friend Theodore Roosevelt's independent campaign for president in 1912. Faced with a choice between a Democratic progressive and a Republican one, the Anaconda Company solved its gubernatorial dilemma in 1920 by making a political deal with the devil—or more correctly with the lesser of two devils. The company got behind Dixon, making a calculating decision that the Republican would be more reasonable and more easily controlled. Dixon's campaign was suddenly awash with publicity and money.[26]

Dixon skillfully acted out his role in this political drama by having it both ways: attacking Wheeler as a radical—his hyperbole was effective—and soft-pedaling his own progressive instincts. Elect Wheeler, Dixon said, and Montana would embrace "revolutionary government . . . only the kindergarten course in the full program that Lenin and Trotsky have put into . . . effect in Russia." To a critic who complained that Dixon seemed to be abandoning progressivism, he replied:

> Let me just give you a little lesson in practical politics. . . . Do you think I
> could get anywhere in this election by trying to out–Nonpartisan League Burt
> Wheeler? . . . the Company didn't want me nominated, and they don't want
> me elected. But . . . they just can't take Wheeler. . . . Now my job is to carry
> on this campaign in a way that promised [the Anaconda Company] nothing.
> You haven't seen me giving anything away. But on the other hand, I've got to
> get the votes of the conservative element . . . or I won't be elected. That's all
> there is to it.[27]

Newspapers and political operatives who had once denounced Dixon as a dangerous radical now embraced him as the embodiment of "the Americanism of Montana" in contrast to Wheeler's "red tide." Montana Power Company, Anaconda's "twin," employed a sophisticated strategy to assist the Republican. The power company purchased nine different full-page advertisements that appeared in more than two hundred Montana publications during the height of the election campaign in September, October, and November. The ads touted the company's service to Montana, clearly suggesting that a Wheeler win would put that in jeopardy. Wheeler counterpunched gamely, but he was short of money, and the anti-Wheeler press routinely ignored his speeches and ideas while slamming his character and deploring his radicalism.[28]

The most astounding charge leveled against Wheeler, the charge most likely to gain wide public attention as well as the most difficult to refute, was the allegation that somehow followers of the Nonpartisan League advocated "free love." The charge presumably meant, at minimum, that NPL advocates condoned sex outside of marriage. The "free love" canard apparently originated in North Dakota during the tenure of League-backed Governor Lynn Frazier when a book advocating a "free love" doctrine showed up in a public library. The book was cited as proof that libertine sentiments were running wild across the North Dakota prairie and threatened to pervert Montana too. The "free love" charge was also leveled in 1920 against the League-backed candidate for governor in Minnesota.[29]

Wheeler tried to make light of the silliness by turning the allegation back on his Republican opponents. "In Billings," he recounted in his memoirs, "I decided to have some fun with the 'free love' rumor. I brought up the name of Charles Bair, a Republican, a wealthy sheepman, and part owner of the *Billings Gazette*."

"You all know Charley Bair," Wheeler told his listeners. "Now, let me ask you something: if there was free love in North Dakota, do you think Charley Bair would still be in Montana?" Many voters remembered that Wheeler had unsuccessfully prosecuted Bair for "white slavery"—taking a woman across a state line for "immoral purposes." The joke worked well enough that Wheeler started using it regularly.[30]

Despite his aggressive effort to portray the election fight as between the "special interests" and "the people," the relentless negative attacks on Wheeler—free love advocate, Bolshevik Burt, socialist, red, radical, destroyer of Montana's economy—were outrageous but effective. Tom Walsh, somewhat belatedly, sought to keep Montana Democrats united in support of Wheeler by declaring that his friend was an honorable man with the courage to "defy the most powerful political and business interests in the state." But when Democratic senator Henry Myers abandoned the party and condemned Wheeler's followers as representing "the very worst elements of our society . . . bent on ruination, class warfare, destruction of American principles, assault on vested rights, confiscation of property and some of them even on bolshevism, with its terrors," Wheeler's candidacy was effectively doomed.[31]

Walsh's chief political advisor in Montana, his law partner C. B. Nolan—no friend of Wheeler's—wrote to the senator in early October that the campaign was going to end in a Democratic rout. Senator Myers's allegation that the Democratic ticket amounted to "a Bolshevist crowd endeavoring to sovietize our government" was, in Nolan's view, politically fatal. That prediction was spot on. While Wheeler ran well ahead of the national Democratic ticket in Montana, he won only seven counties, including barely scratching out a win in his home county, Silver Bow, but, perhaps not surprisingly, ran well in the "red corner" of Montana. Wheeler won an impressive 60 percent of the vote in sparsely populated Sheridan County, where the *Producers News* provided lavish coverage of his campaign. But he was routed nearly everywhere else. In Beaverhead County, where Wheeler had spent the night in a boxcar, he lost to Dixon by a four-to-one margin. The election was the worst defeat since statehood for a Montana gubernatorial candidate and amounted to a Republican sweep of historic proportions. Montana Democrats won just 9 of 108 seats in the state house of representatives, and only ten League-endorsed candidates were elected to the legislature. Despite this, the ballot measure to confirm elimination of the direct primary—the position Wheeler had opposed and the Company supported—was rejected handily.[32]

"Butte Kicks out the Reds and Elects Americans to Office," proclaimed the *Anaconda Standard*. "A candidate cannot expect to climb into power by attacking one of its leading industries," the newspaper said. "Mr. Wheeler, an accident in politics, chewing the end of bitter reflection today, found this lesson an expensive one . . . no doornail was ever more dead than Townleyism."[33]

Historian Richard Ruetten has correctly attributed Wheeler's defeat to four major factors: the national Republican landslide that carried Warren Harding into the White House made 1920 an extraordinarily difficult year for Democrats, Wheeler received scant newspaper support and generally what notice he did receive was punishingly negative, his campaign was woefully short of money, and the defection of Senator Myers made it easy for rank-and-file Democrats to abandon the entire Democratic ticket. Wheeler also encountered in Joe Dixon the most capable opponent he would face until his final campaign, in 1946.[34]

There was one additional and perhaps overridingly important reason for Wheeler's historic defeat. He was defined—or perhaps could not help being defined—as a frightening, threatening, un-American candidate at a time when Montana voters were seeking stable, sober, serious leadership. Wheeler's opponent Joe Dixon and Dixon's supporters helped voters imagine a political monster, and then they proceeded to destroy the monster at the ballot box.

Wheeler wished Dixon well and returned to his law practice in Butte, comfortable in the belief that the new governor would be no patsy for the Anaconda Company. A month after the election Wheeler was standing on a street corner in Butte when a company official, D'Gay Stivers—"head of the Company's goon squad," as Wheeler later wrote—approached him. Without provocation, at least in Wheeler's telling, Stivers, a former Texas Ranger and Spanish-American War veteran, hit him in the left side of the head, blackening his eye and knocking him to the ground. Wheeler pressed charges, but Stivers was acquitted of assault after the assailant explained why he had thrown the punch. On the eve of the 1920 election during a rally in Butte, Wheeler had rhetorically asked a crowd of his political supporters, "Who hanged Little? Ask Colonel Stivers—he knows." The judge found that under those circumstances—Stivers said Wheeler was "a liar and character assassin"—throwing a punch at an ex-candidate seemed entirely justified. Wheeler was disgusted by the verdict, but what recourse did he have? He was a loser at the ballot box and even in court.[35]

Immediately upon taking office, Governor Dixon encountered real trouble: the slumping Montana economy created a large state budget deficit and forced a major fight over new tax revenue. The governor's response, imposition of a tax on mine profits, immediately alienated the Anaconda Company. Dixon also advocated establishment of a state tax commission, wide-ranging reforms of the tax structure, and legislation to aid farmers and mine workers, but he got nothing of importance through the legislature. The company's political influence simply crushed Dixon's reform agenda. When the legislature finally adjourned, perhaps merely to underscore where the real power in Montana resided, the Anaconda Company completely suspended industrial operations in the state, throwing thousands out of work and further depressing the state's economy.[36]

Recalling the dire predictions of what his election would mean for Montana's economy, Wheeler could not resist taunting his recent tormenters. Asked to say a few words at a banquet in Butte, Wheeler quipped that he must be in the wrong place. "When I read in the papers that the mines are closed, farm prices are falling and farms foreclosed, I said to myself, 'I am sure I must have been elected governor and that I should be living in Helena.'"[37]

Wheeler came away from his disastrous 1920 gubernatorial campaign a much-changed politician, if not a much-changed man. The hard lessons learned in a bitter and poisonous campaign helped prepare Wheeler for what he would face nearly continuously during his twenty-four year career in the U.S. Senate, a career that remarkably began just two years after the defeat in the governor's race. If Wheeler's battles as U.S. attorney had constituted an undergraduate degree in politics, then the 1920 campaign for governor had been a graduate-level course. Wheeler would never again demonstrate the level of hostility toward Montana's economic powers that he displayed in 1920, and the seeds of Wheeler's later fierce anticommunism can be found in the drubbing he took in the governor's race. Never again would he allow himself to be defined as Bolshevik Burt and never again would he stake his political future on opposing Montana's economic interests. Wheeler would remain a Democrat but essentially an independent, never tying his own prospects too tightly to any party, movement, or other politician. The bitter campaign and humiliating defeat Wheeler suffered in 1920 taught him how to win future elections, and he now turned his attention to getting even with Henry Myers, the man who helped usher him from federal office and then helped end his gubernatorial hopes. Myers's Senate seat would be the centerpiece of the next Montana election, in 1922. Wheeler kept right on campaigning. Rarely has American politics seen a more improbable comeback.

——————

Convinced that his opponents at Anaconda would be preoccupied trying to thwart Governor Dixon and his reform agenda in Helena and therefore would spend little time and attention on the 1922 Senate election, Wheeler saw a path to joining Tom Walsh in the Senate. The company's ambivalent attitude regarding Wheeler's prospective Senate candidacy was confirmed by no less an authority than the loyal editor of the company's newspaper in Butte, who, Wheeler told Walsh, was "more interested in the Legislature than he was in a candidate for the United States Senate." Wheeler's candidacy received a further boost when Senator Myers, damaged by his rejection of the party in 1920, announced his retirement. Suddenly the Senate contest was wide open. Wheeler seized the mantle as the most experienced candidate in the field and wisely said he would refuse to run if the Nonpartisan League insisted on endorsing him.[38]

Wheeler ran an effective primary campaign in a four-candidate field, focusing almost exclusively on national issues, including highlighting mounting evidence of corruption in the Harding administration, particularly in the management of the Justice Department under Attorney General Harry M. Daugherty. Wheeler also blasted the high railroad freight rates impacting Montana farmers that were, he said, a direct result of the controversial Esch-Cummins Act. Wheeler won the Democratic primary going away, burying his closest opponent by more than fourteen thousand votes and polling more votes than his three opponents combined. Congressman Carl W. Riddick, a Fergus County rancher who represented eastern Montana in the U.S. House of Representatives, won the Republican primary.[39]

For the first time, Wheeler seemed to have the unqualified support of the frequently warring factions in the Montana Democratic Party. Even old foes like Governor

Stewart and Bruce Kremer took to the stump to speak for him. The state party convention stressed party unity, while, as Wheeler had predicted, the Anaconda Company concentrated on more pressing political problems with Governor Dixon in the state capitol. "The Company strategists realized they could not expect to openly attack me," Wheeler wrote in his memoirs, "and at the same time hope to achieve the Company's goal of electing a Democratic legislature which would defeat Governor Dixon's tax program." Wheeler did his part by avoiding attacks on the company.[40]

What a change from just two years earlier. Company-controlled newspapers were now covering Wheeler's speeches. Crowds at rallies, which now featured the candidate's politically astute wife, were big and enthusiastic—twenty-three hundred at one event in Billings, for example. The *Great Falls Tribune* noted that Wheeler received the greatest ovation accorded any politician in the city since William Jennings Bryan had campaigned there in 1900. Wheeler also benefited from a lackluster opponent who, even given his substantial political experience, proved an inept candidate. Attempting to appeal to the state's hard-pressed farmers, Riddick began referring to himself as "the only dirt farmer" in Congress, a claim that turned to dust when Democrats pointed out that Riddick did not own a single acre of farmland. Riddick's attempts to resurrect Wheeler's Nonpartisan League ties also backfired when it was discovered that, unlike Wheeler, Riddick actually had been a card-carrying, dues-paying member of the League. When Riddick attempted to attack Wheeler's performance as U.S. attorney, Judge George Bourquin released a public letter calling Wheeler an "able, diligent, and conscientious prosecutor in a most trying period in our country's history." The *Butte Miner,* a reliable barometer of the thinking of the state's business interests and a newspaper that had eviscerated Wheeler two years earlier, branded the Republican candidate an "intellectual pigmy." As in 1920, Montana's business interests were wedged between a political rock and an electoral hard spot, not particularly enthusiastic about Wheeler's political resurrection but calculating that he would likely win under any circumstances against the hapless Riddick. They may also have hoped that a strong showing by Wheeler would sweep enough Democratic legislators into office to thwart the Republican governor's agenda. It was a triple-bank-shot strategy that proved less than perfect, with Wheeler winning in a landslide and Republicans maintaining control of the state legislature, which served to nominally strengthen Governor Dixon's hand.[41]

Less than four years after being forced from office under fire and then after being buried in a historic landslide, Wheeler crushed his Republican opponent in the Senate race with a plurality of nearly 19,000 votes. He polled over 13,500 more votes than he had two years earlier. Counties that Wheeler lost by twenty points to Dixon in 1920 he won by twenty points against Riddick in 1922.[42]

The outcome left Wheeler jubilant, his victory amounting, he later wrote, to "a repudiation of the reactionary policies of the Harding Administration." Montana people, he wrote, "are progressive and want to join with progressives of other states in waging a battle for some constructive legislation in the interest of the average citizen." Wheeler specifically declined to say that his victory amounted to a defeat of Montana's corporate interests. It seemed that the old adversaries had either declared a truce, or, as his critics would maintain, Wheeler had sold out to the company. The truth is more nuanced. What took place was a calculating and uneasy political armistice that, as Richard Ruetten has written, was "marked by distrust on both sides." As historian John Anderson puts it, "The gambler in him had finally realized that in the Anaconda-owned political casino that was pre–New Deal Montana, the house always won, and so he had taken his substantial winning and walked away from the gambling tables, headed elsewhere to play for higher stakes." Wheeler subtly shifted his emphasis from localized Montana concerns to a larger, national agenda, from Montana industry to Wall Street. The radical impulses were downplayed but hardly abandoned, while a new independent progressive began to emerge.[43]

3 THE INVESTIGATION
AND THE FRAME-UP

Senator Wheeler is one of those political mistakes
the American people make from time to time.
—EDWARD DOHENY

The new senator from Montana was officially sworn in as a member of the U.S. Senate
in March 1923, but Congress immediately adjourned until December. For perhaps
the first time in his life B. K. Wheeler had time on his hands and few commitments.
Apparently on the spur of the moment, Wheeler wired his wife, Lulu, asking her to
arrange care for the children—there were now five youngsters in the family—and to
join him in New York City where they would sail for Europe for two months of travel and
sightseeing. For a politician who had devoted virtually all of his attention to domestic
concerns, the European tour was an eye-opener. It was the first of many foreign trips
Wheeler would take, usually with Lulu, during the 1920s and 1930s. In his first years
in the Senate, Wheeler visited Europe twice and traveled to Central America, China,
and the Philippines. The grand European tour in 1923 included a visit to the "Follies" in
Paris, where Lulu's Methodist sensibilities were genuinely shocked, and continued on
to Rome, Venice, Vienna, and finally Berlin. In the German capital a chance encounter
between the Wheelers and other American travelers prompted a spontaneous decision
to attempt to secure visas to enter Russia. In relatively short order the paperwork was
processed, and the Wheelers went by slow and uncomfortable train to Riga, Latvia,
and then on to Moscow, the capital of Lenin's new Soviet state. Wheeler was among
the first American politicians to visit Russia after the Bolshevik Revolution.[1]

Wheeler slept in a Moscow villa that had once been the home of the head of the
czar's sugar trust. During a meeting with Soviet foreign minister Georgy Chicherin,
an aristocratic Bolshevik who had spent years living outside Russia, Wheeler discussed
the issue of diplomatic recognition of the communist government and pressed the

Soviets to honor their debt commitments. Two years earlier Wheeler had been incorrectly dismissed by many in Montana as a dangerous radical, "Bolshevik Burt." Now, having seen the communist experiment firsthand, he concluded that the promised workers' paradise was an illusion and that the Soviet regime's centralized controls and harsh restrictions on free expression ensured its eventual if not immediate failure. Nonetheless, Wheeler encouraged pragmatic engagement with Moscow, convinced that the best policy for the United States would be to bury the Soviet Union in food and consumer goods produced in a free society. On that he was clearly well ahead of his time.[2]

Returning to Washington, Wheeler took up the cause of U.S. recognition of the Soviet government. "This Government is going to stay in power whether recognized or not," Wheeler told the New York Times, "and withholding recognition simply imports a hardship on the 160,000,000 million Russian people, which is contrary to enlightenment and humanitarian principles." Wheeler was convinced that the Soviet government was willing to discuss issues like the country's debt but that the country's leaders would react negatively if the United States simply made demands.[3]

Wheeler's position on diplomatic recognition of the Soviet government prompted harsh criticism in Montana. The Red Lodge, Montana, newspaper said that a politician with Wheeler's views ought to be deported, while the National Civic Foundation, a group of prominent business and political leaders opposed to Soviet recognition, said Wheeler had been taken in by communist propaganda. Undeterred, Wheeler spent the summer of 1923 making a series of speeches across Montana pressing the case that U.S. farmers could do well by doing good and feeding starving Russians.[4]

———

More than a year after his election, Wheeler finally engaged directly in legislative business when the Senate convened on December 3, 1923. He joined a fractious body—fifty-one Republicans, forty-three Democrats, and two Farmer-Laborites from Minnesota. Often the balance of power was held by a handful of progressives in both parties who, if they acted together, could influence Senate procedure and legislation. Majority Leader Henry Cabot Lodge, a Massachusetts Republican, experienced the power of the united progressive bloc in early December when from a back row seat the forty-year-old freshman senator from Montana stood at his desk and boomed out across the Senate floor, "I object!"

On his first day in the Senate, Wheeler courted controversy and immediately established himself as a maverick by refusing to agree to a unanimous consent request regarding a proposed slate of committee chairmen, an unusual objection by any senator but particularly unusual coming from a new senator. "From that moment,"

Washington State democrat Clarence Dill would remark, "Burton K. Wheeler was an outstanding character in the United States Senate." The *New York Times* predicted that Wheeler—"technically a Democrat," the newspaper said—would be difficult for his party or the Senate to control. Republicans confronted a similar problem in attempting to work around the "technically Republican" Robert M. La Follette, who, like Wheeler, was really an independent progressive. The *Times* forecast that Wheeler would be "second in command of the radical progressive group," in effect La Follette's deputy.[5]

Wheeler's objection to the unanimous consent request set off a series of tense discussions and a month of political maneuvering that resulted, for the first time in Senate history, in the majority party electing a member of the minority to serve as a committee chair. Republican senator Albert B. Cummins of Iowa, the senior member of the Senate, was, under seniority rules, entitled to become chair of the important Interstate Commerce Committee. But Cummins, who also served as Senate president pro tempore, had earned the enmity of Senate progressives for sponsoring the controversial Esch-Cummins Act (the Transportation Act of 1920), the measure Wheeler had denounced during his campaign as damaging to Montana farmers. Esch-Cummins was an attempt to end government management of the nation's railroads after World War I, but critics of the law, including Wheeler, maintained that its real purpose was to allow railroads to dramatically increase freight rates. The law also contained a "no strike" provision that, as one historian has noted, "came dangerously close to requiring... government arbitration of labor disputes—a thing that in an era of conservative federal administration would hold little promise for workers."[6]

Even before the Senate had convened in 1923, the progressive bloc, led by La Follette, had pressured Cummins to surrender his committee chairmanship while retaining the position of president pro tempore. If Cummins had agreed, La Follette, the ranking Republican on the committee, would have become chairman, and the committee would have had a leader more sympathetic to labor and more skeptical than Cummins of the railroads. It was a shrewd political gambit, but the Iowa senator refused to step aside, insisting he had a right to continue hold both positions. (The president pro tempore job had become more powerful and lucrative following President Harding's death in August. Calvin Coolidge became president and the vice presidency was left vacant. By continuing in the role of Senate president, Cummins could command the higher salary of the vice president.)

Efforts to arrive at a compromise over the chairmanship involved hours of quiet talks and bargaining among senators, and by the time Wheeler voiced his objection to the unanimous consent request the progressives were prepared to concede defeat, convinced that they had failed in the effort to make La Follette chairman. However, Wheeler, the untested and inexperienced freshman, was not convinced that the moment had arrived to abandon the fight, and he insisted on a vote on whether Cummins should retain the chairmanship of the committee.[7]

"My theory was that the progressive Republicans could never vote for Cummins," Wheeler said, "and that the Democrats would be obliged to vote for their senior member on the Interstate Commerce Committee, the colorful Ellison D. ('Cotton Ed') Smith of South Carolina. I made it clear that this was not a personal fight against Cummins but an ideological one." Wheeler also knew that Smith, the Democrat, opposed the controversial railroad legislation that carried Cummins's name and that Smith might be acceptable as chairman to Republican progressives in the Senate. Despite his inexperience, Wheeler had astutely assessed the internal politics of the Senate.[8]

The standoff over the chairmanship continued for weeks, with regular Republicans, who disliked La Follette, refusing to budge and Republican progressives holding out for their leader or at least another progressive. Democrats also held firm in "fear of Wheeler's tongue," one newspaper reported. La Follette, who had been confined to his sick bed during much of the ruckus, finally returned to the Senate floor in early January 1924 and convinced five Republican progressives to switch their votes to support Democrat Smith. The thirty-second vote on the chairmanship broke the deadlock and also made Senate history and shattered precedent. Smith, a member of the minority, became chairman. La Follette publicly gave Wheeler a "large share of the credit for the successful issue of the Progressive fight." The battle over the Interstate Commerce Committee leadership marked the beginning of the La Follette-Wheeler political friendship, with Wheeler often saying that he considered the Wisconsin senator "one of this country's greatest statesmen." Wheeler became a member of the Interstate Commerce Committee, a perfect vantage point to observe the effects of his political handiwork and the first step on the path to his own chairmanship of the committee.[9]

Wheeler's auspicious start in the Senate began to establish his national profile. His next move, leading an investigation involving the attorney general of the United States, made the rookie senator one of Washington's most prominent and controversial politicians virtually overnight.

———

"When the corruption in the Harding Administration was first exposed," historians Michael Genovese and Victoria Farrar-Myers write, "American humorist Will Rogers called it the 'great morality panic of 1924.' It would, in the end, be much more than that. Indeed, during and immediately after Harding's brief presidential tenure, a trail of fraud, bribery, criminal conspiracy, cover-up, and even suicide became ever more visible."[10]

Warren Harding's most significant contribution to the nation's political history may be his embarrassments. Two major congressional investigations, each conducted by a

Attorney General Harry Daugherty, Wheeler's target in
his 1924 investigation of corruption at the U.S. Justice
Department. (*Library of Congress Prints and Photographs
Division Washington, D.C.*)

Montana senator from the minority party, led to the resignation of Harding cabinet
officers. While Tom Walsh unraveled the administration's corruption in handling
oil leases in Wyoming—the Teapot Dome scandal—Wheeler set out to examine the
misdeeds concocted by members of the "Ohio Gang," the collection of scoundrels,
hacks, and political hangers-on that Harding brought with him into the government,
particularly the Justice Department.

Attorney General Harry Micajah Daugherty, the man more responsible than any
other for helping Warren Harding reach the White House, was the leader of the Ohio
Gang and a Harding confidant. A jowly small-time Ohio lawyer with a gruff demeanor,
Daugherty had been mostly unsuccessful as a political candidate but was a skilled
backroom political operator. "Daugherty's insight into men was something of an art,"
historian Robert Murray has said. "Instinctively he knew just when to cajole, when to
bluster, when to seize the initiative, when to retreat."[11]

Daugherty was among the first, and among the few, who had identified a presidential
opening for his handsome, genial friend, Warren Harding, when Harding was relatively
unknown. Daugherty has often been credited with predicting that Harding's selection

as the Republican presidential candidate in 1920 would take place in a "smoke-filled room" in the Blackstone Hotel in Chicago. There was no "smoke-filled room," and Daugherty's actual quotation is not quite as colorful, if no less prescient. "I don't expect Senator Harding to be nominated on the first, second, or third ballot," Daugherty said. "But I think we can well afford to take chances that about eleven minutes after two o'clock on Friday morning at the convention, when fifteen or twenty men, somewhat weary, are sitting around a table, some one will say, 'Who will we nominate?' At that decisive time the friends of Senator Harding can suggest him and afford to abide by the result." Executing a political strategy devised primarily by Daugherty, who served as his campaign manager, Harding captured the nomination over more seasoned and serious opponents. With the country longing for a "return to normalcy," Harding's promises for this helped ensure a landslide win.[12]

Once installed as attorney general, Daugherty almost immediately came under fire for his slipshod management of the Justice Department and for the staff he installed around him. Daugherty was also widely criticized for favoring his political friends and ruthlessly punishing his enemies. During his campaign for the Senate in 1922, Wheeler frequently raised the issue of corruption at the Justice Department under Daugherty and suggested that an investigation was necessary. Others in Congress agreed. La Follette criticized Daugherty for not aggressively prosecuting Chicago meat packers accused of corrupt practices. Senator Thaddeus H. Caraway, an Arkansas Democrat, charged that Daugherty had received $25,000 for improperly arranging the release of a prisoner from a federal penitentiary. Daugherty was even attacked by Cabinet colleagues, commerce secretary Herbert Hoover included, for seeking a federal court injunction against striking railroad workers that "was so unfair that it bordered on the malicious." Minnesota Republican congressman Oscar E. Keller, demonstrating growing GOP concern about Daugherty, introduced an impeachment resolution detailing a long list of the attorney general's alleged misdeeds, including failure to prosecute war fraud cases, lavishing special favors on corporations and individuals, and appointing an unscrupulous head of the Bureau of Investigation. Keller's effort failed to gain traction largely because he failed to substantiate his allegations but also because Daugherty continued to enjoy the friendship and confidence of Harding. Daugherty retaliated by ordering Justice Department agents to search Keller's office in hopes of finding incriminating material.[13]

With calls for various investigations mounting and some newspapers demanding Daugherty's resignation, Harding seemed oblivious to the political damage his long-time pal was causing him. Daugherty too seemed unmoved by the criticism, telling the *New York Times* in mid-1922: "I wouldn't have given 30 cents for the office of Attorney General, but I wouldn't surrender it for a million dollars."[14]

Under near constant attack, the attorney general maintained a good front, but the pressure was obviously affecting him. Daugherty's biographer James Giglio writes that by early 1923, "Overwork and mental strain taxed his nervous system and weakened him to the point that he could no longer do his job." Suffering from high blood pressure and close to a breakdown, Daugherty would have been well advised to step down, but he refused to consider this. Then in July 1923 the bottom dropped out of Daugherty's political life when Harding fell ill and died. It is hard to fathom now, given subsequent assessments of Harding's presidency, but his death occasioned great national mourning, and his policies and personal style received widespread praise. Sensing the levels of public goodwill toward the dead president, Calvin Coolidge, who became president, pledged to maintain his predecessor's approach to foreign and domestic affairs and vowed to retain Harding's cabinet, including the controversial attorney general.[15]

Scant attention was paid by either Coolidge or Republican leaders in Congress to demands by Wheeler and others that Daugherty resign. Typical for him, Wheeler refused to let up. He proposed a Senate resolution demanding that Coolidge fire his attorney general. Senate Republican leaders publicly dismissed the resolution as nothing more than a partisan attack, even as several influential GOP senators—William E. Borah of Idaho and Henry Cabot Lodge among them—quietly pressured Coolidge, urging that he could put an end to the controversy by dismissing Daugherty. Coolidge acknowledged the pressure in a letter to a Republican advisor but stuck by the attorney general. "I am satisfied that you are right," Coolidge wrote. "The people would be pleased, the party would be helped, my campaign would be advanced, by the summary removal of Mr. Daugherty." But, Coolidge continued, "we have to bear that burden. Regarding being afraid to dismiss Mr. Daugherty, I can assure you that if the attorney general does any act I regard as wrong while I am president, he will be removed."[16]

Unable to force the president to act, Wheeler adopted a new tactic and began a campaign to build support for a Senate investigation. After consulting with La Follette, he proposed a resolution calling for the Senate Judiciary Committee to investigate the Justice Department and Daugherty specifically for failing to pursue alleged antitrust violations and for taking no action against former Interior Secretary Albert Fall and his alleged coconspirators in the Teapot Dome affair. Again Wheeler's effort stalled, but again he kept pushing, demanding early in 1924 that the Senate create a special five-member select committee to investigate Daugherty. Wheeler's proposal, by suggesting the specific membership of the special committee—including himself—violated Senate protocol. Appointments to the kind of committee Wheeler was suggesting, he was reminded by old Senate hands, was a prerogative reserved for the Senate's presiding officer. Again the Montanan was not deterred and pressed ahead, certain that a link existed between Daugherty and the oil-leasing scandal still under investigation by Walsh.[17]

"Recently when the oil scandal first developed it appears the Attorney General's name was mixed in it," Wheeler said as he pushed for the Senate investigation. "It appears, if you please, that he was a friend of Ned McLean [one of the alleged conspirators with Interior Secretary Fall]. Everybody knows that he is a friend of [Edward] Doheny [another oil speculator implicated in the scandal]. Everybody knows that these three men met in the apartment of the Attorney General from time to time. Everybody knows that Jess Smith [a close Daugherty friend], who was brought from the State of Ohio and had an office in the Department of Justice, and who was not on the payroll, was accepting cases that arose in the Department of Justice."[18]

For weeks Daugherty simply ignored the growing tempest in the Senate. But eventually the political pressure became too great for even the dismissive Daugherty, and he began to mount a defense and issued a sweeping denial of any impropriety. Daugherty next threatened, "If a few of these Senators don't resign today," Daugherty blustered, "I may have a statement to make that will cause some splash in Washington."[19]

Newspapers reporters, Daugherty suggested, would be prudent to ignore allegations of corruption in the Justice Department and concentrate instead on the motives of his accusers. What Wheeler really desired by attempting to bring him down, Daugherty asserted, was to push a communist agenda—the old smear was back—that would ultimately bring down the government. Daugherty called Wheeler "the Communist leader of the Senate" and insisted that attacks on him were not the work of a "responsible political party," since "Wheeler is no more a Democrat than Stalin, his comrade in Moscow."[20]

Daugherty's suggestion that Wheeler was doing Moscow's bidding was a monumental red herring, so outrageous a claim that it likely damaged Daugherty's case more than it impugned Wheeler's motives. Still, Wheeler was furious. Daugherty was threatening the Senate, Wheeler said, and he wondered, "which one of the Members of the Senate he thinks he has something on, that he can force to resign." He would find out rather quickly.[21]

From the moment Daugherty learned that Wheeler was close to securing sufficient Senate support for a full-blown investigation of his department and of his own conduct, the attorney general went on the attack. Daugherty ordered the Bureau of Investigation (predecessor of the FBI) to dig up dirt on Wheeler, and he mobilized the substantial resources of the Republican National Committee in an effort to smear, intimidate, and silence Wheeler and remove him from the Senate. The resulting attack on the character and integrity of a U.S. senator, including the widespread misuse of the power of the Justice Department, has been rivaled on few occasions in American history.

Daugherty's most outspoken Republican critic, Senator Borah, went to the White House in late January 1924 expecting to talk one-on-one with Coolidge about Daugherty's resignation, but to Borah's surprise the attorney general was there for the meeting. "Don't let my presence embarrass you," Daugherty snapped at Borah, a successful trial lawyer before his election to the Senate in 1906. "I think I should be the least embarrassed person here," Borah responded. The two men raised their voices as they jousted back and forth regarding Daugherty's job, with Coolidge quietly listening while puffing on a cigar. Daugherty eventually stormed out of the meeting, still refusing to resign, Coolidge having refused to demand that he do so. Other prominent Republicans, including the widely respected secretary of state, Charles Evans Hughes, also implored the president to rid himself of his troubled attorney general. Hughes went so far as to suggest to Coolidge that could he arrange for all Cabinet members to submit their resignations, allowing Coolidge to pick and chose who would remain. "No, don't do that," Coolidge protested, "it might leave me alone with Daugherty."[22]

Republican opposition to Wheeler's demand for a Senate investigation collapsed in the wake of Borah's White House visit, and on March 1, 1924, a resolution authorizing a special committee to investigate the Department of Justice passed the Senate by a margin of sixty-six to one. Assisted by La Follette's quiet coaching, Wheeler succeeded in organizing the investigative committee precisely as he wanted. With Republicans in control of the Senate, a Republican would chair the new committee, and Smith Brookhart, a progressive Republican from Iowa and no friend of Harding or Daugherty, was named chair. Wesley L. Jones of Washington, a moderate, and George H. Moses, a conservative from New Hampshire, were appointed as additional Republican members. Apparently La Follette suggested that Moses should serve in order to avoid criticism that the committee was stacked with Daugherty opponents. The Democratic members were Henry F. Ashurst, an independent-minded former prosecutor from Arizona, and Wheeler. While Republicans technically controlled the committee, an anti-Daugherty majority, led by Wheeler, would largely determine how the investigation would unfold. Daugherty immediately hired legal counsel, and his lawyer demanded that he be able to subpoena and cross-examine witness, but Brookhart granted only limited rights to cross-examination and said any subpoenas would be issued by the committee. Brookhart officially chaired the committee, but newspaper reports soon referred to the panel as "the Wheeler Committee," since it was clear that the Montana senator would effectively conduct the investigation or, as some pro-administration newspapers called it, the "persecution."[23]

Wheeler had few resources with which to pursue the investigation. Little staff was provided the committee, and even office space was meager. Nonetheless, comfortable again in the role of prosecutor, Wheeler launched aggressively into the probe, lining up witnesses and attempting to compel Daugherty to produce documents. Unlike Walsh's plodding, systematic, document-driven probe of the oil-leasing scandals, which was finally coming to an end after two years of work, Wheeler's investigation would be propelled by witnesses—a colorful, quotable, circus-like cast of characters. Wheeler was criticized at the time, and has been since, for wanting to "duplicate the success of his fellow Montanan" by ferreting out Harding administration corruption but doing so with a much more theatrical and undisciplined approach than Walsh's. It is legitimate criticism. The investigation at times involved more gaudy political showmanship than dogged investigation. Due process and conclusive evidence frequently gave way to investigative liberties that led to sensational headlines.[24]

A case in point was Wheeler's handling of California millionaire oilman Edward Doheny. Shortly before the hearings convened, Wheeler said he intended to show a connection between figures like Doheny, who were implicated in the Teapot Dome scandal, and wrongdoing at the Justice Department. Wheeler was never able to conclusively establish the link, and Doheny, who amazingly was later acquitted of offering the $100,000 bribe for government oil leases that Secretary Fall was convicted of receiving, reacted with fury. "Senator Wheeler is one of those political mistakes the American people make from time to time," Doheny fumed. "He is merely the deplorable result of a wave of blind radicalism which some time ago swept the State of Montana. He is far more fit to sit in the Soviet parliament in Moscow than in the Senate of the United States." Wheeler had been called worse, of course, and criticism of the investigation and his methods seems only to have increased his determination to expose Daugherty's corruption.[25]

The public phase of the investigation opened on March 12, 1924, in room 410 of the Senate Office Building. Wheeler arranged for the best—or at least the most scandalous—to come first, stage-managing the appearance of the investigation's most sensational witness. Wheeler described the woman as "a statuesque redhead, with the figure of a showgirl." Roxy Stinson, the divorced wife of Daugherty's longtime Ohio crony and frequent Harding golf companion Jess Smith, proved to be more than a comely attraction for the press photographers.[26]

Jess Smith, before he died under decidedly suspicious circumstances in May 1923, had been Daugherty's closest friend and also his roommate at Washington's Wardman Park Hotel. The official explanation for Smith's death was suicide by gunshot wound, a story many of Smith's friends found difficult to accept because they remembered him frequently mentioning his strong dislike of firearms. Adding to suspicion of foul play was the detail that right-handed Smith had reportedly shot himself in the left temple. Also, after the fatal gunshot wound, Smith had somehow managed to fit his head into a wastebasket in his bathroom. It was also deemed curious that one of the first people on the scene after Smith's alleged suicide was Bureau of Investigation director William J. Burns, who did live, however, downstairs from Smith's apartment. Burns then promptly misplaced the suicide—or murder—weapon. No autopsy was performed on Smith, and his body was sent quickly back to Ohio for burial. It also came to light that Smith had destroyed his personal papers before his death, burning everything but leaving behind a will written in his own hand and placed on the desk in his room. Smith, it was said, had suffered a variety of physical ailments but had also been deeply despondent in the days before his death about allegations of corruption in the Harding administration, allegations that seemed to be getting ever closer to implicating his friend Daugherty and perhaps even the president. While never an employee of the Justice Department, Smith kept a desk outside the attorney general's office and was generally regarded as Daugherty's gatekeeper, errand boy, and chief political operator. Naturally, some suggested that Jess Smith simply knew too much about corruption in the administration and had "been taken care of" to prevent him talking about all he knew.[27]

Smith's death, coming just a few months before Harding's own death, was a stunning development that should have provided Harding with gruesome, conclusive evidence that things were badly off the rails at the Justice Department and that the president's grip on his own political fortunes was being undone by what Harding once called "my God-damned friends." Now, facilitated by Senator Wheeler from Montana, Smith's ex-wife stepped out of the shadows to answer Wheeler's questions about just what those friends of the president had been doing.[28]

———

Wheeler recounted many years later that he had been delighted upon hearing that Roxy Stinson possessed intimate knowledge of the secret shenanigans of Harding, Daugherty, and their Ohio friends. Immediately upon learning about Stinson and what she might tell the Senate committee, Wheeler boarded a train for Columbus, Ohio, to personally deliver a subpoena and escort Stinson quietly to Washington so that she could be questioned in public session. Wheeler checked his star witness into the Washington Hotel across the street from the White House and left his Senate office manager and sister, Maude Mitchell, with Stinson, both to keep an eye on her and to keep her away from any Daugherty associates who might try to intimidate her before she could offer what Wheeler expected would be sensational testimony.[29]

Under Wheeler's gentle prodding, Stinson described in detail what could only be described as her unusual relationship with her ex-husband. "Wearing rimless glasses and looking somewhat like a schoolmarm—a contrived image which enhanced her credibility before the committee," and with reporters craning to catch every word,

Roxy Stinson, ex-wife of a member of Warren Harding's
"Ohio Gang," was a sensational witness in Wheeler's Justice
Department investigation. (*Library of Congress Prints and
Photographs Division, Washington, D.C.*)

Stinson unspooled a story worthy of a supermarket tabloid. Even after her marriage
to Smith broke up, Stinson told Wheeler, Smith regularly visited her in Ohio and
continued to share intimate details of his friendship with his roommate, the attorney
general of the United States. Stinson testified to "deals" that Daugherty and Smith
had been cashing in on, including an audacious scam to exhibit nationwide a film
of the 1921 world heavyweight championship fight between Jack Dempsey and the
French champion Georges Carpentier. Under interstate commerce rules of the day
the fight film could not legally be shipped from state to state, but, as Wheeler said,
"the imaginative Daugherty clique found a loophole."[30]

Stinson said that Smith claimed that he and Daugherty had made a great deal of
money on the fight film because they had been able to find exhibitors in many states
who were willing to pay a small fine for receiving an illegal shipment of the film in

exchange for being able to screen the fight in front of a paying audience. In turn, Daugherty and Smith would pocket a "fee" for helping make the arrangements. In some states, Stinson said, Daugherty and Smith would find a friendly judge who would quietly "fix," with a wink and a nod, any legal problems associated with screening the film. Stinson told Wheeler that her ex-husband also trafficked in bootleg liquor, helped Daugherty arrange paroles of federal prisoners for a price, and participated in various kickback schemes.

Stinson testified that Daugherty's brother, Mally S. Daugherty, an Ohio banker with an unforgettable name, had cheated her out of $11,000 that her ex-husband had deposited for her use before his death. Daugherty, it was alleged, also tried to frame Stinson. Before being subpoenaed by Wheeler, but knowing that she might be required to testify, Daugherty produced "evidence" of her promiscuity. A male friend of Stinson's, apparently paid by Daugherty, asked Stinson to meet him at a Cleveland hotel allegedly to discuss a business opportunity. The man, A. L. Fink, signed the hotel register as if he and Stinson were married and sharing the same room. This was done," James Giglio says, to have the ability to blackmail Stinson into withholding her testimony before Wheeler's committee. Stinson's testimony, as well as the documents she shared, failed to incontrovertibly show a connection between the attorney general and the mountain of circumstantial evidence, not to mention salacious rumors, suggesting Justice Department and personal corruption. There certainly was little in Stinson's testimony that might have stood up in court, and indeed Daugherty was never convicted of anything. Stinson's motives for testifying as she did were also more than a bit suspect. Still, Wheeler believed the copious amounts of smoke proved the existence of a fire, and it helped that Stinson's testimony was delivered with just enough poise, conviction, and compelling detail to make it seem credible. She was questioned for five sensational days, and her testimony was daily front-page news across the nation.[31]

Wheeler's role in making the case against Daugherty gave the young senator his first taste of what life can be like in the glare of unrelenting national press attention. For the rest of his Senate career Wheeler would never be long out of the national spotlight. "Senator Wheeler is a clean-cut, energetic, youngish man, with an interesting trace of the Yankee accent of the Massachusetts in which he was born," *Collier's* magazine reported during the investigation. "He has a reputation in Montana as a vigorous prosecutor, and evidently does not intend that it shall acquire rust. Looked at from the purely artistic point of view, he overstresses his points a bit, and has too much of the air of always being about to hurl the lie into somebody's teeth." The *New Republic* described Wheeler as "an outdoor sort . . . with wind-roughened cheeks, thin hair of nondescript color, and a general appearance of having been battered by life and of having given it something of a battering in return. He assumes easy western attitudes as he works—now with a whole fist jammed into the armhole of his waistcoat, now standing up with one foot on his chair, and elbow on his knee and the index finger of that hand erect and wagging at the witness."[32]

Republicans, concerned about the damage Wheeler's investigation might be doing Coolidge's election prospects in 1924 and mindful that Wheeler's national stature was growing, mounted a vigorous counterattack, slamming Wheeler and his investigation. The Republican National Committee carefully orchestrated the campaign, with one of its news releases headed: "What Everybody Should Know About Senator Wheeler and His Montana Gang." The attack piece alleged that during the war Montana "became a hotbed of treason and sedition" because U.S. Attorney Wheeler had failed to prosecute war protesters and other "radicals."[33]

The *Los Angeles Times*, at the time a reliable mouthpiece for the Republican Party, was particularly vigorous in denouncing Wheeler, calling him a traitor and offering a rehash of old Montana allegations. "Senator Wheeler's record as Federal district attorney in Montana during the war reminds one of that of Benedict Arnold. He lent aid and comfort to disloyalists, to the IWW that sought to destroy our government through violent means.... Preparing himself for his assault on representative government in the United States, Senator Wheeler went to Russia to study the methods of the Soviets ... and he returned equipped with Soviet ammunition for his raid on the Attorney General's office." The Republican assault on Wheeler no doubt helped blunt any political damage the Daugherty affair inflicted on the still-new Coolidge administration, but the president was also mostly successful in distancing himself from the storm raging around the attorney general. However, once Wheeler's investigation began to preoccupy Washington and became daily fodder for news coverage, Daugherty found he had few defenders in Congress and no reservoir of goodwill to sustain him in the capital.[34]

The investigation's next astounding witness was Gaston B. Means, a special agent for the Department of Justice, a former private detective and one-time agent for the German government. One account described Means as "round and ruddy with a head too large for his mobile face." Another said Means was "a sleuth, a professional investigator, and wrecker of reputations." He was all that and more, a truly extraordinary character, with emphasis on "character." Following the brief notoriety he gained as a witness before Wheeler's committee, Means spent most of the rest of his life in and out of federal prisons, finally dying behind bars in 1937. Among other exploits, Means wrote a sensational book claiming that Harding had been murdered. He also did jail time after being convicted of providing false information to investigators of the Lindbergh kidnapping case in the 1930s. Means appeared before Wheeler's committee while under indictment for mail fraud and violation of Prohibition laws. Given his reputation, Means could in no way be considered a credible witness, but his testimony, like that of Roxy Stinson, was convincing enough to further damage the attorney general's standing.[35]

Through many committee sessions Means, officially a witness, sat near Wheeler, smiling in "constant, irrepressible glee," as one account put it, ready to lean forward and whisper his "advice and suggestions" to the senator. Means's testimony corroborated many of the tawdry tales Stinson had told the committee, most importantly confirming that Jess Smith was a key figure, along with Daugherty, in a variety of nefarious schemes. At one point Means told Wheeler off-handedly that he would gladly work for anyone with money, "just like a lawyer." He boasted that he had been indicted for every crime in the book, including murder, but had never been convicted. Wheeler pressed him to explain allegations that while under orders from the Justice Department he had ransacked the offices of members of Congress searching for information that Daugherty might use against his political enemies. Means confirmed that he had indeed done such things.

"Haven't been through mine, have you?" Wheeler asked.

"No, but I will, sir, if someone will assign me to it," Means replied.

Wheeler later claimed that his Senate office had been "rifled during the hearings on several occasions," and there were credible reports that Justice Department operatives were busy in other parts of the Senate Office Building where the offices of other members of the committee were also ransacked.[36]

As shocking and newsworthy as the testimony of Stinson and Means was, it still only indirectly implicated Harry Daugherty. The one common thread connecting all the testimony was a dead man, Jess Smith, who was unable to answer for himself. Wheeler's questioning certainly confirmed that Smith had been Daugherty's principal agent and that Daugherty had surrounded himself with a host of unsavory characters. As historian Richard Ruetten has noted, "Apparently, Wheeler's strategy was to prove Smith's criminality, show the intimate relations that existed between Smith and Daugherty, and thereby leave the implication of Daugherty's guilt by association." Wheeler's approach, unconventional and occasionally slipshod, was his only feasible option while investigating an attorney general who refused to participate in the inquiry and took extraordinary steps to cover his tracks. The evidence may have been circumstantial, but it was still compelling. "A half-a-dozen trails of corruption" lead straight to Daugherty, Bruce Bliven wrote in the *New Republic*. The attorney general's intimate associates were "in turn the intimate associates of bootleggers, illicit drug vendors, [and] criminal conspirators" who bribed their way to the prevention of their prosecution.[37]

Coolidge, for so long steadfastly stubborn and reluctant to act on matters implicating his attorney general, finally reached the breaking point two weeks into the Senate
hearings and fired Daugherty. The attorney general was ultimately caught in the
web of his own rhetoric as much as by any evidence Wheeler produced. Daugherty
originally promised to cooperate fully with Senate investigators, but when Brookhart
formally requested documents related to the Justice Department, the attorney general
refused to turn them over. Daugherty's explanation sounded eerily like that of every
government official, before or since, who has tried to keep potentially damaging
government documents out of the hands of investigators. "These reports [sought by
Brookhart] are a part of the intelligence files of the Bureau of Investigation which are
very confidential in their nature and their presentation . . . would be inimical to the
public interest," Daugherty said.[38]

Three days after Daugherty wrote Brookhart, refusing to produce documents,
Coolidge wrote his own letter to Daugherty requesting his resignation. It had become
clear, Coolidge wrote, "that you are placed in two positions, one your personal interest,
the other your office of Attorney General, which may be in conflict." Coolidge assured
Daugherty that he was not questioning his "fairness or integrity," but of course he was.
It was a perfectly acceptable, if narrowly technical, reason for Coolidge to rid himself
of a troublesome associate. Chief Justice William Howard Taft, watching the entire
affair unfold, commented that Coolidge's letter to Daugherty was the letter of a lawyer.
But Coolidge's demand was also timely, since his 1924 election campaign was about
to begin in earnest. Daugherty complied with the resignation request but not before
chastising Coolidge for establishing a "dangerous doctrine" that would threaten to
drive others from government service, "no matter how malicious and groundless" the
charges against them might be. That would have been a better argument had Daugherty
enjoyed any support on Capitol Hill, which clearly he did not. Members of Congress
too had made up their minds about the attorney general.[39]

Daugherty left Washington immediately, apparently intent on reestablishing his
law practice in Ohio, but his rapid departure did not prevent the Senate from voting
70–2 to censure him. From the friendlier confines of Columbus, Ohio, the former
attorney general took a parting shot at the senator from Montana, again accusing
Wheeler of being a dupe of communists. The files he had refused to surrender to the
Senate committee, Daugherty said, contained "abundant proof of the plans, purposes
and hellish designs of the Communist International." "Bear in mind," Daugherty
continued, "that the files . . . were demanded by Brookhart and Wheeler, two United
States senators who spent last summer in Russia with their Soviet friends."[40]

Public reaction to Daugherty's departure was generally relief, with the *New York
Times* saying that he "went not one day too soon." The *Cleveland Press* called the

resignation inevitable. The pressure of public opinion, the newspaper said, had become too great "for even this hardened, dogged veteran, whose contempt for public opinion enabled him to withstand the shocks that would have been politically fatal to most men."[41]

It is possible to conclude that political expediency and partisan motives, a desire to wrap the "Harding scandals" around Coolidge's neck and harm his election prospects in 1924, drove Wheeler's investigation of the Justice Department. Coolidge biographer Robert Sobel concludes this, saying that Wheeler's real target was Coolidge, but that assertion is belied by Wheeler's extensive criticism of Daugherty and Justice Department corruption during his Senate campaign in 1922, while Coolidge was still vice president. Still, Wheeler and other detractors believed that Coolidge knew about the corruption and even abetted the wrongdoing until it became a political embarrassment.

It is fair to ask whether Wheeler relied too much on sensational testimony from witnesses like Roxy Stinson and Gaston Means, who had ample reason to shade the truth or invent facts. Wheeler's investigative methods suffer in comparison to Walsh's careful and systematic probe of Teapot Dome, which carefully accumulated facts by assembling critical documents and following the money trail. Wheeler was, with some fairness, accused of employing the "dragnet" method of investigation. One Harding biographer says Wheeler "brought in an enormous mass of undigested, ill-assorted testimony, some of which had the most tenuous connection with the subject." Robert K. Murray, in his sympathetic biography of Harding, criticizes Wheeler's attraction to the sensational. "Obviously the fatal flaw in Wheeler's investigation was the nature of his important witnesses," including a bootlegger, a divorcée with questionable motives, and an admitted crook. Yet Murray concludes, "There was just enough truth hidden among all the lies to cause legitimate suspicion."[42]

Wheeler's counter to criticism of his handling of the investigation was typically blunt. "Daugherty didn't associate with preachers," he said. "The witnesses were not friends of the committee. They were called because they had dealings with Daugherty and his close associates. The character of the witnesses in a hearing of this kind is determined largely by the character of the central figure."[43]

Subsequent events, including extensive efforts to frame Wheeler and drive him from public office, would verify significant abuse of power and corruption involving Harry Daugherty.

———

Daugherty never testified on his own behalf, and it was undoubtedly a mistake on Wheeler's part not to attempt to compel his testimony. When Wheeler did belatedly ask Daugherty to appear before the special committee, perhaps to counter Daugherty's argument that he had not been afforded a chance to confront his accusers, Daugherty refused, citing as an excuse legal problems confronting his brother. That flimsy evasion further eroded Daugherty's credibility and confirmed the widespread impression that he had a good deal to hide.[44]

Roxy Stinson soon vanished from public view, eventually remarried, and refused all overtures to speak again publicly about her knowledge of the Harding scandals. She occasionally hinted that she knew a good deal more than she had told Wheeler, but a rumored cache of sensational papers she had reportedly hidden in a bank vault never materialized after her death in 1973. As for the dependably unreliable Gaston Means, he later, as Richard Ruetten colorfully puts it, "repudiated his testimony, disavowed his repudiation, retracted his disavowal, and finally landed in prison, a vivid testimonial of his character." Wheeler would remark years later that Means "had a brilliant mind and could have distinguished himself if he had used it in constructive channels. But you never knew when he was lying."[45]

Widely respected Republican newspaper editor William Allen White, who knew all the principal players personally, perhaps best summarized the general sentiment regarding Daugherty and the scandals when he wrote a generation later that "cheap and sometimes corrupt little men were using the powerful leverage of Daugherty's name for unbelievably corrupt semipublic transactions. The spy service of the Department of Justice was set upon those who protested against the dubious transactions of the Attorney General, or indeed upon those who protested against any irregular practices anywhere in the Federal government."[46]

———

Coolidge accepted Daugherty's resignation on March 28, 1924, and on April 2 Harlan Fiske Stone, the former dean of the Columbia University Law School, was nominated as the new attorney general. Hugely respected in legal and business circles, Stone was a sophisticated lawyer who would later distinguish himself as the chief justice of the U.S. Supreme Court. Stone's first task in his new job was to polish the tarnished image of the Justice Department and, not incidentally, enhance Coolidge's election prospects. Stone soon discovered that he had also been bequeathed an investigation, well under way in Montana, that seemed destined to implicate Wheeler in his own corruption scandal. On April 8, days after the Senate confirmed Stone as attorney general and while the Senate investigation of the Justice Department continued, Wheeler was indicted by a federal grand jury in Great Falls, Montana. He was not entirely surprised, having received a tip that the Justice Department was up to something in Montana. Still, "it was the first time in my life," he would write, "that I had been accused of doing something illegal."[47]

The Montana indictment involved three damaging allegations. Wheeler was accused of unlawfully agreeing to "receive a large sum of money" following his election to the Senate in exchange for providing legal services to a client related to business before the Department of the Interior and the General Land Office. Two additional counts related directly to the first allegation and charged that Wheeler had received two separate $2,000 payments in connection with legal services rendered for a client before federal agencies. Such activities by a sitting U.S. senator were a violation of federal law, which stated: "No Senator, Representative, or Delegate, after his election and during his continuance in office ... shall receive ... any compensation ... for any services rendered ... in relation to any proceeding, contract, claim, controversy, charge, accusation, arrest, or other matter or thing in which the United States is a party."[48]

Wheeler was specifically accused of receiving money in return for legal services in connection with oil and gas prospecting leases under the control of the Department of the Interior. His client, Gordon Campbell, a Montana oilman, geologist, and speculator, had been doing oil exploration work since 1920 near Kevin, Montana, and when Campbell finally struck oil in 1922 he was required, under regulations then in effect, to obtain federal permits and leases. The grand jury indictment charged that Wheeler illegally agreed to represent Campbell in obtaining the necessary permits and leases.[49]

The indictment created a national media sensation. Republicans and Republican-leaning newspapers gloried in the irony of Daugherty's "persecutor" being charged with the very offense that the former attorney general was alleged to have committed: improperly benefiting from his public office. The *St. Paul Dispatch* observed that Wheeler "stands in exactly the same relation to these charges that Mr. Daugherty did to those brought against him by Senator Wheeler when the investigation opened." The newspaper added, "Daugherty declared that he had been framed for political and other reasons" and Wheeler now "declared that he had been framed for political and other reasons." The *New York Times,* saying that Wheeler's arrest was imminent, quoted sources saying the indictment had nothing to do with the Daugherty investigation. Not everyone agreed. The *Brooklyn Eagle* saw the indictment as pure payback for Wheeler's investigation. "The motive inspiring the prosecution of Senator Wheeler was purely political," the paper said. "There was nobody behind the prosecution except the narrow partizan [sic] influences that instigated it. Never would it have been undertaken except for the fact that the committee, of which Senator Wheeler was the guiding spirit, was delving into affairs which these same partizan influences desired to keep undercover."[50]

The day after the indictment was handed down, Wheeler stood on the Senate floor to defend his integrity and begin a fight to save his political career. Daugherty was clearly behind the indictment, Wheeler said, and he challenged the Senate to conduct its own investigation of his conduct, a risky strategy, but one that ultimately benefited Wheeler immensely. The Montana indictment, he told the Senate, was the "culmination of a campaign, backed by the Republican National Committee, to get me because of my activities . . . in connection with the graft and corruption in the Department of Justice." Wheeler noted that the foreman of the Great Falls grand jury, N. T. Lease, was a longtime political foe who, Wheeler said, was "one of the most bitter political enemies I have in the state." Lease, the one-time mayor of Great Falls, had been a member of the Montana Council of Defense when that group interrogated Wheeler while he served as U.S. attorney.[51]

Notwithstanding Wheeler's assessment of the motives behind his indictment, the circumstances of his legal engagement with Gordon Campbell seemed both complicated and problematic. When Campbell retained Wheeler to represent him late in 1922, his business affairs were a mess. Campbell had more than forty separate legal actions pending against him and a network of businesses and partnerships with which he was involved. Wheeler and his law partner, James H. Baldwin, apparently agreed to take Campbell on as a client under two conditions. They would represent him only in state courts, avoiding conflict with the federal statute, and they would require a hefty $10,000 annual retainer. The size of the retainer would later become a issue, but, considering the complicated state of Campbell's oil and land enterprise, the retainer, even by 1922 standards, doesn't seem out of line. Soon after going to work for Campbell, Wheeler and Baldwin produced a significant legal victory for their client in state court when they prevailed in a receivership case that went some distance toward sorting out Campbell's jumbled business affairs. Four other cases followed, all in state court.[52]

Wheeler immediately made plans to return to Montana to defend himself against the apparently serious charges but was dissuaded by advice from Supreme Court justice Louis Brandeis, among others. Wheeler was counseled to stay in Washington and cooperate fully with the Senate investigation that he insisted be conducted. That investigation commenced quickly, chaired by William Borah, who, fortuitously for Wheeler, became both exonerator and long-term political friend.[53]

Borah, a progressive and the Senate's most gifted orator, was in his third term in 1924 and had presidential aspirations. Borah was also no friend of Daugherty, having voiced misgivings when Harding appointed him and later having tried to force Daugherty out after Coolidge became president. The select committee assembled under Borah's leadership included Republicans Charles McNary of Oregon and Thomas Sterling of South Dakota and Democrats Claude Swanson of Virginia and Thaddeus Caraway of Arkansas. Borah had a reputation for seriousness and fairness, and he undertook the Wheeler investigation—he later called it "the unpleasant task"—in a straightforward,

Wheeler (*left*) and Idaho progressive Republican
senator William E. Borah at about the time of
Wheeler's Montana indictment. The two were close
friends, staunch noninterventionists, and worked
together to thwart Franklin Roosevelt's plan to
expand the Supreme Court. (*Library of Congress
Prints and Photographs Division, Washington, D.C.*)

expeditious manner, largely devoid of sensationalism or rumor. Borah's approach was
simply to call key witnesses who had already testified before the Montana grand jury
that had returned the indictment against Wheeler. He also planned to allow Wheeler
to call his own witnesses and present testimony in his own behalf. But Borah quickly
discovered that his committee would not be able to rely on evidence presented to the
Montana grand jury. The judge presiding over Wheeler's case informed the senator
that the evidentiary record had been impounded and could not be released, even to
the U.S. Senate. It was later discovered that the grand jury records could not be shared
because no formal record of the proceedings existed.[54]

It is clear from the records of Borah's committee that Wheeler and his client had
been in communication on Campbell's oil leases and permit problems after Wheeler
had taken his seat in the Senate. Wheeler made referrals for Campbell, and the senator's
secretary had helped arrange meetings for Campbell with officials at the Department

of the Interior. A critical legal question centered on whether these activities were performed while Wheeler served as Campbell's lawyer or whether they merely amounted to the kind of service a senator might reasonably be expected to undertake for a well-connected constituent.[55]

After hearing from a number of witnesses, most of whom had presented testimony before the grand jury in Great Falls, the Borah committee concluded that the charges against Wheeler were "unsupported by the facts." The committee report, issued in May 1924, concluded that "Senator Wheeler was careful to have it known and understood from the beginning that his services as an attorney for Gordon Campbell, or his interests, were to be confined exclusively to matters of litigation in the state courts of Montana, and that he observed at all times not only the letter but the spirit of the law."[56]

Four of the five committee members signed the report, while Senator Sterling, a lawyer and former law school dean, insisted on drafting a minority report in which he stressed his belief that the Senate had no business investigating the Wheeler matter while an indictment was pending against the senator in Montana. While refusing to pass judgment on Wheeler's guilt or innocence, Sterling contended the Senate committee's conclusions could not help but influence the outcome of Wheeler's Montana trial.[57]

In great detail, consuming three full days of Senate business, Borah reviewed the testimony about Wheeler's relationship with Gordon Campbell and concluded that none of the witnesses to any of the events involving Wheeler and Campbell had even hinted at impropriety on Wheeler's part. As to the paper trail, Borah said, "If you take the documentary evidence and look it over, upon its face there is no suggestion whatever of any improper conduct."[58]

Borah also dismissed any question about the hefty retainer Wheeler received from Campbell. As a well-compensated attorney in Idaho, Borah had often represented timber and mining interests, and he told the Senate that Wheeler's fee was not unreasonable given the complexity of the litigation and the stakes involved for Campbell, stakes that Borah estimated involved millions of dollars. Borah was particularly impressed with the credibility of key witnesses, particularly Campbell. "He was an exceedingly frank witness," Borah told the Senate. "He willingly waived immunity. He made no claims that he might incriminate himself, but stated that he was there to give the facts and all the facts and supply any documentary evidence that was in his possession." In a less than subtle reference to Daugherty's refusal to turn over documents during Wheeler's investigation of his conduct, Borah noted that Campbell's offer to turn over documents to his committee "had some weight with me in these days when there seems to be a great familiarity upon the part of a large class of people with the provision of the Constitution of the United States which enables them to claim privilege from incriminating themselves."[59]

Members of the U.S. Senate Select Committee on Investigation of Charges against Burton K. Wheeler. *Seated at table, left to right*: chair William Borah, Claude Swanson, Thaddeus Caraway, Charles McNary, and Thomas Sterling. (*Library of Congress Prints and Photographs Division, Washington, D.C.*)

Sterling, the South Dakota Republican, mounted a half-hearted defense of his minority report, questioning again whether it was proper for the Senate to investigate one of its members who was under indictment in a federal court. At one point during his remarks Sterling was asked if he thought Wheeler was guilty of the charge leveled against him. In reply Sterling seemed to suggest that Borah's committee had not sought all the available evidence against Wheeler. That comment set off a fierce exchange with committee member Swanson, who demanded to know, "What evidence does the Senator know of that ought to have been before the committee that was not before it?" Sterling responded defensively. "I do not think I should be asked to go into that question at the present time," he said. "I know what evidence was before the committee, and what evidence was before the committee that was before the grand jury; and my statement was that if the evidence before the committee was the same as the evidence before the grand jury it was sufficient to warrant the grand jury in returning the indictment. As to the guilt or innocence of the defendant, that will depend upon the evidence produced at trial." Swanson concluded the heated exchange by saying that he was "satisfied that the junior Senator from Montana is entitled to a vote of confidence and to the adoption of the majority report."[60]

Wheeler received his vote of confidence. The Senate vote to approve the Borah committee's report was fifty-six in favor and five opposed, with senators voting "no" generally agreeing with Sterling that the Senate should let the Montana justice system run its course before effectively exonerating Wheeler. In any event, most of Wheeler's colleagues agreed that he had been the victim of a Daugherty-inspired Justice Department frame-up and they spoke empathically in his defense, even as press reaction was mixed.[61]

"The Senate has gone as far as it could go toward directing a verdict in the trial court," the St. Paul Dispatch said, "and has done everything it could do to place Senator Wheeler above the law." But the New York Journal of Commerce made a larger point, saying that the new attorney general should give the Justice Department a major overhaul and "discontinue the proceeding against Senator Wheeler. This has nothing to do with what we may think of Wheeler or his methods; it is a question of protecting individual rights against invasion." The Brooklyn Eagle agreed with most members of the Senate when it asserted that Wheeler had been framed and that he had "performed a public service in showing up the Department of Justice in its true colors."[62]

Swanson made essentially the same point during Senate debate when he recounted the testimony of a private investigator, Blair Coán, who had been sent to Montana by Daugherty, his expenses paid for by the Republican National Committee. "He candidly admitted," Swanson said of the investigator, "that he was employed to go to Montana to see if he could not find something against Wheeler and, he implied, against the other Senator from Montana also [Walsh], who were conducting investigations against this administration."[63]

While the Borah committee settled the issue of Wheeler's guilt for most of his Senate colleagues, the Montanan's ordeal was far from over. Wheeler would be embroiled in his legal quagmire in Montana and in Washington, D.C., for eighteen long months.

———

For obvious reasons Wheeler wanted a speedy commencement of his Montana trial, but that was not to be. On April 28, 1924, he attempted to have the trial moved from Great Falls to Butte, believing that a hometown jury would treat him better. There was no response to the request from Attorney General Stone or anyone else at the Justice Department. A later request that the trial begin immediately was referred to John L. Slattery, the U.S. attorney in Montana, a Republican appointed in 1921, who clearly was in no hurry to try the case. Stone, meanwhile, struggled with the Wheeler case, telling an associate, "I have had doubts from the first whether there was sufficient evidence to secure a conviction in this case and I think the chances of securing the conviction have now been very much diminished by the action of the Senate." Slattery, the prosecutor, harbored no reservations, but he told the attorney general that it was impossible to schedule Wheeler's trial immediately. "Naturally," Slattery wrote, "Senator Wheeler feels that it would be to his advantage to press the trial of his case at once, so that it would follow closely upon the heels of the whitewashing given by his colleagues in the Senate, but, in this instance, he is dealing with a tribunal which is provided for by the Constitution and by the laws of our country."[64]

Further efforts by Wheeler to expeditiously schedule the trial came to nothing, but then out of the blue in late August the *New York Times* reported that a September 1 start date for the trial had at last been selected. This timing was too perfect to be coincidence. The first day of September, as was well known in Washington political circles, was the date Wheeler had selected to kick off, in New England, the presidential campaign of the Progressive Party, for which he was the vice presidential candidate. If evidence was needed of collusion between the Justice Department and the Republican National Committee, this scheduling detail seemed to supply it, and Wheeler was convinced that the date had been chosen to disrupt his campaign. Fortunately for Wheeler, both of Montana's federal judges, owing to long associations with the defendant, recused themselves from presiding at his trial. An Idaho federal judge, Frank Sigel Dietrich, was finally assigned the case, and he set the Wheeler trial for April 16, 1925, in U.S. district court in Great Falls.[65]

Both Wheeler and Tom Walsh, who was now acting as Wheeler's legal counsel, picked up rumors in Washington that the Justice Department, under orders from Attorney General Stone, had launched a new separate investigation of Wheeler. In the late summer of 1924, William J. Donovan, a newly appointed assistant attorney general, was given the entire Wheeler case file for what Stone later called "fresh consideration and re-examination." Donovan's "fresh consideration" concluded in late November, and Stone ordered that the information gleaned from the reexamination be presented to a second federal grand jury, this time sitting in Washington, D.C.[66]

On January 5, 1925, before the new Wheeler investigation became a matter of public knowledge, Coolidge nominated Stone to fill a vacancy on the Supreme Court. Stone's appointment was generally well received, and the Senate Judiciary Committee quickly made a unanimous recommendation that he be confirmed. Two days later, when news reports appeared of Stone's plans to pursue a second case against Wheeler before a Washington, D.C., grand jury, the attorney general's smooth path to the high court suddenly encountered serious opposition. Senators Walsh and Borah each requested a delay in Stone's confirmation vote, and several senators shuttled to the White House to confer with Coolidge about the new developments. The new Wheeler investigation had the potential to cause problems not only for Wheeler, but also for the Supreme Court nominee, the White House, and Senate Republicans.[67]

The White House conference resulted in a decision to send Stone's nomination back to the Judiciary Committee, where the nominee would be given a chance to explain why a second grand jury was needed to look into the actions of the senator from Montana. It was the first time in Senate history that a Supreme Court nominee appeared in person before the committee, and Stone turned in a masterful performance, testifying that Donovan's "fresh consideration" had convinced him that Gordon Campbell might have committed a different crime than had been alleged in Montana. It was possible, Stone said, that Campbell and his associates, and by implication Wheeler, had concocted a "scheme to defraud the United States of its public lands and of the oil and minerals underlying those lands."[68]

Stone testified that Wheeler was inevitably caught up in the allegations against Campbell and "in fairness to him and with view to the due and orderly administration of justice the opportunity should be given to him to explain his connection with the transaction." Stone continued: "But independently of [Wheeler's] connection . . . there had apparently been a crime committed within the District of Columbia, and the case could not be submitted to a Grand Jury without developing the part Senator Wheeler had taken in it."[69]

Stone's explanation did not satisfy Walsh, a member of the Judiciary Committee, who pressed for more details. Was it true that the Justice Department was unfairly delaying Wheeler's trial in Montana, Walsh wanted to know? And did not a second indictment in Washington, D.C., constitute double jeopardy for Wheeler? Stone skillfully fended off the questioning by suggesting that a further airing of the allegations against Wheeler was simply a matter of fairness to all concerned. Walsh and several other senators remained unconvinced, but it was also becoming clear that the controversy about Wheeler's situation would not prevent the full Senate from confirming Stone. Numerous senators opposed Stone's position on a second Wheeler grand jury, but they were not willing to make those concerns the sole reason to bring down an otherwise highly qualified nominee. Lengthy debate on Stone's confirmation followed in the Senate, and Walsh again used the opportunity to raise questions about the Justice Department's handling of the Wheeler affair. Walsh conceded that Stone was a man of "high character," but he said the Justice Department still reeked of the influence of Harry Daugherty. "Whatever may be the disposition of the Attorney General," Walsh said, "he had breathed the mephitic atmosphere of the Department of Justice for the last year, permeated . . . with the influence of Daugherty, whose malevolence toward Senator Wheeler was, I think, the occasion for the bringing of this indictment." Borah voted for Stone's confirmation but not before voicing objections to the attorney general pushing ahead with the second Wheeler investigation. Stone may have a legal right to conduct the investigation, Borah said, but "fundamentally it is a wrong policy." Stone was confirmed, nearly two months after his appointment was announced, by a vote of seventy-one to six. Wheeler and Walsh abstained.[70]

On February 25, 1925, Wheeler testified briefly before a Washington grand jury and, while there is no record of what was said, he emerged from the courthouse in good humor and joshed with reporters. It seemed to many observers that Wheeler was convinced that no second indictment would be forthcoming. The grand jury adjourned, and when days and then weeks passed with no word about an indictment and no leaks concerning the case, it seemed likely that Wheeler was right. But he was again rudely surprised. On March 27 new indictments were handed down naming Wheeler, Campbell, and Interior Department solicitor Edwin S. Booth on charges of conspiring to illegally obtain government oil and gas permits. The indictments claimed that the conspirators would use "dummies"—other persons to shield the identity of the lawbreakers—in order to obtain leases in excess of the number any one person could legally hold. Wheeler, it was alleged, had "agreed to use his influence as a Senator to obtain the permits."[71]

Wheeler and his supporters were flabbergasted by the second indictment, and he blasted the Justice Department and the Republican National Committee for continuing to target him. "The Administration seems determined," Wheeler said in a press statement, "to chastise everyone who has the temerity to criticize or oppose the illegal practices of those in authority in Washington." Wheeler made special mention of Republican operative Blair Coán, who, he said, "was sent to Montana by the Republican National Committee to get me in order to stop the Daugherty investigation."[72]

———

Facing a sensational trial in his home state, reeling from a second indictment in Washington, and knowing that legal expenses would become an issue, Wheeler more than ever needed friends. Help came in the spring of 1925 with the hasty organization of the Wheeler Defense Committee, an eclectic and impressive collection of political activists, reformers, progressives, socialists, and defenders of the Constitution. The committee eventually raised $15,000 to help defray the costs of Wheeler's defense and publicize the case. Perhaps the greatest benefit Wheeler derived from the committee was the weight of the credibility of the names on its letterhead. Norman Hapgood, an influential New York editor and columnist, became the group's chairman. Other members included the Kansas newspaper editor William Allen White, a Republican; political and social commentator H. L. Mencken; social reformer Jane Addams; Chicago lawyer and future secretary of the interior Harold Ickes; labor leader Sidney Hillman; Socialist Party leader Norman Thomas; Roger Baldwin, the founder of the American Civil Liberties Union; and Harvard Law professor and future Supreme Court justice Felix Frankfurter.[73]

———

Tom Walsh's leadership of the defense team gained assistance from Sam Ford, Wheeler's former assistant and the former Republican attorney general of Montana. Walsh, a superb litigator with a reputation for personal integrity and well known to prospective jurors, was the perfect lawyer to lead the defense. Walsh also knew his client, including Wheeler's strengths and weaknesses. Still, Wheeler tried to convince Borah, another respected trial lawyer, to help in the courtroom, but the Idaho senator politely declined, saying, no doubt correctly, that if he helped he would merely be seen as defending his report. With the trial scheduled to commence, dozens of newspaper reporters descended on Great Falls, and a "swarm" of federal agents prowled the town. Wheeler said it looked like a Justice Department convention, with as many as thirty federal agents in Great Falls.[74]

U.S. Attorney Slattery told reporters a few days before the trial began that the one man who had done more than any other to create trouble for Wheeler, Republican operative Blair Coán, would not be called to testify. But Slattery hinted that he had a surprise in store. As the trial began on the morning of April 16, Slattery told the jury that he would prove Wheeler had conspired with an as-yet-unnamed eastern attorney in a million-dollar fraud scheme, and the prosecutor said that the evidence would convince the jury to convict Wheeler. But first the prosecution would lay the foundation for its case by calling a series of witnesses whose testimony essentially mirrored the material pored over by Borah's Senate committee.[75]

Edward Harvey, a stockholder in Campbell's oil development syndicate and the man who had helped precipitate some of the original charges against his business partner, took the stand as a principal witnesses for the prosecution, but to Slattery's consternation Harvey's testimony turned out to be helpful to Wheeler. Harvey testified that Campbell had retained Wheeler's legal services solely to represent Campbell's interests in Montana courts, not what the prosecution wanted to hear. Several other witnesses offered uncompelling performances on the stand, with some providing inconclusive testimony and others flatly rejecting the prosecution's contentions. Slattery's case appeared rather quickly to be coming apart, so he shifted direction and called his surprise witness.[76]

Slattery had been able to keep the identity of this witness, New York attorney George B. Hayes, secret because he had not had to issue a subpoena compelling Hayes's testimony. Slattery's witness was a surprise for Wheeler and Walsh, who immediately set about discovering what incriminating testimony Hayes might offer to the jury. Under questioning by Slattery, Hayes wove a complex story of political and legal intrigue dating back more than two years. He testified that in the late afternoon of March 16, 1923, he had met Wheeler in the lobby of the Waldorf-Astoria Hotel in New York City. During that meeting, Hayes said, Wheeler had proposed that Hayes represent him as part of a million-dollar deal before the federal government on matters pertaining to Gordon Campbell. In effect Hayes said he had been asked to act as Wheeler's front man, while Wheeler pocketed a large fee and stayed in the background. Hayes appeared to be a credible witness able to recall minute details of the New York meeting, and he seemed to have no obvious ax to grind. The date of the New York meeting—March 16—was critical because the Wheelers were scheduled to sail for Europe the next day on the trip that eventually took them to Russia. Hayes said that Wheeler had seemed desperate to get someone to handle Campbell's legal affairs while he was away from Washington, which clearly suggested that Wheeler had indeed been violating the law by representing Campbell before the federal government and now needed someone to cover for him while he was out of the country. Hayes further said he had gone to the meeting at the hotel after receiving a long-distance call from Edwin Booth, the Interior Department solicitor and an old friend of Wheeler's. The implication was that Booth was also in on the conspiracy. In order to confirm that Booth and Hayes knew each other, the prosecution produced three telegrams between the two men, seemingly conclusive proof that they were acquainted. Hayes's testimony raised serious issues and, no doubt, questions in the minds of jurors about Wheeler's conduct. But the crafty Walsh now engineered his own surprise.[77]

Walsh called Booth to the stand, and Booth testified that he had never made a phone call to Hayes and that the only communication between the two men—the three telegrams—had focused solely on an effort to get Hayes involved in financing Campbell's oil operations. Suddenly the prosecution's entire case hung on conflicting testimony of the two attorneys: Hayes's account versus Booth's. But Walsh had more. He produced his own telegram from a Bell Telephone Company official in Washington, D.C., which confirmed, after a check of phone records, that there had been no telephone call from Booth to Hayes. The prosecution's surprise witness had invented a compelling and seeming credible story, but Walsh produced evidence proving it was a lie. All that was left, it seemed, was for Wheeler himself to drive a stake in the Justice Department's case against him, and he did just that during his own testimony.[78]

"The Senator's traits, which caused one of the nationally known magazine writers to once say that Wheeler's foremost characteristic was his combativeness, is easily apparent in his cross examination," reported the Great Falls Tribune. "A thrust from District Attorney Slattery is met with a return equally vigorous from the Senator.

Exchanges between the Senator and the prosecutor, though always in moderate tones, occasionally hint of rising temperatures. 'On the occasion when you landed in Washington'—once began the attorney. 'I did not land in Washington; I arrived there,' retorted the Senator. 'Perhaps I have that mixed with when you landed from Russia,' acknowledged Slattery. 'I did not land from Russia; I landed from England,' Wheeler answered."[79]

Wheeler acknowledged that indeed he had been in New York City on March 16, 1923, but he denied having met Hayes. He and his wife, he said, had spent much of the day shopping for clothes they needed for their European trip. Later they had gone to dinner with several friends, including Colonel Edward House, Woodrow Wilson's confidant. Wheeler testified that he had not met Hayes in the lobby of the Waldorf-Astoria and confirmed other testimony that his one and only encounter with Hayes had occurred during the Daugherty investigation in 1924 when the New York lawyer had been summoned by the Senate special committee to testify regarding his knowledge of lax Justice Department enforcement of liquor laws. Wheeler also vigorously denied that he had made any effort to represent Campbell before any federal agency.[80]

Wheeler briefly took the stand for a second time on the final day of the trial, and the defense rested without rebuttal from Slattery. Walsh's closing statement was contemptuous of the government's case. "There is nothing whatever in this evidence on which you would hang a dog," Walsh told the jury. Judge Dietrich appeared to agree and instructed jurors to ignore nearly all of Hayes's testimony. The judge also said that he found that the government had produced no evidence indicating that any agreement existed between Wheeler and Campbell regarding the senator representing Campbell in Washington, D.C. The jury was that told the prosecution's case rested "wholly on inferences" and that acquittal was required unless the jurors specifically found that Wheeler's retainer from Campbell covered legal services before the federal government.[81]

Wheeler wrote years later, obviously delighting in the memory, "The jury took two votes. The first was to go to dinner at the expense of the government. The second was to acquit me." What happened next might have come from the overactive imagination of a Hollywood scriptwriter. Seconds after Wheeler's acquittal was announced he was handed a telegram announcing the birth of his sixth child, a girl born in Washington, D.C. The baby was christened Marion Montana Wheeler: "Marion" after Robert Marion La Follette and "Montana" for Wheeler's adopted state, where he had just been granted a new lease on political life.[82]

"All the Daugherty gang could produce at Great Falls was a lot of testimony so palpably nonsensical and perjured that the jury laughed at it," H. L. Mencken wrote in the *Baltimore Sun*, effectively summing up the entire episode. With the Montana trial concluded, Wheeler could turn his full attention to the second indictment in

Washington, and he must have hoped, as many predicted, that the Justice Department would now drop all charges. It was not to be, however, and new rumors surfaced of yet another Wheeler indictment in the works, this time in Spokane, Washington. Wheeler reacted to the rumors with pithy humor, suggesting that the Justice Department ought to consider winter indictments in California and Florida, while reserving its summer indictments for cooler, northern locations.[83]

A series of legal maneuvers aimed at quashing the second Wheeler indictment launched in the fall of 1925. Walsh again provided the legal guidance, pressing the argument that a second indictment amounted to double jeopardy for Wheeler. When the Justice Department refused to challenge Walsh's assertion, it became clear that the government's case against Wheeler had finally come undone. Four days after Christmas 1925, more than a year and half after the first indictment was returned in Montana, federal district judge Jennings Bailey concluded that Wheeler had violated no law, and the judge quashed the second indictment. The Justice Department officially dropped all charges a month later.[84]

The *Nation* magazine estimated that the Justice Department had spent a quarter of a million dollars pursuing the Wheeler indictments and that Coolidge and Stone, in particular, should have known better. The magazine concluded that the whole episode "was nothing more or less than a deliberate conspiracy to drive Senator Wheeler out of public life." Wheeler, of course, agreed. "I hope my enemies will have had enough and will leave me alone," he said. "The whole thing has been a retaliation for my investigation of Harry Daugherty." The prolonged legal fight, painful and full of hard lessons, was finally over. Wheeler had been twice indicted, and the Bureau of Investigation had dug deep, picking over every detail of his personal and public life in order to discredit him. He had been assaulted in the press as a reckless radical, a communist who had pursued Daugherty for purely partisan reasons. Yet, typical of Wheeler, he had not buckled or backed down. He fought through the controversy, and a jury of his Montana constituents had acquitted him.

Wheeler's one-time client Gordon Campbell did not fare as well. A few days after Wheeler's acquittal in Great Falls, Campbell was convicted of fraudulent oil promotion and mail fraud following twenty-nine hours of jury deliberation. Judge Bourquin sentenced Campbell to two years in prison and imposed a $1,000 fine. Campbell served his time and was paroled in 1927.[85]

Harry Daugherty, meanwhile, twice escaped conviction for his alleged transgressions at the Department of Justice. His first trial, in 1926, resulted in a hung jury when jurors could not decide on Daugherty's guilt or that of one of his alleged coconspirators. During a second trial, early in 1927, a Daugherty associate was found guilty of "conspiracy to defraud the United States of his unbiased services" and was sentenced to eighteen months in a federal penitentiary and fined $5,000. Daugherty, thanks to one of the twelve jurors holding out for his acquittal, walked away a free man. In both cases the charge against Daugherty and various associates contended that they had received $7 million in kickbacks on the recovery of alien property. The funds were supposedly held in trust by the Justice Department as a result of seizure during World War I, and bonds traceable to the $7 million were found in the bank accounts of Daugherty and others, but Daugherty went unpunished. Daugherty explained away the money as a legitimate payment of political expenses, and he declined to take the stand in his own defense. His attorney said, "It was not anything connected with this case which impelled him to refrain from doing so. . . . He feared that [the prosecutor] would cross-examine him about matters political that would not involve Mr. Daugherty, concerning which he knew and as to which he would never make disclosure."[86]

It would appear from that statement that Harry Daugherty, once the chief law enforcement officer of the United States and one of the closest political associates of the president, simply knew too much about the political shenanigans—or crimes—of the Harding administration, and his testimony might have implicated a dead president. In a written reply to a federal judge seeking information to submit to a federal grand jury in New York, Daugherty said that as the one-time personal attorney for Senator and Mrs. Harding; as attorney for his brother, Mal; as attorney for the Midland National Bank of Washington Court House, Ohio, and as attorney general of the United States under two presidents, whom he said he had served in a most confidential manner, he would refuse to testify and answer questions. The former attorney general took the Fifth, saying: "I refuse to testify and answer questions put to me, because: The answer I might give or make and the testimony I might give, might tend to incriminate me."[87]

"What was so significant about the Daugherty verdict," James Giglio has written, "was not that one juror had voted for acquittal but that eleven had favored conviction. Because vindication had been so overwhelmingly denied, Daugherty received an enormous psychological blow. For the rest of his life, he would seek almost obsessively to restore his damaged reputation." In an interview on the occasion of his eightieth birthday Daugherty claimed he would not have changed a thing about his public life. His conscience, he said, was clear. Daugherty left a sizeable estate when he died in October 1941. In his will he left his papers to his daughter, but he apparently thought better of that decision and destroyed them shortly before he died.[88]

———

This much seems sure from B. K. Wheeler's brush with Harry Daugherty: he would never have been indicted had he not insisted on an investigation of the attorney general. Mabel Willebrandt, the assistant attorney general responsible for enforcing Prohibition during

Daugherty's tenure, recalled years later that Daugherty instantly became concerned when Wheeler and the Senate began investigating the Justice Department. "Daugherty came to the Department," Willebrandt said, "summoned Burns [the Bureau of Investigation chief] and other investigators ... and worked feverishly with ... political appointees to bring an indictment against Wheeler before *Wheeler* brought his whispered charges out in the open."[89]

There are at least two lasting legacies of the clash between Daugherty and Wheeler in 1924 and 1925. The first was Daugherty's use of the Bureau of Investigation, later the FBI, in order to intimidate or smear an opponent. J. Edgar Hoover, who became director of the bureau in 1924 when then–attorney general Stone fired William Burns, was instructed by Stone to focus on investigating violations of federal law and to end the bureau's practices of targeting political enemies, rifling congressional offices, and manufacturing indictments. Hoover, just twenty-nine, promised to obey, but he would go on to perfect the use of the bureau as a political instrument, available to presidents—and Hoover personally—for spying, intimidation, harassment, and blackmail. As Tim Weiner, a historian of the FBI has written, "Harlan Fiske Stone stayed on for nine months before ascending to the Supreme Court. Hoover lasted for forty-eight years."[90]

It can be argued that the Wheeler case marked the beginning of Hoover's long and controversial career that saw him become, as Weiner says, "the architect of the modern surveillance state." Hoover's efforts directed against Wheeler involved coordinating Justice Department and Bureau of Investigation actions with the political activities of the Republican National Committee. The Republican political operation effectively became an extension of the Justice Department. Hoover deployed a battalion of federal investigators on a vast fishing expedition aimed at turning up any detail that might reflect badly on Wheeler, and he made certain that his tracks would be well covered. In late April 1924, Hoover dispatched a telegram to F. A Watt, a bureau agent in Great Falls, advising him of the importance of secrecy in reporting information about Wheeler: "It is suggested that you make frequent reports as to information gathered [about Wheeler], but do not use either of the telegraph companies except in cases of emergency. In that event, it is suggested that it might be well for you to proceed to some point other than Great Falls and send your wire from there. All reports submitted should be on plain paper and should be enclosed in plain envelopes bearing postage." Wheeler's FBI file contains several "investigative" reports from far-flung places like Idaho Springs, Colorado, and Wolfeboro, New Hampshire. In each case the information collected turned out to be routine, even boring. Still the Bureau pressed ahead in search of something that might be used against Wheeler. Apparently a good deal of the agents' time was spent tracking down anonymous rumors, including a report that Wheeler had been thrown out of a hotel in Great Falls with a woman not his wife, that he had received a $25,000 bribe while serving as U.S. attorney, and that he had had purchased the Grand Hotel in Butte for $100,000 in cash after settlement of a particularly notorious case. Not a single rumor panned out, and agents seem to have spent the bulk of their time sitting in Montana hotel lobbies awaiting fresh orders from Washington.[91]

It is not surprising that Hoover, the staunch anticommunist, focused investigations on Wheeler's 1923 trip to Russia or that Harry Daugherty used Wheeler's Russia trip to smear him even after investigators found no evidence of Wheeler's ostensible communism. One Bureau of Investigation informant reported that while Wheeler and his wife were returning by ocean liner from their 1923 European trip, the senator spoke openly with passengers about what he had seen in Russia. Apparently hoping to gather damning intelligence confirming that Wheeler praised the Soviet system, bureau agent E. B. Hazlett tracked down and interviewed the captain of the ship (ironically the SS President Harding). The captain, Paul C. Grenning, reported to Hazlett that Wheeler "was not impressed with the present government of Russia and that it was his opinion that it could not exist for any great length of time."[92]

In the early 1930s Wheeler may have had the opportunity to end Hoover's career at the Bureau of Investigation but passed up the opportunity. "Some Democrats," Wheeler later wrote in his memoirs, "suggested after Franklin D. Roosevelt was elected in 1932 that had I objected to . . . Hoover he would [have been] replaced as director of the Bureau of Investigation." Hoover got wind of "this talk and came to see me," Wheeler wrote. "He insisted he had played no part in the reprisals against me. I had no desire to ask for Hoover's head on a platter—and I'm glad I didn't." Wheeler, usually the skeptic, was not skeptical enough when it came to assessing the full extent of Hoover's involvement in the effort to frame him. One can only speculate how U.S. history over the next forty years might have been different had Wheeler made a different calculation about Hoover in 1932.[93]

Wheeler's Senate investigation of the Justice Department has at least one other legacy—the establishment of a legal precedent for every subsequent congressional investigation.

The role of Attorney General Daugherty's brother, Mal Daugherty, in the Justice Department investigation might have been but a minor footnote in the entire affair were it not for Wheeler's dogged determination to get to the bottom of the Daugherty brothers' corruption. Mal Daugherty was the president of the Midland National Bank in Ohio, and his brother Harry, before leaving to head the Justice Department, had been the bank's legal counsel. Among other things, Mal Daugherty was accused by Roxy Stinson of conspiring with his brother to cheat her out of an inheritance left to her by her ex-husband, Jess Smith. When, as part of the Senate investigation, Wheeler subpoenaed records from Daugherty's bank, the brothers refused to turn documents over to the committee. Mal Daugherty simply ignored the subpoena. The Senate voted to hold Daugherty in contempt and sought to compel his testimony. Daugherty in turn sought an injunction to set aside the Senate's contempt citation, and an Ohio judge ruled in his favor, holding that the Senate lacked legal authority to compel his appearance or the production of records. The Senate then took, as Wheeler recounted, "the highly unusual step of itself employing counsel to appeal the decision to the Supreme Court." In January 1927, long after most Americans had put Harry Daugherty, his brother, Jess Smith, and Harding's Ohio gang out of their minds, the Supreme Court handed down a landmark decision in the case involving Mal Daugherty.[94]

Justice Willis Van Devanter wrote for a unanimous court: "We have given the case earnest and prolonged consideration because the principal questions involved are of unusual importance and delicacy. They are (a) whether the Senate—or the House of Representatives, both being on the same plane in this regard—has power, through its own process, to compel a private individual to appear before it or one of its committees and give testimony needed to enable it efficiently to exercise a legislative function belonging to it under the Constitution; and (b) whether it sufficiently appears that the process was being employed in this instance to obtain testimony for that purpose." The Supreme Court concluded, "The power of inquiry—with the process to enforce it—is an essential and appropriate auxiliary to the legislative function." The decision in *McGrain v. Daugherty* established the legal underpinnings for all subsequent congressional investigations and is one of Wheeler's most significant and lasting contributions to U.S. politics.[95]

4 THE PROGRESSIVE CAMPAIGN

Senator Wheeler has never assumed to be a
dyed-in-the-wool and blown in the bottle Democrat.

—*DAILY MISSOULIAN*, 1924

The *Nation* magazine accurately described B. K. Wheeler in 1924 when it said, "He
has an iron heart and a brass forehead. Also one of the most charming of smiles—a
boyish smile, a cool and deadly smile . . . there is something soft in many reformers.
There is nothing soft in Wheeler." Often a risk taker and flouter of convention, Wheeler
willingly abandoned the Democratic Party, at least temporarily, in 1924 to become
Robert La Follette's vice presidential running mate on the Progressive ticket, and he
did so while under indictment in Montana. The campaign was a quixotic adventure,
but the experience was perfectly tailored for the unconventional politician Wheeler
had become. As Mike Mansfield, another powerful Montana senator would say years
later, the Progressive Party campaign would define Wheeler for the remainder of his
career as "sometimes a Democrat but always an independent."[1]

A U.S. presidential campaign based on peace and prosperity is rarely a loser. Had the
economy been less than robust or had the country faced an international crisis in 1924,
the taint of the Harding scandals might have made Calvin Coolidge something other
than a prohibitive favorite to keep the White House in Republican hands. The country,
riding high with a booming stock market, was comfortable with the motto "Stay
Cool with Coolidge," and the taciturn president presided over a united Republican
Party in contrast to quarreling Democrats who were badly divided on several issues.
The Republican National Convention in Cleveland in early June 1924 was much like
the quiet man in the White House: businesslike and even a bit dull, reassuringly so

for voters wanting a candidate who was understated, predictable, and conservative. Republicans nominated Coolidge with little fuss and selected Charles Dawes, a retired general and Harding's budget director, as his running mate.[2]

What little excitement existed at the Republican convention came when the Wisconsin delegation, partial to Senator La Follette, demanded the Platform Committee adopt proposals that amounted, at least in the eyes of many Republicans, to unwarranted attacks on business. Wisconsin's Republicans, like their leader, considerably more progressive, labor-oriented, and reform-minded than Coolidge and the business-friendly mainstream of the Republican Party, had their ideas shouted down by convention delegates. The venerable composer and conductor John Philip Sousa helped stifle any vocal protest when he led convention's band in rousing version of "Hail, Hail the Gang's All Here." "All here but Wisconsin," some in the crowd shouted back. La Follette and many of his followers concluded that there was no room for them in the GOP.[3]

Democrats opened their convention in New York ten days after the Republicans nominated Coolidge, and they were anything but businesslike and far from united. Wheeler, perhaps anticipating the chaos that descended on the convention, declined to be a delegate but instead attended the gathering in what was for him a new capacity— columnist for William Randolph Hearst's International News Service. In interviews and in several columns Wheeler maintained that only by uniting behind a progressive candidate—someone like his friend La Follette—and adopting a progressive platform could Democrats have a chance to appeal to liberals in both parties and defeat Coolidge. "If the Democrats nominate a reactionary Wall Street-controlled Democrat, the Democratic Party will lose every state west of the Mississippi river and north of Arkansas," Wheeler wrote in a Hearst article that appeared the day the Democratic convention opened.[4]

As Wheeler likely anticipated, the 1924 Democratic convention was a disaster, rivaled only since then by the party's 1968 convention in Chicago that split over the Vietnam War. In 1924, Democrats were divided, nearly irreconcilably, over Prohibition, religion, and the Ku Klux Klan. Democrats who were "wet" on the liquor question battled those who were "dry." Southern Baptists disliked urban Catholics. The solidly Democratic states of the old Confederacy were suspicious of immigrants and wary of organized labor. Democratic progressives, like Wheeler, dismissed the party's conservative old guard as hopelessly wedded to the past. And Democrats confronted one especially divisive issue that seemed insoluble—the Klan, the white supremacist, anti-Catholic, anti-immigrant movement that dominated or greatly influenced politics in states in every region of the country. The Klan's political influence reached the zenith in 1924, and the fight to exert that influence played out on the floor of the Democratic convention. Some Democrats demanded that the party repudiate the

Klan and its followers, while others insisted that the best course was to ignore the movement. Some believed that quiet acquiescence might entice Klan followers to support the Democratic presidential nominee. Ultimately it became impossible for Democrats to finesse all the deep divisions, and their disastrous convention—"the snarling, cursing, tedious, tenuous, suicidal, homicidal rough-house in New York" in the words of journalist Arthur Krock—helped spawn a serious third party, the Progressives, while also ensuring the Democratic candidate would lose in November and that Coolidge would stay in the White House. The 1924 Democratic convention lasted longer than any other in American history, so long that humorist Will Rogers observed, "This thing has got to come to an end. New York invited you people here as guests, not to live." Wheeler blamed the great divides and the convention debacle on "the boodler-reactionary-standpat element, who know no religion, no racial pride and no party." In other words, he was blaming the party's mostly conservative leadership.[5]

Democratic Party rules in 1924 required a two-third-majority vote of the delegates to nominate a candidate, and that was a barrier that the party's major contenders—New York governor Al Smith, an anti-Klan Catholic, and former treasury secretary William Gibbs McAdoo, a southerner with Klan support—could not overcome. After more than a week of deadlock and dozens of inconclusive ballots, a compromise candidate finally emerged. John W. Davis, a conservative former congressman from West Virginia, former ambassador to Great Britain, and Wall Street lawyer, was at last able to command a super-majority of the delegates after Democrats had suffered through an unprecedented 103 ballots. Few Democrats were happy with the outcome, and Wheeler immediately condemned both parties and their chosen candidates, observing that Democrats had labored for sixteen days to bring forward John Davis, "the attorney for the House of Morgan, the attorney for the Standard Oil Company, a director of the Santa Fe Railroad." Coolidge, the Republican nominee, was in Wheeler's estimation little better. "You have on one hand the silent friend of the House of Morgan and on the other hand you have got the attorney for the House of Morgan."[6]

One of the few Democrats to stumble away from the mess with reputation intact was the convention's chairman, Wheeler's friend and mentor Senator Tom Walsh, who somehow commanded respect from all the warring Democratic factions. "Symbolic of the plight of the Democratic Party in this campaign was Walsh's pounding gavel," Walsh's biographer has written, "pounding, pounding, pounding—trying to silence the discordant voices, the anger and the hatred which threatened to tear the party to pieces." Davis, an easterner with strong ties to Wall Street and big business, hoped to balance the Democratic ticket with a progressive westerner as his running mate. Walsh would have been a logical choice. He was Catholic, which might help ease the sting of the party's failure to repudiate the Klan, and Walsh's Teapot Dome investigation, while criticized by some, had raised his national visibility. But Wheeler helped convince his friend, who faced a reelection battle for his Montana Senate seat in 1924, to reject the offer of the second spot on the ticket. When Walsh asked whether he should run with Davis, Wheeler replied, "What would you rather be—a defeated candidate for Vice President or a re-elected Senator?" Walsh immediately broke up the meeting in his hotel suite, telling the others present, "That ends it." When the convention reconvened the next evening Walsh had disappeared, presumably hoping to avoid a movement to spontaneously draft him for vice president. He asked the convention's acting chairman, Kentucky representative Alben Barkley, to read a letter removing him for consideration. "How ironic it was that this convention," historian Robert Murray has written, "after suffering through ten days of acrimonious controversy based in part on religious grounds, should have literally begged a Catholic to be Vice President, with only his refusal preventing it."[7]

Davis and the delegates eventually settled on Charles W. Bryan, the governor of Nebraska and brother of three-time losing presidential candidate William Jennings Bryan, as the vice presidential candidate. The Republicans derisively referred to the younger Bryan as "Brother Charley." Wheeler was too unimpressed. "This was the best they could do as a sop to the populist vote of the West," he groused, promptly declaring that he could not support the Democratic ticket.[8]

The progressives—and there were progressives in both political parties in 1924—who eventually embraced La Follette's campaign were a diverse and quarrelsome bunch, often united more by affection for their candidate than any issue or overriding ideology. La Follette's supporters came from the farm and the city, business and labor, and from the Republican and Democratic Parties. Trust in "Fighting Bob" united the Progressive movement, and supporters embraced the Wisconsin senator's call for sweeping social and economic reforms, with particular emphasis on the interests of farmers and workers rather than the concerns of big business.[9]

The La Follette–controlled Conference for Progressive Political Action took place in Cleveland even as Democrats were still fighting over a nominee in New York. From the same hall where the quiet, disciplined Republicans nominated Coolidge less than a month earlier, the Progressives embraced La Follette and his platform. The La Follette delegates were generally younger than the Democratic and Republican delegates who nominated Davis and Coolidge—a majority were under forty, and many were students hailing from the likes of Columbia, Harvard, Yale, and Vassar. They included William Jennings Bryan–era Populists, Minnesota Farmer-Labor Party supporters, social reformers, intellectuals, and socialists. Many La Follette supporters agreed with Herbert Croly, an intellectual leader of the progressive movement and a founder of the *New Republic*, when he wrote in 1924: "The welfare of the American people demands in my opinion the accomplishment by peaceful agitation under the forms of law of certain radical changes in the structure and functions of their national economy and government." That summarized La Follette's approach well—radical change brought about by peaceful means at the ballot box.[10]

Anticipating that both parties would nominate conservative candidates, La Follette had been making preparations for months to run. He strategically ignored suggestions that he announce the creation of a new national party simultaneously with the launch of his presidential campaign—some saw a model in the British Labour Party—by insisting that the immediate campaign took precedence. La Follette's strategy involved finding a suitable running mate, announcing a carefully crafted progressive platform, completion of the tedious but essential grunt work needed to gain ballot access in all states, the mounting of a nationwide campaign that could take the fight to the two major parties, and then wining election by drawing both Republican and Democratic votes. There would be time later, he believed, to form a truly progressive national party that could succeed in permanently drawing disenchanted liberals away from the two established parties. It proved easier to articulate the strategy than to carry it out.[11]

By 1924, La Follette had been a fixture, an increasingly controversial one, in national politics for more than twenty years. Beginning as a reform governor of Wisconsin, La Follette was pro-farmer, pro-labor, anti-monopoly, and antiwar. As much as anyone could have, La Follette succeeded in consolidating leadership of the Progressive movement after Theodore Roosevelt's failed Bull Moose campaign in 1912. La Follette had hoped to lead that election's insurgency himself and pointedly had not supported Roosevelt's candidacy. Roosevelt's brand of progressivism, a vigorous nationalism and an aggressive, interventionist foreign policy, was out of sync with La Follette and his followers. La Follette was a classic Midwestern noninterventionist who in 1917 had separated himself even more from the mainstream of both parties by opposing U.S. entry into World War I, a position even some of his friends found hard to fathom. La Follette's antiwar stands led to his effigy being burned in the public square of one Texas town, at the Massachusetts Institute of Technology, and at the University of Wisconsin, his alma mater, where the faculty overwhelmingly endorsed petitions condemning his "disloyalty."[12]

La Follette acquired the "Fighting Bob" nickname for good reason. To friends he was tough, determined, courageous, and principled. To foes, many of whom regarded it as a badge of honor to oppose him, La Follette was a dangerous radical and a demagogue. As historian Kenneth MacKay observes, "He hated and, in turn, was hated ... one was either 'for' La Follette or 'agin' him. With the possible exception of Teddy Roosevelt and William Jennings Bryan, Robert La Follette provoked more emotional thinking and irrational attacks than any American statesman of his time." This may explain why Wheeler and La Follette became close friends.[13]

The critical issue facing the nation, La Follette maintained, was that "Life, Liberty and Happiness all have been sacrificed upon the altar of greed." Every other issue flowed from that problem, he concluded, and since both the major parties had nominated candidates who, at least as La Follette perceived it, worshiped at the altar of big business greed, he would take that issue to the country in 1924.[14]

The Progressive platform did not mention the Klan or foreign policy but concentrated almost exclusively on economic and social issues. The platform's preamble read, in part, "It is our faith that we go up or down together—that class gains are temporary delusions and that eternal laws of compensation make every man his brother's keeper." The platform condemned "private monopoly" and called for public ownership of electric generation, conservation of natural resources, widespread tax reform (including taxation of excess profits, dividends, and "rapidly progressive taxes on large estates and inheritances"), reform of the Federal Reserve system, and guarantees that farmers and labor unions could organize and bargain. It called for federal marketing of farm products, control of the meatpacking industry, repeal of the Esch-Cummins Act, public ownership of railroads, abolition of injunctions in labor disputes, ratification of a child labor constitutional amendment "to protect children in industry," an end to discrimination against women, independence for the Philippines, election of federal judges, legislation to authorize a referendum to curtail the power of the Supreme Court to overturn acts of Congress, and requirement of a public vote to authorize U.S. participation in war. The Progressives also pledged "a complete housecleaning in the Department of Justice, the Department of the Interior, and the other executive departments."[15]

La Follette and his followers advocated a fundamental shift in national priorities and envisioned a country substantially different from visions advanced by Coolidge Republicans or Davis Democrats. It was a vision that would, in considerable detail, come to pass before long, and it was a vision shared by B. K. Wheeler.[16]

———

The Progressive convention, warmed by affection for La Follette and giddy about his platform, adjourned without naming a vice presidential candidate to run with their hero. That decision was left to the national executive committee, which meant La Follette alone would decide. La Follette initially hoped Supreme Court justice Louis Brandeis might join the ticket. The two men held compatible views on economic policy and a shared concern about the evils of bigness, but Brandeis was reluctant to leave the court and declined. La Follette and a group of his key advisers then called on Wheeler at his Washington home to gauge his interest. The meeting took place on July 13, shortly after the Cleveland convention, and Wheeler immediately said he was not interested. Wheeler questioned whether any third-party effort could be successful, and he knew his ongoing legal problems in Montana would become a campaign issue. The Portland *Oregonian* and other papers reported on the meeting, and most observers believed Wheeler had definitively removed himself from consideration. However, when a second delegation called on Wheeler a few days later, he gave a much different answer. He would think it over, he said. The next day he agreed to accept the vice presidential nomination and run with La Follette, but in doing so he insisted that he still considered himself a Democrat. The *New York Times* quoted Wheeler, forty-two years old and in his second full year in the Senate, as saying, "Between Davis and Coolidge there is only a choice of conservatives to make."[17]

"In accepting the call, I do not abandon my faith in the Democracy of Thomas Jefferson," Wheeler said. "I am a Democrat, but not a Wall Street Democrat. I shall give my support and whatever influence I may possess to those candidates for office who have proved their fidelity to the interests of the people wherever they may be found, but I shall oppose every man on whatever ticket he may appear who bears the brand of the dollar sign."[18]

What prompted Wheeler's change of heart? He would later write that Attorney General Daugherty and his own legal problems led him to reconsider and accept La Follette's offer. Having picked up rumors of a second indictment related to the Montana corruption allegations, Wheeler asked Ray Baker, an experienced Democratic retainer who had served as director of the U.S. Mint in the Wilson administration, to check the rumors through Baker's Republican connections. Baker apparently did check and reported back that his sources indicated that there would be no additional indictment if Wheeler declined the offer to run with La Follette. On that basis, Wheeler always insisted, he reconsidered La Follette's offer. "I changed my mind because I refused to let Daugherty and his crowd blackmail me the rest of my life," Wheeler wrote in his memoirs. "I determined not only to run but to make a major issue out of what I knew personally of the crookedness and general corruption in the Justice Department—the very thing, apparently, that the GOP feared. I admired La Follette but he never knew that I changed my mind because of Baker's report." Wheeler's explanation, particularly given the attention he placed on the corruption issue during the campaign, seems plausible and is certainly in keeping with his independence and combative attitude, not to mention his ambition.[19]

Wheeler was, in many ways, a perfect complement to La Follette. They were compatible on issues, both relished a good political brawl, and they shared many of the

Wheeler and Wisconsin Republican senator Robert M. "Fighting Bob" La Follette confer in July 1924 shortly after Wheeler agreed to join the Progressive Party ticket as the vice-presidential candidate. (*Library of Congress Prints and Photographs Division, Washington, D.C.*)

same enemies. By asserting that he was not abandoning the Democratic label but only rejecting his party's nominee, Wheeler brought a patina of bipartisanship to the ticket, and his youth and energy were assets due to La Follette's age and increasingly frail health. Additionally, Wheeler came from the West, where the Progressive ticket would have to do well in order to win. La Follette also clearly liked the blunt, candid young Montanan and frequently praised Wheeler's absolute fearlessness in investigating the Justice Department and the attorney general.[20]

Reaction to Wheeler joining the Progressive ticket split predictably along partisan lines. Those who backed La Follette, Minnesota Farmer-Labor senator Henrik Shipstead, for example, believed "the selection of Wheeler for vice president . . . a master stroke." The *New York Times*, on the other hand, dismissed what the ticket offered and suggested that a third-party campaign would only further fragment U.S. politics. The *Times* accused Wheeler of meeting himself coming and going, pledging to remain a Democrat while battling his party and also vowing to support Tom Walsh's reelection in Montana. The newspaper predicted Wheeler would "fall into a sublime fury about Wall Street and the predatory interests" rather than discuss the inconsistency of his own position.[21]

William Hard, writing in the *Nation*, which, under the editorship of liberal crusader Oswald Garrison Villard, became a major publicity tool for the Progressive cause, predicted that the "tail" of the La Follette-Wheeler ticket would offer the sting in the coming campaign. Calling Wheeler "hard-boiled, hard-bitten, hard-headed, hard-fisted," the magazine pointed out that La Follette was the oldest candidate in the field and Wheeler the youngest, and it concluded, "Old men for counsel. And young men for war? Well, war, one of your names certainly is Wheeler."[22]

As the humid August heat descended on Washington, the Wheelers, children in tow, decamped to a rented a house on Cape Cod to vacation and to prepare for the fall campaign. The respite gave Wheeler an opportunity to craft the speeches he would use when the campaign began in earnest in September. While in Massachusetts, Wheeler developed an unlikely but lasting friendship with Boston millionaire Joseph P. Kennedy, who, while publicly supporting Davis for president, was attempting to remain on good terms with all the candidates. During one visit to Wheeler's vacation cottage, Kennedy offered Wheeler use of his chauffeur and luxury Stevens-Duryea automobile for Wheeler's September campaign swing through New England. Wheeler would later write in his memoirs that Kennedy also provided the Progressive campaign with a $1,000 contribution, being careful to obscure the source of the money. During the working vacation Wheeler met with campaign advisors, including law professor Felix Frankfurter, and labored to address organizational and financial challenges inherent in creating a national political campaign from scratch. The problems were serious and difficult.[23]

Most significantly, the campaign encountered ballot access problems in nearly every state as officials struggled to understand a jumble of legal requirements that varied from state to state. In Georgia and Virginia, for example, securing a ballot line was as simple as filing notice with state election officials, while in Nevada qualifying the Progressive ticket for the ballot required a petition with signatures from 10 percent of voters in the last election. The ticket failed to secure a spot on the West Virginia ballot when the filing deadline was missed. California, potentially a large electoral prize, was among the most difficult states in which to qualify. The California Supreme Court finally upheld a bizarre feature of the state's election law that prevented the La Follette–Wheeler ticket from calling itself "Progressive" or "Independent." The ticket finally won a place on the California ballot under "Socialist," which created no end of problems for the candidates and their supporters. In some states, New York, for one, the ticket appeared on ballots under two different names. Ultimately the ticket appeared under a variety of ballot labels—Progressive, Independent, Independent-Progressive, and Socialist.[24]

Money to organize and wage an effective national campaign was also a major problem. The hard-pressed farmers and workers who turned out for Progressive rallies were unable to contribute much cash, and La Follette and Wheeler had little appeal to business interests who were, in most cases, financially backing the established parties. The American Federation of Labor did endorse the Progressive ticket, but that support came with few of the resources that organized labor endorsement provides today. The campaign, in the main, relied on individual contributions of a dollar here and five dollars there and literally passed a hat for donations at speeches and rallies. Not surprisingly, Progressives were swamped in the money race. Republicans reported spending more than $4.2 million on the 1924 election, Democrats just over $900,000, and the Progressives barely $220,000.[25]

Villard, the *Nation* editor, served as assistant treasurer of the Progressive campaign, a job that consumed so little of his time that he was able to travel for long stretches with Wheeler. On a trip to Chicago, Villard, while making an appeal to Harold Ickes, a major supporter of the Bull Moose campaign in 1912, lamented the campaign's dire financial situation. "It is absolutely disheartening the little money we are getting—not $2,000 a day from all over the country," Villard wrote. "Every state organization is starved for lack of cash and literature. If you can help won't you do so *soon*." Ickes, who would later become a fierce Wheeler critic, helped with fund-raising and endorsements, and the future secretary of the interior was at his curmudgeonly best bashing Coolidge. "I will not vote for the political bell-hop who is at the present moment masquerading as a President. Davis is at least an upstanding man and when he serves the House of Morgan he charges for his services. Coolidge is an even more facile servant of the same master, but he does it for nothing."[26]

While problems with ballot access, lack of money, and poor organization were all significant, the Progressive ticket was able to secure endorsements from an impressive collection of supporters, including several elected officials. Republican senators Lynn Frazier and Edwin Ladd of North Dakota and Smith Brookhart of Iowa split with their party and endorsed the ticket, as did congressman Fiorello La Guardia of New York. Ickes, another Republican, was instrumental in convincing the prominent social worker and reformer Jane Addams, nationally known for her work at Chicago's Hull House, to endorse La Follette and Wheeler. Addams, widely condemned by conservatives as a dangerous, radical reformer, confided to Ickes that she was supporting the ticket even though she thought campaign attacks on Coolidge a bit nasty. "I always wince a little over the terms of political abuse," Addams wrote Ickes, "even when men deserve them." The sculptor Gutzon Borglum, who would soon start work on his monumental shrine to democracy, Mount Rushmore, created a handsome bronze relief medal of La Follette and Wheeler that became a popular campaign symbol.[27]

W. E. B. Du Bois, the civil rights activist and a founder of the National Association for the Advancement of Colored People (NAACP), initially criticized but then endorsed the Progressive ticket. Writing in the NAACP's magazine, Du Bois said that La Follette and Wheeler were "unusually honest and straight-forward men. I believe in them." Helen Keller, the pioneering educator and humanitarian, endorsed the Progressives, as did philosopher and educator John Dewey. Norman Thomas, who was running for governor of New York in 1924 and later ran six times for president on the Socialist ticket, supported the Progressives, and Wheeler returned the favor by campaigning for Thomas. Ernest Gruening, who had been the managing editor of the *Nation* and would later be one of Alaska's last territorial governors and then one of Alaska's first two U.S. senators, joined the campaign as national publicity director, "cheerfully," he said, happy to tell "the two old parties to go to the devil." High-profile endorsements were, however, no substitute for a broad-based political organization, a problem never adequately addressed during the campaign. "In many places," Villard said, "We found the merest skeleton of what a fighting political force should be. And in some states we had no organization whatever and could not get on the ballot."[28]

Two well-known and well-regarded progressive Republicans senators with national followings, William Borah of Idaho and George Norris of Nebraska, might have substantially enhanced the Progressive campaign effort with an endorsement. But both men were waging reelection campaigns in 1924 and, while each harbored misgivings about Coolidge and worked diligently to keep a distance from the Republican ticket, they declined to endorse La Follette and Wheeler.[29]

The Klan issue that had so bedeviled Democrats at their convention became a particularly delicate matter for Wheeler since the Klan had established a significant foothold in Montana and exercised a degree of political influence with, by one estimate, more than 5,000 members. Wheeler was sensitive to how any comment he made about the Klan might reflect on the reelection efforts of his Catholic colleague Tom Walsh. Nevertheless, in early August, La Follette, much to his credit and unlike candidates in the major parties, issued a strong condemnation of the Klan. Saying he had always been opposed to discrimination based on race, class, or creed, La Follette said he was "unalterably opposed to the evident purposes of the secret organization known as the Ku Klux Klan." Wheeler wrote immediately to his running mate saying he felt the "statement was a fine one" but then added, "after second thought felt it was just as well that I give out nothing on it unless asked further." The "Imperial Wizard" of the Klan responded to La Follette's repudiation by telling Klan members they should feel comfortable supporting either Coolidge or Davis, but he labeled La Follette "an arch enemy of the Klan."[30]

At the end of August, still not properly organized or funded, the Progressives began the active stage of the national campaign. La Follette would launch this with a speech broadcast on radio from Washington, D.C., while Wheeler began his campaign in his native state with a major speech just down the hill from the Massachusetts statehouse.

As Wheeler began campaigning on a muggy Labor Day with a speech to a crowd of eight thousand Bostonians, the *New York Times* reported that interest in the three-way presidential race was substantial. As evidence the newspaper announced the birth of triplets, three boys born to "Mr. and Mrs. Roy Lee" in Benton, Illinois. The Lees, clearly following the political news closely, named their three sons George La Follette, Thomas Coolidge, and Ralph Davis.[31]

———

Labor Day thunderstorms dumped two inches of rain on Boston, and by the time the city's mayor, the corrupt, colorful, and politically successful James Michael Curley (also the Democratic candidate for governor), introduced Wheeler the temperature was near ninety degrees and the humidity just as high. "There is but one issue before the country today," Wheeler told the crowd on Boston Common. "It is: Shall the control of the government be left in the hands of a small group that has cornered the national wealth and exploited the people? Or shall the control of the government be returned to the representatives of the people, to be administered in the interest of the masses, to be so administered that the right of every man, woman and child to food and clothing and shelter and health and happiness is placed above property rights and the claims of profits?" Wheeler spoke for an hour and a half and left the stage on the shoulders of some of his supporters, his shirt wringing wet.[32]

The *New York Times* and other newspapers gave the campaign kick-off prominent coverage. "Again and again in his main address Senator Wheeler criticized President Coolidge," the *Times* reported, referring to Coolidge as the "mythically strong, courageous, silent, watchful man who occupied the Presidential chair." He also poked fun at the Republican vice presidential candidate for his "gallant service in war on organized labor." Wheeler dismissed the Democratic candidate as "a man who would be willing, it seems, to out-Coolidge Coolidge as a servant of Wall Street."[33]

By the time of his Boston speech, Wheeler had concluded that Davis could not win the election and that Progressive efforts were best spent carrying the fight to Coolidge, an approach Wheeler embraced with a vengeance. He made Republican corruption the centerpiece of his stump speeches. "In all my studies of political history," he said, "I cannot recall an administration more venal, more corrupt, more destructive of the rights of the people than the administration of the Republican Party during the last three and a half years."[34]

In the comfort of Kennedy's touring car, Wheeler set off for a brief tour of New England before arriving in New York City on September 6 for an evening speech at historic Cooper Union. He spoke from the same spot where, in 1860, Abraham Lincoln delivered the speech that made him a presidential contender, but on this evening Wheeler was no Lincoln. He drew a tremendous crowd and when introduced was cheered for "four and a half minutes," but he was, according to one account, "clearly tired out. He departed frequently from his prepared speech, repeated himself, and faltered in his utterances many times." It was the performance of a green, still untested national candidate who, while no stranger to long, difficult days on the Montana campaign trail, was still seeking his marks on a national stage. Wheeler did incorporate in his New York speech what became his standard denunciation of Republican corruption, declaring "a vote for Coolidge is a vote for the Little Green House on K Street," a reference to the scene of many of the alleged misdeeds of Harding and his cronies.[35]

Wheeler was a quick study and worked hard, often delivering several speeches a day. Gradually he became a more polished and effective speaker. Just a week after Wheeler's underwhelming New York debut, Villard, who was traveling with Wheeler, wrote to La Follette that his running mate was "doing extremely good work, quiet, modest, and unassuming, yet dramatic to a remarkable degree by his simple straightforward narrative of Teapot Dome and the Daugherty scandals. I have never seen audiences more fascinated, or that listened more closely." At the same time, Villard lamented that campaign organization and advance work was often badly done, which often produced only small audiences.[36]

Notwithstanding the serious difficulties facing the Progressives, it appeared to many observers that the La Follette–Wheeler campaign was gaining real traction by mid-September. Wheeler said he had received reports, from Kennedy among others, that Democratic leaders were becoming worried about La Follette's strength in New England. The Hearst and Scripps-Howard newspapers reported on polls indicating that La Follette and Wheeler could carry six to nine states. There was constant newspaper speculation that the three-way contest might end in an Electoral College deadlock, with none of the candidates commanding a majority, forcing the House of Representatives to select the president.[37]

Editors of the *Nation*, hoping perhaps to create a self-fulfilling prophesy and with their bias for the Progressive ticket on full display, went so far as to speculate that the House of Representatives might also become deadlocked, leaving the Senate to choose a vice president, who would then assume the presidency. "In the absence of a president, the Electoral College and the House having failed to choose one, the vice president under the Constitution would act as president and Burton K. Wheeler would enter the White House . . . this is very likely what will happen," the magazine predicted.[38]

Wheeler was in Ohio—Cleveland, Cincinnati, and Columbus—in mid-September, Harry Daugherty's home ground. "A tall, blond, deep voiced, and youngish looking man of 42 spoke words that stirred a crowd that squeezed into every inch of space at

Engineers Auditorium last night," the *Plain Dealer* reported. "Few baseball crowds ever yelled louder than Senator Wheeler's audience last night . . . he was akin to a revivalist at the rally." Wheeler, of course, denounced Daugherty, particularly in Columbus, the former attorney general's hometown. "Wheeler has come and gone," Daugherty said in response, "and Columbus still stands." He dismissed Wheeler as "a common liar." Wheeler's traveling secretary, A. B. Melzner, reported after the Cincinnati rally that "police turned away more than 2,000 as standing room was occupied three times over." He confidently told La Follette, "Ohio is going to give you 24 electors on November 4."[39]

During a speech before a crowd of 5,000 in Des Moines, Iowa, Wheeler employed for the first time what would become his most effective campaign tactic—debating an empty chair. Insurgent Republican Smith Brookhart, who officially headed the Daugherty investigation but ceded leadership of the investigation to Wheeler, introduced the candidate. In a study of Wheeler's campaign oratory, historian Donald Cameron describes the scene: "Employing the techniques of a dramatic actor, Wheeler directed a series of questions at the imaginary occupant, concluding with the plea, 'Tell us, Mr. Coolidge, where you stand upon one single solitary issue concerning the American people in this campaign.' After a dramatic pause, he would comment, 'There, my friends, is the usual silence that emanates from the White House.'" Through the remainder of September, Wheeler draw large, enthusiastic crowds, and Villard predicted that "wherever Burton K. Wheeler goes, he will make votes, he will stir the hearts and minds of his listeners . . . he will help the ticket, help it immensely."[40]

By the time Wheeler headed to the Far West in late September he had honed his stump speech to focus almost exclusively on Republican corruption, including sweeping denunciations of the Teapot Dome and Daugherty scandals. Occasionally he took a direct swipe at Coolidge or his running mate, accusing Coolidge of having illegally authorized deposits of state money in a Boston bank while serving as governor of Massachusetts. Wheeler charged that the bank's president made a $6,000 contribution to the 1920 Republican campaign even though Massachusetts law limited such contributions to $1,000. Wheeler also contended that the Republican vice presidential candidate had been involved with questionable banking transactions in Chicago, and at one point he produced a sheaf of papers, apparently documents substantiating the allegations. Newspapers reported Wheeler's charges, often without much detail, but did little to corroborate or refute the substance of the attacks. The Republican strategy was to essentially ignore Wheeler's sniping. Coolidge stayed in the White House, often silent, refusing to take to the hustings, but effectively used the radio and newsreels. To the chagrin of some Republican strategists, Coolidge never responded to the Boston bank allegations, and Dawes, who did take to the campaign trail to attack La Follette and Davis, offered only the curious observation that the charge related to his bank dealings "leaves only a bad smell."[41]

Wheeler hardly mentioned Davis, the Democratic candidate, and rarely touched on the specifics of the Progressive platform. On one occasion he felt compelled to address the Progressives' proposed reforms of the Supreme Court, an issue he would revisit in detail in 1937. The Progressive platform advocated amending the Constitution to create a process to permit Congress to vote to overturn Supreme Court decisions. Explaining the intent, Wheeler said, "We do not propose that Senator La Follette, when elected President, shall by executive order attempt to impair the authority of the courts. We know he could not, even if he were so disposed. We do not intend, when we have control of the Congress, to meet in secret session and devise some scheme for crippling the courts. All we propose is that the extent to which courts shall have the right to nullify acts of Congress shall be settled by the people themselves." It was a controversial proposal, difficult to explain, and the Republican campaign took full advantage of what they portrayed as an attack on the integrity of the court.[42]

The Republican campaign, meanwhile, both sharpened its message and narrowed the political battlefield, essentially conceding the "solid South" to Davis, who would almost certainly win the dependably Democratic states of the old Confederacy. Republicans concentrated on the industrial Midwest and Far West, attempting to blunt a perceived Progressive surge there. Republican attacks on La Follette intensified, with Dawes, the vice presidential candidate, accusing him of being an agent of "red radicalism." La Follette's tenure as Wisconsin governor was picked over, and his vote against war with Germany was rehashed. Republicans also suggested that the sixty-nine-year old La Follette was simply too old to be president. Each line of attack had some resonance with voters, but nothing worked as well as merely labeling La Follette and Wheeler "radical" and implying that the Progressive ticket was cloaked in socialism. The election came down to a stark choice, Republicans said: "Coolidge or Chaos."[43]

———

Like most politicians, Wheeler had a handful of stories or anecdotes he relished telling and retelling on the stump and during interviews. One favorite story recounted advice he had received after being elected to the Montana legislature in 1910. As Wheeler related, he had been warned by a prominent Butte businessman that he should be very careful during his service in the legislature not to antagonize the big economic interests in Montana lest they punish him and force him to "walk out of Montana" with his career in tatters. The businessman had reminded the rookie legislator that he would be walking the tracks while the "captains of industry" rode out in their private railroad cars. "That warning given by the businessman was recalled here today," the *New York Times* reported from Billings in 1924, "when Senator Wheeler returned to Montana not walking the railroad ties, as had been predicted, but riding in a private railroad car as a member of the Senate and nominee of the Progressive Party for Vice President."[44]

Wheeler had three objectives during his campaign swing through Montana. He aimed to win the state's small but still coveted electoral votes; he hoped to assist Walsh with his Senate reelection bid; and he intended to defend himself in front of his constituents against the indictment, still pending in Montana, that accused him of improperly benefiting from his office. In Billings on October 1, his first appearance in months in Montana, Wheeler took what he called the "frame-up" head on. "There are lots of persons here," the *Times* noted in its story, "who do not believe the prosecution of Senator Wheeler will ever be pressed by the Department of Justice under Attorney General Stone, and think that talk of such prosecution is kept going merely as an effort to embarrass the running mate of Senator La Follette and they give him [Wheeler] unstinted applause." Wheeler blamed his legal problems on "crooked politicians," and he blasted corruption in the Republican administration.[45]

Significant portions of the speeches Wheeler delivered during three Montana appearances—in Billings, Butte, and Missoula—were devoted to a full-throated endorsement of Walsh, who was facing both Republican and Progressive challengers. "I should be an ingrate if I did not stand by him," Wheeler said, "and I am here to do it. I ask you to support him because he deserves your support." Walsh was a true progressive, Wheeler insisted, and his defeat "would be looked upon by the country as a repudiation of his magnificent fight against corruption in the Capitol at Washington." Walsh's political position was seriously complicated by his junior partner's bolt from the Democratic Party, since Montana Democrats had not fully recovered from the Nonpartisan League debacle four years earlier when then-senator Henry Myers left the party to oppose Wheeler's election as governor. Walsh's steadfast support of the national Democratic ticket and his broad appeal to the many factions in the state party had seemed a sure way to strengthen Montana Democrats up and down the ballot, but then Wheeler joined La Follette, a move reinforcing the notion that Wheeler was a bit too independent to be completely trusted by rank-and-file Montana Democrats. Even with Wheeler's unqualified endorsement, Walsh was grumbling privately to friends about Wheeler's lack of loyalty to the Democratic Party. Wheeler "ought not, after this, to complain much about want of regularity on the part of Henry Myers," Walsh wrote to one constituent. "It seems to me that if [William Jennings] Bryan could afford to be regular this year [Wheeler] might."[46]

Hundreds who hoped to hear Wheeler speak at Butte's Broadway Theater—the hall had more than twenty-one hundred seats—were unable to elbow in and were turned away. With his wife joining him on the platform, Wheeler was introduced as "Montana's fighting senator who drove America's most corrupt gang [from Washington]." One of those in the capacity crowd was a young veteran of the Great War and a future majority leader of the U.S. Senate. Mike Mansfield, working in a Butte copper mine as a mucker—a miner doing the hardest work, shoveling loose ore—was just becoming interested in politics. Decades later Mansfield would vividly recall getting his first glimpse of Wheeler. He dominated the stage, Mansfield remembered, pacing back and forth, firing questions at an empty chair "as if it were a living person." Mansfield said it was impossible to live and work in Butte and not be swept up in political discussion around Wheeler and his role in the national campaign. Already a staunch Democrat, Mansfield remembered Wheeler, not entirely sympathetically, as "a very independent senator. I was certainly following his career."[47]

In Spokane, Washington, Wheeler was warned that a crowd of sixty-five hundred at the city's National Guard armory would include hecklers. He took this head-on, asking before launching into his speech if anyone had a question. An elderly fellow far in the back of the hall stood and shouted, "Is it true that everyone who votes the Republican ticket gets some oil stock?" The crowd roared, and Wheeler continued, unbothered by any heckling. In another show of his independence, Wheeler took advantage of the Spokane appearance to endorse Republican senator Borah's reelection in Idaho, and he spoke warmly of Washington senator Clarence Dill, a Democrat, who was not up for reelection.[48]

An enthusiastic crowd estimated at ten thousand greeted Wheeler at the Washington State fairgrounds in Puyallup on October 5, but Progressive supporters also read an unwelcome headline in the anti–La Follette *Seattle Daily Times*: "A Vote for La Follette Is a Vote for Hard Times." Republicans and the financial interests supporting them had "gone mad" with fear that La Follette might actually win, Wheeler said, and Republicans were resorting to a campaign of intimidation. There was a measure of truth in the charge. The Washington State Republican Party vice chairman implored "the patriotic people" of his state to beat La Follette. "This is not a question of partisanship—the flag itself is in danger," John Gellatly said. Meanwhile, poolroom bookies quoted 10–7 odds that Coolidge would carry the state. On the day of Wheeler's appearance, bets totaling $10,000 were placed at various establishments in Seattle.[49]

The peak of Wheeler's western swing came in Los Angeles, where the campaign was denied access to a downtown venue and rented instead the cavernous Hollywood Bowl, more typically used for musical performances, for a massive rally. Wheeler delivered one of his best campaign performances, before an audience of close to twenty thousand. "No prima donna, no golden throated tenor, no orchestra leader with a magic wand has ever known the depth of applause that reverberated through the Hollywood hills about the Bowl when Senator Wheeler was finished," reported the *Los Angeles Examiner*. The *Los Angeles Times*, typically a Republican paper and a critic of Wheeler's Justice

Department probe, also seemed in awe of his performance. The paper headlined its story: "Greatest Acclaim Ever Given Performer at Hollywood Bowl."[50]

The western swing continued with Wheeler speeches in Long Beach and San Diego, then Tucson, El Paso, and eventually Wichita, where a telegram from La Follette was waiting. The presidential candidate announced an abrupt, and in retrospect damaging, change in campaign strategy. La Follette was on the verge of embarking on his own western campaign tour, mirroring Wheeler's swing, but, rather than sticking with that plan, La Follette told his running mate that things appeared to be going so well in the Midwest and Rocky Mountain states that he was turning his attention back to the East. "Every advice I have received from Pacific Coast and Rocky Mountain states confirms your assurance of success there. I am confident the people of the West will carry on," La Follette said. "I am therefore turning east from Omaha."[51]

La Follette's decision was dictated, at least in part, by money problems and the candidate's fragile health, but altering the schedule proved a serious mistake. The western states Wheeler had just traversed were, along with Wisconsin, the Progressive base. The big crowds Wheeler drew, as well as evidence of Republican concern about the ticket's strength in states like Washington and California, indicated that by mid-October the Progressive ticket was building genuine momentum across the West. The campaign needed La Follette to close the electoral sale in the wake of the opening Wheeler had spent three weeks creating. Charles Michelson, a respected Democratic campaign strategist was one who believed that several western states were moving toward the Progressives, and he thought La Follette and Wheeler might win 120 votes in the Electoral College. Had Progressives won those votes, questionable under any circumstances, there would have been no Electoral College winner, and the presidential decision would have rested with the House of Representatives. What is clear is that La Follette's change in strategy, turning east rather than going west, stalled the ticket's political momentum at a critical moment.[52]

Meanwhile, Wheeler moved on to Oklahoma, where he attacked Republicans for maintaining a political slush fund and for shaking down well-heeled executives for campaign contributions. The charges contained more than a little truth since at the same moment Wheeler's friend Borah was in the midst of conducting a Senate investigation into campaign contributions. Borah's investigation produced, at minimum, circumstantial evidence of significant contributions to the Republicans that could be linked to lax prosecution by the Justice Department of various antitrust cases. "You already understand what happens when a manufacturer, profiting by a high tariff[,] gives a large sum to the campaign fund," Wheeler said in Oklahoma City. "You know he does so to maintain the tariff that enriches his pockets at your expenses. That is abominable. That is bad government."[53]

One reporter observed that Wheeler's campaign speeches seemed "best when they were delivered to an antagonistic crowd. He was most brilliant when heckled." Wheeler's well-developed sense of humor also helped him win over a crowd, as in Oklahoma City when he quipped that "the only difference between a reactionary Democratic Senator and a Republican Senator was that one came from the south and one from the north."[54]

By the time Wheeler returned to the Upper Midwest at the end of October, Republican attacks on the "radical" Progressives had become a daily feature of the campaign. Coolidge was still largely out of view, but his surrogates were everywhere and on the attack. Secretary of state Charles Evans Hughes, for example, told Chicago-area voters that the nation's economy was fragile and that it would not take much of La Follette's radicalism to destroy economic prosperity. Wheeler responded to Hughes during a stop in Flint, Michigan, accusing him of "ward politician" tactics. "We no longer have a free America if we permit men and women to be intimidated by threats such as those voiced by Mr. Hughes and by the representatives of a few wealthy barons," Wheeler said. "It is an old, old threat Mr. Hughes is making. It is made every four years by the party in power."[55]

Wheeler's travels during the campaign were the most energetic effort by any of the candidates on the three national tickets. Wheeler campaigned in eighteen states over a period of five weeks, made more than fifty major speeches, and gave dozens of other talks in smaller settings. By election eve Wheeler had been on the trail for sixty-four straight days, traveling more than seventeen thousand miles, and had spoken to audiences estimated at a quarter of a million voters. Had La Follette been able to campaign even half as aggressively, the steady drift of support to the Republicans over the last few weeks of the campaign might have been blunted. Wheeler closed out the campaign in Baltimore, the twenty-sixth state he had visited since Labor Day. Lulu and all five children were on hand to hear Wheeler rather solemnly end the campaign. "No man in this country can honestly be sure tonight," he said, "how the country is going. You have wild predictions by the Republicans, the Democrats and the Progressives. Yet, the fact is: every one of these people has a chance: Mr. Davis because he has the 'solid South' and Senator La Follette because he has the West." Yet when the votes were counted La Follette had only Wisconsin. Outside the states of the old Confederacy, Coolidge ran the table and won both a popular vote and Electoral College landslide. The Progressive ticket, as small consolation, ran second to Coolidge in eleven western states. The five million votes the Progressives tallied represented 16.5 percent of the popular vote. It would be 1992 before another third-party presidential candidate drew a greater percentage of the popular vote than La Follette and Wheeler in 1924.[56]

Coolidge and the Republicans ran a nearly flawless campaign, offering a consistent message of peace and prosperity, while constantly raising questions about the "radical" policies proposed by the Progressives. Money and organization were critical factors that also contributed to the outcome. As the *Nation* noted late in the campaign, Republicans enjoyed a huge financial advantage over the Progressive and Democratic campaigns. "Already, the Republicans admit, more than 200 individuals have contributed to the party chest more than $1,000 each," the magazine reported. "William Wrigley, the chewing-gum man, gave $25,000; Mortimer Schiff, of Kuhn, Loeb & Co., gave $15,000; two members of the firm of J. P. Morgan & Co. gave $5,000 each."[57]

The Progressive candidates also violated a basic political rule by failing to articulate a consistent message. La Follette spent most of the campaign denouncing monopoly and the concentrated power of big business, while Wheeler talked almost exclusively about Republican corruption. In fact, La Follette and Wheeler concentrated so heavily on attacking their opponents that they failed to offer a compelling, positive rationale for how their approach to addressing the nation's problems was superior to what Republicans or Democrats were offering. Republican claims that a vote for La Follette and Wheeler might force the presidential selection into the House of Representatives, with attendant uncertainty about who might emerge from that process, also damaged the Progressives. La Follette's 1917 antiwar vote was a factor with some voters, and the popular journalist Mark Sullivan thought the ticket's stand on the Supreme Court was central to their undoing. Sullivan wrote that voters looked at a photo of the staid, solid, predictable, dignified justices of the Supreme Court and then looked at a photo of "Fighting Bob" La Follette, he of the "pompadour hair that suggests emotional excitability," and opted for stability. Finally, it seems that both La Follette and Wheeler were hobbled by their own pervasive sense of political dissatisfaction. Hope usually beats despair, and in 1924 dissatisfaction played poorly with voters who preferred to believe that a business-friendly Republican in the White House would keep the country permanently on an upward trajectory. The Progressive candidates belonged, as Kenneth MacKay has noted, "to an age of discontent [while] this was an age of acquiescence."[58]

Wheeler's statement after the election betrayed more than a hint of bitterness. He admitted no surprise at the outcome but lamented that "exposure of corruption in Washington has apparently made no impression" on the voters, who had voted "for reactionary policies." Nonetheless, Wheeler admitted that voters had spoken clearly. "We all wish President Coolidge and General Dawes a successful tenure of office, and it is the duty of the Progressives to help make it such."[59]

Even while hampered by serious organizational and financial problems, the sheer size of the vote for La Follette and Wheeler and the enthusiasm demonstrated for a fresh reform agenda signaled that the country's political landscape was changing. While the

Progressive campaign did not spawn, as some thought possible, a new political party that might have combined the liberal or progressive elements of the two established parties into an Americanized version of left-leaning, European-style democratic socialism, the movement did give voice to bold new ideas and helped usher in new and ultimately lasting political realignments. In many ways the Progressive campaign of 1924 laid the foundation for what just eight years later would become Franklin Roosevelt's enduring New Deal coalition—farmers, organized labor, and ethnic and urban working-class voters. By the mid-1930s much of the La Follette–Wheeler platform of 1924 had been adopted, modified, or plagiarized by Roosevelt. "The Progressives get no credit line," historian MacKay has written, "for the TVA [Tennessee Valley Authority], the 'rapidly progressive' income [and inheritance] tax schedules, the Wagner Labor Relations Act, the various New Deal aids to agriculture, the Securities and Exchange Commission and the abolition of child labor. Yet all these demands, and others later incorporated as part of the body of New Deal legislation, are to be found in the Progressive platform of 1924." The staying power of the Progressives was not lost on Indiana Republican senator James Watson, who wrote in his memoirs in 1936: "If one will take the trouble to examine the platform of 1924 on which Robert M. La Follette ran . . . [one] will find very many of the identical propositions embodied that are now being put into execution by the administration of Franklin D. Roosevelt."[60]

La Follette's physical and political decline began almost immediately after the election. Conservative Republicans controlling the Senate were not tolerant of his apostasy, and he was drummed out of the Republican Party early in 1925, along with the three Republican senators who had endorsed the Progressive ticket. La Follette's censure had little practical effect since he died following a series of a heart attacks in June 1925. Wheeler, who had named his youngest daughter after La Follette, would always consider Fighting Bob a great politician and a role model.[61]

There were rumors that Senate Democrats might punish Wheeler for bolting, but he quickly and quietly slipped back into the party with little obvious difficulty. Still, after 1924, Wheeler was never again a dependable party regular, and he was "determined to carry on the fight" to make the Democratic Party a liberal party, rather than, as he said, a "sectional party representing only the solid South."[62]

Within a few months Wheeler was again displaying his political independence and defying the party by campaigning for and helping elect progressive Republicans. He went to Wisconsin in the summer of 1925 to help Robert La Follette Jr. win election to replace his father in the Senate. Young La Follette, running as a progressive on the Republican ticket, became, as his father had been, a close Wheeler ally in the Senate. When Republican Smith Brookhart, who had openly supported the Progressive ticket, was being ousted from his Iowa Senate seat in 1926 following a contested election,

Wheeler encouraged those who had organized the "Wheeler Defense Committee" to send the money remaining in the fund to aid Brookhart. As it turned out, Brookhart would soon return to the Senate. He ran for Iowa's other Senate seat that year and was elected after first winning a primary against incumbent Albert Cummins, the senator Wheeler had prevented from chairing the Interstate Commerce Committee in 1923. Wheeler also went to North Dakota in 1926 to campaign for progressive Republican Gerald P. Nye, who also was elected to the Senate and would become one of Wheeler's closest allies in the foreign policy fights prior to U.S. entry into World War II.[63]

Having experienced the national limelight during a remarkable first two years in the Senate, Wheeler was determined to expand his activity, particularly on foreign policy issues, even while burnishing his reputation as a very independent Democrat.

5 A SON OF THE WILD JACKASS

Party bonds still hold Wheeler lightly. A passion for justice,
whether for the farmers, the miners, or the Montana Indians
who back him solidly, remains his political inspiration.

—RAY TUCKER AND FREDRICK R. BARKLEY,
SONS OF THE WILD JACKASS

Historian William Leuchtenburg has observed that during the 1920s a political transition
occurred among the nation's progressives. The movement shifted from a focus on "old
system evangelical reform," exemplified by William Jennings Bryan and "Fighting Bob"
La Follette, to a new "liberal" politics that centered on urban and immigrant voters.
B. K. Wheeler, representing a sparsely populated western state with an economy based
on agriculture and natural resource extraction, never completely made that transition. Wheeler's ideal government existed to protect individual freedom and prevent a
concentration of economic or political power. "History tells me," Wheeler said in 1929,
"that Egypt and Babylon and Rome . . . did not fall until the grasping greed of their commercial classes had destroyed agriculture and reduced the sturdy and once contented
farmers to an idle and turbulent proletariat." Gradually during the tumultuous decade
of the 1920s, and particularly after the stock market crash of 1929, Wheeler modified
his views, for both political and practical reasons, and supported a substantial degree
of federal government intervention in the economy, but he never found centralized
or concentrated power acceptable, whether on Wall Street or in the White House.[1]

And Wheeler maintained a passion for reform. "Wheeler is essentially a fighting
man," journalist Ray Tucker said. "His hormones leap most vigorously when he faces an
overweening beneficiary of social injustice. He can smell corruption when those around
him are plucking roses. He moves fastest in an uphill charge, where entrenched and
powerful interests leer over the ramparts ahead." Wheeler's reputation and influence
with the Senate's bipartisan progressive bloc—Tom Walsh and William Borah were
central figures—grew following the national campaign in 1924, and he increasingly

assumed a leadership role among the progressives, particularly on foreign policy. Still political independence was often more important to Wheeler and other progressives than coordinated group action. Effective leadership of the Senate's progressive bloc was difficult and often proved impossible. Republican senator Peter Norbeck of South Dakota, who occasionally aligned with the progressive bloc, praised the group as the most intelligent and fair-minded in the Senate but also said, "the progressives will not work together, they are jealous of each other . . . they are so individualistic you know." Others, including Senate conservatives, were even more critical. Wheeler and Senate progressives were, in the words of New Hampshire Republican George Moses, nothing more than "sons of the wild jackasses," irresponsible political rabble-rousers bent on forcing a radical agenda on the country.[2]

Wheeler never served on a Senate committee that afforded him a direct role in formation of foreign policy, but in the 1920s he both solidified his foreign policy views—favoring Philippine independence, international trade, diplomatic recognition of the Soviet Union, and opposing U.S. military intervention in Central America, for example—and engaged fully in Senate debates. Wheeler was comfortable in the company of the group that has been termed the Senate's "peace progressives," opposing imperialism and military interventionism and supporting disarmament, all positions from which he never wavered. Wheeler's critique of U.S. foreign policy in Central America in the 1920s offered a foretaste of the debates that would consume policy makers for another sixty years, and his views of World War I would greatly influence his stance before and during World War II. In Wheeler's opinion the Great War of 1914–18 had not made the world safe for democracy, as Woodrow Wilson had famously proclaimed, but rather had impeded the advance of democracy, preserved British imperialism, and enriched bankers and munitions manufacturers. (Wheeler was one of only ten senators who voted in 1931 in favor of a "sense of the Congress" resolution to disavow the provision in the Treaty of Versailles "to the effect that Germany alone was responsible for the war.") Congressional progressives had been split over U.S. entry into the war in 1917, with La Follette, George Norris, and Montana's Jeannette Rankin, for example, all voting against the declaration of war against Germany, while Tom Walsh, Hiram Johnson, and William Borah, with varying degrees of enthusiasm, supported U.S. involvement. But by the mid 1920s, Senate progressives, with Wheeler often in the forefront, were united in believing that U.S. involvement in any future European war must be avoided. Wheeler's views on international issues were also informed by what for the time was considered extensive travel, including to Russia for a second time, to Romania for an international political conference, and to Central America, the Philippines, China, Korea, and Japan.[3]

BURTON K. WHEELER

This caricature by R. G. List accompanied the
chapter on "Montana Maverick" Wheeler in
the 1932 book *Sons of the Wild Jackass*. (*Copy
in author's collection*)

Wheeler returned from a Far East tour in 1927 calling for immediate action on
Philippine independence, although he worried that duty-free Philippine sugar would
be detrimental to Montana sugar beet growers. Nevertheless, he said, "It is inconceivable to me that the people of the United States would want to keep the Philippine
Islands, except those Americans who are located in the Philippine Islands." Philippine
independence did not occur until 1946.[4]

During his Asian trip Wheeler also traveled to Nanking for an audience with
Chiang Kai-shek, the nationalist Chinese political and military leader, who failed to
impress the Montanan. Wheeler wrote in a newspaper article that Chiang "did not
seem big enough for the stupendous tasks he had before him" and observed, long before
it became apparent to many other Americans, that the Chinese leader reminded him
of a "tin-horn gambler—slick, suave, cunning, and insincere."[5]

Turmoil in Mexico and then in Nicaragua was the foreign policy preoccupation
of the Coolidge administration. U.S. marines were deployed to Nicaragua early in
1927 when the administration chose sides in the country's internal political conflict.

U.S. policy was aimed at propping up a friendly regime and protecting U.S. business interests. Wheeler objected loudly to what he considered a kind of U.S. imperialism in Central America. The United States was "simply bullying the Nicaraguan people because Nicaragua was a small nation," he said, and he ridiculed conservative arguments that U.S involvement in Central America was needed to prevent the spread of communism in the hemisphere. "Only those simple-minded souls who still believe in a Santa Claus can be fooled by such hypocrisy," Wheeler said, adding that the State Department would benefit from more enlightened thinking. "I am wondering whether Secretary [Frank B.] Kellogg has become so infected with the Gilbert and Sullivan fever that is now sweeping the country that he is going to stage an American version of the 'Pirates of Penzance' on the little state of Nicaragua."[6]

Wheeler joined other Senate progressives in assailing the Wall Street–inspired "dollar diplomacy" of the 1920s, and he sponsored resolutions calling for an investigation of U.S. policy and for withdrawal of the marines, who eventually numbered 2,500. "Certainly, 'dollar diplomacy' is the only phrase which accurately describes our almost uninterrupted record of interference with the internal affairs of Nicaragua for the last 18 years," Wheeler wrote in a long article printed in the *Congressional Record*. "And when the whole sordid story of our relations with Nicaragua is written every American who holds true to our traditions will hang his head in shame." In Wheeler's view, Americans who intended to do business in an unstable political environment simply had to accept the risk of doing so without the illusion that the U.S. military would bail them out when trouble occurred. Furthermore, Wheeler argued, the Nicaraguan adventure actually harmed U.S. business prospects in Central America by signaling to other nations in the region that they too might be subject to military intervention. Wheeler also objected that Congress, without regard to political party, was too willing to acquiesce to the executive branch on matters of foreign policy. It was, he said, unconstitutional for the executive branch to usurp the congressional prerogative to declare war by dispatching U.S. troops at the sole discretion of the president. "History is strewn with the wreckage of great empires which sought to subjugate smaller states," Wheeler said. "Imperialism inevitably leads to ruin. After all, the universe in which we live is a moral universe. In the end, right and not might, justice and not injustice, and truth instead of lies, prevail."[7]

Wheeler said, "After visiting [Nicaragua], and after seeing those people, I would not give the life of one American Marine for the whole damn country down there." Wheeler voted for a 1928 amendment to a naval appropriation bill—the amendment failed—that would have cut off funding for the marine deployment. Under public and congressional pressure, Coolidge eventually softened his Central America policy, and Senate progressives, including Wheeler, are due some credit for encouraging a U.S.

approach to the region that relied more on diplomacy and less on military intervention, an approach that Franklin Roosevelt later termed a "good neighbor policy." Still, it was not until 1933 that the last marine left Nicaragua, a deployment that Wheeler often condemned as both morally and legally reprehensible, and, as he predicted, the United States would continue to intervene in the region for decades.[8]

Wheeler always maintained, his noninterventionist beliefs notwithstanding, that he supported an adequate national defense, but he also consistently argued that the principal mission of the U.S. military was protection of the continental United States. A military large enough to entertain imperialistic adventures was also capable of repressing internal political dissent, so Wheeler routinely supported efforts in the Senate to reduce military and naval appropriations. Along with other Senate progressives—Borah, young Bob La Follette, Nye and Frazier of North Dakota, Shipstead of Minnesota, and Dill of Washington—Wheeler endorsed the 1930 London Naval Conference, believing it might help control an international naval arms race. Wheeler also voted for the Borah-inspired Kellogg-Briand Treaty to outlaw war as an instrument of international diplomacy. That idealistic treaty was approved with only one dissenting vote, and then the Senate immediately turned to consideration of a $274 million naval appropriations bill, which was promptly approved, over Wheeler's objection.[9]

Wheeler regularly called for diplomatic recognition of the Soviet Union and reemphasized this after a second visit to Russia in 1930. Accompanied by Senators Bronson Cutting of New Mexico, a Republican, and Alben Barkley of Kentucky, a Democrat, Wheeler spent nearly three weeks in the Soviet Union, visiting rural areas near Moscow, observing collective farms, and meeting several high-level officials.[10]

Wheeler returned even more convinced that the United States should recognize the communist government. Without normalized relations, he said, the United States had little opportunity to influence Russian behavior or capitalize on the potential of vast export markets. "Russia is the greatest potential market for American goods in the world," Wheeler said, "and we are just a bunch of suckers, to use a slang expression, if we do not recognize them." Wheeler said recognition need not imply "moral support" for the communist regime, but diplomatic normalization made economic sense because "from a commercial standpoint we are losing millions." In a series of articles in the *Washington Herald,* Wheeler wrote that it would be a mistake to judge the Soviets by "American standards." Joseph Stalin, he wrote, ruled "with an iron hand" supported by a notorious secret police, but so had the czar. Wheeler contrasted the "extravagance" of the old regime with its "poverty, filth, disease, and ignorance of the masses." Russian history, Wheeler argued, helped explain "the reason for some of the excesses, some of the superstitions, some of the murders that have been committed since the proletariat became the ruling class in Russia." Wheeler predicted that eventually Russian leaders would be "forced to modify their views" and embrace more democratic alternatives. In a piece written in 1930 for *Nation's Business*, he expressed optimism that the Soviet government would eventually allow greater individual freedom. "The major social fermentation in Russia today is in the direction of a growing realization that the program of the Communist Party gradually must take into account more and more the awakening sense of individualism encountered in so many phases of life in the new Russia."[11]

Support for U.S. acceptance of the Soviet government grew steadily from the time Wheeler first advocated recognition after his 1923 trip to Russia, but the idea remained extremely controversial, and not until Franklin Roosevelt entered the White House in 1933 was diplomatic recognition extended. Wheeler grew increasingly anticommunist over the course of his Senate career, in part, he said, because he came to fully appreciate the nature of Soviet expansionism during and after World War II. It also seems likely, given the vicious criticism Wheeler sustained early in his career, routinely being condemned as a radical or a Bolshevik, that he was determined to never again be put in political jeopardy by being labeled "soft on communism." At the same time, Wheeler's consistent advocacy of recognition of Russia, particularly in light of the criticism he received for that stand, is a testament to his courage. Wheeler's opposition to U.S. military intervention also never gave way to concerns about the expansion of global communism. His non-interventionism was consistent, and even later, when out of office, he would publicly oppose U.S. involvement in Korea and Vietnam even as those conflicts were portrayed as vital efforts to stem communism in Asia.

According to one analysis of the Senate's key European-related foreign policy decisions from 1923 to 1933, Wheeler voted in support of Harding, Coolidge, and Hoover administration policies only 11 percent of the time. His support for Republican domestic policies was similarly minimal. He opposed Republican administrations on farm policy, tariff legislation, and Supreme Court appointments, and he frequently supported proposals advanced by fellow progressives—federal power development at the Muscle Shoals site in Alabama, for example—that Republican presidents opposed.[12]

With an eye on home-state politics and his own reelection in 1928, Wheeler backed the complicated (and some contended socialistic) McNary-Haugen Farm Relief Act because it was among the few proposals considered by Congress that appeared to offer some hope of relief for hard-pressed Montana farmers. McNary-Haugen was intended to drive up agricultural prices by requiring the government to purchase surplus crops at pre–World War I prices and then sell those commodities in overseas markets, at a loss if necessary. A fee assessed on agricultural producers would fund the program. Wheeler brushed aside criticism of McNary-Haugen, saying, "In a crisis such as confronting the American farmer and all America I am willing to resolve the doubt in favor of the farmers." Wheeler's preferred solution to ending the persistent depression in farm country was to expand exports of American agricultural products, while adopting an inflationary monetary policy that he was convinced would enhance farmers' purchasing power. Wheeler would have to wait for Franklin Roosevelt's New Deal to see the adoption of meaningful reform of agricultural policies, and those efforts were primarily aimed at limiting production (unfortunate in his view).[13]

While Wheeler's positions on legislation rarely prevailed in the 1920s, he proved to be an effective advocate for a vast array of progressive causes. He participated for several months in investigations of working and living conditions in the coalfields in Pennsylvania, Ohio, and West Virginia and was sharply critical of mining company treatment of miners. He pressed for a Senate investigation of working conditions in southern textile mills, including whether workers were paid "wages insufficient to permit a human being to live in decency." He accused the Hoover administration of lax enforcement of the Pure Food and Drug Act because, Wheeler said, the administration was under political pressure from the drug manufacturers. "Our jails are filled with bootleggers," he pointed out, "while these purveyors of impure drugs go free . . . and [are] even allowed to resell their impure products."[14]

Wheeler also continued to battle the railroads and champion the cause of railway labor unions, opposing an Interstate Commerce Commission recommendation to consolidate the Great Northern and Northern Pacific Railroads, the two main rail routes across Montana. "Such a consolidation would mean in my home state undoubt-edly the loss of employment to a great many individuals," Wheeler said. "It would undoubtedly mean in a very short time that various communities would be without any adequate transportation facilities, and in general it would be very disastrous." Instead Wheeler advocated a planned and coordinated system of coast-to-coast railroads, a system that he said would preserve both jobs and service.[15]

With growing seniority on the Interstate Commerce Committee, Wheeler cham-pioned the development of radio broadcasting, but his enthusiasm for the popular new medium was tempered by his innate skepticism concerning just who would benefit financially and how effectively the airwaves and broadcasters could be regulated. He feared that control of the rapidly expanding industry might become concentrated in too few hands. "I felt that since the air space was owned by the public those who used it had a responsibility to the public and should not look upon it as a private preserve to be exploited solely for profit," Wheeler said. He enthusiastically supported the efforts of Senator Dill to create a Federal Radio Commission, the forerunner of the Federal Communication Commission. After the commission was established in 1927, Wheeler watched with concern as President Hoover staffed the new agency with functionaries Wheeler thought unqualified. Wheeler's work on early radio legislation prompted a life-long interest in communications and led to a lasting and important friendship with a Montana and national broadcaster pioneer, Ed Craney of Butte. Craney became a political confidant to Wheeler and a source of expert information about the nation's broadcasting industry.[16]

Like many other Americans who had once embraced the great social experiment of alcohol prohibition, Wheeler's position on control of liquor gradually evolved during the 1920s. When first elected to the Senate, conscious of strong anti-liquor sentiment in Montana, Wheeler adopted the pragmatic political position of most western progressives—he was a "dry," a public if not especially enthusiastic supporter of prohibition. Wheeler's gradual transformation on the issue began with a demand for an investigation into lax and ineffective enforcement of prohibition laws, then moved on to a conviction that outlawing liquor was unenforceable and eventually to favoring outright repeal of the constitutional amendment that outlawed alcohol. In September 1930 Wheeler publicly called for repeal of the Eighteenth Amendment as "the only solution [to] the very bad condition that has developed. I think we must let the states control themselves."[17]

Always leery of the power of government to interfere in the lives of individuals, as Prohibition had attempted for more than a decade, Wheeler opposed a Hoover administration plan to force aliens to register with the government. The scheme was un-American, Wheeler told a Jewish group in New York, and "with its proposal to make all aliens submit to annual inspections, and to be issued cards with their photographs attached, [it] savors too much of the third degree and the rouge's gallery to be acceptable to real Americans." At the same time, Wheeler favored broad restriction on immigration, arguing that Mexican immigrants were coming to Montana to take jobs held by "white miners, American citizens."[18]

———

Indicating his increasing interest in foreign policy, Wheeler brashly (and rather foolishly from a political standpoint) declared during his 1928 reelection campaign that he was "going out of the business" of being focused on home-state issues. He was done with being Montana's "messenger boy," as he put it. "I have been traveling around portions of the world," Wheeler said, "and studying world questions. . . . I mean to devote myself to these big problems. . . . If it's a messenger boy you want, send someone else to the Senate." Predictably the charge that Wheeler was ignoring Montana issues and focusing too much of his attention on foreign affairs would cause problems in subsequent campaigns.[19]

Poster from Wheeler's 1928 reelection
campaign. He won a second term, defeating
old foe Joseph Dixon by stressing his
independence. "I am not going to bend my
knee to suit the policies of anyone," he said.
(*Copy in author's collection*)

Wheeler continued to value the personal and political support of his old friend Tom
Walsh, one of the most respected men in Washington, and Walsh warmly endorsed
Wheeler's reelection in 1928. But during his six years in the Senate Wheeler had com-
pletely stepped out of Walsh's shadow and established a national reputation rivaling
that of his mentor. Mike Mansfield, remarking on the relationship between the two
Montana senators, observed, "Wheeler started out as Tom Walsh's protégé, but then
Wheeler became Wheeler's protégé." When Walsh made a half-hearted run for the
Democratic presidential nomination in 1928, Wheeler supported him. But when Walsh's
effort faded, Wheeler endorsed the eventual Democratic nominee New York governor
Al Smith, perhaps wanting to dispel concern about his party loyalty among Montana
Democrats, before announcing his own reelection plans. Wheeler's endorsement—he
called Smith "a liberal in the best sense of the word"—made the front page of the *New
York Times,* and the paper made much of the endorsement of a politician who had so
recently bolted the Democratic Party.[20]

Wheeler had good reason to concentrate on his own campaign in 1928. His effort to display Democratic loyalty did not prevent a primary challenge. Although Wheeler easily defeated former governor Sam Stewart, his old adversary from the Montana Council of Defense, who ran with support from the Anaconda Company, his real test came in the general election against Republican Joe Dixon, who had decisively thrashed Wheeler in the governor's race eight years earlier.[21]

Wheeler focused his reelection bid on support of the McNary-Haugen farm legislation and his fight to lower railroad freight rates in Montana, and he rarely failed to mention that he had exposed Justice Department corruption and driven Harry Daugherty from office. Wheeler enjoyed broad, impressive, bipartisan support in his first reelection campaign, including endorsements from Republican senators George Norris and Bob La Follette, both of whom came to Montana to campaign. Norris said he considered it "the highest brand of patriotism to support men whom we believe to be right, regardless of the artificial partisan tag which any one of them may carry." He said he would be for Wheeler even if his own father were running against him. William Green, president of the American Federation of Labor, told Montana labor leaders that "Senator Wheeler's record in Congress has been 100 percent favorable to labor and the people." After Wheeler dispatched Stewart in the primary, several former political enemies embraced his candidacy, including Bruce Kremer, the Anaconda lobbyist and an antagonist from the Montana Council of Defense episode. Even Helena newspaper editor Will Campbell, an often-vicious Wheeler critic, signaled that he was favorable to a second Wheeler term when he printed Wheeler's speech to the state Democratic convention under a positive headline. Increasingly Wheeler was able to win over or at least silence some of his biggest critics.[22]

Former senator and governor Dixon apparently decided to challenge Wheeler after having convinced himself that persistent rumors were true that Wheeler had struck a quiet accommodation with Montana's big business interests and as a result had abandoned his progressive principles. The *Miles City Star*, a newspaper not controlled by the Anaconda Company, observed during the campaign that Wheeler had said during his 1920 gubernatorial contest against Dixon that "if ever you see the *Butte Miner*, the *Anaconda Standard* or any of the trust [company] newspapers supporting me you will know I have sold out to the Anaconda," and now Wheeler's speeches and activities were reported in those newspapers with some regularity. Wheeler countered the rumors of a sellout by constantly stressing his independence. He told a crowd in Havre that his job in the Senate was "to protect the ordinary man and woman of Montana from being robbed and exploited by the few selfish interests who think only of their own interest . . . I am not going to bend my knee to suit the policies of anyone. No one can tell me what to do."[23]

Rather than a sellout to Montana business interests, it is more accurate to say that Wheeler, like Walsh before him, had concluded that some accommodation with Montana's business interests was a pragmatic necessity. Accommodation, however, was hardly capitulation, and Wheeler would continue to behave, as he said, with the attitude that no one could tell him what to do. It also seems likely that the choice between keeping Wheeler in the Senate, a politician who now generally refrained from attacks on Montana business interests and increasingly devoted himself to national and international issues, or having the Anaconda Company's implacable opponent Dixon in the Senate presented no choice at all. The company opted to acquiesce to another Wheeler term. There was no political quid pro quo or deal, the two major political forces in Montana merely agreed to stay out of each other's way.

The campaign and speaking skills Wheeler had honed during the 1924 national campaign served him well in 1928. Lee Metcalf, who later served twenty-five years as a Democratic representative and senator from Montana, was a teenager in 1928, but years later he still vividly remembered Wheeler on the campaign trail and marveled at his effectiveness. "He was a tremendous speaker," Metcalf said. "I remember he would put empty chairs on the platform and point at them and talk to them—calling them Daugherty and Fall and Doheny and so on. He would fire questions at them and the audience loved it. He was a great showman."[24]

Election Day produced one of the largest turnouts in Montana history, and voters split their ballots. Wheeler bested Dixon by a margin of 12,500, capturing more than 53 percent of the vote and winning thirty-five of Montana's fifty-six counties. Wheeler ran up impressive margins in Silver Bow County and his hometown of Butte, as well as Deer Lodge and Cascade Counties. There were more ballots cast in the Wheeler-Dixon Senate race than in the Hoover-Smith presidential contest, which Hoover won nationally and by nearly 45,000 votes in Montana. Smith won only three Montana counties. After 1928 Wheeler never again faced a serious Republican challenger or a serious challenge from the conservative wing of the Montana Democratic Party.[25]

The 1928 election marked Joe Dixon's last hurrah in Montana electoral politics, but he remains one of the state's most impressive political figures. After his defeat, Dixon accepted appointment as assistant secretary of the interior and would play a curious role in the fate of a controversial Supreme Court appointee who Wheeler opposed.[26]

―――

On October 22, 1929, following several days of nervous trading on the New York Stock Exchange, General John J. Pershing, U.S. military hero of World War I, cabled his New York financier friend Bernard Baruch: "Would you hold, sell or buy Anaconda?" Baruch replied, "I would stand pat." Selling would have been the better play. That week Anaconda Copper, a "blue chip" stock of the day, closed at $96 a share, but the market began to crash on October 24. By the summer of 1932 a share of Anaconda stock would be worth $4. Despite Wheeler's frequent indictment of the House of Morgan, big business, and Wall Street power, like millions of other Americans he fell victim to the uncontrolled speculative fervor that drove the stock market to dizzying heights in the 1920s. "Father, like so many others, had borrowed heavily to invest in stocks," Wheeler's daughter Elizabeth would remember. "When the crash came, he not only lost those stocks he had bought on margin, but was deeply in debt in bank loans. Mother was worried." The Wheelers responded by economizing at home, and the senator expanded his outside income by lining up regular bookings on the paid lecture circuit, a practice then both legal and common.[27]

As the national and Montana economies deteriorated following the market crash, Wheeler railed against the Hoover administration's ineffective agricultural and economic policies, and he caucused, the only Democrat to do so, with insurgent Republican progressives to plot strategy to derail efforts by conservative Republicans to increase tariffs. Wheeler generally advocated trade policies that he believed would improve the economic plight of farmers by creating robust foreign markets, and he frequently, although not completely, rejected the Republicans' high tariff approach, which he believed protected eastern manufactures at the expense of western farmers. This fundamental economic policy struggle played out in Congress during 1929 and 1930 and eventually reached a climax with the adoption of the protectionist Smoot-Hawley tariff, which Wheeler called "one of the most sordid pieces of legislation ever presented to a legislative body."[28]

Named for the Republican chairmen of the Senate Finance Committee, Reed Smoot of Utah, and the House Ways and Means Committee, Willis Hawley of Oregon, the tariff legislation represented a sweeping assault on free trade that raised tariffs on hundreds of imported goods, from chemicals to mustard seed, to historically high levels. As historian Douglas Irwin writes, "Members of Congress spent an enormous amount of time debating innumerable commodities that most of them had little information about." Smoot-Hawley, passed as the world economy fell deeper into the Great Depression, is now widely regarded as an unprecedented economic blunder, precisely the wrong prescription at the worst possible time.[29]

Wheeler participated extensively in the long Senate debate on the tariff measure and correctly forecast the damaging economic consequences of higher rates. When, for example, the Senate debated a proposed higher tariff on rayon filament in January 1930, Wheeler attacked the proposal, the big manufacturers who would benefit from the measure, and a Republican Party embracing protectionism. "If the rates proposed by this bill are allowed the rayon corporations will get back every cent they paid into the Republican campaign coffers," Wheeler said. "Rayon prices are higher in the United States than in any other place in the world," he said. Our high tariffs are responsible for that situation." Wheeler's proposed amendment to lower the rate was defeated.[30]

At one point Wheeler charged that Smoot-Hawley, championed by two westerners, was "bereft of aid to the important agricultural west, while it [spread] a veritable feast for the industries of the east already overstuffed with protectionist benefits." Wheeler foreshadowed trade debates of later generations when he concluded, "What this country needs is not higher tariffs, but to develop markets outside the United States." Wheeler predicted that Hoover would eventually sign the tariff bill—more than one thousand economists urged him not to—rather than offend eastern manufacturing interests who, Wheeler charged, were contributing "liberally to Republican campaigns."[31]

During the months of debate on tariff legislation, Wheeler developed a deep personal dislike for Reed Smoot. A stiff, formal man, Smoot was an apostle of the Mormon Church and had nearly thirty years earlier battled discrimination against his religion in order to assume his Senate seat. By 1930 Smoot styled himself the Republican Party's expert on taxes and trade and his influence on financial issues was immense. Wheeler told Smoot's biographer in a 1940 interview that "Senators recognized that Smoot had two gods, the Mormon Church and the Republican Party, and . . . they used that knowledge whenever possible." Wheeler recalled an occasion when Tom Walsh attempted to convince Smoot to support an appropriation for a reclamation project in Montana. Smoot was unmoved by the plea from a Democrat, but he reacted differently when Walsh pointed out that the influential Utah-Idaho Sugar Company, controlled by the Mormon Church, had expressed an interest in land adjacent to the proposed Montana reclamation project. "How much?" Smoot asked after Walsh supplied the additional important information. Wheeler considered Smoot undependable, even unethical, in floor debate and contended that Smoot "used subterfuge, misstatements, and, bluntly, lies, when rattled or stirred by opposition."[32]

In addition to hiking tariffs on hundreds of products, Smoot contended that his tariff legislation should also include language authorizing U.S. Customs officials to seize "obscene or seditious" materials entering the country. The conservative Utahan specifically suggested D. H. Lawrence's novel *Lady Chatterley's Lover* and said such "grossly indecent" plays as *King Lear, Hamlet,* and *Romeo and Juliet* should be banned in the interest of protecting public morals. Lawrence was of "a diseased mind," Smoot said during the tariff debate, with "a soul so black that he would even obscure the darkness of hell." New Mexico Republican Bronson Cutting, a favorite of Wheeler's, argued on behalf of the Senate's progressives against Smoot's book-banning provision. "The attempt to suppress individual books simply promotes their circulation and reputation," Cutting argued. Wheeler endorsed Cutting's views when he later wrote, "It is a question of whether the Congress of the United States thinks the morals of the people of the country are going to be corrupted because a few pieces of literature come in, that, in many instances, are classics . . . if the morals of the people of the

United States are so easily corrupted, then surely the keeping out of a few volumes of classics and works of that kind is not going to save them." The final version of the tariff legislation permitted customs officials to identify suspect imported literature, but a ban could be imposed only after a federal court ruled on the offending material. That provision was considered at the time a victory for free speech advocates.[33]

Wheeler and other Senate opponents to high tariffs could only complain and engage in "we told you so" denunciations after Smoot-Hawley became law and the U.S. and international economy continued a downward spiral. "We have had no leadership during the past year and a half from the President of the United States in this great emergency," Wheeler said early in 1931. Returning from an international conference in Bucharest, he was pessimistic. "It seems to me no great progress can come to Europe until there is general disarmament; until the tariff barriers are down and until one country stops trying to dominate other countries because she temporarily has the power to make vassal states out of some of the countries of Europe." Wheeler wondered whether "capitalism throughout the world [could] survive carrying the financial loads of armaments, trade barriers, like our own high tariff walls, and war debt reparations."[34]

Wheeler's answer to easing the disastrous impacts of the Great Depression involved relief for farmers and small business owners but not for the directors of railroad combinations or utility conglomerates. He opposed, for example, creation of the Reconstruction Finance Corporation, believing it would only benefit big business. Wheeler told a radio audience: "The western progressives are fighting against the domination of Congress by men who represent selfish corporate interests, because they believe sincerely that unless the growing concentration of wealth and power is checked this Nation will soon be converted into a plutocracy where a few supremely rich men will rule and the rights of the common man will be trampled under foot." Wheeler lamented the wave of business mergers and the still-new phenomenon of chain banks and retail stores, and, while he regretted the need for more government intervention, Wheeler said it was time for government to do more to regulate big business. "As much as I detest bureaucracy in Government, realizing the inefficiency, and, in many instances, the utter incompetence," Wheeler said, "the price these great combinations are going to have to pay is federal regulation by a bureaucracy."[35]

———

As the economy continued to slide downward, paralysis gripped the government. "The Senate is now almost unable to function," Henry Ashurst, the Arizona Democrat, confided to his diary. "This condition has, intermittently, prevailed in the Senate since Mr. Hoover became President." Republicans commanded a "paper majority" in the Senate, Ashurst noted, but in reality thirteen "radical Republicans" frequently joined more moderate Democrats to constitute a majority of the "negative" that, while unable to advance any program, was particularly good at criticizing Hoover. "Chaos reigns," the Arizonan wrote.[36]

Chaos certainly reigned in 1930 when the Senate considered two Hoover Supreme Court nominees—Charles Evans Hughes and John J. Parker. Wheeler voted against both nominees, believing that the ideology of a judicial nominee trumped experience. "When Democrats vote to place upon the Supreme Court of this Nation a man, no matter how honest he may be, no matter how brilliant he may be, who holds the economic views of Mr. Hughes, they are voting against every tradition of the Democratic Party," Wheeler said. "I know that Mr. Hughes' ideas upon economics are diametrically opposed to mine. As a Democrat and a liberal I propose to take this occasion by my vote to show that I do not approve of his economic views, and I am not going to be party to placing him upon the Supreme Court of the United States of America." Senate progressives all opposed Hughes, a former New York governor, presidential nominee, and secretary of state, whose resume also included previous service on the court. Hughes was confirmed and would later play a central role in Wheeler's efforts to prevent Franklin Roosevelt's expansion of the Supreme Court.[37]

Wheeler was in the Senate majority opposing confirmation of federal court of appeals judge John J. Parker of North Carolina. In an odd twist, Senate rejection of Parker's nomination was inadvertently aided by Joe Dixon, Wheeler's two-time Montana political opponent. Dixon, a native of North Carolina, now working at the Department of the Interior, wrote, apparently unsolicited, to White House assistant Walter Newton, offering his perspective on the Supreme Court vacancy. Dixon noted, "North Carolina gave President Hoover [a] 65,000 majority" in the last election and "carries more hope of a permanent alignment with the Republican Party than any other of the southern states. The naming of Judge Parker ... would appeal mightily to the state pride. It would be the first distinctive major appointment made from the south ... [it] would be a master political stroke at this time." Dixon suggested that this letter, which he believed would be held in strict confidence, might be shared with the president as he considered an appointment to the Supreme Court.[38]

A week later, perhaps following Dixon's advice or perhaps acting entirely on his own inclination, Hoover nominated Parker, whose views on race immediately drew fire. As a candidate for governor of North Carolina in 1920, Parker had said political participation by black voters was "a source of evil and danger to both races and is not desired by the wise men of either race or by the Republican Party of North Carolina." Wheeler, cognizant of this, announced in a letter to National Association for the Advancement of Colored People that he would oppose Parker's nomination to the court. Other progressives, including several Republicans, expressed similar sentiments, casting doubt as to whether Parker could be confirmed.[39]

Hoover, desperate to save his appointee, badly needed southern Democrats to support Parker, and many southern Democrats were conflicted. They were reluctant to support a southern Republican nominee for the court, but they were mindful that Parker might be the best nominee they could hope to see with a Republican occupying the White House. For reasons that have never been fully explained, Dixon's letter extolling the benefits of a Parker nomination found its way into a large stack of documents forwarded to the Senate in support of the Parker nomination. Senator Kenneth McKellar of Tennessee, one of the southern Democrats who opposed Parker, discovered the letter in the pile of White House documents and released it to reporters. The letter became an immediate sensation. The *New York Times* said Dixon had urged Parker's appointment as "a political move" that would create an opportunity for Republicans to win the South. The "master political stroke" Dixon advocated suddenly became a fatal blunder and gave southern Democrats ample reason to oppose Parker's confirmation.[40]

Seventeen Republicans eventually bucked the White House and joined Wheeler, Walsh, Dill, and twenty other Democrats in voting not to confirm Parker. The rejection marked the first time since 1894 that the Senate had refused to confirm a Supreme Court nominee. Not until Richard Nixon's 1969 nomination of another southern judge, Clement Haynsworth, would the Senate reject outright a Supreme Court nominee. Dixon never admitted even a little embarrassment over the role his letter played in denying Parker a seat on the Supreme Court. The letter was "a confidential note," Dixon said, not intended for public release, and after rereading the letter he said he was rather "proud of its contents." Judge Parker's friends were not so sanguine. The misstep "that killed us was the Dixon letter," a friend wrote to Parker. "How in the name of all that is Holy such a faux pas could have been made passes all human understanding."[41]

With another presidential election approaching, Wheeler considered it unlikely that Hoover could be reelected in 1932. The miserable state of the U.S. economy and the president's often-tepid response to the crisis provided Democrats with a genuine opportunity to capture the White House for the first time since 1916. During a national radio address delivered April 26, 1930, in front of a crowd of two thousand of the Democratic Party's elite, Wheeler once again seized the national political spotlight by endorsing his candidate two and half years in advance of the presidential election. "When I saw the bottles on the massed tables and the rapidly liquefying politicians crowded into the ballroom, I was glad I planned to speak for only fifteen minutes," Wheeler later wrote, recalling the scene at the Hotel Commodore in Manhattan. "Also I took the precaution of issuing a press release before the dinner began. I had a serious message—I was coming out for Roosevelt for President."[42]

6 A LONG AND BUMPY RELATIONSHIP

> Montana played a greater role in national politics
> in this eventful year [1932] than any other time,
> before or since, in its history.
>
> —MICHAEL P. MALONE

In the spring of 1930, with the national economy and Herbert Hoover's popularity in free fall, B. K. Wheeler was determined to see his party unite behind a progressive candidate who could recapture the White House for Democrats in 1932. Before it became politically fashionable to climb aboard the Franklin Roosevelt bandwagon, Wheeler became the first member of the U.S. Senate to endorse Roosevelt's candidacy, doing so even before Roosevelt won reelection to a second term as governor of New York. He expected that his early and unequivocal endorsement, his political spade-work helping Roosevelt secure the nomination, and his effective work on the stump would lead to a prominent position, perhaps even the vice presidency, in a Democratic administration. He would be sorely disappointed.

The two ambitious politicians—Roosevelt and Wheeler—never established personal rapport, and eventually animosity and deep mistrust came to characterize their relationship. For his part Wheeler became embittered by Roosevelt's treatment, and his was "a long and bumpy relationship" with the man who would dominate U.S. politics for the rest of Wheeler's tenure in the Senate.[1]

———

As much as Franklin Delano Roosevelt's twelve-year presidency has come to define the era of the Great Depression and the Second World War, it was less than a sure thing that FDR would even be the Democratic nominee for president in 1932. Neither party chairman John J. Raskob, a top executive of the DuPont Corporation and a board member of General Motors, or his chief lieutenant Jouett Shouse, a former congressman and the party's executive director, supported Roosevelt. Both men were supporters of New York governor Alfred E. Smith, who sought to avenge his 1928 defeat by running again in 1932. Given Raskob's and Shouse's desire to advance Smith while also enhancing the fortunes of fellow conservative Democrats, it is difficult to understand why the party leaders provided a western progressive like Wheeler with a prominent platform at the party's big Jefferson Day dinner in New York in April 1930. The Democratic power brokers certainly knew that the Montana senator was unpredictable and disdainful of party leadership and that Wheeler regularly attacked big business, banks, and Wall Street. Wheeler was a liberal in a party led by conservatives. Predictably he had a surprise in store.[2]

"As I look about for a General to lead the Democratic Party on the two issues, the tariff and control of power and public utilities, I ask to whom we can go," Wheeler said before a crowd that included both New York senators, the governor of Virginia, two of New York's most influential political bosses, and a big delegation from the city's Tammany Hall machine. Democrats need a candidate, Wheeler answered his own question, who could lead "a reunited, militant progressive party" in 1932. After considering all the potential candidates, Wheeler said, he could not help "but fasten my attention upon your Governor." "I say if the Democrats of New York will re-elect Franklin Roosevelt Governor, the West will demand his nomination for President and the whole country will elect him." As the New York Times pointed out the next day, "Governor Roosevelt, who was one of the speakers at the dinner, was not present when Senator Wheeler placed him in nomination for the Presidency amid cheers. The Governor, who said he had signed or vetoed 750 bills in the last week and had worked until 3 o'clock every morning, pleaded fatigue and asked to be excused." In fact, Roosevelt had been tipped off that Wheeler was going to anoint him as the Democrat's best hope in 1932 and decided it would not be appropriate to be sitting in the hall while his prospective candidacy was discussed. Wheeler had heard Roosevelt's speech to the Jefferson Day crowd and approved of his attack on concentrated economic power, his foreshadowing of future legislative battles with the electric power industry, and Roosevelt's reference to Thomas Jefferson's aversions to a "concentration of economic power." Wheeler's speech, the Times reported, "launched a boom" for Roosevelt, and there was little doubt that Wheeler, who was becoming a master of political theater, had stirred up the Democratic race two and a half years before the 1932 election.[3]

Roosevelt waited five weeks before sending Wheeler a carefully crafted thank-you note, warm with flattery and cool with political calculation. "I have been meaning to write to you for the past month," Roosevelt said. "I want to tell you that personally I was made very happy by your reference to me at the Democratic Club dinner, for the very good reason that I have always thought of you as one of the real leaders of the progressive thought and action in this country. Therefore, to be considered as [a] real progressive by you means something to me." As for the next presidential race, Roosevelt said it was too early to consider running, even though his lieutenants were already plotting his campaign. "I am in a somewhat difficult position," Roosevelt told Wheeler, "first, of having no personal desire to run for national office"—a disclaimer few would have believed—"and, secondly, because I feel that the more I get into the national limelight the more it is going to hurt my present work as Governor of New York." Wheeler immediately acknowledged Roosevelt's letter, emphasizing the importance he placed on the New Yorker's progressive credentials. "You more nearly typify the progressive thought of the Nation than anyone else," Wheeler said.[4]

Wheeler's very early endorsement of Roosevelt—whom he barely knew—was based on at least three calculations: he believed Roosevelt was electable, he was convinced that the New York governor was the most progressive of the likely Democratic candidates, and he thought getting on board with Roosevelt early would enhance his own influence with a new administration. Wheeler also worried that a second nomination of Al Smith, the Catholic who had lost badly to Hoover in 1928 and ran poorly in Montana, would make a Democratic victory more difficult. "The religious issue was raised so bitterly at that time that I didn't want to see it raised again," Wheeler said. "I thought our best candidate would be Roosevelt."[5]

While Wheeler threw himself headfirst into the fight to help Roosevelt capture the Democratic nomination and then win the White House, he came to experience the same kind of problems with Roosevelt that Smith had experienced after Roosevelt replaced him as governor of New York. Roosevelt and Smith had once been close, enjoying an almost mentor-protégé relationship, but the camaraderie had not lasted. "Do you know, by God," Smith said of Roosevelt, "that he has never consulted me about a damn thing since he has been Governor? He has taken bad advice and from sources not friendly to me. He has ignored me!" Wheeler came to know the feeling.[6]

Roosevelt and Wheeler shared similar political résumés but had vastly different personalities. And, as historian Richard Ruetten has noted, Wheeler was "a progressive first and a Democrat second; with FDR . . . the reverse was true; these differences, accentuated by diverse personalities, would lead eventually to disagreement." Both men were native northeasterners, born in the same year—1882. Both studied law, were elected to their respective state legislatures in 1910, and embraced reform. And both lost office two years later, Wheeler thanks to the manipulations of the Anaconda Company and Roosevelt due to maneuverings of Tammany Hall politicians. Both young politicians won appointments during the Wilson administration in 1913, Wheeler as U.S. attorney in Montana and Roosevelt as assistant secretary of the navy in Washington, D.C. Both men mounted comeback attempts in 1920, and both suffered the worst defeats of their careers, Wheeler losing the governorship of Montana and Roosevelt, running for vice president on the Democratic ticket, defeated in the Harding landslide. After his gubernatorial thrashing, Wheeler was a disgraced loser, out of office, and possessed of few prospects. Stricken with polio in 1921, Roosevelt too seemed to have a bleak political future. Yet by 1924 both of these confident, attractive, well-spoken, and still young men were back on the national stage—Wheeler running for vice president on the Progressive ticket and Roosevelt, setting aside his crutches and willing his way to a Madison Square Garden podium to deliver one of the great speeches in American political history—the "Happy Warrior" nominating speech for his then-friend Al Smith.[7]

Wheeler and Tom Walsh at one point encouraged Roosevelt to run for the Senate from New York, but in a revealing comment Roosevelt bluntly said he was not interested in being a legislator. "I am temperamentally unfitted to be a member of the uninteresting body known as the United States Senate," Roosevelt said. "I like administrative or executive work, but do not want to have my hands and feet tied and my wings clipped for 6 long years."[8]

Roosevelt was, in the words of biographer Frank Freidel, "a master of carrying water on both shoulders; he was deliberately trying to straddle the whole country" in 1932. The Roosevelt straddling had its detractors. Influential *New York Herald Tribune* columnist Walter Lippmann was one observer who thought, and Wheeler would soon agree, that Roosevelt was too slick, too eager to please, too political, and too calculating. "He has never thought much, or understood much, about the great subjects which must concern the next President," Lippmann said. He called Roosevelt a "kind of amiable boy scout."[9]

Nevertheless, in the dark early days of the Great Depression, Wheeler was eager to get on board with an optimistic candidate who held the real prospect of becoming a winner and who displayed at least some progressive inclinations. For the moment and in the interest of winning an election, the two eventual rivals would conduct themselves as the nation's foremost humorist, Will Rogers, suggested rival Democrats must. Bury the hatchet, Rogers said. Bury it "in the Republican President."[10]

Early in 1931 four Senate progressives—Democrats Wheeler and Edward Costigan of Colorado and Republicans George Norris and Bronson Cutting—issued a call for a national conference of progressive leaders that would develop legislative proposals for next Congress. The conference opened in Washington on March 11, 1931, with an impressive group of the nation's progressive leaders in attendance, including Harold Ickes, soon to become Roosevelt's interior secretary; historian Charles Beard; journalists

Lincoln Steffens and Bruce Bliven; labor leaders Sidney Hillman and William Green; and newspaper tycoon Robert P. Scripps. Roosevelt was invited to participate but begged off, citing a busy schedule, although he sent a supportive message. New York Republican congressman Fiorello La Guardia, also unable to attend, provided the conference with a detailed brief on the need to modernize economic policy.[11]

The conference debated a variety of proposals, all of which would eventually receive attention when Roosevelt occupied the White House, including unemployment relief, industrial stabilization, public utility regulation, and tariff reform. Still, Norris, a respected elder in the group, admitted the obvious. Little progress was possible on progressive legislation while Hoover, whom Norris called "the engineer," was still in office. "What we do need," Norris said to great applause, "is another Roosevelt in the White House." Without a champion, the work of the progressive conference languished, and critics, including philosopher and education reformer John Dewey, accused the group of being too timid and "paralyzed" to make a difference. Some pointed out that, while the progressives were fair-minded and forward-looking, they lacked a forceful leader, a unifying vision, and a concrete plan to turn their proposals into law. The bipartisan conference did, however, confirm what Wheeler had been saying—a presidential candidate with progressive ideas could appeal to reformers in both parties.[12]

"If the Democratic Party wants to win it must name a progressive candidate in 1932," Wheeler said early that year. If Democrats were to "nominate some reactionary," he forecast a repeat of 1924, with a third party attempting to appeal to progressives in both parties. But with little interest among progressives in again attempting to run a third-party candidate, most of Wheeler's friends in and out of the Senate were coming to the position he had staked out in endorsing FDR: Roosevelt was the only candidate all progressives could get behind. Still there were skeptics, including Wheeler's friend Oswald Garrison Villard, who expressed doubts about whether Roosevelt was a true liberal. Wheeler assured Villard that Roosevelt was liberal enough. "He probably would not go as far as I would go," Wheeler wrote Villard, "but we cannot always get as candidates, people who entirely agree with our views. If Governor Roosevelt is not the man to lead us in the present crisis, name some man upon whom the liberals would agree at the present time who would have the slightest possible chance of receiving the Democratic nomination."[13]

Roosevelt's 1932 campaign took shape under the careful guidance of two of his closest friends: a former newspaperman, Louis McHenry Howe, and the chairman of the New York Democratic Party, James A. Farley. Farley made a whirlwind western tour in the summer of 1931 to firm up early support for Roosevelt and found that little work was needed in Montana. "The Fourth of July found me at a luncheon in Butte, Montana," Farley would write in his memoirs, "given by such outstanding party workers as Senator Burton K. Wheeler, James E. Murray, afterwards elected Senator [at the time Murray was chairman of the Silver Bow County Democratic Party], J. Bruce Kremer, the national committeeman, Thomas J. Walker, brother of Frank C. Walker [a former Butte attorney, the party's national treasurer, and a future postmaster general], and Dr. T. J. B. Shanley. They were all such ardent Roosevelt backers that there was little for me to do except make arrangements to keep in close touch during the pre-convention period."[14]

By the fall of 1931 Wheeler was confidently predicting a first-ballot nomination for Roosevelt and his eventual election, a prediction based, at least in part, on his observation of the steadily deteriorating economic conditions. "The situation of the farmers in parts of the Northwest which suffered from a tremendous drought are deplorable," Wheeler said. "A large number of farmers are now being assisted by the Red Cross. Many more will have to be assisted this year. Conditions in that section are much worse than last year, many farmers being unable even to pay their taxes, owing to low prices." Wheeler pleaded with the Hoover administration for a national farm relief program. "Something will have to be done to help these farmers. Funds will have to be raised by the government, either by taxation or by a bond issue. I should prefer to have them raised by taxation but that cannot be done now so a bond issue will become necessary."[15]

Even as Roosevelt's presidential prospects brightened, there were telltale signs that the Democratic convention might again dissolve, as it had in 1924, into a long, bitter, and politically damaging struggle. Bosses in Chicago, Newark, and New York City and conservative party leaders like Raskob and Shouse were determined to stop Roosevelt. While few Democrats wanted a repeat of the convention fiasco of eight years earlier, the party's two-thirds rule requiring a supermajority of the delegates to secure the nomination remained a significant hurdle for any candidate, and the New York governor had competition for the nomination. Smith and Speaker of the House John Nance Garner of Texas were serious contenders, while Maryland governor Albert Ritchie, Oklahoma governor William Henry "Alfalfa Bill" Murray, and Newton Baker, the secretary of war in the Wilson administration, might emerge from a deadlocked convention. Wheeler predicted, "There is going to be a determined effort within the Democratic Party to prevent the nomination of Governor Roosevelt by a lot of bosses in the East because they think he is a liberal," Wheeler said. "Democrats can win with Roosevelt or lose without him. They can take their choice."[16]

On January 22, 1932, Roosevelt formally declared his intention to seek the presidency by requesting that his name be entered in the Democratic primary in North Dakota. Roosevelt immediately encountered opposition from a shrewd, agrarian populist who tested FDR's appeal in the farm belt. Alfalfa Bill Murray, lanky and rumpled, with a soggy black cigar perpetually stuck beneath a bushy moustache, entered the North Dakota primary hoping to capture votes from the state's notoriously independent farm voters. Murray, nicknamed in recognition of his devotion to, and knowledge of, alfalfa as a farm crop—leavened his prairie radicalism with more than a dash of cornpone speech. Next to Roosevelt, Murray was the best-known governor in the country, and rarely has America seen a better campaign slogan: "Bread, Butter, Bacon and Beans."[17]

"The people want me, that is the plain people," Murray told one North Dakota crowd. It was so cold at one of his stops that ice formed in his shaggy moustache as Murray unspooled his prairie populism, ranting against Republican policies and big banks. Roosevelt's managers immediately recognized the threat Murray presented and issued a slightly panicked call for help. Wheeler stormed out of Montana to the rescue, delivering an effective radio speech on Roosevelt's behalf that was broadcast on several North Dakota stations. He had nothing against Murray, Wheeler told voters, but they needed to understand that the quirky Oklahoma governor was not a true national candidate but merely a stalking horse for "a corrupt gang in the east, which for lack of a better name, might be called the Wall Street crowd," the forces determined to deny Roosevelt the nomination. In effect, Wheeler claimed that Murray, a politician far more accustomed at attacking Wall Street than Roosevelt, was an unwitting tool of the very interests Murray opposed. Wheeler's spin was effective. News coverage of Wheeler's radio talk helped blunt Murray's appeal in North Dakota and give credence to Roosevelt's promise, the first he had made during the campaign, to support new farm relief programs when elected. A record number of North Dakotans voted in the primary, and Roosevelt won with more than 62 percent of the vote, taking nine of the ten convention delegates. The results provided the first real evidence that the Farm Belt was ready to desert Herbert Hoover, not for a hardcore populist like Alfalfa Bill Murray but for a liberal like Roosevelt who enjoyed support among prominent western progressives. Murray campaigned energetically in several other primaries but won only twenty-one more delegates all from Oklahoma.[18]

Wheeler returned to Washington, D.C., in late March confidently predicting that Washington, Oregon, Idaho, Montana, Wyoming, Wisconsin, and the Dakotas were lining up behind Roosevelt. "All you have to do to become convinced is to go out in that country and listen to what the people are talking about. Mr. Hoover is in bad out there; don't doubt that for a minute," Wheeler said. The farm economy was in awful shape, he declared, with "some of the stories about the troubles of the farmers almost beyond belief, but just the same they are true."[19]

Also in March, Wheeler proposed creating a refinancing program for farmers, a move Hoover had resisted. "President Hoover's course has been directed at helping those at the top, the railroads, the banks and the insurance companies, and none of the program is likely to help the farmer or the small business or laboring man," Wheeler said. Wheeler's timely intervention in North Dakota and his regular critiques of Hoover's response to the economic collapse clearly advanced Roosevelt's campaign, but his most important contribution was yet to come.[20]

Wheeler first met Louisiana governor Huey P. Long in 1929 in Shreveport, while Wheeler was participating in hearings conducted by the Senate Committee on Indian Affairs. Wheeler and Long shared a mutual dislike of big business, and the Montanan immediately took a liking to the flamboyant governor who already had designs on a seat in the U.S. Senate. "I liked him," Wheeler remembered. "I think he was sincere in espousing welfare programs—some of them admittedly pretty radical—to do something for the kind of poor people he sprang from. Perhaps he fancied himself a kind of Robin Hood of the bayous."[21]

Long was not precisely another "son of the wild jackass," but he embodied many of the characteristics of that group of independent, colorful politicians. Long's epic battles with Standard Oil in Louisiana resembled in intensity Wheeler's fights with the Anaconda Company in Montana, and both styled themselves as advocates for the common person. Wheeler admitted that Long could be politically ruthless and was perhaps even corrupt, but Long also displayed one characteristic that Wheeler came to value above almost any other. "Huey never lied to me," Wheeler said, "and I had no evidence that he was a crook. Of course, there were a lot of stories about him. But after the way I had been maligned in Montana I knew enough not to believe the worst about a politician just because it was being passed around."[22]

By 1932 Long's political influence was growing across the South, with many voters enjoying his showy, humorous speeches and embracing his programs, including free textbooks for Louisiana schoolchildren, new public hospitals, and road and bridge construction. Wheeler, along with other progressive senators, including Norris and La Follette, mostly ignored allegations of Long's corruption when the Louisianan arrived in the Senate that year. Wheeler, who quickly became Long's best friend in the Senate and was a frequent guest for dinner at the Wheelers' home, immediately helped educate the flamboyant "Kingfish" about the rituals and personalities of the institution. Not all of the tutoring worked. Long delighted in flouting Senate rules, and his stock in

trade was insulting, often in a highly quotable way, his political adversaries. Of the
Senate's progressives, Long admired Wheeler and George Norris above all, saying
they "were the boldest, most courageous men" he had ever known.[23]

Early in 1932, Wheeler and Long had dinner at Congressional Country Club in
Washington, where Long had taken up residence. During dinner Wheeler pressed
his new friend to support Roosevelt for the Democratic presidential nomination,
no doubt using the same argument he had used to convince other progressives to
support FDR: Roosevelt was not only the best available candidate for progressives,
but he could also win the Democratic nomination and defeat Hoover. Long needed
convincing. Shortly before taking his Senate seat, Long had told reporters that he
considered Roosevelt a likely loser to Hoover in 1932. There were stronger White
House contenders, Long thought, including fellow southerners like Speaker of the
House Garner, Senate Democratic leader Joe Robinson of Arkansas, and Senator Pat
Harrison of Mississippi.[24]

As the dinner progressed, Wheeler grew steadily more persuasive, and at one
point Long asked whether George Norris was supporting Roosevelt. Wheeler assured
him that indeed the Nebraska senator was in Roosevelt's camp. Long responded
that he would check with Norris, and if Wheeler was correct then he too would
back Roosevelt. A short time later, with Wheeler helping engineer the conversation,
Norris confirmed his support for Roosevelt, and Long immediately headed back to
Louisiana to make certain he could deliver the state's delegation to FDR at the Chicago
national convention. Long's commitment to Roosevelt remained solid throughout
the convention, but he also told Wheeler that his support was grudging. "I don't like
your son of a bitch," Long told Wheeler, "but I'll be for him." Given his power and
political influence in Louisiana, it still required considerable effort on Long's part
to make certain the state's delegation committed to Roosevelt, and the Kingfish
barely succeeded. Quarreling Louisiana Democrats eventually sent three different
delegations to Chicago, each claiming to be the state's official representatives. The
handpicked Long delegation was eventually seated but not before a bitter convention
fight. Long biographer William Ivy Hair argues that Long's support for Roosevelt
had more to do with Huey maintaining his iron grip on Louisiana politics than with
nominating Roosevelt, but for whatever reason Long kept his word to Wheeler.
And, as events unfolded, Long's support proved critical to keeping other southern
delegations in line for Roosevelt.[25]

———

On Sunday June 5, 1932, a select group of politicians who would manage Franklin Roosevelt's fortunes during the Democratic National Convention scheduled to convene in
twenty-two days—began arriving at the small train station in Poughkeepsie, eighty-five

Longtime pals and Democratic operatives Homer
S. Cummings (*left*) and Butte attorney J. Bruce
Kremer. Wheeler harbored a strong dislike for both.
(*Library of Congress Prints and Photographs Division,
Washington, D.C.*)

miles north of New York City. Reporters were calling the group "BC men"—supporters
of Roosevelt "before Chicago"—but journalists did not know about the gathering. The
politicians were driven the six miles from the train station to Springwood, Roosevelt's
beloved birthplace and family home situated on a bluff above the Hudson River in Hyde
Park, New York. Five U.S. senators attended this historic strategy session—Cordell
Hull of Tennessee, John S. Cohen of Georgia, Dill, Walsh, and Wheeler—as did former
Wilson administration attorney general A. Mitchell Palmer, former party chairman
Homer S. Cummings of Connecticut, and the national committeeman from Montana,
Bruce Kremer. Roosevelt's closest political advisers, Farley, Howe, Bronx Democratic
leader Edward Flynn, and Robert H. Jackson, the national committeeman from New
Hampshire, also took part.[26]

The "BC men" had come to Roosevelt's home united in their desire to secure the
nomination for FDR, but as they filed into the living room on the south side of the
big house—a large yet cozy room filled with books, antiques, and nautical prints the
complicated relationships and in some cases open hostility among the participants must

have been obvious to everyone. Most Roosevelt biographers have given scant attention to this pre-convention strategy session that was critical to Roosevelt's candidacy. That such a diverse—and rivalrous—group of politicians were uniting behind Roosevelt is a testament to both his appeal and to how badly these men wanted a Democrat to win the presidency.

The three Montanans at the Hyde Park meeting were lawyers, and Walsh and Wheeler, it was commonly known, detested the urbane, handsome, and much more conservative Kremer. Kremer, still on retainer to the Anaconda Company, had little use for Walsh or Wheeler, who likely wondered why a mining company lobbyist had been invited to such a meeting. Kremer was a good friend of another lawyer present, Cummings. The two men had become close during the more than twenty years each had been involved in national party politics. Both Kremer and Cummings also had close connections to the candidate, knowing Roosevelt better than Wheeler or Walsh did.

Most of those at the meeting must have been thinking about their own political futures as well as Roosevelt's. It was an open secret that Walsh had almost certainly secured a position in a future Roosevelt cabinet, likely as attorney general. Should Roosevelt win and should a Walsh appointment occur, the Montanan would need to resign his Senate seat, and Kremer, known to be interested in a political office, may have been thinking about how to get himself appointed to replace Walsh. "Bolshevik Burt" Wheeler and former attorney general Palmer must have eyed each other with some discomfort. Palmer's controversial raids aimed at rounding up and deporting alien "radicals" during the postwar "red scare" had helped spawn the poisonous political environment in Montana in 1920 and at least indirectly contributed to Wheeler's shellacking that year in the governor's race. Dill, Hull, and Wheeler were all ambitious senators, vice presidential or cabinet material perhaps, and each believed he deserved special consideration from Roosevelt.

A pivotal decision was quickly made to abandon a "gentlemen's agreement" Roosevelt forces had made that would have allowed the party's executive director, the anti-Roosevelt Jouett Shouse, to serve as permanent chair of the convention. Nearly everyone gathered in Roosevelt's living room believed that his chances of prevailing on contested convention issues could come down to rulings by the chair, and they were convinced that Shouse could not be trusted. Wheeler bluntly told Roosevelt, "If Shouse becomes chairman you will not become President!" The group agreed, and it was decided that Walsh, who had chaired the unruly convention in 1924 and briefly bid for the party's nomination in 1928, would become the Roosevelt team's candidate for permanent chair. It was a wise strategic decision but required Roosevelt to renege on a personal commitment made months earlier. Shouse, who had been less than forthcoming about his efforts to stop Roosevelt, now suffered his own double-crossing by the candidate. Walsh's sterling reputation for integrity and fairness, however, made going back on a commitment somewhat easier for Roosevelt. Still, as historian Steve Neal has written, "There were few decisions more badly handled by the Roosevelt camp than those involving the leadership of the convention."[27]

The strategists next decided that Kremer would have responsibilities for dealing with individual state delegations, as well as chairing the convention's Rules Committee, a decision that had the effect of placing Montanans in two of the convention's most important roles. Discussion next turned to whether Roosevelt forces should challenge the controversial two-thirds rule, which had nearly destroyed the party during the 103-ballot marathon eight years earlier. Most Roosevelt's advisors agreed with Wheeler that the rule had to be changed, but they also knew the that supermajority requirement, a legacy of historic demands by southern Democrats that their region effectively maintain a veto over the party's nominee, was considered sacred by many party faithful. The session adjourned without a firm decision on how to handle the two-thirds rule and with Roosevelt delegating Farley to manage the issue in Chicago, where a final resolution about challenging party tradition, a decision fraught with danger and drama, could be made on the eve of the convention.[28]

FDR biographer Frank Freidel notes what might have been one of the few light moments during the Hyde Park gathering. He writes that Wheeler recalled that at one point Roosevelt's formidable mother, Sara Delano Roosevelt, no fan of her son's taste for a cocktail, remarked that she did not care to see her son nominated for president of the United States on the basis of abandoning support for Prohibition. Apparently no one said anything in response to Mrs. Roosevelt's remark, and the candidate's mother was left unaware that it had been decided that Roosevelt would support a platform advocating repeal of Prohibition.[29]

————

The Democratic National Convention convened on June 27, 1932, in cavernous Chicago Stadium, later home of the Chicago Bulls and Blackhawks and the venue for scenes in the political thriller *The Manchurian Candidate*. Two weeks earlier, in the same Chicago hall, in an environment approaching political despair, Republicans had nominated Herbert Hoover for a second term during a listless, colorless convention. "To the Republicans," Anne O'Hare McCormick wrote in the *New York Times*, "politics is business, while to the Democrats it's a pleasure." But any pleasure Democrats were feeling as they convened was tempered by the realization of how enormous the stakes were for the party. Owing to the two-thirds rule, a divided convention might still nominate a weak candidate who could lose in the fall. Roosevelt's team entered the convention claiming commitments from half the convention delegates, but that represented a tenuous grip on the nomination. Roosevelt would need many more votes to win. Anything might happen.[30]

Three of the previous five Democratic conventions had gone through at least forty-four ballots before producing a nominee, and since the Civil War no Democrat entering the convention as the front-runner had gone on to win the nomination if voting continued beyond four ballots. Four days before the convention opened, well aware of the history of Democratic nominating battles, Jim Farley, Roosevelt's campaign manager, invited an unwieldy group of sixty-five Roosevelt partisans to a strategy session in the presidential suite on the eleventh floor of the Congress Hotel in downtown Chicago. The group's purpose was to settle on a strategy to address the two-thirds rule, but Farley would later write that he immediately realized the meeting was a mistake, a violation of his own long-standing rule against large meetings. "What started out to be a friendly get-together developed into a sort of noisy town-meeting," Farley remembered.[31]

Wheeler argued forcefully for abandoning the long-standing supermajority rule. Huey Long and Cordell Hull supported him. Kremer observed that a rule change would have to go to the full convention for vote, but most felt confident that Roosevelt's forces controlled a simple majority of the delegates and therefore could accomplish the historic rule change. The meeting broke up with agreement to push for the change and with a commitment to try to nominate Roosevelt on the first ballot by a majority vote of the delegates. Farley was stunned—it felt "like a blow on the nose," he later wrote—that the meeting had gotten away from him. Ruled by emotion, a large and unruly group had made a strategically vital decision that ought to have been decided calmly by a small group able to consider all the ramifications for the candidate. Roosevelt now faced what Farley knew would be a major rules fight on the convention floor.[32]

Almost immediately word of Roosevelt's strategy began to leak, and southern delegates and Al Smith partisans voiced violent objections. Both groups charged that a Roosevelt power play was afoot—it clearly was—that would abandon decades of tradition. The depth of the revolt became clear when Roosevelt's home-state delegation voted to oppose any rule change and respected Democratic leaders (Sam Rayburn of Texas, for one), said it was a simple matter of fairness not to tamper with the rules in the middle of the nomination process. The *New York Times* called the dust-up over a rule that had governed Democratic conventions since Andrew Jackson "the most sensational development in a national convention since 1912."[33]

Support for the rule change eroded rapidly, and Roosevelt, ever the pragmatist, ordered a halt. "I decline to permit either myself or my friends to be open to the accusation of poor sportsmanship or to the use of methods which could be called, even falsely, those of a steamroller," Roosevelt said in a message to Farley that was publicly released. If he were to win the Democratic nomination, Roosevelt would have to do it in the old-fashioned way, winning the votes of two-thirds of the convention delegates.

This capitulation, intended to head off a fight that might have doomed Roosevelt's chances, left some FDR supporters, including Wheeler, feeling that they had gone out on a limb only to see it cut.[34]

Roosevelt fared better on a series of votes to determine the seating of Long's Louisiana delegation, and Long celebrated the win by grabbing the Louisiana standard and waving it about while standing on a chair on the convention floor. Walsh's role as permanent chairman of the convention was also secured by a comfortable if not overwhelming margin.[35]

After three ballots Roosevelt held a comfortable lead in the race for the nomination, but his delegate count was still well short of two-thirds, and increasingly another deadlocked Democratic convention appeared forthcoming. Again Wheeler's friend Long helped save the day. "Several times in the months since I had wrangled his pledge for Roosevelt," Wheeler would later write, "Long had begged me to release him. He actually favored Garner. But now he did more than keep his word. He worked over the two state delegations [Arkansas and Mississippi] with all his red-necked eloquence."[36]

It was during voting on the third ballot, Wheeler recalled, "when it looked like Roosevelt would have to win quickly or be through, [that] the Mississippi delegation voted to withdraw support for Roosevelt. We got hold of Huey and sent him to their meeting and he held them off until the next ballot when [William Gibbs] McAdoo [chair of the delegation] brought California in and it was all over." In this case Long's "red-necked eloquence" was a bald-faced threat. Long told Mississippi senator Pat Harrison that if Harrison was not able to keep his delegation in line for Roosevelt by continuing to observe the so-called "unit rule" (that binds an entire state's delegation when a majority favor a particular candidate or position), there would be hell to pay. "If you break the unit rule, you sonofabitch," Long fumed at Harrison, "I'll go into Mississippi and break you." Mississippi continued to support the unit rule.[37]

"If it hadn't been for Huey Long," Wheeler recalled years later, "Roosevelt wouldn't have been nominated at the convention, because [Long] had power. The southern politicians were afraid of Huey Long." Long had saved the day, in Wheeler's view, "but conveniently some of the Roosevelt people forgot what he had done for them." Wheeler harbored lingering resentment about the slight. Roosevelt's convention manager Farley acknowledged Long's role—and indirectly Wheeler's—noting in his diary, "To me the most vital moment of the convention was the seating of Huey Long's delegation."[38]

Roosevelt eventually secured the nomination by engineering a classic deal. The California delegation, controlled by former treasury secretary McAdoo and influenced by newspaper tycoon William Randolph Hearst, and the Texas delegation, controlled by Garner, switched support to Roosevelt. Garner eventually received the vice presidential nomination as part of the agreement, and McAdoo was promised a voice in cabinet appointments and a major role in determining patronage in California.[39]

Garner's nomination for the second spot on the ticket made sense, since the Texan had delivered his delegates to Roosevelt at a critical moment and Garner's place on the ticket would balance the slate geographically and philosophically, but several other Roosevelt supporters, Wheeler included, had believed they deserved the role. "Some of our most enthusiastic supporters were asking that we have a conference without delay to pick a man for second place on the ticket," Farley recalled. "There were a number of candidates being urged for the place, including Senator Dill, Governor [George] Dern of Utah, and Senator Wheeler."[40]

Wheeler's interest in the number two spot received public notice the day the convention opened and in advance of the intense maneuvering to secure Roosevelt's nomination. The *Chicago Examiner* reported, incorrectly, that Wheeler had been offered the vice presidency, which must have flattered him, at least until Roosevelt quickly scotched the rumor. In a telegram to Farley, Roosevelt said he had "asked no one to become my running mate" and that "no one has been authorized to do so on my behalf." The *New York Times* reported the same day that many are "mentioned for the vice presidency" but that "the strategy of the Roosevelt forces requires the vice presidential nomination to be kept open until after the nomination for president is made, if that is possible, because half a dozen of the Roosevelt leaders in various parts of the country have vice presidential aspirations."[41]

Wheeler never admitted to desiring the vice presidency in 1932, but few politicians admit to coveting the position, even though fewer still turn down the opportunity when it is offered. Wheeler had certainly positioned himself to be considered. His early endorsement of Roosevelt, his diligent pre-convention work, his hand-holding of Huey Long, his efforts to draw sharp distinctions between the Roosevelt forces and the Democratic Party's conservative leadership, and his obvious appeal to western progressives were all reasons, at least in his mind, to be considered. There are also numerous reasons why it did not happen. Wheeler was still widely viewed as a maverick Democrat who abandoned his party with some regularity. The conservative, business-oriented wing of the party did not trust him. While it is true that Wheeler would have brought regional balance to the ticket, Garner, who was both well known and had a large following in the national party, had more to offer as a running mate. Additionally, Montana's miniscule four electoral votes argued for someone other than Wheeler as the vice presidential candidate. Roosevelt also had in mind a senior role in his administration for Tom Walsh, and it would have been unprecedented to tap both of Montana's senators for top positions. Consequently there is no evidence that Wheeler received serious consideration by Roosevelt, which may have actually deepened his disappointment. While only one can be selected, many can be consulted, and some can be considered. If Wheeler was not considered for the vice presidency, it is also clear that FDR did not consult with him.

Some Democrats, including the party's finance chief Frank Walker, thought that Wheeler "wanted the vice presidential nomination desperately." Walker claimed that Wheeler "had never quite recovered from the sting of his defeat when he was the vice presidential candidate with the elder La Follette on the Progressive ticket in 1924." Newspaperman and Democratic operative Charles Michelson also believed that Wheeler "thought he ought to have the second place on the ticket," writing more than a decade later that Wheeler "has been grouchy ever since." The Walker-Michelson theory is entirely plausible, and as Roosevelt intimates both men were in a position to know the inside story. Walker was clearly convinced that being passed over wounded Wheeler and that the hurt of being snubbed lasted. Walker wrote in his autobiography that Wheeler "being passed over in 1932 was what originally soured [him] on Roosevelt. He never was wholeheartedly for him after that."[42]

———

Republicans in 1932 were caught, as historian James MacGregor Burns put it, "neatly in a cul-de-sac" of their own making. Hoover had campaigned four years earlier on the promise of continuing prosperity, and now a Republican administration was presiding over of a nation of bread lines and soup kitchens, with countless thousands of jobless Americans living in makeshift shantytowns that everyone took to calling "Hoovervilles." In Montana, miners in Butte, smelter workers in Anaconda, and lumberjacks all across the western half of the state were out of work. One study pegged the number of malnourished children in Montana at five out of six. Governor John Erickson toured the farm country of eastern Montana during the summer of 1931 and wondered if anything could be done to ease the suffering. Montana's agricultural economy had yet to return to prewar conditions, and prolonged drought made conditions worse. The people, Erickson said, are "in rather desperate condition." Unable to get any real assistance from the state or the national government, half of Montana's fifty-six counties petitioned the American Red Cross for disaster relief.[43]

Roosevelt visited Montana during a post–Labor Day tour of the west. The carefully orchestrated campaign swing was aimed at nailing down a Democratic sweep of the Northwest and western states, a strategy Wheeler advocated. When Roosevelt's train arrived in Butte on September 19, Roosevelt was greeted by what a New York Times reporter called "one of the largest and most enthusiastic crowds" the candidate encountered during the western tour. Senators Wheeler, Walsh, and Nevada's Key Pittman were on Roosevelt's train to schmooze with local politicians and, as Farley said, "to make sure that responsible party leaders were let aboard."[44]

Walsh introduced the candidate, and Roosevelt spoke in general terms about agriculture and mining, but, more importantly, at least to Wheeler, Roosevelt suggested that he would work to include silver as a component of his overall monetary policy and would push to convene an international conference to address the world economic crisis. Roosevelt also, as he was pragmatically prone to do, left himself plenty of flexibility, saying that improving the condition of silver "must be done with the pledge of the platform in mind that sound currency be maintained at all regards. This must and shall be done." Roosevelt was having it both ways on a delicate monetary policy issue that had taken on great importance to Wheeler and other western progressives. Roosevelt came close to promising to push for a more inflationary monetary policy, but he was also saying, in a kind of political shorthand, that he would be sensitive that inflating currency might upset the business community.[45]

Roosevelt's comments in Butte amounted to astute politics and were typical of his approach during the campaign. Roosevelt was all about balancing proposals that could appeal a little here to conservatives and a bit there to liberals. "The candidate found himself in the center of a triangle of advice," as Arthur Schlesinger Jr. put it, with one group recommending centralized planning of the economy, another advocating a balanced budget, and a third group, including Wheeler, focused on an inflationary monetary policy, tighter controls on monopolistic practices, and tougher regulation of business. Roosevelt was looking for ideas that appealed broadly to voters, even if the details were at times inconsistent. Most of all Roosevelt wanted to avoid the appearance that he was under the sway of any one group or faction, while giving all the competing constituencies reason to believe that he actually embraced their ideas.[46]

Nevertheless, conservative commentators pounded on the theme that Roosevelt was most influenced by "economic radicals" whose proposals would ruin the country and destroy capitalism. Journalist Mark Sullivan, supportive of Hoover's candidacy to the bitter end, worried about the "frightful specter of a national Administration dominated by Huey Long, Burt Wheeler, and Mrs. Hattie Caraway [the Arkansas Democrat close to Long]." The Nation responded that Sullivan and his ilk simply could "not see how bolshevism could be avoided if those two millionaires, Franklin Roosevelt and John Garner, were elected." Hoover, feeling a second term slipping away, adopted a similar line of attack. Twice in the last week of the campaign Hoover mentioned Wheeler by name as one of the "radicals" influencing Roosevelt. In a radio speech broadcast on the CBS and NBC networks and delivered before twenty-two thousand supporters at Madison Square Garden, Hoover charged that Roosevelt and his supporters were proposing "revolutionary changes" in the American system, changes totally at odds with "the traditional philosophies of the American people." Four days later Hoover sharpened his attack during a speech in St. Louis. "The people deserve to know," Hoover said, whether Roosevelt "will support or repudiate Messrs. Wheeler, Norris, Huey Long, W. R. Hearst, and others, in their long-continued efforts to put the government into large business undertakings."[47]

Wheeler ended his own campaigning for Roosevelt with a blistering radio speech in Salt Lake City that undoubtedly helped Roosevelt in Utah and contributed to Democrat Elbert Thomas's defeat of Wheeler's tariff battle adversary Reed Smoot. Wheeler said that if Smoot, chairman of the Senate Finance Committee, "worked as hard for the remonetization of silver as he did for the Smoot-Hawley tariff bill we would have made some headway." He also reminded Utah voters that Smoot opposed unemployment relief but favored bailout loans to big banks. Thomas defeated Smoot, a five-term incumbent, by thirty thousand votes, and Smoot refused to speak to Wheeler when the two met during the post-election lame duck session of Congress.[48]

Roosevelt's historic landslide win against Hoover—he won 472 electoral votes to Hoover's 59—helped produce a nearly complete Democratic sweep in Montana. Governor Erickson, "a gentle, sleepy, colorless conservative," in the view of one commentator, but also a Wheeler ally, won a third term in a tight race, capturing less than 50 percent of the vote. Democrats also won both Montana congressional seats.[49]

Wheeler, likely confident that his own role during the convention and the campaign would be rewarded, traveled to Warm Springs, Georgia, in late November for conversations about the shape of Roosevelt's cabinet and other issues immediately confronting a new administration. Wheeler urged the appointment of his friend Ed Keating of Colorado as secretary of labor. Keating had often used his liberal *Labor* publication to back progressive causes, and Keating had actively supported the La Follette–Wheeler ticket in 1924. Roosevelt responded that he needed to avoid too many Catholics in the Cabinet. Farley, a Catholic, would serve as postmaster general, and Roosevelt was determined to convince Walsh, another Catholic, to become attorney general.[50]

Roosevelt asked Wheeler's reaction to Frances Perkins as a possible labor secretary. She had served as New York's industrial commissioner under both Al Smith and Roosevelt. Wheeler said he did not know Perkins but thought it would be a mistake to appoint a woman, presumably because a woman would find it difficult to succeed in an environment so completely dominated by men. Perkins, of course, would become the first woman appointed to a Cabinet position and serve with considerable distinction and skill throughout Roosevelt's administration. Roosevelt also told Wheeler that he was hoping that Republicans George Norris, possibly at the Agriculture Department, and Hiram Johnson, an Interior Department possibility, would join the Cabinet. Wheeler said he was convinced that both would want to stay in the Senate, which they did.[51]

There is some evidence that Roosevelt thought, however briefly, of a spot in the cabinet for Wheeler, perhaps at the Department of the Interior. Washington senator Clarence Dill wrote in his memoirs that Roosevelt told him in January 1933 that Wheeler and Hiram Johnson "would not take" the Interior Department position. Perhaps Roosevelt really did not want Wheeler in the cabinet or concluded Wheeler would refuse the job or focused on the complication of appointing both Montana senators to top jobs. For whatever reason, Wheeler was offered no position, although its possible Roosevelt raised the issue during the Warm Springs meeting.[52]

Wheeler, for a complex set of reasons, was also less than enthused by the prospect of Walsh leaving the Senate to become attorney general. "The President-elect asked me to talk to Walsh about taking the Attorney Generalship," Wheeler would later write, and, when he spoke with his onetime mentor, Walsh had expressed no interest in the job and insisted that Wheeler should get the appointment. "I told him I wasn't interested," Wheeler wrote, "for the simple reason that the Roosevelt Administration undoubtedly would want me to do certain things politically as Attorney General that I would not do." Wheeler's Warm Springs visit left him disappointed again. He was offered nothing, his suggestion regarding Keating was rejected, and he was asked to convince Walsh to take a position that he was not sure was a good idea.[53]

A further indication of Wheeler's thinking about a Walsh appointment was his suggestion, neither generous nor necessarily fair, that the seventy-three-year old Walsh was not up to the strenuous job of running the Justice Department. Wheeler mentioned in both a 1959 interview and in his memoirs that Walsh was slipping both mentally and physically in 1932. Wheeler almost certainly was also considering who might replace Walsh in the Senate should he become attorney general and how that process might affect him, a potentially unsettling development in the Montana political landscape.[54]

Walsh eventually agreed to become attorney general because, as he told Wheeler, Roosevelt promised that he would be first in line for appointment to a vacancy on the Supreme Court. Walsh told Wheeler that he could turn down one appointment but not two, particularly since Walsh had long harbored an ambition to sit on the high court. It also seems clear, due to Walsh's sterling reputation and his rectitude, that Roosevelt convinced Walsh to accept the attorney general position by guaranteeing him a role in the cabinet as a first among equals.[55]

News of Walsh's appointment was greeted with near universal approval, but tragedy quickly followed the announcement. A few days after being named attorney general, Walsh shocked almost everyone who knew him, particularly Wheeler, when he stole off to Havana, Cuba, and married a vivacious, younger widow, mother of two sons, with the audacious name of Mina Nieves Perez Chaumont de Truffin. Hardly a Don Juan, the buttoned-down Walsh had been a widower for fourteen years, and his sudden marriage came as a complete surprise to his friends. When Wheeler and his wife heard rumors of the pending marriage both dismissed the idea as preposterous. An even bigger shock came on March 2, 1933, just two days before Roosevelt's inauguration, when news reached Washington that Walsh had died, apparently of a heart attack, in a Pullman car not far from Rocky Mount, North Carolina. Walsh and his new wife were en route to Washington to begin a new life together, with Walsh joining the cabinet. The circumstances of Walsh's death have never been conclusively determined. Witnesses said he looked ill before collapsing. No autopsy was conducted.[56]

Walsh's death shocked the nation. "I am grieved beyond words," Wheeler said. "He has been almost a father to me. His advice and counsel was so much needed in this time of stress." The New York Times, once harshly critical of Walsh's investigation of Teapot Dome, now praised his "unblemished honor" and "unflinching courage." Roosevelt called Walsh's death "a grievous loss," but the president-elect also moved quickly to replace him by making what was, in many ways, a fateful appointment, one that would bedevil Wheeler for years to come. With little consultation Roosevelt designated former party chairman Homer S. Cummings to become attorney general.[57]

Wheeler disavowed any interest in replacing Walsh—there is no evidence Roosevelt considered him—but he was not happy to see Cummings appointed since it would give his rival Bruce Kremer, a close Cummings friend, even more access to the new administration. Kremer, meanwhile, had bigger things in mind and went to work immediately, even before Walsh's funeral, maneuvering to secure appointment to fill the vacant Senate seat. The New York Times mentioned Kremer as a likely replacement and called the Butte attorney "a close friend" of Roosevelt's. Wheeler was forced to move just as quickly, some might say ruthlessly, in order to head off Kremer's appointment, a decision that would be made by Montana's governor John Erickson. The rapid high-stakes maneuvering produced one of the great stories in Montana political history.[58]

Precisely what Wheeler did to thwart Kremer's chances and influence Governor Erickson's decision about the Senate vacancy is impossible to know for sure, but Wheeler's own account of what happened seems entirely plausible. Wheeler's objective was twofold: keep Kremer out of the Senate and get someone appointed to fill Walsh's seat who would be a friend, not a rival. Wheeler frequently remarked of his extreme distaste for Kremer's backslapping style and what he considered the Butte lawyer's dubious ethics. "Walsh, who hated few people, hated Kremer," Wheeler said. "[He] had opposed both of us politically and I didn't like him any better than Walsh did." Wheeler knew that top officials of the Anaconda Company and Montana Power would lobby Erickson, with whom they enjoyed a close relationship, to appoint Kremer, who had been working on their behalf for years.[59]

To Montana's big-business interests, Kremer seemed an ideal choice to balance Wheeler's influence in Washington, in Montana, and within the state's Democratic Party. Kremer was also from Butte, which might also serve to limit Wheeler's influence there in the Anaconda Company's home base. Wheeler responded aggressively to the prospect of Kremer joining him in the Senate, letting it be known that a Kremer appointment would be tantamount to a declaration of war by Montana business interests, thus renewing Wheeler's old battles with Anaconda. "When you have Kremer appointed," Wheeler told Frank Kerr, the president of Montana Power, "you'll be serving notice on me that you want a fight. I'm coming up for election in two years and that'd be a good time to test just how much power you really have." The next day, Wheeler would recount in his memoirs, "representatives of Anaconda informed me it had withdrawn its support for Kremer." Just to make certain that everyone involved in the appointment was hearing the same message, Wheeler summoned Governor Erickson and representatives of Anaconda and Montana Power to a meeting in his Helena hotel room, where Erickson heard firsthand that his business friends had abandoned support for Kremer.[60]

It also seems likely that Wheeler encouraged Walsh's politically sophisticated daughter, Genevieve Walsh Gudger, to lobby Erickson against a Kremer appointment. Wheeler claimed that Walsh's daughter, dressed in mourning clothes, called upon the governor in his office in the Montana statehouse. So the story goes, Walsh's daughter slowly lifted the black veil from her face and told Erickson that she was speaking for her dead father in saying "he doesn't want Bruce Kremer appointed to the United States Senate." Wheeler said Erickson later told him it was "one of the eeriest experiences he ever had." As Wheeler dryly noted, "That ended Kremer's chances."[61]

Wheeler next put in motion a bold scheme that reworked Montana's political landscape for years to come and more firmly cemented his own grip on political power. "I then persuaded Erickson to resign as governor," Wheeler matter-of-factly explained, "and let the lieutenant governor, Frank Cooney, appoint him as Walsh's successor in the Senate." Erickson apparently needed little encouragement—Erickson's wife also liked the idea—and the governor eagerly agreed to switch offices. Erickson submitted his resignation on March 13, 1933, and eleven minutes later Governor Cooney appointed him to fill Walsh's Senate seat until a special election could be held in 1934.[62]

Wheeler's maneuvering, assuming it happened more or less as he recounted (there are apparently no other contemporary accounts of the events involving Kremer and Erickson), amounted to the most calculating political hardball, and Wheeler accomplished objectives important to him. He made certain a Senate seat was denied to an old enemy, and in Erickson he gained a compliant, even lazy junior colleague, one not from Butte, who Wheeler correctly believed would never become a political rival. With Walsh dead, Kremer sidelined, and friends in the Senate and governor's office, Wheeler now completely dominated Montana politics. Ironically, engineering the Erickson-Cooney switch also served to placate the Anaconda Company, which accepted the conservative Erickson more easily than it would have any liberal in the Wheeler mold. "The deal," as it was called ever after, went down less easily with

Montana voters, and as is usually the case with such transparent schemes, it did not reflect well on anyone involved.[63]

Erickson, three times elected governor before Wheeler helped him engineer his appointment to the Senate, never again won an election. Cooney died of a heart attack in 1935, never overcoming the taint of his role in the deal. For his part, Wheeler was forced to defend his involvement in the Erickson appointment on the Senate floor, where harsh criticism from his old courtroom adversary and occasional judicial helpmate George Bourquin forced a debate about the propriety of seating Erickson given how his appointment came about. Bourquin wrote to every member of the Senate blasting the Erickson-Cooney deal and Wheeler's role in bringing it about. The judge condemned what he called the "huckstering, horse trading, barter and sale of great public office." Wheeler defended Erickson by pointing out that Montana law permitted the appointment even if it had been done in an unorthodox way. Wheeler also questioned Bourquin's motives for raising the issue, alleging that the judge intended to run for the Senate, likely against Wheeler in 1934, and was therefore "seeking the limelight." After a quick review, the Senate seated Erickson.[64]

Bruce Kremer's political fortunes also took a sharp turn. With his close friend Cummings now attorney general, Kremer packed up his law practice in Butte and relocated to Washington, where he became the capitol's go-to lawyer for those wanting to transact business with the Justice Department. However, early in 1934, Kremer had to give up the position he held for twenty-five years on the Democratic National Committee when Roosevelt decreed that holding party office was incompatible with also lobbying the administration or Congress. Roosevelt, with Kremer and several other lobbyists in mind, told reporters that he intended "to sweep the back door entrance to the White House clean of political-influence vendors." Kremer's substantial influence in Montana politics began to wane almost immediately, although he continued, much to Wheeler's dismay, to exercise influence over Montana political patronage by virtue of his close relationship with Cummings.[65]

Never before or since has Montana played a larger role in national politics than in the pivotal year of 1932. With his man in the White House, Wheeler could turn his considerable energy and independence toward improving the crippled U.S. economy while helping to secure the larger progressive agenda he hoped to see Franklin Roosevelt's new administration advance. Almost immediately, however, Wheeler's optimism gave way to disillusionment with Roosevelt, and the two men faced off over an almost constant series of personal and political disagreements.

7 NEW DEAL IRREGULAR

Wheeler disliked the government almost as much as
big business, for repression had come from both.

—RICHARD T. RUETTEN

"This nation calls for action and action now," Franklin Roosevelt declared as he took
the oath of office on March 4, 1933, and during the frantic first hundred days of the
new administration Roosevelt delivered. After declaring a bank holiday, which paused
some of the economic panic, a special session of Congress approved, at Roosevelt's
behest, a bill reducing government spending and legalized low-alcohol beer. On
March 16 the new administration sent Congress legislation that would become the
Agricultural Adjustment Act (AAA), designed to increase farmers' purchasing power,
ease mortgage pressure, and control production. Between March 21 and June 16, 1933,
Congress handled a dizzying array of legislation, creating the Civilian Conservation
Corps, establishing a system of unemployment relief for the states, mandating federal
supervision of security sales, authorizing the Tennessee Valley Authority, protecting
homeowners from foreclosure, granting the Interstate Commerce Commission more
authority over the nation's railroads, rewriting the nation's agricultural policy, and
approving the National Industrial Recovery Act (NIRA), a stunningly ambitious
effort aimed at a planned reordering of the national economy.[1]

No president had ever proposed so much so quickly, and never had a Congress
acquiesced so completely. The headlong flurry of political activity, generally viewed
favorably by the public, also sowed the seeds of a backlash. "Conservatives, whose
most cherished ideals were under attack," historian Adam Cohen has written, "started
to speak out, objecting that Roosevelt was trying to become a dictator, and that his
programs were un-American. The more time passed, the more outspoken these critics became." Republican senator William Borah, who supported much of the early

Roosevelt's program, nonetheless complained, "No one man can execute all the powers we have given him." Republican senator Lester Dickinson of Iowa wondered, "How much longer are we going to continue this delegation of power?" And B. K. Wheeler also became a critic, clashing with the administration on issues as diverse as monetary policy and the authority of the Bureau of Indian Affairs. Wheeler was particularly critical of the growing concentration of power in the executive branch and what he saw as a disturbing tendency for the new president to assume near dictatorial powers, while the authority of Congress shrank.[2]

The idea, Wheeler said, "of giving power to some of the executive departments is running riot." Typical of this concentration of power, he said, was authority granted to the Department of Agriculture as a result of the Agricultural Adjustment Act, legislation that Wheeler with great reluctance supported and then often criticized.[3]

The AAA was based on the theory of domestic allotment, a system that limits production in order to drive up prices. The domestic allotment concept originated with a little-known but widely influential Montana State College economist and reformer, Milburn L. Wilson. A "mild man with wild ideas," a friend said of Wilson, who served as a top advisor to agriculture secretary Henry Wallace early in the Roosevelt administration and eventually became undersecretary of agriculture and head of the Extension Service. Despite the central role played by a Montana economist in developing the policy behind the AAA, Wheeler was convinced the farm bill was the work of eastern academic theorists with little clue about conditions on a Montana farm.[4]

"The Department of Agriculture and the few professors up there, who sit around the office and never saw a bushel of wheat in their lives," Wheeler fumed during a Senate speech, "see fit to send down to the Senate certain legislation and say to us, 'jump through the hoop and vote for this bill . . . and ask that we shall give the Secretary of Agriculture the greatest amount of power that has ever been granted in any bill in the history of the United States." Still, farm conditions were so bad in Montana in 1933 that it was unthinkable that Wheeler, even with profound misgivings, would oppose a proposal touted by Roosevelt and many national farm leaders as the salvation of American agriculture. The AAA ultimately provided $10 million a year in desperately needed benefits to Montana farmers but rarely without controversy.[5]

While at best a reluctant supporter of the administration's farm programs, Wheeler was a thoroughgoing opponent of the NIRA, which Roosevelt predicted would be remembered as "the most important and far-reaching legislation ever enacted by the American people." Far-reaching it was, as well as controversial, and ultimately the Supreme Court struck down much of the law. "The [NIRA] was supported by the so-called liberals," Wheeler said years later, "solely because it was proposed by Roosevelt, even though it permitted price fixing that otherwise would have violated the Sherman Anti-Trust law. They wouldn't have been for it if a conservative had sponsored the legislation, but Roosevelt could lead the 'liberals' anywhere." In addition to concerns about the NIRA skirting antitrust laws, Wheeler objected to very idea of industry leaders huddling together to formulate agreements about how to operate entire segments of the economy. The centerpiece of Roosevelt's economic program was, in Wheeler's view, proof of the evils of bigness and monopoly.[6]

As the first hectic phase of the New Deal came to an end, Wheeler believed the flurry of legislation proposed by Roosevelt and approved by Congress was still not adequate to turn the economy around. "I was struck by the pessimism of Senator Wheeler and Senator [Elbert] Thomas [of Utah]," Harold Ickes confided to his diary after having dinner with the senators in April 1933. "They both think the economic situation is getting worse rapidly and they look for a very serious situation unless something is done speedily." Specifically, Ickes noted, the westerners wanted an immediate large-scale public works program.[7]

Wheeler's economic reform agenda also included more trade, which he believed had been strangled by the Smoot-Hawley tariff, as well as recognition of the Soviet Union, which he called "the greatest potential market in the world." Wheeler's free trade attitude did not, however, extend to Montana copper, for which, bowing to home-state considerations, he demanded more protection. Wheeler also wanted more direct relief for the unemployed and a farmers' reconstruction finance corporation that he believed could provide needed capital for hard-pressed farmers.[8]

Wheeler's principal economic reform idea, remonetizing silver, which he repeatedly said would benefit the economy "quicker than anything else," was never fully realized, and the issue put him at odds with Roosevelt. Throughout 1933 and 1934 Wheeler danced a complicated minuet with the White House on the issue, first courting Roosevelt's support for his own silver proposals and then shifting to a critique of the president's more conservative approach. Ultimately Wheeler found Roosevelt much too timid on monetary policy, and he became deeply disillusioned by his near-complete lack of influence with the administration on economic policy. At the same time Wheeler introduced in the Senate and worked hard to pass the administration's legislation regarding Native American nations, the Indian Reorganization Act, although he later repudiated the effort. By the time of Wheeler's reelection campaign in 1934, the frayed relationship between the president and the Montana senator had become difficult to conceal. He indeed became a New Deal irregular.[9]

———

"My interest in the subject [silver] went all the way back to a debate in Hudson, Massachusetts High School during the McKinley-Bryan campaign of 1896," Wheeler wrote in his memoirs. "I took the side of William Jennings Bryan—and it converted

NEW DEAL IRREGULAR   139

me to the Democratic Party. I had been for the remonetization of silver ever since."
Wheeler said that his first real "rift" with the new president was over the question of
silver, and the dispute left bitterness that never went away. At least since 1873, when
Congress officially removed the silver from dollar coins and limited its role as legal
tender, silver had been a potent political issue, particularly in the U.S. West. Silver
advocates took to calling the congressional anti-silver action the "Crime of '73," and
Bryan found a national audience—and a presidential nomination—with his famous
"Cross of Gold" speech during the Democratic National Convention in 1896. Bryan
centered his populist campaign that year on a demand for the "free coinage of silver"
at a ratio to gold of sixteen to one, while Republican William McKinley promised
sound currency backed by gold. When he began pushing his inflationary silver policy
proposals in 1933, Wheeler certainly had Bryan's 1896 question to the Democratic Party
in mind: "Upon which side will the Democratic Party fight; upon the side of 'the idle
holders of capital' or upon the side of 'the struggling masses'?"[10]

Wheeler's motivation in pushing so hard for so long for a role for silver in national
and world monetary policy was arguably the product of an oversimplified but genuine
belief that "labor and capital" would benefit from remonetization and that "content-
ment, happiness, and lucrative occupation would be substituted for discontentment and
despair." Never a profound economic theorist, Wheeler viewed monetizing silver and
encouraging an inflationary monetary policy as the quickest, surest way to stimulate
the economy, particularly the farm economy, and he remained almost religiously
attached, as Bryan had been, to the gospel of silver. As a silver advocate Wheeler was
not acting merely on behalf of home-state mining interests as other westerners, Nevada
senator Key Pittman for one, clearly were, but rather his concern was to find some
means to help economically distressed small farmers and business owners. Wheeler's
view of the vital center of the U.S. economy—farmers, small merchants, and working
people—represented, in many ways, nostalgia for a simpler time, a Jeffersonian America
that increasingly did not exist in the rapidly globalizing 1930s. Wheeler believed that too
often the American economy worked only for big corporations or for those attempting
to monopolize an entire industry. As a result, Wheeler approached the silver cause
with the zeal of a revivalist and was a true believer that gold, as Arthur Schlesinger Jr.
has written, "was the rich man's metal, the creditor's metal, the banker's metal," while
silver was "the poor man's metal, the debtor's metal, the worker's metal."[11]

Bankers and eastern industrial interests generally opposed the inflationary monetary policy Wheeler supported, advocating instead sound money and a minimum of
inflation, as most conservatives had embraced even before McKinley firmly linked the
Republican Party to gold in the 1890s. Wheeler complained that even "the great mining
companies are openly opposed to remonetization of silver because most of them are
controlled by the big banking interests of New York." But the mining company Wheeler

knew best, the Anaconda Company, actually urged the Senate Finance Committee to take some action on silver, likely motivated by a desire to inflate the price of the metal, a by-product of the company's copper-mining operations in Montana, while also acknowledging the substantial political support that existed for Wheeler's silver position in the state.[12]

In January 1932, with the Depression deepening and before Roosevelt had even announced his candidacy, the *New York Times* had reported that Wheeler was planning to reintroduce Bryan's free coinage of silver proposal—essentially the old "sixteen to one" measure—as a means of putting more dollars in circulation and improving the nation's trade prospects with the Far East. Wheeler confidently predicted the proposal would bring about an increase in the money supply, a tripling of commodity prices, and lower unemployment.[13] "What my bill proposes to do," Wheeler told the Senate, "is to put more dollars in circulation; make it possible for us to regain our lost trade in the Orient by increasing [Chinese and Japanese] purchasing power[,] and make it possible for the debtor classes to pay their debts with dollars of the same value as when they borrowed the money." Wheeler was certain that "both labor and capital would be benefited." It was a compelling if simplistic explanation. A handful of western senators, most notably Democrats Pittman and William H. King of Utah, supported Wheeler's bill, but his proposal languished and eventually died in the Senate Finance Committee, chaired by Utah Republican Reed Smoot. Wheeler predicted the worst with the demise of his silver proposal. "One of two things is going to happen in this country," he said. "We will have bimetallism or we shall have bolshevism in the United States of America."[14]

Roosevelt's election emboldened Wheeler to again push his silver proposal during the lame duck session of Congress in January 1933, but again the legislation faltered. Nevertheless, forcing a Senate vote on silver marked the first time in forty years that a bimetal proposal had gotten that far in the legislative process. Having a debate and a vote on silver, even a losing vote, heartened Wheeler even as many sympathetic with his objectives worried over the political consequences of again stirring up the old Bryan-era regional animosities over silver policy. Pittman, not an inflationist and never as radical on the silver issue as Wheeler, begged his fellow westerner not to press the issue further since "it would turn the whole east against us." Wheeler complained, with Pittman no doubt in mind, of westerners who "have always pretended" they were for remonetization "when speaking to the voters" but behaved differently when given a chance to actually put silver at the center of the nation's economic policy.[15]

Wheeler's next opportunity to advance his ideas came in April during debate on the administration's agricultural legislation when he proposed an amendment to effectively remonetize silver. As the Senate debated what became the AAA, Wheeler recalled that then-candidate Roosevelt had seemed to endorse the need to address silver policy during his Montana campaign appearance the previous September. "We all know that the President of the United States, in his speech in my home city of Butte, Montana, declared emphatically that he was for rehabilitating silver," Wheeler said. "We know that since that time he has uttered statements to the effect that he wanted to do something about it. Let us show him that the Senate of the United States is going to back him up in that statement." Roosevelt had certainly mentioned silver during the campaign stop in Butte, but he had not committed to a specific action. Roosevelt and Wheeler almost certainly discussed the silver issue during Wheeler's post-election trip to Warm Springs, but there is no evidence that Wheeler received any specific assurance of support from Roosevelt for his approach. In fact, since his election Roosevelt had heard a good deal about silver from his economic advisors, and to a person they counseled that he not embrace what one newspaper called "the false Gods of Bryan." Now as Wheeler attempted to invoke Roosevelt's words to build support in Congress for an inflationary monetary policy, the White House frantically maneuvered behind the scenes to thwart his efforts.[16]

As the Senate debated Wheeler's silver amendment, Roosevelt advisor Raymond Moley fielded phone calls from the Senate cloakroom and counseled senators on how to respond to Wheeler. Moley told several lawmakers who worried about how opposing Wheeler would play back home that they simply should not vote on Wheeler's proposal or at the very least be strategic in deciding if home-state political considerations really required an affirmative vote. "All told," Moley calculated, "we knew that well over ten senators either voted 'No' on the Wheeler amendment or refrained from voting on it altogether, despite the fact that they were prepared to support inflation of some sort."[17]

Wheeler's amendment was defeated by a vote of 43–33, with the ten or more votes Moley influenced obviously critical to the outcome. Nevertheless, the vote was close enough that the White House knew something had to be done to tamp down the ruckus Wheeler and his silver supporters were creating. Knowing that another vote on a similar proposal might well succeed, Roosevelt concluded that he could quiet the clamor by embracing something far less radical than Wheeler's measure, some approach that provided the administration with options and broad discretion that might or might not be exercised. Roosevelt ultimately cut a deal with Elmer Thomas, an Oklahoma Democratic senator, to support an approach granting the administration near total control over the timing and scope of any action related to silver. Roosevelt worked out the details in a White House meeting that included several of his key economic advisors, as well as Senators Thomas and Pittman. Wheeler was neither invited nor consulted, and he was seriously miffed when he heard about the gathering.[18]

Father Charles Coughlin, the Michigan Catholic priest who had been using his wildly popular Sunday radio program to demand greater action on the economy, including action on silver, told Wheeler about the White House tête-à-tête. Meeting Coughlin at Washington's Mayflower Hotel, Wheeler must have immediately realized that the priest had better sources of information at the White House than he did. The deal worked out by Roosevelt would not include remonetization of silver, Coughlin told him. Wheeler, perturbed, promised to fight for his approach and if necessary offer his own amendment to any bill that came up. Wheeler added in his memoirs, as if it were not obvious, "I was quite critical of Roosevelt."[19]

Word quickly got back to the White House that Wheeler was upset at not being consulted and determined to fight the president's proposal in the Senate. Frank Walker, the Democratic Party official and a Montanan who knew Wheeler, was detailed to call him and implore him to avoid an open break with Roosevelt. Wheeler was unmoved, telling Walker that he would break with the White House whenever he wanted to and on any issue. Walker pressed harder, and Wheeler finally snapped: "You take a message to him. You tell him he can go to hell." Then he slammed down the phone. Realizing the extent to which Wheeler felt insulted and worried he might act on his anger on the Senate floor, Roosevelt invited him to the White House, hoping his legendary ability to charm might convince the Montanan to support the administration's silver proposal. Wheeler told Roosevelt that he felt slighted and that as a leader in the cause to remonetize silver he was entitled to be consulted on any silver legislation. "I had a right to be included in any conference on the subject," he would later write in his memoirs. "We've been friends," Wheeler told Roosevelt, adding, "I don't like it and I just won't take it." Roosevelt's only reply, as Wheeler later remembered, was to say, "Burt, Bryan killed the remonetization of silver in 1896." Considering what lay ahead between Roosevelt and Wheeler, the head-butting over monetary policy in the president's office was prophetic, the beginning of the end of any real political alliance between the two men. Wheeler left the White House reluctantly agreeing to support legislation to permit but not require the administration to remonetize silver. The proposal eventually passed, and Roosevelt gained the policy discretion he desired. Wheeler, temporarily outflanked, found himself on the outside of the new administration that seemed to care little about his opinions on an issue he believed was of overriding importance to the country.[20]

Certain that he was correct and could eventually convince the Senate and the administration of the wisdom of his position, Wheeler continued to press at every opportunity for additional action on silver. As Roosevelt prepared to send a U.S. delegation to the World Monetary and Economic Conference in London, Wheeler pushed a Senate resolution—it passed unanimously—instructing U.S. delegates to "work unceasingly for an international agreement to remonetize silver" on a sixteen-to-one basis. The administration and the U.S. delegation quietly ignored Wheeler's resolution, and, when the mostly unproductive conference ended after adopting an ineffectual silver purchase agreement, Wheeler was again disillusioned. He called the London action the "most backward step that has been taken by the United States since the demonetization of silver in 1873."[21]

"We do not have much faith that the [silver] agreement reached in London will do much good," Wheeler wrote in a candid yet somewhat conciliatory letter to Roosevelt at the end of July 1933. Roosevelt replied two weeks later with a "Dear Bert" letter—the White House habitually misspelled Wheeler's first name—"It was good to get your note and I am glad things are doing pretty well in the Northwest." Roosevelt made no mention of silver nor did he ever use the authority Congress granted him to monetize it.[22]

Wheeler's last big push on the issue came early in 1934 when the western silver bloc ratcheted up demands that the government institute a program to purchase silver, with Wheeler insisting that the administration should ignore the advice of bankers, most of whom counseled the administration to do nothing about silver. While the administration actively consulted with several proponents of a silver purchase policy, Wheeler was again left out of those discussions. When Wheeler had gone to the White House to lobby for action on silver in January, Roosevelt had been unmoved, later telling Senate majority leader Joseph Robinson of Arkansas that Wheeler's efforts were "wholly contrary" to what the administration favored. Roosevelt had apparently concluded that Wheeler simply could not be dealt with, at least on monetary policy, and he was not going to waste time trying.[23]

Wheeler, for his part, took some credit for the passage in June of the Roosevelt-endorsed Silver Purchase Act of 1934. "I wasn't successful in expanding the money supply by remonetizing silver," he would say years later, "but I forced President Roosevelt to move in that direction by increasing the price of gold and going off the gold standard. These measures helped to alleviate the plight of debt ridden farmers and to encourage businesses to expand." Most historians of the New Deal have been critical of the efforts of Wheeler and others in the silver bloc, while acknowledging that the Silver Purchase Act of 1934 did, for example, spur expansion of the money supply and thereby modestly contribute to a general economic recovery. But the verdicts were decidedly mixed, with treasury secretary Henry Morgenthau commenting that the administration's silver policy "is the only monetary fiscal policy that I cannot explain or justify." Arthur Schlesinger Jr. has written that "Roosevelt surrendered to political blackmail on the part of the silver bloc" by even accepting a watered-down measure. Apparently Roosevelt feared that the continuing silver debate could damage other administration priorities and impact the 1934 Congressional elections, and primarily for those reasons the president agreed to some action. Other critics dismiss Wheeler and other silver advocates as parochial westerners merely packing water for the region's mining interests, with historian Alonzo Hamby calling the Silver Purchase Act "a textbook example of narrow-interest legislation" that raised the world price of the metal, thereby enriching silver producers, while "destabilized the currencies of the two major silver standard nations, Mexico and China."[24]

Wheeler's frustration over his failure to influence the administration on economic policy led him to increasingly view Roosevelt as lacking core convictions on big issues. Roosevelt, Wheeler believed, was a deal maker rather than a serious policy maker, a coldly calculating, transactional politician with little compunction about slighting or ignoring allies. In his memoirs, for example, Wheeler recounts a White House meeting with Roosevelt in 1933 where the two discussed construction of the proposed Fort Peck Dam in northeastern Montana. Wheeler explained the benefits of the massive $75 million project during a session that lasted no more than fifteen minutes. At the conclusion of the conversation Roosevelt simply declared that the huge flood-control and navigation project on the upper Missouri River would be built with funds under Roosevelt's direct control. Wheeler was certainly pleased by the decision but still troubled by Roosevelt's motives. He was convinced that he had received the go-ahead for the huge project less for its merits than because Roosevelt was attempting to make up for having opposed Wheeler on the silver issue. "The simple fact was that when FDR wanted to help a senator he built a dam for him," Wheeler said. "He built one on the Columbia River in Oregon for Republican leader Charles McNary because he needed his support. He did the same thing in the state of Washington for Senator Clarence Dill, a Democrat . . . in the Depression, all Roosevelt had to do, if he felt like wooing a legislator, was to dip into the federal treasury on his own and allocate some of the millions granted him under the Public Works Administration." It is a cliché but also true that Roosevelt authorized the huge Fort Peck Dam with the stroke of a pen, and construction commenced months before a formal Army Corps of Engineers report justifying the project was delivered to Congress. As historians David P. Billington and Donald C. Jackson note in their book on dam building during the New Deal, "The speed with which Fort Peck Dam was approved and authorized for construction under provisions of the National Recovery Act occurred completely outside of the more traditional legislative mechanism involving the corps [of engineers] and Congress."[25]

———

In early February 1934, during the time Wheeler was jousting with the White House over silver, a senior official of the Bureau of Indian Affairs (BIA) delivered a document to Wheeler's office. Wheeler was chair of the Senate Indian Affairs Committee, and the document was a draft of the Roosevelt administration's proposed Indian Reorganization Act—"the Indian New Deal," a sweeping rewrite of law regulating the relationship between Native American nations and the federal government. Simultaneously BIA commissioner John Collier delivered the draft to the office of Nebraska Democratic congressman Edward Howard, Wheeler's counterpart in the House of Representatives. Among other features, the legislation proposed to end the practice of allotment of tribal land that had been established by the 1887 Dawes Act, also known as the General Allotment Act. Allotment to individual tribal members was supposed to have encouraged assimilation and help end Native American poverty, but in reality tribal governments were weakened under the law, and vast amounts of native land were transferred to white owners. The administration's proposal also created a mechanism to provide federal recognition of tribal constitutions and attempted to enhance Native American self-determination. After making only a cursory effort to digest the contents of the complex legislation, both chairmen immediately introduced the bill in their respective chambers. The legislation would consume Wheeler for many weeks and again bring him into conflict with the administration.[26]

Wheeler had been an active member of the Indian Affairs Committee since his earliest days in the Senate, developing legislation, conducting field hearings, advocating on behalf of Montana tribal interests, and providing oversight of the BIA. Wheeler had also been acquainted for some time with Collier, the crusading social worker Roosevelt appointed in 1933, upon the recommendation of Interior Secretary Ickes, to run the BIA.[27]

Small of stature, sporting an unruly mop of hair, and fiercely driven, Collier disdained the bureaucrat's uniform of suit and tie in favor of a baggy sweater. He habitually smoked a corncob pipe, and it was rumored that he frequently carried a pet frog in his pocket. Collier's quirky, intense personality meant members of Congress often did their best to avoid him, even as many admired his passion for reform of the federal-tribal relationship.[28]

In 1926 Collier, out of government at the time, wrote a flattering letter to Wheeler saying he believed "every Indian welfare body and all Indians look to you as one of the two or three men in the Senate who most disinterestedly and thoroughly care about justice to the Indians." It was a fair characterization. In a Senate speech that same year Wheeler outlined some of his thinking about national policy related to Native Americans. "The Congress of the U.S. has violated in many instances every provision of these Indian treaties, and has treated them . . . as a mere scrap of paper . . . we have taken their land, we have turned it over to whites, we have appropriated their money, and we have treated them in a shameful manner." In his Montana legal practice Wheeler had represented tribal governments, and his experience as U.S. attorney provided firsthand knowledge of how federal policy and tribal interests intersected. As his 1926 Senate speech shows, Wheeler was genuinely interested in how government policy impacted tribes and individuals, but his confidence that Native Americans could manage their own affairs was limited. Wheeler had many Indian acquaintances and enjoyed strong political support among Montana Native Americans, yet his paternalism, not uncommon among politicians then or now, was frequently on display.[29]

When Roosevelt, for example, considered appointing an Indian to head the BIA, Wheeler thought it was a bad idea because and said, "I know of no Indian competent to handle the job." He also remarked that his legal practice had given him the ability to tell when an Indian was lying on the witness stand. "If he talked with an expressive use of his hands, in the traditional fashion, he was sure to be telling the truth," Wheeler said. If a witness's hands were quiet, resting in his lap during the cross-examination, that meant one was lying.[30]

Paternalism and stereotyping notwithstanding, Wheeler insisted on adequate compensation for a tribal government in a protracted controversy over power development on the Flathead Reservation in northwestern Montana, and in 1925 he pushed a bill—ultimately vetoed by Calvin Coolidge—that would have permitted Native Americans to sue the federal government over treaty violations. In a 1929 speech, Wheeler focused on a major problem in Indian County when he called for a "business-like accounting system," including quarterly financial statements, that would provide regular accountability of tribal funds held in trust by the federal government. Government mismanagement and accountability for tribal funds was a problem that had bedeviled tribes and the Interior Department for decades and led to countless lawsuits. Wheeler also believed Native nations ought to have a greater say in decisions about leasing tribal property, and he was consistent in one overarching belief: big oil, timber, and energy companies exploited individual Native Americans and tribal governments in the same way those interests exploited white Americans.[31]

As Wheeler's Senate experience grew, he became a persistent and vocal critic of the BIA, seeing the agency as a sprawling, inefficient bureaucracy often uninformed about tribal conditions. With strong support from Ickes, Collier promised to address such shortcomings by turning "the administration of Indian affairs on its head." He promised tribal governments greater resources to improve Indian health, education, and economic conditions, and he promised that Native Americans would be able to preserve and celebrate their culture and tribal identity. But Collier's well-intentioned desire to benefit tribes through more enlightened public policy often foundered in implementation.[32]

Wheeler would later admit that he had introduced the administration's—more correctly Collier's draft—of the Indian Reorganization Act without having read it, reserving his prerogative as chairman to make changes when hearings on the legislation took place. "When I began looking over the original draft, there were many provisions

I didn't like," Wheeler later remembered, and he began to work on changes. When presidential assistant Stephen Early called Wheeler shortly after the legislation was introduced to say that Roosevelt hoped for speedy action on the bill, Wheeler told Early to make certain Roosevelt had read the bill, "because there are some things in it I'm sure he won't favor."[33]

In early March 1934, Roosevelt wrote Wheeler expressing thanks for his work on the legislation, and Wheeler positively gushed in replying. "I am deeply affected to receive your kind and gracious little letter commending me for my bill to be presented in behalf of the Indians." The bill would become known as the Wheeler-Howard Act, but its draft was totally Collier's work on behalf of the administration, an important distinction that Wheeler would stress as he eventually rewrote major portions of it. Wheeler's "My dear Mr. President" letter to Roosevelt was uncharacteristically saccharine, and of extant Wheeler correspondence it is in a category alone. There is no evidence that Wheeler ever again used such a tone with Roosevelt: "A friend of mine said the other day the smile of Franklin D. Roosevelt is one of the most precious assets the American people have. When I know what a multitude of duties are pressing in upon you from all parts of the world, and yet you find time to send such a courteous and friendly little note, I can only say that if my friend had enlarged his statement to include all your superb qualities, it would have been an under-estimate. May I again assure you of my continued esteem?"[34]

Wheeler's over-the-top flattery is so uncharacteristic that it requires analysis. The exchange of notes between Roosevelt and Wheeler occurred as Wheeler and others in the Senate's silver bloc were hoping to convince the president to embrace something closer to their views on monetary policy. Wheeler's missive to the president was surely part of a short-lived charm offensive. It did not work, and Wheeler, as we have seen, eventually settled for much less than he wanted.

Shortly after composing his fawning letter, Wheeler shifted tactics. The Indian New Deal was no longer "my bill" but the handiwork of John Collier. He criticized the proposal as too top-down, too bureaucratic, in essence a power grab that concentrated far too much authority in the BIA and by extension the commissioner. Rather than encouraging Indian self-rule, Wheeler said, the proposal would make Native American self-sufficiency *less* likely, and he was particularly agitated about a proposal to create a new legal entity, "a court of Indian Affairs," a provision that Wheeler determined had to be eliminated from the legislation.[35]

Collier, aware of the building animosity in Congress and in Indian County, organized and held a series of "congresses" with tribal leaders, hoping apparently to smooth passage of the legislation by demonstrating that he had undertaken widespread consultation with Native American leaders. But, as historian Vine Deloria Jr. has noted, concerns among tribal leaders and politicians only grew and soon reached a climax when Collier sat before Wheeler's committee.[36]

No single law would cure the problems of Native Americans, Wheeler insisted as congressional hearings began. "It is not a question of the laws that you have upon the statute books as much as it is to have somebody who has sympathy with the Indians and knows something about [their conditions and] is able to [act effectually on their behalf]." Collier, under withering criticism from members of Wheeler's committee and from adversaries both outside and inside the BIA, scrambled to preserve the essence of his legislation. The commissioner was also under intense pressure to get the proposal approved before Congress adjourned in advance of the 1934 mid-term elections. Making a last push to move the legislation, Collier sought help from Roosevelt and Ickes. On April 28 Roosevelt sent identical letters to Wheeler and Representative Howard offering his personal endorsement of the legislation and urging quick action. Roosevelt termed what was now being referred to in the press as the Wheeler-Howard Bill "a measure of justice that is long overdue" and said the nation should "extend to the Indian the fundamental rights of political liberty and local self-government and the opportunities of education and economic assistance that they require in order to attain a wholesome American life." Two days later, also at Collier's behest, Ickes sent a bluntly worded memorandum to all BIA employees, some of whom had been working behind the scenes to thwart his efforts. Ickes warned BIA staffers to cease their opposition. "If any employee wishes to oppose the new policy, he should do so honestly and openly from outside of the Service," Ickes wrote. "This would mean resignation. Any other course is unscrupulous." In the event any federal employee missed his point, Ickes said the purpose of his memo was "to notify all those engaged in this scheme to defeat our program that a continuance will be under penalty of dismissal from the Service."[37]

With the administration intent on pushing the legislation through Congress, Wheeler committed to securing its passage but only after making significant changes. The final bill was half as long as Collier's draft—the original was fifty-two pages—and it substantially revised the way tribes could opt out of the legislation's provisions. The Senate ultimately approved the revised Indian Reorganization Act on the last day of the congressional session in June. Wheeler took to the Senate floor to summarize the act's provisions and to remind his colleagues and Collier, "There is nothing in this bill which in any way gives the Department of the Interior the right to impose its will upon the Indians on any reservation." He added that successful implementation of the legislation ought to, in time, eliminate the need for the Bureau of Indian Affairs.[38]

As historian Graham Taylor has written, the final version of the Wheeler-Howard Act, in addition to completely eliminating the court provision Wheeler found so offensive, "repealed the allotment laws, permitted the restoration of surplus reservation lands to tribal ownership, and provided for voluntary exchanges of restricted trust lands for shares in tribal corporations." The legislation also appropriated $2 million for purchase of non-Indian lands to consolidate tribal holdings and established a revolving loan fund to help fund tribal corporations. Additionally it set forth the means to establish new tribal governance systems, with approval required from the secretary of the Interior. The law also required within one year (later extended to two years) that each recognized tribe, by secret ballot, either endorse or reject the terms of the law before it would go into effect for an individual tribe.[39]

A majority, 172 tribes, with about 130,000 members, eventually endorsed the terms of the law, 93 adopted constitutions, and 73 accomplished incorporation. However, 73 other tribes with a total of nearly 90,000 members refused to adopt provisions of the Indian Reorganization Act. In Montana, the Crow, Assiniboine, and Sioux of Fort Peck declined to adopt of the terms of the act.[40]

Almost immediately Wheeler began criticizing Collier for mishandling implementation of the new law, and he soon concluded that he had been wrong to support the legislation. Earl Old Person, a Blackfoot leader, remembered that Montana tribal elders had confronted Wheeler saying, "What about this law? We do not see how it is working for us, even though it might be working for a few people." Wheeler was particularly critical of Collier's moves to enhance the authority of the BIA bureaucracy. "I thought it was going to work for the Indian people," Wheeler said, "but it has been administered in a bad way." Collier also dramatically increased many salaries at the BIA and personally assumed a significant role in overseeing tribal land transactions and the reorganization of tribal governments and courts, all to Wheeler's dismay. Collier was particularly heavy-handed in the administration, some would say manipulation, of the tribal referendums conducted to affirm or reject the new law. For example, the BIA determined that for purposes of the referendums, abstentions would be counted as yes votes. Congress amended the law to correct that interpretation in 1935 but not before seventeen tribes where the no votes outnumbered the actual yes votes (not including abstentions) were brought under the terms of the law.[41]

"The main objection of Wheeler and other congressional critics," Taylor has written, "was that the reorganization program seemed directed less toward developing Indian self-sufficiency than toward setting up tribal corporations as permanent controls over Indian resources. Since the corporations relied largely on bureau advisors, the opportunity for eliminating the bureau in the near future seemed remote." For his part, Collier dismissed his congressional critics as advocates for "cattle interests, timber interests, oil interests, and other substantial corporations and regional interests" who, in Collier's view, were naturally opposed to any measure of additional Indian self-government. That may well have been a fair criticism of some of his critics, but Collier's analysis did not accurately describe Wheeler.[42]

Wheeler's relationship with Collier continued to deteriorate even after Wheeler left the chairmanship of the Senate Indian Affairs Committee early in 1935. Wheeler's frustration led him to cosponsor legislation early in 1937 to completely repeal the law that unofficially carried his name. The law "did not do what it was intended to do, and, more than that, the Indians didn't want it," Wheeler said. "They tell me they want to be prepared and permitted to take their place in the world and make their way like any other American citizen."[43]

During hearings to consider repeal of the Indian Reorganization Act, Wheeler ripped into Collier, accusing him of spreading the story that Wheeler's true motive for seeking repeal was to assist whites intending to exploit Indian land. "My only reason for trying to get this Act repealed is because the Indians don't like it," Wheeler thundered. "That's the only reason I am opposing it, and anybody who says anything else is a damn liar." With Collier sitting red-faced at the witness table, Wheeler continued, "If you said these things—if you said what I think you said—then all I can say is you are a low cowardly liar." And he went on:

> There is not one word of truth in the things I think you said. I haven't read your statement myself. But I want to know from you—all I want to know—is on what grounds you said or implied that I was motivated by pressure from local interests; because—don't interrupt me—it is a dirty lie; it is a damned low thing to do and just about what I expect from you, Collier. . . . You can't tell me you didn't say these things. I know you so well, Collier. I know just how you have gone about this thing. No one is better able to cast implications than you are. I know you through and through. You deliberately said things about me that aren't true and that you know aren't true. You haven't any respect for anybody on God's earth.[44]

Collier wisely did not respond to Wheeler's angry outburst during the hearing, but he answered later in writing. "I could not at the hearing meet your animus with like animus. No word of mine has been personal or invidious. And surely I have not been, as your remarks at the hearing seemed to imply that I ought to be, deterred by dread of your wrath."[45]

Ickes's biographer T. H. Watkins dismisses Wheeler's allegations against Collier as unfounded, and indeed Wheeler's rage may have been misplaced. What is certain is that Wheeler had come to completely distrust Collier, and he viewed the BIA, in microcosm, as a prime example of what he increasingly disliked about the Roosevelt administration. Collier, in Wheeler's view at least, was a bureaucrat run wild: too powerful and certainly not respectful or in any way deferential to Congress as a coequal branch of the government. It is worth noting that Wheeler's biting words about Collier came at the very peak of his 1937 brawl with Roosevelt over enlarging the Supreme Court, and it is not hard to imagine that Wheeler, feeling under attack on that front, lashed back at the handy administration target Collier presented. The Senate would defeat Wheeler's repeal attempt in 1937, but he would never give up on trying to eliminate the law.

Vine Deloria Jr., a Standing Rock Sioux, has written, "Collier's Administration can be regarded as the high-water mark of federal bureaucratic supremacy in policy making. Although Senator Wheeler had substantially reduced the powers of self-government that Congress was willing to grant Indian reservations when he wrote the final version of the Indian Reorganization Act, John Collier proceeded as if his original proposal had been passed intact by Congress. The number of solicitor's opinions issued during the Collier years testify to the propensity of the Bureau of Indian Affairs to make policy in the absence of Congressional initiative and perhaps even without Congressional knowledge and understanding." This was, of course, precisely Wheeler's complaint with Collier and more broadly with the Roosevelt administration.[46]

It is a rare occasion in American politics when a state selects two senators during the same election. It happened in Montana in 1934. Wheeler was seeking a third term, something only Tom Walsh had accomplished up to that point in Montana history. In addition a special Senate election would be held to fill the remaining two years of Walsh's term. Wheeler won renomination easily in the Democratic primary in July, beating a little-known challenger by a nine-to-one margin, the most lopsided primary win of his career. Former governor John Erickson, quietly occupying Montana's other Senate seat thanks to the self-nomination he engineered at Wheeler's suggestion the year before, lost in the primary, finishing third in a race that drew half a dozen candidates.[47]

Wheeler expected and wanted Erickson to win, in part because Erickson, a native of Kalispell in northwestern Montana, would not reinforce the impression that only politicians from Butte could rise to the top of Montana Democratic politics. Wheeler had little regard for the Democrat who beat Erickson in the Senate primary, former Silver Bow County attorney James E. Murray. Wheeler considered Murray not particularly bright (a view shared by Lulu Wheeler) and, more importantly, a potential rival threatening Wheeler's new hold on political dominance in Montana. Murray, a millionaire thanks to his law practice and inheritance, displayed no inclination, as Erickson had, to defer to Wheeler. With his wealth and many friends, the handsome

Canadian-born politician of Irish heritage indeed became a Wheeler rival. Murray was also among Franklin Roosevelt's most devoted supporters in Montana—Roosevelt had appointed Murray to the Montana advisory board of the Public Works Administration—and he became a staunch New Dealer in the Senate in contrast to Wheeler's frequent criticism of Roosevelt and his policies.[48]

Wheeler's disdain for Murray was matched by his dislike for another up-and-coming Montana Democrat and potential rival, twenty-five-year-old Jerry O'Connell, who was elected to the Montana Public Service Commission in 1934. Over the next several years both Murray and O'Connell worked to end Wheeler's dominance of Montana politics, and each would have been delighted to see, indeed plotted to accomplish, the senior senator's defeat. Wheeler's wife, Lulu, frequently even more outspoken about her husband's adversaries than Wheeler himself was, also disliked Murray and O'Connell and likely helped reinforce what eventually became bitter public feuds.[49]

At a time when voters were looking for liberal or progressive candidates committed to aggressive action to combat the Great Depression, Montana Republicans in 1934 nominated staunch conservatives and implacable foes of the New Deal as challengers to Wheeler and Murray. Wheeler's opponent was seventy-one-year-old George Bourquin, a twenty-two-year veteran of the federal bench, the judge who had defended civil liberties during the turbulent war years. More recently Bourquin had been critical of Wheeler's role in 'the nefarious deal" that put Erickson in the Senate. With something approaching Old Testament fury Bourquin said his campaign against Wheeler's role in the Erickson episode "would arouse the outraged citizenry of the state, irrespective of party, to pour out the vials of their wrath upon the hucksters until they call upon the mountains to fall upon and cover them with shame." But Bourquin, astute and courageous on the bench, was out of his depth as a candidate, particularly against an accomplished campaigner like Wheeler.[50]

Bourquin miscalculated badly in believing Montana voters would punish Wheeler rather than Erickson for the appointment scheme. Had the Republican candidates been more capable—Murray's opponent, former congressman Scott Leavitt, was also a lackluster campaigner—having candidates from Butte in three of the top four spots on the Democratic ticket might have been more damaging. Wheeler, Murray, and the Democratic candidate for Congress in the First District, Joseph P. Monaghan, were all Butte residents, as was incumbent Governor Cooney. Montana's Republican Party chairman chided Wheeler during the campaign for heading a ticket that looked "like the Butte telephone directory," and Republicans tried to capitalize on their claim that Butte enjoyed entirely too much power in Montana politics, controlling 92 percent of the most important elected and appointed offices while home to only 8 percent of the voters. Bourquin also misfired when he attacked the New Deal—the judge dismissed the Fort Peck Dam project as creating "a nice duck pond"—and what he called the Roosevelt administration's "alarming and dangerous departure from Constitutional government." In the end, Roosevelt and the New Deal were the only real election issues in Montana in 1934, and, with the New Deal delivering for Montana, its popularity would be confirmed at the ballot box.[51]

The state ranked only behind Nevada in per capita relief spending flowing directly from New Deal programs. Fort Peck Dam, in many ways the symbol of the New Deal in Montana, was a major conduit for federal spending. At its peak the project created ten thousand construction jobs, pumped $110 million into economically depressed eastern Montana, and created a structure 20,000 feet long and 250 feet high. Briefly setting aside his concerns about Roosevelt and the New Deal, Wheeler ran for reelection as a committed supporter of the administration, praising the benefits Roosevelt's programs brought to Montana. He even heralded the NIRA and the AAA, initiatives he had often questioned in Washington. Wheeler also praised Roosevelt publicly, describing him as "warm blooded, big hearted, [and] high minded" and a "charming and lovable personality." He said FDR was the "man who has done more than any living person to alleviate suffering and rekindle the spirit of America."[52]

Roosevelt toured the Fort Peck Dam construction site in early August 1934 as part of a weeklong western political trip intended to bolster Democratic fortunes in advance of the November elections. Wheeler joined the presidential train in eastern Washington and traveled with Roosevelt across Montana, with stops at Glacier National Park, Havre, and Fort Peck.

In contrast to Wheeler's public praise of the president, not once in prepared or informal remarks during the Montana trip did Roosevelt mention Wheeler by name, not even to urge his reelection. There was no word of praise for his Senate service or his work on behalf of Montana, no acknowledgement of Wheeler's early support for Roosevelt or acknowledgment that Wheeler had convinced other prominent progressives to endorse his candidacy. Roosevelt did not mention Wheeler's votes in favor of New Deal legislation or even his legislative leadership on the recently approved Indian Reorganization Act. Considering Roosevelt's enormous political sensitivities and his consummate attention to detail, it is impossible to not conclude that the slights were intentional.[53]

The snubs by Roosevelt stung and would be remembered, but Wheeler had other frustrations too, including a beef with the White House over Montana patronage. Wheeler believed his old political adversary Bruce Kremer was capitalizing on his relationship with Attorney General Cummings to exercise a good deal more influence

Franklin D. Roosevelt addresses a crowd at Fort Peck, Montana, August 6, 1934. Wheeler is
on the right, in front of Roosevelt's press secretary, Stephen T. Early. (*Franklin D. Roosevelt
Presidential Library*)

over Montana appointments than Wheeler himself. The patronage situation drew
complaints from Montana Democrats, with one local official telling Wheeler that "the
Republican organizations are laughing at us here, and rightfully they should" since
many Federal Land Bank and other New Deal agency positions were being handed
to leading Republicans. Wheeler passed the complaint on to Roosevelt, adding in a
letter that "this is typical of the situation as it exists throughout Montana." There is
no record of the White House having responded.[54]

Wheeler was secure enough in his own reelection and independent enough of his
own party to briefly abandon the Montana campaign trail in early October to travel
to Milwaukee to speak in support of the reelection of Bob La Follette, a nominal
Republican, who was running on the Wisconsin Progressive Party ticket. The trip
was a statement once again of Wheeler's political independence, and he again floated
a third-party trial balloon. Stumping for La Follette, Wheeler predicted that a new
national party would spring up if reactionaries in either party were to be successful
in thwarting additional economic reforms.[55]

Wisconsin's Robert La Follette Jr. (*left*), the son of "Fighting Bob" La Follette, and North Dakota's Gerald P. Nye (*front*), both progressive Republicans, were two of Wheeler's closest allies on foreign policy prior to World War II. (*Library of Congress Prints and Photographs Division, Washington, D.C.*)

Wheeler broke with tradition and ended his campaign in Lewistown rather than going home for a final appearance in Butte. "Some of the Irish in Butte were pretty sore at first at your father's audacity," Lulu Wheeler wrote daughter Elizabeth shortly after the election, "but he didn't care how they voted knowing that the balance of the state was with him. However the Irish always have more respect for the person who dares to snap their fingers in their faces and so they voted for him to the tune of 9,500 majority, only lost one precinct by 35 votes and that was where the Montana Power crowd reside. It has been a wonderful campaign and I have enjoyed every moment of it."[56]

Wheeler's 1934 victory was enormous, and the coalition he put together formidable. He captured votes from Republican farmers in eastern Montana and Democratic laborers in western Montana, carried every Montana county, and captured more than 70 percent of the vote. Wheeler's most lopsided margin came in northeastern Montana's Valley County, where the county seat, Glasgow, is less than twenty-five miles from Fort Peck Dam. Wheeler's election to a third term removed any doubt about who had become Montana's most powerful elected official. As a political force

Wheeler now eclipsed even the Anaconda Company. Wheeler, with Senator-Elect Murray and future adversary Jerry O'Connell the only real exceptions, had friends in key positions, and he had assembled the elements of an unprecedented bipartisan machine. Yet reigning over Montana had not earned Wheeler favor or influence with the president of his own party. Wheeler and Roosevelt would work together in the next Congress to break up the nation's massive utility companies, but it would be the last time they would truly cooperate.[57]

8   DEFEATING THE POWER TRUST

The only way we can save capitalism in this country is to
encourage a decentralized system of moderate-sized businesses.

—BURTON K. WHEELER

When the new Congress convened in January 1935, B. K. Wheeler's seniority allowed
him to assume the chairmanship of the Committee on Interstate Commerce, one of
the Senate's most powerful committees, with wide-ranging responsibility for communications, transportation, and energy policy. Wheeler's committee included some
of the Senate's most effective members—New York liberal and labor advocate Robert F.
Wagner, future Supreme Court justice Sherman Minton of Indiana, future majority
leader and vice president Alben Barkley of Kentucky, and Wheeler's colorful friend
Huey Long—as well as newcomer Harry Truman of Missouri. The committee minority
was led by Michigan Republican James Couzens, a millionaire who had been a top
official at Ford Motor Company, mayor of Detroit, and the progressive governor of
Michigan. The committee chairmanship provided Wheeler with a platform from which
to investigate and legislate widely, with a purview that ranged from railroads to radio,
and from tariffs to telephones. Wheeler assembled a stellar committee staff, including
chief counsel Max Lowenthal, a brilliant lawyer who enjoyed a close friendship with
Supreme Court justice Louis Brandeis and would later be an influential advisor to
President Truman. Other committee staffers included Telford Taylor, later a top
prosecutor at the Nuremberg war crimes trials, and Alfred Bernstein, a Columbia
University law professor who later became a successful union organizer and lawyer.
Bernstein's son, Carl, would be one of the *Washington Post* reporters who exposed the
Watergate affair during the Nixon administration.[1]

Taylor, the committee's assistant counsel in 1935, remembered Wheeler as "a man
of enormous personal force, but he was not highly educated; his grammar occasionally

fell down. In a curious way he was like an English barrister. He could pick up anything with very little preparation . . . he was a real power. I had great admiration for him; he was an old rogue." John A. Carver Jr., an eighteen-year-old college student and part-time messenger for Wheeler's committee in the 1930s and much later undersecretary of the interior in the Johnson administration, remembered the committee as "a top-flight outfit, a liberal outfit," where hearings were well-planned and crisply conducted, with Wheeler often leading the questioning.[2]

The chairmanship gave Wheeler the opportunity to make what was arguably his greatest contribution to New Deal legislation, the successful effort to reform the nation's electric utilities, including dismantling the massive utility holding companies that dominated the industry before 1935. Roosevelt's fight against the "power trust" while serving as New York governor was a major factor in Wheeler's early endorsement of Roosevelt as presidential candidate. The opportunity to join forces against the utility industry in 1935 prompted both men, temporarily at least, to put aside most of the distrust that had become a feature of their relationship. The resulting battle royal pitted utility reformers against the most powerful business lobby in the nation, led to a sensational investigation of lobbying practices, and ultimately succeeded in the historic breakup the holding companies.[3]

The nation's electric energy industry grew rapidly in the 1920s, often through complicated mergers that created enormous, highly lucrative, and largely unregulated empires. Between 1917 and 1927, more than thirty-seven hundred individual utility operating companies were subsumed into fewer than twenty sprawling, often multistate holding companies. By the early 1930s, the six largest holding companies controlled 70 percent of the privately owned electric utility industry in the United States, and three of those companies, including Electric Bond and Share, of which Montana Power Company was an operating asset, controlled near half the industry. In Wheeler's view, few things could be worse for the country and for utility consumers than such enormous concentration of control over a critical national industry. The utility holding companies were for Wheeler the very epitome of monopoly.[4]

With little state regulation and even less logic as to how the holding companies were organized geographically and economically, the conglomerates had license to grow and grow. Twenty-four states had no provisions at all for regulating holding companies, and many other states' utility commissions had only minimal regulatory authority. The largest of the holding companies, Commonwealth and Southern Corporation, was a combination of 165 operating entities geographically spread over ten states from Ohio to Alabama. These mostly unregulated entities were a tremendous vehicle for concentrating corporate wealth. Holding companies typically issued publicly traded stock, but prior to the creation of the Securities and Exchange Commission (SEC) in 1934 there was little independent oversight of the stock offerings, a situation creating vast opportunities for fraud. Holding companies also frequently charged significant management, engineering, and accounting fees to the operating companies under their control and typically bled off a percentage of revenue those companies generated. Occasionally these empires were constructed of multiple layers of holding companies, with the companies at the top squeezing cash out of the only assets with real value—the operating entities at the very bottom of the pyramid, where the electricity was generated and transmitted and where customers were served.[5]

Wheeler contended that this opaque and complex scheme was little more than a monopolistic mechanism that drove up ratepayer costs, while fabulously enriching a few Wall Street investment houses and extremely well-paid holding company executives. With little transparency as to how the companies operated it was nearly impossible to determine how costs and revenues were apportioned across a single utility empire, a circumstance that stoked a widespread belief that holding company stock was heavily watered down. Even the most astute investors had little ability to determine the real value of these entities. Additionally, as historian Robert Caro notes, the holding companies often provided shoddy or nonexistent service to customers. "Because holding companies saw little profit in rural electrification," Caro writes, "which required the building of long power lines into sparsely populated areas, in 1929 more than 6 million of America's 6.8 million farms did not have electricity." A generation or more after electricity had become a common feature of urban life, most of the nation's farms and ranches—including most in Montana—remained without modern conveniences like electric pumps and washing machines. After dusk in rural America, light often still came from a wood stove or a kerosene lamp.[6]

As is often the case in U.S. politics, it took a high-profile scandal—the collapse of Samuel Insull's vast midwestern utility empire—to make regulation of utility holding companies an urgent national issue. Insull had built his massive holding company by relentlessly focusing on growth—growth in utility customers, growth in number of operating companies he controlled, and growth in political influence. Insull dominated the Illinois utilities commission and influenced public opinion through state and national "committees on public utilities information." While Insull did help pioneer relatively cheap and abundant electricity for millions of Americans, he was also a ruthless and shrewd businessman, once telling a questioner who had asked if more enlightened workforce policies at his plants might improve efficiency, "The greatest aid to efficiency of labor is a long line of men waiting at the gate." During a Senate speech in 1931, Wheeler predicted the collapse of Insull's empire. The sprawling

Chicago-based empire was a fraud, Wheeler said, and its eventual demise would cost "Uncle Sam and the people" between $500 million and $1 billion dollars, although he admitted no one really knew the extent of Insull's financial manipulation or what the cost would be when the empire crumbled. When Insull's empire finally did implode in 1932, the impact on Wall Street and in Washington was staggering. Overnight the issue of holding company regulation was thrust into the middle of the Roosevelt-Hoover presidential campaign, heightening calls for reform and regulation. With Insull's empire in bankruptcy and Roosevelt in the White House, the political environment was primed for action against the holding companies.[7]

Eager as Wheeler was to regulate or even dismantle the utility empires, a major legislative fight involving one of the most important industries in the nation had the potential to create serious political problems for the senator in Montana, including renewal of old battles with Montana Power Company. Additionally, many of Wheeler's constituents owned stock in the Montana utility, and those shareholders might hold their senator responsible if legislation impacted, or even seemed to impact, their investments. Neither consideration caused Wheeler pause.[8]

Roosevelt began developing options for regulating utility holding companies in 1934 when he created the National Power Policy Committee. The committee, chaired by Interior Secretary Ickes, included representatives of the Bureau of Reclamation, the Army Corps of Engineers, the newly created Tennessee Valley Authority (TVA), the Federal Power Commission, and the SEC). The committee received a sweeping mandate from Roosevelt to recommend "national policy in power matters" in the interest of making electricity "more broadly available at cheaper rates." The committee was also instructed to "consider what lines should be followed" in shaping legislation dealing with holding companies and the regulation of utilities in interstate commerce.[9]

During its first meeting committee members agreed to use the legal and bill-drafting skills of a quiet, scholarly, brilliant young Harvard Law graduate, Benjamin V. Cohen. Cohen was an employee of the Public Works Administration, an agency supervised by Ickes, and a close confidant of his former Harvard professor Felix Frankfurter. He was also a close friend of another bright, energetic young New Deal attorney and political operative, Thomas Corcoran. Corcoran—nicknamed "Tommy the Cork" by Roosevelt—had by 1935 played a major role in drafting much of the New Deal's legislation, including that which established the SEC. Corcoran, personable and well-spoken, was a consummate Washington insider with ready access to Roosevelt and important members of Congress. He was on good terms too with Wheeler.[10]

As the power policy committee worked on specifics, Roosevelt quietly cranked up pressure on the power industry by, among other things, conducting his own background briefings for reporters. In these ostensibly off-the-record sessions Roosevelt candidly discussed his view of the evils of holding companies, and details inevitably showed up in newspaper coverage, precisely as the administration intended. Laboring through the late summer and fall of 1934, the committee considered a variety of approaches to holding company regulation, but time and again members returned to discussion of total abolition as opposed to mere regulation. Cohen eventually produced legislative language that would be described as a "death sentence" for utility conglomerates, a provision authorizing the SEC to compel dissolution of holding companies unless it could be shown that an operating company "cannot be operated as an independent system without the loss of substantial economies" resulting from its control by a holding company. The "death sentence" became the central issue in the legislative fight.[11]

On January 5, 1935, near the end of Roosevelt's annual State of the Union speech, the president directly addressed the holding company issue and did something rare for such a gifted public speaker—he misspoke. Roosevelt's prepared remarks called for "the abolition of the evil features of holding companies," but, in a Freudian moment, while delivering the line Roosevelt inadvertently dropped the word "features." To members of Congress and those listening on radio Roosevelt seemed to be calling for the complete elimination of holding companies. Roosevelt attempted to correct himself during a news conference the next day, but the message seemed clear: the administration was planning an all-out attack on the utility industry.[12]

Roosevelt had not yet detailed the scope of his legislative proposal when he agreed to a late January 1935 White House meeting with a small group of utility executives. The gathering included, among others, the dynamic president of Commonwealth and Southern, Wendell Willkie. The utility empire Willkie headed was based in New York, and, while Commonwealth and Southern was among the best-run of the holding companies, it was also a prime example of a massive enterprise that had come to dominate the electric industry in a vast swath of the country.

The meeting did not go well. Roosevelt, as he typically did in such settings, dominated the conversation, regaling the utility executives with a litany of holding companies' abuses. Willkie, a plainspoken Indiana-born lawyer and future Republican presidential candidate who had worked his way to the top of the utility world, finally heard enough and interrupted. David Lilienthal, a TVA commissioner who sat in on the meeting, recorded what happened. Lilienthal wrote in his diary that Willkie pulled his reading glasses from his coat pocket and jabbed them in Roosevelt's direction. It was "as if Willkie had suddenly produced a gun and started shooting," Lilienthal remembered of Willkie's potshots at the president's arguments. Roosevelt quickly declared further discussion to be futile, and the meeting ended with the battle lines between the administration and the industry even more sharply drawn.[13]

Wheeler prepared his own proposal addressing holding company issues and had the legislation ready for introduction shortly after Roosevelt's State of the Union speech, but Cohen and Corcoran, acting at the behest of the White House, persuaded him to set aside his proposal in the interest of presenting a single bill. Wheeler was told he would not need to work on the legislation immediately because the White House wanted the bill to start in the House of Representatives, where Sam Rayburn, Wheeler's counterpart as chair of the House Interstate Commerce Committee, would call the shots. "I agreed to go along," Wheeler would later write, noting that the Cohen-Corcoran bill "was more carefully drafted than mine." But Wheeler's ego was bruised again by the realization that Roosevelt was entrusting legislative strategy on such an important issue to Rayburn rather than to him. "He was deliberately turning the job over to Sam and ignoring me," Wheeler wrote in his memoirs, claiming to have forgotten why he was "not in too good grace with FDR at the time."[14]

Roosevelt believed that he could convince the House, with its huge Democratic majority, to quickly approve what was certain to be controversial legislation, as had been demonstrated repeatedly in 1933 and 1934. A quick, decisive House vote would then create pressure on the Senate to follow suit. Following review by Attorney General Cummings, who opined that the legislation could withstand constitutional review, Wheeler and Rayburn introduced the administration's bill in their respective chambers on February 6, 1935. "This bill is intended to whittle down and ultimately eliminate public-utility holding companies," Wheeler told the Senate. "Its spirit is the spirit of the bill I propose for a Federal tax on bigness . . . both these bills are essentials in what I consider the only program that can eventually restore us to the reality of that theory of economic and political democracy by which we fondly think this Nation lives." Congress had to be willing to reform and regulate concentrated economic power, Wheeler continued, or it would see the country inevitably move toward repressive economic and political systems, including even fascism or communism.[15]

Utility interests, bankers, various business groups, and insurance companies that owned significant utility stock immediately prepared, as Arthur Schlesinger Jr. writes, "to defend the holding company system as if it were the ark of the American covenant." A huge, unprecedented lobbying effort was launched to defeat the holding company legislation and destroy any momentum toward comprehensive regulation. Rayburn's biographers write: "Through newspaper, magazine, and radio advertising and through zealous, fear-inducing letter-writing campaigns, the utilities sought to marshal public opinion. Millions of stockholders were misled into believing that the bill threatened their entire investment. Lists of stockholders were compiled by congressional district and distributed to each member of Congress to emphasize the bill's adverse effect on constituents." Ben Cohen called the utility campaign "foolish and harmful" but also extremely effective in its objective to alarm and influence "many honest congressmen."[16]

Congressional offices were buried in mail from worried constituents. The Western Union manager in Washington, D.C., estimated that his office handled four thousand telegrams an hour during the holding company debate, with most of the telegrams featuring nearly identical language. The deluge of public comment worked as planned on the members of House committee, and the legislation quickly stalled, even as Rayburn insisted on continuing hearings. The utilities, Rayburn would later remember, did "an excellent job of having the right calls made to congressmen from bankers, for example, who told them: 'You don't realize what an effect this bill will have on the estate I am planning.' They really alarmed many honest congressmen." With the legislative effort stalled in the House, the political focus shifted to Wheeler's Senate committee, where the lobbying became even more intense.[17]

At one point Wheeler accepted delivery of a huge postcard, five feet long and a foot wide, that made the remarkable claim that every American opposed the bill except for Roosevelt, Wheeler, Rayburn, Cohen, Corcoran, "and a few who have long had a prejudice against the public utilities and are advocates of government ownership." Wheeler's Montana colleague Jim Murray complained that lobbyists "get me . . . at the entrance to the floor of the Senate, at my office, and on the street." Utility interests in Missouri mobilized the state's Pendergast political organization to apply pressure on Harry Truman, who received thirty thousand pieces of mail and claimed to have "burned them all." Mississippi Democrat Theodore Bilbo, also deluged by mail from back home, was also unmoved. "These holding companies are mere leeches," he wrote a constituent, "veritable parasites feeding upon and sucking the life blood of that class of industries you seek to protect."[18]

The files of Wheeler's committee contain thousands of letters and telegrams received between February and the summer of 1935, nearly all opposing the legislation and most carrying a nearly identical message. Hundreds of pieces of mail, all originating in Pennsylvania, carried the same heading—"PROTEST." Typical of the letters is one signed by Irene Engard of Philadelphia who identifies herself as "a citizen, and a customer of Philadelphia Electric Company" who "protests against the unfairness of the proposed Wheeler-Rayburn Utility Holding Company Bill. It is viciously and rankly socialistic, and I am firmly convinced that its adoption will delay the return of prosperity to this country. I don't want politicians running the company supplying me with electric service." Dozens of letters to Wheeler and his committee featured the same phrasing—"viciously and rankly socialist"—indicating the level of coordination and message discipline involved in the lobbying effort by utility interests.[19]

Letters to the committee and to Wheeler personally came from professionals, academics, and executives, even the vice president of the Pittsburgh Pirates baseball team. The president of the Harrisburg, Pennsylvania, chamber of commerce complained to Wheeler that "many businessmen . . . feel that [the proposed legislation] is driving private business out of the field of employment and that it is tending toward Government ownership." Wheeler received ten letters on the same day all on the letterhead of the St. Louis office of the American Surety Company of New York, each praising the Union Electric Light and Power Company and opposing the Wheeler-Rayburn Bill. Tina Hakala, a Wheeler constituent in Butte, apparently hoped to get the senator's attention by detailing her objections to the legislation in a note written on hot pink stationary. Hakala said she was "a small stockholder in the Montana Power Co. . . . and from the letters I have received from them I am convinced that the Rayburn Bill . . . is very detrimental to the interests of us small stockholders."[20]

As that and other correspondence in the files of Wheeler's committee shows, Montana Power Company coordinated opposition to the legislation among the company's Montana shareholders but took care not to attack Wheeler directly. Company spokesmen regularly referred to the legislation as "the Rayburn bill," even as Montana Power president Frank Kerr implored stockholders to tell Congress that "every dollar" of the $20,000,000 Montanans had invested in his company "will be jeopardized" if the legislation passed. The legislation, Kerr said, was an "unparalleled" attack on investors and would likely lead to "nationalization" of the utility industry.[21]

Wheeler largely ignored the flood of correspondence he received from across the country, but he paid close attention to the concerns of his Montana constituents. Committee files contain copies of dozens of letters Wheeler wrote to Montanans like Mr. and Mrs. E. L. Stackhouse of Thompson Falls. The Stackhouses had sent Wheeler a telegram protesting the legislation, and in his answer—he addressed the Stackhouses "My dear friends"—he made a careful, if somewhat evasive distinction regarding the origin of the legislation. "This is an Administration bill," Wheeler wrote, "and we have been holding hearings on the same, and everyone has had an opportunity to be heard. Holding companies in many instances have been just a form of legalized theft. They are now calling upon their victims to defend them. I am sending you . . . a copy of my speech on this bill, and hope you will take the time to read it, instead of listening to the false propaganda put out by the holding companies." In his standard letter to constituents Wheeler explained the distinctions between "holding companies" and "operating companies." The legislation, he maintained, "will not destroy the value of Montana Power stock, which is an operating company. Much false propaganda has been and is being put out all over the country against this legislation."[22]

It is perhaps an indication of the intensity of the heat being generated that Wheeler told constituents that the legislation carrying his name was "an Administration bill," while Roosevelt did his best to preserve the fiction that the controversial proposal was actually the work of Congress. It was not until March 12, more than a month after the legislation was introduced, that Roosevelt finally and definitively endorsed his own proposal. "I am against private socialism or concentrated private power as thoroughly as I am against governmental socialism," Roosevelt said as he released the report of his National Power Policy Committee. "The one is equally as dangerous as the other; and destruction of private socialism is utterly essential to avoid governmental socialism." With Roosevelt finally acknowledging the paternity of the Wheeler-Rayburn Bill, columnist Walter Lippmann proclaimed that the political battle was now fully joined, a "revival of old fashioned, 100% American trust busting."[23]

With the exception of the Scripps-Howard newspaper chain, press reaction to the holding company legislation was generally negative, and the near-unanimous newspaper opposition made the direct mail and the unprecedented lobbying effort even more effective. Wheeler fought back, moving to counter what appeared to be widespread opposition to the holding company regulation during a scathing two-hour Senate speech on March 28. Every citizen has a right to complain to Congress, he said, "but there is a common-sense difference between the right of fair petition and a high-powered selling campaign of canned propaganda which makes power-company employees obtain signatures to form letters at the risk of their jobs."[24]

Wheeler continued his counteroffensive five days later in a radio speech laced with sarcasm. Wheeler began the half-hour talk by noting that as Senate sponsor of the legislation he had received more mail from Philadelphia in the preceding weeks than he had received from Montana in the preceding two years. "Nice chummy letters, too," Wheeler said. "They call me everything from such high-class terms as 'rogue' and 'rascal' on down the scale. Most of them show the fine hand of the United Gas Improvement Company [one of the larger holding companies]. The best of them could have been written by Gertrude Stein: 'It makes me sick to think how sick I get when I think about you.'" Wheeler said he was surprised not to have the same kind of letters from Chicago, where the fallout over the Insull bankruptcy was still playing out. "It must be that that city has been Insull-ated against my charm," he quipped. After cataloging the worst abuses of the holding companies, detailing the lack of regulation on a national scale, and condemning the "desperate, insidious . . . misleading" lobbying effort on behalf of "widows and orphans," Wheeler attempted to reassure utility investors that the legislation would not destroy their investments but instead preserve them. The reorganized holding companies would, Wheeler said, be forced to adopt "safeguards which will, in fact, protect the investor." At the end of his occasionally bitter speech Wheeler spoke of his own economic philosophy and again invoked a Jeffersonian ideal of the U.S. economy. Lamenting the decline of small businesses, Wheeler called the holding company "an instrument by which a few men have been able to set up a system of private socialism, which has crowded . . . individual enterprise and local initiative out of one of the most important of our industries." For Wheeler, always at his best in political brawl, the fight over the holding company legislation became nothing less than a struggle for the future of American free enterprise. He would, he said, continue the fight to contain "bigness," rein in the influence of Wall Street, and cut the power of "a few men" down to size.[25]

In mid-April, with Rayburn's House committee hopelessly bogged down—the lobbying effort was working on House members—Wheeler began its own hearings. His committee, he said, intended to give utility representatives ample time to make their case, but he was not going to permit the hearings to drag on indefinitely, and considering the complexity of the proposal he ultimately handled the legislation with considerable speed. Senate testimony was completed in two weeks, with Wheeler driving the hearings with his typical vigor while also serving as the chief defender of the legislation. When witnesses complained that the proposal would hurt investors, he reminded them that the Senate's job was "to legislate for the greatest good to the greatest number." When it was suggested that the bill would inevitably lead to government ownership of utilities, Wheeler said that precisely the opposite was true. "I think if you have strict regulation," he said, "you are much less likely to have Government ownership and operation of these utilities." While Wheeler confessed that he was not eager to give more "dictatorial power to various bureaus and departments" to regulate industry from Washington, he also said that the massive economic power of holding companies and their interstate configurations left only one alternative, "and that is government regulation." Wheeler had a particularly testy and telling exchange with George B. Chandler, the secretary of the Columbus, Ohio, chamber of commerce. Growing exasperated with Chandler's testimony, Wheeler finally asked Chandler if he had even read the legislation he opposed:

> Chandler: Yes sir; I have also read the figures prepared by the
>   Edison Institute.
> Wheeler: That is an institute controlled by the utilities?
> Chandler: It is made up of educated and scientific men, they are—
> Wheeler: Owned and controlled—
> Chandler: The figures are published and subject to criticism if they
>   are inaccurate.
> Wheeler: I contend that they are inaccurate.[26]

Willkie, the articulate, personable head of the largest holding company, became the most effective spokesman for the utilities and assumed a lead role in defending the industry. In testimony before both House and Senate committees, Willkie argued for regulation of holding companies but not dissolution. "Stop us where we are, don't dismember us," he pleaded. Then a registered Democrat, Willkie had supported Roosevelt's election in 1932 but almost immediately took issue with the creation of TVA, which put the federal government in the power-generation and distribution business squarely in the middle of Willkie's holding company territory.[27]

At one point during Willkie's appearance before Wheeler's committee the utility executive expressed admiration for an industry colleague, referring to him as an idealist. Wheeler interrupted and asked Willkie, who had made his way to the top of corporate America from the humble circumstances of his Indiana upbringing, "You started out that way, too, didn't you, as an idealist?" Willkie, ever quick, replied, "And I hope I still am, Mr. Chairman, I still have my western views." Willkie's engaging testimony helped put a human face on the utility industry, whose leaders were often characterized, not without some justification, as greedy, power-hungry, and largely anonymous men.[28]

Wheeler ended Senate hearings in late April and took his committee into executive session to mark up the legislation, a task that consumed most of the next month. During this period his efforts received a powerful endorsement. The popular radio priest Father Coughlin, who had agreed with Wheeler's position on silver legislation a year earlier, told his national audience that they should ignore the utility public relations campaign and join the fight to break up the holding companies.[29]

Finally, on May 29, with Ben Cohen parked on the Senate floor next to Wheeler's desk, the Montanan opened debate on the landmark legislation, spending most of the day explaining provisions of the complex, 151-page bill. Title I granted broad new power to the SEC to simplify and restructure holding companies along both economic and geographic lines. Section 11 of Title I—the "death sentence" provision—both the heart of the legislation and source of greatest controversy, empowered the SEC to break up holding companies that refused to dissolve voluntarily. Title II focused on operating companies and delegated to the Federal Power Commission the job of defining regional systems determined by operational efficiency rather than by financial investment. Wheeler and Cohen occasionally exchanged a whispered aside during the long presentation, but it was clear that Wheeler had mastered the huge subject, and he floor-managed the bill through what all observers knew would be contentious Senate debate.[30]

Wheeler's efforts were complicated by a unanimous Supreme Court decision, rendered just two days before Senate debate began, striking down large portions of the National Industrial Recovery Act. The court held that the centerpiece of the New Deal's effort to create a planned national economy in fact provided the president with "unfettered discretion" to create "new law" without congressional approval. The NIRA, justice Benjamin Cardozo wrote, amounted to "delegation run riot."[31]

Wheeler was neither upset nor surprised by the Supreme Court decision. He had opposed the NIRA legislation in 1933, primarily because he feared the industry-sponsored codes of fair competition authorized by the law would inevitably favor big business and provide a legal shield for monopoly. He also had concerns about the "unfettered discretion" the legislation granted to the president. Nevertheless the timing of the court decision complicated Wheeler's task related to the holding company legislation. Supreme Court rejection of a key part of the president's economic reform strategy handed opponents of the utility legislation a new argument with which to attack what they perceived as one more example of Roosevelt's regulatory overreach.

Opponents also attempted to show that the complex legislation had been hap-hazardly thrown together, a charge also leveled at the National Industrial Recovery Act. Critics noted that wholesale changes had been made between introduction of the legislation and Senate floor action, and Wheeler had to admit that the proposal had been altered to such a degree that he deemed it "advisable to report a substitute bill." Two opponents—a Republican, Wallace White Jr. of Maine, and a Democrat, William H. Dieterich of Illinois, both lawyers—claimed that the Senate, and indeed the members of Wheeler's own committee, barely knew what was contained in the legislation. Dieterich demanded that the legislation be returned to Wheeler's commit-tee for more consideration, including hearing more testimony from utility interests, a move that clearly would have delighted opponents, given the utilities more time to lobby, and likely would have killed the bill. "I've given a fair hearing to the bill," Wheeler snapped, "but I do not propose to stand idly by and let statements go unchallenged about treatment given the public utility companies. Things could be said that would not be complimentary to them." Looking directly at the burly Dieterich, a veteran of the Spanish-American War, Wheeler said that if the senator failed to comprehend the bill it was his own fault since "he came to the committee meetings only for a few minutes each day" and only then to "complain that members of the Commission were present." The reference was to Roosevelt's National Public Policy Commission and the constant presence in the hearing room of Ben Cohen and Tommy Corcoran, both of whom were closely identified with the commission's work.[32]

Wheeler received valuable support a few days into the debate when his friend Repub-lican senator Norris of Nebraska, the godfather of the Tennessee Valley Authority, spoke for five hours in defense of Wheeler's legislative handiwork. "Armed with a schoolmaster's pointer," as the *New York Times* described the scene, Norris "traced, step by step, the ramifications of the holding companies drawn on large maps. These great charts showed the pyramiding of the holding concerns, their interlocking relationships . . . all the intricacies of the financing." Norris's essential point, which he made with eloquent precision, "was that he had been unable to find a single instance where a holding company in the second degree, a corporation that controlled another holding company in addition to integrated operating companies, was of any benefit to society." Regulating holding companies was the most important issue before the Congress, Norris contended, and among the most important in his forty years in Washington. Approval of the legislation would open "the eyes of the people of the United States to the wrongs and ills they have suffered from greedy corporations."[33]

Hastings and Dieterich led the bipartisan opposition, repeatedly questioning whether Wheeler's legislation was constitutional, particularly in light of the recent Supreme Court decision. Both men also claimed the bill would devastate utility industry investors. "The vicious part of this bill is section 11," Dieterich said, "giving the Securities Commission, following its whim, without any fixed rules, the absolute power to destroy and fix the time when the destruction shall be wrought. That is a death sentence."[34]

A week into the Senate debate Wheeler scrambled to respond to nearly seventy amendments, many offered in an effort to stall action, others hoping to dilute or defeat the legislation. He ultimately agreed to several changes, most importantly accepting language that specified that the "death sentence" would not apply to holding companies that operated primarily within a single state, but he refused to abandon the principle of breaking up multistate, multiregional holding companies even as it seemed possible that this most contentious provision might doom passage of any reform proposal.[35]

On the morning of June 6, with the fate of the holding company legislation in doubt, Wheeler made a trip downtown to the White House to solicit help directly from Roosevelt. While the president had made a strong statement in favor of comprehensive holding company regulation when he released his commission's report, Roosevelt had not explicitly endorsed the "death sentence." Some in Congress interpreted this silence as a signal of quiet opposition. Like all visitors who needed to see Roosevelt before ten in the morning, Wheeler was ushered into the president's second-floor bedroom, a room, as Frances Perkins recalled, too large to be cozy and not large enough to be impressive. Wheeler found Roosevelt propped up in his narrow bed, still wearing pajamas. The president had the morning newspapers spread around his bed with the breakfast tray still waiting to be removed.[36]

Wheeler got directly to the point: was Roosevelt for the "death sentence" or not? If Roosevelt supported dismantling the biggest utility holding companies, Wheeler said, he needed to let the Senate and the country know immediately. The visit was fruitful.

Before Wheeler left Roosevelt's bedroom he had in his pocket a handwritten "Dear Bert" letter—FDR again misspelled Wheeler's name—confirming the president's unqualified support for the "death sentence" provision. Roosevelt told Wheeler to use the note in any manner he deemed appropriate, and Wheeler determined that he would hold on to the valuable piece of paper for use at the moment of maximum political advantage.[37]

Roosevelt realized that the holding company legislation had become more than just another piece of his economic reform agenda. Approval of the legislation had become a litmus test of his political strength. With the House of Representatives and its huge Democratic majority in disarray regarding the proposal, a circumstance not before confronted during Roosevelt's presidency, the president now had to rely on the more independent Senate to adopt legislation addressing holding company abuses. Additionally, as evidenced by the fierce opposition of Dieterich and several other Democrats, the "death sentence" provision had divided Democrats. By endorsing the most controversial portion of the legislation and empowering Wheeler to use the endorsement as political leverage, Roosevelt signaled that he was fighting to secure the reforms Wheeler, Norris, and other Senate progressives were determined to pass. White House aide Raymond Moley was convinced that prior to Wheeler's visit the president had been prepared, if it became necessary, to use the "death sentence" as trading stock in order to get some type of utility reform legislation through Congress in 1935. But now Roosevelt tied his immediate legislative fortunes to Wheeler's ability to move the holding company bill through a skeptical Senate. If Wheeler succeeded in passing the strongest possible bill, the House might still be forced to act and Roosevelt might continue a nearly unbroken string of legislative victories.[38]

Meanwhile, the political terrain shifted again, with some supporters of the legislation—Norris, Washington's Homer Bone, and Huey Long most prominently—suggesting that efforts to compromise with utility interests had gone too far. Long had not been active during committee consideration of the bill, in large part because he was spending most of his time in Louisiana stage-managing a special session of the state legislature. But with the fight nearing a climax, the Louisiana senator was determined to have his say. Decked out against the humid heat of the Washington summer in a white serge suit and pink shirt and necktie, Long attacked the White House for not proposing even tougher legislation. Not content with regulation of electric utilities, Long advocated including the nation's gas and telephone monopolies under the provisions of Section 11.[39]

"The Senator from Montana and his colleagues on the Senate Interstate Commerce Committee apparently have realized that the whole force of fraud was too big to fight in one battle," Long said. "They have realized that these brigands and high binders, all

combined, are too powerful for Congress to engage in one single battle with them."
Alluding to his battles with Standard Oil in Louisiana, Long acknowledged that
taking on big interests was "pretty tough," but nonetheless he contended that the bill
under consideration had been compromised too much. "It is not strong enough," Long
insisted, "it is not half strong enough." Wheeler stood by and listened to the tirade,
convinced that Long's real objective was merely to cause discomfort for Roosevelt.[40]

As historian Philip Funigiello has written, "the Montana Democrat was put in
the difficult position of trying to balance contending interests" in the Senate, and the
competing positions—Long agitating for tougher legislation, southern Democrats
worried about protecting state prerogatives, other senators questioning the constitutionality of the proposal, and still others hoping to kill the bill outright—required
from Wheeler the skills of a master political juggler. When debate resumed on June 11,
Dieterich finally offered an amendment to eliminate the "death sentence," which, as
Wheeler knew, was the vote that would determine the overall fate of the legislation.[41]

"This bill," Dieterich said, "instead of regulating and correcting evils that exist
in holding companies, is an effort to bring about public control of all utilities in the
United States. . . . I say this with all due respect to the Senator from Montana, because
at one time he was a candidate for Vice President on a platform which declared for
the public ownership of utilities." Wheeler was perfectly entitled to hold that view,
Dieterich said, but senators should have no doubt that passage of legislation with the
"death sentence" intact would be "the beginning of an effort to accomplish" public
ownership.[42]

Dieterich scored points by highlighting the public ownership position Wheeler
had once advocated but no longer embraced, but the Illinois senator also stumbled
into the trap Wheeler had rigged by obtaining Roosevelt's written endorsement of
the "death sentence." When Dieterich unwisely asked if the president really supported the controversial provision, Wheeler dramatically producing Roosevelt's
handwritten note from his coat pocket. With senators now giving him their complete
attention, Wheeler read Roosevelt's unambiguous endorsement. "I am very clear in
my own mind," Roosevelt had written, "that while clarifying or minor amendments
to the section cannot be objected to . . . any amendment which goes to the heart of
major objective of section 11 would strike at the bill itself and is wholly contrary to
the recommendations of my message."[43]

To any wavering Democrat, Roosevelt's words were precise. Wheeler was doing
the bidding of the president in pushing the "death sentence," and a vote against
Wheeler's approach would, in effect, be a vote against Roosevelt. Wheeler added his
own emphasis by reminding the Senate that the only real advocates of eliminating the
"death sentence" were the holding companies themselves. "When they vote for this

[the Dieterich] amendment they vote to kill the bill," Wheeler said. "When they vote for this amendment they are voting as the lobbyist up in the galleries, representing the Power Trust, want them to vote, because the lobbyists want them to vote to kill the bill." Dieterich's amendment dramatically failed by a single vote, decided at the last moment when Peter Norbeck, a once-in-a-while progressive Republican senator from South Dakota, voted with Wheeler to keep the "death sentence" provision in the legislation. Yet, despite Wheeler's impassioned arguments and Roosevelt's eleventh-hour endorsement, twenty-nine Democrats, many of them southerners, voted against the "death sentence" provision. The Senate rather anticlimactically approved the full holding company legislation later that same day by a 56-to-32 margin, with eighteen Democrats defying the White House. From Hyde Park that evening Roosevelt wired his thanks to Wheeler: "Tried to get you on the phone tonight to thank you for your splendid victory today. Will see you Thursday to discuss next steps."[44]

The next steps involved getting the legislation moving again in the House of Representatives, where, despite constant effort since February, Sam Rayburn had lost control of his badly divided committee. Enthusiasm in the House for holding company regulation had been dulled by the intense utility lobbying effort and what appeared to be a massive outpouring of public opposition. Ironically it was the Roosevelt administration's own effort to lobby House members, led by the ebullient Irishman Tommy Corcoran, that precipitated a sensational Senate investigation that finally illuminated the extent of the industry's deceptive efforts to defeat regulation. Maine Republican representative Ralph Owen Brewster prompted the investigation when he charged Corcoran with threatening to eliminate Public Works Administration funding for a dam project in Brewster's state if the congressman refused to support the holding company legislation. Corcoran vehemently denied the charge, and the subsequent investigation, Corcoran's own testimony, and other firsthand accounts indicated that no precise threat had been issued.[45]

Nevertheless, Brewster's allegation, combined with other accusations that the intense utility lobbying effort had bordered on fraud, prompted the Senate to commission a full inquiry. The subsequent revelations convinced many House members who had been prepared to abandon the legislation to reconsider and stiffened the resolve of many senators.

Cohen and Corcoran tried to convince Wheeler to lead the Senate probe, but he wisely refused, arguing that his time was already consumed managing the legislation. Wheeler also must have known that his well-deserved reputation as the Senate's chief critic of the utility industry would be seen as tainting any investigation before it began. Alabama senator Hugo Black, another critic of holding companies, a staunch New Dealer, and a future Supreme Court justice was finally chosen to head the Senate investigation. Black's committee bore deep into details of the utility industry's activity and unearthed evidence that the utilities had conceived, organized, and financed a vast lobbying campaign of at least $1.5 million (more than $26 million today) against the Wheeler-Rayburn Bill. These were hardly startling revelations since most members of Congress had personally experienced the intense pressure of the campaign, but what scandalized Congress and titillated the press and public was the degree to which the utilities used deception, including funding various front organizations to spread their message. These groups appeared to be independent advocates for concerned constituents or utility shareholders, but it was ruse. Black's investigation unearthed a letter and telegram campaign that appeared to be a spontaneous outpouring of public concern but was in fact carefully organized, financed, and implemented on a massive scale by the utilities.[46]

The American Federation of Utility Investors (AFUI), claiming to be independent of utility companies and purporting to represent worried investors, produced huge amounts of printed material aimed at discrediting the bill and supplied it to the utility companies who, in turn, distributed it to customers and stockholders. The material was "purchased" from AFUI by utilities at rates sufficiently above what it cost to produce, a tactic that generated the substantial resources required to operate the front organization. Black's investigation also disclosed that most of the 250,000 letters and telegrams directed at Congress had been generated by the utilities with names of signers often copied directly from city directories or telephone books.[47]

Direct lobbying of Congress, which complemented what appeared to be a grassroots letter-writing campaign, was bankrolled and directed by the Committee of Public Utilities Executives and the Associated Gas & Electric Company (AG&E). The utility interests hired several well-placed Democrats, including former presidential candidate John W. Davis and Woodrow Wilson's onetime assistant Joseph P. Tumulty, to directly lobby Democratic members of Congress. Bruce Kremer, the former Butte lawyer and Anaconda lobbyist, was on retainer serving both the utility executives and AG&E.[48]

The utilities' campaign pioneered some of the earliest and most effective public relations techniques. What the utilities attempted in 1935 was both innovative and, to many, underhanded and deceptive. Industry PR men placed articles favorable to utilities in dozens of newspapers and aggressively courted columnists and editorial writers who, it was hoped, would attack the legislation. To broaden the impact of the effort, investment bankers and insurance executives were mobilized. Direct advertising was used, particularly in Chicago, New York, and Washington, D.C., where local utility companies were instructed to replace their regular advertising with messages attacking the Wheeler-Rayburn Bill. A memo unearthed by Black's committee said in part, "If every operating company will run the same message . . . the newspaper publishers throughout the country will recognize this as a united effort of truly national character." Utility ratepayers, of course, were footing the bill for the campaign, which one analyst described as "a striking example of the degree of political manipulation available to the holders of concentrated economic power."[49]

The testimony of nineteen-year-old Elmer Danielson, a Western Union messenger from Warren, Pennsylvania, illustrated the lengths to which the utility companies had gone to defeat the legislation. Decked out in his best clothing, young Elmer testified before Black's committee that he received three cents from Associated Gas and Electric for every signature he produced on a telegram opposing the holding company bill. He lined up six telegrams in all, he said, including messages signed by his mother, a friend, and a neighbor. "Did you tell them what they were signing?" Black asked the young man. "I explained the Wheeler-Rayburn Bill," he said, grinning, while those in the hearing room broke into laughter. When Black asked Elmer his current position on the legislation, the young man said to more laughter, "Well, I guess I'm neutral now."[50]

Black was forced to compel the testimony of Howard C. Hopson, the investigation's most sensational witness and the man who had built the Associated Gas & Electric holding company into a vast enterprise from which he received millions in salary and dividends. Hopson's empire "offered for sale three classes of common stock, six of preferred, four of preference, seven issues of secured bonds and notes, twenty-four classes of debentures, and four series of investment securities" all from an interconnected group of 160 companies. Hobson resisted Black's subpoena for two weeks before finally appearing as a witness and confirming the extent of the industry's deception. As *Time* magazine noted, Hobson dug "a pit into which the utility tycoons of the United States fell and writhed in despair."[51]

Influential editor William Allen White succinctly summed up what the utilities had done in hopes of stymieing regulation: "It was pure fake," he said. Black's investigative methods, particularly the blanket subpoenas the committee issued, received widespread criticism, but as historian Arthur Schlesinger Jr. observes, the investigation "seemed to bear out George Norris's old thesis that the utilities were the source of all corruption and David Lilienthal's contention that the power trust was out to take over the government."[52]

Hugo Black's headline-grabbing investigation refocused attention on the holding company legislation, and a somewhat weaker version of the Senate bill, without a "death sentence" provision, passed in the House by a lopsided vote of 321–81. One House member complained about "Wheelerism," an apparent reference to public ownership of utilities.[53]

While the House vote was widely interpreted as a defeat for the White House, House and Senate versions of the legislation were not markedly different except for the critical "death sentence" provision, and a House-Senate conference committee was charged with attempting to reconcile the competing versions. Wheeler led the Senate conference, which included four other members of his committee, Democrats Barkley of Kentucky and Fred Brown of New Hampshire, Henrik Shipstead, a Farmer/Laborite from Minnesota who frequently voted with Senate progressives, and Republican Wallace White of Maine. Wheeler, Barkley, Brown, and White were lawyers. The Senate conferees were under instruction to maintain the "death sentence" provision contained in the Senate bill, but if the conference became deadlocked it was agreed that the full Senate would revisit the issue.[54]

Almost immediately a nasty argument broke out in the closed conference committee over Wheeler's insistence that Benjamin Cohen and Federal Power Commission staffer Dozier DeVane be permitted to participate as "expert advisers" in the meetings. Wheeler demanded that he have his own experts in the conference room, in part because he feared that the principal House opponent of the "death sentence," Alabama Democrat George Huddleston, who had adroitly managed House debate on the legislation, would "pull the wool over Rayburn's eyes," resulting in weak bill from the House conference.[55]

Huddleston, slight of build, with a shock of red hair, was a smart, well-spoken Birmingham lawyer who professed outrage that Wheeler was bringing outsiders into the conference to "lobby." The rhetoric became heated when Wheeler suggested that a bigger problem than the presence of his advisers was Huddleston's coziness with utility lobbyists. Thus goaded, Huddleston responded by calling the Montanan a "four-flushing bluffer." Not surprisingly the first meeting of the conference committee ended poorly. Days of hassling over who could or should be in the room continued until finally a compromise was worked out allowing Cohen and DeVane to park themselves in an adjacent anteroom, while the conferees continued to try to fashion a compromise behind closed doors. The wrangling continued into the hot, humid third week of August, with Wheeler growing nervous that Roosevelt, eager to get any bill that would allow him to claim another legislative victory, might actually abandon the "death sentence" and settle for a weak bill.[56]

On August 18, with pressure building to adjourn Congress, Roosevelt called House and Senate leaders, Wheeler included, to the White House to consider what options were available to salvage the legislation. No option seeming particularly attractive, but Wheeler insisted that, whatever was done, the intent of the "death sentence" could not be sacrificed. Roosevelt confidant Felix Frankfurter finally proposed an alternative that would authorize the SEC to leave undisturbed a holding company that managed more than a single integrated utility if it could be shown that related systems could not survive economically if forced to stand alone. Frankfurter also proposed that the commission be instructed to consider issues such as local management, the level of existing regulation, and the benefits of efficiency. And the SEC was to attempt to simplify integrated systems and permit no more than two holding companies to exist above their subsidiary operating companies. The future Supreme Court justice's ideas pleased neither Roosevelt nor Wheeler, since exception to holding company regulation would expand beyond what was included in the Senate bill. Roosevelt reportedly complained at one point that "Felix sounds just like John W. Davis," the influential New York lawyer and former presidential candidate lobbying for utility interests. Still, with no obviously better option that might break the legislative deadlock, it was decided that Barkley, a less polarizing figure in the conference committee than Wheeler, should present the compromise.[57]

Huddleston now found that he had to manage shifting political momentum in the House, where many members were now more accepting of a compromise that would feature some form of the "death sentence." On August 21, with the oppressive Washington heat helping the push toward adjournment, Rayburn read a letter from Roosevelt to members of the House, a letter Wheeler later claimed that he and Cohen authored. The president argued that the Senate had made real concessions on the "death penalty" that and the House should agree to the changes, end the debate, and pass the bill. The next day, more with a whimper than a bang, and with the *New York Times* observing that many House Democrats had "switched positions they had first taken," the Public Utility Holding Company Act of 1935 received final approval in both houses of Congress.[58]

Several factors account for the outcome of what was the most ferociously fought legislative battle of Roosevelt's first term. The revelations of Black's lobbying investigation had real impact with the public and with Congress. Roosevelt's willingness to fight for the toughest possible bill was also important to the outcome. Even as his grip on the Democratic supermajority in Congress was slipping in 1935, Roosevelt never signaled, at least publicly, a willingness to settle for anything less than the type of bill Wheeler wanted, one including a "death sentence." Wheeler's ferocious fights, first in the Senate and then in the conference committee, provided the leadership and determination to push the proposal forward.

George Norris, still not entirely satisfied with the final legislation, nonetheless singled Wheeler out for his "patience, ability, ingenuity and courage" in steering the bill to passage. On August 26, 1935, Roosevelt signed the holding company bill and called it his greatest legislative victory. The holding company legislation represented the third and final piece of Roosevelt's plan to create effective national economic

Franklin Roosevelt signs the Public Utility Holding Company Act of 1935 (Wheeler-Rayburn Act) on August 26, 1935. *Standing, left to right*: Senator Alben Barkley of Kentucky; Wheeler; Senator Fred H. Brown of New Hampshire; Dozier DeVane, solicitor, Federal Power Commission; Representative Sam Rayburn of Texas; and attorneys Benjamin Cohen and Thomas Corcoran. (*Everett Collection Historical/Alamy Stock Photo*)

regulation. The landmark Securities Act passed in 1933, the Securities and Exchange Commission Act in 1934, and the Public Utilities Holding Company Act in 1935 worked together to create a mechanism to ensure a preeminent role for the federal government in regulating big business. Taken together the effort was not, as some critics suggested, "creeping socialism" or an assault on free market capitalism but rather a recognition that preserving capitalism, particularly during a time of enormous economic upheaval, required a modernizing approach to regulating the American economy, with an emphasis on transparency and accountability. As Benjamin Cohen put it in a private letter to Wendell Willkie, "I wish you could dispassionately try to understand what we are trying to do . . . if we want to avoid the sort of regulation which we both abhor, we have simply got to simplify the rules of the game."[59]

The major utility holding companies did not, however, fall easily or quickly into line. Utility interests immediately challenged the constitutionality of the Public Utilities

Holding Company Act, and it was not until March 1938 that the Supreme Court upheld Wheeler's work. The SEC, with a small staff and with careful attention to the interests of utility investors, slowly and deliberately reorganized the nation's utility industry in what is generally regarded as the most significant task of its kind ever undertaken by a governmental agency. Not until 1952 did the commission report that the job had been completed. Widespread claims that the legislation would destroy private utilities or decimate stockholders were specious. By the early 1950s the SEC reported that the financial integrity of nation's utility industry was actually stronger than it had been in 1935. Nonetheless, Wendell Willkie said he regretted not spending even more money to "prevent this destructive act from being passed."[60]

———

Even as B. K. Wheeler cooperated with the Roosevelt Administration in 1935 to pass landmark legislation to regulate utility holding companies, he was also constantly sparring with the administration. Wheeler's disenchantment with Roosevelt and the New Deal, well known in Congress and among journalists, prompted almost constant speculation about whether he might repeat his revolt of 1924 and become part of a third-party challenge to the president in 1936. He had, in many ways, the ideal profile for such a move. Wheeler never tried to develop or lead a mass movement as his friend Huey Long did, but his independence and outspoken leadership on economic issues made him politically appealing to supporters of Long's "Share the Wealth" movement, Father Coughlin's economic nationalism (what the priest called "social justice"), and California physician Francis Townsend, the apostle of an old-age pension scheme that took his name. By the end of Roosevelt's first term, each of these self-styled reformers, Wheeler included, was expressing increased disenchantment with the president. Revolt was in the air, and, as Arthur Schlesinger Jr. has written, Wheeler's "shrewd, sharp prosecutor's mind and his vigilante's audacity and ruthlessness" made him "the most formidable of the Senate radicals."[61]

As a contemporary observer noted, Wheeler was "one of the most effective stump-speakers in the country," and his "powerful grip on his home state of Montana" allowed him "to take chances in national politics":

> Wheeler possesses the apparatus for a hook-up of some kind with most of the actual or potential deserters from the Roosevelt camp. In addition to this fact, he is "respectable," impeccably so. Huey Long has openly talked of running Wheeler for President . . . and in the belief that Huey could deliver his own strength to Wheeler. There has also been talk of a Long-Wheeler ticket, but Burt is not the man to take second place again on a Third Party ticket with anybody. Wheeler has so far not given any indication of how he will play his hand. . . .

[B]ut if 1936 looks like a good gamble for a man with nothing to lose, look out! His past political record shows he has dramatic abilities which might make history if he decides to employ them to break down Roosevelt."[62]

Interior secretary Harold Ickes warned Roosevelt late in 1935 of the political dangers lurking for the president among his populist critics when he observed that "the general sentiment in the country is much more radical than that of the Administration." Roosevelt, weary of the often-bitter attacks on his policies, on him, and on his family, complained he was "fighting Communism, Huey Longism, Coughlinism, Townsendism . . . to save the capitalist system" from "crackpot ideas." Always the skillful politician, Roosevelt responded to radical ideas with his own legislative agenda—the Second New Deal— including Social Security, in no small part, a response to the Townsend plan, and tax, banking, and utility regulation aimed, at least partly, at blunting the populist messages of Long and Coughlin.[63]

Huey Long's assassination in September 1935 eliminated one potential radical threat to Roosevelt, but the White House never ceased worrying about the threat presented by the radical from Montana. Journalist George Creel, well connected in the Roosevelt administration, observed in the summer of 1935, even as Wheeler worked with the administration on the utility legislation, that the administration was "beginning to cock its ears at every mention of Senator Wheeler's name, betraying an almost feverish interest in his state of mind." The White House worried, for example, that Wheeler might use a Senate investigation of the nation's railroads to embarrass Roosevelt, and presidential aides strategized about the appointment of a U.S. attorney in Montana who might "crimp" Wheeler at home. Wheeler remained as independent as ever, regularly speaking his mind about the administration's shortcomings, but he never seriously contemplated a direct challenge to Roosevelt in 1936. Rather Wheeler would fight his battles—and the president—from the Senate.[64]

When Roosevelt advocated U.S. membership in the World Court, for example, Wheeler said such a move would again unnecessarily embroil the country in European affairs. Members of the World Court, he said, were "the same countries we saved from destruction during the World War and who repudiated their debts which they owe us." Wheeler complained of a White House tendency to "crack the whip" on the Senate, demanding approval of legislation precisely as written by the administration, and he condemned Roosevelt's failure to remember his friends. Wheeler and other Senate progressives were outraged in 1934 when Roosevelt refused to back the reelection of Republican progressive Bronson Cutting in New Mexico. Cutting not only knew Roosevelt from prep school days but also had crossed party lines to endorse FDR in 1932. Like a number of progressive Republicans, Cutting also provided bipartisan support for much early New Deal legislation. Nevertheless Roosevelt withheld any endorsement during the campaign, and after Cutting prevailed in a very close and bitter race against Democrat Dennis Chavez, the White House encouraged Chavez to challenge the outcome. To Cutting's friends, including Wheeler, it was a double betrayal by the president. When Cutting subsequently died in a plane crash while returning to Washington to manage the legal effort to defend his Senate seat, Wheeler, Norris, Hiram Johnson and other progressives felt that Roosevelt shared responsibility for the tragedy. The entire episode provided additional proof, at least for Wheeler, that Roosevelt was often a callous, ungrateful politician willing to cast off a friend without a thought.[65]

Shortly after Cutting's death, and while Wheeler was managing the holding company legislation in the Senate, Roosevelt invited the Montana senator as well as Senators Norris, Johnson, Bob La Follette, and Edward Costigan of Colorado to the White House to clear the air and, he hoped, repair the growing breach with the Senate's progressive bloc. Wheeler and La Follette did most of the talking, according to Ickes' notes of the meeting, and "they did a pretty good job" of candidly telling Roosevelt that his legislative program was foundering and the country was demanding stronger leadership. "At one point," Ickes recorded, "the President asked Wheeler why he hadn't come to give him an opinion that he had just expressed. Senator Wheeler said that he was never able to see the President; that [White House assistant Marvin] McIntyre always reported that [Roosevelt] was bogged down and wouldn't give him an appointment. The President said that he could get in to see him any time within twenty-four hours, but Wheeler insisted that he couldn't get in at all. Then the President told him the next time he should call Miss [Missy] Le Hand," Roosevelt's confidential secretary. The meeting allowed Wheeler to vent but did not placate him or address his mounting grievances.[66]

In July 1935 Wheeler clashed again with the White House over administration plans to target progressive Republican William Borah of Idaho. Postmaster General Farley, also chairman of the Democratic National Committee, told reporters that "the Democratic Party is justified in doing everything it can to defeat Borah." Wheeler took immediate umbrage and, displaying his political independence, once again declared his support for a Republican friend. "I will go to Idaho and campaign for Senator Borah if he wants me to," Wheeler said. "Regardless of politics, Senator Borah deserves reelection." The White House wisely backed off, and Borah was reelected easily in 1936.[67]

Wheeler's major role in Roosevelt's 1932 campaign was but a distant memory four years later, and it was a measure of Wheeler's essential lack of enthusiasm for a second Roosevelt term that he sought no role for himself in the 1936 campaign. He would endorse a few Montana Democrats, most notably Jim Murray and Congressman Roy Ayers, who was running for governor, but otherwise, as he told a Montana supporter, he would "go to Montana and hope to be able to remain there until the convening of Congress. This has been a strenuous session and I'm extremely weary." However, when the presidential campaign began in earnest in September, it was Roosevelt who came seeking Wheeler's help for his reelection bid. It is telling that the president did not personally ask Wheeler to hit the campaign trail on his behalf but rather implored Farley and Congressman Rayburn to "please beg Senator Wheeler to start speeches [in] key places at once and this is my request—Will you tell him?"[68]

In response Wheeler briefly joined an October presidential campaign swing through the Midwest before undertaking his own speaking tour through Iowa, Minnesota, South Dakota, Nebraska, Kansas, and Wyoming. Wheeler reported to Roosevelt after his tour that he was "certain you will carry every one of these states and every state west of the Mississippi River not because I've been here but because the people believe you are on their side against the overlords of finance." The Republican candidate—Kansas governor Alfred M. Landon—"won't carry ten states," Wheeler said in Spokane just days before the election, and "Roosevelt will win in a landslide." Roosevelt responded with appreciation for "the splendid work you are doing out there." Back in Montana just before the election, Wheeler admitted that he occasionally disagreed with Roosevelt but praised him publicly. Not everyone thought he meant it.[69]

Roosevelt's 1936 victory over Landon was one of the great landslides in American political history, and in Montana Roosevelt's long coattails carried the entire Democratic ticket into office. Murray won his race for a full Senate term by a more than a two-to-one margin, Ayers was elected governor, and twenty-eight-year old Jerry O'Connell captured the western Montana congressional seat. "President Roosevelt now has a mandate from the people to carry forward on his reform program," Wheeler proclaimed, knowing he had again contributed to a Roosevelt landslide. Wheeler could not have anticipated the role he would play in stopping Roosevelt's next big reform effort.[70]

9 NINE OLD MEN AND WHEELER

I am going to spring a bombshell.
—FRANKLIN D. ROOSEVELT

Near the end of the 1936 presidential campaign, former president Herbert Hoover asked some questions that would prove prescient. With FDR's domestic reform program having been undercut time and again by adverse rulings from the Supreme Court, what, Hoover asked, was Roosevelt planning to do with the court in a second term? "Why not tell the American people before the election what changes he proposes?" Hoover asked. "Does he intend to stuff the Court itself? Why does the New Deal not really lay its cards on the table?"[1]

Roosevelt would never mention the Supreme Court during the 1936 campaign, even in the face of the court's rejection in 1935 and 1936 of substantial elements of the New Deal. In whole or in part the Supreme Court struck down the National Industrial Recovery Act and the Agricultural Adjustment Act; limited use of the Constitution's commerce clause as a tool to reduce overproduction, regulate competition, and provide collective bargaining for workers; and voided a New York law regulating wages and hours for women and children. Inevitable legal challenges to other Roosevelt programs, including Social Security, the utility holding company legislation, and the National Labor Relations Act were sure to come during a second Roosevelt term.[2]

But seeking a second term, as historian William Leuchtenburg has noted, "Roosevelt maintained a studied silence on the question [of the court] despite counsel from different sides that he urge action to alter the federal judiciary or that he assure the country that he would not pack the Court." It was, as New Dealer Rexford Tugwell noted, "a kind of twilight war" in which politicians of the Left and Right knew of the president's distaste for the court, but Roosevelt insisted on keeping his own counsel about what—if anything—he intended to do during a second term.[3]

Roosevelt had not always been so circumspect. In an unusually spirited news conference in the wake of the Supreme Court's rejection of much of the National Industrial Recovery Act, Roosevelt called the ruling more important than any "probably since the Dred Scott decision." With a hundred or more reporters crowded into his office, Roosevelt vented for an hour and half, all off the record, on the implications of the case, but the only phrase press secretary Steve Early allowed reporters to quote directly was Roosevelt's comment that "we have been relegated to the horse-and-buggy definition of interstate commerce."[4]

Newspaper columnists Drew Pearson and Robert Allen, picking up on Roosevelt's "horse-and-buggy" metaphor, blamed the "nine old men"—the average age of members of the court was then seventy-one—sitting in the marble isolation of their magnificent new $9 million Supreme Court building for thwarting effective action to address the crisis of the Depression. As Pearson and Allen saw it, the court was eager to rein in the New Deal, attacking "laws extending to the vitals of the nation. Child labor laws, pension laws, workmen's-compensation laws, minimum-wage and maximum-hour laws, laws to curb utility rates and profits, to prevent monopoly, to tax corporate interests, to protect investors from fraud and deception, to ensure honest weights and measures and purity of product, to safeguard the health and safety of users of public conveyances, to succor agriculture from a disastrous depression and to secure for labor the right to organize collectively—all went down the ravenous maw of the Nine Old Men."[5]

Emboldened by his landslide reelection, Roosevelt believed he possessed both public and congressional support to push back aggressively against the old men on the court. It was a historic miscalculation. The post-election confrontation over the future of the Supreme Court, where Wheeler played the central and critical role opposing Roosevelt, effectively marked the end of any further collaboration between the two, confirmed once again Wheeler's independence, and, in retrospect, marked the beginning of the end of the Montanan's political career.

—————

Roosevelt's plan to "pack" the Supreme Court and greatly expand the nation's federal district courts was conceived in near total secrecy in the days immediately after the 1936 election. On February 2, 1937, three days before Roosevelt sprang his plan on the nation, with his most trusted members of Congress totally in the dark about it, the president entertained seven members of the court, the attorney general, and several legislators at the annual White House dinner for the judiciary. It was a purely social evening of light conversation, and Roosevelt, smiling and jovial as usual, offered no hint that he was about to attempt a fundamental reshaping of the Supreme Court and a realignment of political power in the federal government. Roosevelt was "enjoying one of those ironical little moments which he dearly loves," Joseph Alsop and Turner Catledge wrote in their 1938 account of the court battle. "At his table he had assembled all but two of the justices of the court he was preparing to subjugate, and all of the men who had worked with him to prepare its subjugation." It was, as historian Kenneth Davis has noted, "akin to the Duchess of Richmond's famous ball the night before Waterloo."[6]

The following Friday at ten in the morning, Roosevelt summoned his cabinet, the Speaker of the House, the House and Senate majority leaders, and the chairmen of the House and Senate Judiciary Committees to the White House. Roosevelt hurriedly explained that he was about to meet with the White House press corps and would submit court reorganization legislation to the Congress that very day. As his audience sat in stunned silence, Roosevelt read the message that would accompany his legislation and then abruptly left the room, accepting neither questions nor comments. The plan Roosevelt outlined was both simple in detail and grandiose in impact, appointment of a new judge to the federal courts whenever a judge who had ten or more years of service failed to retire within six months of reaching the age of seventy. The immediate effect would be to create six new positions on the Supreme Court and forty-four new appointments to other federal courts.[7]

The proposal had been prepared by Attorney General Homer Cummings, and its stated rationale was that "the personnel of the Federal Judiciary is insufficient to meet the business before them." Cummings cited as proof of this assertion the relatively small number of cases the Supreme Court had accepted on appeal the previous year. The implication was clear. The "nine old men," by Cummings's reasoning, simply were not able to keep up with their work.[8]

Criticism of the sweeping and unprecedented proposal was immediate, scathing, personal, and bipartisan. Representative Hatton Summers, a Texas Democrat and chair of the House Judiciary Committee, denounced the proposal immediately, telling colleagues, "Boys, here's where I cash in my chips." Should Roosevelt succeed with this plan, columnist H. L. Mencken wrote, "the Court will become as ductile as a gob of chewing gum, changing shape from day to day and even from hour to hour as this or that wizard edges his way to the President's ear." Dorothy Thompson, the influential *New York Herald Tribune* columnist, said the court-packing plan seemed to offer proof of Roosevelt's lust for power and "pure personal government." Kansas editor William Allen White, invoking a world where democracy seemed everywhere on the run from dictators wrote, "Surely, Mr. Roosevelt's mandate was to function as the President, not Der Fuehrer."[9]

Wheeler was in New York City when Roosevelt's bombshell detonated in Washington. Like most every other member of Congress he read about the court plan in the newspaper. "I was flabbergasted," Wheeler wrote in his memoirs. "Here was an unsubtle and anti-Constitution grab for power which would destroy the Court as an institution. I felt I had to do everything I could to fight the plan." Returning to Washington, Wheeler informed his wife, he later would write in his memoirs, that he "intended to oppose the President on the Court-packing and that it would no doubt mean my elimination from politics." Wheeler may well have made up his mind as quickly as he remembered many years later, but he held his rhetorical fire—or perhaps more fully assessed his options—until February 13, eight days after Roosevelt exposed his plan.[10]

Wheeler had been aware for some time that the president and his closest advisors longed to find a way to liberalize a Supreme Court that remained very much a creation of Roosevelt's Republican predecessors. Early in 1936, Tommy Corcoran and Ben Cohen, draftsmen of New Deal legislation and Wheeler's partners in the holding company fight, had approached him about delivering a speech they had drafted on the court. The speech, as Wheeler remembered, "criticized and—by implication—warned the Court to watch its step." Wheeler listened to the request, which surely had the blessing of Roosevelt, but never gave the speech.[11]

In May 1936, Corcoran appealed again, asking that Wheeler introduce legislation to expand the court by adding three new members. Wheeler told Corcoran the idea was so dangerous that it could "defeat the President in the 1936 election," and he reminded Corcoran of the 1924 campaign and his own need to defend the Progressive ticket's proposal for a constitutional amendment to reform the court. The court was "like a religion to the American people," he told Corcoran, who almost certainly had been dispatched again by Roosevelt to sound Wheeler out. A few days after Roosevelt unveiled his court plan and before Wheeler had gone public with his opposition, he met with Corcoran again, this time in a quiet corner of the Dodge Hotel dining room. As Alsop and Catledge recounted the meeting, relying on contemporary sources, including perhaps Wheeler himself, "Corcoran opened the conversation, and Wheeler's understanding of the opening, vague as it had to be in such a delicate matter, was that Corcoran promised him he might nominate two or three of the new justices if he would go along on the Court plan. Wheeler declined the offer." Over lunch the two men sparred back and forth over Roosevelt's plan and whether it could gain congressional approval. No minds were changed, with Wheeler finally telling Corcoran that he would have to oppose the president.[12]

On February 13, Wheeler finally released a statement to the press making clear his opposition. The *Washington Post*, recognizing the impact of Wheeler opposition, reported that "a pillar of New Deal strength in the Senate" was abandoning the president over the Supreme Court issue. "Wheeler's defection from the program, significant in view of his extreme liberalism and unstinted support of the president [not an accurate assessment, as many knew], came as another progressive, Senator Robert M. La Follette, Jr. of Wisconsin, broadcast a radio defense of the White House program." La Follette's speech, the newspaper noted, "Was the first clean break in the Progressive senate opposition to the plan."[13]

Wheeler's statement, issued on a Sunday, dominated Monday's newspapers. Wheeler's opposition, he attempted to make clear, was based on defending the principle of separation of powers:

> I am, always have been, and will continue to be opposed to the usurpation of legislative functions by the courts; I am, have been and will be opposed to usurpation of legislative and judicial functions by the executive branch of government.
>
> The usurpation of the legislative functions by the courts should be stopped. But to give to the executive the power to control the judiciary is not giving the law-making power back to the branch of the government to which it rightfully belongs, but rather is increasing the dangers inherent in the concentration of power in any one branch of our government.

Wheeler noted his disagreement with many of the court's recent opinions, but he said that "the issue is not whether the Court in the opinion of litigants, Congress or the Executive is wrong. The issue is: How are we going to prevent in the future this usurpation of the legislative power by the courts?" Roosevelt's plan, Wheeler said, did not address that. "You cannot correct the fundamental evil by merely adding new faces to the court," Wheeler maintained. "At best the President's proposal is a mere stop-gap which establishes a dangerous precedent." Progressives, Wheeler said, would never tolerate such a scheme if Harding, Coolidge, or Hoover had made the suggestion. "The progressives would have said, and rightly so, that it is fundamentally unsound, morally wrong, and an attempt to set up a dictatorship in this country. . . . If this administration can increase the Supreme Court to make it subservient to its wishes, another Harding administration can do the same thing." Wheeler ended with a plea that Roosevelt support a constitutional amendment to accomplish court reform. "With the backing of the President of the United States I think that it could be promptly obtained."[14]

At nearly the moment Wheeler's statement was released to the press, Democratic Party publicist Charles Michelson, an old friend, walked into Wheeler's Senate office.

"I explained to him," Michelson wrote seven years later in his memoirs, "that I was acting on my own volition, that nobody had sent me, that my sole purpose was to see if there was some way we could avert further hostilities." If he could arrange it, Michelson wondered, would Wheeler come to the White House for dinner and talk over the court proposal with Roosevelt? "His reply was to hand me a copy of the statement," Michelson said, "which he had already given to the press." Wheeler had a similar recollection of the conversation but would claim in his own 1962 memoirs that he also told Michelson that Roosevelt "ought to save the plate for someone who persuades more easily. . . . I heard no more about dinner at the White House."[15]

In the view of reporters Alsop and Catledge at the time, the Supreme Court controversy in 1937 highlighted a dominant Wheeler character trait—suspicion. "Essentially [Wheeler's] liberalism is based on a sincere passion for good government," Alsop and Catledge wrote. "He had always disliked the strong personal flavor of the President's administration, which seemed wrong to him. Confronted with the court plan, he instantly saw what it implied—a heavy alteration of the whole governmental balance of power in favor of the White House—and, being suspicious, he feared there might be more to it than that." Roosevelt's approach seemed proof of the president's desire to accumulate ever-greater personal power and foreshadowed a dangerous slide toward an American dictatorship. This became a theme Wheeler returned to again and again during and after the court debate. Wheeler's own solution to a Supreme Court stuck in the horse-and-buggy era was to march on the complex, time-consuming, but well-established path of amending the Constitution, a remedy Roosevelt expressly rejected.[16]

Wheeler had additional motives, both personal and political, for opposing Roosevelt's plan. He distrusted the plan's architect, Attorney General Cummings, and considered him incompetent. Wheeler's strong-willed, opinionated wife harbored a visceral dislike for Roosevelt that dated back at least to 1932, and she certainly influenced his thinking. Lulu had warned her husband that Roosevelt was prone to "making too many promises," and she predicted that when FDR had gotten what he needed from Wheeler he would discard him. Now those warnings seemed prescient. *Chicago Tribune* reporter Walter Trohan, who knew the Wheelers well, contended that Roosevelt blamed Lulu Wheeler more than her husband for the senator's biting opposition to the court plan. Trohan wrote that Roosevelt privately referred to Lulu Wheeler as "Lady Macbeth," the evil influence behind the senator.[17]

Wheeler was also surely calculating—it would be unusual for any ambitious politician to withstand the temptation—his own possible trajectory to the White House in 1940. Wheeler had certainly arrived as a major national figure, but he was still only one of many pretenders to the Democratic nomination in 1940 when, as everyone expected, Roosevelt would respect the historic two-term limit and retire to

Hyde Park. By establishing his appeal to the conservative, southern base of the party while also keeping one foot planted in the progressive camp, Wheeler's leadership in the court battle might demonstrate that he possessed the broad appeal, the political independence, and the liberal credentials to make him a worthy candidate in the next presidential election. Wheeler also read the public mood correctly with regard to the court plan. At the end of February a Gallup poll found 53 percent of respondents opposing Roosevelt's plan and 47 percent in favor.[18]

But the most critical factor influencing Wheeler's opposition was personal experience. As he led the months-long Senate opposition to Roosevelt's plan in 1937 he frequently recalled his experiences as U.S. attorney in Montana and "the hysteria of the First World War," when an independent federal judiciary was one of the few institutions defending free speech and tolerating dissent. "Only the federal courts stood up at all," Wheeler said, "and the Supreme Court better than many of them."[19]

Wheeler's willingness to buck the White House alarmed and infuriated Roosevelt and his principal advisors because, as historian Jeff Shesol writes, "only Wheeler, among the bill's initial opponents, had the skills and stature to instigate a large-scale rebellion," one that could unite both Democrats and Republicans against the president. Wheeler brought to the fight a demonstrated ability to work with Senate Republicans, including minority leader Charles McNary of Oregon, a progressive Republican who Wheeler had once endorsed for reelection. McNary wisely counseled fellow Republicans to hold their tongues and allow Wheeler and other Democrats to publicly bash Roosevelt's proposal. Throughout the fight Wheeler was in constant contact with McNary and his old friend Borah, the ranking Republican on the Judiciary Committee, sharing intelligence, assessing strategy, and strengthening bipartisan cooperation. An unintended consequence of Roosevelt's court proposal was to unite many conservative southern Democrats with Republicans on a range of issues. The grand coalition that carried Roosevelt to two landslide election victories was weakened by controversy over the court, with the president fighting not just Republicans but fellow Democrats as well.[20]

The White House, too slowly as it turned out, recruited Bob La Follette, the Wisconsin progressive, to line up liberal support for the court plan, but Wheeler had already outflanked his friend and frequent collaborator. Before La Follette could make his appeal on behalf of Roosevelt, Wheeler had already spoken with Republican progressives Gerald Nye and Lynn Frazier of North Dakota, both of whom announced opposition to the Roosevelt's plan. Minnesota's Shipstead and Hiram Johnson, the California Republican, also quickly sided with Wheeler. Johnson, who had twice endorsed Roosevelt, viewed the president's plan much as Wheeler did, saying he opposed the "sinister grasp of power." During a bipartisan strategy session at the home of Maryland Democratic senator Millard Tydings—the meeting took place more than a week after Wheeler's opposition became public—Wheeler was formally acknowledged as the Senate leader of the anti–court packing forces. "Wheeler is absolutely essential to us in this fight," Michigan Republican Arthur Vandenberg said after the session. "He has taken a courageous stand against the President and is entitled to any co-operation we can give him."[21]

Still, some Wheeler critics, even some who joined him in opposition to Roosevelt, worried that his spirited defense of the Supreme Court and separation of powers amounted to little more than shrewd political posturing. Texas Democratic senator Tom Connally, for example, never completely trusted Wheeler's opposition to the court plan even after the two discussed strategy around Tydings's dinner table. "In view of his many speeches on the bill," Connally would recount in his 1954 memoirs, "[Wheeler] was widely regarded as the leader of our group. Actually, he wasn't, since we were never sure where he stood. Wheeler was always looking for a compromise solution.... Above all he wanted to avoid the position of being on the losing side." Connally, whose strong personal dislike for Wheeler was reciprocated, was correct that Wheeler did not want to lose but incorrect in suggesting that he was prepared to negotiate a compromise that would cut the legs from under Roosevelt's opponents. It was never Wheeler's style to compromise; once engaged he never quit fighting. Nevertheless, Wheeler understood the necessity of offering a viable, competing solution to the problem of a Supreme Court that had repudiated so much New Deal legislation. His preferred solution was to revisit the constitutional amendment that the La Follette-Wheeler Progressives had advocated more than a decade earlier. A proposed amendment was introduced in 1937, sponsored by Wheeler and Democratic senator Homer Bone of Washington and based on the 1924 Progressive platform. The amendment proposed changing the Constitution to permit Congress to override judicial rejection of a statute by a two-thirds vote but only after an intervening national election. It was a profoundly democratic but hardly conservative idea. The Wheeler-Bone proposal envisioned that when the Supreme Court invalidated a law passed by Congress, a robust national debate on the merits of the court decision should occur. That debate, preceding a regular national election, would allow, for example, candidates for Congress to take positions on the court's decision. After the debate and following the election, Congress would have the opportunity, by a supermajority vote, to reverse the court decision. *New York Times* columnist Arthur Krock wrote that the concept was seriously discussed in Washington but only because it was an "interesting political development" and not because anyone thought it stood much chance of being adopted. Krock dated the essence of the idea to 1912, when Theodore Roosevelt had advocated a similar proposal during his insurgent Bull Moose presidential candidacy.[22]

As leader of the forces opposed to Roosevelt's court plan, Wheeler received offers of help from unusual and unfamiliar sources that in other circumstances would have made him uncomfortable. Wheeler's new allies came from Wall Street and included old guard Republicans, bankers, corporation executives, and Democratic conservatives. Corporate lawyer John W. Davis, the man Wheeler had considered too conservative and too close to Wall Street to be the Democratic Party's standard bearer in 1924 and who had opposed Wheeler on the utility legislation in 1935, now offered his help to fight Roosevelt. Republican newspaper publisher Frank Gannett, a major supporter of Borah but no particular friend of Wheeler's, dumped nearly $50,000 of his own money into the anti–court packing campaign and raised another $150,000 from business friends.[23]

As Wheeler discovered new allies, he dismayed old friends and many Montana constituents with his fierce opposition to the president and his apparently easy alignment with the "economic royalists" he had so often opposed in the past. Many wondered if the old progressive champion had finally gone over to the dark side. The *Nation*, long a champion of Wheeler and his causes, now warned ominously that his opposition to Roosevelt courted danger. "The soil of economic chaos out of which fascism grows has been supplied by the Court's refusal to allow national action for economic control," the magazine ominously declared. In Montana, for the first time in his career, Wheeler's position on the court proposal placed him at cross-purposes with longtime allies in organized labor. After hearing from both Wheeler and Congressman O'Connell, who enthusiastically backed the court plan, labor councils in Butte, Anaconda, and Great Falls voted to publicly support Roosevelt. Not wanting to openly condemn Wheeler, the few pro-administration newspapers in Montana instead praised his political independence while broadly approving of Roosevelt's objective to liberalize the court. Newspapers dominated by the Anaconda Company, rarely in the past praising Wheeler for anything, now gave his position substantial and favorable coverage.[24]

"We get a lot of fun out of the antics of some local democrats," editorialized the Republican-leaning *Dawson County Review*. "Many of the staunch supporters of the President were for his court proposals instanter and sooner, but when Burton K. said his little piece they sure didn't know what to say! Now they are silent. It's sure rough when the gods on high Olympus get to quarreling!"[25]

"We had better have no Supreme Court at all than to have a Supreme Court which is subservient to any one man," Wheeler declared in a national radio address on February 21, 1937. "Not only does the President want to make each and every one of the branches of the government subservient to him—as subservient as the Congress is—but now he proposes to make the Supreme Court subservient to him." Wheeler lamented that Roosevelt was "not thinking this thing through" and had been "unduly influenced" by the attorney general.[26]

On the same day, without directly mentioning the court proposal, Father Coughlin, once a supporter of the president but now firmly in the anti-Roosevelt camp, used his weekly radio broadcast to endorse the type of constitutional amendment Wheeler proposed. "Let me remind you," the priest told his listeners, "that in the Declaration of Independence one of the charges against the dictator George III was that 'he has made judges dependent upon his will alone for the tenure of their offices.'"[27]

Meanwhile, while Roosevelt remained supremely confident that he would eventually prevail in Congress, the White House political team consistently underestimated the determination of Wheeler and his supporters and over-estimated the ability of the president to force Democrats to close ranks. Roosevelt's son, James, who joined the White House staff as an assistant to his father early in 1937, illustrated how flawed the administration's strategy was and how fundamentally the president's team misread Wheeler. Young Roosevelt noted in his diary—the date was February 15, a few days before Wheeler's first nationally broadcast radio attack on the court plan—"We are ... going to do some heavy work on Senator Wheeler in the hope that we can swing him back in line." Roosevelt, usually in firm command of political strategy, was surprisingly slow taking the offensive to push his plan, waiting nearly a month after announcing his proposal to launch a real campaign to sell the idea, an effort he termed "a grand fight." Roosevelt ultimately turned for support, as he so often had in the past, to proven political allies—congressional Democrats, organized labor, and farm groups, but this time the old coalition would prove inadequate. Still, at the Democratic victory dinner in Washington on March 4, Roosevelt delivered one of his most famous speeches, a fighting and defiant talk that signaled a new and bitter phase of the court battle.[28]

"Here is one-third of a Nation ill-nourished, ill-clad, ill-housed—NOW!" Roosevelt told a national radio audience. "Here are thousands upon thousands of farmers wondering whether next year's prices will meet their mortgage interest—NOW! Here are thousands upon thousands of men and women laboring for long hours in factories for inadequate pay—NOW!"[29]

Tying the Supreme Court's rejection of his legislative proposals to urgent national needs, Roosevelt lamented the lack of child labor laws and called labor conditions in the country unacceptable. Even spring flooding and the Dust Bowl were problems demanding action. "If we would keep faith with those who had faith in us, if we would make democracy succeed, I say we must act—NOW!"[30]

Roosevelt followed up his fighting speech five days later with a more measured fireside chat from the White House, and during that talk he unsubtly shifted the focus of his argument, directly challenging members of the court. "Our difficulty with the Court today," Roosevelt said, "rises not from the Court as an institution but from human beings within it. But we cannot yield our constitutional destiny to the personal judgment of a few men who, being fearful of the future, would deny us the necessary means of dealing with the present." This second Roosevelt speech, specifically singling out individual members of the court as the problem that needing fixing, stood in contrast to FDR's brawling, partisan talk at the victory dinner, but taken together the two speeches—appeals both to congressional Democrats and the country at large—were quite effective. Support for the court plan reached its highest point in mid-March.[31]

Wheeler countered Roosevelt's speeches with his own stinging rebuttal in Chicago on March 10. The occasion was a debate with James M. Landis, chairman of the Securities and Exchange Commission and a designated spokesman for the administration's position. Landis proved to be no match for the Montanan. Employing a bitter and often personal tone, Wheeler pressed his argument that Roosevelt was engaged in a one-man power grab, and he charged the president with overstating the threat posed by the court. "Crisis, power, haste, and hate was the text from which the President preached," Wheeler said, dismissing the argument that the court was behind in its work or that the age of the justices was a factor in the court's performance. Wheeler also mocked Roosevelt's "ill-housed, ill-nourished, ill-clad" arguments by pointing out they were made "at the $100 a plate victory dinner in the Mayflower Hotel."[32]

"I am in complete accord with the President in his desire to secure economic freedom for the wage earner, small-business man, and the farmer of this country," Wheeler said. "Those objectives have a reality to me which only a life-time of hardship, struggle, and service can give. I was for them in 1920 and in 1924 at the sacrifice of party loyalty, and, if necessary, I will do it again. Real liberals charter a course that may take them outside of party lines. I will be fighting for democracy with a small 'd' when many of the office-holding liberals of today will desert the New Deal ship for fat jobs with economic royalists in the caves of Wall Street." Wheeler, indignation growing in his voice, took particular exception to Roosevelt's contention that opposition to the court plan involved "substantially the same elements" that had opposed Roosevelt during two national elections and the first four years of the New Deal. Reminding his listeners that he had been among the earliest supporters of Roosevelt, Wheeler named other progressives who had supported the president's reelection but opposed his court plan. "The point of disagreement in this controversy is not between those who want social and economic reform and those who do not want it. It is on the method of getting reform and whether that reform will be sham or of a real and permanent character." In his closing comments Wheeler took direct aim at Roosevelt, quoting the liberal Justice Brandeis: "Experience should teach us to be most on guard to protect our liberty when purposes of government are beneficent. Men born to freedom are naturally alert to repel invasion of their liberty by evil-minded persons. The greatest dangers to liberty lurk in insidious encroachment by men of zeal, well-meaning, but without understanding."[33]

FDR delivers a fireside chat on the Supreme Court, March 9, 1937, and tells the nation "we cannot yield our constitutional destiny to the personal judgment of a few men." The president's speech was effective, and the controversial court plan enjoyed its highest approval immediately after the nationally broadcast address. (*Library of Congress Prints and Photographs Division, Washington, D.C.*)

Harold Ickes recorded in his diary, "Charlie Michelson [the Democratic Party publicity chief] frankly admits that Senator Wheeler put it all over James Landis in their joint appearance recently in Chicago before a big women's meeting." Ickes wrote that Michelson identified a need "to repair that damage" done to Roosevelt's proposal "and at the same time reach out for new support." That would prove to be a tall order.[34]

Senate Judiciary Committee hearings on Roosevelt's court plan began on March 10, 1937, in the ornate Senate caucus room where Tom Walsh had investigated Teapot Dome and where Sam Ervin would one day preside over the Watergate hearings. Attorney General Cummings led off for the administration and offered the rationale for Roosevelt's plan, including the argument that the aged justices were not keeping up with the court's casework and that crowded dockets created unacceptable delays in dispensing justice. The administration's strategy, managed primarily by Tommy Corcoran, was to present a steady flow of favorable witnesses—law school deans, labor and farm leaders, and various legal experts—who, it was believed, would help solidify Democratic support for the legislation. A decisive vote in the committee would then speed the proposal to the full Senate. But the opposition had its own strategy. Committee Democrats, including particularly Texan Tom Connally and Edward Burke of Nebraska, questioned each administration witness at length and often combatively. Judiciary Committee chair Henry Ashurst of Arizona, publicly in support of the proposal but in fact quietly and very consciously aiding the Wheeler forces, made certain the hearings moved at a deliberate, at times even glacial pace. The go-slow strategy provided ample opportunity for the warts on Roosevelt's proposal to be exposed.[35]

With the American Bar Association providing much of the research needed to effectively cross-examine administration witnesses, supporters of the court plan often proved to be less than helpful, with many witnesses being confronted with something said or written in the past that directly contradicted their now favorable testimony. The opposition's handling of witnesses proved so effective and consumed so much time that White House strategists decided to prematurely end testimony favoring the court legislation after less than two weeks of hearings. As a result nearly half the witnesses lined up to defend Roosevelt's plan never had a chance to appear before the committee.[36]

Wheeler was not a member of the Judiciary Committee, but he was quarterbacking the opposition full-time. Daily he checked signals with Borah, who actively participated in the hearings, as well as with other Judiciary Committee members, including Burke, Connally, and Indiana's Frederick Van Nuys. The three were also members of an informal Democratic "steering committee" that Wheeler chaired. Still, even as they faced organized, effective, and highly motivated opponents, Roosevelt and his men went confidently forward, signaling no willingness to compromise and believing that eventually a sufficient number of Democratic senators would surrender to a plea for party loyalty and support the White House. Interior Secretary Ickes, intently following all the political moves, confided to his diary that Corcoran, as the chief White House strategist and vote counter, was certain that pro-administration testimony had weakened the resolve of the opposition. "Tom believes that sooner or later [for Democratic senators] a line of retreat will be found back to safe land. Some, like Wheeler and Connally and Burke simply went over board and couldn't climb back now even if they wanted to." Corcoran and the president's advocates, as was so often the case during the court fight, misread the situation. Wheeler was about to give any wavering senator a powerful reason to stand pat.[37]

———

Wheeler, as usual puffing on a Robert Burns panatela, settled into the Judiciary Committee's witness chair on Monday morning, March 22, 1937. He was the lead witness against a proposal from the president of his own party, the most prominent actor in

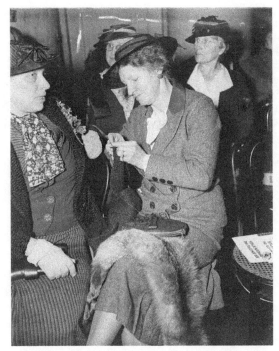

Lulu Wheeler (*knitting*), her husband's chief supporter and advisor, listens to his Judiciary Committee testimony on the court-packing legislation. (*Library of Congress Prints and Photographs Division, Washington, D.C.*)

a political drama that now dominated life in the capitol. A *Washington Post* reporter captured the atmosphere: "Like the French women of another day, who knitted placidly around the guillotine that creaked and crashed down on the royalist of the time, the knitting ladies of Washington have knitted placidly for two weeks in the Senate caucus room. Yesterday there were dropped stitches for the first time; there were purls where knits should be . . . when Senator Burton K. Wheeler of Montana began to read a long letter with the scrawled blue signature, 'Charles Evans Hughes' the echoing white marble walls heard no other sounds than the edged voice of the lean-chiseled liberal."[38]

Playing the moment for all its theatrical impact and with his wife sitting nearby knitting with other women in the audience, Wheeler began his testimony with an acknowledgment that he had not always agreed with the court and had long advocated reform. Then he dramatically reached into an inside coat pocket and produced a letter from Supreme Court chief justice Charles Evans Hughes and began reading it to the

Wheeler moments before his testimony on March 22, 1937, as the lead witness in opposition to Roosevelt's plan to expand the Supreme Court. (*Library of Congress Prints and Photographs Division, Washington, D.C.*)

members of the committee and the hushed audience. In a town not known for its ability to keep a secret, Wheeler had managed a surprise that caught the White House flat-footed. "In all the sessions since the President first proposed his plan to pack, repack or unpack the Supreme Court (choose one, according to your point of view)," wrote the *Post* reporter, "there has been no sensation to equal this second-handed speech from the Olympian heights."[39]

Hughes's nine-page letter, addressed to Wheeler, began: "In response to your inquiries . . . the Supreme Court is fully abreast of its work." Hughes cited an impressive volume of material to back his contention that Roosevelt was simply mistaken about the justices being behind in their work. Moreover, Hughes wrote, "An increase in the number of Justices of the Supreme Court, apart from any question of policy, which I do not discuss, would not promote efficiency of the Court . . . there would be more judges to hear, more judges to confer, more judges to discuss, more judges to be convinced to decide. The present number of Justices is thought to be large enough so far as the prompt, adequate and efficient conduct of the work is concerned." Hughes, with Wheeler as his messenger, had with a few sentences cut the heart out of Roosevelt's original rationale for enlarging the court.[40]

Roosevelt's recent speech to the Democratic victory dinner had signaled a strategic shift away from the argument that the court's aging justices were not keeping up with their work, but Hughes refused to acknowledge any new rationale for expanding the court. "It was good tactics," Ickes noted. "The episode proves again the mistake of going to court with a weak case ... we abandoned that ground [aging justices behind in their work] some time ago, but shrewdly Hughes chose to fight his skirmish where we were the weakest."[41]

Wheeler fielded pointed questions from administration supporters on the Judiciary Committee, but the questions seemed anti-climatic in the wake of Hughes's surprising and effective letter. Many close observers, assistant attorney general Robert Jackson for one, believed Hughes's letter "pretty much turned the tide" against the court proposal. The *New York Times* reported that the letter had arrived with "an authority and suddenness which took administration forces by surprise and sent them scurrying to strengthen their defenses." Legal scholar Richard Friedman has argued that the Hughes letter, while dramatic and headline-grabbing, was not, as it seemed at the time, the turning point in the debate over the court, but since Wheeler was attempting to influence not only committee members but also the public and the press, the dramatic letter helped, at a minimum, to change perceptions of what was at stake with Roosevelt's proposal. The chief justice, a longtime pillar of the Republican establishment, had now spoken on Roosevelt's court proposal, and a prominent liberal Democrat had been his messenger. The Hughes letter may have been just one more rock lobbed at the president's plan, but it was a very big rock. Franklin Roosevelt was now even more on the defensive, his plans upset by two of the most unlikely allies in any Washington political battle.[42]

———

Precisely how Wheeler came to have the Hughes letter for use during his testimony has long been a matter of some confusion. The documentary evidence is thin, and accounts from the various participants vary. In his own account, for example, Wheeler fails to mention a meeting and follow-up telephone conversation he had with Hughes three days before the chief justice presented him with the letter, and he makes the sequence of events surrounding the letter appear to be a series of remarkable coincidences. Hughes's version of the story differs slightly from Wheeler's, and the account of Elizabeth Wheeler Colman, who played a supporting role in the mini-drama, is slightly different still.

This much is known for sure: On Saturday March 20, 1937, Alice Brandeis, wife of the venerable justice, drove across the Potomac River Bridge to Alexandria, Virginia, to visit Elizabeth Colman to deliver a gift to Elizabeth's new baby, Senator Wheeler's first grandchild. After her brief visit, Mrs. Brandeis remarked to Elizabeth that she should "tell your father I think he's right" with regard to the court battle. Elizabeth, displaying her keen political instincts, immediately telephoned her father, who in turned placed a call to Justice Brandeis. The two old friends met at Brandeis's California Street apartment that afternoon and apparently discussed how Wheeler might obtain a letter from Chief Justice Hughes. Brandeis eventually called Hughes, who invited Wheeler to visit him. By the time Wheeler left Hughes's home he had a promise that he would have a letter to use during his Judiciary Committee testimony in two days time. The differences in details regarding the origins of the Hughes letter do not detract from the fact that two senior members of the Supreme Court, Hughes and Brandeis, eagerly conspired with a U.S. senator to undermine a legislative initiative of the president. In the long history of American politics, the plotting of the three was not an unprecedented collaboration between politicians and justices, who are usually portrayed as being above such political gamesmanship, but it certainly was unusual, and that may help explain why the story has been told and retold with various interpretations. In any event, Wheeler must have known well in advance of his face-to-face weekend meeting with the chief justice that he could have a letter that would help his cause if only he requested it. The meeting provided the opportunity for Wheeler to ask for a document that undoubtedly Hughes had already begun to compose.[43]

Whatever the precise details, there has rarely been a meeting that better epitomized the adage that politics makes strange bedfellows. Wheeler, one of the most outspoken opponents of Hughes's nomination as chief justice in 1930, had long viewed the patrician New Yorker as an overly partisan, ultraconservative Republican in thrall to big business and high finance. One can only speculate as to what Hughes thought of Wheeler, the former prosecutor who had often opposed the interests that Hughes had identified with during his public life. In Roosevelt the two found a common enemy. When Wheeler returned to Hughes's home to pick up the finished letter on Sunday, the chief justice handed him the document, saying, "The baby is born."[44]

In his memoirs Wheeler would recount a long Sunday-afternoon conversation with Hughes during which the chief justice expressed concerns about the integrity of the court as an institution if Roosevelt's proposal were adopted. Wheeler said Hughes was also highly critical of Attorney General Cummings, blaming the court's rejection of New Deal legislation on inept legal work at the Justice Department under Cummings's leadership. As he left Hughes's sitting room with the letter in hand, Wheeler later remembered, the chief justice had said, "I hope you'll see that this gets wide publicity." Wheeler had come close to laughing.[45]

Four major court decisions affecting New Deal legislation, including validation of the National Labor Relations Act, were handed down between late March and early April 1937. In what appeared to be a dramatic reversal of the court's view of the New Deal, each of the decisions affirmed significant portions of Roosevelt's domestic agenda. However, by winning cases before the Supreme Court, Roosevelt lost ground in the effort to make dramatic changes in the court. Wheeler applauded each of the decisions and did his best to capitalize on what appeared to be a moderation of the court's views regarding the New Deal. "There cannot be any excuse left for wanting to add six new members to the Supreme Court," Wheeler said in response to the rulings. "The court enlargement proposal will certainly be defeated. A number of Senators have told me privately that if the court upheld the [National Labor Relations Act], they did not see how they could vote for the court enlargement measure."[46]

Roosevelt quietly fumed over the court's sudden swing toward the New Deal, but he vowed to keep fighting for his proposal, and he would do so using tactics both orthodox and arguably underhanded. One bizarre controversy involved Wheeler and the Kansas State Board of Review, a state agency established to review and censor motion pictures. In April 1937, the board banned a *March of Time* newsreel featuring Wheeler's critique of the court plan. A board member—a Democrat and Roosevelt supporter—ordered Wheeler's remarks, which she said were "partisan and biased," cut from the film before it could be shown in Kansas. Wheeler reacted predictably, charging Kansas officials with behaving like dictators and censoring his comments. The board eventually reversed its decision but not before Wheeler claimed, with scant evidence, that the censorship was orchestrated by the Roosevelt administration and particularly Postmaster General Farley. Farley adamantly denied the charge.[47]

At about the time of the newsreel flap, Attorney General Cummings quietly launched two different Justice Department reviews involving Wheeler. Cummings directed Assistant Attorney General Carl McFarland, a University of Montana Law School graduate and future president of the university who may have helped Cummings draft the court plan—to look "at the legislative history" of the lease granted in 1930 to Montana Power Company for a hydropower project on the Flathead Indian Reservation in northwestern Montana. Cummings, clearly looking for an issue that might be used against Wheeler in Montana, said he wanted to "know something about the background of this legislation with a view to ascertaining who promoted it and what the purposes were." It was widely known in Montana that Wheeler, along with Senator Walsh, had been intimately involved in the lease deliberations and that Wheeler and Walsh had taken positions on the issue beneficial to Montana Power Company. A detailed report on the lease deal was returned to Cummings nineteen days after the attorney general made his request, and the report contained no indication that Wheeler had done anything improper with regard to the lease. The report did mention that Cummings's old friend and Wheeler's old adversary Bruce Kremer, legal counsel for Montana Power Company when the Flathead lease was created, had been involved in reviewing the final terms of the agreement.[48]

Three weeks later, Cummings ordered a Justice Department review of Montana patronage. The attorney general noted in his request, directed to his assistant Joseph Keenan, "[I have] heard, though I do not assert, that one of the reasons for Senator Wheeler's dislike for the Department of Justice grows out of the claim that he has not been fairly treated in the matter of patronage so-called. My impression is that he has been given all, or even more, consideration than would be called for by matters relating to senatorial courtesy." Cummings thought it "worthwhile" that "a check up be made of all appointees in the State of Montana who have been appointed by the Department of Justice, to ascertain whether [Wheeler] endorsed them or not." The subsequent report, fourteen pages long and including a memorandum from FBI director J. Edgar Hoover, concluded that virtually every major Justice Department appointee in Montana had received Wheeler's endorsement. The list of those who had applied for positions with the department but had not been hired included the senator's son Edward. The ubiquitous Kremer was also mentioned as having recommended a number of the Montanans who received appointments.[49]

Cummings was clearly interested in Wheeler's motives for opposing the administration, but the White House was willing to go even further, including punishing Wheeler's independence with public actions designed to damage his standing in Montana. Wheeler had long been the principal congressional champion of construction of the $17 million Buffalo Rapids irrigation project in southeastern Montana, an initiative Wheeler termed "the most worthwhile project in Montana." Wheeler, who had once facilitated a meeting between Roosevelt and project supporters, argued that Buffalo Rapids was justified as both a water resource project and as a creator of jobs. But in May 1937, while Cummings was conducting his intelligence gathering and with the court bill under consideration by the Judiciary Committee, Roosevelt told Wheeler that the Buffalo Rapids project was just too costly to construct and "under present conditions the prospects for this project are not encouraging." The rejection was a major blow to Wheeler. Roosevelt's decision was not really about project viability but instead a message about who was in charge. Once the court battle was resolved, Roosevelt quickly reversed course and authorized the release of funding for Buffalo Rapids. Senator Murray, who ultimately supported expanding the court and thereby stayed in favor at the White House, was given the choice assignment of announcing that the Montana project was back on track. Murray made that announcement after a well-publicized visit with Roosevelt at the White House.[50]

Additional evidence of the administration's fixation with Wheeler is contained in a striking notation in Harold Ickes's diary. Roosevelt, Ickes wrote, wanted Wheeler's income tax returns examined. "The President told me," Ickes wrote late in 1937 after the court issue had been resolved, "that Senator Wheeler had paid $21,000 to the

Public Printer for reprints of his speeches during the Court fight and that these were sent to millions of voters in all parts of the country under this Senatorial frank. He wonders who furnished this money and whether Wheeler will account for it in his income tax return. He thinks that it is a close question whether these contributions will be taxable income, but he observed that it will be interesting to have a look at Wheeler's return when it is filed next year." The White House apparently did not follow up and examine Wheeler's tax returns, or, if the issue was pursued, the returns may have contained nothing out of the ordinary. The money for the mailing of Wheeler's speeches likely came from newspaper publisher Frank Gannett, who Senator Borah had enticed to financially help the anti–court packing forces. Gannett's help allowed opponents of the court proposal to, as Jeff Shesol notes, send 500,000 pieces of mail to opinion leaders across the country.[51]

On May 18, 1937, the same day Roosevelt sent his letter to Wheeler delivering the bad news about the Buffalo Rapids irrigation project, the court plan absorbed a staggering combination punch. The first blow landed with the announcement that Supreme Court justice Willis Van Devanter, a stalwart of the conservative bloc on the court, was resigning. Borah, with assistance from Wheeler, prompted Van Devanter's decision and strategized the timing of the announcement to ensure maximum political impact. Once news of the resignation became public, Wheeler quietly suggested to the White House that it was now time to broker a compromise. Roosevelt, Wheeler argued, could now appoint a liberal replacement for Van Devanter, accept some compromise legislation—perhaps the Wheeler-Bone constitutional amendment—and end the increasingly bitter debate within his own party. The White House flatly rejected the idea.[52]

The second punch landed later that morning when administration supporters lost every vote in the Judiciary Committee and a bipartisan group of senators voted 10–8 to recommend to the full Senate that Roosevelt's court bill "not pass." Roosevelt learned of Van Devanter's resignation just minutes before hearing about the Judiciary Committee vote. The committee action prompted more suggestions that the time was ripe for the White House to give ground and embrace one of the alternative proposals under discussion. Yet, even when presented with the opportunity to name a liberal justice to replace a conservative, and even in the face of the political significance of the Judiciary Committee vote, Roosevelt and his attorney general refused to budge. Asked what impact the Van Devanter resignation would have on his legislation, Roosevelt told reporters dismissively, "I have no news on that subject today."[53]

Roosevelt's willingness to consider any compromise was undoubtedly complicated by a promise he had made to Majority Leader Joe Robinson—a promise well known in the Senate—that the well-liked but quite conservative Arkansan would recognize his lifetime ambition and be appointed to the Supreme Court as soon as Roosevelt had a vacancy. When news of Van Devanter's resignation reached the Senate, Robinson's colleagues surrounded his desk, slapped him on the back, and jovially referred to him as "Mr. Justice Robinson." Senators Borah and McNary wrote Roosevelt urging Robinson's quick appointment to the Supreme Court, but Roosevelt hesitated, even as it became clear that appointing Robinson might help heal the deepening division in the Senate. Roosevelt's disdainful reaction to the Van Devanter resignation and his refusal to act quickly and appoint Robinson was the fumbling away of yet one more chance to exit the political thicket created by the court plan, another political miscalculation by a politician who rarely made one.[54]

Wheeler, meanwhile, feeling a different kind of political pressure, hustled home to Montana to fend off growing criticism for having turned so dramatically against Roosevelt.

———

"I helped nominate Mr. Roosevelt in 1932—and again in 1936—and supported much of the New Deal legislation, but I refuse to let him or any other man make the court subservient to his will," Wheeler told graduates of the Montana School of Mines in Butte as he began a home-state damage control tour. In a well-crafted speech Wheeler invoked recent Montana history—a not so thinly veiled reference to the Montana Council of Defense in 1918—to make the case about the role of courts in American democracy. "Let us not forget that legislatures have sought to deny the guarantees of freedom and religious worship, freedom of education, freedom of speech, freedom of assemblage, and that they were saved to us only by an independent Supreme Court."[55]

Explaining his position on the court legislation, Wheeler delivered major speeches in Butte and Great Falls, labor centers of Montana, and made several brief stops in eastern Montana. The appearances were primarily an attempt to repair relations with old allies in organized labor and the state Democratic Party, but Wheeler also needed to respond to pointed and oft-repeated criticism he was receiving from Jerry O'Connell. Congressman O'Connell seized on Wheeler's opposition to the court proposal to stake out political turf to the left of Wheeler, and the young congressman was already making noises about a future challenge to the senator in a Democratic primary. In his own talks to labor groups O'Connell referred to Wheeler and other Roosevelt opponents as "decoy liberals" and "decoy Democrats." Wheeler was a "pseudo-liberal," O'Connell said, and he grouped Wheeler with the "economic royalists" who Roosevelt said were behind efforts to defeat his court plan. "For the first time in the Senator's long career," historian Richard Ruetten has written, "a politician threatened his support [with]

Wheeler (*left*) with Nebraska Democratic senator Edward R. Burke on
May 18, 1937, as they celebrate the report from the Judiciary Committee
recommending that the Senate not approve Roosevelt's court proposal. Allies
on this occasion, Wheeler and Burke would later clash over the establishment
of the first peacetime draft in the nation's history. (*Library of Congress Prints
and Photographs Division, Washington, D.C.*)

labor. And the prospect of a divided Democracy was equally disturbing; in a matter
of days, O'Connell had shattered the outward unanimity of the party, something
Wheeler had nurtured carefully since 1924."[56]

Most Montana newspapers, particularly those controlled by the Anaconda Company, reported favorably on Wheeler's speech to graduates in Butte, where he offered
a lawyerly rationale for his opposition to the president. From Roosevelt's earliest days
in the White House, Anaconda newspapers were almost always hostile to Roosevelt,
just as they had often been antagonistic to Wheeler. The Supreme Court battle abruptly
changed that dynamic, at least for Wheeler. The company-controlled paper in Helena,
for example, printed the full text of his speech at the School of Mines and featured a
large photo of Wheeler on its front page. Once the best that Wheeler could hope for
from company newspapers was to be ignored. Now the same papers lavished praise
for his opposition to the president and printed his photograph.[57]

Labor leaders, as well as rank-and-file workers, struggled to understand Wheeler's
fierce opposition to a president many union men worshiped as their great champion.

Wheeler's detailed explanation of his position helped, at least temporarily, to bring about an uneasy truce. Montana labor leaders continued to support Roosevelt and his court plan, while acknowledging the sincerity of Wheeler's opposition. "Not in a long while have the graduating students of the Montana State School of Mines listened to as liberal a talk," the *Montana Labor News* said in an editorial. "Senator Wheeler is unquestionably sincere in his attitude toward the President's proposal to reorganize the Supreme Court." Sincere perhaps, even politically courageous, but in the minds of many Montana labor leaders and Roosevelt partisans, Wheeler's position on the court proposal was simply wrong, and he was doubly wrong to criticize Roosevelt so vehemently. This was a political apostasy that organized labor in Montana would not forget.[58]

At least one newspaper, the *Lewistown Democrat-News*, downplayed Wheeler's break with his old-time supporters when it editorialized that the senator deserved to be called "an elder statesman" and asserted that "there is no man in Montana capable of rendering the services for his state and the nation that he has been able to render." Judging by the newspaper reaction, Wheeler's political base-covering in Montana was at least a short-term success, but it was also obvious that Wheeler had badly bruised many home-state political relationships. Postmaster General Farley gleefully reported to Roosevelt on a letter he had received from well-placed Montana Democrat and a former Wheeler law partner. At about the same time Wheeler was trying to mend fences in Montana, H. L. Maury of Butte reported to Farley that as a result of the court fight "the Wheeler balloon here is badly punctured."[59]

———

As Senate action on the court bill approached a climax, Majority Leader Robinson, among others, became increasingly desperate to identify a compromise that might head off even more damaging intra-party warfare. The need for compromise became starkly apparent on June 14 when the Judiciary Committee issued its formal majority report—Wheeler had provided some of the most incendiary passages—arguing that Roosevelt's court plan had to be defeated in order to save the Constitution. The report said that Roosevelt's proposal violated "every sacred tradition of American democracy" and would foster a government "of men rather than one of laws." The plan would destroy the Supreme Court, the committee reported, "the only certain shield protecting individual rights." One commentator noted that authors of the report accused Roosevelt of practicing deceit and that "history-minded persons who have delved into the records were unable to discover an instance where a President was so scathingly indicted in a congressional committee report."[60]

Rather than seeing the bipartisan denunciation as fresh evidence of the need for political compromise, Roosevelt launched a charm offensive that he hoped would turn congressional Democrats back in his direction. With Robinson's help, Roosevelt organized a weekend of socializing, recreation, and political small talk at the exclusive Jefferson Island Club on Chesapeake Bay. All 407 Democrats in the House and Senate were invited and most made the trip, in a somewhat less than convincing show of party unity. Roosevelt joked and charmed fellow Democrats while drinking beer and holding court under a shade tree, but the socializing had little effect in easing intra-party tensions. Savvy lawmakers sensed that the president, instead of dealing with the substance of his legislation, was offering them a pleasant social outing to camouflage an increasingly blunt and uncompromising appeal for party unity. Roosevelt's interaction with Wheeler was confined to the final day of the gathering and consisted of no more than a "Hello, Burt!" from Roosevelt and a "Hello, Mr. President" from Wheeler.[61]

The two men had a longer but no more constructive conversation on the morning of July 6, at literally the eleventh hour before the full Senate was scheduled to take up the court bill. Homer Bone, the Washington Democrat and Wheeler's constitutional amendment cosponsor, phoned Wheeler from the White House saying that Roosevelt wanted him to come downtown for a visit. Wheeler protested that he was busy with last-minute preparations for the Senate debate, but Bone persisted, and Wheeler finally relented, hailed a taxi, and presented himself at the White House at eleven o'clock. It was Wheeler's first visit to the White House since the introduction of the court bill, and it would be his last visit for a long time to come. Alsop and Catledge called the meeting "the strangest scene in the whole long drama of the court fight."[62]

"Burt, I want to give you a little background on the Court matter," Roosevelt reportedly told Wheeler as he was ushered into the president's sun-splashed office. Bone was there waiting. This was the same office, Alsop and Catledge wrote, where Roosevelt had made the decision to pack the court and in the process "gamble his prestige, his power in his party and his absolute command of Congress with perfect confidence that he would win." Now Roosevelt sat face-to-face with his most determined Senate opponent, "with the ugly possibility of defeat staring him in the face." Roosevelt, as Wheeler knew, had finally and grudgingly agreed to a compromise and had authorized Majority Leader Robinson to suggest a plan to the Senate that would allow the appointment of an additional judge for every member of the court over age seventy-five but limit appointments to one in a calendar year. If approved, the compromise would give Roosevelt three appointments in short order, one to replace Van Devanter, another for 1937, and a third in 1938.[63]

After weeks during which Wheeler and the president sniped back and forth over the air and in the press, Roosevelt now attempted to cajole and convince Wheeler. He wanted a reformed court system along English lines, Roosevelt said, flexible and quick, and he wanted Democrats, particularly liberal Democrats like Wheeler, to step back from the fight and allow Republicans to lead the attack during the Senate debate. Wheeler was having none of it. In fact, Roosevelt irked Wheeler, the former prosecutor and long practicing lawyer, with what Wheeler considered Roosevelt's ignorance of the Supreme Court's function and inner workings. Wheeler was also upset by Roosevelt's dismissal of objections to the court plan raised by Justice Brandeis, whom Wheeler counted as among the greatest progressives in the country and a genuine friend of much of the New Deal.[64]

Wheeler, his quick temper kicking in, replied pointedly that Roosevelt was wrong about the court and said that he would not back off his leadership of the opposition to the president. "The Supreme Court and the Constitution are a religion with a great many people in this country," Wheeler said, repeating what he had told Tommy Corcoran weeks earlier, "and you can't keep bitterness out of a religious fight."[65]

Wheeler would always contend that he was confident that the votes existed to defeat any plan to expand the court, but nevertheless he went to the White House with something to offer. If Roosevelt dropped his proposal, Wheeler said, there would almost immediately be additional resignations from the court. Borah had apparently convinced Wheeler that other resignations would happen quickly once it was clear that the plan to enlarge the court was dead, but justices contemplating retirement were not willing to quit if it might appear that they were leaving under duress and while the legislative fight continued. "How can I be sure?" Roosevelt demanded to know. "You can be just as sure as Senator Borah and I giving our word," Wheeler replied. Roosevelt was unmoved.[66]

Wheeler's parting shot was a prediction that he immediately shared with reporters waiting outside the White House. "This will kill your popularity," he told Roosevelt. As Alsop and Catledge described the drama: "The pair parted coldly, as men must when a truce was ended and they go to fight again." Neither Bone nor Roosevelt commented publicly on the testy White House meeting, but Wheeler had no reservations about providing details. He was quoted the next day as telling Roosevelt that only an enemy of the president would help him pass the court legislation, and Wheeler said he was a friend. The court bill represented a stark choice for Roosevelt, Wheeler maintained. FDR could drop his proposal and be regarded as a "great president" or persist in pushing the idea and be judged "a bad one." Roosevelt reportedly ended the meeting telling Wheeler, "Well I want it, and I'm going to get it."[67]

As Wheeler left the White House, debate on the court bill began in the Senate. It had been five months and one day since Roosevelt had dropped his bomb. Amid predictions that the Senate debate would rival an earlier generation's political battle over the League of Nations, Majority Leader Robinson offered his substitute legislation, appointment of one new judge a year for each member of the court over age seventy-five but limiting the appointments to one in a calendar year. Robinson argued vigorously and at length for the compromise, frequently punctuating his angry rhetoric by pounding a fist on his desk and cutting the air with flailing arms. At one point during his long rant, Robinson, clearly tired and frustrated by the political mess he was trying to manage, threatened to keep the Senate in session indefinitely, even if senators were forced to miss the Major League All-Star Game scheduled for the next afternoon in Washington.[68]

The essence of Robinson's argument was that justices were legislating from the bench and not showing appropriate deference to the legislative branch. The court's role, Robinson said, was to interpret and apply the law, but the Supreme Court had "entered the realm exclusively ascribed to the Congress by the Constitution—the realm of defining public policies." Roosevelt's proposal would cure that problem, Robinson said, by gradually installing "on the bench those who respect, as a primary consideration, the limitations of their own authority." New Mexico Democrat Carl Hatch supported the majority leader, observing that Robinson's compromise was similar to a plan once endorsed by conservative justice James McReynolds. Wheeler pounced on that claim and, mocking Hatch, said he never expected to see the day "when the Senator from New Mexico would be following Justice McReynolds." Hatch snapped back, "If the Senator from Montana is surprised to see the Senator from New Mexico following Justice McReynolds, imagine the astonishment of the Senator of New Mexico when he observes the crowd the Senator from Montana is running with."[69]

With the gallery overflowing with visiting Boy Scouts and summer tourists, senators abandoned, one reporter observed, "their time honored decorum and indulged in nearly two hours of shouting and charging as the thermometer rose to new levels over the court reorganization issue." The raucous debate brought out one of Wheeler's true strengths—he was a highly skilled legislative tactician. He consistently out-maneuvered and out-debated his opponents who were unable to persuade on the merits of the court legislation and were reduced to pleading for party loyalty from Democrats who, it was argued, owed it to Roosevelt to support his plans. Kentucky Democrat Marvel Logan at one point accused Wheeler of "turning his back" on fellow Democrats and "giving aid and comfort to the enemies of the President." Wheeler bounded to his feet, demanding a chance to respond to a remark that was "not in accord with the truth." He was not anti-Roosevelt or lacking gratitude for what Roosevelt had done for the Democratic Party, Wheeler said. In fact, if anyone was guilty of ingratitude it was Roosevelt who insisted on absolute party loyalty while turning against some who had helped elect him in 1932. "I know men who left their party in order to support the present President," Wheeler said, "then I saw the present administration send speakers to New Mexico to fight the late Senator Cutting, notwithstanding the fact that he had left his party to campaign for Roosevelt." The *New York Times* characterized the debate "as the bitterest Senate session in recent years."[70]

Using language that almost certainly infuriated Robinson, the majority leader could scarcely conceal his contempt for Huey Long, even though Long was no longer alive. Wheeler said, "When we talk about ingratitude, when we talk about breaking hearts, I know another man who was largely responsible for the nomination of the President, and but for whose support the President could not have been nominated at the Chicago convention; yet I saw this same administration go into his State and carry on a persecution against that man never equaled except in the days of Daugherty, and Gaston Means, and President Harding." Gratitude should play no role in politics, said Wheeler, who had often been stung by Roosevelt's lack of gratitude. "The only thing one gets in politics," Wheeler said, "is the comfort derived from the knowledge that he is doing what his conscience tells him to do. The idea of gratitude . . . should never be entertained."[71]

Wheeler's full-throated vilification of the court proposal came during a three-hour Senate speech on July 9 that included a furious indictment of the administration's motives and tactics. Turner Catledge, the *Times* reporter, said Wheeler "warned the other side that those 'who rode into office' on the President's coat tails would 'ride out on the President's coat tails, if that is the only reason you are here. Thank God I did not ride in on the coat tails of the President!'" Wheeler's summer-weight white suit was soggy with perspiration—the Washington temperature was in the nineties and the humidity just as high—but he went on in high dudgeon, pausing only briefly to sip lukewarm milk from a paper cup perched on his desk. The nation was sliding toward a dictatorship of the executive branch, Wheeler said, since "no man in the history of the country," not even George Washington, "had proposed such vast and extraordinary power." Wheeler ridiculed the accusation that his opposition to Roosevelt proved he had abandoned liberalism. "I know it is being whispered around that Senator Wheeler has changed his economic views, that he has gone back on the President; but I will be fighting the liberal cause when many of the so-called officeholding liberals who are now in Washington will have gone back to the caves of Wall Street to work for the economic royalists."[72]

Wheeler had sharp exchanges with two fellow Democrats during the debate, testy spats that illustrate the gaping divide the court proposal created in the Democratic Party. Wheeler pointedly asked Mississippi senator Theodore Bilbo why he was going along blindly with every presidential demand. "Is that what the people of Mississippi sent you here for? Were Senators sent here to say 'yes,' or were they sent here to think?" After Senator Logan quipped that he had some dead cats, metaphorically speaking, that he intended to throw, Wheeler said to go ahead: "I've had lot of things thrown at me that smelled worse than dead cats."[73]

"It was a characteristic Wheeler performance," Jeff Shesol writes, "self-righteous, belligerent, defensive, defiant. He answered, one after another, the charges that had been made against him, sometimes striding up to an accusing senator's desk and wagging his finger in the man's face." It was an extremely effective, feisty, and colorful performance that further undermined the administration's position. One reporter noted Wheeler had "it all over Robinson when it comes to a supporting cast. Most of the keen minds in the Senate are on his side. The Montanan is in the position of a coach with a surplus of bench strength."[74]

The political tide, running against Roosevelt at least since the unfavorable vote in the Judiciary Committee, grew to a flood on July 14, when Joe Robinson's maid found the majority leader, clad in pajamas and sprawled on the bathroom floor of his tiny apartment near the Capitol, dead of a heart attack. A copy of the previous day's *Congressional Record* lay nearby. Robinson had left the Senate two days earlier not feeling well, and his death stunned Washington and altered decisively the final trajectory of the court fight in the Senate. The bitter battle continued for several more days, but without Robinson's leadership, insider knowledge of the Senate, parliamentary skills, and personal relationships, Roosevelt's cause lacked an effective champion. Wheeler recognized immediately, indeed much more quickly than Roosevelt, that Robinson's death was a decisive turning point in the court fight, but, perhaps feeling overconfident, he committed a major gaffe. "Joe Robinson was both a political and personal friend of mine," Wheeler said. "Had it not been for the court bill he would be alive today. I beseech the President to drop the fight lest he appear to fight against God." It was an appalling comment, and Wheeler paid for it. In her newspaper column Eleanor Roosevelt answered Wheeler with barely concealed contempt. "The gentleman seems to feel that he was so receptive to information from the Almighty that he knew the reason for whatever might happen on this little planet of ours."[75]

Ickes thought Wheeler's comment "positively ghoulish," and Alben Barkley, the Kentucky senator who eventually replaced Robinson as majority leader, found Wheeler's comments in "unbelievably bad taste," bordering on "sacrilegious." Wheeler's tasteless remark about the cause of Robinson's death prompted Barkley, serving as the acting majority leader, to inform Roosevelt firsthand of the increasingly nasty Senate atmosphere and the fact that the fight now involved only Democrats. As Barkley prepared to leave the White House after conferring with Roosevelt on the next steps in the battle, the president hastily composed a tone-deaf letter addressed to "My Dear Alben." It was the "duty" of Congress, Roosevelt said in the letter, to act quickly to thwart those determined to use Robinson's death for political advantage. The "Dear Alben" letter was immediately perceived as an order to the Senate to continue the court debate and a sign that Roosevelt was endorsing Barkley in the contest to determine who would replace Robinson. (Mississippi senator Pat Harrison was also a candidate.) Roosevelt's move, another costly stumble, was broadly resented by Democratic senators who viewed the president's actions as an unprecedented degree of meddling in the Senate's internal deliberations.[76]

Roosevelt's letter further incensed Wheeler, and he hit back hard, perhaps in part because of the criticism he was taking for seeming to politicize the Robinson tragedy. "I cannot believe the President wrote such a letter," Wheeler said.

> It would not be in character for the man who is the leader of our party, the President of our country and the man other liberals and I triumphed with in 1932 and 1936.
>
> I cannot believe President Roosevelt would make political capital out of a tragedy of this sort, but if it is so he must have accepted poor counsel in an hour when men who have lost a friend are particularly susceptible.
>
> When Joe Robinson passed away I cancelled all engagements and forgot the Court Bill completely. After Tuesday [when senators were scheduled to be back in Washington after Robinson's funeral] I hope we will all take counsel with one another for the good of the country.[77]

A special train carried most members of the Senate to Little Rock for Robinson's memorial services, and raw politics—"one continual bicker" according to Jim Farley—mixed with genuine mourning as the train swayed across the south. Roosevelt declined to make the trip to Arkansas, another political misstep that angered many senators, but Vice President Garner, who had some weeks earlier deserted Washington to avoid involvement in the intra-party hostility, quickly made his way to Little Rock and rode the train back to Washington, assessing the political situation during the trip. Garner concluded that Roosevelt was beaten, a message he delivered in person to the president on the morning of July 20.[78]

The recriminations came quickly. "The fight in the Senate was bungled from the beginning," presidential assistant Harry Hopkins wrote of Roosevelt's crushing defeat. "The message itself was weak—we had no adequate line of communication with the leaders—the President's messengers were incompetent and perhaps disloyal. I tried to keep Senator Wheeler in line but he hated Cummings and walked out on us." Hopkins was hardly alone in criticizing the attorney general and the handful of others who advised Roosevelt from the beginning of the battle. Cummings, however, accepted little responsibility for the debacle. "There was no moment during the controversy when we did not have the battle won up to the time of the death of Senator Robinson," Cummings claimed. "It must be confessed, however, that . . . when the Senator's death occurred the margin was too small to stand the shock. It is also clear that there never was a moment when we could not have compromised advantageously." But Roosevelt could not bring himself to give even a little until the very end of the battle, and then it was too late.[79]

On July 21, by a one-vote margin, Senate Democrats elected Barkley majority leader. There is no record of how Wheeler voted in the leadership election, but he almost certainly voted for Pat Harrison, if only because it was clear that Roosevelt was maneuvering to put his man, Barkley, in the leadership position. Garner waited until the contentious leadership battle was settled before walking over to Wheeler's office—room 421 in the Senate Office Building—to negotiate, at Roosevelt's behest, the terms of White House surrender.[80]

"Burt, you can write your own ticket," Garner told Wheeler, meaning that the Montanan could determine exactly what would happen next. "But for God's sake and the sake of the party," Garner pleaded, "be reasonable." As several other senators, including Judiciary Committee chairman Ashurst and the new majority leader, gathered in Wheeler's office, Garner declared the court legislation a plague on the country and the Democratic Party. Garner asked Ashurst to serve as the "undertaker." The courtly Arizona's bowed theatrically and said, "Gentlemen, I am at your service."[81]

It was agreed that a motion to recommit the bill to the Judiciary Committee would be made, a quick procedural move that guaranteed the demise of the proposal and also had the benefit of ensuring there would be no more heated debate among Democrats. The Judiciary Committee met for two hours on July 22—the 168th day of the court fight—and agreed to the strategy. On the Senate floor, Senator Logan fumbled and mumbled his way through a confused explanation of the significance of the motion to recommit. Finally an exasperated Hiram Johnson, one of Wheeler's staunch allies in the fight, hauled himself to his feet and demanded to know if the motion meant that "the Supreme Court [was] out of the way." Logan replied, "The Supreme Court is out of the way." Half under his breath, but with enough intensity that his raspy voice carried to gallery, Johnson punctuated the end of the Supreme Court fight by declaring "Glory be to God." Senate rules require the presiding officer to gavel down any applause from the gallery, but Garner allowed the loud clapping from onlookers to end naturally, and the ayes and nays were called. By a vote of 70–20, Franklin Roosevelt's plan to pack the Supreme Court died with a whimper. Wheeler and Murray joined 51 other Democrats and all the Senate's Republicans in support of the motion to recommit.[82]

Roosevelt took the defeat hard. Legislative rejection of one of his proposals was a new experience, and he apportioned blame among those Democrats, Wheeler in particular, whom Roosevelt felt should have supported him but instead had done the most to doom his plans. He began plotting retribution. The court fight further soured Roosevelt's relationship with his vice president, who, the president complained, had not even attempted to bargain with Wheeler on the terms of surrender.[83]

Wheeler (*back right*) displays a half-smile at the decision to recommit, or send back to the Judiciary Committee, Roosevelt's court legislation. Standing next to Wheeler is Henry Ashurst of Arizona, chairman of the committee, and standing at the far left is Senator James H. Hughes of Delaware. Seated (*left to right*): senators George McGill of Kansas and Marvel Logan of Kentucky, Vice President John Nance Garner, and Majority Leader Alben W. Barkley. (*Library of Congress Prints and Photographs Division, Washington, D.C.*)

"I never disagreed with the objectives of the President's plan to liberalize the Supreme Court," Wheeler often said after the bitter battle. "The thing I objected to was the method by which it was sought to be done." Wheeler also claimed, not without cause, that Roosevelt eventually, even though he had lost the legislative battle, attained his real objective—a liberalized Supreme Court. Wheeler delighted in pointing out that Roosevelt had liberalized the Court "through the method I once pointed out to him—by regular appointment when vacancies arose in the normal way." Wheeler would later claim to be "happy that the long controversy over the Supreme Court has ended in its liberalization."[84]

Initially Wheeler's political standing in Montana seemed to suffer little from his fight with Roosevelt, but subtle warning signs portended future problems. The *Bozeman Chronicle* suggested, for example, that Wheeler, perhaps because of his presidential ambitions in 1940, had now aligned with "the economic royalists, the vested interests." Wheeler would soon need to hold off a challenge from the Left in the person of Congressman O'Connell, try to repair relationships with organized labor, and reassure the state's pro-Roosevelt Democrats that he had not abandoned them or liberalism. While an American Institute of Public Opinion poll in Montana in September 1937 found that 60 percent of the state's voters endorsed Wheeler's position on the court legislation, tellingly only a bare majority of Democrats said they supported his position.[85]

———

President Roosevelt visited one more heated controversy on the Senate before the summer of 1937 ended. He appointed Alabama senator Hugo Black, a liberal Roosevelt loyalist and supporter of the court plan, to replace Van Devanter on the Supreme Court. Black had supported Roosevelt's plan to the bitter end, casting one of the twenty votes against recommitting the bill, and once on the court Black was likely, as Wheeler said, to "vote the New Deal line." Black's biographer has written that the appointment "dropped like salt into already raw political wounds." Wheeler claimed not to be surprised by the choice and considered Black's appointment Roosevelt's way of thumbing his nose at the Senate, which the president knew would be hard-pressed to reject the appointment of one of its own. Amid rumors of his membership in the Ku Klux Klan, rumors Black refused to discuss directly, the Alabaman won quick confirmation, with Wheeler and a dozen other senators recorded as not voting. Even after receiving Senate approval, questions about the new justice's connection to the Klan persisted, and, when a reporter uncovered conclusive evidence of Black's Klan membership, there were immediate calls for his resignation as well as for a Senate investigation. Black eventually saved himself in a nationally broadcast radio speech in which he claimed he had ended any connection to the Klan before coming to the Senate. Wheeler, who had expressed his own concerns about whether Black had been completely forthcoming about the Klan issue, seemed satisfied, more or less, with the explanation. "I think he satisfied the people generally," Wheeler remarked rather unconvincingly.[86]

During the remainder of his presidency Roosevelt appointed eight justices to the Supreme Court, more appointments than any president since George Washington. His appointments of William O. Douglas, Stanley Reed, Robert Jackson, and Frank Murphy, among others, remade the court along the ideological lines Roosevelt sought with his court-packing scheme. It was widely believed that Roosevelt had lost a battle but won the war to liberalize the Supreme Court. Still, the battle inflicted many lasting wounds. New Deal historian James T. Patterson, the authority on the conservative backlash against the New Deal that only increased after the Supreme Court controversy, correctly contends that the court fight was a major turning point for Roosevelt, for Congress, and for those politicians who bucked the president. "Having left the New Deal fold once, they were marked men who would find it easier to do so again," Patterson wrote in his authoritative *Congressional Conservatism and the New Deal*. "The court plan undermined Roosevelt's powerful senatorial coalition; it alienated many western progressives and moderate Democrats; it helped to unite Republicans and to transform their strategy; and it led conservatives of both parties to begin to work together in bipartisan fashion."[87]

Every degree of Wheeler's political independence was on display in his victory over Franklin Roosevelt in the court fight, a battle royal involving the bedrock principles of separation of power and the independence of the Supreme Court, and the fight was layered with political complexity and marked by personal ambition. Wheeler's willingness to buck the immensely popular president of his own party and alienate many of his friends and supporters over a matter of such importance may indeed constitute Wheeler's most enduring contribution as a U.S. senator. Wheeler's independence, however, came with a steep price. The court fight, even in victory, made Wheeler an even bigger target for a growing list of political enemies.

10 PURGE

Who does Roosevelt think he is? He used to be just one
of the barons. I was baron of the Northwest, Huey Long was
baron of the South … he's like a king trying to reduce the barons.

—BURTON K. WHEELER

Having lost the bitter fight to expand the Supreme Court, Franklin Roosevelt resolved
to even the score with those he considered responsible for the biggest defeat of his
presidency. Roosevelt set out to purge the Democratic Party of what the president called
"outspoken reactionaries," particularly southern Democrats but also those politicians
who, as Roosevelt put it, "say 'yes' to a progressive objective, but who always find some
reason to oppose any specific proposal designed to gain that objective." After the court
fight, Roosevelt sought a fundamental realignment of the two parties—a strictly liberal
Democratic Party and an unabashedly conservative Republican Party—and he would
pursue this realignment even if Democratic Party fratricide played out very publicly.
B. K. Wheeler, who had so often straddled the partisan divide, was an obvious target
of Roosevelt's purge.[1]

Since Wheeler would not face Montana voters again until 1940, in the near term
Roosevelt could go after the Montanan only indirectly. His principal tactic was to
deliberately ignore Wheeler, casting him as not a real Democrat, while lavishing praise
on other members of the state's congressional delegation, including in particular the
left-leaning firebrand from Butte, first-term congressman Jerry O'Connell. "Wheeler
a Target for Court Revolt," a New York Times headline announced as the dust from the
court fight settled. "The understanding here was that Senator Wheeler was chosen as
the first target of the Administration because he is looked upon as the 'key man' in
the Democratic opposition against the court bill." The same brief article reported that
O'Connell had been selected by the White House "to tilt the first lance in Montana
in opposition" to Wheeler.[2]

———

Brash, chubby, baby-faced Jerry O'Connell—"a baldheaded bundle of left-wing tenden-
cies," according to journalist Richard Neuberger—was an ambitious politician with a
passion for the attack. Born in Butte in 1909 and a graduate of Carroll College, a Catholic
liberal arts college in Helena, O'Connell was barely twenty-one when he won his first
election to represent Silver Bow County in the Montana House of Representatives.
Reelected to a second term, O'Connell became, even by the standards of Montana
liberals in the 1930s, an outspoken opponent of "local monopolistic corporations," by
which he meant the Anaconda Company and Montana Power. O'Connell was also a
divorced and remarried Catholic, a circumstance that eventually contributed to his
political demise. After two terms in the state legislature O'Connell was ready in 1934
to step up to statewide office—he was admitted to the bar the same year—and he was
elected to a seat on the Montana Public Service Commission, the state's utility regulator.
Two years later, at twenty-eight, O'Connell became the youngest member of the U.S.
House of Representatives. Already positioned to the left of Wheeler on many issues,
he enthusiastically backed Roosevelt on the court issue. O'Connell's support among
Butte's working class created complications for Wheeler, giving the senator another
hometown rival popular with organized labor. In the wake of the court fight, O'Connell
systematically set about casting himself as a more liberal, more pro–New Deal, and more
pro-Roosevelt alternative to the senator. O'Connell's criticism of Wheeler threatened
to split the Montana Democratic Party into a pro-Roosevelt faction (including both
O'Connell and Jim Murray) and a pro-Wheeler faction. Ironically, O'Connell was helping re-create the Montana Democratic Party divide of 1920 but this time with Wheeler
cast as a reactionary conservative rather than a dangerous radical. His ultimate objective,
which O'Connell did little to disguise, was to take Wheeler out in the Democratic
primary in 1940, when the senator would be up for reelection.[3]

Neuberger described O'Connell's political appeal when he wrote about the assertive
congressman in 1938: "Besides being a militant New Dealer, he is a champion of the
Spanish Loyalists and a defender of the [Congress of Industrial Organizations]. . . .
O'Connell's father died from a combination of silicosis, contracted in the mines, and
a wound suffered in a strike, all of which gives young O'Connell a closer bond with
the miners than Wheeler ever had."[4]

And Neuberger, generally sympathetic to Wheeler, analyzed the political challenge
the senator confronted in Montana after leading the forces that destroyed Roosevelt's
plan to expand the Supreme Court:

> In his own State Wheeler today is, like Mohammed's coffin, suspended between
> heaven and earth. He is bitterly hated by the New Dealers and is still regarded

by the conservatives as too radical to be supported. One newspaper editor I spoke to went into a state of verbal ecstasy over Wheeler's leadership of the anti-Court bill forces but showered imprecations on him in the next breath for sponsoring a measure to forbid newspaper control over radio stations. Whatever support Wheeler has won in Montana because of his recent behavior is largely of a passive variety. This is not true of the antagonism he has incurred. Miners and railroad men insist they will never vote for him again.

One mine union leader carried around a clipping from the *New York Times* describing a speech by Wheeler before the Maryland Bar Association. "He'll be takin' dinner with the du Ponts next," the union man said. The statement that has lost Wheeler the most ground in Montana was his mawkish observation after the death of Senator Robinson that the President had better drop the Court plan lest he appear to be fighting against God. This demagogic remark disgusted many of the Senator's erstwhile supporters and definitely created the impression in Montana that his opposition to the New Deal had moved out of the liberal perspective within which he had promised to confine it.

The Bonanza State voters aroused to anger and indignation because Wheeler was largely responsible for the bogging down of the President's judiciary legislation are voters who otherwise would be militant Wheeler followers. A ragged fellow selling a labor paper near an A.C.M. [Anaconda] shaft said he had distributed Wheeler's literature in 1934. "But I'd roast in hell before I'd do it again," he cried vehemently.[5]

The White House hit list for 1938 contained the names of a half-dozen Senate Democrats. All had opposed Roosevelt on the court plan. While Wheeler was careful to excuse Roosevelt of any direct responsibility for undertaking what became known as "the purge," he lit into the president's advisors, labeling them "a little group of outsiders, little fellows from New York and Washington, with no political experience, [who] are going around trying to stick knives into the backs of senators who will not 'go along.'" This little crew, Wheeler contended, "is leading the party straight to defeat and they ought to be ashamed of themselves." When conservative Democrat Frederick Van Nuys of Indiana, an opponent of the court bill, announced plans to mount what was widely expected to be a difficult reelection bid, Wheeler immediately pledged his help, promising to campaign in any state where an incumbent Senate Democrat who had opposed Roosevelt was threatened. "Their attempt to pack the Court failed and their attempt to pack the Senate will fail," Wheeler said. That was an astute prediction as it turned out, but much political blood was spilled before the purge ran its course.[6]

———

Pennsylvania senator Joseph Guffey, chair of the Democratic Senatorial Campaign Committee, identified some of the targets of Roosevelt's purge during a radio speech in which he predicted defeat for those who had crossed the president. Guffey included Wheeler on his list, as well as senators Edward Burke of Nebraska and Joseph O'Mahoney of Wyoming. "I dislike political ingrates and ingratitude," Guffey thundered. "I believe that the twenty-seven million who voted for Mr. Roosevelt likewise dislike ingrates and ingratitude and that they will bury in the oblivion of defeat those now public men who come within these classifications." On the Senate floor the next day—the last day of the 75th Congress—Wheeler lashed back at Guffey, accusing the senator from Pittsburgh of being a tool in the White House strategy of retribution against fellow Democrats. "I feel highly honored," Wheeler sneered at his fellow Democrat, "that the Senator from Pennsylvania has singled me out as one of three members of the Senate for the purpose of broadcasting a speech which everyone knows he did not write and which everyone knows he would not have dared to deliver on the floor of the Senate." Wheeler was referring to the Senate rule that prohibits a senator speaking "disrespectfully" of another on the floor, but with his own remarks Wheeler came dangerously close to violating the rule. In what *Time* called "a very bitter scene of personal animosity," Wheeler shook "a long lean finger at his enemy, [and] croaked: 'Lay on MacDuff and damned be he that first cries Hold, Enough.'"[7]

Wheeler, as usual, refused to back away from the budding intra-party fight, and he confidently predicted the reelection of two southern Democrats—Millard Tydings of Maryland and Walter George of Georgia—who were on the White House hit list. He also praised Michigan Republican Arthur Vandenberg for opposing the court legislation and mocked a Roosevelt plea that Republican voters not cross over and participate in Democratic primaries in 1938. "Why should the President be worried about Republicans voting in Democratic primaries?" Wheeler asked. "He was delighted to accept the aid of Senators Johnson, Norris and Cutting, Republicans, in 1932." Wheeler chided Roosevelt for being a sore loser, saying, "It's not an easy thing to disagree with the President of your party. But there comes a time, James Farley notwithstanding, when you've got to place your country first."[8]

Wheeler found himself in an odd position, as the *Saturday Evening Post* noted in a generally flattering article in November 1937, "President Tamer": "His leadership of the court battle left him with new-found friends and new-found enemies. The enemies are helping him and the friends are hurting him."[9]

Wheeler's high-profile enemies—administration hard-liners in and out of the Senate and Roosevelt himself—helped enhance his national standing, which was magnified by widespread and generally flattering news coverage. At the same time,

Wheeler's new political friends—southern conservatives, prominent figures from Wall Street and the financial world, Republicans, and even powerful, conservative economic interests in Montana—were hurting him at home with his traditional supporters— liberals, farmers, miners, and organized labor. "After hating him for twenty-five years," the *Saturday Evening Post* noted, conservatives "have fallen desperately in love with him. Bankers, conservative men, lawyers, even Old Guard Republicans of Montana are damning him with loud praise. Wheeler's title of 'demagogue' has been changed to that of 'statesman'; his subtitle of 'the most dangerous man in public life' has been changed to that of 'the man who saved the nation.' Certain newspapers which are house organs of the copper industry used to print editorials against Wheeler which were worth thousands of votes to him; today they print eulogies."[10]

———

With adjournment of Congress in the fall of 1937, Roosevelt embarked on a campaign-style trip to the Midwest and Far West, hoping to reconnect with voters. Those voters had less than a year earlier returned him to the White House in a landslide, but now, thanks to the controversy over the court plan, many were harboring doubts about the president. Jim Murray assured Roosevelt that the court fight had not hurt the president's standing in Montana and that he would receive a warm welcome when he visited. Wheeler, on the other hand, as Murray wrote, was engaged in "frantic efforts to recover his lost prestige." Roosevelt did attract large crowds, shook hands, lavished attention on supporters, and offered folksy little talks from the back platform of his rail car. The trip was a success, in no small part because Roosevelt touted his accomplishments and punished his opponents by ignoring them. Tipped off by an administration source that Roosevelt would ignore him in Montana, just as he had done during his 1934 trip to the state, Wheeler went on the offense. He wired Roosevelt his own invitation "to visit Montana either going to or returning from the west coast," and then, certain that Roosevelt would publicly snub him, Wheeler found a plausible excuse to be out of state—legal work in California—when Roosevelt's train crossed Montana.[11]

With Wheeler conspicuously absent, others in the Montana delegation—Murray, O'Connell, and eastern district congressman James F. O'Connor—were welcomed aboard Roosevelt's eastbound train at Spokane, Washington. When the president's train stopped in Havre, a wire from Wheeler, already released to the Associated Press in Helena, was waiting. Wheeler's message made it sound as if relations with Roosevelt were in fine shape. "I regret exceedingly that an important engagement makes it impossible to join the people of Montana in welcoming you to the State," Wheeler's carefully phrased telegram said. "I can assure you all the people are profoundly grateful to you for what you have done and are doing to assist them." Wheeler then made news of his own by lobbying Roosevelt to tell Montanans "that power development at Fort Peck will go forward immediately," a position he had been pushing on the administration with little success for months. (The Fort Peck project was developed as a flood control and navigation project, and only later was power generation added.) With his apparent graciousness and attention to an important local issue, Wheeler succeeded in taking some of the sting out of Roosevelt's calculated indifference toward him. At the same time, he was able to tweak Roosevelt on the Fort Peck power issue, which Wheeler knew to be of great interest in eastern Montana. As historian Richard Ruetten has noted, "When the President mounted the podium at Fort Peck, he could not bring himself to proclaim the possibility of public power; Wheeler already wore the laurels."[12]

After a quick tour of the shantytowns where thousands of Fort Peck construction workers lived—one town was named Delano, another Wheeler—Roosevelt delivered remarks to a large crowd, noticeably avoiding any mention of Wheeler. Those who opposed his policies, Roosevelt said, "are the kinds of people who can't understand the interest, my interest, Jim Murray's interest, Jim O'Connor's interest, Jerry O'Connell's interest, in the development of the Yellowstone River, the Milk and the Gallatin and the Big Horn, and a lot of other rivers right in this state." *New York Times* reporter Robert Post took note of the obvious: "It would appear that the public embracing of only three Democrats in connection with a state affair on which all four members of Congress are agreed would certainly make the President's unquestioned popularity in the state work against Mr. Wheeler."[13]

Wheeler surveyed an unsettled political and personal landscape at the beginning of 1938. Challenged almost daily in Montana from the left by O'Connell, out of favor with the national party and the White House, his once undisputed leadership of the state party threatened, Wheeler responded by doing what he did best. He went on the attack, quietly mobilizing his political network in Montana to oppose O'Connell's reelection to the House.[14]

O'Connell, although only a first-term representative from a sparely populated western state, like Wheeler possessed a knack for generating national publicity, which both helped and hurt the young congressman. In May 1938, police in Jersey City, New Jersey, arrested O'Connell—whose picture then appeared in the *New York Times*—for leading a protest against Jersey City's authoritarian mayor Frank Hague, who was also a vice chairman of the Democratic National Committee. Hague unconstitutionally banned all demonstrations by the Congress of Industrial Organizations (CIO), on grounds that communists had influenced the labor organization. O'Connell twice went to Jersey City to criticize Hague's tactics and oppose constraints on free speech. The national

Montana congressman Jerry O'Connell and his wife Mazie talk to reporters shortly after the legislator was arrested in Jersey City, New Jersey. O'Connell, raising his profile in order to challenge Wheeler in 1940, was detained for defying Jersey City mayor Frank Hague's order banning protests by the Congress of Industrial Organizations. (*Collection of the U.S. House of Representatives*)

publicity helped position the congressman as a gutsy defender of organized labor against conservatives in his own party. O'Connell also garnered substantial attention, as well as condemnation from the Catholic Church, for his alleged communist sympathies. He was an outspoken supporter of the leftist Republican cause in the Spanish Civil War and made a well-publicized trip to Spain to express solidarity with forces who were receiving assistance from Stalin's Russia. The Catholic Church officially backed General Francisco Franco's nationalist forces in the civil war, even though Franco received extensive military and economic assistance from Nazi Germany and fascist Italy. Returning from Spain in 1938, O'Connell was summoned to appear before the Dies Committee—later the House Un-American Activities Committee—and accused of offering "the clinched fist salute of communism," a charge O'Connell dismissed as "simple, silly, idiotic." Eager not to offend Catholic constituents in Montana with his foray into international politics on the opposite side of his church, O'Connell told the bishop of Helena, Joseph P. Gilmore, that he was "not a Communist," and he defended

222   POLITICAL HELL-RAISER

his support for Spanish Republican Loyalists. O'Connell also told the bishop that his well-publicized divorce and remarriage comprised a "private, personal affair, to be discussed, as Canon Law teaches, in the secrecy of the confessional."[15]

With O'Connell elevating his national profile and continuing his attacks on Wheeler—he repeatedly referred to Wheeler as "a Tory"—the senator's Montana political operatives Barclay Craighead and George Shepard recruited a credible challenger to face O'Connell in the July Democratic primary. Helena school superintendent Payne Templeton, a man with an impressive résumé but little political experience, agreed to run against O'Connell after being convinced that he would receive Wheeler's active support. However, that support never fully materialized. Despite his considerable animus toward O'Connell—Wheeler complained to a Montana friend that the congressman had "viciously attacked" him—he was reluctant to personally campaign against a fellow Democrat, worried no doubt about the political backlash.[16]

Craighead later remembered spending two long hours pleading with Wheeler to grant Templeton a public endorsement, but it was only after Lulu Wheeler said she was "going to do something; I'm going out and talk against O'Connell to the women of Montana," that Wheeler committed to a degree of personal involvement in the effort to defeat O'Connell. Still, he steadfastly refused to provide a public endorsement of the congressman's challenger. As Ruetten recounts, "In the few days remaining [before the primary election], Wheeler darted across the western district in a gumshoe campaign, prodding his lieutenants to support Templeton openly while he remained in the background." Voters in O'Connell's district found letters in their mailboxes, posted with Wheeler's frank, exposing the "false statements of Congressman Jerry J. O'Connell." Templeton, the novice candidate, discovered he had the support of "many business and industrial organizations," as well as that of the governor, Roy Ayers, Wheeler's Democratic ally. O'Connell meanwhile touted his unstinting support for the New Deal and benefited from the strong backing of traditional Montana Democratic constituencies, organized labor, miners, smelter workers, and farmers. Senator Murray, now disliking Wheeler nearly as much as Wheeler disliked O'Connell, was solidly in the O'Connell's camp. Murray appealed for support for O'Connell and the New Deal in a speech in Butte on the eve of the primary election. "Repudiation of O'Connell would be repudiation of Mr. Roosevelt," Murray said. "It is our duty to stand loyally behind Mr. Roosevelt and the men who stand behind him." O'Connell used his last speech before the primary election to again attack Wheeler. "President Roosevelt told me," O'Connell related to a crowd in Butte, "to go out there and fight like hell to defeat Wheeler's machine so he wouldn't be back in 1940."[17]

Templeton made a respectable showing, particularly for a first-time candidate, but O'Connell won the Democratic primary by just over sixty-four hundred votes. After the election Wheeler scoffed at O'Connell's claim that Roosevelt had encouraged the congressman's attacks on him, and he disingenuously denied involvement in the primary. "Of course President Roosevelt never told Jerry O'Connell anything of the kind," Wheeler said. "Even if the President wanted me beat, and I'm sure he doesn't, he would never pick on Jerry O'Connell to do it."[18]

O'Connell's primary victory seemed to indicate the success of his effort to broaden the divide between Wheeler and the large bloc of Montana Democrats who continued to revere Roosevelt. The primary win also positioned O'Connell for what appeared would be an easy general election victory against a virtually unknown Republican opponent, Jacob Thorkelson, a Butte physician. Newspapers were already forecasting a bloodbath in 1940, when Wheeler would face O'Connell in a contest where Wheeler's tepid support for Roosevelt and the New Deal would be the principal issue. Wheeler needed to engineer a miracle if he hoped to stop O'Connell's rise. Using his uncanny ability to outmaneuver his political opponents, that is precisely what he did.[19]

Amid the twists, turns, and detours of Montana's colorful history, there has never been a more unlikely candidate for high public office than Jacob Thorkelson. Born in Norway, Thorkelson left home to go to sea at the age of fifteen and eventually commanded some of the last large commercial sailing vessels. He enlisted in the U.S. Navy during the Spanish-American War and eventually became a naturalized U.S. citizen. After graduating with honors from the University of Maryland's medical school, Thorky, as friends called him, made his way to Montana to establish his medical practice. After short stays in Dillon and Anaconda, Thorkelson settled in Butte in 1920. A dozen years later, Thorkelson and a partner undertook an unusual business venture, particularly unusual for Butte and for a future political candidate. They opened a nudist colony. The partners purchased a house, remodeled it into a medical clinic, and landscaped the surroundings to make the grounds suitable for nude sunbathing. The camp's policy of segregating male and female clients perhaps made it a less viable business than it otherwise might have been, and the camp lasted only two years before the clinic burned down under mysterious circumstances.[20]

Wheeler never openly endorsed Thorkelson in his campaign against O'Connell, even though they held nearly identical positions on Roosevelt's court plan and both advocated a noninterventionist foreign policy, but Wheeler did place the full force of his Montana and national political network behind the Republican candidate. Wheeler's trusted political and personal friend, Butte broadcaster Ed Craney, effectively managed Thorkelson's campaign and put his radio network, stretching across the congressional district, to work for the Republican. By 1938 Craney had in effect become an extension of Wheeler's Senate staff, employing his extensive business and political contacts on Wheeler's behalf. When Roosevelt made his 1937 visit to Fort Peck and publicly snubbed Wheeler, Craney made sure the president's remarks received little radio play. "The rest of these goofy stations in the state wanted to broadcast from Fort Peck the other day," Craney wrote Lulu Wheeler, "but I said no and got the telephone company to say they didn't have any facilities . . . so consequently the Fort Peck visit was a pretty quiet one."[21]

Craney prepared a detailed memo and sent it to Thorkelson immediately after the primary, outlining for the first-time candidate who he should see, where he should go, and what he should say during the campaign against O'Connell. "Be against the world court and all entangling alliances," Craney wrote the former nudist camp owner. "Get the fact out that if Jerry was 100% for Roosevelt, then why did he vote against the Soldier Bonus . . . why was he for remonitorzation [sic] of silver when the President was against it." Most important, Craney pointed Thorkelson to Democrats who would "help out on finances" and are "very bitter against Jerry."[22]

With Craney orchestrating Thorkelson's campaign, both Wheelers set about working their political connections, the senator on the stump and Lulu quietly making the rounds of Montana women's clubs. "I dislike disagreeing with my President," Wheeler said somewhat disingenuously in August. "I dislike it especially when he is a personal friend, but I must fulfill the duties of a senator as the constitution outlines." During a speech to the Montana Bar Association, Wheeler joked with fellow lawyers about the threat O'Connell presented. "Of course, if my young Congressman friend has his way about it . . . I'll be back practicing law with you . . . when Jerry gets through with me." The lawyers responded with a resolution praising Wheeler's "courageous efforts" to maintain bedrock principles of the U.S. Constitution.[23]

Stopping in Montana in early August, Interior Secretary Ickes made a diary notation concerning the intensity of the Wheeler-O'Connell feud and noted that O'Connell was pressuring him for help. "When the Great Northern train on which we were traveling reached Shelby, Montana," Ickes wrote, "Congressman Jerry O'Connell was waiting for me on the platform . . . he was very anxious for me to make a speech in his district before election day. Senator Wheeler is bitterly opposed to him and O'Connell has frankly accepted the Wheeler issue. . . . O'Connell anticipates that Wheeler will do everything he can to help his Republican opponent, and this is probably true. I told him that what, if anything, I might do in the campaign would have to be determined by the President, indicating that if the President wished me to do so, I would be glad to return to Montana later in the year for a speech." Ickes never gave the speech, and apparently Roosevelt never requested that he do so.[24]

Democratic Party chairman Jim Farley did not approve of Roosevelt's purge strategy, calling it "stupid politics," and on his own September trip to Montana—Farley was already thinking about seeking the 1940 Democratic presidential nomination—he went out of his way to embrace Wheeler, even staying at Wheeler's cabin in Glacier National Park. "It was not the copper millionaire's chateau of New Deal Senator James Murray, or the Butte house of New Deal Representative Jerry J. O'Connell which sheltered Farley," *Life* magazine reported. "It was the summer camp of shrewd, troublemaking Burt Wheeler, who the president detests as he detests few others." During his trip Farley told Montana Democrats, "You've got a fine party out here, but you ought to stop squabbling and get behind your natural leader, Burt Wheeler."[25]

As the campaign intensified, O'Connell doubled down on his criticism of Wheeler, repeatedly saying that Wheeler had abandoned his old radicalism and sold out to Montana's business interests. It was almost as though O'Connell were running against the senator instead of his Republican opponent. In a rambling Labor Day speech in Butte, defending his own record and attacking Wheeler's, O'Connell stressed that his reelection was actually a referendum on whether Montana supported Roosevelt. He supported the president, O'Connell said, but Wheeler no longer did. "He [Wheeler] doesn't belong to you anymore," O'Connell said, noting that Anaconda Company–controlled newspapers now provided Wheeler with regular and favorable coverage. O'Connell also appealed for support from organized labor, not knowing that Wheeler had quietly convinced several national labor leaders to abandon O'Connell. Wheeler also shut O'Connell out of any meaningful role at the state Democratic convention in September. The convention should have been a preelection tune-up for O'Connell, but, as former congressman and newspaper editor Tom Stout noted, "through some peculiar oversight, none of O'Connell's adherents were named to any of the committees. They had but a meek and futile voice in the work of the convention and they finally abandoned the idea of even offering a candidate for the chairmanship."[26]

Wheeler also worked quietly and skillfully to exploit the tensions that existed between the very liberal O'Connell and the conservative leadership of the Catholic Church. Wheeler, who rarely, if ever, attended any church, later admitted to seeking and obtaining a private meeting in Helena with Bishop Gilmore. During the meeting Wheeler encouraged the bishop, who likely needed little prompting, to attack O'Connell. "On the Sunday before the election," journalist George Seldes wrote in his book *The Catholic Crisis*, "O'Connell was denounced in each of the seventeen Catholic pulpits in his own district. Priests instructed congregations to vote against O'Connell. In Butte the hierarchy additionally organized a telephone campaign among Catholics . . . which was particularly effective in keeping all Catholics from voting for O'Connell." Seldes may well have overstated the impact of the Church's efforts, but there is little doubt they had some effect. Meanwhile, Craney used his radio stations in Butte, Helena, and Bozeman to blanket O'Connell's congressional district with a steady barrage of anti-O'Connell commentary. Third-party attacks on O'Connell—earlier-day independent expenditure campaigns—reinforced Thorkelson's message that the congressman was a far-out radical, not "100 percent for Americanism" but "a stooge for communism" and "a cringing, creeping creature" who was "Montana's disgrace."[27]

As O'Connell felt the heat, his speeches, which Anaconda Company–controlled newspapers rarely reported, became increasingly shrill. He said he was for "the New Deal, not the Nude Deal" and predicted that his defeat would be portrayed nationally as a repudiation of Roosevelt. O'Connell's attacks on Wheeler also became more desperate, and at one point he termed Wheeler a "traitor to Roosevelt" and "a Benedict Arnold to his party."[28]

Three other developments in the closing days of the campaign, two Wheeler's doing, the other perhaps serendipitous, sealed O'Connell's fate. While many local Montana labor leaders endorsed O'Connell's reelection, major national union figures, including William Green of the AFL and John L. Lewis of the CIO, likely at Wheeler's request, declined to endorse the congressman. Despite those snubs, O'Connell remained confident that he maintained union support in Montana. He received a rude surprise. Just days before the election a special edition of *Labor*, the weekly newspaper of the influential railroad unions, began landing in Montana mailboxes. The paper contained a blistering attack on O'Connell. "He might have been a useful member of the House," *Labor* said of O'Connell, "but his hunger for publicity and his intemperate utterances on and off the floor completely destroyed his influence." Wheeler's longtime friend Ed Keating, the man Wheeler recommended Roosevelt appoint secretary of labor, was the editor of *Labor*. Wheeler almost certainly prevailed upon Keating to launch the last-minute attack on O'Connell, and he clearly cashed in chits with other friends in organized labor to make certain union support for O'Connell withered. The labor attack on O'Connell was particularly effective because it came suddenly, unexpectedly, and hit the candidate at the very spot where he seemed to be the most secure.[29]

A second blow fell on O'Connell when Thorkelson received the endorsement of old age pension advocate Francis Townsend. Despite many questions regarding the economically suspect scheme he promoted, Townsend enjoyed a significant following in Montana, and his acolytes paid close attention to his political endorsements. Townsend's endorsement of Thorkelson was as great a shock to O'Connell as the unexpected broadside from organized labor. O'Connell had consistently endorsed the Townsend plan and supported Townsend-backed legislation. Nonetheless, Townsend praised Thorkelson, a fellow physician, as a man of "statesmanship and ability," and he called O'Connell "untrustworthy."[30]

Lulu Wheeler delivered one more blow to O'Connell's reelection prospects by quietly connecting with hundreds of women voters across western Montana. Wheeler acknowledged years later that his wife and a politically active friend, Rose Bresnahan, had traveled across O'Connell's congressional district, with Wheeler aide Bailey Stortz serving as their driver. The under-the-radar campaign put the two women in front of dozens of women's church groups—Methodists, Baptists, Lutherans, and Catholics. It is not difficult to envision the politically astute Mrs. Wheeler quietly chatting with women voters about O'Connell's well-publicized divorce and his open conflict with his church at these understated but potent political gatherings.[31]

On November 8, 1938, Montana experienced one of the biggest political upsets in the state's history. The virtually unknown Republican congressional candidate, a onetime nudist colony operator from Butte, defeated an incumbent Democratic congressman who enjoyed the backing of a popular president and who nearly everyone believed was just beginning a long political career. It was a stunning reversal of fortune for Jerry O'Connell and effectively removed him as a future threat to Wheeler. Two years earlier O'Connell had carried each of the seventeen counties in Montana's First Congressional District, but in 1938 he lost thirteen of those counties, and Thorkelson enjoyed a victory margin of just under eight thousand votes. O'Connell did manage to carry Silver Bow County and his home base of Butte, but the percentage of the vote he received in the organized labor center of Montana fell dramatically, from the 69 percent he polled in 1936 to just 54 percent against Thorkelson. Nearly everywhere else in his district, O'Connell's margin from two years earlier was reversed.[32]

Not yet thirty, Jerry O'Connell may not have fully realized that his career as an elected official was over. He had fallen victim to Wheeler's shrewd political maneuvering, but he also committed the kind of political faux pas that is often fatal. He picked a very public fight not with his opponent but with a skilled politician who was not even on the ballot. O'Connell's objective in 1938 was to defeat the certifiably odd Jacob Thorkelson, a seemingly easy target, but instead he devoted precious campaign time to attacking Wheeler, a battle-tested politician who exploited every one of the young man's vulnerabilities. O'Connell's secretary and campaign manager, John E. Kennedy, blamed the congressman's defeat on "the powerful copper-power-Wheeler-Ayers machine" and admitted that O'Connell lacked organization and money. Kennedy contended that Wheeler was so determined to defeat O'Connell that he "went so far as to visit Montana bars and buy drinks while urging the defeat [of his rival]." Kennedy clearly was not aware that Wheeler had often employed the old Montana political tactic of buying drinks for the house, while talking politics. Wheeler learned that effective tactic nearly thirty years earlier while running his first campaign for the state legislature.[33]

O'Connell was defiant in defeat. "I extend my heartiest congratulations to my opponent for the victory of the Anaconda Copper Mining Company . . . and bounding

Bertie [sic] Wheeler." His defeat, O'Connell said, would give him two years "to prepare for something bigger in 1940." But there would be no comeback. O'Connell did secure the Democratic nomination for his old congressional seat in 1940 but lost the general election to former congresswoman Jeannette Rankin, who defeated Thorkelson in the primary and engineered her own remarkable resurrection after being away from electoral politics for more than twenty years. O'Connell kept his hand in politics, editing a newspaper for a time, practicing law in Butte, and eventually becoming executive secretary of the Washington State Democratic Central Committee. O'Connell worked for the Progressive Party presidential ticket in 1948, returned to Montana in 1950, and practiced law in Great Falls until his death in 1956 at the age of forty-four.[34]

Wheeler waited years before acknowledging his decisive role in the defeat of a fellow Democrat. There is no mention in his memoirs, for example, of the O'Connell-Thorkelson election, but Barclay Craighead's papers, now in the manuscript collection of the Montana Historical Society, make it clear that O'Connell's political career was cut short as the result of a carefully executed strategy implemented by Wheeler and his lieutenants. Four days after Thorkelson's election, Father Patrick Casey, editor of the official newspaper of the Catholic Diocese of Helena—who worked directly for Bishop Gilmore, to whom Wheeler had appealed for help defeating O'Connell—wrote to congratulate Craighead on the election outcome. "Our greetings are somewhat belated but this is accounted for by the enthusiasm which this entire community celebrated your victory," Casey wrote. "You will always know of our keen interest in your every welfare and success and whatever little we endeavored to do—I can assure you it was a pleasure." Craighead sent letters to a number of labor union leaders notifying them of O'Connell's defeat and to say "thank you for your help." *Labor* editor Keating, whose last-minute repudiation of O'Connell was also a critical factor in the election outcome, wrote to Craighead: "I was afraid we got into the game a little too late, but evidently all the voters needed was the right kind of leadership. The Democratic Party will be stronger without O'Connell."[35]

Keating likely came to regret those words. Thorkelson was a one-term congressional wonder. He immediately acquired a reputation in the House of Representatives as a crank, an anti-Semite, and a fellow traveler with some of the most disreputable elements of the pro-fascist American Far Right. Thorkelson inserted dozens of long harangues on the Constitution, the gold standard, and immigration into the *Congressional Record*, so many inserts that the House attempted to revoke his privileges to get material into print. Thorkelson bizarrely defended Nazi Germany's treatment of Jews, saying on one occasion, "I question the truthfulness of many of the statements published in our newspapers, for I find upon investigation that German-Hebrews are in a better position in Germany than many of our people in the United States." Montana historian

Jon Axline has written, "It is difficult to determine if 'Thorky' actually believed the gibberish he had presented in the *Congressional Record*. Time after time he was unable to respond to questions about those insertions. Congressman Thorkelson probably was neither a true fascist nor a Nazi, but he was definitely clueless," and very likely he was a clueless tool of pro-Nazi propagandists in the United States.[36]

Wheeler's purge of a Montana political rival was substantially more successful than Franklin Roosevelt's purge of Democrat opponents of his court plan. Senators George in Georgia, Tydings in Maryland, and Ed Smith in South Carolina all won reelection in 1938 despite Roosevelt's active support of their primary opponents. Smith was asked after he had won reelection if Roosevelt was his own worst enemy. "Not as long as I'm alive," the crusty South Carolinian responded. In Iowa, where Roosevelt confidant Harry Hopkins became embroiled in a nasty intra-party feud over the reelection of Senator Guy Gillette, another Democrat who had bucked Roosevelt on the court plan, the outcome was no different. Gillette won easily in an election Wheeler termed a "vindication for democracy and repudiation of the backseat drivers here in Washington." Democratic primary outcomes showed clearly, Wheeler said, that "the people do not want rubber stamps in Congress" but rather "men who do their own thinking and are truly ambassadors from their respective states."[37]

In the larger context of the midterm elections of 1938, O'Connell's loss was not a huge surprise. Republican strength in the House nearly doubled, while the GOP picked up eight seats in the Senate and more than a dozen governorships. As James MacGregor Burns has observed: "A shift had taken place in the spirit and temper of the people. In many races the issues were not the standard old reliables like prosperity, security, reform, and peace, but vague and fearsome things such as state rights, the 'rubber stamp' Congress, presidential power, the purge itself."[38]

By eliminating O'Connell as a threat to his own reelection in 1940, Wheeler had gone some distance in reestablishing firm control over the Democratic Party in Montana, and he demonstrated that he could still command support from left to right across the political spectrum, a skill he would continue to perfect to the point of establishing in 1940 a genuine bipartisan machine. Roosevelt, unsurprisingly, had a different explanation for Wheeler's success and positioning. "You know," Roosevelt told Democratic Party chairman Farley, "I have come to the conclusion that Wheeler is not a progressive or liberal at heart, but a New England conservative, the same as Calvin Coolidge. He moved out to Montana and had to go along with the progressive ideas that were in evidence in that section of the country, but his heart was never in them. Of course, he is tremendously ambitious and wants to be president. His wife is even more ambitious for the White House and it's a well-known fact that she runs him. He can't control her."[39]

Roosevelt's assessment is curious in that it demonstrates that this typically astute analyst of politicians and their motives never really understood Wheeler and certainly did not understand the central features of his personality—his independence and lack of regard for party labels. With regard to Lulu Wheeler's influence over her husband, Roosevelt was closer to the mark. She did share her husband's ambition, toughness, and willingness to fight. She was also more politically conservative, which may have enhanced any enjoyment she felt in helping engineer O'Connell's demise. "I've never known Wheeler well, nor Mrs. Wheeler," Farley says he told Roosevelt when the president made his comment about the Montana political partners, "but more than one man has had trouble controlling his wife on political matters." That remark, of course, might have been applied as well to Roosevelt.[40]

11 MR. WHEELER GOES FOR THE WHITE HOUSE

Great principles don't get lost once they come to light;
they're right here! You just have to see them again.

—JIMMY STEWART AS SENATOR SMITH IN
MR. SMITH GOES TO WASHINGTON

October 16, 1939, was officially "Mr. Smith Day" in Washington, D.C., so designated in celebration of director Frank Capra's sentimental, slightly sappy, and ultrapatriotic film *Mr. Smith Goes to Washington*. Jimmy Stewart starred in Capra's Academy Award–nominated movie as an idealistic western senator battling the wicked forces of political corruption. Against all odds, Smith prevails and, of course, wins the plucky young woman (played by Jean Arthur) as the credits roll.

The Wheelers—the senator, Lulu, and youngest daughter Marion—were honored guests for the film's premiere, invited to sit with Capra in his box, an invitation that Wheeler readily accepted since the film, at least some suggested, was loosely based on his career. As Capra recalled the evening, he and his wife were escorted to the best box in the hall and introduced "to Senator and Mrs. Burton K. Wheeler and their teenage daughter. Mr. Smith, in the film, allegedly came from Montana, so it was thought fitting that Montana's Senator Wheeler should sit in the official box with us."[1]

A who's who of Washington—members of Congress, the cabinet, the judiciary, Georgetown hostesses, four thousand people in all—knotted black ties and slipped into evening gowns to attend a gala pre-movie dinner at the National Press Club. The club broke with long tradition and allowed women to attend the dinner. The crowd then adjourned to the grand surroundings of Constitution Hall, the bailiwick of the Daughters of the American Revolution, to view the much-anticipated film, touted as Capra's greatest. The trailer noted that the director had won three previous Academy Awards but asserted that with *Mr. Smith* he had produced the "most timely, vital and most significant film to ever come out of Hollywood." But the premiere did not go as planned.[2]

Many critics now consider *Mr. Smith* a classic, a staple of the Hollywood genre in which the naïve reformer helps good triumph over evil, but in 1939, official Washington, senators particularly, hated Capra's film, and many left the premiere feeling lampooned, even scandalized. Even Washington reporters, depicted in the film as being a bit too fond of a cocktail on duty and off, took exception to Capra's movie.

"The ominous signs that strike terror into the hearts of filmmakers—whispering and fidgeting—became evident about two-thirds of the way into the picture," Capra wrote in his autobiography. "When Jimmy Stewart started filibustering, the whispering swelled into a provoked buzz. To me it was the rolling of distant tumbrils. Mrs. Wheeler and her daughter withered us with hostile glances, then whispered into Senator Wheeler's ear." By Capra's reckoning "by the time *Mr. Smith* sputtered to the end music, about one-third of Washington's finest had left. Of those who remained, some applauded, some laughed, but most pressed grimly for the doors. The Wheeler family, having courteously stuck it out, now rose and huffily left our box: but not before Senator Wheeler had thrown me a polite, but curt, over the shoulder 'Good evening.' He was not amused."[3]

The next day Senate majority leader Alben Barkley, speaking, he said, for all his colleagues, condemned Capra's film as a "grotesque distortion" of what the U.S. Senate was really like. The film, Barkley said, was "as grotesque as anything I have ever seen." Years later, Marion Wheeler remembered little of the controversy about *Mr. Smith* or that her father had been compared to Jimmy Stewart's character. "I had no clue that it had anything to do with father," she said, but she did recall, as most fourteen-year-old girls would, that her parents got her a new dress for the big occasion of the film's premiere.[4]

Some who disparaged Capra's film worried that it would be fodder for anti-American propaganda, a not insignificant worry since war in Europe, sparked by the German invasion of Poland, had broken out six weeks earlier. Political critics notwithstanding, *Mr. Smith* was a major box office success and received a nomination for Best Picture, which perhaps indicates that moviegoers got a message from the film that Washington missed. Official Washington saw the film linking government to corruption, while the movie viewing public enjoyed Capra's celebration of American ideals—idealism, courage, and fighting the odds.

For Wheeler, film controversy notwithstanding, the movie's storyline conveniently helped advance his ambition—he was increasingly focused on a 1940 bid for the White House—and for the rest of his career he made the most of his personal story being favorably compared to *Mr. Smith*. Making note of Wheeler's presidential ambitions a few weeks after the release of Capra's movie, the *Washington Sunday Star* noted that the Jimmy Stewart character in the already-popular film "was based in part on the

tempestuous career of Senator Wheeler . . . [but] Burt Wheeler's career is studded
with episodes more lurid than any in Frank Capra's film."[5]

———

Wheeler was debating with himself—occasionally even in public—about his own and
Franklin Roosevelt's political future as the presidential and Montana Senate election
year of 1940 approached. Roosevelt first encouraged one potential candidate and then
another, suggesting to several hopefuls that they might receive his blessing. At the
same time the president concealed his own intentions, never decisively rejecting the
possibility that he might seek a tradition-shattering third term. Like other potential
candidates, Wheeler was both guessing and hoping regarding Roosevelt's intentions. During an interview in June 1939 Wheeler predicted Roosevelt would be the
Democratic nominee in 1940, but by fall he was contradicting himself, likely because
he had come to the conclusion that he was ready to try for the nomination if Roosevelt
actually decided to retire. "I have never believed that the President is going to be a
candidate again," Wheeler told the *New York Times* in November. "The President is a
very good politician in addition to being a very good President. He must realize that
the two-term tradition is deep-seated in the minds of the American people." Even
Roosevelt, Wheeler believed, would have difficulty breaking with a tradition that had
held since George Washington's time.[6]

In addition to Wheeler, many Democrats harbored 1940 presidential ambitions.
Vice President Garner and Jim Farley were widely seen as contenders, as were Secretary
of State Cordell Hull and former Indiana governor Paul McNutt. Roosevelt seemed
to give particular encouragement to Commerce Secretary Harry Hopkins, a former
top aide to the president. In fact, as historian Susan Dunn has written, "Roosevelt
was directing and starring in an intricate Machiavellian political drama, in which
he was shrewdly maneuvering for control and playing for time. By not throwing his
hat in the ring, he could play the role of president, not candidate; and by refusing to
state publicly that he would not run again, he managed not only to remain a potential
candidate but also avoid the weakened and politically impaired status of a lame duck."[7]

Wheeler, convinced that two Roosevelt terms were more than enough, had no
choice but to quietly plot his own strategy while waiting for a decision from the
president. Any hope he had of mounting a successful campaign to replace Roosevelt
hinged on three factors, and each involved presidential action beyond his control.
First, and most importantly, the still very popular Roosevelt had to disavow a third
term and mean it. If Roosevelt wanted the Democratic nomination, few believed that
the party would deny him, even if he waited until the last possible moment to make
his intentions known. Second, if Roosevelt did step aside he would have to forego

Wheeler in his Senate office in December 1939, when
he was the subject of intense press interest as a possible
presidential candidate in 1940. (*Library of Congress Prints
and Photographs Division, Washington, D.C.*)

the temptation to anoint a successor. Roosevelt's endorsement, particularly with
no obvious heir apparent waiting in the wings, would likely prove decisive for any
Democratic aspirant. Wheeler certainly knew that there was no chance that he would
be Roosevelt's handpicked successor. Finally, Wheeler had to believe it was possible
that he could bridge the divides that since the court fight and the purge campaign
of 1938 had separated the Democratic Party into warring factions. To be successful,
Wheeler would have to find a way to keep Roosevelt's coalition—organized labor,
farmers, big-city ethnic voters, and southern Democrats—united, while also reaching
out to more conservative, business-oriented Democrats who, by the beginning of 1940,
had lost faith in the New Deal. Privately Wheeler admitted that he too had lost faith.

   Wheeler was tired of Roosevelt, tired of the president's most ardent supporters,
and ready to see the end of the New Deal. "These radicals—these so called New Deal
liberals—are all intolerant," he wrote his daughter Elizabeth. "Agree with me 100
percent or off goes your head politically . . . the world is built upon intolerance I am
afraid. The New Deal is slipping—they are rudderless—its piteful [*sic*]—it's the price it

pays for intolerance—and bad judgment." Concerns about Roosevelt's accumulation of power in the executive branch at the expense of Congress—Wheeler's chief complaint about the New Deal—fueled his White House aspirations, as did FDR's handling of the court controversy, his effort to purge his opponents, and the president's increasingly internationalist foreign policy. Lulu Wheeler's profound dislike for Roosevelt was also certainly a factor in her husband's White House ambitions. "Mother is fine," Wheeler wrote to daughter Elizabeth early in 1939, "same old fighting intolerant spirit." On another occasion he admonished daughter Marion, "Don't tell your mother, but I voted with the President today."[8]

Historian James T. Patterson notes that as Roosevelt approached a potential third term, he "still had sixty-nine Democrats in the Senate. But at least twenty, and often as many as thirty, would be cool or downright hostile to any extensions of the New Deal." Wheeler was firmly in the 'downright hostile" faction, and when he and other disaffected Democrats united with twenty-three Senate Republicans, as Patterson has written, the Senate threatened to "split down the middle on controversial legislation," which is what happened with the sweeping government reorganization proposal Wheeler opposed. Wheeler enjoyed respect and friends among all the Senate factions, but he had few friends at the White House. "The President on the surface is friendly," he wrote Elizabeth early in 1938, "but underneath he still has his grudge."[9]

———

In spite of Roosevelt's "grudge" and his frustration with what he saw as Roosevelt's inattention to domestic affairs as international tensions grew, Wheeler worked hard to write comprehensive transportation legislation during the 76th Congress. The chaotic legislative sessions of the 1930s had produced a vast hodge-podge of transportation legislation enacted against the backdrop of widespread railroad mergers and bankruptcy. By 1937, crippled by "inept corporate managers and rapacious Wall Street financiers," the nation's railroads were near total collapse, with widespread bankruptcies hampering efforts to consolidate the industry. Economic chaos ruled as labor fought management, shippers protested ever-increasing rates, and shareholders worried about imperiled investments.[10]

Wheeler and Missouri senator Harry Truman, a close Wheeler friend and colleague on the Interstate Commerce Committee, conducted a nearly continuous series of investigative hearings on the railroad industry from 1937 to 1939. Wheeler and Truman probed the complicated, convoluted financing of the nation's railroads and studied how rail lines were organized. It was tedious, time-consuming, important work. While the investigation did not receive the public attention or the industry opposition that accompanied the utility holding company fight in 1935, the issues confronting rail carriers and their customers were every bit as confusing and controversial as those Wheeler encountered when he worked to dismantle the holding companies. Wheeler and Truman, senators from rural states where access to markets depended on reasonable rail shipping rates, were devoted allies, and their investigation was aided greatly by the committee's brilliant counsel, Max Lowenthal, who had worked for Wheeler since he became chairman of the committee in 1935. "Wheeler instinctively knew that all railroads were guilty of something," Truman biographer Robert Ferrell has written, and Truman shared his belief. As the lengthy hearings unfolded, both already skeptical senators were astounded by the breadth and depth of financial chicanery practiced by railroad executives and by the tactics employed by the big financial backers of the rail lines. Wheeler reserved special scorn for the battalions of lawyers and bankers who profited handsomely when the eventual railroad receiverships occurred. At Wheeler's request, Truman chaired many of the hearings, including particularly contentious hearings on the Milwaukee Road, with Truman at one point comparing rail financiers to the legendary train robber from Truman's home state, Jesse James. The infamous Missouri bandit, Truman told the Senate, used a gun to rob the Rock Island Line, while the "gentlemen" in charge of the Milwaukee road in the 1920s and 1930s "used no guns but ruined the railroad and got away with seventy-million dollars or more. They did it by means of holding companies." Jesse James was "a piker," Truman said, compared to such thieves.[11]

"This [railroad] legislation is getting me down," Wheeler wrote to his daughter Elizabeth as the investigation slogged forward. "Every selfish interest is pulling and hauling until you feel what's the use—no leadership at the other end [the White House]—all he thinks about is European affairs—that Hitler is going to take over America. To me it's silly." The railroad legislation, officially known as the Transportation Act of 1940 (sometimes called the Wheeler-Lea Act after the Senate and House committee chairmen who managed the legislation), was signed into law by Roosevelt in September 1940, but only after Wheeler and Truman scrambled to placate last-minute concerns about job protection for members of the powerful railway unions. In keeping with Wheeler's concerns about the evils of concentrated economic power, the law, as historian Alonzo Hamby has written, "bound errant bankers and lawyers to stricter business ethics," improved oversight of rail mergers, and for the first time brought water transportation under the purview of the Interstate Commerce Commission. The law, "the most ambitious effort to establish a national transportation code ever undertaken," constituted a major legislative accomplishment for both Wheeler and Truman. The depth of Truman's commitment to the effort, as well as his affection for Wheeler, is evident in the fact that the future president always referred the law as the Wheeler-Truman Act.[12]

As he contemplated a third term, Franklin Roosevelt was increasingly preoccupied with foreign affairs, even as serious domestic challenges continued to confront his administration. The White House fought with Congress over relief spending, reorganization of the executive branch, and housing legislation, among other issues, even as Roosevelt began 1939 by advocating repeal of the arms embargo stipulations in the Neutrality Act, his response to worsening conditions in Europe.[13]

Wheeler, sketching out a line of argument he would pursue until the Japanese attack on Pearl Harbor in December 1941, acknowledged that a "very grave crisis" faced the world in 1939, but he rejected the idea that the United States should attempt to "be the guardian of all the people of the world in whatever country they may be found." In a radio speech Wheeler recalled the defining period in his political development:

> Some twenty-one years ago the United States entered the World War "to make the world safe for democracy." Though moved by this political idealism, and though we emerged from that conflict as one of the victors, the world today enjoys less democracy and suffers more dictatorship than ever before. The people of the United States know this. They are keenly aware of the futility of war. They can remember all too clearly the sacrifices of human life, and they know full well of the costs in terms of human misery as well as the unlimited expenditure of money.... As a member of the United States Senate, and regardless of what hysteria might sweep this country, I want you to know that I will never vote to send a single American boy to fight upon foreign soil unless this nation is attacked.

Wheeler argued that "conflicting economic interests" had created the international crisis. "England and France are not seeking to preserve democracy, but rather to maintain their existing trade areas, their present territorial boundaries and their imperialistic empires." Americans needed to stay calm and unemotional, he argued, to avoid being swayed by "a tremendous propaganda campaign" using newspapers, radio, and films to build sympathy and support for Britain and France. Wheeler warned that U.S. involvement in another European war could mean the end of U.S. constitutional government and the disappearance of civil liberties. The world would witness, he predicted, "even more widespread dictatorship," and he asserted that "the intelligence of the American people must and will prevent our entry into another world war."[14]

Congress initially balked at Roosevelt's proposed changes in the Neutrality Act in 1939, but after the German invasion of Poland the president summoned Congress into special session to try again. "The Executive Branch of the Government did its utmost, within our traditional policy of non-involvement, to aid in averting the present appalling war," Roosevelt said in his message opening the special session. "Having thus striven and failed, this Government must lose no time or effort to keep our nation from being drawn into the war." Wheeler saw Roosevelt's action as leading to an opposite outcome. Making U.S. arms available, Wheeler was convinced, would surely bring the United States closer to war, and he joined twenty-nine senators, primarily noninterventionist Republican progressives from western states, including Borah, Nye, McNary, Johnson, and La Follette, to oppose repeal of the arms embargo.[15]

"It is hard to tell what is going to come out of this war," Wheeler wrote to his son Richard, a student at Dartmouth. "A good many people think there will be a revolution in Germany, but I rather doubt it, for a while anyway. I feel quite positive that we will not get into the war. In my travels around the country I find sentiment quite overwhelmingly against it. This is true among the farmers, the mothers, and is also true among the businessmen. I have scarcely found a business man in the country who wants us to get into it." War, Wheeler reminded his son, always brings about inflation and economic controls.[16]

As his 1940 Senate reelection approached in Montana, complicating his White House aspirations, Wheeler's public statements made note of the no-third-term tradition, but he also avoided direct criticism of Roosevelt. Wheeler was playing a careful game, effectively preparing to run for president without quite admitting so. "The old forth-right fighter is now the soft-speaking peacemaker," wrote *Cut Bank Pioneer Press* editor Dan Whetstone, a prominent Montana Republican and no friend of Wheeler's. "His political prescience and ability to suddenly shift positions is the despair of his enemies and the joy of his admirers. Watch this fellow in days to come. You will witness a scintillating exhibition of dexterous maneuvering by the nation's cleverest political practitioner."[17]

Columnist Raymond Clapper also took note of Wheeler's political skills and his White House ambitions when he wrote, "There is no more skillful politician in the Senate than Burton K. Wheeler of Montana." Noting Wheeler's complicated political calculus in 1940—a Senate campaign in Montana, uncertainty about Roosevelt's plans, and therefore uncertainty about a White House bid—Clapper said Wheeler's most serious problem remained his refusal "to go along on the supreme court fight. For a few weeks during that controversy he was catalogued . . . as a New Dealer turned tory, which is listed as a crime second only to beating your mother-in-law."[18]

In October 1939, Wheeler was welcomed home to his Hudson, Massachusetts, birthplace, and the warmth that greeted him there, along with the effusive praise he received during the trip, prompted even more speculation about a presidential candidacy. Four thousand people turned out in a "lashing rain storm" and "cheered wildly when [Wheeler] opposed lifting of the arms embargo" and promised again "never to vote to send a single American boy overseas to fight on foreign soil." Massachusetts senator David I. Walsh, the Democratic chair of the Naval Affairs Committee and like Wheeler an ardent opponent of lifting the arms embargo, introduced Wheeler, saying, "There is none more worthy of the highest office in the land."[19]

Montana's miniscule four electoral votes argued against Wheeler as a presidential candidate, but favorable reaction to his public appearances indicated substantial national appeal across the political spectrum. Democratic senators Edwin Johnson of Colorado, Elmer Thomas of Oklahoma, D. Worth Clark of Idaho, and Patrick McCarran of Nevada all said Wheeler would enjoy widespread support in the party if Roosevelt passed on a third term. Father Coughlin, the once-powerful radio priest, was a much-diminished player in national politics by 1939, but he also touted Wheeler's presidential prospects on the front page of his *Social Justice* newspaper, an endorsement of mixed benefit since Coughlin was now widely condemned for his anti-Semitic speeches and writing.[20]

"You have the friendship of a large, liberal, progressive element within the state, most of which is perhaps found within the ranks of the so-called Nonpartisan League," North Dakota's Democratic governor John Moses wrote Wheeler late in 1939. "The stand you have taken of late on public matters has insured for you the very friendly feelings of conservative people in North Dakota, people who perhaps have never supported a Democrat for national office." Wheeler wrote back: "I feel quite sure now that President Roosevelt is not going to be a candidate," and since he was not ready to declare his intentions, Wheeler cautioned the governor that his comments about Roosevelt were "strictly confidential."[21]

Frank Knox, a prominent Republican internationalist who had been the GOP vice presidential candidate in 1936, somewhat surprisingly also approved of a Wheeler candidacy. "Personally, I was delighted to read Senator [Edwin] Johnson's comment suggesting consideration of yourself as a possible Democratic candidate, Knox wrote. "While I am a Republican as you know, if I had to live under another Democratic administration, I know of no other Democrat whom I would rather it would be than yourself."[22]

Writing to a Democratic friend in Minnesota, Wheeler acknowledged that "things have been moving much better than I expected. Some friends of mine wanted me to announce my candidacy, but I felt it would be a mistake to do so. Some wanted me to challenge Roosevelt. I feel positive that Roosevelt is not going to be a candidate, although of course the inner circle are doing everything they can to get him to be a candidate, and are trying to create a demand for him. I do not want to be a stalking horse, or part of a movement to stop Roosevelt, and I am not going to be, but if he is not a candidate, then I would not hesitate at all about challenging McNutt, or any of the rest of them."[23]

Not so impressed by Wheeler's presidential aspirations was the editor of the *Iowa Legionnaire* magazine who denounced Wheeler for alleged past sins, including a lack of patriotism and sympathy for radical labor organizations during World War I. "Because of your attitude in 1918 when we were actually at war I don't feel you are the man to be the Democratic nominee for President," Frank Miles wrote after Wheeler complained to him about negative coverage in Miles's magazine. "Moreover, your bolting the Party and going to the self-styled Progressives in 1924 is simply unpardonable in my mind." Never one to surrender the last word, Wheeler fired back saying he had been called lots of names, with Montana corporate interests and their press allies long ago labeling him "pro-German and an I.W.W. and everything else," while "Jerry O'Connell . . . and all the communist crowd are accusing me of being an ultra-conservative . . . it is amusing to me to find an apparently intelligent person in this day and age writing articles about me such as the one you printed in the *Iowa Legionnaire*. If you get any satisfaction out of it, go to it."[24]

Wheeler's presidential ambitions, as well as his attractiveness to various factions in the Democratic Party, were regularly discussed in the press during 1939. "Such recognition for a man from the small and remote state of Montana—politically speaking—cannot be discounted," syndicated columnist Ray Tucker wrote in December. "It may be only the Christmas spirit—or momentary political madness—but the Wheeler movement appears to have substance. Rate him high in your winter books—for win or place." Frank Kent, writing in the *Wall Street Journal,* said Wheeler was a serious possibility for the Democrats despite Montana's lack of electoral clout and Wheeler's party bolting sixteen years earlier. "Time has mellowed him to a considerable degree," Kent wrote, but "he is still the implacable foe of 'entrenched greed,' still friendly to organized labor, still opposes the concentration of wealth in a few hands, still concerned about the plight of the farmer."[25]

Yet when the *New York Times* reported just before the end of 1939 that Wheeler had reached a definite decision to enter the New Hampshire primary early the next year, Wheeler instantly fired off a telegram to publisher Arthur Hayes Sulzberger denying any such plan. "I have repeatedly stated that I will be a candidate for re-election to the United States Senate in Montana. I have neither made nor authorized any statement that I would enter the Presidential Primaries in any State."[26]

Wheeler had to be careful not to appear to take his Senate reelection in Montana for granted while he entertained larger ambitions. It was a wire walk, yet Wheeler thought his balance was sure enough that he finally authorized aides to develop plans to roll out "Wheeler for President Clubs" early in 1940. "I've been asked to run," Wheeler told a Jackson Day Dinner crowd in Denver in early January 1940. "I haven't made up my mind," he said, but in fact he had made up his mind. He would run if Roosevelt declined a third term and left the Democratic field open.[27]

Wheeler's presidential candidacy boomlet received a major boost late in January 1940 when the powerful but also controversial United Mine Workers president John L. Lewis invited him to address the fiftieth-anniversary convention of Lewis's large and well-financed union in Columbus, Ohio. As Lewis's biographers note:

> Lewis' preference for Wheeler was neither accidental nor gratuitous. In January 1940 the two men shared many beliefs concerning foreign affairs and domestic policies. Both Lewis and Wheeler remembered World War I with regret. To them it had been a time when a reform president, Woodrow Wilson, had misled the nation into an unnecessary foreign war and allowed reactionary businessmen and politicians to repress labor and persecute radicals in the guise of national security. In 1940 Franklin D. Roosevelt seemed likely to repeat Wilson's mistakes of 1917–1918, to involve the United States in someone else's quarrel, to terminate the New Deal and domestic reform, as Wilson had earlier gutted the New Freedom. Roosevelt, argued Wheeler and Lewis, must be stopped.[28]

"It was a great show in Columbus," Wheeler wrote to Elizabeth. "I shook hands with 2500 miners and their wives." He said he was "very much pleased" over the publicity he had been getting, considering the fact that he had "no organization, and no money, outside of the little that was collected in Montana for the Montana [Wheeler for President] Club." Wheeler also told his daughter that Aubrey Williams, the federal relief official and chief deputy to Roosevelt confidant Harry Hopkins, had "just returned from a trip thru twenty-seven states, and he reported to the President and Mrs. Roosevelt, that I was the strongest person who could be nominated outside of the President.[29]

Wheeler continued to accumulate impressive near-endorsements early in 1940 in addition to that from Lewis. The leaders of the railway unions, the American Federation of Labor, and several prominent progressives, including George Norris, Bob La Follette and his brother Philip, and Colorado senator Edward Costigan encouraged Wheeler's presidential ambitions, even if most pledges of support were conditioned on Roosevelt not running.[30]

Wheeler's skeletal presidential campaign organization eventually managed to raise about $15,000, with active volunteers in eleven western states. Longtime aides J. Burke Clements and Barclay Craighead put together the printed materials, including 100,000 circulars with the headline "That Man Wheeler." The brochures emphasized Wheeler's independence and featured statements on everything from foreign policy

242   POLITICAL HELL-RAISER

("we cannot undertake to regulate the internal affairs of other people") to farm issues ("greater cooperation between government, industry, farmer and labor would hasten the return to national prosperity"). The materials were mailed, with a cover note from Clements, to Democratic precinct committee workers in several western states. Clements stressed that Wheeler "is *not* a candidate for the presidency" and would file for reelection to the Senate, but then added, "There is no western candidate; no other man in the country who can appeal alike to conservatives and progressives; no other man who can unite the democratic party [*sic*], Roosevelt and anti-Roosevelt people. If President Roosevelt does not himself become a candidate for reelection, no other man appears to have a better chance for the nomination."[31]

As the national guessing game about Roosevelt's intentions continued, Wheeler received substantial and mostly favorable press attention over the spring and early summer of 1940, including major profiles in the *Nation*, the *New Republic*, the *Washington Star*, and the *Christian Science Monitor*. "Burton K. Wheeler has what it takes to make a good gambler: the shrewdness to gauge chances and the nerve to take them," reported the *Nation*. "Bold enough to be a flaming liberal in the early twenties, when only 'Bolsheviks' were liberal, he was daring enough to lead the anti-Roosevelt forces in the middle thirties, when only 'economic royalists' were anti-Roosevelt. In both cases he staked his political fortunes on a hunch that public opinion was about to shift. His hunch in the twenties despite his initial defeat, was to gain him a star role in the Senate for seventeen years; his hunch in the thirties may win him or lose him the Presidency of the United States."[32]

Even *Time*, a publication that rarely praised a progressive Democrat, described Wheeler in an edition that featured his photo on the cover, as "a lanky, rumpled man who walks with a rapid shamble, smiling quizzically, his glance a friendly, direct glare through octagonal spectacles, smoking a cigar with the superb nonchalance of Groucho Marx." *Time* called the fifty-eight-year Wheeler "not just another cow-country Senator but a Washington landmark." Wheeler was favorably compared to popular sports and entertainment personalities: "Carl Hubbell is a ballplayer's ballplayer; Count Basie is a swing artist's swing artist; bounding Burt Wheeler is a Senator's Senator."[33]

Journalist Richard Neuberger wrote the best informed and most insightful of the many Wheeler profiles that appeared prior to the 1940 Democratic National Convention. Neuberger, whose piece appeared in *Harper's* in May, a month before the convention, knew Montana, had solid sources in the state, and admired Wheeler's political independence and slashing style. He also marveled at the political comeback Wheeler appeared to have engineered since his open break with Roosevelt over the Supreme Court three years earlier. Yet, sympathetic as Neuberger's profile was, the shrewd political analyst detailed Wheeler's shortcomings using crisp and critical language, taking particular note of the senator's "slipshod action" in supporting an embarrassing Republican against an incumbent Democrat in 1938.

"He backed [Jacob] Thorkelson without finding out enough about him," Neuberger wrote.

Thoroughness has never been the senator's forte. He prefers the drama of the rostrum to the humdrum grappling with figures and statistics. He is lazy. His knowledge of economics does not match his good intentions because research and heavy reading bore him. Samuel Hopkins Adams [a celebrated muckraking journalist and writer] salutes the courage with which the scandals of the Harding Administration were probed, but points out that "Wheeler lacked Senator Walsh's patient talent for accumulating and collating facts. He had not the same power of discrimination between the essential and the non-essential. . . . He brought in an enormous mass of undigested, ill-assorted testimony."

But being a glutton for work and study has never been essential to occupancy of the White House—not as essential, for example, as coming from a state with a big chunk of electoral votes.

Neuberger noted that Montana was "a hard state," with Butte's cemeteries full and the relief rolls in Silver Bow County growing.

Yet there is hope. Montana's rivers are white-capped and lusty. Thousands of its acres need only water to bloom. A dam can store water and generate electricity to pump it into irrigation canals. The money gathered by the non-resident capitalists, who own the minerals and timber and railroads of Montana, is gradually being returned in Federal appropriations for reclamation and waterway projects.

From this background can a man go to the presidency? No chief executive has ever come from the vast hinterland, which forms so large a part of the nation's territory. Acreage does not cast votes. Montana is third in the Union in areas, but thirty-ninth in population. To come from Montana may be a grave liability in view of the fact that Democrats have never won a nomination from the west.

Yet precedents have been broken before, and the decision will presumably be up to a man for whom precedents have slight meaning, indeed. The Democratic convention may very conceivably confront Mr. Roosevelt with three alternatives: (1) A third term, (2) a conservative southerner hostile to the New Deal at home, but sympathetic with the foreign policy, and (3) Burton Kendall Wheeler, the senior Senator from Montana.

What will F.D.R. do then?[34]

With the Democratic convention approaching and still no signal of intentions from Roosevelt, Wheeler had to devote some attention to his reelection campaign in Montana. Montana attorney general Harrison J. Freebourn, a prominent liberal whose tenure was dogged by accusations of corruption, announced against Wheeler. Freebourn was not an ideal candidate, having barely survived a 1939 effort by the Montana House of Representatives to impeach him, and he announced for the U.S. Senate shortly after being indicted on income tax evasion charges. But, like Jerry O'Connell and even Wheeler at one time, Freebourn built his political career around opposition to the Anaconda Company and Montana Power, never an unpopular position with most Montana Democrats. Like O'Connell, Freebourn attacked Wheeler from the political left, calling him a tool of big business and even suggesting that Wheeler and the Anaconda Company had somehow engineered his tax evasion indictment. While Freebourn was a deeply flawed candidate, he did enjoy some support on the left of the Montana Democratic Party, including that of twenty-nine-year-old Lee Metcalf, an assistant in the state attorney general's office and a future congressman and U.S. senator. Metcalf was also a leader among Montana Democrats who hoped to see Roosevelt elected to a third term, and he was determined to prevent a Montana delegation going to the national convention pledged to support Wheeler for president. Metcalf, both to help his boss Freebourn and to support Roosevelt, set about, as he put it, to "offset the work the Wheeler stooges are doing throughout the state."[35]

Even with the machinery of the state party organized to his benefit and with national labor leaders remaining supportive, Wheeler's support among Montana union members was softer in 1940 than it had ever been. The left-leaning Montana Progressive Council, including representatives of organized labor and the Farmers' Union, sent a message to Wheeler when the group endorsed Freebourn just days before the Democratic primary. Former congressman O'Connell used his *Montana Liberal* newspaper to bash the senator in front-page tirades, alleging again that Wheeler had abandoned liberalism to become a stooge of the Anaconda Company. Another liberal writer echoed this, pointing out that Wheeler "has uttered not a syllable of criticism of the dominion over Montana on the part of the Company machine."[36]

Wheeler refused to respond to the attacks, confident that he still enjoyed substantial Democratic support and could attract election support from Republicans as well. The state party convention ultimately passed a resolution commending Wheeler's "wise and courageous leadership" and instructed Montana's national delegates to support him for president if a Roosevelt third-term nomination failed to materialize. The resolution was passed after Wheeler told the convention that he would not oppose a third Roosevelt term, a statement that clearly left the impression with the president's Montana supporters that Wheeler would only make a play for the nomination if it

Wheeler addresses a gathering of more than eleven hundred antiwar activists in Washington, D.C., a little over a month before the 1940 Democratic convention. (*Library of Congress Prints and Photographs Division, Washington, D.C.*)

became clear Roosevelt was not running. Wheeler ended his own speech to the state convention with praise for Roosevelt's intelligence and insisted that the country needed to stay out of the worsening war in Europe.[37]

The war became the dominant political issue as both parties headed to conventions to nominate their presidential candidates. In early May, Germany invaded the Low Countries and France, and within a month 340,000 British and French troops were hastily evacuated from the beleaguered port of Dunkirk on the French coast. British prime minister Winston Churchill defiantly promised to fight on, even though the French government soon capitulated to the Nazis. Churchill ended his most famous speech in the House of Commons—promising "we shall never surrender"—with an appeal that the "New World, with all its power and might" might come to the rescue of the old. Wheeler was moved by neither Churchill's eloquence nor his plea that the United States provide aid. Wheeler used the period between the state party convention in Montana and the national party convention in Chicago, with an eye carefully fixed on the primary challenge back home, to deliver a series of bluntly worded speeches restating his unwavering opposition to assistance that might involve the United States in another European war. While always claiming that he did not want to see Germany prevail, Wheeler contended that every small step Roosevelt took to offer assistance to Hitler's foes was a step toward American involvement. Opposing the administration's plan to call up National Guard units for a year of active duty, Wheeler told the Senate in late May, "My sympathies are with the Allies," but he said that this sympathy did not involve U.S. assistance. "I have repeatedly said that I am not in favor of getting this country into war or to sending American boys across the waters. Not only that, but I do not want to give any President of the United States, in the absence of Congress, the right to mobilize the Army or anything else and take away the power that should rightfully rest with the Congress of the United States."[38]

Addressing a meeting of the Women's International League for Peace and Freedom in Washington, D.C., Wheeler said he subscribed to a foreign policy that no longer considered "this country a British colony." He criticized Roosevelt administration plans to sell "officially obsolete" rifles, field guns, and ammunition to Britain and France and said, "I want to do everything to help the Allies stamp out the brutal forces which seek to dominate Europe and perhaps the rest of the world, but setting the United States on fire will not help cut out the fire in Europe." He would not, Wheeler said, "want to see the youth of this country killed and maimed on the battlefields of Europe." Britain was fully capable of turning back the Nazis, Wheeler said. "Why is it necessary to give the Allies anything? The British empire alone covers one-fourth of the earth's surface."[39]

A few days later, no doubt with Wheeler in mind, Roosevelt issued a stinging reply to "those who talk and vote as isolationists." The isolationists, Roosevelt said, "hold to the obvious delusion that we of the United States can safely permit the United States to become a lone island in a world dominated by the philosophy of force."[40]

At about this time, as recounted in his memoirs, Wheeler received a visit in his Senate office from Rear Admiral Stanford C. Hooper, a pioneer of early radio technology that earned him the title "father of naval radio." Wearing civilian clothes, Hooper warned Wheeler that "the man at the other end of [Pennsylvania] Avenue is going to get us into the war." Hooper was particularly dismissive of increasing talk of German air attacks on the United States, a threat frequently mentioned by proponents of greater American intervention in the European hostilities. Hooper encouraged Wheeler "to go out and make a lot of speeches" that countered Roosevelt's calls for American support for Britain. "You licked him once on the Court issue and you can lick him again," Hooper told Wheeler, who in turn asked the admiral to supply him with information he could use in speeches, which Hooper agreed to do. "My position was the same as it had been in the first war," Wheeler later wrote in his memoirs. "While I am of English ancestry

Republican newspaper publisher Frank Knox during his Senate confirmation hearing in 1940. (*Library of Congress Prints and Photographs Division, Washington, D.C.*)

and was always pro-ally, I felt that this was not our war. When I was U.S. District Attorney for Montana during the World War I, the hysteria over possible invasion even in that remote area was so great that I had to resist pressure to prosecute for sedition Montanans who were guilty of nothing more than having a foreign name. I wanted to see the American people keep their heads this time." Shortly after the admiral's visit, Wheeler was visited by a second military officer, an Army Air Corps captain whose identity Wheeler never disclosed, who told him that the United States did not have "a single, solitary plane that's fit for overseas service." As Admiral Hooper had, Wheeler said the air corps captain provided material on military readiness and the extent of the military threat to the United States that Wheeler incorporated over the next eighteen months in dozens of speeches advocating a U.S. policy of nonintervention.[41]

Meanwhile, Roosevelt, still being coy about his reelection plans, inflamed Wheeler and other noninterventionists when he announced, on the eve of the 1940 Republican convention, the stunning appointments of two prominent, interventionist Republicans to his cabinet. (Positions were open in the wake of FDR's firing of Secretary of War Harry Woodring and the resignation of Secretary of the Navy Charles Edison to run for governor of New Jersey.) Roosevelt picked Henry Stimson, a former secretary of state and war in Republican administrations, to head the War Department, and Frank Knox, a Chicago newspaper publisher and Alf Landon's 1936 running mate, the man who praised Wheeler's presidential possibilities just a few months earlier, became secretary of the navy. The timing of the bipartisan appointments was brilliant since it contributed to Republican division between the party's interventionists and isolationists on the eve of the GOP convention and, as historian Lynne Olson says, "positioned FDR as a unifying, nonpartisan figure interested only in the public good." Also by bringing outspoken interventionists into his cabinet—men even more publicly identified with aid to the Allies than Roosevelt himself—the president was straddling the pragmatic middle in the increasingly contentious foreign policy debate, rejecting isolation and styling himself as a reluctant belligerent, even as his new cabinet members began preparing for war. Many Republicans, unsurprisingly, were shocked that such prominent members of their party would join a Democratic administration. Wheeler, speaking for noninterventionists, characterized the appointments as Roosevelt's creation of a "war cabinet," which was precisely the president's intention.[42]

Despite Wheeler's increasingly harsh attacks on Roosevelt's constantly evolving foreign policy in 1940, some Democrats, up to the very eve of the Democratic convention, amazingly and unrealistically hoped that a Roosevelt third-term ticket might include the senator from Montana. The vice presidency was discussed at a Washington dinner party that the Wheelers attended in June, and Wheeler believed that this discussion was sanctioned by the White House, since four prominent administration officials, including Benjamin Cohen, attended the dinner. All agreed that Wheeler could have the vice presidential nomination if he desired. He told the group that he was not the least bit interested.[43]

Rather than an effort to test Wheeler's availability for the vice presidency, the dinner party seems more plausibly to have been an effort to keep Wheeler off balance and encourage him to tone down his foreign policy criticism heading into the Democratic convention. Evidence points more surely in the direction of Roosevelt wanting nothing to do with Wheeler. Harold Ickes recorded in his diary that the vice presidential overture was not authorized by the White House, and Ickes noted that Roosevelt told Jim Farley, himself a presidential hopeful, early in 1940 that, "if Wheeler should be nominated for President, I'd vote for a Republican." Farley objected that Roosevelt, as leader of the Democratic Party, could do no such a thing. "Oh, yes, I could," Roosevelt replied.[44]

Roosevelt had still made no comment about his availability to be drafted for a third term when Republicans convened in Philadelphia for one of the most extraordinary major party conventions in U.S. history. Republicans nominated the darkest of dark horses, the moderately interventionist Wendell Willkie, Wheeler's adversary from the utility holding company battles, as their standard-bearer. Wheeler immediately condemned Willkie as "an acknowledged Wall Street lawyer" who "openly espoused the policy of American intervention in Europe's bloodbaths." Republicans had abandoned, as Wheeler saw it, any claim to being the peace party by adopting a platform that merely paid "lip service to the idea of keeping the United States out of war."[45]

It was now up to Democrats, Wheeler said, to be a real peace party or face a third-party challenge over U.S. involvement in the European war. On July 2, still in advance of the Democratic convention, Wheeler let go his pent up frustrations with Roosevelt, Republicans, and the war in Europe. In a speech to a boisterous crowd at the national convention of Townsend pension plan advocates, Wheeler predicted that a peace-oriented third party would emerge if Democrats failed to stand fast against war. Without a clear peace declaration from Democrats, Wheeler said, there would be "no difference" between Democrats and Republicans in 1940. Montana Townsend delegates—"some dressed as cowboys with boots, gold-colored silk shirts and bandanas"—lead a raucous demonstration after Wheeler's speech, and labor leader John L. Lewis, publicly supporting Wheeler, shouted over the turmoil that "only one man in the Democratic party can take the nomination for president of the party this year." *New York Times* coverage of Wheeler's speech ran under a headline—"Wheeler Will Run Even if Roosevelt Seeks Third Term"—that ignited an immediate firestorm in Montana.[46]

Perhaps the *Times* reporter got the story wrong, or a headline writer conjectured too much, or perhaps Wheeler did suggest that he would run regardless of Roosevelt's decision. Whatever the explanation, when the news landed on Montana front pages the next day, Wheeler appeared to be contradicting what he had told the state's Democrats just days earlier. Lee Metcalf, the Roosevelt partisan and assistant to Wheeler's primary challenger, pounced. Wheeler "is going to be a candidate against Roosevelt and is going to oppose him at the convention," Metcalf said in a letter he immediately sent to Montana Democratic leaders. "Such an outrageous breach of faith cannot be justified on any ground," he said, and Metcalf reminded Democrats that Wheeler once before had "refused to support his party's nominee and bolted the ticket. He has consistently opposed President Roosevelt until he has been called the leader of the fifth column in Democratic ranks. . . . On July 16th when we go to the polls to select our nominee for United States Senator from Montana we can select one who is a Democrat, who is for Roosevelt and who will still be a Democrat in November. Let Wheeler run for President but nominate H. J. Freebourn for United States Senator."[47]

Wheeler scrambled to contain the damage and issued a hurried statement saying he stood by his promise not to oppose a third term, and he issued a scathing response to Metcalf. "I do not blame you for being loyal to your boss [Freebourn]. You should be," Wheeler wrote. "I would not respect you if you did otherwise. But on the other hand, the spreading of false and malicious propaganda with reference to me goes far beyond any loyalty you owe to anyone."[48]

The next day "Wheeler for President" headquarters opened quietly at the Congress Hotel on Chicago's Michigan Avenue, with aide Burke Clements on hand as Wheeler's chief convention organizer. Veteran Washington reporter Marquis Childs described the scene: "Three or four rooms were hung with photographs and posters. Pretty girls passed out Wheeler buttons. But the senator himself took all this with a certain cynicism." Wheeler expressed his real feelings to Jim Farley on the opening day of the convention, which also happened to be the eve of his Montana primary election. "We have a primary in my state Tuesday and I can't say anything until it's over," Wheeler groused to the party chairman. "If this were not an election year [for the U.S. Senate], I would raise hell for the presidency."[49]

Rather than the presidential nomination, Wheeler had to content himself with a lopsided Senate primary win in Montana, a victory that appeared to provide a convincing mandate but actually contained the elements of Wheeler's eventual political defeat. He carried every Montana county, but Freebourn made a much stronger showing than had Wheeler's primary opponent six years earlier, and caution flags appeared in Silver Bow County and Butte, Wheeler's longtime political base. Wheeler won just 55 percent of the vote in Silver Bow County, a respectable showing but far below the 79 percent he commanded in 1928 and the 87 percent he amassed in 1934.[50]

———

In Chicago, Democrats finally nominated—or drafted—Roosevelt, but many delegates felt, as Susan Dunn has written, "sour and frustrated . . . that they had been used . . . that the convention had been all sewed up before it began." Wheeler felt the same and was left to publicly demand, and work feverishly behind the scenes to accomplish, changes in the Democratic platform related to foreign policy. "It is not sufficient to say we will not send troops to fight in Europe's war," Wheeler said. "We must make it clear that we will not participate in those wars in any way whatsoever. If they don't write a plank satisfactory to me and those who share my views you can bet your last dollar there will be a fight on the floor of the convention." The White House–prepared draft of the party platform was an unabashedly liberal document, but Wheeler and other noninterventionists, principally Senator Walsh of Massachusetts and Senator Pat McCarran of Nevada, found the foreign policy plank, in Wheeler's words, "ambiguous" and "wholly unsatisfactory." They insisted on different language.[51]

"We will not participate in foreign wars, and we will not send our army, naval or air forces to fight in foreign lands outside the Americas," was Wheeler's proposed language. After discussions with Harry Hopkins, who was handling the delicate platform negotiations for Roosevelt, the president suggested an additional phrase be added—"except in case of attack." Wheeler agreed to the modification and claimed victory on the issue of war and peace. "The principles of peace, for which I stand, have been incorporated in the platform," he said in a statement. "That is the real victory."[52]

Wheeler's presidential aspirations ended with a whimper. Other contenders, Farley and Garner, for example, were nominated and received delegate votes, but as journalist Marquis Childs wrote, "When the time came for nominations ... Montana was silent. Wheeler had stepped aside ... apparently he felt that the weak compromise plank on foreign affairs had been triumph enough." By not being nominated, Wheeler also stood by his pledge to Montana Democrats not to challenge Roosevelt.[53]

For a moment in the wake of Roosevelt's nomination, Wheeler was again the subject of speculation about the number two spot on the ticket, and he hastily abandoned earlier reluctance to consider becoming the vice presidential candidate. Wheeler was interested enough in the prospect of the vice presidency that he dispatched Montana congressman Jim O'Connor, a trusted friend, to sound out Interior Secretary Ickes about his chances. Ickes may not have been the best sounding board, since he was also being mentioned as a candidate, and, as he recounted in a lengthy passage in his diary, he poured ice water over the idea that Roosevelt and Wheeler might run together:

> I told [O'Connor] frankly that while the President had not yet sent word as to his choice, I did not believe it would be Wheeler. I said that if Wheeler were nominated for Vice President no one would guarantee that he would not be taking issue with the President the next week. I told [O'Connor] that I liked Wheeler personally and that he had been a good friend to my department but that he had gone out of his way to fight the President and in a manner that was bound to give offense. I didn't object to the fight so much as the manner in which it was carried on.[54]

Roosevelt eventually selected Agriculture Secretary Henry Wallace as his running mate, a selection that did not excite Wheeler because of Wallace's internationalist foreign policy views. To end speculation that he would not support the ticket, Wheeler promised loyalty to the party and said he would vote for Roosevelt in November.[55]

Did Wheeler ever really believe he could capture the Democratic nomination? Reflecting on the prospect many years later, his youngest daughter was not convinced he ever believed winning either the nomination or the presidency was likely. On the other hand, his wife very much encouraged his aspirations. "Mother took [a presidential candidacy] very seriously," Marion Wheeler Scott remembered, to the point that Lulu subscribed to a clipping service in order to have her own source of information about how Wheeler's prospects were unfolding across the country. Whether he was ever serious or not, Wheeler had a plausible campaign strategy: maintain the Roosevelt coalition of labor, farmers, westerners, and southerners and present himself to this coalition as a liberal, a fighter, and an antiwar noninterventionist. A Wheeler candidacy would also certainly have focused on his progressive ideas about economic security and staying distant from the worsening international crisis. But in 1940 the Democratic Party still belonged to Roosevelt, and his desire for a third term left no room for Wheeler.[56]

Two questions dominated the 1940 presidential election. Would voters sanction a third term for Franklin Roosevelt? And how far should the United States go in preparing for war? The second question played out in late summer as Washington became consumed with the question of whether Congress would authorize the first peacetime draft in the nation's history. The proposal again put Wheeler at cross-purposes with the Roosevelt administration. Wheeler fought tenaciously against the conscription legislation—both Roosevelt and Willkie endorsed the measure—suggesting at one point that the issue be settled by a national referendum. "If the proponents of conscription are in favor of democracy and feel it is necessary to have conscription in order to save democracy, they ought to be willing to submit the question to a referendum because that would be the democratic way to ascertain the public's reaction," Wheeler said. Congressional supporters of the draft and the White House rejected out of hand the idea of a referendum.[57]

On August 13, Wheeler warned that a peacetime draft would create a vast and costly permanent military establishment, an issue he contended both his critics and newspaper editorialists were ignoring:

> When we talk to the Congress of the United States about putting people on relief, giving hungry women and children in this country something out of the Treasury of the United States, and giving farmers the benefit payments—which even Mr. Willkie has recently endorsed—when we talk about doing some of those things, some said, "You will wreck the Government. Why do you not balance the Budget?" Every little chamber of commerce from one end of the country to the other, and every great metropolitan newspaper in the country was clamoring, "Why do you not balance the budget?" I wish to call the roll. When we wanted to feed the poor, help the farmer, and do something for the underprivileged every single one of such newspapers was crying for balancing the Budget. They said, "Balance the Budget or you will wreck the country."
>
> Now every single one of these great newspapers, and every single one of the great economic royalists who has been clamoring about balancing the Budget,

has forgotten about it and thrown it out the window. They say, 'Let us set up a Military Establishment in the United States.' Why? Not for national defense. No—let us be frank about it—that is not the reason. The reason is that they want to impose upon our country a militarism the like of which is not to be found in any democratic country in the world. It is found only under Mr. Hitler in Germany, Mr. Mussolini in Italy, and Mr. Stalin in Russia.[58]

Two days later in a speech on the NBC radio Blue Network, Wheeler expanded on his antidraft, antiwar message:

Enact peacetime conscription and no longer will this be a free land—no longer will a citizen be able to say that he disagrees with a government edict. Hushed whispers will replace free speech; secret meetings in dark places will supplant free assemblage; labor and industry, men and women, will be shackled by the chains they have themselves forged. And all this, mark you, while this last great democracy is still at peace. Is that the sort of society for which our forefathers shed their blood? Is this the goal for which we strive?

If this bill passes—it will slit the throat of the last democracy still living— it will accord Hitler his greatest and cheapest victory. On the headstone of American democracy he will inscribe, "Here Lies the Foremost Victim of the War of Nerves."[59]

Wheeler's friends in Montana, including Governor Roy Ayers and former congressman Tom Stout, warned him that opposition to the draft was hurting him with voters at home. Stout admitted his own misgivings about instituting a draft but said he was concerned "that if Hitler defeats Britain, we are sure to be the next attempted victim of his ambition of world domination." Ayers told Wheeler, "Opposition to the Conscription Bill is decreasing as the German attacks on Britain are increasing." Another friend, Montana Internal Revenue director Lewis Penwell, told Wheeler his position was "not popular in those portions of the state where I have been—and I think this is generally true all over the state." Penwell warned Wheeler that onetime supporters of the senator were now "inclined to criticize you because they think you are hampering the President in his preparedness program." Wheeler was unmoved by the warnings, telling Ayers, "I am afraid I would be opposed to [the draft] even though sentiment in Montana was for it," and he added, "It looks to me as though we are going to get into this war. If we get into the war, we will have a dictator, and the Lord knows whether we will get out of it very soon."[60]

"Peace time conscription, to me is contrary to every principle of democracy," Wheeler wrote to a Montana constituent. "They have [had] peace-time conscription in Europe for generations, and it has brought nothing but war, misery, and dictatorship.

I am opposed to getting into this war." Wheeler offered a final attack on the draft proposal—he returned to his theme of a too-powerful government constraining individual liberty—in Senate remarks on September 9, 1940. Local draft boards, he said, would wield a club "over the heads of all workingmen in all communities of the United States.... It will mean for the laboring people that if they do not do as they are told to do they may be drafted into the Army." Just days earlier Roosevelt had bypassed Congress to consummate a deal to send fifty aging American destroyers to Britain in exchange for long-term leases on military facilities in the Western Hemisphere. Wheeler condemned the destroyer deal as illegal and one more step toward war.[61]

The Senate approved a conference report on the draft legislation in mid-September by a vote of 47–25. Draftees were required to serve twelve months, with the legislation specifying that no draftee would serve outside the Western Hemisphere other than in U.S. territories and possessions. The law doubled the army's size to nearly 500,000 and increased the authorized strength of the National Guard. Public opinion polls indicated broad support for the move, leaving Wheeler, as his Montana friends had warned, out of sync with popular sentiment. But Wheeler evidenced little concern that his foreign policy views were increasingly marginalized. Writing to historian Henry Elmer Barnes three days after Roosevelt signed the draft legislation, Wheeler seemed upbeat. "I feel we have made a good fight and that it has not been in vain," he said.[62]

On September 27, Germany, Japan, and Italy announced the Tripartite Pact, formalizing an agreement of mutual cooperation and pledging united action should the United States enter the war. Wheeler's response to the agreement was to gain approval for a Senate Interstate Commerce Committee investigation of the extent of German ownership, control, and influence of the U.S. defense industry. Wheeler may truly have believed such an investigation was necessary, but its also possible that the dynamics of the moment, including his reelection campaign in Montana, dictated the need to propose some positive action rather than be seen as constantly voicing opposition to the administration. In any event, little came of the investigation.[63]

———

Late in the 1940 campaign, with a Gallup poll showing Willkie closing to within four points of Roosevelt, the president and his advisers became anxious that an election that since summer had seemed certain might actually be slipping away. On October 30, as the campaign neared its climax, Roosevelt tried to reassure an electorate nervous about war and concerned that the United States might soon be involved. Before a boisterous crowd at Boston Garden Roosevelt proclaimed, "I have said this before, but I shall say it again and again and again. Your boys are not going to be sent into any foreign wars." Listening to the speech on radio, Willkie immediately understood the impact of

Roosevelt's words. "That hypocritical son of a bitch," he said. "This is going to beat me."[64]

Roosevelt's reassuring antiwar statements—disingenuous campaign rhetoric to Willkie as well as Wheeler—may not have decided the election, but the president's words undoubtedly resonated with many worried voters. Willkie won just ten states to Roosevelt's thirty-eight, and the Electoral College went overwhelmingly for the president—449 to 82. As historian Robert Dallek has noted, "Roosevelt was greatly relieved by the outcome. For weeks he had worried about a defeat which, in spite of Willkie's internationalism, could be interpreted as a victory for anti-British, pro-appeasement forces in the United States." Wheeler had a much different interpretation, fearing, correctly as it turned out, that Roosevelt's victory would loosen political constraints on the president and smooth the way for additional U.S. support for Britain.[65]

Wheeler's Senate reelection in Montana, meanwhile, was a cakewalk. His intense opposition to the draft and criticism of Roosevelt seemed hardly to register with voters. Wheeler aide Bailey Stortz ran the campaign, while Wheeler mostly stayed in Washington, focused on the intensifying foreign policy battles. "The people of Montana know my record, and there is nothing I can add to it or take away from it," he said in explaining his non-campaign. Wheeler's opponent, E. K. Cheadle, a former state Republican Central Committee chairman from Shelby, barely mounted a campaign because an active-duty assignment with the Montana National Guard took him out of the state. Wheeler's margin was nearly 110,000 votes, a commanding 73 percent and 30,000 votes more than Roosevelt's total in Montana. The victory margin, in terms of percentage, was the largest to that point in Montana history. "I carried every county and every city in Montana and received almost 3 votes to 1 for my opponent's and carried my home city 4 to 1," Wheeler bragged in a letter to Majority Leader Alben Barkley. Wheeler carefully avoided direct involvement in other Montana races in 1940 but used his influence and that of his loyal staff to provide behind-the-scenes help to two Republican candidates. Former congresswoman Jeannette Rankin, sister of Wheeler's friend Wellington Rankin, defeated the embarrassing incumbent Jacob Thorkelson in the Republican primary. Rankin, who generally shared Wheeler's foreign policy views, then spoiled Jerry O'Connell's comeback in the general election. Wheeler also worked quietly to help elect his old assistant, Republican Sam Ford, the former Montana attorney general, as governor. Wheeler had supported Democrat Roy Ayers in 1936 but did nothing to help Ayers in 1940. Ford won by fewer than five thousand votes.[66]

Despite pledging to support Roosevelt and the Democratic ticket in 1940, Wheeler cast his own presidential vote for Socialist Party candidate Norman Thomas, who shared Wheeler's noninterventionist views.[67]

Wheeler's overwhelming reelection win in 1940 was misleading. Republican opposition was virtually nonexistent, and disaffected Democrats, many of whom had demonstrated their disapproval of Wheeler during the primary, simply had no place to go to register disapproval during the general election. The enormous national attention Wheeler generated during 1940 also clearly provided a publicity boost at home that, when combined with weak opposition and his own effort to appeal to voters in both parties, gave Wheeler an opening to form an effective bipartisan coalition with the new Republican governor. The Wheeler-Ford partnership (in which Jeannette and Wellington Rankin also participated) dominated Montana politics in the early 1940s, with Ford appointing Wheeler partisans to state positions and the Democratic senator largely deferring to the Republican governor on home-state issues. This open embrace of nonparty politics, however, exacted a price. In the future, Wheeler's most committed Montana opponents, convinced that he had changed his political stripes from liberal to reactionary, came from the ranks of the very Democrats who had flocked to support him in the 1920s and 1930s. His bitter fight to keep the country out of war soon overshadowed every other issue, and the continuing conflict with Franklin Roosevelt grew more intense. Almost immediately after winning in a landslide in 1940, Wheeler's political standing in Montana began to deteriorate, and within a few months, with his positions on foreign policy constantly in the news and steadily more controversial, many of Wheeler's constituents would come to regret their vote for the man they had now sent to the Senate four times.

Wheeler traveled to Hawaii after the election for rest and relaxation, and while on Oahu he toured the massive U.S. naval base at Pearl Harbor, home base of the Pacific Fleet. Everything, he wrote to daughter Elizabeth, was about "preparing for defense and war."[68]

12 AMERICA FIRST

> There is only one way to avoid [further economic and
> political collapse]—stay out of war and correct the
> conditions that make 10,000,000 men idle and jobless.
>
> — BURTON K. WHEELER

A kind of "national schizophrenia," as one historian has described it, gripped the country at the beginning of 1941. The Gallup Poll reported that when Americans were asked whether it was more important to keep out of a European war or help Britain hold off Nazi Germany, 60 percent favored helping, even at the risk of war. But when the same Americans were asked how they would vote on the question of going to war against Germany and Italy, 88 percent of those surveyed said they would vote to stay out of the war. Given the national mood—conflicted, worried, confused—newly reelected and very popular Franklin Roosevelt (the Gallup Poll placing his approval at 71 percent) faced a daunting challenge: how to maneuver public opinion and Congress in the direction of aiding Britain while not running headlong into Americans' desire to avoid war.[1]

Roosevelt knew from his frequent and secret contacts with Prime Minister Churchill that Britain was in desperate shape and required vast economic and military aid to continue to resist the Nazis. Roosevelt was also keenly sensitive to allegations from noninterventionists like B. K. Wheeler that any action he might take to provide assistance would set the country on the road to another war. Roosevelt's answer to this dilemma—he dubbed his proposal Lend-Lease, an effort to provide massive aid but still avoid war—sparked a vicious debate, the first of many foreign policy and preparedness debates in 1941, that would pit Roosevelt against Wheeler. The Montanan believed that what Roosevelt *appeared* to be doing to keep the country out of war was at cross-purposes with what the president was actually doing. Further, Wheeler was convinced that Roosevelt was purposefully misleading Americans and deceiving

Congress about what his policies would accomplish. "Can anyone be certain now that the United States could have stayed out of World War II," Wheeler wrote in his memoirs in 1962. "Obviously not. What I am certain of is that FDR, from whatever motivations, never tried to keep us out of war—while deliberately misleading the people into thinking that he was."[2]

Repeatedly during 1941 Wheeler accused Roosevelt of being "a warmonger" and acting like "a dictator," while the senator's critics questioned his patriotism, condemned him as a Nazi sympathizer, and called him anti-Semitic. Meanwhile, the FBI stepped up its surveillance of Wheeler and his family, and press coverage became more critical, even as his attacks on Roosevelt and his policies generated massive national attention. This "great debate" ultimately led to an erosion of Wheeler's political support in Montana and would become the critical factor in his eventual defeat. Yet, at least early in 1941, it appeared that Wheeler's antiwar position enjoyed broad public support. A Gallup poll months earlier had reported that 68 percent of those surveyed felt U.S. entry into World War I had been a mistake. By resisting the president's foreign policy the Montana senator seemed to be fulfilling his often-made promise to oppose the kind of intervention in European affairs that he was convinced would only repeat the mistakes of the earlier war. From the beginning of Roosevelt's third term, Wheeler became a sort of shadow president, the administration's chief Senate critic, and the de facto leader of one of the largest—and most controversial—grassroots political movements in American history, the America First Committee.[3]

College campuses in the 1930s and up until the attack on Pearl Harbor in December 1941 were centers of America's antiwar sentiment. Eric Sevareid, a student at the University of Minnesota and later a protégé of CBS broadcaster Edward R. Murrow, later remembered the period as "the peak of the intellectual revulsion against the First World War. We felt ashamed for our fathers and uncles . . . we were young, and to those just beginning to taste the wonderful flavors of life the idea of death is a stark tragedy of unutterable horror . . . we began to detest the very word 'patriotism.'"[4]

It was therefore no surprise that the antiwar America First movement began on a college campus. Robert Douglas Stuart, a twenty-four-year old Yale Law School student, was the early organizer of the movement. "Most of us of our generation," Stuart later recalled, "who were in any way thoughtful about history and international affairs learned that the U.S. didn't accomplish very much in committing troops to the First World War, which was a terrible slaughter of talent of the western world. Therefore, we'd be smart if we stayed the hell out of the conflagration that seemed to be emerging by the time we were all talking up at law school." From the University of

Chicago to Harvard, from Columbia to the University of Missouri, students by the thousands passionately opposed American involvement in another war. They wrote anti-interventionist editorials in college newspapers declaring "the Yanks are not coming," they signed a version of the "Oxford Oath" of resistance to war, and they organized, most effectively first at Yale, to contest the foreign policy of the Roosevelt administration.[5]

Wheeler met Robert Stuart in Washington, D.C., a month before the 1940 Democratic convention. Stuart, son of a Quaker Oats Company executive, had spent the previous weeks organizing students opposed to U.S. involvement in the European war that in May had reached a new crisis point with the German invasion of France. Stuart counted among the earliest backers of this new movement several Yale law students, including future president Gerald R. Ford, future Supreme Court justice Potter Stewart, and future Yale president Kingman Brewster.[6]

Wheeler encouraged Stuart to try to convince Robert E. Wood, the chairman of the giant retailer Sears Roebuck, to serve as chair of the fledging antiwar organization. Wood, a nominal Republican who had supported Roosevelt in 1932 and 1936, had built Sears into a merchandising powerhouse, and his military background was stellar—West Point graduate, retired brigadier general, and onetime army quartermaster general. Wood seemed an ideal choice to lead an organization committed to a strong national defense but even more strongly opposed to involvement in the European war. Wood initially resisted overtures to get involved but eventually agreed and began to address the details involved in developing the grassroots movement. On September 5, 1940, the America First Committee formally announced its national leadership and opened headquarters in Chicago, in the heart of midwestern isolationist sentiment. The committee's leadership, a broad, impressive, bipartisan group of business, academic, political, and former military figures, included Avery Brundage, future head of the International Olympic Committee; Alice Roosevelt Longworth, the outspoken daughter of Teddy Roosevelt and cousin of FDR; and Jay C. Hormel, president of the meatpacking company bearing his name. Other early members of America First included Hanford MacNider, an Iowan, World War I veteran, former ambassador to Canada, and onetime commander of the American Legion; General Hugh Johnson, a West Pointer and the head of the National Recovery Administration until a falling out with FDR; George H. Whipple, winner of the 1934 Nobel Prize for Medicine; Eddie Rickenbacker, the decorated World War I ace; Albert W. Palmer, president of the Chicago Theological Seminary; and Ray McKaig, a close friend of William Borah.[7]

Wheeler never formally became a member of America First, but he was the committee's most sought after speaker in 1941 and became closely identified with the group's eventual controversies. Lulu Wheeler, on the other hand, was an active member of the organization's national board and served as treasurer of the Washington, D.C., chapter. "I take full charge of the finances, pay all the bills, keep the cash book, bank the money, send out membership cards and a button to every new member," Lulu wrote to her daughter Elizabeth. "In addition, I write a note of thanks to every contributor who is already a member so that every penny is entered in the book and acknowledged. You have to run these headquarters in a business-like way." Another Wheeler, son John, a Los Angeles attorney, chaired the committee's Southern California chapter.[8]

America First eventually boasted 450 official chapters and as many as 850,000 members. As Wayne S. Cole, a historian of the noninterventionist movement, has written, "Nearly two-thirds of the membership was located within the three hundred mile radius of Chicago," not coincidentally the circulation area of the ferociously isolationist, anti–New Deal *Chicago Tribune*. The *Tribune*'s influential and imperious publisher Robert McCormick was never a member of America First, but, hating Franklin Roosevelt, he provided vast coverage of the group's antiwar and anti-Roosevelt activities. The *Tribune* had once called Wheeler "a radical Democrat of notorious ill fame," and on one occasion the publisher had objected to too favorable treatment of Wheeler, demanding to know if his Washington correspondent had "hired out to be a press agent for Wheeler." But Wheeler's antiwar position and anti-Roosevelt rhetoric trumped any past animosity, and McCormick and the *Tribune* lavished favorable coverage on America First and Wheeler.[9]

At about the time Wheeler met the student organizers, he had his first encounter with the aviator Charles Lindbergh, whose historic solo flight of the Atlantic in 1927 had made him an international celebrity. Wheeler and Lindbergh—a reserved mid-westerner married to the daughter of wealthy Republican businessman and politician Dwight Morrow, Calvin Coolidge's ambassador to Mexico—would never become real friends, but they did share a profound distrust of Roosevelt as well as a belief that his policies would lead the country to war. The two met in June 1940 when they joined Senators Robert La Follette Jr., Bennett Champ Clark of Missouri, and Robert Reynolds of North Carolina, all strong noninterventionists, to discuss, as Lindbergh noted in his dairy, "plans for counter acting war agitation and propaganda. Everyone is very much worried about Roosevelt and feels he is leading the country to war as rapidly as he can."[10]

World War I, Wheeler believed, had smoothed the way for Hitler's rise to power in Germany and Mussolini's in Italy, and the "money crowd," as he put it, as well as the common people in both countries had willingly embraced dictators. "I sometimes wonder," he fretted, "whether or not the American people are any different from the people of these other countries." Wheeler and Lindbergh, hoping to shape U.S. public opinion in 1941 to oppose intervention in Europe, used the America First Committee, including its fund-raising and publicity capability, as an expedient vehicle to try to stop the drift toward war. Apparently neither man gave much thought to the fact that the movement would also attract some of the nation's most disreputable anti-Roosevelt, anti-Semitic, pro-Nazi elements and become a lightening rod for controversy.[11]

"There have been a number of fierce national quarrels in my lifetime," historian Arthur Schlesinger Jr. writes in his memoirs, "over Communism in the later Forties, over McCarthyism in the Fifties, over Vietnam in the Sixties—but none so tore apart families and friendships as the great debate of 1940–1941." What Schlesinger called the "searing personal impact" of this turbulent period involved bitter political brawls over whether the United States should arm and feed the British (and later the Russians), whether American naval ships should undertake convoy duty in the North Atlantic, inevitably producing armed clashes with German U-boats, and whether the United States should prepare for instituting a peacetime draft. The first great debate involved Roosevelt's plan to mobilize America's "Arsenal of Democracy" to aid the beleaguered British. Wheeler's approach to the conflict in Europe was much different.[12]

Early in 1941 Wheeler wrote his friend Norman Thomas, the Socialist Party leader, that the only "sensible thing to do," given the war in Europe, was "to try and bring about a negotiated peace. Of course, a negotiated peace is not going to be satisfactory. No peace terms are entirely satisfactory, but sometime a peace is going to have to be negotiated, and I think those who are encouraging Britain to keep on fighting are doing her a real disservice." Wheeler expressed this idea publicly as well, maintaining that a negotiated peace was a better alternative than the "loss of a million America youth." Critics, including Roosevelt, immediately rejected the concept as unworkable, and the New York Times ridiculed Wheeler's naïveté in an editorial.[13]

Did a negotiated peace imply, the Times editorial asked, that "the heel of the conqueror is lifted from the prostrate Holland, Denmark, Norway, Belgium, Poland, France and Czecho-Slovakia, with restitution made for damage done and adequate assurance given for the future?" And where "in the record of Hitler's broken promises and his savage treatment of the countries he has conquered can they find the slightest scrap of evidence to indicate that such a peace is possible?"[14]

Wheeler persisted and eventually developed an eight-point agenda that he said should form the basis for a negotiated settlement of the war: restoration of Germany's 1914 boundaries and an autonomous Poland and Czechoslovakia; restoration and independence for France, Holland, Norway, Belgium, and Denmark; return of Alsace-Lorraine to France; return to Germany of her colonies; protection of all religious and racial minorities; internationalization of the Suez Canal; no reparations or indemnities;

and a limitation on armaments. Roosevelt wanted nothing to do with negotiations. He had something much different in mind.[15]

"I have been thinking very hard about what we should do for England," Roosevelt remarked to Treasury Secretary Henry Morgenthau. "It seems to me the thing to do is to get away from a dollar sign. I don't want to put the thing in terms of dollars or loans," he said. If the United States dramatically stepped up production, Roosevelt said, it could then say to England "We will give you the guns and the ships you need, provided that when the war is over you will return to us in kind the guns and ships we have loaned to you." Roosevelt's folksy description of what would become his Lend-Lease proposal—a simple loan of tanks, ships, and planes that would one day be returned—is one of the best of many examples of Roosevelt's remarkable ability to explain complex, controversial ideas in understandable, everyday language. During a White House news conference late in 1940, Roosevelt offered a compelling example of how Lend-Lease would work. He compared the program to lending a neighbor a garden hose to put out a fire. Once the fire was out, Roosevelt said, a good friend would not say: "Neighbor, my garden hose cost me $15; you have to pay me $15 for it." Rather, the president said, you would want your garden hose back. He intended to replace the "silly, foolish, old dollar sign" with a "gentlemen's obligation" on the part of the British "to repay in kind."[16]

On December 29, 1940, Roosevelt fleshed out his proposal during his first fireside chat since May, one of the most consequential speeches of his presidency. The speech was not, Roosevelt said, "a fireside chat on war" but rather "a talk on national security." In what would be known ever after as the "Arsenal of Democracy" speech, Roosevelt explicitly rejected Wheeler's negotiated peace proposal as nothing more than fantasy by those the president called "American appeasers." If Britain were defeated, Roosevelt said, the United States would be next:

> Some of us like to believe that even if Britain falls, we are still safe, because of the broad expanse of the Atlantic and of the Pacific. But the width of those oceans is not what it was in the days of clipper ships. At one point between Africa and Brazil the distance is less than it is from Washington to Denver, Colorado, five hours for the latest type of bomber. And at the north end of the Pacific Ocean, America and Asia almost touch each other. Why, even today we have planes that could fly from the British Isles to New England and back again without refueling. And remember that the range of the modern bomber is ever being increased.[17]

Roosevelt declared that America needed to be "the great arsenal of democracy," throwing its economic and moral weight behind the fight against Nazi Germany since the country and the world faced "an emergency as serious as war itself."[18]

Wheeler had offered a starkly different view of the stakes during a speech just the night before. Speaking over a telephone hookup to a meeting of the National Youth Anti-War Congress in Madison, Wisconsin, Wheeler said that those advocating aid to Britain were not real Americans but rather the "international banker or a wealthy lawyer with European clients, or a publicist who has lived most of his life in Europe, or a social dowager whose life ambition was fulfilled when she knelt before royalty." These internationalist elites had nothing "in common with the great mass of Americans" whose simple desire was to stay out of the war. During an NBC radio appearance on December 30, the evening Roosevelt unveiled the first details of his aid proposal, Wheeler mocked the idea that the United States was vulnerable to foreign attack. "If Hitler's army can't cross the narrow English Channel in seven months, his bombers won't fly across the Rockies to bomb Denver tomorrow."[19]

Despite immediate criticism from Wheeler and others, Roosevelt's "Arsenal of Democracy" speech was popular with the public. The White House reported that messages ran 100-to-1 favorable. "The ingredients of Roosevelt's success seem clear," historian Robert Dallek writes. "The 61 percent national approval for the talk was close to the number of people favoring help to Britain even at the risk of war, while the overall 9 percent disagreement with the speech suggests that Roosevelt's emphasis on assuring peace through expanded aid disarmed the fears of many who felt it more important to stay out of war than help Britain win."[20]

Following his own radio speech, Wheeler also claimed overwhelming support for his position, with a thousand telegrams arriving at his Washington office, 93 percent of which, he claimed, were favorable. The *Times*, without questioning White House claims of the level of support for Roosevelt's speech, dismissed Wheeler's count as unrepresentative of broad public opinion. "People who send telegrams to a public speaker are like the people who send telegrams to a concert singer or the author of a new play. Only those who are pleased with the performance take the trouble to wire. The others obviously refrain from spending their good 25 cents after the bad $4.40 for a seat."[21]

Roosevelt's proposed Lend-Lease legislation signaled a dramatic turn in U.S. foreign policy by authorizing the president "to sell, transfer title to, exchange, lease, lend or otherwise dispose of any defense article for the government of any country whose defense the President deems vital to the defense of the United States." Germany was now clearly defined as the enemy, and U.S. policy was being reordered in an attempt to ensure Britain's survival, which now became unequivocally linked to U.S. interests. Wheeler certainly believed that Lend-Lease represented a fundamental shift in U.S. policy, but, even more important, he thought Roosevelt's proposal was both unconstitutional and a virtual declaration of war against Germany.

Negative reaction from other noninterventionists was blistering. California Republican Hiram Johnson said Lend-Lease would "create a dictatorship" in the United States, with the president able to bypass Congress and effectively wage war. Ohio Republican Robert Taft said of Roosevelt, "The words of his mouth were smoother than butter, but war was in his heart," and Taft compared lending war equipment to lending chewing gum. "We certainly do not want the same gum back," he said. Wheeler waited until two days after introduction of the actual Lend-Lease legislation before launching his own sustained counterattack. In two different radio debates on January 12, 1941—the first a face-off with liberal newspaper editor Ralph Ingersoll—Wheeler expounded on the argument that Roosevelt sought "dictatorial powers" and "a blank check" that would inevitably pull the country into war.[22]

During the debate with Ingersoll, Wheeler said he genuinely hoped Britain would prevail against Hitler's Germany, but the country's first order of business was to solve its domestic economic problems, while remaining secure behind two vast oceans. Hitler was "crazy," Wheeler said, but as long as the United States maintained its defenses and stayed away from entanglements in Europe's chaos, the country would be secure.[23]

Wheeler debated for a second time on January 12 as one of four participants in the radio program *American Forum of the Air*. During that broadcast he uttered what was perhaps the most memorable, certainly the most widely quoted, phrase of his career, a bitter, cutting remark that was afterward quoted in nearly every history of the period. "The Kaiser's blank check to Austria-Hungary in the first World War was a piker compared to the Roosevelt blank check of World War II," Wheeler said. "It warranted my worst fears for the future of America, and it definitely stamps the president as war minded. The lend-lease-give program is the New Deal's triple-A foreign policy; it will plow under every fourth American boy." It was a clever, if incendiary (and many thought outrageous) comparison of Lend-Lease to the controversial New Deal agricultural policy—the Agricultural Adjustment Act (AAA)—that sought to limit commodity production by plowing under a portion of farmer's crops.[24]

At a White House news conference two days later Roosevelt was asked by a reporter, without mention of Wheeler, if Lend-Lease, as critics asserted, provided the president with a blank check on foreign policy matters, particularly aid to Britain. "Yes, I suppose so," Roosevelt said. "The easiest thing is, write me [another piece of legislation] that you would not put the [blank check] label on that would accomplish the same objective. That is the perfectly good answer to all these people. That is not the answer to those, at all, who talk about plowing under every fourth American child, which I regard as the most untruthful, as the most dastardly, unpatriotic thing that has ever been said. Quote me on that." Then, as if to underscore the importance Roosevelt attached to countering Wheeler, the president said, "That really is the rottenest thing that has been said in public life in my generation."[25]

Wheeler admitted years later that his comment had crossed the line. "When I had written these words in longhand that Sunday afternoon at home, I thought little about them. But when I spoke the phrase over the network that night, I must confess it did sound somewhat harsh." Wheeler's mail, at by his count, continued to run overwhelmingly in support of his tough stand against Lend-Lease. His public criticism of Roosevelt, he said, only brought more favorable reaction.[26]

———

Immediately after the Lend-Lease fireside chat, Wheeler complained to Paramount News, a major producer of newsreels shown in American movie theatres, and to the Motion Picture Producers and Distributors of America (MPPDA), the Hollywood studio trade group, that he was being denied equal time in which to make the case for a noninterventionist foreign policy. He also charged that Hollywood was turning out pro-war propaganda, an accusation he would return to later in 1941. "The propaganda for war that is being waged by the motion picture companies of this country is reaching a point at which I believe legislation will have to be enacted regulating the industry in this respect unless the industry itself displays a more impartial attitude," Wheeler said. The industry reacted sharply to the threat of regulation, with MPPDA president Will Hays, a former Republican congressman, national committee chairman, and Harding administration postmaster general, categorically rejecting Wheeler's assertions. "The facts utterly deny the merit" of the charges, Hays wrote to Wheeler. Hollywood's top lobbyist also gave Wheeler a detailed analysis of the content of newsreels and feature films, including movies now considered classics—Charlie Chaplin's *The Great Dictator* and Alfred Hitchcock's *Foreign Correspondent*, for example—before concluding that only a tiny fraction of Hollywood's output dealt with "international politics or current events in Europe." Hays sent the White House a copy of his response to Wheeler, which Roosevelt saw on January 17. The president responded with his own two-sentence letter to Hays. "Thank you so much for letting me see that correspondence. Why do you say at the end of your letter to Wheeler 'With kindest personal regards?'"[27]

———

On February 14 Senate debate began on the Lend-Lease proposal, in legislative terminology "H.R. 1776," an appropriate number for an administration seeking to portray the issue as one of patriotism. Wheeler assumed a major role managing the debate and huddled with Lend-Lease opponents to prepare amendments, including amendments prohibiting convoying and the transfer of the U.S. Navy to the British.[28]

Even as he fought against the proposal, Wheeler and his noninterventionist allies knew that defeating Lend-Lease was a long shot. Steered by Majority Leader Barkley, the administration pulled together a bipartisan Senate majority that appeared able to pass a bill agreeable to the White House even if opponents mounted a filibuster. Nevertheless, Wheeler and his followers believed they had a slim chance to derail the legislation, and three lines of attack seemed available: slow the Senate to a crawl with procedural actions constituting a filibuster in practice if not in name, offer amendments to weaken the bill and make it at least less objectionable, and take the fight off the Senate floor and to the country. As the debate unfolded, all three approaches were employed.[29]

The lengthy Lend-Lease debate, full of drama, emotion, outrage, partisanship, even occasionally facts and reason, reminds us of why the Senate has been called the world's greatest deliberative body. Both sides attempted to use the heated talk in the Senate chamber to sway opinions, but the real point was to take arguments to the public. Wheeler's major speech during the debate—he titled it "The American Enabling Act of 1941"—spanned the better part of two days, including a Saturday session. He savaged the proposal from a dozen angles, breaking down the specifics, dissecting the ambiguities, and repeatedly questioning the wisdom of putting so much unchecked power in the hands of any president. Repeatedly interrupted by questions, Wheeler responded deftly and often humorously, which the crowded gallery enjoyed. Vice President Wallace, presiding over much of the debate, repeatedly admonished onlookers not to applaud and once threatened to clear spectators. Discounting any "grave and imminent danger," Wheeler said a grant of unprecedented authority to Roosevelt "set up a dictator, concentrating enormous powers in his hands," and he worried that the American people had "been duped into signing away their charter of civil liberties and their civil rights for a mess of pottage" with no "control over their purses, their swords, or the lives of their sons."

An American dictator, he said, would surely erode civil liberties as had happened in Montana during the Great War. Wheeler called out "international bankers" and conservative business interests, once Roosevelt's bitterest enemies, who, he now said, were presidential allies, pushing America into war. Wheeler's contempt for the British Empire was on display when he predicted that the level of assistance being contemplated for Churchill's government would strip the United States of its own defenses while underwriting British imperialism. "Talk about slavery," Wheeler thundered. "I have been to India. Go there, if you will; go to Bombay, and you will see tens of thousands of people sleeping on the sidewalks, more poverty-stricken than the people in any other place in the world, with nothing under them except the cement and boards, and nothing over them except the British flag. They are starving in misery, and we are going to keep up that exploitation." Wheeler, admitting he was worn out, ended his debate by quoting Isaiah: "They shall beat their swords into plowshares and their spears into pruning hooks; nation shall not lift up sword against nation, neither shall they learn war no more."[30]

Fellow Democrats responded contemptuously to Wheeler's debate. Scott Lucas of Illinois, a future majority leader, said opponents of Lend-Lease were using the Senate debate "as a springboard to make the headlines and create panic and fear among the American people." Jim Murray, once a noninterventionist like Wheeler but now fully onboard with FDR's foreign policy, offered a damaging critique of Wheeler's position in a radio speech that received notice in Montana. "It is not an easy matter for me to take issue with my Senatorial colleagues who are possessed of far more political experience than I am," Murray said, but, "arguments against the bill are not based on reason but on appeals to passion and hate" that "confuse and mislead" the public.[31]

───────

During the dozen years that Wheeler and Murray served together—Murray was first elected in 1934—the two repeatedly demonstrated the accuracy of the maxim that no relationship in politics is more complicated than that between senators from the same state. Wheeler and Murray were, of course, both Democrats, but that detail in no way prevented the two from engaging in a personal and political rivalry marked by utter contempt, constant suspicion, and continual jockeying for attention and dominance in Montana.

Wheeler and Murray had first taken notice of one another in the early 1930s, when Wheeler, always comfortable working a crowd and accustomed to delivering a tub-thumping stump speech, began to regularly disparage Murray's speaking ability—the junior senator was not polished speaker—as well as Murray's political acumen. Wheeler came to believe that Murray was little more than a useful tool of the Roosevelt White House, favored with patronage and publicity, and forced to rely for advice and political success on his son (lawyer and later judge William Daniel W. D. Murray). The two senators engaged in a major brawl in 1935 when Wheeler pushed the appointment of a friend, Republican Ray Hart, to head Montana operations of the Works Progress Administration (WPA), the relief agency pumping millions of dollars of Depression-era spending into the state. Hart immediately appointed several fellow Republicans to top positions, even before he had received Senate confirmation. Not surprisingly, both senators received protests from Montana Democrats. (Wheeler, even though he had suggested and supported the nominee of a Republican to a plum patronage position, complained that the White House needed to pay closer attention to such issues.) Wheeler nevertheless stood by Hart's appointment, which Murray might have stopped in the Senate by availing himself of the unwritten tradition that permits an individual senator to stop an objectionable home-state appointment, but for whatever reason Murray did not act. When the Senate confirmed Hart by a voice vote—a testament perhaps to Wheeler's influence at the time and Murray's lack thereof—Murray drew criticism in Montana for his inability to influence such an important appointment. The appointment controversies only accelerated over time, reflecting poorly on all the participants, with Murray, as his biographer has written, guilty of "playing politics with the Works Progress Administration in Montana." Hart eventually resigned early in 1936, and Murray and Wheeler buried the hatchet long enough to agree on a new director both found acceptable. But before long Wheeler was complaining again that politics infected the work of the relief agency, and he accused Murray and his family—Murray's sons were active politically—of interfering with both the WPA and the National Youth Administration, particularly in Butte where Wheeler said political interference in the relief effort by the Murray clan left "a stench in the nostrils of decent people of the state." "I think the way politics has been played with the WPA in the state is a scandal," Wheeler complained on the Senate floor. His criticism was directed at both Murray and the Roosevelt administration.[32]

More damage was done to the Wheeler-Murray relationship during the Supreme Court fight in 1937. Murray adopted what his biographer has called an "awkward position," squeezed between his desire to be a Roosevelt loyalist yet not relishing a public feud with Wheeler on a high-profile issue. Murray essentially tried to lie low, quietly supporting Roosevelt's plan to enlarge the court but not once during the long fight speaking publicly on the issue. Wheeler simply wrote Murray off as lacking independence and courage, while Murray quietly fumed that Wheeler was doing everything possible "to embarrass and disrupt the Democratic Party and discredit the President."[33]

Wheeler clashed late that same year with W. D. Murray. Wheeler and the younger Murray shared a platform at a Montana Young Democrats meeting at Butte's Finlen Hotel, and the Supreme Court fight was on both their minds. Murray's remarks offered general criticism of Roosevelt's opponents but without mentioning Wheeler by name. When Wheeler took the podium it was clear he had been stung when he caustically asked, "What the hell are you trying to do, start a fight? If your father wants one I can take care of him in this state." Mike Mansfield, who knew both men, said years later, "Wheeler had a very strained relationship with Jim Murray. They were on opposite sides on many occasions. Murray was a one hundred percent Roosevelt New Dealer."[34]

"We have no Democratic organization in our State," Murray complained in a personal October 1941 letter to the publisher of the *Glasgow Messenger*, not intended for print. "Wheeler never wanted one. He has always had the big head, and thinks he is so big and important that he can be elected without any organization. . . . He has always wanted to play both ends from the middle. He caters to Republicans and has always got the big Republican vote. . . . He caters to the big corporations—Montana Power and the A.C.M.—and always has their support. . . . He succeeded in ousting the Democratic State administration and installed his stooge, Sam Ford. It is about time the people of Montana got next to Wheeler." Having vented his frustration, Murray beseeched the publisher, "It would be unwise to quote me in this matter, so I trust you will keep this letter confidential."[35]

Wheeler and Murray diverged most dramatically on foreign policy issues after 1939. On every major foreign policy issue before Pearl Harbor the Montana senators effectively canceled each other's vote. Their fundamental differences are illustrated by how the two men viewed U.S. support for the Soviet Union. Wheeler's anticommunism became steadily more strident before U.S. entry into the war, and he came to believe that Stalinist Russia presented a threat to the United States nearly equal to Hitler's Germany, while Murray thought accommodation and cooperation with the Soviet Union was possible and ought to be a centerpiece of U.S foreign policy. When Wheeler advocated for the United States to stay out of the war and let the "dictators fight it out," Murray called for closer relations with Stalin's government and praised the Soviet Union as a "young, vigorous, and mighty republic" unlikely to seek territorial expansion in the postwar period. At one point, Murray even praised Lenin in comments reported in a pro-Russian publication.[36]

The Wheeler-Murray feud, as it was often called, continued unabated even after Wheeler left office.

A final Wheeler radio appeal—he called this speech "The Road to War"—had little impact on the Lend-Lease vote. That Roosevelt would prevail had been obvious for some time, but Wheeler knew, as did the White House, that more battles lay ahead. "Mr. Roosevelt can and will likely take us to war if [Lend-Lease] passes," Wheeler said. Hostilities were being foisted on the country, he maintained, because American business interests were agitating for war to preserve "investments in India, Africa and Europe. . . . What hypocrisy! What sham! And you people are urged, through the motion picture, by radio commentators, and through the columns of some papers, to accept it! Are you going to listen to these political and economic royalists or will you heed those Americans who stand for peace?"[37]

The historic Lend-Lease legislation passed the Senate by the anticlimactic vote of 60–31, with Wheeler one of thirteen Democrats voting no. The final vote in the House of Representatives was 317–71. Roosevelt signed the legislation on March 11. Secretary of State Cordell Hull summed up the import of the measure, calling Lend-Lease, "one of the most revolutionary legislative actions in American history," and it was. It also represented, as one diplomatic historian has noted, "a huge step toward war" that skated past existing neutrality provisions in U.S. law and ignored statutes prohibiting loans to belligerents. For good reason the *Economist* called Lend-Lease a "Declaration of Interdependence." On March 24, the first $7 billion was appropriated to finance the initial wave of aid to Britain. Churchill, while recognizing both the practical and symbolic importance of the legislation, still hoped, as he said, "to get [Americans] hooked a little firmer, but they are pretty well on now."[38]

Roosevelt, clearly pleased by the overwhelming congressional support, was nevertheless unforgiving about the personal attacks he had endured from Wheeler and others. A day after signing the Lend-Lease legislation Roosevelt had dinner at the White House with a small group of his closest advisers, including Harry Hopkins, who would manage the logistics of Lend-Lease, and speechwriter Robert Sherwood. After dinner, as Sherwood later recounted in his book *Roosevelt and Hopkins*, Roosevelt began dictating a speech he planned to deliver at the upcoming White House Correspondents' Association dinner. "It was one of the most scathing, most vindictive speeches I have ever heard," Sherwood recorded, as Roosevelt relieved himself of the animus he felt toward Wheeler and others who, Roosevelt believed, had unfairly attacked him. Having vented and cooled off, Roosevelt eventually discarded the blistering speech, but he certainly did not forget or forgive his critics. "The debate unleashed by Lend-Lease did not end with its passage," historians James MacGregor Burns and Susan Dunn write. Indeed the intensity of the prewar debates only increased in the months ahead as the prospect of war became more serious.[39]

While the Lend-Lease Act solved the problem of how Britain would finance the material the United States was now prepared to supply, a practical and vexing question remained: how to get American goods past German U-boats and into British ports. Wheeler and America First leaders were convinced that the next major battle would focus on whether U.S. Navy ships would be used to convoy supplies across the North Atlantic. Some noninterventionists were profoundly discouraged by the prospect of that fight. Robert Wood briefly considered resigning his leadership of America First, convinced that the organization had failed in not stopping Lend-Lease, while Kingman Brewster, one of the early organizers at Yale, did resign, saying that America

First clearly had no ability to influence policy except to obstruct it, adding, "I cannot be part of that effort."[40]

Wheeler was certainly disappointed but not discouraged, and he kept offering alternatives to administration policy and continued criticizing of Roosevelt. Preparing in early April for a national speaking tour organized and paid for by America First, Wheeler cosponsored a Senate resolution calling for a national referendum in advance of any congressional action to deploy U.S. troops outside the Western Hemisphere. The resolution went nowhere. On April 3 he convened an informal conference—all congressional opponents to Lend-Lease were invited—to coordinate strategy for the next fight. In Wheeler's statement after the meeting he expressed hope that "representative citizens who are determined to keep this country from the catastrophe of war will arrange mass meetings, invite speakers to discuss the fallacies back of the arguments for our entry into war, and offset the propaganda of the war-mongers who are urging war upon us for their own selfish reasons." Wheeler would headline many of those mass meetings.[41]

Beginning his nationwide tour with a rally in Detroit on April 7, Wheeler predicted that Roosevelt was on the verge of ordering the navy, as indeed the president was contemplating, to convoy merchant ships across the Atlantic. "I am here to ask you to save your sons from the slaughtering pens of Europe, Africa and Asia by keeping the United States out of a foreign war." The war makers, Wheeler said, "are advocating convoys because they know such a course means war." Those who attended the rally were given envelopes and asked to make a donation to support America First's work.[42]

On April 15 Wheeler was in Denver, where he said two high-profile supporters of Roosevelt's foreign policy—an old nemesis from the Coolidge-era Justice Department, William J. Donovan, and Wendell Willkie, both of whom were representing Roosevelt on missions to Europe—"should be recalled from Europe and returned to their haunts on Wall Street."[43]

In Salt Lake City the next evening Wheeler again attacked the motion picture industry for producing newsreels and feature films that he said were "cleverly directed for passion-arousing effect, and to bring an overwhelming call for convoys." A day later in Spokane, Washington, Wheeler rejected the idea than any U.S. president should try to influence events around the world. The country does not need, he said, "a President of the universe." The American people should grasp, he said, the "chance to keep out of war and save this country as the greatest nation in all the world, a nation that, if we remain at peace, can lead the world out of chaos. And it is an opportunity we will accept." In St. Paul, Minnesota, on April 24, Wheeler forecast, "Britain can't win unless we actually get in," adding, "It looks now like sentiment will never permit that."[44]

Meanwhile, in early April, Roosevelt quietly authorized the navy to prepare for Atlantic convoy duty, just as Wheeler feared he would, but then the president hesitated in implementing the policy. While he never admitted it publicly, it seems clear that Roosevelt had concluded that the United States would eventually enter the war, but having arrived at that conclusion the president remained conflicted about the next steps. Treasury Secretary Morgenthau related that Roosevelt told him that "he wanted to be pushed into the war rather than lead us into it," a sentiment Roosevelt expressed at a cabinet meeting on May 23, when several of his advisors admonished him to declare his intentions more forcefully. "I'm not willing to fire the first shot," Roosevelt responded. With his political radar carefully modulated, Roosevelt was reading the public mood with something approaching scientific precision. In early May, Gallup again asked whether Americans would vote to go to war, and 79 percent of respondents said they would vote to stay out.[45]

Wheeler read the same poll results and sought to keep the debate focused on his best argument—Americans did not want to go to war, even if Roosevelt did. The Hearst newspapers' political columnist George Rothwell Brown, writing in the spring of 1941, said Wheeler had become the most important peace advocate in the country, a worthy successor to the late Senator Borah, delivering "a series of addresses, which must be counted as among the most remarkable crusades in our political annals." While Wheeler possessed little of Borah's eloquence, Brown said he displayed the same "deep sincerity and courageous fighting heart . . . there is an intellectual honesty about him that commands respect." Robert Wood, the America First chairman, agreed, telling Wheeler in early May, "If we win this fight you will be the biggest man in the country and you deserve anything that might be given to you."[46]

———

A huge America First rally in New York's Madison Square Garden on May 23, 1941, was both the high-water mark for the antiwar movement and the largest live audience Wheeler ever addressed. A capacity crowd twenty-two thousand jostled and elbowed its way inside the hall, while as many as fourteen thousand stood in the streets outside listening via loudspeakers. The CBS, Mutual, and NBC networks broadcast speeches by Wheeler, Lindbergh, Norman Thomas, and novelist Kathleen Norris, at the time the country's most popular writer of fiction for women. The *New York Times* featured the rally on its front page, with several photographs, and noted that Wheeler and Lindbergh "received an enthusiastic reception from a standing, cheering, flag-waving crowd when they made their entrance on the platform . . . the ovation continued for five minutes. When it stopped the crowd in the north balcony started a chant, 'We want Lindbergh,' repeated over and over, during which Mr. Lindbergh rose and bowed. Then it began, 'We want Wheeler,' and continued until the Senator rose and waved."[47]

Left to right: Wheeler, aviator Charles A. Lindbergh, novelist Kathleen Norris, and Socialist Party leader Norman Thomas at the May 23, 1941, America First rally in New York City. (*Associated Press*)

Following remarks by the other major speakers, Wheeler took the podium, bathed in a brilliant spotlight. Cutting a striking figure in a cream-colored double-breasted suit and dark bow tie and clutching a half-smoked cigar, Wheeler offered the massive crowd a wide-ranging critique of the "war makers" who were, he said, determined to take the country "into the hell of war."

"I speak to you tonight," Wheeler said, "not as a Democrat—not as a Republican—but as a plain ordinary citizen who is deeply interested in this country of ours. I am here to urge you to muster the courage to fight as you have never fought before—to fight to save your sons from the bloody battlefields of Europe, Asia and Africa—to fight against one-man government in the United States.

"Peace is not a partisan issue—it is an American issue," Wheeler insisted, recounting his speaking tour and visits with "workers in Denver, farmers in Sioux Falls, miners in Butte," while condemning "British imperialists" and what he called the "imaginary threats conjured up by those who want to take us into a jolly war." He continued:

I am afraid that if President Roosevelt repudiates his election pledges to the American people, not to take us into a foreign war, that the American people will lose faith not only in their President but in their government.

I am afraid that if our national debt grows greater and greater we will resort to debt repudiation of inflation. I am afraid that if the President accepts the advice of that little coterie who surround him—most of whom have never faced an electorate, or met a payroll, or tried a lawsuit and many of whom are impractical dreamers—he will wage an undeclared war. And then Constitutional democracy will end.

I am afraid that when American boys return from Singapore, Dong-Dang, Bombay, Dakar and the Red Sea—armless, legless, maimed and insane—and when other American boys return to seek jobs when there are no jobs—they will be embittered and disheartened. Some of them will seek those who said election pledges of peace were mere campaign oratory.

I fear the aftermath of war. A post war period is far more threatening and dangerous to this democracy than any foreign military or naval force. When we enter the conflict we would become at that moment a regimented nation. We as individuals would be subordinated to one person, the Commander in Chief, and to one objective—the waging of war. From such a state democracy could hardly be restored. Our men and women—disillusioned, disheartened and even destroyed mentally and morally—amid economic chaos and social dislocations would turn to the man on horseback. Then, and not before, would there arise little American fuehrers and from them would come the native fuehrer—an American Il Duce, an American Hitler.

Wheeler, repeating the demand he had made since the beginning of the year, called upon Roosevelt to become an international peacemaker, but on this night at least he abandoned his typically hard-line criticism of the president in favor of a moral appeal:

Tonight the warmongers and their satellites demand that President Roosevelt assume leadership of their crusade of blood and destruction. They decry his leadership. Why? Because he has merely taken us to the brink of war. These sordid romanticists—jingoistic journalists and saber-rattling bankers in New York criticize the President for barely keeping his promises. Only war—blood, sweat, tears and destruction—can satisfy their lust.

The workers, the farmers, the business and professional men—people from every walk of American life look to the President for leadership—for another brand of guidance. They are not alone. The people of the world look to Franklin D. Roosevelt. They look to him with upturned faces, with prayers on their lips and hope in their hearts. They see him, a symbol of liberty, a champion of the down-trodden—they see him as their knight, a leader for peace.

These people are realists—they are not dreamers. English mothers, Italian mothers, German mothers know what it is to have sons fighting, killing, destroying. Certainly all thinking people the world over understand the cost and futility of war. They want peace—peace before all the people of the world and civilization are doomed—before they sink in a common grave.

The President of the United States could appeal to the world for peace—he could appeal not to Hitler or to Mussolini or Churchill but to the people of Germany, Italy and England. He could demand that the war makers, the Hitlers of Germany, the Churchills of England and the Knoxes and Stimson[s] step down and out. I believe he could dictate the peace of the world if he would. But first he must rid himself of those war makers who surround him—who refuse to understand the wishes of the people.

And Wheeler invoked the "tremendous power . . . of the United States lent to the cause of peace":

With the destiny of mankind in the balance the time has come to act—to act for a just peace not in the interest of British tories or imperialists, not in the interest of power or land-hungry dictators but in the interest of all the people in the world.

Tonight most of the world is engaged in bloody battle. I ask on behalf of millions that the President of the United States—at the risk of being called an appeaser—appeal to all the people of the world to stop War—now—before it is too late.[48]

Lindbergh, who sat nearby during Wheeler's speech, thought it "one of the best addresses he has yet made." But Newbold Morris, the president of the New York City Council who also attended the rally, had a much different reaction. In a letter to the *Times* Morris said the crowd reminded him of an earlier Madison Square Garden rally for the pro-Nazi German American Bund. "In 1938, George Washington was their patron saint . . . now they are using Senator Wheeler and he doesn't seem to mind."[49]

Anne Morrow Lindbergh sat between Wheeler and Alice Roosevelt Longworth at a pre-rally dinner at the Waldorf-Astoria Hotel and recorded in her diary:

[Wheeler] talks all the time—a nice slow drawl. He just radiates a healthy American confidence, courage, and taking-it-in-stride. I like him very much and trust him. He has integrity, like C[harles].

He tells me, I mustn't let it get under my skin (the criticism) and he tells about all the things they've said of him in different campaigns—how he was slandered, chased out of town, defeated, smeared. And of his wife sticking by him, urging him on, never minding. "If you can stand it, I can." There is a wonderful pride in him about his wife.

American—American—American, I kept feeling as I talked to him.

Anne Morrow Lindbergh also recorded her observations of Lulu Wheeler, who also attended the dinner and rally. "Mrs. Wheeler—blonde, overdressed (a little), nice, honest, loyal, outspoken, 'American.' I liked her, too." Not surprisingly, Lindbergh's wife said she favored her husband's speech over Wheeler's, but she offered warm praise for the Montanan's character. "I felt he had the makings of a great leader in him," she wrote. "His intellect and his emotions are blended. And there is a cord between him and the people, a confidence. He is rooted in the people. I felt better about America when he stopped speaking. The basic emotion in him is love and not hate. Although he exudes an American confidence he is, I think, without personal vanity."[50]

―――――

As early as the spring of 1940, Franklin Roosevelt and many of his advisors had come to regard Wheeler, Lindbergh, and other of the most outspoken nonintervention-ists as not simply misguided critics of administration policy but also adherents to beliefs that were disloyal, un-American, indeed borderline treason. In response the administration mounted an aggressive campaign to discredit Wheeler, a campaign that in its use of the FBI bears resemblance to the bureau's efforts to frame Wheeler during the Daugherty investigation nearly a generation earlier. Roosevelt's personal and persistent demands that the FBI act in effect as the White House intelligence service was strongly conditioned by his desire to smear his opponents and call into question their loyalty.

In May 1940, FBI director Hoover, with the backing and encouragement of the White House, began widespread surveillance of Roosevelt's critics, including Wheeler. It bears noting that, at the time the FBI surveillance began, Wheeler was still a serious candidate for president. William Sullivan, for more than thirty years a top FBI official, later confirmed that the bureau tapped Lindbergh's phone (Wheeler's was likely tapped too), and FBI informants spied on members of Wheeler's family. Roosevelt and others in the White House issued broad instructions, Sullivan said, to investigate the activities of those opposing the administration's foreign policy, not unlike how later "administrations had the FBI look into those opposing the conflict in Vietnam."[51]

FBI surveillance, particularly of America First activity, increased dramatically during the congressional fight over Lend-Lease when White House press secretary Stephen Early requested an FBI report on the committee. Hoover also sent a "personal and confidential" memorandum by "special messenger" to Roosevelt's chief of staff, Major General Edwin "Pa" Watson, in February 1941 reporting on the activities of

Wheeler's son John. Hoover's memo, identifying young Wheeler as "Chairman of the America First Committee of Los Angeles," reported that Wheeler and his wife had been present at a party where persons with German names "who are under investigation by this Bureau" were also in attendance. John's wife, Helene Albright Wheeler, according to Hoover's memo, attacked the "contemplated Lend Lease Bill" in a fashion that "indicated she had become imbued with pro-German sentiment."[52]

In a March 1941 memo, labeled by Hoover "strictly confidential," the director reported that the America First Committee would undertake national tours "for the purpose of opposing any plans that the President might have in bringing this country into war." "Apparently," Hoover reported, "there are sufficient funds on hand to complete this program. General Robert Wood and Senator Burton K. Wheeler are to be known as leaders of this plan." Hoover's "strictly confidential" information was hardly a state secret. America First and Wheeler activities were reported on a near-daily basis in most major U.S. newspapers, and any FBI agent able to read and clip an article could have assembled a good deal of the "intelligence" the bureau routinely passed on to the White House. But reading and clipping newspapers was not the extent of FBI surveillance.[53]

Douglas Charles, a historian of the FBI's activities in this period, concludes that the bureau's surveillance of Wheeler, Lindbergh, Senator Gerald Nye, and others was essentially political in nature, aimed at advancing the administration's congressional and foreign policy goals, and had little if anything to do with national security or the loyalty of those under surveillance. The bureau's efforts, Charles says, sanctioned at the highest level of the administration and directly involving the president, used a variety of tactics, including "informers, illegal wiretaps, illegal trespass, mail covers, [and] official investigations." Agents "perused organizations' private files; collected derogatory intelligence; provided public opinion leaders with FBI-obtained political intelligence (using blind memoranda); likely liaised with British intelligence about the anti-interventionists; and sought to develop cases against them that would have discredited their efforts in the courts. Hoover also recommended to his superiors the use of the grand jury that, despite its work being technically secret, would invariably draw public attention through leaks to create pressure that would serve to cast doubt on the legitimacy of the president's critics." As historian Wayne S. Cole bluntly concludes, "President Roosevelt was not reticent in trying to use government investigative and legal powers to crush isolationists."[54]

Roosevelt attempted to employ "the loyalty issue" against Wheeler early in 1941 by invoking, rather bizarrely, a comment in the diary of a deceased former U.S. ambassador to Germany. During his time in Berlin from 1933 to 1937, William Dodd kept a regular diary that would be posthumously published at about the time the Lend-Lease debate galvanized the country. One diary entry refers to a February 1935 dinner Dodd said he attended while on a visit to Washington, D.C. A member of Roosevelt's "brain trust," Rexford Tugwell, who was then serving as assistant secretary of agriculture, hosted the dinner at his home. Dodd recorded that a "certain well-known senator," later identified as Wheeler by Dodd's son, who edited his father's diary, bitterly denounced Roosevelt during the dinner. Wheeler and Dodd also reportedly exchanged sharp words over the recent Senate defeat of legislation that would have authorized U.S. participation in the World Court. That legislation had been backed by Roosevelt and opposed by Wheeler. Dodd noted in his dairy that he told the unnamed senator that U.S. rejection of the World Court would surely lead to another war. The day after the dinner, while visiting Roosevelt at the White House, Dodd apparently reported the gist of the dinner conversation to the president, who, it seems, filed the story away for future use. The opportunity came nearly six years later. During one of his regular news conferences, and apparently relying on his memory for the details, Roosevelt recalled that Dodd had indeed told him of this conversation and that the dissident senator had been Wheeler. As he bantered with reporters, Roosevelt confirmed that Dodd had told him that Wheeler expressed a belief that Nazi domination of Europe was "inevitable." A reporter pressed Roosevelt on the word "inevitable." Had Wheeler really said he "favored" Nazi domination, the reporter asked, or had he simply said it was "inevitable?"

"Well, what does one do if he has made up his mind that a thing is inevitable?" Roosevelt replied. "That's a pretty comprehensive word—the word 'inevitable.'"[55]

The *Chicago Tribune* reported the exchange the next day under the headline "President Aids Attempt to Tag Wheeler as Nazi." As the newspaper reported, "The President today was obviously trying to pin a pro-Nazi tag on Wheeler although he insisted that the newsmen do the talking and that he would merely confirm it. When a reporter told the President that the word 'inevitable' did not necessarily mean that Wheeler favored such domination, the President asked the reporter what the word 'inevitable' meant and added that the thought it was a pretty broad word." Roosevelt also claimed that Dodd had told him that Wheeler believed the security of the United States, in the event of Nazi domination of Europe, rested with the U.S. "taking over—Canada and Mexico and the five Central American Republics," a comment that, given Wheeler's long history of opposition to military intervention in the region, seems unlikely.[56]

Wheeler was deeply offended by Roosevelt's bantering with reporters and denounced as absolutely false "this slanderous attack on me—attributed to a dead man." He denied even having been at the dinner Dodd described in his diary and said Roosevelt had resorted to "a desperate attempt to discredit me because I stand unalterably for American peace and against the entry of the United States into any foreign war." It was also reported that Virginia senator Carter Glass had attended the

Tugwell-hosted dinner, but Glass denied his attendance too, saying, "I never was in the home of Rex Tugwell in my life." Journalist John Franklin Carter, who did attend the dinner, recorded his own account of the events. Carter thought Wheeler and Dodd had simply demonstrated "that there was complete irreconcilability between the Wheeler nationalistic view and the Dodd internationalist view. Each believed that his way was the way to prevent war and that the other way would involve us in war." Tugwell, who by 1941 was no longer part of the Roosevelt administration, issued his own statement confirming that the dinner had taken place but said, "As a host, I am of course unable to repeat any of the conversation." The fact that an unspecific six-year-old anecdote in the diary of a dead former diplomat could spark such a sharp exchange illustrates how poisonous the political atmosphere had become between Roosevelt and Wheeler. Neither man displayed any tolerance of the other's position, with Roosevelt making little effort to distinguish between principled dissent and actual disloyalty and Wheeler regularly labeling his opponents, including the president, as warmongers.[57]

In the bitter contest to shape public and congressional opinion during 1941, Franklin Roosevelt had significant advantages over his opponents. Roosevelt possessed the ultimate bully pulpit and was able, as the Dodd diary incident illustrated, to command public attention at any time. Additionally, many of the most influential voices in the American press, encouraged by a sophisticated public information campaign managed from the White House, either endorsed the president's policies or saw little merit in the position of the noninterventionists. No one enjoyed a larger national following or did more to assail Roosevelt's opponents than Walter Winchell, the wildly popular columnist and radio personality who displayed a particular loathing for Wheeler.[58]

"Calling Winchell a mere gossip writer is like calling Lindbergh a mere aviator or Gene Tunney a mere prizefighter," the New Yorker said in a 1940 profile of the celebrity columnist and broadcaster. By one estimate fifty million Americans—a significant percentage of adults in the country—tuned into Winchell's weekly radio show or read his syndicated column that appeared in hundreds of newspapers. Winchell developed his considerable influence by virtue of what one observer called the "largest continuous audience ever possessed by a man who was neither politician nor divine." Winchell's approach to the news, gossipy items about celebrities with a sprinkling of caustic opinions about items from the headlines, was among the earliest examples of "journalism as entertainment, celebrity gossip as news, opinion-making as reportage."[59]

A "genius of resentment" by one account, Winchell was a relative latecomer to the interventionist cause, but once he embraced Roosevelt's view of how to support Britain he embraced it fully. "Appeasement has taught America its lesson," Winchell opined in 1940. "We know now that a nation that gives up an inch of its soil gives up all of its soul . . . a nation which appeases insult abroad—will suffer outrage at home." As his biographer Neal Gabler has written, Winchell used his radio and newspaper platform to aggressively push "a military buildup and a two-ocean navy but, clearly acting with the administration's blessing, confronted Congress itself, challenging those senators and representatives who opposed the buildup." Wheeler was a favorite target.[60]

Winchell went after the Montana senator both directly and indirectly. The two men, Gabler writes, "jousted for months, Walter calling Wheeler an obstructionist who would prevent America from defending itself, Wheeler calling Walter an 'alarmist' who advocated that the country 'immediately join the Allies and help them not only in materials, but that we actually get into the war.'" Wheeler became convinced that Winchell was, at minimum, a well-placed, sympathetic, pro-British mouthpiece closely coordinating his opinions with British propaganda efforts in the United States. More likely, Wheeler believed, Winchell was on the British government's payroll. His suspicions were not completely far-fetched. Ernest Cuneo, a longtime Winchell friend, legal advisor, and ghostwriter, also served as a liaison between British intelligence agents in the United States and the Roosevelt administration during the period when Winchell was regularly accosting Wheeler in print or over the air. Cuneo's relationships with the administration—he worked for the Democratic National Committee in the 1930s—as well as his contacts with British officials gave him access to newsworthy items that he passed along for Winchell's use. The information often came directly from British intelligence operatives determined to advance Britain's interests before a U.S. audience.[61]

Cuneo compared the verbal brawling between Wheeler and Winchell to a fight among longshoremen, as brutal as any between a news commentator and a politician. Cuneo also believed that Winchell's full-throated defense of American intervention, combined with Winchell's contention that certain noninterventionists, Wheeler prominently among them, were disloyal Americans, helped grow public support for Roosevelt's foreign policy. Wheeler, in turn, attempted to make Winchell the issue, saying the broadcaster was "blitzkrieging the American people into this war." Blunting the impact in Montana of Winchell's harsh attacks, Wheeler received timely help from his broadcaster friend Ed Craney. Winchell's weekly radio program was simply taken off the air at Craney's stations after Winchell's criticism of Wheeler became routine.[62]

Wheeler engaged in several other high-profile press feuds, including clashes with New York Herald-Tribune columnist Dorothy Thompson, a fierce critic of Nazi Germany and an advocate of closer cooperation between the United States and Britain. Thompson's three-times-a-week "On the Record" column was syndicated in 150 newspapers, and she appeared regularly on NBC radio. The columnist's popularity and impact

Dorothy Thompson, popular syndicated columnist and
radio commentator, leaving the White House after visiting
President Roosevelt in May 1940. A frequent critic of
Wheeler's foreign policy positions, Thompson was also close
to First Lady Eleanor Roosevelt. (*Library of Congress Prints
and Photographs Division, Washington, D.C.*)

were such that in 1939 *Time* called her the second most influential woman in the
country behind Eleanor Roosevelt. Thompson was a political analyst, the magazine
said, who "appealed to women because she wrote like a woman," and appealed to
men "because, for a woman, she seemed [to them] surprisingly intelligent." The *Time*
profile claimed that powerful men were known to quake in Thompson's presence. In
a 1941 column datelined London and under the headline "The Unexplainable Senator
Wheeler," Thompson wrote: "Now, I do not believe Senator Wheeler is a traitor or that
he wishes anything but the best of fortune for the United States. He is only a stubborn,
bitterly resentful man, provincial in outlook, abysmally ignorant of world policies and
absolutely convinced that he is trying to spare the country of the terrors of war. Even
the Nazis do not count on Senator Wheeler as reliable in their councils. They merely
count him as useful." Thompson said Wheeler was not the type of leader the Nazis

wanted to come to power in the United States because Wheeler was, as she correctly said, "opposed to concentrations of the power of supertrusts, economic consolidations or dictatorship." The real danger in Wheeler's views, Thompson concluded, was that he advocated "no foreign policy at all."[63]

Wheeler, Nye, and other noninterventionists found Thompson so stridently pro-British that they publically suggested that she be investigated to determine whether she was operating as a British agent. The columnist complained to J. Edgar Hoover about the accusations and appealed for help in heading off what she called "a program of abuse and vilification" by Wheeler and other "ostriches" in Congress. Whether Hoover took any action on her request is not clear.[64]

Wheeler's criticism that carefully disseminated British "propaganda" regularly found its way into news columns, radio broadcasts, and Hollywood films was widely dismissed at the time, but he was more correct than not. The British government did establish, as historian Nicholas John Cull has documented, "a network of middlemen ... seemingly unconnected with the British to place stories and some twenty rumors each day with the 'leading home reporters on the New York and Chicago papers' and such commentators as Dorothy Thompson [and] Walter Winchell."[65]

Cull's research into British propaganda efforts in the United States prior to and during World War II relied on British government documents and firsthand recollections that detail a massive, sophisticated, and "concerted British propaganda policy," the evidence of which, "after the war, the British government seems to have tried to destroy." The "British Political Warfare Executive," created in July 1941 as part of the British Foreign Office, focused on disseminating "subversive propaganda" aimed at influencing columnists, editors, politicians, and even the White House. "The full effort," Cull has written, "stands as one of the most diverse, extensive, and yet subtle propaganda campaigns ever directed by one sovereign state at another." A clear subtext of the British campaign, which also mirrored the Roosevelt administration's essential message about the noninterventionist movement, was that Wheeler and others of like mind were hopeless appeasers doing, consciously or unconsciously, the bidding of Nazi Germany, while encouraging the growth of a domestic pro-fascist movement that was a danger to the United States.[66]

The avalanche of criticism directed at noninterventionists was unrelenting. The *New York Post*, for example, compared Wheeler to Benedict Arnold and noted that his comments opposing U.S. naval assistance to Britain-bound Atlantic convoys would "fulfill the hopes of Berlin" and would be applauded by the pro-Nazi German-American Bund. The legendary editor of Greenville, Mississippi, *Delta Democrat-Times*, Hodding Carter II, while chastising those who questioned Wheeler's loyalty, still referred to Wheeler as "a badly misguided man, but an honest one." Carter thought Wheeler was "way off base in his personal feud with the President," but not disloyal, while CBS correspondent Eric Sevareid called Wheeler an "irresponsible man" whose criticism of Roosevelt had made him "a sort of opposition president."[67]

As historian Wayne Cole notes: "In addition to the verbal attacks, the America First Committee and its leaders were the victims of discrimination and pressure. . . . [T]he Committee [often] found it difficult or impossible to secure public buildings or parks in which to hold mass meetings. The city council of Charlotte, North Carolina, expressed its feelings by changing the name of Lindbergh Drive to Avon Avenue. Economic pressure was brought to bear on some Committee supporters. A few lost jobs or found it difficult to secure new ones because of their noninterventionist activities."[68] In San Diego the city council divided four to two over whether to allow the use of the Balboa Park amphitheater for an America First rally. Councilman Al Flowers strongly dissented from the majority that voted to allow the meeting to go forward. "They're [America First] tearing down our government and they ought to be in a concentration camp," Flowers said. "Not on your tintype will I vote to let them use the park bowl or a city building owned by the people." Councilman Fred Simpson agreed. "Both Lindy and Wheeler are doing this country irreparable damage, and I'm against it," he said.[69]

One particularly odious assault on America First came from a group calling itself Friends of Democracy, a self-described "non-partisan, non-sectarian, non-profit, anti-totalitarian propaganda agency." In the wake of the Lend-Lease debate the group distributed a pamphlet titled "The America First Committee: The Nazi Transmission Belt." The pamphlet declared that America First was "a Nazi front! It is a transmission belt by means of which the apostles of Nazism are spreading their antidemocratic ideas into millions of American homes!" While claiming not to "question the integrity of the leadership and membership of America First," statements by Senators Wheeler and Nye were run side by side with quotes from Hitler's speeches. The group's leader, Leon M. Birkhead, a former Unitarian minister, contended that America First was "run by very naïve, simpleminded people."[70]

During his national speaking tour Wheeler also received several credible personal threats, including one in advance of an appearance in Rockford, Illinois, in April. In a letter signed by "A Citizens Committee of 100 Per Cent Americans," Wheeler was issued "a timely warning . . . as you schedule your address in this city: A number of us citizens have discussed and decided that our city is not disposed to listen to your poisonous, anti-Roosevelt, anti-American traitorous fifth column activities. If you set foot anywhere near here . . . well, you shall have no one to blame for what might happen to you—and other copperheads trailing you." Wheeler spoke as planned in Rockford, and the event came off without incident, perhaps because, as the *Chicago Tribune* reported, nine local police officers were assigned to protect Wheeler.[71]

———

In a "fireside chat" national radio talk on May 27, Roosevelt seemed almost to heed Wheeler's warnings against the navy undertaking convoy duty in the North Atlantic. Instead of announcing a new policy, Roosevelt merely amended the "limited" national emergency he had proclaimed in 1939 to declare that now an "unlimited" emergency existed, still an unprecedented declaration by an American president. America First's Robert Wood hailed the president's speech as "the least warlike of any of his utterances since the election. It bears unmistakable evidence that he has begun to listen to the American people." Wheeler, however, remained skeptical, warning during a speech in Indianapolis that Roosevelt was echoing "the sentiments of the war makers—our Rockefellers, Morgans, Dorothy Thompsons, Stimsons, Knox[e]s, Walter Winchells," the people ready to "plunge this Nation into war either because of their hate or fear of the little paperhanger from Berlin." A day after Roosevelt's speech, and during a rally in Washington, D.C., sponsored by the Keep America Out of War Congress, another antiwar group, Wheeler complained that Congress had become merely a rubber stamp for the administration's foreign policy and "might as well go home." Congress, he said, "is now just a sounding board for President Roosevelt, almost the same as the Reichstag is for Hitler."[72]

———

The war continued to go badly for Britain in mid-1941, and the U.S. foreign policy debate further intensified. German troops entered Athens in late April, foreshadowing the eventual British defeat on Crete. The Luftwaffe continued murderous night-time raids on British cities, including a raid on London that damaged the House of Commons. German U-boats and surface raiders had by mid-1941 sent 900,000 tons of allied shipping to the bottom of the Atlantic. Sixty-eight British merchant ships were lost to enemy action in February alone. Roosevelt, knowing that U.S. ships and sailors were now regularly in harm's way, warned that "unless the advance of Hitler is checked now, the Western Hemisphere will be within range of the Nazi weapons of destruction." Declaring an "unlimited" national emergency required, the president said, "the strengthening of our defenses to the extreme limit of our national power and authority," yet Roosevelt remained unwilling, as he told his cabinet, to be seen as the aggressor.[73]

On May 21 a dramatic incident, illustrating how close the nation was to war, occurred in the South Atlantic when a German U-boat torpedoed and sank the SS *Robin Moor*, a merchant freighter flying the U.S. flag and bound for South Africa. It was the first time a U.S. ship had been sunk by the German navy. There was no loss of life, but the crew suffered greatly, bobbing about in lifeboats on the open sea for two

Clifford Berryman cartoon from the *Washington Star*, May 1941. Navy
Secretary Frank Knox, Secretary of War Henry L. Stimson, and former
presidential candidate Wendell Willkie, all Republicans, bucked leaders of
their own party—and Democrats like Wheeler—and called for decisive
action in supporting war-ravaged Britain. (*Library of Congress Prints and
Photographs Division, Washington, D.C.*)

weeks before being rescued. The sinking of the *Robin Moor* indicated the inevitability
of similar incidents in the future and, as Wheeler knew, offered dramatic evidence that
an undeclared war had begun at sea. Harold Ickes, for one, urged action that would
get the county "into this war somehow, by hook or crook," but he concluded that "the
President didn't have the nerve" to go through with actions that would precipitate
open hostilities. Instead, in a June 20 statement to Congress, Roosevelt condemned
the sinking of the freighter as the "act of an international outlaw," contending that
Hitler had taken "a first step in assertion of the supreme purpose of the German Reich
to seize control of the high seas."[74]

Wheeler's statement reacting to Roosevelt's message was dismissive. "It was just
another bitter and warlike diatribe against Germany. No one can defend German
treatment of the survivors," Wheeler said. "It was cruel—but the President did not
tell the American people that 70% of the *Robin Moor*'s cargo was contraband of war

and—as such—was subject to seizure or destruction by belligerents." The America First Committee's statement on the incident insisted that Roosevelt's call for "freedom of the seas" was actually a demand to "help one country at war defeat another." Echoing much the same message, Wheeler said, "It was apparent that the President was trying to arouse the war spirit of the American people."[75]

Americans awoke to more shocking news on June 22—Hitler's invasion of Russia. The *New York Times* reported that "the outbreak of war between Germany and Russia appeared . . . to have made American isolationists more isolationist than ever and American interventionists more convinced than ever that their views were right." Wheeler commented on the developments while in Dubuque, Iowa, where he was delivering yet another speech. The German invasion was "a favorable development for America," Wheeler said, since it would likely "forestall actual participation" in the fighting by the United States. "Now we can just let Joe Stalin and the other dictators fight it out."[76]

During a June 25 speech in Hartford, Connecticut, Wheeler went even further. The European war was not, he said, "a war to make the world safe for democracy" but rather a fight between "Nazi Germany and Fascist Italy" on the one hand and "Imperialist Britain and Communistic Russia" on the other. By lumping all the belligerents together Wheeler attempted again to explain the war as just the latest chapter in the old saga of European great power politics, a simple case of economic and military competition pitting rival empires against one another. The United States had no business being involved and simply had to keep its distance. Wheeler's comments incensed the easily incensed Harold Ickes, who recorded in his diary that Wheeler "was particularly nasty" in implying that Roosevelt and Churchill were "sleeping in the same bed with Stalin." But before long the United States was providing Lend-Lease assistance to Stalin's hard-pressed Red Army.[77]

Writing to Robert Wood on July 1, Wheeler was uncharacteristically upbeat. "I think the sentiment is growing in our favor, and the President knows it," Wheeler wrote. "They would like to create the impression that [war] is inevitable, and are doing everything they can along that line, but the people are just not fooled by the Cabinet members, and are just not going to war, if they can prevent it."[78]

That same day Wheeler demanded the resignation or impeachment of one of those cabinet members, Navy Secretary Frank Knox, who had argued in a speech that U.S. policy in the Atlantic ought to be to shoot at German naval vessels on sight, a comment that may well have been a trial balloon for what Roosevelt was contemplating. Wheeler said that Knox had gone back on a pledge made a year earlier that the United States would offer only moral and economic aid to Britain. By advocating military action, Knox had completely reversed position. The America First Committee called for

Knox's resignation on July 12, saying the navy secretary had acted unconstitutionally in advocating a naval war in the Atlantic without approval of Congress. Lulu Wheeler, continuing to devote time and energy to committee work, said she agreed with many America First supporters who were not only demanding Knox's resignation but that of the president too. Yet she admitted to her daughter, "Your father thinks it is a little premature to start on the President." Roosevelt ignored the clamor about Knox, and the controversy quickly subsided.[79]

On July 3 Wheeler was on the attack again. This time his target was the army chief of staff, General George Marshall, who formally asked Congress to extend the term of service for those drafted under the 1940 conscription legislation. Marshall also asked Congress to end restrictions prohibiting U.S. military deployment beyond the Western Hemisphere. Wheeler immediately condemned the request and, relying on his well-placed sources in the military, said he had reliable information indicating that Roosevelt had already secretly decided to order U.S. military occupation of Iceland, with U.S. troops scheduled to ship out July 23 or July 24. Wheeler's public discussion of apparently sensitive national security information, including details about troop movements, prompted Roosevelt's press secretary to suggest that Wheeler had put the lives of American servicemen at risk. Criticism of Wheeler was again searing, even after it became clear that the movement of U.S. troops had been completed before Wheeler publically commented on the deployment to Iceland. "I have always disagreed with Senator Wheeler's views on foreign affairs, but until now I tried to think of him as a sincere but misguided American," said the Episcopal bishop of Cincinnati, the Right Reverend Henry W. Hobson, who chaired the strongly interventionist Fight for Freedom group. Wheeler's disclosure of the Iceland occupation, Hobson said, "obliged me to change my mind."[80]

While the Senate debated extending the terms of draftees—Wheeler tried to change the administration's bill to encourage voluntarily enlistments and ultimately voted against the legislation just as he had in 1940—controversy arose over the use of his Senate franking privileges, and again Wheeler was accused of damaging the nation's military preparedness. This controversy dated to early July when General Marshall received letters from a handful of active-duty military personnel protesting a postcard mailing the soldiers received from Wheeler. The America First Committee paid for the printing of the postcards that urged Americans to "write today to President Roosevelt, at the White House, in Washington, that you are against our entry into the European war." The cards were signed "Senator Burton K. Wheeler." The message side of the card reprinted Roosevelt's "no-foreign-war" pledge from the end of the 1940 campaign, as well as quotes from Lindbergh, former president Hoover, former ambassador Joseph P. Kennedy, Wheeler, and Nye.[81]

Using Wheeler's Senate franking privilege, the postcards were sent to more than a million addresses from a list that included names from Wheeler's own correspondence file as well as a commercial list maintained by a former Democratic National Committee operative. It was later revealed that the commercial list contained the names of several active-duty military personnel, and at least two of them complained to Marshall about what they considered the inappropriate nature of the mailing. Assuming the worst regarding Wheeler's motives, Secretary of War Stimson concluded that Wheeler was trying to influence congressional debate on the draft extension legislation by purposely targeting the mailing to military personnel. This possibility worried Marshall and enraged the secretary of war, who wanted to confront Wheeler publicly but, before doing so, checked with Roosevelt. The president, unsurprisingly, sanctioned a broadside. Roosevelt urged Stimson to say that Wheeler's action "came very near the line of treason." Stimson went immediately to the press, telling reporters that Wheeler's postcards "necessarily have the effect of impairing . . . discipline and impairing our defense against danger which now confronts the country. Without expressing legal opinions I will simply say that I think this comes very near the line of subversive activities against the United States, if not treason."[82]

Predictably Wheeler responded in kind, making it clear that the mailing had been sent before the draft extension legislation had even been proposed. Wheeler also asked, "Has [it] come to pass in the United States that we cannot oppose legislation affecting millions of people without being accused by some Cabinet officer of being guilty of treason or carrying on subversive activities?" Refusing to let anyone, particularly a Republican internationalist like Stimson, question his loyalty, Wheeler called on the secretary of war to resign since "everyone in Washington knows that the old gentleman [Stimson was seventy-three] is unable to carry on the duties of his office, and some go so far as to say that he has reached the point where—to use the expression of a Britisher—he is ga-ga." Wheeler said that he would do everything in his power "to keep Mr. Stimson from sending our boys to the bloody battlefields of Europe, Africa and Asia." The New York Times blasted the "indiscretion" of Wheeler's mailing, which if not immediately checked, the paper said, would "lend aid and comfort to the enemies of the United States." Stimson, however, would serve with distinction and remarkable energy at the War Department throughout World War II and not resign until September 1945.[83]

Roosevelt also pounced, telling reporters that he agreed with Stimson's sentiments—after all, he had suggested Stimson's key talking point—as well as with the Times editorial. This time Wheeler had gone too far, Roosevelt said. Privately, at a cabinet meeting, Roosevelt was considerably more pointed. Ickes recorded in his diary that Roosevelt was "all worked up" about Wheeler's mailing. "The President was worried about Wheeler's activities," Ickes wrote, "and it was suggested that some people ought to be sent out to answer his speeches." Ickes thought it unfortunate that nothing of substance came of the cabinet discussion beyond Roosevelt's venting of steam. "The President has indicated on more than one occasion that he would like to see Wheeler answered," Ickes remembered, "but he not only does nothing about it himself, he is reluctant to have anyone else do anything about it." Ickes was ignoring the fact that Roosevelt and many others had been answering Wheeler but perhaps was also expressing frustration that the response from the administration and its friends in the press had neither tempered nor silenced Wheeler's criticism.[84]

Wheeler said his only regret about the incident was that his postcard would not reach the mailbox of "every mother in the United States." He defended his conduct on the Senate floor, he said, because Stimson sought to deprive him of "freedom of speech and freedom of petition." Furthermore, the secretary of war and his allies in the press had "created the utterly false and spurious impression that I have circulated this franked card principally among selectees [draftees], and that it encouraged these American boys to resist any attempt to keep them in service over a year." Wheeler went on:

> If it is near treason to send out these cards, then every floor speech against war that is made by any Senator on the floor of the Senate and published in a newspaper makes him guilty of near treason. If any man over the radio makes a speech saying that we ought to keep out of war, and the speech happens to be heard by some man in an Army camp, or read in a newspaper, then in Mr. Stimson's opinion the speaker is guilty of near treason.... Which is treasonable—to plunge this country into a disastrous and ruinous war, resulting in the death of perhaps millions of American boys, or to try to maintain peace and democracy in the United States? If when we are at peace we are to be denounced as guilty of treason, or near treason, what would happen after a declaration of war?
>
> Which is subversive—to deny freedom of speech, press and petition or to maintain our civil liberties guaranteed by the Constitution of the United States?
>
> Apparently Mr. Stimson believes that war and the suppression of constitutional government constitute a mark of patriotism. I do not.[85]

As Wheeler returned to his seat, a number of his colleagues rose to offer him support. "For God's sake," fumed Republican Hiram Johnson, "have we reached such a point in this Government that there can be no right of petition to the duly constituted authorities in the land?" Johnson, growing emotional, said to Wheeler, "Stick to it, Brother Wheeler. Stand up; stand out. Never mind how many are with you; never mind who is with you; stand up; there will be at least one with you in the fight.... I am proud of you today, and every man of us should say, 'Hurrah for Wheeler!'"

As the *Congressional Record* noted, there were "manifestations of applause in the galleries" as Johnson finished his comments. Millard Tydings, the Maryland Democrat, said he disagreed with Wheeler on foreign policy but considered him "one of the outstanding men of this body. . . . He ranks well with the outstanding men who have served the Nation in the Senate throughout all its history." Michigan Republican Arthur Vandenberg said he rose "to present my compliments to the distinguished, militant senior Senator from Montana . . . he represents not the seeds of treason, but the preservation of the democratic process under the Stars and Stripes." Republicans Henrik Shipstead of Minnesota (who had been a Farmer-Labor senator but was reelected in 1940 as a Republican), C. Wayland "Curly" Brooks of Illinois, and Robert La Follette Jr. of Wisconsin joined Democrats David I. Walsh of Massachusetts and Dennis Chavez of New Mexico in praising Wheeler for his political courage and rejecting any allegation that he was involved in treasonous activity. Even Majority Leader Barkley, the administration's chief spokesman in the Senate and diametrically opposed to Wheeler on foreign policy issues, felt compelled to acknowledge Wheeler as "one of the ablest and one of the most courageous men in the Senate or the United States or in public life."[86]

Stimson would later describe Wheeler's response as "hot," but Wheeler's comments, as well as the support he received from Senate colleagues, caused Stimson to question whether his allegations had been completely fair. Concluding that he had been wrong, and ignoring the advice of advisers, Stimson issued a public apology. "On the basis of Senator Wheeler's statement in the Senate as to the time and method of the issuance of his circular, I believe that he has shown the absence of any intent on his part to circularize the soldiers in the training camps." Stimson blamed "incomplete information" for causing him to launch his attack, and, of course, he did not mention that Franklin Roosevelt had encouraged him.[87]

Wheeler deemed the apology "a very decent thing for [Stimson] to do," while the *New York Times* wrote off the controversy as "a mistake, made in the heat of debate and best forgotten by all concerned." Officials with the America First Committee (AFC) believed the franking controversy was an orchestrated effort by the administration to draw attention from more important issues. As historian Justus Doenecke has noted, "Page Hufty, AFC director of organization, accused Stimson of attempting to divert public attention from Wheeler's accusation that thousands of American troops had been landed in Suez," a development that the committee subsequently disclosed in one of its regular bulletins. Nonetheless, Hufty told America First chapters to remove the names of all military personnel from the files. Hufty underscored the directive by adding, "As you know America First has always been strongly in favor of adequate national defense and believes that a high morale among the personnel of the armed forces is vital."[88]

While most of the attention in Washington and the nation during the first half of 1941 had been directed toward the war in Europe, in late July developments in Asia assumed new urgency when Roosevelt, responding to new aggressive steps by imperial Japan, froze Japanese assets in the United States, in effect imposing a crippling trade embargo. Additionally the Panama Canal was closed to Japanese shipping, and General Douglas MacArthur was recalled to active duty and placed in command of U.S. and Philippine forces. Uncharacteristically, Wheeler found himself in agreement with Roosevelt's actions. "I think the President did the right thing," Wheeler told reporters. "You may say for me that I agree with him—for the first time." Wheeler said he believed an appropriate U.S. response to an increasingly volatile situation in Asia was to simply quit trading with Japan, but he also worried that war was now more likely with Japan than with Germany. If war did come about in the Far East, Wheeler said, it would be about "preserving the British domination of Asia rather than helping the United States." Britain had vital interests in Asia, he said, and the United States did not, but "only when British possessions and interests are vitally affected does the Administration seem to be greatly concerned about the Orient."[89]

Had Wheeler been able to anticipate the response of Japanese political and military leaders he might well have opposed Roosevelt's policy in Asia, just as he did in Europe. By the end of the summer of 1941, Japan could count on only eighteen months of oil reserves, a realization profoundly impacting strategic thinking within the Japanese high command, which had already begun planning an attack on the U.S. Pacific fleet.[90]

On September 4 the "incident" Roosevelt had long believed was a prerequisite to a further change in U.S. policy regarding convoys occurred off the coast of Iceland. A British aircraft on patrol duty informed the U.S. destroyer *Greer* by radio signal—the destroyer was operating in international waters—that a German submarine, U-652, *had* been spotted ten miles ahead of the American ship. The British plane and the American destroyer proceeded to shadow the U-boat and eventually four depth charges were dropped from the plane. The attack was unsuccessful, and, low on fuel, the plane broke off contact. The *Greer*, meanwhile, continued to stalk the submarine, and two hours later the German captain surfaced his U-boat and fired two torpedoes, both missing the destroyer. The *Greer* responded—the first U.S. warship to fire on a German vessel—with eight more depth charges, and then, after one or perhaps two more torpedoes were fired, the *Greer* dropped eleven additional depth charges. A short time later both vessels broke off the engagement, and each slipped away unharmed.[91]

Pulitzer Prize–winning cartoonist Rollin Kirby depicted Wheeler in
this August 1941 cartoon published in the *New York Post*. Wheeler
maintained, till the eve of the Japanese attack on Pearl Harbor, that
the United States had no reason not to try to "live in peace" with
Japan. (*Courtesy of the estate of Rollin Kirby Post; from Library of
Congress, Prints and Photographs Division, Washington, D.C.*)

In a nationally broadcast radio speech on September 11 Roosevelt ordered a new
policy—the U.S. Navy would now fire on German and Italian ships on sight. "We
have sought no shooting war with Hitler," the president said. "We do not seek it now,
but neither do we want peace so much that we are willing to pay for it by permitting
him to attack our naval and merchant ships. . . . When you see a rattlesnake poised to
strike, you do not wait until he has struck before you crush him. These Nazi raiders
are the rattlesnakes of the Atlantic." The German U-boat, Roosevelt said, had "fired
first upon this American destroyer without warning, and with deliberate design to
sink her." The German action was "piracy—piracy legally and morally." The president
announced what amounted to an undeclared naval war.[92]

Roosevelt's statement—"studied hyperbole" in the words of historian David Kennedy—came despite Roosevelt having been told by the navy two days before his speech that there was "no positive evidence that [the] submarine knew [the] nationality of [the] ship at which it was firing." In fact, the *Greer* was of the same class of destroyer that Roosevelt had transferred to the Royal Navy in 1940. But in his speech Roosevelt offered no such nuance and also made no mention of the fact that the British aircraft had tipped the American destroyer to the whereabouts of the submarine or that the plane and the destroyer had pursued the U-boat for several hours and that the U.S. ship had been involved in the initial attack.[93]

Still, Roosevelt's speech on the *Greer* incident had the effect he must have hoped for, reassuring Americans that the administration had initiated a policy to protect U.S. interests while still avoiding an out-and-out declaration of war. Public opinion in the wake of the speech also seemed to solidify. When the Gallup Poll asked in late September, "In general, do you approve or disapprove of having the United States shoot at German submarines or warships on sight?," 56 percent of those surveyed approved, while 34 percent disapproved.[94]

Wheeler was in Montana when Roosevelt announced the new shoot-on-sight policy, and his first reaction, somewhat surprisingly, was to telegraph former president Hoover and urge him to take part in an America First rally in Los Angeles in late September. "Apparently Mr. Roosevelt intends to take us into a shooting war regardless of Congress or the Constitution and I believe we must take prompt action to arouse the people now," Wheeler wrote. Hoover, perhaps weary of the continuing controversy engulfing America First, declined the invitation, saying he thought he could be more helpful "as a sort of independent voice" attempting to convince what he called "the great group who are of an undecided mind."[95]

Roosevelt's explanation of the *Greer* incident, deceptive and incomplete at best, has often been excused, as have other prewar presidential actions—bypassing Congress on the destroyer-for-bases deal, for example—as both necessary and expedient given the circumstances. After all, the president knew, based on his private communication with Winston Churchill, of the perilous condition of the British war effort, but he also had to deal with an American public fervently hoping to stay out of the war. At the same time, a straightforward call by Roosevelt for a declaration of war, as Wheeler and his noninterventionist allies knew, would not command public or congressional support. Roosevelt, facing these seemingly intractable problems, often fudged, told half-truths, misrepresented, and fundamentally, as Wheeler believed, refused to candidly level with the American people or Congress regarding his ultimate intention—U.S. involvement in the war.

Faced with what he deemed an existential threat to U.S. interests and a worried public, Roosevelt, most historians agree, did what he had to do, even if that meant bypassing Congress and dissembling with the public. To do less, Robert Dallek has argued, "would have been a failure of his responsibility as Commander in Chief." Still, absolving Roosevelt for his approach because his motives were understandable does not diminish the precedent FDR helped establish. Future presidents, arguably for less worthy reasons—Lyndon Johnson with Vietnam and George W. Bush with Iraq, for example—misled the public and Congress on a host of foreign policy issues, often in the interest of shaping public opinion or achieving an outcome that an honest presentation of the facts might have rendered impossible. If Wheeler was guilty, as he has often been judged, of badly, even tragically, misreading the threat represented by Nazi Germany and imperial Japan prior to Pearl Harbor, he did correctly foresee, when many others did not, the danger to democracy when a president, even for worthy reasons, willingly deceives the public and Congress about matters of war and peace.[96]

13 BIG SCREEN, BIG LEAK

> Roosevelt knew that the only way he could fulfill his
> secret commitments to Churchill to get us into the war,
> without openly dishonoring his pledges to the
> American people to keep us out, was by provoking
> Germany or Japan to attack.
>
> —ALBERT C. WEDEMEYER

B.K. Wheeler's national profile in 1941, enhanced by almost daily public appearances and press coverage saturation, could hardly have been higher. Wheeler was a household name, a politician both admired and loathed, his every statement analyzed for hints about underlying motives and political ambition. Wheeler's combative personal style and ability to generate press attention were clearly an asset to the noninterventionist movement that needed a high-profile speaker willing to engage in the constant give-and-take of debate and able to keep the antiwar cause on front pages. But the constant attention, much of it negative and damaging, also began to exact a toll, particularly in Montana, where Wheeler's political support eroded throughout 1941.

A *Life* magazine profile titled "Boss Isolationist" in May that year described Wheeler as "a tall, stooped, rumpled, cigar-chewing man with a clipped Yankee voice, the easy manners of the west and a thin mouth which seems set in a perpetual wry secret smile at the duplicity of mankind." Wheeler, the article said, "has been stumping the country in a curious political campaign. His immediate object is not to get himself elected to any office, but to persuade the people of the U.S. that the President of the U.S. is not to be trusted in the conduct of the nation's foreign policy." If the nation went to war, *Life's* reporter observed, and if the results proved unpopular and again brought about widespread disillusionment as happened after World War I, then Wheeler might well represent the future of the Democratic Party. "Every speech of [Wheeler's] makes plain his belief that America is just as safe from invasion as it was in 1917, that there will be another bad peace, that Americans will again believe they were tricked into war by international bankers, British propagandists and an ambitious President, and that they will again experience the same after-war revulsion which put Warren Harding in the White House and Burton K. Wheeler in the Senate. On those eventualities Burton K. Wheeler, at a hale and vigorous 59, is willing to gamble his political future."[1]

Wheeler truly had gambled his political future, and his leadership of the antiwar movement stretched him thin—virtually every one of the 450 local America First chapters requested him as a speaker in 1941. His speeches required extensive prepara-tion, and they came day after day. His schedule, one speech often followed the same or the next day by another in a city hundreds of miles away, required exhausting travel. Wheeler was in constant demand for interviews, and he regularly appeared on radio. The time needed to attend to issues and relationships in Montana became scarce, and the personal, retail politics that had long served Wheeler so well, allowing him to explain his positions directly to voters, took second place, as one profile said, to serving as "the wheel horse" of the noninterventionist movement. The constant publicity, while certainly valuable to the antiwar effort, also meant constant criticism, and the political damage accumulated. In September 1941, Montana-born James Rowe, a Roosevelt White House assistant, sent the president a newspaper article showing eroding support for Wheeler in Montana. "This latest Montana poll on Wheeler will interest you," Rowe wrote in a note accompanying the clipping. The unscientific poll indicated that many Montanans who voted for Wheeler just a year earlier would be unlikely to support him again. The New York Times featured a similar item headlined "Wheeler Popularity Shrinks in Montana."[2]

Montana should have been fertile ground for the America First Committee in 1940 and 1941, but Montanans never really embraced the movement that became synonymous with Wheeler, perhaps because of his own neglect of Montana issues or perhaps because Wheeler underestimated how polarizing his positions had become even among the voters who had four times sent him to the Senate. For whatever reason, Wheeler did little, considering his clout with the America First Committee, to use the organization to buttress his standing at home. Montana never had more than two chapters of America First.

"We have no headquarters and never had one," Margaret Loughrin, an America First volunteer in Butte, wrote to the committee's national headquarters. (The letter was sent at about the time Wheeler was engaged in his public spat with Henry Stimson.) "We have no membership rolls for the reason that most of us here or at least those of our working group are low bracket working people, and have neither the time nor the means to belong to any membership of any kind." The overwhelmed Loughrin predicted that fifty thousand Montanans could be mobilized by America First but not without help from the Chicago headquarters. "Something will have to be done," she cautioned, "as the few of us who have taken the lead here are pretty well worn out."[3]

Jim Murray, having jettisoned foreign policy views that were at one time similar to Wheeler's, also became a more effective political counterpoint to Wheeler in Montana. Murray's outspoken defense of administration policy, particularly his support for aid to Britain, angered some of his Irish constituents, especially in Butte. The Butte Miners Union, for example, criticized Murray's support for Lend-Lease, and Butte's mayor claimed that the legislation gave Roosevelt the authority to "give America back to England." But, even in the face of such criticism, once Murray embraced Roosevelt's policies he remained as adamant about his position as Wheeler was about his. Noninterventionist sentiment remained strong, but increasingly more Montana voters felt comfortable with the Roosevelt and Murray approach to foreign policy than with Wheeler's. The intense personal rivalry between the two senators from Butte defined the fault lines in Montana politics, further divided Democrats, and put Wheeler increasingly on the defensive. During a nationally broadcast speech from Helena, without mentioning Wheeler by name but clearly with his colleague in mind, Murray said that the America First Committee and its allies were "unconsciously serving as Hitler's tools in America." Such people, Murray said, deserved "Nazi medals for subversive activities." Without acknowledging his own support for neutrality legislation prior to 1940, Murray chided those in Congress who had followed an "ill-considered policy of absolute isolation."[4]

The late summer and fall of 1941 was a bitter time for Wheeler and America First. The charge that the movement and Wheeler were abetting anti-Semitism became more pronounced and more difficult to dismiss. An ill-considered Senate investigation of Hollywood "propaganda" went badly off the rails, and the debacle played into the hands of Wheeler's critics, as did a historic blunder by Charles Lindbergh. And Wheeler, succumbing to desperate measures, engineered a monumental leak of sensitive war-planning documents, hoping that the revelations might prevent involvement in World War II.

———

No charge leveled at Wheeler or the America First Committee did more damage to the antiwar cause or had more staying power than the allegation that the organization and its followers were anti-Semitic. Despite Wheeler's lifelong commitment to civil liberties, his frequent calls for tolerance, and his long friendship and collaboration with leading members of the American Jewish community, including Louis Brandeis and Max Lowenthal, the anti-Semitism label has stuck to his legacy. It is clear that he did too little to refute the charges or, perhaps even worse, discounted the allegations.

In a September 1941 memo, FBI director Hoover circulated a report that explicitly attached the anti-Jewish label to America First. Hoover wrote that "a tremendous Jewish group" backing America First "withdrew all financial support from the committee" in part because "Mrs. Wheeler, the wife of the Senator, Colonel McCormick, owner of the [Chicago] *Tribune*, and Harry Jung, head of the American Vigilante Intelligence Federation [an allegedly pro-fascist, anti-Semitic group], are using the America First Committee as a sounding board for anti-Jewish propaganda." Hoover was reporting hearsay, but it was hearsay with just enough credibility to hurt.[5]

It was obvious to America First leaders, including Robert Wood, who worked for a Jewish family, the Rosenwalds, owners of Sears, Roebuck, that pro-Nazi, anti-Semitic groups had infiltrated the organization. "Because it was to Germany's advantage for the United States to stay out of the war, it was inevitable that America First would be accused of pro-Nazism," the committee's Washington director Ruth Sarles acknowledged years later. "There is no doubt," Sarles said, "that there were anti-Semites among the rank-and-file members." America First national leaders implored local chapter leaders, not always successfully, to avoid association with such groups and their representatives. Former Montana congressman Jacob Thorkelson, more outspokenly anti-Semitic after his defeat in 1940, addressed an America First–sponsored rally in Salt Lake City in 1941. National headquarters learned of Thorkelson's appearance after the fact, and he was blackballed as a future speaker, but the impression persisted that America First, whatever its intentions, had become a vehicle for anti-Semitism.[6]

Father Charles Coughlin's rabidly anti-Semitic newspaper *Social Justice* endorsed America First, causing more problems. A committee leader warned chapters in the eastern United States, "It is of particular importance that none of these [Coughlin] supporters be permitted to inject anti-Semitism into the work of the chapter. We have the support of many Jewish people, and will not abide intolerance as a part of this movement." Nevertheless, in the summer of 1941, *Social Justice* printed letters from both Wood and Lulu Wheeler in which each made the case that Coughlin's followers and America First shared the goal of keeping the nation out of war. The mere fact that letters from such prominent America First leaders appeared in a publication widely viewed as anti-Semitic reinforced the impression that the antiwar group was also anti-Jewish.[7]

Some Wheeler friends warned him that he was being defined precisely as critics were defining America First. Norman Thomas implored Wheeler "to avoid even the suspicion of racial implication" in his speeches. He should avoid references to "international bankers," Thomas said, which might be interpreted as code for "Jewish bankers." Thomas suggested that Wheeler always speak of "the House of Morgan" or "the Chase National Bank." Wheeler, belatedly and not particularly effectively,

fought back against the allegations and began to pay closer attention to where and
to whom he spoke. Wheeler declined an invitation to appear at a rally organized by
the anti-Semitic preacher and Huey Long disciple Gerald L. K. Smith, and America
First in turn refused Smith's request to become a member. Wheeler also increased his
outreach to American Jewish leaders, including writing a lengthy and defensive letter
to Charles Schwager, an executive with the General Insurance Company in New York
and a respected leader of the American Jewish community. "All my life I have hated
intolerance and bigotry," Wheeler wrote. "I am concerned with human beings, not
with their race, creed, or color." He continued:

> During my 30 years in public life I have always fought for the under-dog—for
> those who are economically and socially under-privileged. I am concerned
> with what is an obviously rising tide of intolerance in this country. That is a
> backwash from what is happening in Europe, I have no doubt. I am of the firm
> conviction that we are not going to stamp this out by embroiling ourselves in
> the quarrels of Europe, even if the objective of the present war is to crush a
> European madman. I say this because I believe that Hitlerism was born in the
> degradation and poverty that was visited on the German people after the last
> World War. Political and social changes, history proves, come from within a
> nation and generally are born of economic difficulties. I have no fear of America
> adopting fascism or communism as a result of outside pressures, military or
> otherwise, so long as the American people live better under our democratic
> system than they will under some other system. The danger to America lies
> within—it lies in the fact that large numbers of our people are still ill-fed, ill
> clothed, and ill-housed.
>
>   Democracy means little to the man who is hungry or who sees no future for
> his family and himself. It is among these people that the spirit of frustration
> gives rise to bitterness which in turn breeds intolerance and bigotry toward
> other groups in the population.[8]

Wheeler wrote Schwager early in 1941, long before the worst of the characterizations
of anti-Semitism had been leveled. For example, Rabbi Sidney Goldstein, an opponent
of American entry into the war, made a public show of canceling his participation in
a major conference of antiwar activists in May 1941 rather than appear on the same
platform with Wheeler in light of what the rabbi called the senator's private and public
"anti-Jewish statements."[9]

By not addressing the allegations of anti-Semitism more forcefully—perhaps he
thought his record spoke for itself—Wheeler left damning personal charges largely
unanswered. Wheeler wrote in his memoirs that he "publically condemned the Nazis'

racial and religious persecutions" and often denounced what he called "organized prejudice." All true, but his condemnations were often lost amid the barrage of criticism Wheeler leveled at Roosevelt and other "warmongers." Acknowledging that the antiwar movement had, at least to some degree, offered safe haven to bigots and home-grown fascists, Wheeler wrote years later that "the haters were as hard as maggots to shake off."[10]

Apparently without giving great thought to what a Senate investigation of the big Hollywood studios might involve or what the consequences might be, Wheeler approved an inquiry by his committee into what America First termed the "brazen war propaganda" of American moviemakers, propaganda, it said, of the kind "that created the hysteria for entrance into the last war." Wheeler put his friend John Flynn, head of the New York America First chapter, in the role of chief investigator, and Flynn coordinated his work closely with the larger antiwar movement. But inept handling of the hearings and allegations that the investigation was motivated by anti-Semitism—many top film industry executives were Jewish—combined to create an avalanche of negative publicity for Wheeler and the noninterventionist cause in the fall of 1941. The Hollywood investigation was a major blunder, an amateurish sideshow to the more important foreign policy debate but ultimately significant for what it seemed to say about the motives of many of the noninterventionists.[11]

Wheeler often criticized what he believed to be a pro-intervention bias in the film industry, at one point complaining that a "little clique of Wall Street bankers, together with the motion picture industry, are trying to stir up sentiment to take us into war." That particular charge came shortly after Helena-born Gary Cooper's patriotic portrayal of Sergeant York, the backwoods Tennessee hero of World War I, reached the big screen. The movie, a huge box office hit in 1941, earned Cooper an Academy Award and the real Sergeant Alvin York an invitation to the White House, where Roosevelt praised the movie and posed for photos with the former soldier. York made it clear that he supported Roosevelt's policies and condemned "appeasers" like Wheeler—York called the Montanan "Neville," a reference to the former British prime minister—saying such people ought to be turned out of office. Wheeler also objected to what he considered the pro-administration, pro-interventionist "propaganda" in newsreels, the short, timely, news-oriented motion pictures that routinely preceded feature films. Wheeler was particularly critical of The March of Time series, a product of the communication empire of committed internationalist Henry Luce, who often used his short subjects to emphasize a political point of view. March of Time newsreels regularly attacked noninterventionists.[12]

Wheeler knew, as historian M. Todd Bennett has demonstrated in his authoritative history of Hollywood and World War II, that motion pictures were powerful tools to shape public opinion. "Each week from 1939 to 1941," Bennett has written, "tens of millions of moviegoers consumed a steady diet of newsreels, shorts, and features that articulated pro-British and interventionist themes and rarely if ever expressed opposing points of view." The Gallup organization reported that by overwhelming margins moviegoers viewing pro-British films were more inclined to support greater assistance to the British war effort.[13]

The big studio chieftains—Samuel Goldwyn, the Warner Brothers, and Darryl Zanuck, among others—began to embrace a more assertive pro-interventionist, pro-administration line after distribution of Hollywood films was officially banned in Germany in 1940. Moreover, Harry Warner, whom one historian called Roosevelt's man in Hollywood, and Walter Wanger, president of the motion picture academy, were major West Coast financial benefactors of the pro-British Fight for Freedom Committee, and, as Bennett writes, "industry leaders established a quid pro quo with the White House by which the Roosevelt administration insulated the major studios from antitrust litigation in exchange for pictures supportive of the president's ever more internationalist and specifically pro-British foreign policy."[14]

"Here's the program," John Flynn, wrote to the America First Committee's Douglas Stuart, explaining how the rollout of the motion picture investigation would be conducted.

A. Wheeler sounded off in the Senate on Thursday, [July 31] denouncing the movies. B. Nye delivered a speech over the radio Friday night, which we prepared as part of this drive. C. Friday afternoon Bennett Clark and Nye jointly offered a resolution in the Senate for an investigation of war propaganda in the movies and radio. The plan here is to have this referred to Wheeler's Interstate Commerce Committee.... Wheeler is appointing ... a committee to hold hearings on the resolution. We'll present the case that way, getting the benefit of the publicity, and we plan to summon the movie moguls to Washington.[15]

The publicity rollout heralding the Senate investigation was more skillfully managed than anything that followed. As planned, Wheeler did launch the campaign in a Senate speech charging Hollywood with "destroying democracy" ("Shame on them; they should be in a better business"). Senators Nye and Clark then introduced a resolution calling for an investigation of propaganda in the motion picture industry, and, again as Flynn planned, the resolution was referred to Wheeler's committee. Nye, in a radio speech, then attacked motion picture companies as "gigantic engines of propaganda in existence to rouse the war fever of America and plunge the Nation to her destruction."

Americans, Nye asked, "[Are you] ready to send your boys to bleed and die in Europe to make the world safe for this industry?" The stage was set for an investigation.[16]

Wheeler handpicked the members of the subcommittee to investigate Hollywood propaganda, and he tapped a junior member of his committee, Democrat D. Worth Clark of Idaho, to chair what technically was to be a preliminary review that would determine if a full-blown investigation was warranted. That subterfuge was a not particularly well-disguised effort to avoid seeking Senate approval for the investigation, and from the outset the distinction between a preliminary review and an actual investigation was lost on all the participants. Clark, at thirty-nine one of the youngest members of the Senate, was from a prominent Idaho political family but had no experience handling such a high-profile assignment. His basic qualification seems to have been that he shared Wheeler's foreign policy views, as did three other members of the subcommittee, Democrat Homer Bone of Washington (who did not participate due to illness) and Republicans Charles W. Tobey of New Hampshire and Curly Brooks of Illinois. The fifth member of the subcommittee, and the only administration supporter, was freshman senator Ernest W. McFarland, an Arizona Democrat, who became an important ally of the film industry and was, in many ways, the star of the hearings.[17]

Even before the committee was formally organized, and well in advance of its first meeting, a torrent of criticism descended on the investigation. Interventionists, pointing to Nye's speech naming Jewish studio heads as controlling "considerably more than half of the motion picture industry," charged that the investigation was motivated by anti-Semitism and tainted by a pro-Nazi bias. Wheeler was blasted for his "bitter, unsubstantiated accusations" against Hollywood and accused of an "error in judgment and discretion that is all too common in congressional circles" in launching the investigation. Columnist Dorothy Thompson said the investigation would set off "an anti-Semitic movement in the United States" that would result in stopping "all attacks on Hitler and Hitlerism on the ground that criticism of the Nazi regime in war-mongering." Thompson called the hearings the "American Dreyfus Case."[18]

The Motion Picture Producers and Distributors of America (MPPDA), which might have been expected to assume a defensive posture in response to a congressional investigation, instead seized on the hearings as an opportunity to tell the industry's story, casting studio executives as patriotic defenders of freedom of expression. The industry group retained Wendell Willkie, who had by now become an outspoken interventionist, to represent the studios. The MPPDA's president, Will Hays, who had clashed before with Wheeler, said that the industry welcomed the chance to defend itself against "a challenge to the fundamental principles of free expression," an ironic statement coming from the man who was Hollywood's official censor.[19]

On the eve of the first hearing, Willkie sent Worth Clark a devastatingly effective nine-page letter, refuting the specifics of both the Senate resolution and Nye's "gigantic engines of propaganda" radio speech. Willkie's preemptive attack immediately shifted the spotlight from the moviemakers to the investigators. "After reading the resolution and Senator Nye's speech with care," Willkie wrote, "I have come to the conclusion that your sub-committee intends to inquire whether or not the motion picture industry, as a whole, and its leading executives, as individuals, are opposed to the Nazi dictatorship in Germany. If this is the case, there need be no investigation." The industry and its executives plead guilty, Willkie said, to abhorring "everything which Hitler represents." He also admitted that the industry was doing all it could possibly do, as all patriotic Americans were, to support the national defense program. Then Willkie played his best card. "If the committee feels that the racial and geographic background of American citizens is a condition to be investigated, there is no need for an investigation. We frankly state that in the motion picture industry there are ... both Nordics and non-Nordics, Jews and Gentiles, Protestants and Catholics, native and foreign born. This industry, with many others in the country, demonstrates that neither race, creed nor geographic origin is an essential qualification to participate in American business." Willkie warned Clark of "the very genuine dangers involved in this type of investigation," since free expression was under attack. "From the motion picture and radio industries, it is just a small step to the newspapers, magazines and other periodicals. And from freedom of the press, it is just a small step to the freedom of the individual to say what he believes." For good measure Willkie suggested that the subcommittee was likely proceeding on dubious legal grounds since the Senate had not formally approved any investigation but only consideration of whether an investigation was warranted.[20]

Thanks to Willkie's framing of the issues, the hearings would not focus on the arguably legitimate question of whether Hollywood was engaging in a coordinated effort with the Roosevelt administration to present one-sided treatment of the intense national debate over foreign policy. Instead, as Willkie skillfully managed perceptions, the investigation would consider the motives of the investigators—dark, sinister motives that appeared to include pro-Nazi sympathies, anti-Semitic beliefs, and disdain for free expression. At the first hearing, McFarland, a former prosecutor and judge, pressed Nye for specifics on how Congress could accomplish the objective of ending, what Nye had called, "the most vicious propaganda" he had ever seen. "Would that be done by legislation?" McFarland asked. McFarland said he remembered hearing "something about Constitutional guarantees of freedom of speech and press." In another exchange, McFarland maneuvered Nye into admitting that he had not seen most of the films he named as objectionable. As *Variety* reported, "The North Dakota isolationist was tossed around at intervals by Senator McFarland who accused him of trying to gag everyone with ideas different from his."[21]

While Nye and Flynn struggled to keep the hearings focused on Hollywood propaganda and monopoly practices, the sessions dissolved into a disjointed spectacle that wandered far afield of Hollywood bias to touch on employment discrimination and film distribution policies. Wheeler contributed to the confusion by demanding an investigation of "lewd and lascivious" jukebox movies. The investigation sputtered to a crawl thanks to committee bungling, Willkie's effective defense of the industry, McFarland's skill as an interrogator, and an avalanche of negative press coverage. Despite generating considerable circumstantial evidence that indicated industry bias toward the interventionist cause and suggested close coordination between the Roosevelt administration and the studios, the investigation failed to prove conclusively that a conspiracy existed or that British propaganda influenced Hollywood's creative output. In October the hearings were indefinitely recessed without having produced a report.[22]

Why Wheeler, typically a staunch defender of free speech and expression, sanctioned the bungled investigation remains a puzzling question. Perhaps he felt that Clark and the subcommittee, even when forced to rely on circumstantial evidence, could create the kind of sensation he had once caused by investigating an attorney general. But the investigation had no blockbuster witnesses, Clark had no instinct for the political jugular, the Idaho senator was not the kind of prosecutor Wheeler had been in 1924, and Wendell Willkie was no Harry Daugherty. Giving in to his antiwar zeal, Wheeler overplayed his hand badly, allowing the investigation to further taint the noninterventionist movement with the stain of anti-Semitism. It would be an enduring black mark, but something even worse came almost simultaneously. Charles Lindbergh delivered a speech in Des Moines, Iowa.[23]

———

The same evening that Franklin Roosevelt announced, in the wake of the *Greer* incident, his new "shoot on sight" policy in the Atlantic and described German U-boats as "rattlesnakes of the sea," Charles Lindbergh was speaking at an America First rally in Des Moines. Lindbergh had long promised himself that when it became clear that war was eminent he would lob one last powerful rhetorical grenade. Before a raucous crowd at the city's cavernous coliseum he pulled the pin.

Lindbergh provocatively entitled his speech "Who Are the War Agitators?" But rather than expose his opponents as advocates of war, the speech was widely seen as laying bare Lindbergh's own anti-Semitism. The address was a historic blunder not only for the famous aviator but also for America First and the entire noninterventionist movement. Wheeler suffered collateral damage too.[24]

By the fall of 1941, the Wheeler-Lindbergh relationship was the subject of intense curiosity and speculation. Were the two men intent on creating an isolationist third party positioned to challenge Roosevelt or a handpicked successor in 1944? Was Wheeler using the better-known Lindbergh's popularity to again advance his own White House ambitions, or was Lindbergh, a political novice, creating his own political path by identifying himself with Wheeler's political experience and following? *Liberty* magazine, a widely read weekly, devoted four consecutive stories in 1941 to "Why Senator Wheeler and Lindbergh Work Together." Author Frederick L. Collins concluded that both men were deeply committed to the noninterventionist cause and not unaware of the political possibilities, including the White House for one or both. "At the moment," Collins wrote, "Lindbergh draws bigger houses, but Wheeler arouses greater enthusiasm. Lindbergh's long, carefully written compositions are for the library rather than the platform. . . . Wheeler's folksy ways, his cracks out of the old cracker barrel, his rages and, above all, his ability to smile through them—all of these qualities get over to his audience one hundred percent."[25]

As criticism of both men grew more intense Wheeler frequently found himself defending Lindbergh. There is little record of Lindbergh returning the favor. When, for example, Roosevelt called Lindbergh, a colonel in the Army Air Corps Reserves, "a Copperhead," a derisive Civil War era term used to describe northern Democrats who sympathized with the South, Wheeler came immediately to Lindbergh's defense. Roosevelt was engaging in "a smear," Wheeler said, using language "beneath the dignity of the President of the United States." He added, "For anyone to attack Colonel Charles A. Lindbergh as a Copperhead is shocking and appalling to every right-thinking American." Lindbergh's Des Moines speech was beyond defending, however, and Wheeler did not try, but neither did he condemn Lindbergh's language. The omission is glaring and remains difficult to reconcile with Wheeler's willingness in many other circumstances to condemn intolerance.[26]

When Lindbergh somewhat nervously stepped to a podium in Des Moines on September 11, 1941, "no social class in America," as historian Lynne Olson has written, "was immune from the virus of anti-Semitism. It infected Wall Street lawyers along with rednecks, well-regarded statesmen as well as populist extremists." Many American colleges and universities employed strict quota systems that prohibited or severely limited Jewish students, many private clubs banned Jews as members, and many agencies of the federal government—particularly the War and State Departments—were openly anti-Semitic.[27]

Yet when Lindbergh spoke on nationwide radio, daring to say publicly what some Americans only privately whispered, he did so in the middle of the most incendiary

American political debate since the Civil War. The speech ignited a firestorm, as Anne Murrow Lindbergh wrote, as if a match had been "lit near a pile of excelsior." Lindbergh identified three main groups that he maintained were agitating for war—the Roosevelt administration, the British, and Jews. "Instead of agitating for war, the Jewish groups in this country should be opposing it in every possible way, for they will be among the first to feel its consequences," Lindbergh said. What came next ensured that Lindbergh's speech, more than any other single event or action, would define the pre-war noninterventionist movement as un-American and anti-Semitic:

> Tolerance is a virtue that depends upon peace and strength. History shows that it cannot survive war and devastation. A few far-sighted Jewish people realize this, and stand opposed to intervention. But the majority still do not. The greatest danger to this country lies in their large ownership and influence in our motion pictures, our radio, and our Government.
>
> I am not attacking either the Jews or the British people. Both races, I admire, but I am saying that the leaders of both the British and Jewish races, for reasons which are as understandable from their viewpoint as they are inadvisable from ours, for reasons which are not American, wish to involve us in the war. We cannot blame them for looking out for what they believe to be their own interests, but we must also look out for ours. We cannot allow the natural passions and prejudices of other people to lead our country to destruction.[28]

The critics pounced. Lindbergh had called Jews un-American, representing different values and motivated by different interest than "real Americans." The famous aviator was subjected, as A. Scott Berg has written, to "a Niagara of invective. Few men in American history have ever been so reviled." White House press secretary Stephen Early immediately condemned Lindbergh's speech, comparing his words to recent "outpourings of Berlin." Wendell Willkie called the Des Moines speech "the most un-American talk made in my time by any person of national reputation." A San Francisco rabbi said, "Hitler himself could not have delivered a more diabolical speech."[29]

Norman Thomas, who had spoken at many America First rallies, including appearances on the same platform with Lindbergh, condemned the speech and said he would never again speak at events the committee organized. Former president Hoover told a friend, "Lindbergh's anti-Jewish speech is, of course, all wrong. And I fear it will hurt all of us who are opposed to war." John Flynn, the head of America First's New York chapter, was particularly incensed. "It seems incredible to me that Col. Lindbergh without consulting anyone literally committed the America First movement to an open attack upon the Jews," Flynn said.[30]

Lindbergh's speech, as well as the outrage it ignited, demanded an immediate and clear response, but it took the national board of America First nearly two weeks, a virtual lifetime in the evolution of a scandal, to say anything about the Des Moines speech. When the board finally did respond, its statement did more harm than good. Rather than forcefully denouncing anti-Semitism, the unsigned communiqué avoided the obvious and lashed out at critics, deploring what it called the interventionists' effort "to hide the real issue by flinging false charges at the America First Committee and at every leader who has spoken out against our entry into the European conflict." After asserting that Lindbergh was not anti-Semitic, the committee made the odd claim that interventionists had injected "the race issue into the discussion of war and peace."[31]

After Des Moines the noninterventionist movement, particularly America First, stumbled back on the defensive as never before. "As you know, there are some individuals in America First who are anti-Semitic," Wheeler's son, John, wrote to Douglas Stewart shortly after Lindbergh's speech. "They misrepresent the speech just as much as the extreme on the other side for the purpose of justifying themselves by claiming Lindbergh's approval. I can assure you that we can take care of these individuals or groups here and keep them in hand." But the damage could not be contained.[32]

Unlike many others involved with America First, Wheeler never publicly condemned Lindbergh's comments, and there is no evidence he did so privately. His only tangential acknowledgement of the controversy was to voice a halting defense of Lindbergh's right to free speech. There is no mention of Lindbergh in Wheeler's memoirs, an omission hard to fathom, and after 1941 there is no evidence the two men had any communication. Perhaps Wheeler came to feel, as his friend Norman Thomas said, "I honestly don't think Lindbergh is an anti-Semite, but I think he is a great idiot. . . . It is an enormous pity that . . . the Colonel will not take advice on public relations which he would expect an amateur in aviation to take from an expert."[33]

Wheeler was now nearly always playing defense. Hecklers interrupted his speeches, he was denounced at a Rutgers University science seminar for failing to stand up to "evil," and when New York rabbis condemned anti-Semitism in a statement during Rosh Hashanah his name was invoked. On at least two occasions he was pelted with eggs during speeches. A raucous appearance in Billings on September 17, less than a week after Lindbergh's Des Moines speech, came close to getting out of hand, with Wheeler enduring loud jeers and boos as he spoke of Lindbergh's right to free speech and attempted to defend his own record. The mayor of Billings introduced Wheeler for the nationally broadcast speech to a mixture of applause and catcalls. "I'm sure you read about the Billings episode and possibly you heard the broadcast," Lulu Wheeler wrote to daughter Elizabeth. "The following day they arrested the boy that threw the eggs and he admitted that he was paid $5.00 to do it.... So, as usual, the troublemakers hurt only themselves and helped the cause they planned to hurt." Perhaps, but the Billings meeting was an ugly reminder that Wheeler, elected overwhelmingly less than a year earlier, could not now get through a speech in Montana without some of his constituents calling him out. Three weeks later in Tucson, Arizona, while speaking in a high school auditorium, loud boos greeted Wheeler's call for opposition to Roosevelt's foreign policy. The Associated Press reported that an egg "thrown from the balcony, struck a curtain above Wheeler's head and fell beside him."[34]

———

By early October 1941 Franklin Roosevelt had exhausted the opportunities for unilateral action he could take to aid Britain and protect the vital passage of goods crossing the Atlantic. To do anything more, Roosevelt would have to go to Congress and seek changes to the Neutrality Act, the foundational legislation that had shaped U.S. foreign policy since its enactment in 1935. While the Neutrality Act had been modified a number of times, it still prevented arming U.S. merchant vessels, and U.S. ships were prohibited from sailing directly into British ports. Roosevelt asked Congress as "a matter of immediate necessity and extreme urgency" to approve amendments to alter those provisions.[35]

Wheeler, not surprisingly, pledged to fight the amendments even as he knew that the noninterventionist bloc in the Senate lacked the votes to prevail. Interestingly, given the manner in which the filibuster is routinely invoked in the modern Senate, Wheeler, Hiram Johnson, and several other like-minded senators declined to filibuster proposed amendments to the Neutrality Act, even though Robert Wood, among others, believed that the Neutrality Act debate was the last legislative stand of the noninterventionist movement. Wood believed, as he wrote to Wheeler, that after the seemingly inevitable amendment of the Neutrality Act, "our only chance [to shape policy would be] to elect non-interventionist Congressmen and senators in 1942." Wheeler disagreed. "We simply cannot quit and let the people down," he wrote Wood. "If we do, some irresponsible groups will take it up where we left off, and it will throw the leadership into the hands of a group of Communists or Fascists, and the people who seek to stir up religious and racial hatred. That will completely destroy our government. I am confident that history will vindicate our action."[36]

The shooting war in the Atlantic grew more ominous on October 16 when a German submarine attacked the U.S. destroyer *Kearny* and eleven sailors were lost. The next day, by a lopsided margin of nearly 2–1, the House of Representatives amended the Neutrality Act to permit the arming of U.S. merchant ships. Roosevelt would try to broaden the changes in the Senate to allow U.S. ships to enter combat zones. The Gallup

Poll now reported that 72 percent of Americans supported arming merchant ships, but still less than a majority favored U.S. ships carrying war materials directly to Britain.[37]

As the Senate debated Neutrality Act changes, Wheeler and his allies were left struggling to marshal arguments that might stop what they believed was one more step, perhaps the final one, toward war. When some senators proposed the wholesale repeal of the Neutrality Act, Wheeler threatened to attach a provision to the legislation declaring war against Germany, a proposition that America First, as well as Roosevelt, knew could not pass Congress. Senator Tom Connally, the blustery chair of the Foreign Relations Committee and a Roosevelt ally, bristled at the suggestion that Congress should declare war, and he lashed out at Wheeler, accusing him of "carrying on guerilla warfare on our defense program and foreign policy all over the United States." For years, Connally fumed, Wheeler had not been "in sympathy with our efforts to arm the nation for defense and he is not in sympathy now." Connally's charge was a "misrepresentation of my position," Wheeler countered. "I am not opposed to the defense program. I am opposed to the Administration taking us down the road to war."[38]

On October 30, with debate continuing in the Senate, the America First Committee staged one of its last mass rallies, at Madison Square Garden. New York police reported that elaborate security arrangements—750 uniformed officers patrolled outside the arena while 50 plainclothes detectives stood watch inside—were made to "cope with any possible trouble." Wheeler shared speaking duties with the former U.S. ambassador to Belgium John Cudahy, John Flynn, and Lindbergh, who was making his first public appearance since Des Moines. Wheeler spoke last to a crowd estimated at twenty thousand and complained bitterly of the "scorn, abuse and vilification" the "warmongers and propagandists paid with British and Russian gold" had heaped on the noninterventionists. A "disastrous war policy" had unfolded, Wheeler said, while the administration had talked disingenuously of wanting peace:

> Clothed in promises of peace—the Roosevelt Administration has foisted one war measure after another upon a peace-loving and unsuspecting people. The people trusted the President. They accepted his peace pledges. They believed him when he spoke of aid-short-of-war. They accepted conscription and the destroyer transfer. They accepted the lend-lease bill in the name of national defense with definite promises from the Administration leaders of no convoys. But today the Administration is bolder. Gone is the pretext and subterfuge. . . . Franklin D. Roosevelt endorsed legislation to send our ships into a zone where a bloody war rages, knowing as he must that American ships and American sailors must inevitably go to the bottom of the sea.

I charge that enactment of such legislation means war. Believing that—I will oppose it. I will fight it. I will vote against it.[39]

Another incident in the Atlantic, the torpedoing of the U.S. destroyer *Reuben James*, took the lives of 115 American sailors on October 31. The obvious peril facing U.S. sailors and ships was clearly impacting opinion in the Senate and solidifying support for amending the Neutrality Act, but Wheeler pressed ahead with his opposition. Occasionally wiping his perspiring forehead with a towel, Wheeler spoke for five hours in the Senate in opposition to the administration's proposed changes. Invoking World War I, he reminded the Senate that "practically every superpatriot" who had advocated intervention in that war had been defeated for reelection. "I am here to make a prediction now," he said, "that the people will turn against those who vote to put this country into war" because "the catastrophe that will follow this war will be so much worse than that which followed the last one."[40]

On November 7, after what historian Justus Doenecke has called "eleven days of bitter debate," the Neutrality Act revisions, including the provision allowing U.S. ships to enter war zones, passed the Senate by a vote of 50–37. It was a clear win for the administration but also the closest Senate vote on any major foreign policy issue since the war in Europe began in September 1939. The House of Representatives concurred in the Senate version of the legislation but by only an eighteen-vote margin. The country and Congress still wanted to stay out of the war, even as all the momentum took the country deeper into the conflict. Still, neither the naval incidents nor the loss of American lives nor even the president's statement that Nazi Germany had a secret plan to turn Central and South America into a group of client states had changed congressional or public opinion regarding a formal declaration of war.[41]

In a letter to Norman Thomas, Wheeler admitted to being "pretty much worn out" by the end of the Neutrality Act debate. "Of course," he said, "a good many people were disappointed because we didn't win, but the important thing is that we got as far as we did. If anyone had said to me, at the outset, that we could have come as close as we did, I would not have believed it. The Administration was licked the nite [*sic*] before the vote in the House, but with the tremendous pressure they can bring to bear, they were able to put it across." Wheeler was already thinking of his next move to avoid war, including offering a congressional resolution prohibiting the deployment of an American Expeditionary Force (AEF). "My confidential information is to the effect that China was insisting on our sending an AEF to protect the Burma Road, and practically told the Administration, unless they did, they would make peace. There were hurried consultations at the State Department, and the War Department turned thumbs down on it." Wheeler added, as if he needed to do so, that he was "steadfast" in opposition to war with Japan.[42]

U.S.-Japanese relations were nevertheless close to the breaking point, with Secretary of State Hull, at Roosevelt's direction, insisting on negotiating conditions that he knew the Japanese would find unacceptable. Meanwhile, a Japanese imperial conference on November 5 directed that plans to initiate war with the United States, including a surprise attack on Hawaii and other Pacific targets, go forward. "Ironically enough," historian David Kennedy has written, "on that same date of November 5, the American Joint Board of the Army and Navy reaffirmed that the primary objective of the United States 'is the defeat of Germany.' Therefore, the Board concluded, 'war between the United States and Japan should be avoided.'" On December 3 Wheeler told reporters, "The only time the Administration has intimated that we should go to war with Japan is when the British Empire is threatened. Japan has not threatened us."[43]

On Thursday morning December 4, 1941, the front pages of the *Chicago Daily Tribune* and its sister paper the *Washington Times-Herald* carried a blockbuster story. "FDR's War Plans!" screamed a two-inch-tall headline, with a subhead reading, "Goal Is 10 Million Armed Men, Half to Fight in AEF." The newspapers detailed "a confidential report—*The Victory Plan*—prepared by the U.S. army and navy high command by direction of President Roosevelt" providing a "blueprint for total war on a scale unprecedented on at least two oceans and three continents, Europe, Africa and Asia." The top-secret assessment detailed the U.S. military's conclusion that Germany could not be defeated by "the European powers now facing her" and that a British victory would require "the United States to enter the war and employ a part of its armed forces offensively in the eastern Atlantic and in Europe and Africa."[44]

Chesly Manly, the *Tribune*'s well-connected Washington correspondent, broke the huge scoop, a story so authoritative it quoted from the letter Roosevelt had written directing the development of the plans. Wheeler immediately denounced the existence of the war plans, and he believed that Manly's story was the smoking gun proving that Roosevelt and his advisors had been secretly planning for inevitable U.S. military involvement in the war, while repeatedly reassuring the public that they were trying to avoid war. The very name—"Victory Plan"—seemed to confirm Wheeler's contention, repeatedly cited over the preceding year, that the president was purposely misleading the U.S. public about his real intentions.

Fred Burdick, an America First Committee staffer who served as a link between the organization and the House of Representatives, thought publication of the war plans constituted a game changer in the debate between the noninterventionists and Roosevelt. Burdick sent a report on the sensational story to the organization's leadership on December 4: "The article by Chesly Manly astounded most interventionists and non-interventionists on the Hill," Burdick said. "Nearby newsstands were soon sold out of the *Times-Herald* containing the copy-righted story." It was generally agreed, Burdick said, that the story "would result in keeping America out of Europe's war, or at least prove a great contributory factor in that direction."[45]

Roosevelt, not surprisingly, was infuriated by the leak and told his cabinet that a proper response would be "the arrest of those responsible for disclosure, including if possible the managers of the newspapers." Attorney General Francis Biddle agreed, believing the government ought to pursue prosecutions under the Espionage Act and that the main target for prosecution should be Robert McCormick, the *Chicago Tribune* publisher. The *Tribune*'s managing editor was sufficiently concerned about publishing details of the sensitive document that he cleared the decision to go with the story with his boss. McCormick told his editors to spread it across the front page.[46]

The FBI was immediately ordered to investigate the leak, with initial suspicion centering on Colonel Albert Wedemeyer, a senior officer in the War Pans Division of the War Department. Wedemeyer had numerous friends and contacts in the non-interventionist community and harbored some sympathy for the objectives of the America First Committee. As he read the blockbuster story, Wedemeyer said, "It became all too clear that the *Chicago Tribune* correspondent had published an exact reproduction of the most important parts of the *Victory Program*, on which I had been working day and night for the past several months." Wedemeyer knew that release of the plan was "political dynamite" that provided "irrefutable evidence that American intervention in the war was planned and imminent, and that President Roosevelt's promises to keep us out of war were only campaign oratory."[47]

Wedemeyer, his career in the balance, denied involvement in the leak, and no evidence was produced that he had been involved, beyond the circumstantial, which primarily included the fact that Wedemeyer was acquainted with a number of nonin-terventionists. Wedemeyer continued to enjoy the confidence of Army Chief of Staff George Marshall and for the remainder of his career held increasingly responsible military commands. He retired as a four-star general, but even after his retirement Wedemeyer continued to seek information from the FBI in order to unravel the source of the leak. "My efforts to fix responsibility for this episode came to naught," he wrote in 1958.[48]

What Wheeler did not immediately acknowledge, in fact did not admit until the publication of his memoirs in 1962, was that he had leaked the documents to Chesly Manly. Wheeler also never revealed who provided him a copy of the Victory Plan document, other than to say that one of five numbered copies of the extremely sensi-tive plan had been carried to his Washington, D.C., home by a U.S. Army Air Forces captain, likely the same captain who had been a confidential messenger to Wheeler in the past. Wheeler wrote in his memoir that he asked the officer if he harbored fears, presumably for national security reasons, should the document become public. "Congress is a branch of the government," Wheeler recounted the officer saying. "I think it has a right to know what's really going on in the executive branch when it concerns human lives." Wheeler said he briefly considered providing the sensational document to the Senate Foreign Relations Committee, but he worried that the committee "would bury it," and in any event the report was something "the people as well as a senator should know about." Publication of the plan was warranted, Wheeler believed, because its very existence "undercut the repeated statements of Roosevelt and his followers that repeal of the neutrality acts, lend-lease, the destroyer deal, and similar measures, would keep us out of the European conflict." Once he had a copy of the document, Wheeler invited Manly to his home, where the reporter feverishly took notes in order to prepare what he and Wheeler both believed was sure to be a story of stunning importance, and it was for a short time.[49]

Who facilitated the leak to Wheeler has never been determined, but theories abound. Wheeler's son Edward told historian Thomas Fleming that his father always believed the leak of the Victory Plan had been authorized by U.S. Army Air Corps (USAAC) chief Henry H. (Hap) Arnold and that Arnold had used the USAAC captain to make the document handoff to Wheeler. Wheeler apparently agreed, telling Wedemeyer after the war that Arnold "did not approve of this business of going into war until he had raised an Air Force, and he would do all he could to retard it."[50]

Frank C. Waldrop, the managing editor of the *Times-Herald*, agreed that Arnold orchestrated the leak. Waldrop told "of having lunch after the war with the FBI man who had directed the investigation." The agent told Waldrop that the bureau had solved the case within ten days of the leak and identified the responsible party as "a general of high renown and invaluable importance to the war." In a subsequent interview with Waldrop, the FBI agent confirmed that when the investigation reached General Arnold "we quit." Fleming has suggested that Roosevelt himself may have authorized the leak of the war plans. Roosevelt's motive, in this speculation, was to precipitate a German declaration of war on the United States. "Why not leak [the Victory Plan] to one of the antiwar leaders," Fleming writes in his book *The New Dealers War,* "who would undoubtedly leak it to one of the antiwar newspapers, and inspire all these angry people to fulminate against it in their most choleric fashion? When Japanese aggression exploded in their faces, they would be left speechless with embarrassment—and politically neutered. But that would be a minor triumph, compared to the real purpose of the leak: to provoke Adolph Hitler into a declaration of war."[51]

Historian Lynne Olson has advanced the most plausible theory. She suggests, as Edward Wheeler believed, that General Arnold authorized the leak. Olson convincingly shows in her book *Those Angry Days* that Arnold was a skilled practitioner of the strategic leak, as well as an accomplished bureaucratic infighter. After detailing Arnold's less-than-successful efforts inside the War Department to elevate U.S. air power in the military's war planning, Olson describes the USAAC general's motives for leaking the secrets this way: "By leaking the report, he would take his case [for more attention and resources] to the Congress and the American people, hoping to halt the *Victory Program*—and the kind of war it proposed—in their tracks."[52]

When Wheeler disclosed his role in the episode more than two decades later he took care to explain that the leak had not provided "information of value to the axis powers. It was not an operational plan, but it bore out my charges against Roosevelt." While the big leak has largely been forgotten due to the spectacular events that occurred just three days after the blockbuster story was published—the Japanese attack on Pearl Harbor—the existence of the secret plan, which had been under development for much of 1941, does provide additional perspective concerning the beliefs and conduct of Wheeler and other noninterventionists during that pivotal year.[53]

Governments, of course, make all of kinds of plans, often secret ones, all the time in order to prepare for a host of possibilities, and that is obviously what Roosevelt and his planners were doing with the Victory Plan. Still, Wheeler correctly contended that the plan he had leaked displayed a sophisticated level of preparation by the Roosevelt administration for what the president and his military advisers obviously considered to be an inevitable war, a fact the president never came close to acknowledging in public. While it is impossible to know how a U.S. public reluctant to commit to war would have reacted had there been knowledge of extensive war planning and preparation earlier than December 1941, it is at least possible that public awareness of the Victory Plan would have provided additional fodder for a fundamental argument of the noninterventionists: that Roosevelt not only kept vital information from Congress and the public but also was a devious dissembler. One can only speculate on what public knowledge of the secret plan, with its explicit acknowledgment of the huge personnel demands required for a global war, would have meant, for example, to the debate that raged when the draft was established in 1940 and extended the next year. It is at least possible that Wheeler's warnings about drafting and sending "American boys" to fight in foreign wars would have assumed greater public urgency and influenced congressional and public opinion.

By the same token, Wheeler was not entirely convincing in his own defense when he said his leak had provided no "information valuable to the axis." Exposure of the plan did provide German and Japanese war planners with valuable insight into a number of strategic assumptions concerning how the United States intended to wage a world war, including perhaps the most important of all strategic considerations, that the

United States would likely adopt a "Germany first" strategy if confronted with a war involving both Germany and Japan. As Robert McCormick's biographer has noted, a week after the publication of the war plans "the fox in the White House prompted the Berlin crow into a fatal miscalculation. On that date [December 11] Hitler appeared before the Reichstag to declare war on the United States." Hitler justified the step, Richard Norton Smith writes, "As a preemptive measure to forestall the huge invasion described by the *Tribune* and its sister publications."[54]

Wheeler's desperate effort to keep the country out of war by leaking the top-secret war plan entailed great personal and political risk. Had his role been revealed at the time he might well have faced criminal action under the Espionage Act, and it is not difficult to imagine that the Roosevelt administration would have prosecuted him to the fullest extent and delighted in doing so. Wheeler was accustomed to playing for high stakes, even if playing required calculated risk. While he took great pains to keep his fingerprints off the leak, Wheeler still acted to expose what he saw as presidential duplicity, always confident in the righteousness of his position. Wheeler's big leak was truly the last grab for influence in the great debate of 1941, but the incident faded quickly, overtaken by vastly more dramatic events in the Pacific.[55]

14 WAR AND DECLINE

My good isolationist friend Wheeler is a natural purveyor of bad news.

—HARRY TRUMAN

Japanese aircraft in the skies over Pearl Harbor on the morning of Sunday, December 7, 1941, marked both the beginning of a war and the end of an era. West Virginia senator Robert C. Byrd, a great student of Senate history, would say years later that "twenty years of political debate ended in a beautiful Hawaiian harbor, marred by the burning hulls of a fleet of American battleships."

"We remember December 7, 1941, as a day of infamy," Byrd said during one of his lectures on Senate history.

> We mourn the hundreds who died at Pearl Harbor, and the thousands who gave their lives in the war that followed. We might also mourn the abrupt ending of the debate over American foreign policy. While history proved President Roosevelt and his followers more correct than their isolationist opponents, it also buried for decades the warnings of the isolationists that the United States should not aspire to police the world, nor should it intervene at will in the affairs of other nations in this hemisphere or elsewhere. Subsequent events . . . demonstrated that some validity existed in the arguments on both sides of that great debate.[1]

Pearl Harbor marked the beginning of the end of B. K. Wheeler's influence in the Senate and accelerated what had become a steady decline in his political support in Montana. Two days before the attack Wheeler had predicted, "The Japanese are bluffing, and don't want war with the United States." But the war came, and with it some of the bitterness of the previous two years abated, at least publicly. "The only thing now is to do our best to lick hell out of them," Wheeler said in Billings upon

Wheeler (*left*) reading the war news—and erroneous headline—upon his arrival at Chicago's Union Station en route from Butte to Washington, D.C., December 9, 1941. Wheeler was in Montana when the Japanese attacked Pearl Harbor, and he missed the Senate vote on a declaration of war. (*AP Photo*)

hearing the news of the Japanese attack. It was clear, he said, that the Japanese "must have gone crazy" and that Congress had to immediately declare war.[2]

In private Wheeler was despondent and resentful, telling America First Committee chair Robert Wood, "I feel we did everything we could to keep this country out of war. We lost and the warmongers have won. They wanted war, and they have it, and now that they have it, they do not know what to do with it." Future generations would hate those politicians who had opposed nonintervention, Wheeler wrote, "because of the foolishness of the President and his advisors."[3]

When Congress voted on December 8 to declare war on Japan, Wheeler was not in Washington. Travel from Montana caused him to miss the vote and Franklin Roosevelt's famous "day of infamy" speech, although he said he would have voted for the declaration of war. Jim Murray privately chided Wheeler for missing the vote, but by not voting Wheeler conveniently was able to have it both ways—say he supported a war declaration but still not vote, as he repeatedly had said he never would, to send

Americans to fight. Montana's pacifist Republican congresswoman Jeannette Rankin did vote against the declaration of war, the only member of Congress to do so.[4]

The America First Committee issued a statement late on December 7 urging "all those who have subscribed to its principles to give their support to the war effort of this country until the conflict with Japan is brought to a successful conclusion. In this war The America First Committee pledges its aid to the President as commander in chief of the armed forces of the United States." The committee announced a meeting four days later to consider whether to disband or undertake some new effort.[5]

"Well, we find ourselves in a pretty mess don't we after having tried to run everybody else's business in every corner of the globe," Lulu Wheeler wrote to daughter Elizabeth. "We have finally pulled the temple down on our own heads." The militant Mrs. Wheeler was adamant that the America First effort had to continue. "I am voting (by mail) a vigorous 'No' to the proposition of their ceasing all activity. I think we should form a 'loyal opposition' that will always be on hand to prevent the abuses that are sure to arise. I have reason to think that those are the sentiments of the Chicago heads—I hope so."[6]

She was wrong. Despite pleas from some leading congressional noninterventionists, Senators La Follette and Johnson among them, the national board of America First voted on December 11, the same day Germany declared war on the United States, to dissolve the organization. The announcement of the committee's end was among the most eloquent statements the organization produced in its year and half of existence, a fitting epitaph for the organization and a cautionary statement about the future of American foreign policy. Ahead lay vast violations of civil liberties (beginning with the relocation and detention of Japanese Americans), decades of U.S. military interventions from Korea to Afghanistan, the establishment of a worldwide American empire of military bases, and a Congress increasingly unwilling to assert its constitutional role regarding war-making.

"Our principles were right," the committee insisted.

Had they been followed, war could have been avoided. No good purpose can now be served by considering what might have been, had our objectives been attained. . . . We are at war. Today, though there may be many important subsidiary considerations, the primary objective is . . . victory.

While the executive branch of the government will take charge of the prosecution of the war, the fundamental Rights of American citizens under our Constitution and Bill of Rights must be respected. The long range aims and policies of our country must be determined by the people through Congress. We hope that secret treaties committing America to imperialistic aims or vast burdens in other parts of the world shall be scrupulously avoided to the end that this nation shall become the champion of a just and lasting peace.[7]

What, then, can be said of history's verdict on the America First Committee, as well as Wheeler's role in the movement? "At its best America First supplied rationale, and data needed for intelligence decision making," says historian Justus Doenecke, who collected and analyzed the vast written record of the committee. "Some of its arguments, particularly as expounded in its position papers, could—if thoroughly debated—have done much to elevate the public dialogue. But the debate far too often became one big exercise in mud slinging, for which the AFC must bear part of the blame." The belligerent anti-British tone of many America First's materials, along with the often bitter, condemning speeches of Wheeler and Nye and particularly Lindbergh's Des Moines speech, damaged the movement's credibility and reputation. However, it is possible to argue, as Doenecke and others have, that the effort by the Roosevelt administration to intimidate and discredit the movement, including bitter assaults on the patriotism and loyalty of its leading spokesmen, leaves Roosevelt and his associates bearing a heavy historical burden for fostering a political climate where dissent and disagreement was considered tantamount to disloyalty.[8]

Roosevelt and his advisors came to detest their anti-interventionist critics because of the profound policy differences separating the two camps but also in part because the noninterventionists had been quite effective, fighting the administration to a standoff by late 1941. Roosevelt speechwriter Robert Sherwood observed that the president "had no more tricks left. The hat from which he had pulled so many rabbits was empty." Despite Roosevelt's skillful and occasionally deceptive maneuvering, until Pearl Harbor there was no public consensus supporting war. Nevertheless America First failed in its one principal objective—to keep the nation out of war.[9]

A central argument of the committee, that the United States was invulnerable to attack, was certainly discredited by the Japanese attack at Pearl Harbor. But a major concern of Wheeler's, that another world war would change American democracy, and not for the better, did not completely miss the mark. While Wheeler's warnings in 1941 that war would bring about "an American dictator" were wildly overstated, the new and evolving national security state did feature presidentially authorized spying on critics, the wholesale internment of American citizens, a further concentration of power in the presidency, often at the expense of congressional influence, and a diminishment of presidential candor. Roosevelt famously quipped in 1942, for example, that he was "perfectly willing to mislead and tell untruths if it will help win the war."[10]

At the same time, Wheeler and other noninterventionists stand condemned for their apparent willingness to accept, as was the case in 1941, that nearly all of western Europe was destined to live under fascist domination, perhaps for generations. Wheeler's belief that somehow the United States could morally and economically stand apart from that now seems naïve or misguided.

The America First movement did succeed in one important and constructive way, and the same could be said for Wheeler. By contributing to the vigorous and extended national debate regarding a fundamental question—when and how the country makes the decision to go to war—the noninterventionist movement performed an essential democratic function. The kind of intense, detailed debate that occurred in 1941 has been sorely missing in every subsequent decision to commit American arms to combat.[11]

———

Prime Minister Winston Churchill came to Washington in late December 1941 to confer face-to-face with Franklin Roosevelt about the war that had finally made the United States and Britain formal allies. The day after Christmas, Churchill addressed a joint session of Congress held not in the House of Representatives, as would have typically been the case, but in the smaller Senate Chamber. Many legislators were away from the capital for the holiday, and it was deemed best to avoid the image of rows of empty seats greeting Churchill. Still, it was a moment of high drama, and the great orator delivered a bellicose and optimistic performance. "I am glad to be able to place before you, members of the Senate and of the House of Representatives," Churchill said, "at this moment when you are entering the war, proof that with proper weapons and proper organization we are able to beat the life out of the savage Nazi." James Reston reported in the *New York Times*, "House members sat on one side of the chamber, Senators on the other. Senator Burton K. Wheeler, leading opponent of the Administration's foreign policy until the Japanese attack, was on the right aisle with an unlighted cigar between his teeth and, like the rest, he applauded vigorously as the speech went on." Churchill's speech, Wheeler said, was "clever" and appealing "to the average American." But he told a news conference that the country needed "less oratory and more action" and called for creating a single procurement agency to speed the production of war material. "We are not, and were not, prepared for war," Wheeler said. He did allow that Churchill during his speech exhibited "more humor than the average Englishman."[12]

———

The war, even its preliminaries, brought great change to Montana. When many of Wheeler's constituents confronted limited employment prospects during the worst of the Great Depression years, substantial numbers of young men joined the military to receive a meager but regular paycheck. After Pearl Harbor, thousands more enlisted—forty thousand Montana men and women in the first year of the war alone. Another eighty thousand Montanans left the state during the war to work in defense industries. By 1945 more than fifty-seven thousand Montanans had served in uniform, over 10 percent of the state's population, and, as during World War I, Montana sent a higher percentage of its citizens into the fight than almost any other state. As many as twenty-five hundred Montanans died as a result of the war, and only New Mexico recorded more combat deaths per capita.[13]

Once the United States entered the fighting, Wheeler involved himself in the war effort in ways large and small. When leaders in Great Falls asked Wheeler and Murray for help locating a military facility, Wheeler lobbied Hap Arnold. By the spring of 1942 Great Falls had been selected as a training site for bomber crews and became a transit point to move Lend-Lease materials (of the sort Wheeler had opposed) from the United States to Canada, on to Alaska, and eventually to Soviet Russia. Military airfields were also constructed at Cut Bank, Glasgow, and Lewistown. With copper, coal, and farm products critical to the war effort, Montana's mining and agriculture became more important than ever during the war. Wheeler personally intervened late in 1943 to broker an agreement to head off a threatened strike by Butte copper miners, and to address farm labor shortages he helped arrange for thousands of enemy prisoners of war to work on the harvest of Montana sugar beets and wheat.[14]

On February 27, 1942, Wheeler celebrated his sixtieth birthday in typical fashion—he gave a speech. The United States would win the war, Wheeler predicted, but "it is going to be a long, hard, bloody war unless our enemies are more exhausted that we here in the United States know about." He also offered his opinion that the war was sure to change "the good old days," with the country likely headed toward adoption of measures that "would have been looked upon a few years ago as ultra-radical, but in comparison to what will happen in the rest of the world will be conservative." Wheeler pleaded for understanding of different points of view and lamented what he called intolerance by "those who talk the loudest" for unity while condemning those who hold different views. "Out of the welter of debate, discussion, and honest criticism . . . the truth emerges," he said. American democracy, Wheeler said, would be preserved by "patience, suffering, and tolerance—particularly tolerance."[15]

Just before Wheeler's speech, Roosevelt initiated one of the "ultra-radical" actions Wheeler warned against. Under the guise of military necessity, Roosevelt ordered the internment of 120,000 Japanese Americans, almost all of them U.S. citizens living in California, Washington, Oregon, and Arizona. The internment order, now viewed as one of the most egregious violations of civil liberties in U.S. history, enjoyed widespread public support at the time, including support from many elected officials. Wheeler privately protested the internment, but there is no record that he offered any public condemnation, and in that he was not alone. "There was little hysteria in the Second World War," Wheeler would write in his memoirs, "compared to the first one, except on the West Coast, where the United States confiscated Japanese property and interned American citizens because they were of Japanese blood. This was a violation of the Constitution and violated the very principles of the Four Freedoms, for which the President said we were fighting. There was no law on the books to sanction this high-handed action."[16]

"I protested to various high-level government officials," Wheeler wrote,

including the late Secretary of War Robert P. Patterson. I had always had respect for Patterson as a very able lawyer, but when he defended the internment of American citizens as a necessary action under the circumstances, I was surprised and disillusioned.

So far as I know, there was no case of disloyalty ever brought against any of these people. If the federal government can get away with such treatment of citizens of Japanese descent, it can do the same to any minority. It should demonstrate to the American people that there is all too little difference between us and any other people when war or hysteria, or both, grip the nation."[17]

Roosevelt, as Wheeler feared he would, pressed other initiatives aimed at eliminating domestic dissent or what the president considered disloyalty. "Have you pretty well cleaned out the alien waiters in the principle Washington hotels?" Roosevelt asked J. Edgar Hoover early in 1942. "Altogether too much conversation in the dining rooms!" Roosevelt also wanted private transatlantic telephone calls to neutral nations ended, on the theory that such calls might be the source of enemy intelligence, and he ordered widespread monitoring of much official communication. Roosevelt, as his attorney general observed, "was not much interested in the theory of sedition, or in the constitutional right to criticize the government in wartime. He wanted this antiwar talk stopped."[18]

Roosevelt repeatedly urged Attorney General Francis Biddle to crack down on administration opponents, demanding of Biddle during a cabinet meeting, "When are you going to indict the seditionists?" Roosevelt got his wish in mid-1942 when a federal grand jury indicted thirty mostly right-wing activists—"assorted nativists, isolationists, and former leaders of the German-American Bund"—on charges of conspiracy to obstruct the national defense effort and bring about a pro-Nazi, fascist government in the United States. The indictments resulted in a lengthy legal proceeding in 1944, *United States v. McWilliams*, more popularly known as "the Great Sedition Trial." The liberal New York newspaper *PM* said of the defendants, "Seldom have so many wild-eyed, jumpy lunatic fringe characters been assembled in one spot, within speaking, winking, and whispering distance of one another."[19]

William P. Maloney, Biddle's special assistant, was in charge of securing grand jury indictments against the activists, and he was less than scrupulous in observing due process. Maloney, as historian Arthur Herman has written, did "all the things people would later accuse [Joseph] McCarthy of doing. He publicized unsubstantiated charges against political opponents; he leaked grand jury testimony to the press; he indicted [Congressman] Hamilton Fish's legislative aide in hopes that he would implicate his boss as a German agent; and he ceaselessly charged that there was an active conspiracy between conservatives and far right groups like the Silver Shirts."[20]

Wheeler objected repeatedly to the prosecutions, including the fact—and here he might have been recalling the details of his own indictment in 1924—that the defendants were arrested in jurisdictions all across the country but indicted collectively in Washington. Given his own pre-war activity and outspoken opposition to the administration, Wheeler had reason to fear that he might also be under investigation and subject to prosecution. At the very least he believed he would have to endure a smear campaign linking him to the odd assortment of political cranks, anti-Semites, and Roosevelt haters who ultimately were indicted.[21]

Maloney's tactics "smack of an inquisition of bygone days," Wheeler wrote to Attorney General Biddle, and he belittled the contention that any conspiracy existed among those charged:

> I scarcely know any of the defendants—and certainly to not approve of the things which they are charged with saying and writing. I believe that they were mostly the mouthing of irresponsible people. But, however misguided they may have been, I cannot believe that some of them were guilty of a conspiracy to obstruct national defense or break down the morale of the armed forces of America.
>
> It is entirely possible that some individuals and organizations may have had that in view, but to draft a catch-all indictment including patriotic organizations and individuals with unpatriotic organizations for the purpose of smearing them is in itself, to say the least, reprehensible and should not be tolerated in this country.[22]

Biddle responded by saying that a federal grand jury had considered evidence against the defendants for a total of seventy-one days before returning indictments, a contention that did not satisfy the former U.S. attorney. Wheeler said he knew from experience "how easy it is for a prosecuting attorney to indict anyone he wants regardless of the evidence," and he complained that Maloney, the government's point man on the case, "was bantering my name, and other Senators' names, around the court without the slightest foundation for so doing, trying to give the impression that some of us who were opposed to getting into the war were guilty of some crime." Biddle would be well advised to dismiss his assistant, Wheeler said, and install an attorney "who has the respect and confidence of Congress and the people." Maloney was eventually replaced, but the new prosecutor, O. John Rogge, pursued essentially the same approach to the case, and the prosecutions went forward—for months and months.[23]

Rogge took over the prosecution in 1944, and two years later produced an internal Justice Department report that accused Wheeler and several other pre-war noninterventionists of being under German influence. Rogge alleged that German agents had convinced the politicians to use their franking privileges to disseminate pro-Nazi propaganda. When Rogge, in violation of Justice Department policy, referenced the report in a speech, including suggesting that labor leader John L. Lewis had engaged in a vast Nazi-inspired conspiracy in 1940 to engineer Franklin Roosevelt's defeat at the polls, Attorney General Tom Clark fired him. Rogge's report was eventually published in 1961. There is no evidence that Wheeler cooperated in any direct way with German agents, but he may well have been guilty of the occasionally careless use of his frank. He was, after all, merely distributing his own speeches, which, while critical of government policy, contained many of the same arguments he had been making for twenty years. Commenting on his firing during the Truman administration, Rogge reportedly said, "Wheeler was closer to Truman than I was."[24]

The *Washington Post*'s coverage of the sedition trial—one headline read "Wheeler Defends Sedition Suspects, Although Nazis Used Him as a 'Front'"—is an example of the kind of the guilt-by-association reporting that Wheeler not infrequently endured. The newspaper, citing no evidence, said Wheeler's objection to the indictments provided proof that he was an "innocent and unknowing tool of the German propaganda ministry." The *Post* made particular note of the fact that one man indicted in the Justice Department dragnet, Franz K. Ferenz, a California crackpot, member of the German-American Bund, and the owner of a bookstore that sold Nazi materials, had been photographed at America First rallies where Wheeler had spoken. The newspaper provided no evidence of any other connection between the two men. Wheeler blasted the story as "dirty business" and scolded the newspaper for being "nothing but a stooge . . . for the Department of Justice."[25]

Early in 1943, Wheeler denounced another "a smear campaign" against him, this one by syndicated columnist Drew Pearson. Wheeler described Pearson as "that little black animal which has a white stripe up its back." "I am getting sick and tired of sitting here," Wheeler said, "trying to . . . do everything I possibly can to win the war and then having a lot of snipers here peddling out information to some of these columnists." Wheeler challenged Pearson and *Washington Post* publisher Eugene Meyer to produce evidence that he was hampering the war effort. He labeled the press criticism of him as nothing less than "deliberate falsehoods." Still other publications joined in Wheeler attacks, with *Time* and *Life* publishing unflattering photos of Wheeler,

Lindbergh, and Joseph P. Kennedy side-by-side with a profile of Lawrence Dennis, a writer, fascist-oriented propagandist, and one of those indicted in the sedition action. The magazines described Dennis as "America's No. 1 Intellectual Fascist."[26]

The Great Sedition Trial—"the biggest and noisiest sedition trial in U.S. history," according to *Time*—plodded on for months. The government's indictments were so badly drawn that they twice had to be rewritten, and still the prosecution struggled to assemble a case. The trial was finally suspended late in 1944 after the presiding judge died of a heart attack, and finally in 1946 the Justice Department opted to end the prosecution. The *Washington Post*, after originally linking Wheeler and other noninterventionists to the defendants, admitted, even before the trial was terminated, that the whole exercise had been a "mistake" and "that whatever may be the outcome of this trial it will stand as a black mark against American justice for many years to come." And so it did. Dennis and an attorney for another defendant in the sedition trial would later write, "It is . . . to the great credit of Senators Wheeler, [Robert] Taft [of Ohio] and [William] Langer [of North Dakota] and Congressman [Clare] Hoffman [of Michigan], that, during the course of the Trial, they spoke out most effectively on the floor of the Congress in criticism of what the government was doing." Again Wheeler, at considerable peril to his own political and legal standing, stood fast in defense of dissent.[27]

"The Great Sedition Trial left no legal precedent and put no one behind bars," legal scholar and historian Geoffrey Stone has written, "but it did curtail right-wing propaganda during the war, compel thirty American fascists to defend themselves in court for four years, and set an important *political* precedent for the Smith Act prosecutions of Communists during the Cold War, which loomed just around the corner."[28]

It is likely that Wheeler did not fully understand the extent of the administration's efforts to discredit him, even considering his innate skepticism about Roosevelt. Late in 1941, for example, Roosevelt personally instructed the postmaster general, Butte native Frank Walker, to "look quietly into the radio situation in Montana . . . Wheeler has seen to it that a 50,000-watt station has been made possible to a political friend of his out there." At about the time Roosevelt instructed Walker to undertake his review, Ed Craney, the Montana broadcasting entrepreneur and close Wheeler friend, applied to the Federal Communications Commission (FCC) to assume ownership of the fifty-thousand-watt clear-channel frequency of New York's WEAF, the flagship station of NBC's Red Network and one of the most highly regarded radio stations in the country. Reporting on Craney's application to acquire the frequency, the industry publication *Broadcasting* took note of Craney's reputation, which, the publication said, attached "unusual significance to the request. Mr. Craney is regarded as the chief radio advisor to Senator Wheeler (D-Mont.) chairman of the Senate Interstate Commerce

Committee, and is a close personal friend." Whether or not the administration quietly interceded to block the frequency transfer, the FCC rejected Craney's application shortly after Roosevelt ordered Walker to look into the matter.[29]

Another instance of the administration seeking opportunities to embarrass Wheeler involved the Wheeler cabin in Glacier National Park. The cabin occupied leased ground inside the park. In 1941 a fire damaged the summer retreat that Wheeler had purchased in 1916, and Lulu Wheeler, who loved the place perhaps even more than her husband did, managed the construction of a new cabin and other buildings, and work continued into the summer of 1942.

When the Wheeler cabin was placed on the National Register of Historic Places in 1998, the National Park Service noted: "In 1941, Glacier National Park officials found themselves faced with a situation . . . very embarrassing both to the administration of [the] park, the [National Park] Service and the Department [of the Interior]." The embarrassment came about during the course of the cabin rebuild when the Park Service discovered that Wheeler apparently did not have a valid lease for the cabin site. Federal law, the Park Service noted, seemed to prohibit Wheeler from entering into a lease for the cabin site after his election to the Senate in 1922. The Park Service concluded, and with considerable delight Interior Secretary Ickes concurred, that Wheeler had effectively been squatting on federal land for twenty years.[30]

Wheeler went ahead and began the rebuild after receiving approval from Interior Department Undersecretary John Dempsey. Dempsey indicated that he had "no objection [to] remodeling log cabin . . . under present status." Meanwhile Ickes, unaware that his deputy had already granted Wheeler permission to rebuild, suggested in a memo to Roosevelt that he would like to initiate steps to evict "a certain eminent squatter on Glacier Park land." After reviewing this sequence of events just before Christmas 1942—American troops were engaged in combat from North Africa to New Guinea, and presumably Roosevelt was occupied with far more important matters—the president wrote to Ickes, "I am inclined to think that in view of Undersecretary Dempsey's reply to Senator Wheeler permitting remodeling of the log cabin, we are somewhat estopped from taking any further action." Roosevelt continued, "It is my thought that Senator and Mrs. Wheeler should be allowed to live in their cabin during their lifetimes but that this right should not extend to some other member of their family beyond their respective deaths." It was later determined that the cabin could remain in family control as long as direct descendants of senator and Mrs. Wheeler remained alive. The property reverted to the Park Service in 2014 upon the death of Marion Wheeler Scott. The radio license and cabin episodes in the full context of the Roosevelt-Wheeler relationship are perhaps trivial, but each illustrates the administration's attention to any detail, large or small, that might reflect poorly on Wheeler.[31]

The long-running feud between Wheeler and his Montana colleague Jim Murray—one historian has written that their personal animus "has few parallels in modern times"—reached a flashpoint in 1942 when Murray ran for reelection against Wheeler's old Republican friend Wellington Rankin.[32]

Speculation about the hostility between the two senators ran so hot that Wheeler was forced to deny fanciful rumors that he might resign his own Senate seat in order to run against Murray in the Montana Democratic primary. Instead Wheeler adopted the approach he had used successfully against Jerry O'Connell four years earlier. He encouraged an opponent—former Congressman Joseph Monaghan—to challenge Murray in the Democratic primary, and then, after that challenge fell short, Wheeler quietly helped his friend Rankin in the general election. In a speech in Glasgow, anticipating the Senate race, Wheeler said, "I do not care who the people of Montana elect to the Senate [he did care, of course], except that I would like to see them elect someone who will fight for Montana in Washington, and who will be more interested in the problems of our people than in political jobs for a few favorites." That was a swipe at Murray and his involvement with the WPA controversies in the 1930s. Murray fired back hard in a radio speech: "If I am driven out of the Senate of the United States by these conspirators who are rushing up and down Montana seeking to organize what is left of Roosevelt-haters, isolationists, and pro-Nazis, I will at least go out of the Senate with my head erect and my conscience clear."[33]

As the 1942 campaign unfolded, Montana voters must have thought at times that Wheeler and Murray were running against each other. In dueling statewide radio addresses Murray attacked Wheeler for "talking the language of Hitler," and Wheeler responded by saying that Murray was guilty of "cheap politics" and "childish imbecility." He went on: "Those of you who know me—who have voted for me over the years—those of you who have been my friends and in whose homes I have visited—do you believe that I . . . was talking the language of Hitler? My first and only love is the United States and I was denouncing Hitler when Wall Street and Downing Street and Internationalists were supporting Hitler because they wanted him to wipe out the Communists in Russia and the threat of Communism throughout the world."[34]

The nasty language improved little when Murray, totally ignoring his primary opponent, referred to Wheeler as "the man who assumes to be the dictator of Montana politics." Murray also accused Wheeler of using his Senate staff and a "slush fund" to work against him.[35]

Despite Wheeler's open opposition, Murray won the Democratic primary easily, but in the flush of victory he overstated the extent of his victory. In a telegram to Roosevelt Murray said, "I have defeated and discredited Senator Wheeler and restored the good

name of Montana.... Wheeler came here with the conceit and arrogance of a dictator....
He will leave Montana and sneak into Washington a discredited and disgruntled politician
with nothing left but the frazzled remnants of his ruined reputation."[36]

Winning the Democratic nomination merely set up the real political donnybrook for
Murray. Wellington Rankin, a wealthy Helena attorney, rancher, brother of Congresswoman Jeannette Rankin, and a leader of the moderate wing of the Montana GOP, had
been close to Wheeler for years. Rankin boasted an impressive résumé—Harvard Law
grad, Rhodes Scholar, Montana attorney general, Montana Supreme Court justice,
and U.S. attorney—but had a mixed record as a candidate, including losing races for
the state legislature and governor. Rankin had managed both of his sister's successful
congressional races, but he had little of Jeannette's—or Wheeler's—knack for working
a room, mingling with voters, or connecting from the stump.[37]

Still Rankin campaigned energetically, aggressively taking the fight to Murray. As
Murray's biographer Donald Spritzer has written, "From the outset [Rankin] played
on the voters' wartime discontent and threw Murray on the defensive. He charged
the administration with slighting Montana in establishing new war industries. He
repeatedly informed crowds that more Montanans per capita were being drafted
than in neighboring states. The Republican candidate also berated Murray's work on
behalf of small business." That was a particularly damaging charge since Murray was
a member of the Senate's Small Business Committee. Murray fought back against the
charge that he was ineffective in the Senate, and using the power of incumbency he
held hearings on small business concerns in several Montana cities. The face-to-face
politics were critical, since news of Murray's appearances and the content of his speeches
rarely received attention in Anaconda Company newspapers, while Rankin enjoyed
extensive coverage. Murray proved to be most effective when he encouraged voters to
evaluate his challenger on the basis of the voting record of his pacifist sister, a record
Murray deemed "un-American." The attack was damaging since Jeannette Rankin's
vote to oppose a declaration of war against Japan was, as Spritzer says, "still ringing
in many Montanans' ears" in 1942.[38]

Wheeler made no public comments during the general election campaign, but political observers detected the senator and his loyal associates doing everything possible
behind the scenes to help Rankin, effectively mobilizing the bipartisan coalition that
had carried Wheeler and Republican governor Sam Ford to victory two years earlier.
On the stump Murray frequently criticized both the Republicans and the Democrats
opposing him, charging that the Wheeler-Rankin-Ford alliance was attempting to
exert complete political control over Montana. Rankin's wife, Louise, would later
laughingly refer to Wheeler, Rankin, and Ford as "The Unholy Triumvirate," adding,
"And of course Wheeler was a Democrat."[39]

Wheeler wrote to Ed Craney late in the campaign that he was leaning toward the belief that "Murray will be elected but I am not at all sure. He is slippery—he makes a fool out of himself every time he opens his mouth. He has been getting drunk around some of the smaller towns I am told which spreads." Wheeler avoided the Montana Democratic convention in September, telling Craney he was content to "let Murray run it. He wants to be the big boss, let him take it. As far as I am concerned the situation gets better every day—at least that is my thought."[40]

Wheeler, hoping for a Rankin victory but not entirely expecting one, believed his old friend's campaign had "been miserably handled" and that Rankin had not "shown as much courage and guts as he should have." Wheeler especially thought Rankin should have emphasized opposition to drafting eighteen- and nineteen-year-olds into military service. After taking his own political soundings among Montana voters, particularly mothers, Wheeler was convinced that drafting Montana teenagers was a position that was bound "to hurt Mr. Roosevelt and Murray."[41]

Wheeler's bipartisan coalition nearly pulled off a win for Rankin. Democrats lost nine Senate seats in the midterm elections of 1942, but Murray, while suffering a scare, held his seat against that very stiff Republican tide and the opposition of Wheeler. The Murray-Rankin contest was one of the closest in Montana history and by far the closest Senate race in the country in 1942. When Rankin finally conceded three days after the election he trailed Murray by only 1,212 votes. Surprisingly, both candidates won where their opponent should have been the strongest. Murray outpolled Rankin in Helena, where Rankin practiced law, and Rankin won in Butte, Murray's political base. The loss in Silver Bow County may have reflected continuing resentment of Butte's Irish American voters—whom Murray had offended with embrace of Roosevelt's pre-war support of Britain—but it may also have reflected Wheeler's influence in his own political stronghold. In none of his other elections—in 1934 when he was first elected to complete Tom Walsh's term, or in elections in 1936, 1948, or 1954—did Murray lose in Butte or Silver Bow County. Murray typically eked out small statewide margins in each of his Senate races, helped by his ability to accumulate 2–1 margins in Silver Bow County, but not in 1942.[42]

In claiming victory Murray said he had overcome "a strong Republican state organization and the powerful opposition of Senator Wheeler's Democratic machine." Still, Wheeler had the last word, chiding his junior colleague about his loss in Butte. "If I were Senator Murray and had lost my home town, a Democratic stronghold, and only won by such a small margin, I wouldn't do any boasting," he said. Lulu Wheeler told her daughter she believed the election signaled the end of the New Deal, which pleased her, but she was "terribly sorry to see Murray get by."[43]

Murray's biographer correctly notes, "Despite the closeness of the election, Murray had achieved something a powerful New Deal congressman [Jerry O'Connell] and an incumbent governor [Roy Ayers] had failed to achieve. He had won reelection over the opposition of Burton K. Wheeler and his powerful political alliance."[44]

Another big Montana political winner in 1942 was a young history professor from the University of Montana and onetime mucker in Butte's copper mines. Republicans picked up forty-seven seats in the House of Representatives in 1942, but Democrat Mike Mansfield ran against that Republican tide and captured 60 percent of the vote in western Montana's congressional district. Mansfield was helped in his quest to replace Jeannette Rankin—who opted not to run for reelection—by Roosevelt assistant James Rowe. Rowe solicited campaign funds for Mansfield from Speaker of the House Sam Rayburn, pointing out to the Speaker that Mansfield "has carefully kept away from getting into a factional fight with either the Murray or Wheeler factions in Montana." Rowe also touted the young politician to Roosevelt, calling Mansfield "an intelligent New Dealer with an international point of view [who] combines the excellent background of a hard-rock copper miner and history professor." Roosevelt took careful notice of Mansfield as a potential future rival to Wheeler.[45]

In the immediate aftermath of the sizeable Republican gains in Congress, the Senate took up new selective service legislation late in 1942, and Wheeler strongly opposed drafting eighteen- and nineteen-year-olds, as he believed his friend Rankin should have. Wheeler opposed the legislation because, he said, voters in the recent election had shown they were "opposed to having the whole civil population of the country regimented by a lot of bureaucrats in Washington who do not know the problems of the people in the hinterlands. The people voted as they did because they did not want any administration, Republican or Democratic, to have all these dictatorial powers." Early in 1943, with two of his sons on active military duty, Wheeler continued his three-year crusade against the administration's selective service policies by introducing legislation to exempt entirely from the draft men who had become fathers before Pearl Harbor. Wheeler argued that military estimates of the personnel necessary to wage the war were excessive and that drafting fathers would result "in breaking up the home life of many families." Furthermore, he said, there were plenty of able-bodied "government employees, who, like swarms of locusts, infest Washington and every city in the land where Government bureaus have been established." These employees should be transferred to the military, he said. Washington alone, Wheeler argued in a radio speech, could "furnish a full army division of men who are less essential to winning the war than the housewife who saves her kitchen fat." Congress recessed for the summer without acting on Wheeler's legislation, but it eventually agreed to structure the draft so that fathers, though not exempted, were the last called to military service.[46]

Pulitzer Prize–winning reporter Allen Drury was a keen observer of Wheeler in this period. Drury wrote in his classic *A Senate Journal* that Wheeler was "understandably bitter" regarding the outcome of his foreign policy confrontation with Roosevelt and particularly about his characterization at the hands of his adversaries. Nevertheless, Drury said, Wheeler was "a very able man, and his views of foreign policy have little to do with his stature as a senator, which is considerable. In fact, so amiable is he, with such a good sense of humor, that it is hard to reconcile the bitter partisan and the calculating politician who is undoubtedly biding his time in preparation for the reaction he believes will be inevitable." Not everyone agreed. A blistering 1943 article in the *New Republic*, a magazine often sympathetic to Wheeler in the past, criticized his stand on selective service, his lack of support for national defense measures, his criticism of prosecutions of what the magazine called "tinhorn fascists," and his questioning of U.S. military strategy. "It is undeniable that Wheeler today makes no public suggestions except that are harmful to the war effort," the magazine said, before essentially labeling Wheeler a fascist.[47]

Wheeler also publicly took issue with the administration strategy of defeating Germany first before turning fully against Japan. In Wheeler's view such an approach would prolong the war and weaken the U.S. hand in fashioning the postwar peace. Like many Republicans but not many Democrats, Wheeler thought the administration gave too little attention and resources to the U.S. commander in the Southwest Pacific, General Douglas MacArthur. Wheeler may have been motivated in this view because he saw MacArthur as a potential challenger to Roosevelt. Writing to his friend Robert Wood, Wheeler suggested that MacArthur might be the only person who could defeat Roosevelt for the presidency in 1944, an outcome Wheeler privately believed essential.[48]

While congressional attention increasingly focused on what ought to happen after the war was won, Wheeler argued that formulation of postwar strategy, including the shape of a new international organization to replace the League of Nations, was premature and should wait until Americans could gauge "the situation which will exist at the expiration of the war." The Soviet Union, Wheeler thought, presented particular challenges, and he correctly predicted that Stalin's postwar designs on "a large share of Poland, the Baltic states of Estonia, Latvia and Lithuania and a substantial part of the Balkans" would contribute to ongoing international tensions after the war. Furthermore, Wheeler said, Russia had "yet to show a clear-cut demonstration that she is on our side in the Pacific war." And Wheeler continued his skepticism of British war aims, particularly in the Pacific, where he believed British policy was predicated by a desire to preserve or even expand the British Empire. It would be much more in the interest of the United States, Wheeler said, "to proceed primarily with an offensive against Japan, and only secondarily with the allied invasion of Europe, pending the defeat of Japan." U.S. policy was, of course, precisely the reverse, with planning far along on a cross-channel invasion of France that ultimately took place in June 1944.[49]

Wheeler was no more successful influencing Senate consideration of a new postwar international organization. When consensus eventually formed around an approach suggested by the Foreign Relations Committee chair, Texan Tom Connally, Wheeler was one of five senators to vote no. The critical language of what became known as the Connally Resolution called for "the establishment and maintenance of international authority with power to prevent aggression and to preserve the peace of the world." Many pre–Pearl Harbor noninterventionists, including Nye, Taft, and Vandenberg, voted for the Connally Resolution. Wheeler joined three Republicans and one Democrat in offering only ineffective talking points against the proposal and making familiar complaints about unfair attacks on their character and foreign policy views. The resolution placed the Senate unambiguously on record supporting a postwar international organization dedicated to keeping the peace, and it was, as Wheeler knew and lamented, another major step away from nonintervention and toward a postwar internationalist foreign policy.[50]

In a long piece written for the New York Times, Wheeler articulated his concerns about the proposed new organization that he feared might require the United States to contribute to "a world police force," an idea he flatly rejected. Rather than keeping the peace through military force, Wheeler maintained his long-standing faith in open markets and suggested that the United States ought to embrace establishment of "an economic United States of Europe," an idea, broadly speaking, not unlike what would become the European Union:

> It is the scheme of an economic United States of Europe then—an economic union perhaps not inclusive at the start but designed to embrace western Europe, which holds out the best avenue for world peace. One cannot exaggerate the stabilizing effects upon the world that a great free trade area in Europe, the counterpart of the great free trade area of our own country, would create. It would be creating a situation that tended to remove at their very roots the cause of war. And many capable men believe that unless it is brought about Europe will eventually perish in internecine strife.
>
> Through such an economic union it might further be possible to get rid of traditional jealousy and prejudice and create political understanding between the several nations of Europe, soundly founded on the broad base of unrestricted

free trade—an understanding which is demanded not only by the interests of the peoples but by the causes of civilization itself.[51]

Continuing his nearly unbroken streak of opposition to Roosevelt foreign policy positions, Wheeler rejected the administration's policy of insisting on "unconditional surrender" as the only acceptable way to end the war. Wheeler thought the policy too limiting—Churchill also had serious reservations about the policy—since it might discourage a popular uprising against Hitler in Germany. In an open letter to Roosevelt from Helena on September 2, 1943, Wheeler asked for a definition of "unconditional surrender" and suggested that as a "champion of democracy and opponent of totalitarianism" Roosevelt could "now bring about peace in Europe." Roosevelt, as usual, did not respond. When Wheeler again objected to the unconditional surrender policy near the end of the war, Secretary of State Edward Stettinius called his comments "profoundly regrettable" and added, "Senator Wheeler speaks not for the American people, but for a discredited few whose views have been overwhelmingly rejected by their fellow citizens of every party." Public opinion supported Stettinius's view, with one survey indicating that 81 percent of Americans supported the unconditional surrender policy.[52]

———

Attacks on Wheeler's character and patriotism continued nearly unabated in 1943, with the most notable appearing in what became the surprise blockbuster political book of the year. An Armenian immigrant, Arthur Derounian, born Avedis Boghos Derounian and writing under the pseudonym John Roy Carlson, authored the sensational book *Under Cover*. Derounian, hereafter referred to as Carlson, styled himself a freelance journalist and undercover investigator, and his book sold nearly a million copies. One admirer was John Rogge, the prosecutor in the mass sedition trial, who called Carlson the most gifted private investigator in the county. Using various aliases, Carlson had undertaken an "investigation" of Nazi agents who he alleged were at large in the United States. His finding: "Axis agents and our enemies within are now plotting to destroy the United States." The "facts" Carlson assembled frequently included out-of-context quotations or merely lists of participants in allegedly clandestine meetings. These cherry-picked details were carefully organized to create the most lurid and damaging interpretation to support Carlson's premise that a pro-fascist conspiracy existed in the United States. Like all conspiracy theorists Carlson relied on healthy doses of guilt by association and wrote with a level of certainty that gave his potboiler the thinnest veneer of believability. For those already inclined to believe that Wheeler and other pre-war noninterventionists were in fact Nazi secret agents taking orders directly from Berlin, Carlson's book seemed to offer the proof, spread across 544 pages. Closer examination of the "evidence" reveals a hackneyed smear piece, journalism of the type commonly found in a supermarket tabloid.[53]

The index of *Under Cover* contains more references to Wheeler than to any other elected official, with most entries offering a third-party view of Wheeler's personality or positions. The activist Lawrence Dennis, indicted as part of the Great Sedition Trial, was quoted, for example, as saying, "Wheeler is a good fellow, but he can't stand up to Nye." In a chapter titled "Liberty's Hangman," Wheeler's opposition to the prosecution of antiwar activists was cast as a defense of "America's alleged Quislings." For Wheeler and other pre-war noninterventionists, including John Flynn and Norman Thomas, Carlson's book was the latest in a long line of attacks on their character and patriotism, albeit potentially one of the most damaging. In response to the book Wheeler introduced a resolution authorizing a Senate investigation of connections that Carlson reportedly maintained with the FBI, including the allegation that Carlson was or had been a paid investigator or informant for the bureau. "This man [Carlson] is the author of a book which seeks, by inference at least, to smear anyone and everyone who has tried to keep the country out of war," Wheeler said. The resolution gained no traction in the Senate, so Flynn undertook his own investigation and confirmed that Carlson had worked for the pro-interventionist Fight for Freedom group as well as the Friends of Democracy and had, in fact, spent a few months on the FBI payroll. Flynn concluded, with hyperbole just shy of what Carlson used in his book, that *Under Cover* was part of a vast conspiracy to discredit Wheeler and the antiwar movement, a conspiracy directed by the Communist Party USA with at least indirect encouragement from the White House.[54]

Carlson's book can still be found in used bookstores and for sale online, but it is nearly worthless as history of a particularly contentious period in U.S. politics. Still, the book, which commanded a wide audience when it was published in 1943, helped advance the narrative that pre-war noninterventionists were essentially un-American, holding views and taking actions that damaged national security. The book's appearance during the same period as the Justice Department's high-profile sedition trial—even Flynn labeled the defendants in that proceeding "a handful of crackpot[s]"—undoubtedly enhanced the book's impact with the public.[55]

———

The 1944 presidential election presented Wheeler with one more dilemma. He had opposed a third Roosevelt term in 1940 hoping that he might garner the Democratic nomination but then pledged to support the ticket while quietly casting his own ballot for Norman Thomas. In 1944, with the end of the war in sight, it was a foregone conclusion that Roosevelt would seek and likely win a fourth term. Amazingly, rumors persisted among politicians and the press that Wheeler might be drafted to replace Vice President Henry Wallace as Roosevelt's running mate on the Democratic ticket. Wallace had fallen out of favor with party bosses as well as with many in Congress, and it was an open secret that he would be replaced.[56]

The Wheeler-on-the-ticket rumor mill was stoked on May 11, 1944, when the Montanan made his first visit to the White House in nearly seven years. Wheeler had last been in the president's office during the Supreme Court fight in the summer of 1937. This time he ostensibly went to invite Roosevelt to participate in a congressional ceremony marking the hundredth anniversary of transmittal from the Capitol of the first telegraph message. The meeting lasted forty-five minutes, and when Wheeler left the White House he offered little information about what had been discussed. Years later Wheeler remembered that he had warned Roosevelt about Soviet designs on Poland and the Balkan states, and he recalled being shocked when Roosevelt let slip the news that the Allied invasion of Normandy would commence on June 5. (Bad weather eventually postponed the attack till June 6.) Concerned that the top-secret information might leak and that his "enemies would blame me and not the President," Wheeler did not confide the date to anyone, not even his wife. Asked to comment to the press at the time on "how he thought the President looked following his month's rest in the South," Wheeler uncharacteristically declined comment, but he clearly recognized that Roosevelt's health had deteriorated badly. The meeting between the two frequent adversaries, perhaps because it was so unusual and the announced reason seemed so inconsequential, spawned rumors about Wheeler's availability as Roosevelt's running mate, but he never again set foot in White House while Roosevelt was alive.[57]

Wheeler would claim that Roosevelt never raised the issue of the vice presidency but rather that several administration emissaries sounded him out about his interest in the number two spot as well as his views on other potential candidates. It is inconceivable that Roosevelt would have accepted Wheeler on the ticket. There was too much bad blood between the two, not to mention profound differences regarding international relations. Wheeler acknowledged in his memoirs that he "would have had to repudiate" much of what he had been saying about foreign policy in order to run with Roosevelt, but he still flattered himself that the prospect of his joining the ticket had been real. It seems more likely that the wily Roosevelt, even in declining health and confronted with the daily management of a global war, was simply keeping Wheeler off balance, as he had in 1940, encouraging rumors that would never become more than rumors.[58]

Further evidence that Roosevelt would never have accepted Wheeler as his vice presidential running mate is that the president already had identified the young politician—Congressman Mike Mansfield—who he hoped would deny Wheeler a fifth term when he had to run again in 1946. Mansfield had his own meeting at the White House in the fall of 1944 and pitched Roosevelt the idea of sending him as a personal presidential envoy to assess the military and political situation in China. Roosevelt readily agreed to the request, and it was decided that Mansfield's trip, which would be described as undertaken at the request of the White House, would take place immediately following the fall election. Mansfield's biographer Don Oberdorfer writes, "Clearly, FDR had something else in mind in sending a freshman congressman . . . halfway around the world as his personal emissary. The existing evidence suggests that Roosevelt was motivated by political and personal factors—a wish to enhance Mansfield's stature in hopes that in the elections of 1946 two years later the congressman would slay FDR's personal dragon . . . Burton K. Wheeler." Jim Rowe, the Roosevelt confidant who had prompted the president's interest in Mansfield in 1942, may have suggested the China mission as a way to elevate Mansfield's standing in Montana and in Congress. National labor leaders, including Teamsters president Dan Tobin, perhaps acting at White House urging, were quietly beginning to think about whom they might support against Wheeler in 1946, and Mansfield was an obvious candidate, particularly after he easily won reelection in November 1944 and undertook the presidential mission. Upon his return from the Far East, Mansfield personally delivered to Roosevelt a twenty-three-page report on his observations, and he followed up with an hour-long speech on the House floor. The trip and the attention it generated began to cement Mansfield's reputation as a congressional expert on Asia. Later in his career Mansfield famously shunned publicity, but early in 1945, perhaps thinking about his positioning for a future run against Wheeler, "China Mike" Mansfield made the most of the unusual mission. He wrote newspaper articles and sought speaking opportunities across Montana, including appearances outside his congressional district.[59]

Wheeler privately hoped that New York governor Thomas E. Dewey, the Republican presidential candidate, would defeat Roosevelt in 1944. While not particularly enthusiastic about Dewey, Wheeler told Robert Wood that "a change is quite necessary for the good of the country." Roosevelt's victory margin was the smallest of any of his four elections, and he carried Montana by less than twenty thousand votes, with nearly a third of the margin coming from Wheeler's political base in Silver Bow County. Wheeler was heartened by the election of his friend Harry Truman as vice president, as well as by the reelection Governor Ford, his bipartisan partner in Montana. Ford won handily over Montana Supreme Court justice Leif Erickson. A year earlier a *Chicago Sun* reporter had written that Montana was "pretty well controlled by a powerful, smooth functioning bi-partisan political machine—the Wheeler-Ford-Rankin machine," and the reporter had suggested that Wheeler could likely "hold his office as long as he pleases." That analysis was more accurate in the summer of 1943 than in the fall of

1944. A close read of the 1944 election results offered evidence that Wheeler's grip on Montana had weakened.[60]

Erickson, the Democratic gubernatorial candidate, enjoying strong backing from Jim Murray and the pro-FDR faction in the Montana Democratic Party, had been able to consolidate the Democrat vote in Silver Bow, Deer Lodge, and Cascade Counties, population centers where organized labor was a potent political force. Roosevelt also carried those areas with ease. Had Wheeler carefully read the tea leaves, analyzing how easily Mansfield had won reelection with strong labor backing, he would have seen on his political left at least two potential future challengers—Erickson and Mansfield—able to command support from the pro-Roosevelt, pro-labor Montana Democrats, the faction that dominated party primary elections. If a future left-leaning challenger to Wheeler was successful in gaining labor support, or even in splitting the labor vote, he could make a serious run at the incumbent in the 1946 Democratic primary.[61]

Political signs across the country were also ominous. Pre-war noninterventionists seeking reelection in 1944 were decimated. Four of Wheeler's usually reliable foreign policy allies—Gerald Nye in North Dakota, Bennett Champ Clark in Missouri, Guy Gillette in Iowa, and D. Worth Clark in Idaho—lost their reelection bids in 1944. Wheeler lost another ally when Washington senator Homer T. Bone, sensing that he might well not get reelected, resigned from the Senate to accept a court appointment. Even Hamilton Fish, the long-serving Republican and die-hard isolationist who represented Roosevelt's own GOP-leaning Hyde Park district in New York, lost his reelection bid. The Montana machine—Wheeler, Ford, and Rankin—may have appeared to many both well-oiled and unchallenged, but that was an illusion, and the fact that two noninterventionist Democratic senators lost primary elections in 1944 should have been a wake-up call for Wheeler. All the political trends in Montana and the nation were running against Wheeler's brand of noninterventionism.[62]

Increasingly isolated in the Senate, Wheeler remained, in the words of reporter Allen Drury, "determined and unyielding" in his criticism of foreign policy and the conduct of the war. "The vigor of his denunciations reveals that he has not modified in the slightest degree the opinions he held before the war and during its early stages," Drury wrote at the time. Yet Wheeler's critique of foreign policy, including condemning the Yalta conference for its "cynical partition of Poland and for giving Stalin a free hand in eastern Europe," earned him little support. Even old allies had moved on, and his attempts at legislating—Wheeler tried to get the Senate to affirm the language of the 1941 Atlantic Charter primarily as a way to embarrass the administration—gained little support. Wheeler became what he had never before been in his Senate career: ineffective and mostly ignored.[63]

In a letter to General Wood, Wheeler off-handedly noted that during a trip to Montana—he had traveled to Livingston to attend the funeral of Montana congressman James F. O'Connor—he had been "told that certain groups in New York were going to make a fight and spend a lot of money to defeat me." He added, with an air of indifference that would contribute to his downfall, "That doesn't interest me."[64]

———

After observing Franklin Roosevelt, thin, pale, and obviously exhausted, upon his return from the grueling trip to the Yalta conference in February, Wheeler suspected that the president's death was eminent. "To me it was a tragedy indeed that a person in [his] critical condition had attempted to cope with a creature like Stalin at Yalta," Wheeler wrote years later. When Roosevelt died on April 12, 1945, at his Warm Springs, Georgia, retreat, Wheeler had little to say beyond regretting the death of the man he had once so strongly supported. With his friend Harry Truman now president, Wheeler was sure to enjoy the kind of White House access that Roosevelt had never offered him.[65]

Less than three weeks after Roosevelt's death, Adolf Hitler was dead in his bunker beneath the Reich Chancellery in Berlin, and on May 8, 1945 the Nazi government surrendered unconditionally. Just a week later Wheeler was in London at the head of a Senate delegation studying international communication problems in war-devastated Europe. Three Senate colleagues, the chairman of the Federal Communications Commission, top army and navy communications officials, and Ed Craney, who was listed in the official itinerary as the senator's aide, accompanied Wheeler on the trip. High-level meetings were held with Winston Churchill; Lord Beaverbrook, a former British cabinet minister; U.S. generals Dwight Eisenhower, Anthony Patch, and Maxwell Taylor; and Pope Pius XII, among others. The group did assess communications issues during the month-long, sixteen-thousand-mile trip but also undertook a good deal of sightseeing and enjoyed the best available accommodations, including one night at the Ritz in Paris. Traveling via military aircraft, Wheeler's delegation went from London, to Paris, Reims, Frankfurt, Munich (including a side trip to Hitler's mountain retreat at Berchtesgaden), Naples, Rome, Malta, Athens, Cairo, Jerusalem, Tripoli, Algiers, Casablanca, and the Azores. The delegation made a short trip to the Nazi concentration camp at Dachau, although strangely Wheeler made no mention of the scene of some of the worst Nazi atrocities. Wheeler used the European trip, at least in his telling, to press his concerns about Communist aims in Europe, a theme he repeated to the new president on his return stateside.[66]

Wheeler wrote to his daughter Elizabeth that he visited many hospitals and cemeteries and had "seen thousands of boys," including a few from Montana. "They want to come home. Everywhere in Italy, France and England they are alarmed at Russia's action. Every day I feel more strongly than ever that I was right before we got in."[67]

On July 6, one day before Truman left to confer with Churchill and Stalin at Potsdam, the president met at the White House, as he recorded in his private diary, with "Sens. Wheeler, McFarland, [Albert] Hawkes and [Homer] Capehart. They've been oversees, had seen Germany, France, Italy—and knew *all* the answers." (The emphasis appears in the source.) "Anyway," Truman wrote, "their song was that France would go Communistic, so would Germany, Italy and the Scandinavians, and there was grave doubt about England staying sane. The Pope, they said, was blue as indigo about the situation. All of 'em except McFarland assured me that the European world is at an end and that Russia is a big bad wolf." Truman largely dismissed the senatorial gloom and doom as the product of "cursory glances of oratorical members of the famous 'Cave of the Winds' on Capitol Hill. I've been there myself and have been through crisis after crisis in each of which the country surely would disintegrate (and it never did) [so] that 'Senatorial Alarm' doesn't much alarm me." While Truman genuinely liked Wheeler and remembered fondly the friendship and opportunities the Montanan had provided him early in his Senate career, the two men were as far apart on foreign policy as Roosevelt and Wheeler had been. As Truman noted in 1945, Wheeler was "a natural purveyor of bad news" and not a senator likely to help him "win a peace."[68]

Wheeler, rare for him, seemed genuinely confused about his next steps. After directing at considerable length his old-style vindictive argument against the United Nations proposal when it was considered in the Senate, he ultimately and surprisingly joined eighty-eight others in voting for the UN Charter. Still, his affirmative vote came only after he described at length his misgivings, including warnings about future presidents committing the U.S. military without engaging Congress or winning congressional approval.[69]

The president's daughter, Margaret Truman, would take note of Wheeler's vote on the UN in her 1973 memoirs. "To everyone's amazement, all [Senate] opposition to the UN practically melted away. Everyone had expected Senator Burton K. Wheeler to lead the assault on the Charter. He was the man who had killed the Supreme Court revision bill in 1937. He was the Senate's best parliamentarian—and an outspoken isolationist. Everyone waited anxiously for the anti-UN maneuvers they were sure he had up his sleeve. But they forgot that Burt Wheeler was also one of Harry Truman's closest friends. As Dad left the Senate chamber [after calling for approval of the UN Charter] he made a point of shaking hands with him."[70]

Wheeler wrote in his memoirs that he did not want to give internationalists a chance to say, as had been said about the League of Nations, that an international organization had failed "because the United States had not joined." Wheeler's comment ignores the fact that the UN Charter was going to be approved with or without his vote.

It seems more likely that Wheeler, mindful of his upcoming reelection campaign, was maneuvering to have it both ways—raising concerns about how the UN would operate, generating headlines with his debate, but in the end voting for the charter and preserving the ability to tell Montana constituents he had warned the Senate before reluctantly supporting his friend Harry Truman. If that was his political calculation, it may have been too little too late.[71]

Walter Aitken, a Bozeman attorney, sent Wheeler an open letter in 1945 expressing his view that, "whether intentionally not," by his votes, speeches, and positions Wheeler had provided aid and comfort to an enemy during wartime. Montana voters, Aitken claimed, "no longer trust you or believe in your sincerity or loyalty to anything but your own over scrupulous self-aggrandizement and self-seeking." Aitken prophetically added, "You are going to have a hard time fooling them again."[72]

15 DEFEAT

He was convinced he was bigger than
any one party—big enough for two.
—JOSEPH KINSEY HOWARD

B. K. Wheeler's brand of progressivism, still very much flavored by the La Follette era, became seriously dated in post–World War II America. Noninterventionism, once the prevailing foreign policy position in the Senate and the country, was out of fashion in a nation that had become the greatest military and economic power on the globe. So much had happened in the six years since Wheeler's last election: bitter fights over foreign policy, the "plow under every fourth American boy" comment, anti-Semitism allegations, Pearl Harbor, a U.S. alliance with the Soviet Union, continuous squabbles with Jim Murray, sedition trials, and a new world organization created to preserve the new peace.

By 1946, Wheeler's landslide reelection in 1940, the greatest victory margin ever recorded to that point in Montana, was a distant memory. So much had changed. Montanans had once voted for a young progressive, a radical reformer, but now many looked at Wheeler and saw an aging conservative. Wheeler, always at his political best on the attack, was now always on the defensive, reduced increasingly to counterpunching. He now mostly made headlines refighting old battles. Onetime "Bolshevik Burt" now stood accused of stirring up animosity against the country's recent ally, the Soviet Union. The man who once vowed to kick the Anaconda Company out of Montana politics was now labeled a stooge of big business. Wheeler's celebrated independence was now often seen as mere opportunism.

There is a truism in politics: a candidate explaining is a candidate who is losing. Wheeler often blithely told Montana voters "My record speaks for itself," but given his controversial foreign policy positions and feuds with Franklin Roosevelt, voters had to be reminded of that record. He had battled political corruption, championed Fort Peck Dam and the Buffalo Rapids project, broken up the utility trust, and reorganized the nation's railroads, but little about those accomplishments passed his lips in 1946 as he sought a fifth term. Instead Wheeler was constantly explaining himself, often not very effectively.[1]

Rather than drawing sharp contrasts with a young and inexperienced primary opponent, Wheeler wrangled with a growing number of enemies: the Congress of Industrial Organization (CIO) Political Action Committee, communists, and "eastern and Hollywood interests." They were all out to defeat him, Wheeler said, and he was correct, but fighting against "outsiders" rather than appealing to his constituents and engaging his opponent was a losing strategy. Wheeler even got into very public spats with FDR's son James and a left-wing New York tabloid newspaper, a publication that most Montanans had never heard of, let alone read. Wheeler, never before at a loss for words, lacked a compelling message that made the case for his reelection, while his opponents had a simple message: defeat Wheeler. A left-leaning Montana newspaper editor said as much in a letter to Jim Murray in 1946: "The big thing is to defeat Wheeler. Nothing else matters much."[2]

Wheeler, usually an astute political analyst, was also slow to appreciate the peril he faced. The Montana Democratic primary election was held on July 16, and Wheeler really only campaigned for a few weeks prior to the election. His opponents, by contrast, had been plotting Wheeler's defeat at least since the great foreign policy debate five years earlier; they only needed to settle on a candidate willing to take on the incumbent.

———

Many, perhaps even most Montana Democrats wanted Mike Mansfield, the two-term congressman from western Montana, to challenge Wheeler in 1946, and Mansfield seriously considered his prospects, spending weeks taking soundings from prominent Democrats. He received much encouragement. The state Democratic Party chair told Mansfield, "I rarely hear anyone who is plugging for Wheeler, but every day I hear, and my mail brings complaints by Democrats." A union leader in Anaconda told the congressman there was "a definite turn against Wheeler in the industrial counties of the state . . . if anyone is to beat Wheeler it will have to be Mansfield." A Kalispell constituent wrote, "The Democratic Party in Montana has needed a purge for some little time, and I am quite sure this will be the opportune time to get it going. You may rest assured that I will do anything and everything to assist you in your laudable endeavor to rid the State of Bouncing Bertie [sic]. He has had it coming to him for some little time." And a navy veteran from Glasgow wrote Mansfield, "It is the opinion of many World War II veterans of Montana that the infamous, obstructionist

& isolationist Mr. B. K. Wheeler, who has done nothing for international cooperation, should have been beaten a long time ago."[3]

Even with such encouragement Mansfield hesitated, while other potential candidates—Montana Supreme Court justice Hugh R. Adair, former Montana attorney general (and future governor) John W. Bonner, and 1944 gubernatorial candidate Leif Erickson—were frozen in place, waiting to see if the congressman would commit. When asked years later why he had taken so much time to decide and then opted not to challenge Wheeler, Mansfield, typically candid and to the point, simply said, "I didn't think I could win. It was too chancy to run in 1946. I was not dissatisfied with my seat in the House. I decided to wait for a more favorable moment."[4]

Wheeler was certainly not surprised to face a challenge from a fellow Democrat; he had primary challengers in each of his elections since 1922, and his own political soundings had convinced him that he would face either Mansfield or Erickson. Wheeler also knew that "Democratic New Dealers," as one of his chief lieutenants described Wheeler's opponents in the party, and "certain groups in New York and probably the CIO" would try to defeat him. Nevertheless, as the election approached, Wheeler remained confident, too confident.[5]

"Mike Mansfield called me yesterday," Wheeler wrote to a friend, "and said he was not going to run for the Senate . . . and I haven't the slightest doubt but that Erickson will be the one who will run. This ought to make it rather easy." To a friendly constituent Wheeler wrote, "While I have no doubt that I will beat Mr. Erickson, nevertheless I think my friends have to be on the watch and do some work." The *Miles City Star*, a newspaper backing Wheeler's reelection, editorialized that Erickson "is about to commit political suicide by barging into battle with Senator B. K. Wheeler." Erickson, eager, ambitious, and more liberal than Wheeler, did seem to many to be a long-shot candidate, and that may have actually helped him gain a jump on the incumbent.[6]

Wheeler knew Erickson would benefit from support from some elements of organized labor because, as he said, "[Sidney] Hillman [president of the Amalgamated Clothing Workers Union and the chairman of the CIO Political Action Committee] and some of his crowd . . . are very bitter." But Wheeler underestimated both Erickson and the impact of defections from his old labor allies. Erickson had a plan, and he knew precisely what needed to be done to beat Wheeler. "Wheeler can be beaten only by a slugging campaign," Erickson wrote to Mike Mansfield. "Most people feel that whoever beats Wheeler must get right down to cases and call him what he is."[7]

Erickson, a burly former college wrestler with dark, deep-set eyes and a receding hairline, was forty-one years old in 1946. While Erickson was a preteen, his parents settled on a dryland farm near Sidney, Montana. He graduated from Sidney High School in 1924 and later enrolled at the University of Chicago where he won the Big Ten heavyweight wrestling championship and eventually earned undergraduate and law degrees. Returning to Sidney in 1934 to practice law, Erickson was elected Richland County attorney two years later, and in 1938 he won a nonpartisan race to become the youngest person ever elected to the Montana Supreme Court. Montana writer Joseph Kinsey Howard would later quote Wheeler as saying of Erickson, "That boy is coming up fast; he's the only one who can beat me." Wheeler, it appears, recognized Erickson as a threat but discounted that 1946 was Erickson's political moment.[8]

Rather than seek a second term on the court, Erickson entered the governor's race in 1944 and won a three-way Democratic primary, but he then was soundly defeated by Governor Sam Ford. Still, Erickson performed well in Montana's industrialized counties where organized labor maintained substantial influence, a fact that would become critical in his race against Wheeler.[9]

For intelligence and organization in Montana, Wheeler continued to rely on two longtime political operatives: J. Burke Clements, chair of the state Industrial Accident Board, and Barclay Craighead, chair of the Montana unemployment compensation commission. Both men were Democrats, personally loyal to Wheeler, but each held an important position in the Republican administration of Governor Ford, where they helped maintain the bipartisan political organization that Wheeler and Ford rode to office in 1940.[10]

In February 1946, Clements, writing from Helena on his official state government stationery, identified the challenge Wheeler faced in the campaign. "There is no question about the [general] election, if you are nominated," he wrote. Sixty percent of Montana Republicans "want you returned to the United State Senate," Clements said. Clements quoted a "former Republican state chairman and Billings lawyer" as saying "every damn Republican that comes into my office is for Wheeler ... why don't you fellows straighten out some of your Democrats that are around here knocking him." Clements hastened to add that he quoted such statements "merely in an effort to give you a true picture of what the people are saying."[11]

Wheeler's dilemma was obvious: he enjoyed substantial Republican support, but his positions had alienated many Democrats. By 1946, many Montana Democrats identified with Jim Murray and his optimistic support of the United Nations as well as his call for accommodation with the Soviet Union. By contrast Wheeler seemed a grumpy pessimist, a constant critic, fearful of a larger American role in the world, and obsessed

Senator James E. Murray in 1945. A wealthy
Butte attorney and staunch New Dealer, Murray
battled Wheeler for dominance of the Montana
Democratic Party for years. (*Harris and Ewing
Collection, courtesy of Harry S. Truman Library
and Museum*)

with the ostensible communist threat. Erickson's campaign slogan—"Construction
NOT Obstruction"—captured perfectly the challenge Wheeler had to overcome.

Before a largely Republican audience at the Montana Wool Growers Association
convention in Great Falls early in the campaign, Wheeler was even critical of his friend
Truman's management of postwar relations with the Russians. Wheeler would later
write that it was "easy to see why the Communists" had turned against him. "They
had hailed me when I had opposed our intervention in the war—up to the time Hitler
attacked Russia," Wheeler said. But when he continued to advocate nonintervention
after the German invasion of Russia in June 1941, Wheeler believed, American communists, including a small group in Montana who quietly supported the Communist
Party line, wrote him off for good. Wheeler remembered that a Butte constituent had

advised him that he should "get up at just one meeting and say something nice about Russia" and thereby help his campaign, but "of course," Wheeler said, "I couldn't do that."[12]

The 1946 Senate election in Montana, both the Democratic primary and the general election, provided a preview of the type of campaign that has now become routine in U.S. politics—bitter and personal, involving dark money, a scandalous book, and a Senate investigation.

———

The proposed Missouri Valley Authority (MVA), an ambitious, nine-state project to create coordinated, multipurpose resource development along the Missouri River from Great Falls to New Orleans, modeled on the New Deal–era Tennessee Valley Authority, became a contentious issue in Montana in the early 1940s. The MVA figured prominently in the 1946 Senate race. Franklin Roosevelt endorsed the concept and encouraged Jim Murray, the plan's leading advocate, to push the idea in Congress. Murray introduced legislation to authorize MVA in 1944 and received immediate pushback. Governor Ford, along with most Montana Republicans and business interests, including Montana Power Company, opposed the concept as a threat to state sovereignty, potentially adversely impacting energy development and irrigated agriculture. In response to Murray's legislation the Republican-controlled Montana legislature went on record opposing the MVA, and Governor Ford attacked the proposal as a "super-government planning" agency that would be "a long step toward state socialism."[13]

Leif Erickson, like many Democrats, supported creation of a Missouri Valley Authority, and he served as the first chairman of a regional group pushing the idea. The MVA became a major issue during the Ford-Erickson gubernatorial campaign in 1944, and Ford's decisive victory, many observers thought, settled the issue, at least in Montana. But two years later the MVA was still alive. The politics of the MVA, particularly for Democrats, were complicated and problematic. Many Democrats applauded Murray's leadership on the issue, believing river basin–wide planning, managed by a TVA-like commission, was a logical continuation of the type of regional planning the New Deal had tried to advance. At the same time a number of western Democrats, including Mike Mansfield, avoided, to the extent they could, saying anything about MVA, while other Democrats, leery of public concerns about creating a new federal bureaucracy on a regional basis, advocated more modest river development proposals with the Army Corps of Engineers or the Bureau of Reclamation as the lead agency.[14]

Wheeler had supported creation of the Tennessee Valley Authority when his friend George Norris pushed the concept in 1933, but during his 1946 campaign he kept his distance from the Missouri Valley proposal, saying with studied hyperbole that "the CIO, the ultra radical group in the Farmers' Union, and the Communists are behind it." The grand concept of river-basin planning would ensure, Wheeler believed, more bureaucracy and more centralized political and economic power. He wondered if Erickson was "naïve enough to believe that any board which is set up by any administration will let the state with the smallest number of votes dictate to the states which have the larger votes down the river and who are interested in navigation and flood control rather than irrigation and reclamation?" Wheeler's weariness about MVA is also explained, at least in part, by the fact that Murray championed the idea. Carefully navigating the middle ground on an issue like centralized planning and management of a huge river basin, particularly given legitimate concerns about conflicts with downriver states over water rights and other issues, would have amounted to smart politics in a general election where independents, Republicans, and Democrats would be voting. But by voicing concerns about the MVA plan Wheeler complicated his path to a primary victory. His position aligned with Montana Power, the state's big-business interests in general, and Republicans and Wheeler again drifted further from the Democratic legacy of Franklin Roosevelt and the New Deal. None of which was helpful as he courted Democratic primary voters.[15]

An election in the immediate aftermath of World War II naturally meant that the economic, educational, and health concerns of returning veterans were major political issues. Neither Erickson nor Wheeler had served in the military, but both made a determined effort to appeal to veterans. Erickson had been exempted from military service due to his judicial position, but that did not prevent Wheeler from repeatedly reminding voters that his opponent was of draft age during the war and had not served. "I cannot stoop to attack or criticize my younger opponent's war record for he hasn't any," he told one audience. Erickson responded by attacking Wheeler's isolationism, which he said made a third world war more likely. Both men had groups of veterans supporting their candidacies, and, while the group supporting Wheeler tried to appear independent, it was effectively an extension of his campaign.[16]

Willard Fraser, who had chaired the America First Committee chapter in Billings, headed a "Veterans for Wheeler Club" that produced radio commercials, newspaper ads, and brochures attacking Erickson. Wheeler's campaign funded the ads, and the committee raised no money independently. One typical ad appeared in the *Billings Gazette* and asked in reference to Erickson: "Where was this young man when other young men of Montana were doing their courageous bit to defeat our country's enemies? This young man, of military age and supposedly good physical condition, was bravely and courageously fighting the Battle of Last Chance Gulch," the latter comment a reference to the main street in downtown Helena.[17]

A flier carrying the "Veterans for Wheeler" logo outlined what was termed "the cold, hard facts" of Wheeler's record on national defense and veterans' issues and listed dozens of Wheeler's "yes" votes on military appropriations and legislation authorizing veterans' benefits. Omitted, not surprisingly, was any reference to Lend-Lease or Neutrality Act legislation. In a radio speech devoted to veterans' issues, Wheeler touted his record and experience and rejected those who belittled him as an "isolationist." His positions, Wheeler said, were aimed at protecting American farmers and ranchers and advocating a living wage. He insisted that his efforts in the Senate were focused on avoiding war and the sacrifice of "American boys."

"If I am wrong about these things," Wheeler said, "if I stand alone in Montana on these propositions, then I am not the man to represent you in the Senate of the United States."[18]

Erickson was convinced that Wheeler's foreign policy and national security positions had broadly alienated Montana voters and believed that exploiting those issues was the key to victory. He campaigned in support of better veterans' housing, supported a GI Bill of Rights, and called for enhanced widows' and orphans' benefits. A "Veteran's Committee Against Wheeler," apparently organized well before it became clear that Erickson would be Wheeler's opponent, simply advised Montanans to vote "against a fifth term for B. K. Wheeler." The group received financial support from the United Auto Workers and the Maritime Union, and its chairman was Chet Kinsey of Great Falls, an ally of former congressman Jerry O'Connell. One of the group's fliers detailed a series of Wheeler's votes against military appropriations and pointedly noted that the senator "did not vote" on the declaration of war against Japan. The flier proclaimed, "American Dead Deserve a Better Tribute Than Votes for Wheeler."[19]

While many factors, including voter anger about his foreign policy positions, contributed to Wheeler's defeat, perhaps the most important factor was his loss of support among both the leadership and rank and file of organized labor. Wheeler blamed the CIO Political Action Committee for orchestrating labor opposition to his reelection. The powerful union's anti-Wheeler stance was a significant factor in his defeat, but it was individual members of Montana labor unions and their families, the men and women who had once considered Wheeler their champion, who abandoned him in droves.

The CIO's political action arm had been organized in 1944 to undertake a coordinated effort to ensure Franklin Roosevelt's reelection that year. Sidney Hillman, the founder of the Amalgamated Clothing Workers of America and the union's influential president from 1914 until his death five days before the Montana primary in 1946, chaired the CIO Political Action Committee. During the 1944 election Hillman's committee reportedly produced eighty-five million pieces of campaign literature in support of Roosevelt and other Democratic candidates, but Hillman also insisted on old-fashioned, highly effective, and extremely labor-intensive door-to-door canvassing to identify and turn out voters. When training volunteers, the PAC stressed the importance of the "quiet talk of neighbor to neighbor about the issues and the candidates." For his part, Roosevelt both respected and needed Hillman and his political organization, and "the cerebral-looking rabbi of industrial concord," as one writer called him, became widely recognized as the administration's go-to man in the labor movement.[20]

A Jewish immigrant from Lithuania, Hillman was a committed internationalist who believed the United States needed to seek rapprochement with the Soviet Union, and, as a devoted friend and frequent advisor to Roosevelt, he was a passionate New Dealer. Despite what Wheeler characterized as his positive "voting record on labor and other liberal measures," the CIO PAC organized to "purge" him in 1946 because, as Wheeler believed, he had broken often with FDR, was skeptical of the UN, and unwilling to "follow the PAC's internationalist line."[21]

Confronted with the challenge from Hillman's well-financed PAC, something no Democrat would have wanted, Wheeler believed, or said he believed, that shadowy communist elements in organized labor were conspiring against him. While undoubtedly overstating the impact of communist influence in the campaign—Wheeler admitted most Montana labor leaders "were certainly not Communists"—Wheeler was not entirely incorrect about Communist Party–influenced labor activity in Montana and national politics after the war. From 1935 until late 1946, for example, the national president of the International Union of Mine, Mill, and Smelter Workers was Reid Robinson, a labor activist from Butte. Robert H. Zieger, a historian of the CIO, has described Robinson as "a faithful spokesman of the pro-Soviet left," while Robinson's successor at the union, Maurice Travis, was a member of the Communist Party USA. Evidence of Communist Party influence in Montana's labor movement was confirmed in 1950 when the CIO expelled nine unions suspected of being under Communist Party control. Among those expelled were the Mine, Mill, and Smelter Workers union, which had supported Wheeler until 1946, when it switched its endorsement to Erickson.[22]

A U.S. Senate committee reported after the election that Erickson's campaign had been the beneficiary of nearly $8,000 (more than $100,000 today) from the CIO PAC and its related unions. Given the limited campaign resources available to Erickson, the amounts he received from unions were significant, but the "quiet talk of neighbor to neighbor about the issues and the candidates" may well have been even more significant.[23]

Jim Murray, with his own strong ties to organized labor, was also at work to defeat Wheeler. As Murray's biographer has written, the senator was agnostic about who should replace Wheeler. He simply wanted his archrival defeated and made certain that his office "worked in harmony with the state Democratic organization before the campaign in an effort to achieve a unified, well financed party to use against Wheeler." Just as Wheeler had worked quietly behind the scenes to help Wellington Rankin's efforts against Murray in 1942, Murray now "made every effort to avoid personal involvement in the campaign," while still doing all he could to support Erickson's candidacy. Charles Murray, who served as his father's chief of staff and chief political strategist, coordinated efforts between Murray's Senate office and Wheeler's opponents, and, while Murray refused all requests that he campaign openly for Erickson, he did raise money for the challenger, including, as Wheeler believed, "money from wealthy Jewish people" in New York who were angered by Wheeler's pre-war positions. Wheeler deeply resented that Murray, as he saw it, was helping Erickson raise campaign money by suggesting unsubtly that Wheeler was anti-Semitic.[24]

Even though he lost the support of the CIO, Wheeler was not completely lacking in high-profile labor endorsements. William Green, the president of the American Federation of Labor, and Wheeler's old friend John L. Lewis, the United Mine Workers president, issued public endorsements. Senators La Follette of Wisconsin, Johnson of Colorado, McCarran of Nevada, and Walsh of Massachusetts all permitted their names to be used in Wheeler campaign materials. But these endorsements were no match for Erickson's support among rank-and-file Montana Democrats and union members, voters Wheeler once could have taken for granted. The Silver Bow Trades and Labor Association, including both AFL and CIO unions, refused to back Wheeler's reelection, the first time in his career that had happened. The Cascade County Trades and Labor Assembly in Great Falls gave its endorsement to Erickson. Another local labor council claimed Wheeler had ceased being a Democrat. "He is not for Democrats when Ford runs for Governor, when Rankin runs for the Senate, when J. J. [Jerry] O'Connell runs for Congress, or when FDR runs for President," the union leadership said. The Democratic Central Committee in Yellowstone County—Billings was rapidly overtaking Butte as Montana's largest city—passed a resolution essentially reading Wheeler out of the party.[25]

The one endorsement Wheeler coveted and eventually received, that of Harry Truman, ended up hurting more than helping his prospects, with the critical issue again involving organized labor. From coast to coast in 1946, America's unionized workforce was angry and in revolt. The U.S. Bureau of Labor Statistics, as labor historian Jeremy Brecher has noted, called the first six months of 1946 "the most concentrated period of labor-management strife in the country's history." Nearly three million workers were involved in strikes or related labor actions. By the end of 1946, a total of nearly five million workers had participated in strikes impacting virtually every sector of the economy. Tens of thousands of miners, including seven thousand in Montana, went on strike in April, with widespread violence accompanying the work stoppage in Butte. A *Chicago Tribune* story about the violence ran under a banner headline—"Butte Mobs Wreck Homes." The newspaper reported that "a reign of terror" had descended on Butte, with gangs of young men, women, and children attacking the homes of miners who had refused to join the strike. True to form, Anaconda Company officials blamed communist elements in the Mine, Mill, and Smelter Workers union for instigating the mob violence.[26]

Truman's popularity tumbled as he struggled to respond to the coast-to-coast chaos caused by the strikes. The president first sought injunctions to end the strikes, and after three hundred thousand railroad workers walked off their jobs in May, effectively shutting down American commerce, Truman threatening to draft striking trainmen and locomotive engineers. But when the House of Representatives overwhelmingly approved Truman's legislation allowing striking workers to be drafted, organized labor turned on the president. Truman was branded the country's top strikebreaker and denounced for abandoning the labor movement. Prominent labor leaders, including Sidney Hillman, and members of Truman's own cabinet were openly critical of the president. Chesly Manly reported in the *Chicago Tribune* that Truman's heavy-handed tactics with organized labor had "incensed" the union rank and file, most of whom were dependable Democratic voters. It did not help Truman's standing with union members when it appeared that he granted mine workers' leader John L. Lewis, a nominal Republican, a better deal to end a coal strike than he was willing to provide to striking trainmen and engineers.[27]

Wheeler continued to enjoy the support of national rail unions, a significant constituency in Montana given that three major rail carriers crossed Montana, and he refused to support Truman's "draft the strikers" legislation, which was ultimately defeated in the Senate. But against this quarrelsome, violent backdrop, with widespread labor dissatisfaction directed toward Truman and with many Montana union workers already skeptical of Wheeler's loyalty to organized labor and the Democratic Party, Truman's endorsement of Wheeler's reelection backfired—badly. With the exception of his home state of Missouri, Truman originally pledged to stay out of all intra-party Democratic disputes in 1946, but just days before the Montana primary he reversed course and offered his blessing to Wheeler. Truman said Erickson's attacks, including a charge that Wheeler had abandoned the railway labor unions, were "preposterous." In a letter to Wheeler aide Bailey Stortz, Truman said he hoped to put a stop to the "smear campaign against Burt Wheeler," and he made it clear he hoped Montana voters would return his friend to the Senate. Erickson's response to Truman's statement was immediate, politically shrewd, and coldly cynical. "The President is under great obligation," Erickson said, "to Wheeler for his part in trying to put the shackles of slavery on labor." That was a lie, but in the heat of the campaign Erickson was able in one short sentence to link Wheeler to the perceived anti-union actions of the increasingly unpopular president. A coveted presidential endorsement, normally a boost to any incumbent's campaign, became an immediate liability.[28]

———

Under assault by an aggressive opponent and abandoned by many old labor allies, Wheeler also faced coordinated attacks, in more-recent parlance an "independent expenditure campaign," designed to impugn his character and question his loyalty. One relentlessly negative campaign was coordinated by a Minnesotan, Walter E. Quigley, a self-described "political dynamiter," hired by the president of the national Brotherhood of Railway Trainmen, A. F. Whitney, to smear Wheeler. Whitney's motive for attacking Wheeler is difficult to ascertain beyond the fact that Whitney had clashed bitterly with Truman over the national rail strike in 1946, at one point saying of Truman, "you can't make a President out of a ribbon clerk." Whitney apparently believed that Wheeler had become an unreliable ally of labor due both to his foreign policy stands and his friendship with Truman. Quigley's "dynamiting" of Wheeler involved a six-page newspaper—the *Montana News*—that depicted Wheeler as a lackey for the Anaconda Company and a threat to Montana's working class. Quigley, as historian Frank Jonas has written, "associated Wheeler with Germany, Hitler and the Nazis. He made Wheeler appear a self-seeking politician who had voted himself a pay raise." Quigley said years later that as many as 125,000 copies of the *Montana News* were printed in Lewistown, Montana, and distributed by hand in Butte and Great Falls, major labor towns, and mailed statewide. Wheeler, probably incorrectly, later dismissed Quigley's attack as having had little to do with his defeat, but the newspaper repeated powerful and well-known anti-Wheeler attack lines in circulation since before the war and reached a significant number of Montana voters at a critical point in the campaign.[29]

The second smear came in the form of a "lurid, libelous" book—*The Plot against America: Senator Wheeler and the Forces behind Him*—that was widely promoted in a brochure mailed to twenty-five thousand Montana addresses. This potboiler took the allegations against Wheeler contained in *Under Cover*, the hit piece from 1943, to an entirely new level.

"I am getting a great deal of this literature; they are sending it out wholesale," Wheeler wrote to a constituent who sent him the gaudy flier promoting *The Plot against America*. The headlines on the flier—"How Wheeler Hitlerized Montana!" and "A Shocking Revelation of American Nazism in Action"—were mild compared to the sensational language in the book. Wheeler was "Hitler's handyman," a "Benedict Arnold" operating "a dictatorship in Montana," and the "Butte Casanova" who had conducted affairs with Alice Roosevelt Longworth—"Wheeler's elegant confidante"— and Roxy Stinson, the fetching star witness of Wheeler's Justice Department hearings twenty-two years earlier.[30]

Just as the author of *Under Cover* had used an assumed name, the author of *The Plot against America*, David George Plotkin, a Brooklyn lawyer, wrote under the name David George Kin. Plotkin, referred to as Kin below, seems to have practiced law briefly and made his living publishing books with sensational titles and provocative subject matter. Kin's *Rage in Singapore*, published in 1942, purported to tell the story of the Japanese invasion of Malaysia. In 1958 Kin would publish *Women without Men: True Stories of Lesbian Love in Greenwich Village*, a book featuring chapters titled "The Tough-Minded Blonde Has a Secret" and "She Was the Father of Her Child." Where John Roy Carlson's *Under Cover* contained just enough detail to plant doubt about Wheeler's relationships and beliefs, Kin's book was a lurid combination of sex and scandal designed to do more than plant doubt. The *Plot against America* was effectively a lead pipe to the back of the head.[31]

Wheeler was initially inclined, as with the Quigley newspaper, to ignore the outrageous book, telling one constituent, "I can't conceive any intelligent person can be influenced by that kind of stuff," but he was also sufficiently concerned to write J. Edgar Hoover inquiring if the FBI had "a file on this man, David George Kin." Wheeler told Hoover that Kin "is working with John E. Kennedy, who was formerly Congressman Jerry O'Connell's secretary, and is reputed to be a Communist or at any rate a fellow-traveler who is close to him." There is no record of a reply from Hoover. Wheeler's decision to trust the intelligence of Montana voters rather than to strike back forcefully against the outlandish charges was both out of character and a serious mistake. Wheeler, the deft campaigner and skilled counterpuncher, did not appreciate until too late that he was involved in a campaign of attrition, with each new allegation adding to a building mountain of invective surrounding his conduct, politics, and character. He was being hit with exactly the type of campaign that Erickson said would be needed to beat him, a campaign that got "right down to cases" and attacked his character.[32]

On June 27, less than three weeks before the Montana primary, Wheeler filed a formal complaint with the Select Committee on Senatorial Campaign Expenditures requesting an investigation into the origins of the George David Kin book, particularly seeking to discover how the book had been financed. On June 29 the Senate committee, chaired by Allen J. Ellender, a Louisiana Democrat, agreed, in light of the rapidly approaching election, to immediately send investigators to Montana to look into the "allegedly vicious and scurrilous circular announcing the publication of a forthcoming book . . . contended by Senator Wheeler to be an illegal and libelous smear of his candidacy."[33]

Neither Ellender nor any of the other members of the committee, Democrats Burnet Maybank of South Carolina and Ed Johnson of Colorado and Republicans Styles Bridges of New Hampshire and Bourke Hickenlooper of Iowa, attended the three days of hearings in Helena conducted by Robert A. Barker, counsel to the committee. Wheeler attempted, not particularly successfully, to use the hearing to refute some of many allegations in Kin's book, as well as to counter the charge repeatedly made by Erickson that Wheeler had become a tool of the Anaconda Company and Montana Power. The committee eventually published the amounts and sources of contributions to both candidates—nearly $19,000 to Wheeler and $12,800 to Erickson—with the bulk of Erickson's financial support coming from labor organizations outside Montana. Still, Wheeler aide Bailey Stortz complained that investigators had uncovered "not more than ten percent of the money sent into Montana during the past year to smear Senator Wheeler." While Stortz was unable to prove his claim, it stands to reason, given the wide distribution of the newspaper and the publication and promotion of the book, that a great deal more than $12,800 was spent to attack the incumbent. The investigation did expose some of Jim Murray's behind-the-scenes help for Erickson when evidence was presented that two out-of-state checks that ended up in Erickson's campaign account had originally been made out to Murray, who had then endorsed them over to Erickson.[34]

The Senate committee was also able to establish that Kin had written the scandalous book at the behest of the volume's "publisher" John Kennedy, O'Connell's former assistant. Kennedy paid Kin's expenses in Montana and, while the book was being written, a $100 a month salary. Kennedy had hired Kin, it was disclosed, after placing an ad in the Saturday Review of Literature seeking an "experienced writer who because of too frequent contact with John Barleycorn, or other reasons, would welcome new surroundings in Montana."[35]

The committee further concluded that the book's publication, as well as the mass mailing promoting it, had been paid for by Julius Walter Gehring, "the operator of the Coffee Shop in the Palace Hotel in Missoula." Gehring told the Senate committee's counsel that he had parlayed an initial $425 investment in his coffee shop into an enterprise that was "grossing in excess of $20,000 month." Gehring said that he had invested $7,000 of his own money in the publication of The Plot against America and also paid for the flier. To help finance the book's publication, he said, he had also borrowed an additional $1,800 from a Seattle man to whom he had been introduced by O'Connell. The committee concluded, not surprisingly, that "the financial arrangements which made the publication of The Plot Against America possible, were at best of a dubious business nature, [but] no direct connection between the candidate Erickson and either the brochure or the book was established in the record." The committee report noted that Kin and Kennedy had begun work on the book in 1945, well before it was known that Erickson would be a candidate, and therefore any political benefit that resulted from the book's attacks on Wheeler "inured to the benefit of the candidate opposing him, whomever that candidate happened to be." In essence, Erickson was declared not guilty of having any role in the book's publication.[36]

The Senate committee's investigation was necessarily rushed in order to complete the public hearings before voters went to the polls on July 16. As a result, curious, perhaps confused Montana voters read sketchy newspaper coverage of the proceedings that for the most part merely recounted the charges and the countercharges, while leaving many questions about the origins of the attacks on Wheeler and the money that financed them unresolved. On the whole, not unlike the Truman endorsement that became public during the Helena hearing, the totality of the episode did more harm than good to Wheeler's campaign, since the old charges about his being a tool of Montana big business and an apologist for Hitler received one more, high-profile airing, and this time the venue was an official Senate investigation. The final written report of the investigation was not produced until early 1947, long after the election had been decided and long after there was any chance for Montana voters to consider it. Left unanswered was who stood to benefit the most from what the report condemned "as one of the vilest, most contemptible, and obscene pieces of so-called literature ever published concerning a man in public office in the United States."[37]

The one detail in the Senate report that raises the biggest question and most stretches credulity is the testimony of Julius Gehring, the man who claimed to have almost singlehandedly financed the printing of the salacious book and the statewide distribution of the glossy promotional flier. Gehring's sworn testimony that his coffee shop was grossing "in excess of $20,000 a month" and that this business success made it possible for him to invest in a publishing endeavor is, to put it charitably, fanciful. If Gehring was telling the truth to the committee, in twenty-first-century dollars his coffee shop was taking in more than $250,000 a month, a number hard to square with the reality of running a coffee shop in Missoula in 1946. The true source of the money to produce and publicize the Wheeler hit piece remains an unsolved mystery.

It was not disclosed during the Senate investigation, but John Kennedy had attempted to entice the CIO PAC to finance publication of the book. Kennedy wrote an impassioned three-page letter in March 1946 to the committee's New York head-quarters, seeking $8,400 to pay a California printer who was willing to print *The Plot against America* but only if paid in advance. "Unless a suitable guarantee can be made to our printer in the next ten days, our project looks hopeless," Kennedy wrote. He pleaded for an answer from the union within three days. Sidney Hillman's assistant responded in early April and confirmed the PAC's opposition to Wheeler's reelection but turned down the request, saying, the committee would "gladly do anything within our means to get out a heavy vote so the people can express their desires but our own budgetary limitations make it impossible for us to finance the book."[38]

If the Hillman-controlled CIO PAC did not finance publication and the Missoula coffee shop owner's story does not add up, who did finance the book? The trail long ago went cold. It is clear, however, that at some point between Kennedy's mid-March plea to the union and the mid-April arrival in Montana mailboxes of the fliers promoting the book, Kennedy secured, from some individual or organization, the money necessary to launch one of the most outrageous smears campaigns in Senate history. The Missoula coffee shop owner seems to have provided a convenient, if implausible, cover story to obscure the truth about who really paid and why.

———

As if Wheeler did not have enough problems with organized labor, a picture of his middle daughter, Frances, appeared in many of the nation's newspapers three days before the primary election under the headline "Disagrees with Dad." Frances Sayler was pictured walking a picket line in her role as "a field organizer for the CIO United Electrical, Radio and Machine Workers" during a strike in Mount Clements, Michigan. Frances, over her parents' strong objections, had some years earlier married Allen Sayler, an official with the CIO's left-leaning United Auto Workers (UAW). (B. K. and Lulu had even refused to attend the wedding.) Now the UAW was one of the unions financially backing Erickson. Frances was quoted as saying to reporters, "Father and I no longer agree on labor matters."[39]

———

Wheeler had one more run in with a Roosevelt as the primary campaign drew to a close. A left-leaning Hollywood-based group, the Independent Citizens Committee for the Arts, Sciences, and Professions—the group's executive committee included Olivia de Havilland and Ronald Reagan—financed a fifteen-minute Montana radio broadcast featuring the late president's son, James Roosevelt, who called for Wheeler's defeat. The FBI had the Independent Citizens Committee under surveillance in California at the time and noted in a May 1946 report that the group's political endorsements coincided "exactly with [those] made by the Communist Party." Young Roosevelt, who had once served as his father's White House secretary, delivered his anti-Wheeler speech from Southern California, and, as Wheeler would note in his memoirs, young Jimmy "insisted he knew his dead father wanted me defeated." The speech may have had little impact on the race save for the fact that a Roosevelt was once again associated with bashing Wheeler. The senator compounded the impact, however, when he used his own final appeal to offer a muddled response.[40]

Wheeler's closing campaign speech came during a radio broadcast the night before the primary. He termed the campaign "perhaps the most bitter and dirty that I have witnessed in thirty years of politics in this state," which was saying a lot from candidate who had once hidden in a boxcar to avoid being assaulted. Wheeler's angry and defiant speech had the tone of a candidate who likely knew he was beaten. He devoted half of his thirty-minute address to a point-by-point rebuttal of young Roosevelt's "half truths and ... outright falsehoods," with Wheeler repeating several times that James Roosevelt could not possibly know what he had been talking about "because Jimmy wasn't there." The speech failed to offer a comprehensive rationale for a fifth term, and instead Wheeler again said his record was "an open book" and that Montanans who knew him would not "pay this trash any attention." A surviving copy of the speech is heavily edited and badly organized, and Wheeler wanders deep into the rhetorical weeds as he attempts to paint a picture of the forces determined to "besmirch" his character. He mentions his opponent almost in passing. "Poor Lief [sic]—I doubt that even he knows what a dupe he is—he is merely the convenient front for these activities. The object is to get me—the nomination of Lief is purely incidental."[41]

Wheeler's defeat in 1946, even accounting for the sideshow nature of the campaign, including the smears of the Kin book and the hurried Senate investigation, ranks as the most stunning upset in Montana political history. Erickson won 52.6 percent of the vote, outpolling Wheeler by more than 4,900 votes out of nearly 94,000 votes cast in the Democratic primary. Nearly 53 percent of eligible Montana voters went to the polls, a higher-than-normal turnout for a primary election in a non-presidential-election year. Wheeler ran relatively well in rural and agricultural eastern Montana, carrying the state's Second Congressional District, but his modest margin there could not offset the shellacking he suffered in heavily unionized western Montana, including the counties of Silver Bow, Deer Lodge, and Cascade. Stunningly, Wheeler lost his home base, Butte and Silver Bow County—which had sent him to the state legislature and provided large margins in all his previous elections—by nearly 3,300 votes. The opposition of organized labor more than any other single factor prevented Wheeler from winning a fifth Senate term.[42]

Wheeler's friends were thunderstruck. Oswald Garrison Villard, the former editor of the *Nation*, said he was "simply heartbroken by the news" of the defeat of the man he considered "the most valuable in Senate." Robert Wood wrote Wheeler that he was "much upset and distressed," although he thought Montana deserved to "receive condolences rather than yourself."[43]

Wheeler, publicly at least, was gracious, saying the "people of Montana have been very good to me." He told Norman Thomas that his enemies had "done me a personal favor by defeating me." He did not mean it. When he wrote his memoir fifteen years later, the memory of the 1946 defeat still stung. "I hate to lose," he wrote, and "I was not happy about losing or of the tactics used by anti-Wheeler forces to defeat me."[44]

There was short-lived discussion of Wheeler running in the general election as an independent, but he wisely refused, and 1946 turned out to be a big Republican year. Two of the last Senate noninterventionists—Shipstead of Minnesota and La Follette of Wisconsin—also lost in primaries in 1946. Wheeler's son Edward told me decades later that his father had seriously talked about even not running for a fifth term, since a persistent ear infection had bothered him off and on during much of the year, at one point requiring hospitalization. Edward remembered telling his father that he needed to get out to Montana and campaign, but Wheeler had delayed, determined to finish Senate action on legislation important to railroad workers. Edward Wheeler recalled talking with his father shortly after he finally did hit the campaign trail. "I'm going to get beat," Wheeler had told his son. Edward later expressed that his father "had an uncanny ability to see how elections were going to go, a real sixth sense."[45]

Erickson's showing in the general election confirmed Wheeler's view that the Democratic primary had been an "anybody but Wheeler" affair. Riding a national GOP tide that saw Republicans win control of Congress for the first time since 1930, Republican Zales Ecton, a conservative Gallatin County state senator and former state party chairman, crushed Erickson in the general election. Ecton assailed Erickson as a left-winger and successfully attacked the Democrat for "double-dipping," taking his full state Supreme Court salary while also being paid as a mediator for the federal government, an appointment that Erickson had received from President Truman. Ecton became the first popularly elected Republican senator in Montana history, at least in part because connections to Harry Truman hurt both of Montana's Democratic Senate candidates in 1946.[46]

While there are never perfect analogies in politics, Wheeler might have seen what was in store for him in 1946 had he paid close attention to what happened to his North Dakota Republican friend Gerald P. Nye two years earlier. Nye's biographer writes that "those in the Farmers' Union who supported President Roosevelt generally opposed Nye. Substantial opposition to the senator originated outside the state—particularly from the Roosevelt administration, internationalists, and the East. Nye had won labor support in his earlier campaigns, but by 1944 organized labor actively opposed him, particularly the CIO Political Action Committee. During the campaign the opposition distributed many copies of John Roy Carlson's book *Under Cover*, a sensational account of 'the Nazi Underworld of America' which was highly critical of Nye and other isolationists." In his farewell Senate speech after that campaign, Nye had lamented that attacks directed against him "had many honest North Dakotans convinced that if I was not actually on Hitler's payroll, I should have been," and Nye decried that his brand of noninterventionist foreign policy was now equated with "everything that was bad, terrible, un-American, and indecent. The attempt to keep our country out of war had become an unforgivable sin." After the 1946 primary, Wheeler knew the feeling. His opponents had clearly taken pages from the same playbook that had defeated Nye two years earlier.[47]

———

Wheeler would go to his grave denying that he had ever made any sort of deal with the powerful interests at the Anaconda Company and the mining company's "twin," Montana Power. As suggested earlier, it seem clear that Wheeler pragmatically decided at some point relatively early in his political career to forgo open warfare with the state's major economic interests. In turn, the big interests may have accepted a quiet, never officially acknowledged truce. But the question remains: did Montana's economic interests, as Wheeler's liberal opponents contended, actually favor his reelection in 1946 or was something more complicated at play? Two seemingly unrelated bits of information fail to offer a definite answer but add a final note of intrigue to Wheeler's last election.

Four days before the primary two top Montana Republican leaders, Dan Whetstone and Ashton Jones, issued an appeal to the state's Republican voters to remain loyal to their party and not vote in the Democratic primary to either elect or defeat individual Democrats. The appeal likely worked, since there is little evidence of any significant Republican crossover vote that might have helped Wheeler in the Democratic primary.[48]

Much was made after the election of a comment Wheeler had allegedly made during his 1920 race for governor. "If you ever see my picture on the front page of the Company press you'll know I've sold out," Wheeler had reportedly said. In 1946 Wheeler did receive, at least by the standards of Montana newspapers at the time, front-page attention from the Anaconda Company–controlled press. The political operatives at Anaconda headquarters in Butte certainly knew that favorable attention lavished on a Democrat like Wheeler would not be particularly helpful in a hard-fought primary election in which the company, once again, figured as a major issue. So were the big-business interests trying to help Wheeler win reelection in 1946? Or were they employing a type of political bait-and-switch, building Wheeler up so that Democrats would be more likely to deny him renomination at the hands of a more liberal Democrat, thereby paving the way for election to the Senate of a genuinely conservative Republican who had been a dependable pro-business state legislator?

On July 11, 1946, five days before Montanans went to the polls to vote in the primary election, Anaconda's general superintendent of mines received a three-paragraph letter from the head of the company's engineering research department. "Following your instructions the employees whose names are on the attached list were interviewed," J. A. O'Neill wrote to H. J. Rahilly. "The state and local political set-up was discussed with each one and it was pointed out the importance of voting in the Primary in the method as outlined in our conversation. Each employee is 100% for the idea and will work to that end."[49]

There is no list of employees attached to the letter, which is in the Anaconda archives, and no way to know exactly how Anaconda managers instructed their employees to vote in 1946, but instruct them they certainly did.

EPILOGUE

Burton K. Wheeler, a political hell raiser out of Montana...
stamped his distinctive imprint on a score of the most vital
and flammable national issues for three decades.

—*NEW YORK TIMES* REVIEW OF
YANKEE FROM THE WEST

The end of Burton K. Wheeler's political career, *Time* magazine said, "was a strange climax to a strangely twisted career." When *Time* featured Wheeler on its cover in 1940 he was described as "a Washington landmark, not just another cow country Senator" and "first rank Democratic material," but by 1946 the magazine concluded that Wheeler had "wandered off into the dead end of isolationism. Somewhere he lost pace with history." It was a judgment widely shared.[1]

John Gunther, a journalist and best-selling author of popular sociopolitical books, devoted several pages of his *Inside USA*, published in 1947, to an analysis of Wheeler's career and ultimate defeat. "I do not think he ever has, as has often been charged, been an Anaconda tool or puppet, though the company has certainly supported him on occasion," Gunther wrote. It was more likely "that the company recognized him as such an able and dangerous antagonist that it let him win the senatorship [in 1922] in order to get him out of the state. Then for years the two most conspicuous of Montana institutions [Wheeler and the Anaconda Company] watched each other warily." Gunther dismissed Wheeler's "isolationism" as politically expedient, contending that he "was grasping for an issue" rather than acting on deeply held conviction. But Wheeler was not that sort of politician. He held fast to his controversial foreign policy views long after most of his constituents had rejected them, even to the point of seeing those views contribute to his defeat.[2]

Montana writer Joseph Kinsey Howard's insightful postmortem—"The Decline and Fall of Burton K. Wheeler"—written for *Harper's* early in 1947 is among the best assessments of Wheeler's career. Howard, who had observed Wheeler for years, said his overall record "was all the more remarkable because no other senator of his generation had been the center of such violent controversy. Few American politicians since the earliest days of the republic had climbed so swiftly to positions of national eminence; and Wheeler's climb earned him the additional distinction of being the subject of two of the worst books [*Under Cover* and *The Plot against America*] ever written in one man's lifetime. Probably no political figure had ever been more frequently or more prematurely 'counted out.' Surely none had more defiantly flouted the will of his own party or fought more implacably against his party's leader—who in Wheeler's era was the strongest-willed President in modern times."

Howard praised Wheeler for bringing down a corrupt attorney general and for battling and beating the nation's utility monopoly, and he stressed the importance of Lulu Wheeler to her husband's career. "It is significant that when Wheeler was finally beaten both he and his conqueror in post-election public statements attributed the outcome to the veteran Senator's frankly acknowledged contempt for party loyalty," Howard wrote. "And one of the old-timers, Dan Whetstone, Republican national committeeman, wrote this in his Cut Bank *Pioneer Press*: 'I am more inclined to credit his defeat to a factor which is being discussed but little . . . that was his cavalier disregard of party regularity and his very evident ambition to dominate both major parties in the state, employing as an instrumentality a group in the state capitol.'"

Wheeler, Howard concluded, "fell between two stools which were yanked out from under him just when he thought he had them securely anchored and while he was attempting to convert them into a bench. He was convinced he was bigger than any one party—big enough for two." Howard's critical but fair assessment of Wheeler's career surprisingly devoted only passing mention to the senator's foreign policy positions, the issues that now almost exclusively define Wheeler's political legacy.[3]

———

There was speculation early in 1947 that Harry Truman would nominate Wheeler to become attorney general, and the rumors prompted an outraged Montana's Democratic committeeman to object to the appointment of Wheeler to any "high and honorable office." For whatever reason, Truman offered no job to his old friend, and, after briefly considering an offer to work for the American Federation of Labor, Wheeler opened a law office in Washington with his son Edward.[4]

The Wheeler and Wheeler firm was immediately successful, no doubt thanks to Wheeler's years of experience on the Interstate Commerce Committee and his extensive contacts in the federal government. "We take a little bit of everything here," Wheeler told the *Washington Post*. The firm represented railroads, shipping lines, and radio stations, and it defended the Zenith Radio Corporation in various antitrust actions. Wheeler also occasionally handled criminal defense cases, gaining acquittals for a group of defendants charged with violating federal lobbying laws, and he served as counsel to *Washington Times-Herald* publisher Cissy Patterson, an old friend. Wheeler argued cases with some regularity before the U.S. Court of Appeals and on several occasions appeared before the Supreme Court. A 1954 profile described Wheeler as "a brilliant lawyer" and a member of a large group of former politicians who stayed in Washington after leaving office rather than returning home.[5]

Visits to Montana became more infrequent, save for the annual summer vacations at Lake McDonald, but Wheeler still continued to exercise political influence in his adopted state, and, as earlier, he provided good copy for reporters. Twice Wheeler resisted overtures that he again become a candidate for public office, including a 1958 plea from Montana Republicans that he run for governor. He never came close to reconciling with Jim Murray. Wheeler publicly endorsed the prospective primary candidacy of Montana attorney general Arnold Olsen in 1954 when Olsen was considering a race against Murray. When Olsen ultimately decided not to run, Wheeler wrote to friends in Montana letting them know that he opposed Murray's reelection, and he stopped just short of publicly endorsing Congressman Wesley D'Ewart, Murray's Republican opponent. D'Ewart's campaign nevertheless released Wheeler's letter to the press, which is almost certainly what Wheeler intended. Wheeler also made several speeches attacking Murray for, as Wheeler said, "playing the game 1,000 percent with the left-wing internationalist group that has cost us thousands of lives, billions of dollars, and spawned a Communist war machine that is the greatest threat that our country has ever faced." Wheeler wrote to a friend that his old allies in organized labor were "worried about Murray's health, about his drinking, but they said they would rather have Murray drunk than have the Republican sober." Worst of all, in Wheeler's view, "Murray has no influence in the Senate with either the Democrats or the Republicans." Murray won the 1954 Senate race, his last, by fewer than two thousand votes.[6]

Murray also carried on the old feud, writing in 1951, for example, to Harry Truman's White House appointments secretary, Matt Connelly, enclosing newspaper clippings noting Wheeler criticism of Truman's foreign policy. "I think the President should not rely on Wheeler's friendship as he has in the past," Murray suggested. "If you get a chance," he told Connelly, "you might call the President's attention to these clippings which I enclose." Connelly obviously shared the material with the president, who responded with a letter that is vintage Truman. "Matt handed me the clipping from the *Lewistown Daily News* regarding my friend Burt Wheeler," Truman wrote Murray. "He has always been in that [noninterventionist] frame of mind and naturally I understand exactly how he feels. His viewpoint is almost opposite to mine but you must understand that sixteen years ago Burt Wheeler was one of the few Senators in the Senate who was in any way decent to the Junior Senator from Missouri and I can't forget that. That doesn't necessarily mean that he has any influence with me as to policy but I shall continue to like him as long as I live."[7]

Years later, with Lyndon B. Johnson president and another Montanan, Mike Mansfield, increasingly critical of the president's foreign policy, Wheeler could still demand attention inside the White House. LBJ is said to have described Mansfield, not kindly, as one-third Burton K. Wheeler, one-third Jim Murray, and one-third Jeannette Rankin.[8]

––––––

Wheeler faced considerable criticism and discomforted one of his daughters with his defense of Wisconsin senator Joseph McCarthy's investigation of Communist Party influence in the federal government. "Pop is not a McCarthyite," daughter Frances wrote to a friend in 1955, "but I wish he wouldn't act like one because it makes one more thing to explain away." Frances, who shared her father's abiding interest in politics, but was a good deal more left-leaning—her sister Marion said the family believed Frances was a socialist but "may have been a communist"—was eventually subpoenaed to testify about her political activities before the House Un-American Activities Committee (HUAC). Wheeler served as her legal counsel.[9]

Frances was working on her father's biography in this period and wrote to Max Lowenthal, Wheeler's onetime Senate aide, that she was ready to abandon the project because she strongly disagreed with her father's appearance at a pro-McCarthy rally. Wheeler told his daughter that he attended only to voice objection to Senate censure of McCarthy, apparently believing the censure would intimidate future senators and weaken the Senate's investigative function. Frances understood her father's position but still disagreed.[10]

Wheeler's fierce anticommunism after 1940 largely insulated him during the McCarthy era from any personal scrutiny regarding his loyalty or associations, although he shared with friends his concern that he might become a target. Wheeler was convinced that the FBI targeted Frances simply to embarrass him. "If you don't agree with the reactionary conservatives . . . then you are a radical and a Communist. If you don't agree with the Communists then you are a Fascist," Wheeler wrote to Lowenthal, who was also a target of House and Senate investigators in the 1950s, likely because of Lowenthal's book highly critical of the FBI. There is no record that Wheeler spoke out publically, even after his daughter was subpoenaed, against the climate of anticommunist fear in the 1950s, but in addition to representing Frances during her HUAC interrogation Wheeler twice served as counsel to Lowenthal when the New York attorney was questioned by congressional investigators about his political beliefs.

Records of Frances's HUAC appearance indicate that Wheeler was forceful in asserting his daughter's rights before the committee in the 1955, just as he had asserted his own rights in a similar situation in Montana in 1918.[11]

Frances wanted to confront the notorious red-baiting committee by refusing to cooperate, and she wanted to voice her objection to the idea that it was appropriate for a congressional committee to inquire about any citizen's political beliefs. Frances reluctantly deferred to the wishes of her father, while admitting that cooperating with HUAC "is nothing I am proud of." Wheeler essentially insisted that his daughter take the same approach he had taken during his testimony in 1918 when he challenged the Montana Council of Defense by pushing back vigorously against the council's suggestions that he was somehow un-American, but he never refused to answer questions or cooperate, nor did Frances.[12]

Wheeler experienced a brief moment of rediscovery in 2004 with the publication of novelist Philip Roth's book *The Plot against America*. The book centers on President Charles Lindbergh and features a fictionalized Wheeler, an anti-Semitic, civil liberties–abusing, power-hungry politician, as Lindbergh's vice president. The book was a widely admired best-seller that won Roth the Society of American Historians award for "the outstanding historical novel on an American theme in 2003–2004." But Roth's "historic fiction" actually turns Wheeler's story on its head. There was little if any objection, even by historians, to the novelist's portrayal of Wheeler as a ruthless fascist plotting to establish concentration camps in Montana. The *New York Times* reviewer suggested, "You could learn quite a bit about American history from Roth's novel, if only any of this had happened." It did not happen, of course, and the character reimagined in fiction was long gone and unable to offer any rebuttal.[13]

The novelist cited numerous historical sources in a "note to readers" at the end of his book but neglected to mention that its title is precisely the same as the "nonfiction" book published in 1946 in an effort to discredit Wheeler as he campaigned to retain his Senate seat. That version of *The Plot against America* purported to expose Wheeler as a fascist handyman determined to "Hitlerize Montana." At least in that case Wheeler had the chance to defend himself before a Senate committee that, as noted earlier, condemned the book as vile and contemptible.

Frances Sayler died of cancer in 1957 without finishing her father's biography. Her task had been complicated, she said, because the Wheeler family wanted a book that provided "complete acceptance of father's positions on every major issue." Her father,

Frances said, presented "the least problem" in her effort to write a book that was sympathetic but not uncritical, "but he too is not interested in any careful weighing of the evidence but is anxious to get down on the record his side of the argument with Roosevelt on foreign policy and other domestic issues in general in answer to the many memoirs of the New Deal period." Wheeler used Frances's considerable research to write, with the help of coauthor Paul Healy, his memoirs, *Yankee from the West*, a book the *New York Times* called "an absorbing and illuminating look into the political life of a top-flight politician." Cabell Phillips, the *Times* reviewer, said the then-eighty-year-old Wheeler represented a "bridge ... between what seems a banal today and a more glamorous yesterday." Wheeler's book, like most political memoirs, presented an often self-justifying view of events, but to his credit he largely avoided score-settling, and, with a few notable exceptions—failing to mention Charles Lindbergh, for example—he dealt forthrightly with the many controversies that marked his career.[14]

During the Labor Day weekend of 1962, shortly before *Yankee from the West* was published, seventy-eight-year old Lulu Wheeler suffered a fatal stroke at the Wheelers' beloved cabin at Lake McDonald. Wheeler was devastated by the death of his wife and political partner of more than fifty years—"the toughest blow I have ever received," he told Max Lowenthal. Harry Truman, retired and living in Independence, Missouri, was among those who called to express condolences. "I probably would have been a bum—had it not been for her," Wheeler told Ed Craney, and to another old friend, Wellington Rankin, Wheeler wrote, "I am sure that I never could have accomplished whatever I have had it not been for her sterling qualities, her religious devotion, her strong character and her loyalty. In all my bitter fights in Montana and in Washington, she stood loyally behind me." John L. Lewis, the labor leader who endorsed Wheeler for president in 1940, and former Senator Gerald Nye, once a stanch noninterventionist ally, attended Lulu Wheeler's funeral services in Washington, D.C.[15]

Wheeler lived another dozen years after his wife's death, continuing to the end of his life to keep regular office hours and maintain an extensive correspondence. He played golf often, lunched regularly at Washington's Metropolitan Club, and enjoyed winter retreats to the Arizona desert and summertime visits with his children and grandchildren at Glacier Park. By the time of his death from a stroke on January 6, 1975, just shy of his ninety-third birthday, Wheeler had outlived nearly all of his critics, his adversaries, and his allies. He was the last survivor of the once-prominent group of antiwar progressives. Nye, La Follette, Shipstead, Taft, Vandenberg, the Clarks—D. Worth and Bennett—Joe Kennedy, Wood, and Lindbergh all died before Wheeler. So it was with his adversaries—Jim Murray, Jerry O'Connell, Harold Ickes, J. Edgar Hoover, Walter Winchell, and Dorothy Thompson. Wheeler also outlived nearly all his closest political friends, including Harry Truman, Sam Ford, and Wellington Rankin,

B. K. Wheeler (*at right*), youngest son Richard Wheeler (*left*), and family employee Simeon Arboleda display a good day's work at Lake McDonald in Glacier National Park. (*Box 20, folder 15, image 166, Merrill G. Burlingame Special Collections, Montana State University Library*)

and among his close friends only the pioneering broadcaster Ed Craney survived him. When it came time to remember the old fighting progressive, there were few left who had known him at the zenith of his power and influence. In an extensive obituary the *New York Times* noted that "Wheeler perplexed his friends and enemies alike." In public, the newspaper said, he was "a powerful and sharp-tongued speaker, in private he was kindly and courteous." The *Washington Post*, so often critical of Wheeler in the 1940s, called him "a breed rare these days. He was an American original who believed that what he thought mattered and, by heavens, would try to make it stick. Many times he did."[16]

Never for a moment, even after defeat, did Wheeler doubt the wisdom of his foreign policy views, and he continued to the end of his life to speak out against American military adventures around the world. Opposing intervention in Korea, for example, Wheeler told his old friend Robert Wood that "we can be happy in the thought that there's no blood of American boys on our hands." When President Eisenhower condemned British, French, and Israeli efforts to seize the Suez Canal in 1956, Wheeler approved and called Eisenhower's chief of staff, Sherman Adams, to praise Eisenhower's "guts" for demanding that Israeli forces withdraw from Egyptian territory.[17]

In a series of oral history interviews conducted in 1968 and 1969, Wheeler offered a scathing critique of U.S. foreign policy and said "for the past 50 years every President has made commitments and sent troops to various parts of the world without even consulting the Congress." The Constitution, Wheeler said, has been abused and ignored, since only Congress has "the right to declare war." American involvement in Indochina, Wheeler believed, brought the country only "contempt and ridicule." He hoped, even as Americans continued to die in Southeast Asia in 1969, "that Vietnam has so aroused the American people that no President of the United States will attempt to take action which will commit our country to war thereby rendering the war powers of the Congress a nullity. With all the bad things that have come out of this Vietnam war maybe some good may result from the fact that it has aroused the American people."[18]

When, in the face of fierce objections from the Nixon administration, the *New York Times* and *Washington Post* published the Pentagon Papers in 1971, Wheeler supported disclosure of the details of how successive presidents from Truman to Johnson had led, or misled, the country ever deeper into a tragic war. "The people ought to know what's going on. And I can't see how that will affect foreign relations in any way, shape, or form," Wheeler said.[19]

At a critical period in American history—before World War II—with the nation debating questions of war and peace, it would have been politically advantageous for Wheeler to hold his tongue and go along, but he refused, and he paid the price. The noninterventionists of the twentieth century, Wheeler included, it is now easy to see, were often wrong and their rhetoric occasionally foolish. Still, without discounting the faults and misjudgments, many of which now seem credulous or worse, and while acknowledging the validity of at least some of the caustic abuse heaped upon the pre-war noninterventionists, which continues to shape the prevailing verdict on their positions, these dissenters often displayed considerable wisdom. From a twenty-first-century perspective, Wheeler in particular often seemed quite prophetic.[20]

Wheeler warned against what the United States has become: a true global empire not unlike the old British Empire he forcefully condemned, an empire relying on vast military power, an "empire of bases," as historian Chalmers Johnson has written. Yet, given its overwhelming military superiority and the ability to intervene in every corner of the world, the United States regularly confronts, as Wheeler would certainly have understood, the limits of its power. It is possible to detect in Wheeler's now-distant warnings—and his worry that congressional acquiescence on foreign policy would embolden presidential overreach, encourage executive duplicity, and further government secrecy—an eerie echo of contemporary American political debates. Wheeler understood how easily power is concentrated and abused, and like his former running mate Robert La Follette Sr. he understood the folly of a representative democracy that permits massive income disparity, is accepting of vast corporate influence in its politics, and embraces a huge military-industrial complex so deeply intertwined with the U.S. economy that few members of Congress dare question its size or the trillions of dollars spent on its maintenance.[21]

Historians as well as Wheeler's contemporaries have struggled to unwind, analyze, and understand the political hell-raiser from Montana who often perplexed those who tried to define him. Some argue that Wheeler evolved over the course of his political life from a fire-breathing radical to a flinty reactionary, but that analysis is too simple, and conventional political labels never completely explained him. Wheeler argued, of course, that he never really changed and always remained a Jeffersonian Democrat, an old-style independent western progressive, more at home in the age of a Bryan or a La Follette or a Borah than in mid-twentieth-century America. "In the generally accepted grouping today," Wheeler wrote in 1962, "I agree with the 'liberals' when they are on the side of justice for the individual and against the concentration of economic power. I agree with the 'conservatives' in their opposition to the buildup of centralized power in the federal government." Wheeler's individualized political philosophy helped foster the notion that the radical liberal of the 1920s, the man who embraced the nonpartisan movement and campaigned against corporate excess, came to resemble, at least at times, a contemporary conservative who never reconciled to a powerful, constantly growing central government of the kind that developed during the Roosevelt's presidency and continues to this day.[22]

Wheeler loved a fight almost as much as a victory. He remembered slights and held grudges, as Jim Murray, Jerry O'Connell, and Franklin Roosevelt well knew. He could be ruthless in dealing with enemies and was often too quick to condemn an opponent, yet he was also unflinchingly loyal to friends and no one ever doubted his word.

Wheeler was, as one analyst suggested at the time of his death, a man without a sharply defined political philosophy who seemed to be at his best—or worst—when he was raising hell and frothing against the latest outrage. Nevertheless, what Wheeler ushered into law (the break-up of the utility monopoly, the Wheeler-Howard Act), what he influenced (an independent Supreme Court, the mighty Fort Peck Dam project, and forcing a true national debate about foreign policy), and what he exposed (a corrupt Justice Department and executive branch overreach) constitute a record that compares favorably to any of his contemporaries and is decidedly superior to most.

But it is central feature of Wheeler's political life, his astonishing and remarkably consistent political independence that most distinguishes his career and sets him apart. Wheeler's embrace of bipartisanship, evidenced by friendships and alliances with Fighting Bob La Follette, William Borah, Hiram Johnson, George Norris, Sam Ford, and Norman Thomas to name but a few, demonstrated his belief in a practical, constructive, often nonpartisan approach to government, a government where ideas mattered more than partisan labels. His inclination, indeed his eagerness, to buck his party and his president was extraordinary, even at a time when partisan labels were less confining than they have since become. There is no significant politician in the country today—and few in history—who approach Wheeler's level of political independence and who routinely offers support, votes, and endorsements across party lines. Wheeler's regular disregard for partisanship represented an approach to legislating that has virtually disappeared from the modern Senate and more broadly from American politics. During a career that was at various times controversial, instructive, turbulent, impressive, and even destructive, there was a consistent characteristic in Wheeler's public life that citizens in a democracy might well value above all others—the independent politician as one's own person, unconstrained by partisanship, willing to forge alliances without labels, committed to the perceived greater good, and without regard for the consequences.

Neatly summing up on his eightieth birthday, Wheeler wrote, "If my career has brought me more than one man's share of fights, I regret none of them. Incessant conflict made me live life more deeply." Mike Mansfield, another great Montana political figure, provided a fitting Wheeler epitaph: "B. K. left his mark for independence."[23]

NOTES

ABBREVIATIONS

AFC Papers America First Committee Papers, Hoover Institution, Stanford University, Stanford, Calif.

CCOH Columbia Center for Oral History, Columbia University Libraries, New York City

RML Papers Robert M. La Follette Papers, Library of Congress, Washington, D.C.

PREFACE

1. David A. Horowitz, *Beyond Left and Right: Insurgency and the Establishment* (Urbana: University of Illinois Press, 1997).

2. Burton K. Wheeler and Paul Healy, *Yankee from the West* (Garden City, N.J.: Doubleday, 1962), 17; interview with Edward Wheeler, May 4, 2001.

3. Robert David Johnson, *The Peace Progressive and Foreign Relations* (Cambridge: Harvard University Press, 1995); Justus D. Doenecke, "American Isolationism, 1939–1941," *Journal of Libertarian Studies* 4, nos. 3–4 (Summer/-Fall 1982), 214; Wheeler and Healy, *Yankee from the West*, 399, 398.

CHAPTER 1

1. Melvin Dubofsky, *We Shall Be All: A History of the IWW* (Chicago: Quadrangle Books, 1969), 480.

2. Wheeler and Healy, *Yankee from the West*, 180. An account of Frank Little's abduction and murder appears in Arnon Gutfeld, *Montana's Agony: Years of War and Hysteria, 1917–1921* (Gainesville: University of Florida Press, 1979), 23–26. See Jane Little Botkin, *Frank Little and the IWW: The Blood That Stained an American Family* (Norman: University of Oklahoma Press, 2017), 295–311; and Michael Punke, *Fire and Brimstone: The North Butte Mining Disaster of 1917* (New York: Hyperion, 2006), 202–12.

3. Joseph Kinsey Howard, ed., *Montana Margins: A State Anthology* (New Haven: Yale University Press, 1946), ix.

4. Wheeler and Healy, *Yankee from the West*, 38.

5. Ibid., 56.

6. A. W. Chase, *Dr. Chase's Recipes, or, Information for Everybody* (Ann Arbor: R. A. Beal, 1874); Wheeler and Healy, *Yankee from the West*, 51; Elizabeth Wheeler Colman, *Mrs. Wheeler Goes to Washington* (Helena, Mont.: Falcon Press, 1989), 1–17.

7. Joseph K. Howard, *Montana: High, Wide and Handsome* (New Haven: Yale University Press, 1959), 85–86; Michael P. Malone, *The Battle for Butte: Mining and Politics on the Northern Frontier, 1864–1906* (Helena: Montana Historical Society Press, 1995), 217; Dashiell Hammett,

The Novels of Dashiell Hammett (New York: Alfred A. Knopf, 1965), 1. The classic study of the Montana copper industry and its development is C. B. Glasscock's *The War of the Copper Kings: Builders of Butte and Wolves of Wall Street* (New York: Grosset & Dunlap, 1935). Historian Patricia Nelson Limerick offers a fine summary of the Montana Copper Kings and the IWW in her book *The Legacy of Conquest: The Unbroken Past of the American West* (New York: W. W. Norton, 1987), 114–24. In his book *The Butte Irish,* historian David Emmons observes that "Butte was the only one of the western mining camps that became an industrial city." Estimates vary, but Butte's population in 1920 was probably around 60,000, larger than any county in Montana then other than Silver Bow, of which it was the seat.

8. David E. Emmons, *The Butte Irish: Class and Ethnicity in an American Mining Town, 1875–1925* (Urbana: University of Illinois Press, 1990), 148–49; oral history, Dennis "Dinny" Murray, Butte miner, transcribed and edited by Teresa Jordan, 1986, in *The Last Best Place,* William Kittridge and Annick Smith, editors (Seattle: University of Washington Press, 1988), 502.

9. *Copper Camp: Stories of the World's Greatest Mining Town, Butte, Montana,* compiled by workers of the Writers Program of the Works Progress Administration (1943; repr., Helena: Riverbend Publishing, 2002), 303; Dave Walter, *Montana Campfire Tales* (Helena: Twodot, 1997), 149.

10. See Dave Hannigan, *De Valera in America: The Rebel President and the Making of Irish Independence* (New York: Palgrave Macmillan, 2008).

11. *Copper Camp,* 304–306. What eventually became the Anaconda Copper Mining Company was known, at various times, by other names. For sake of clarity, I have elected to use the terms "the Anaconda Company," "Anaconda," and "the company."

12. K. Ross Toole, "A History of the Anaconda Copper Mining Company: A Study in the Relationships between a State and Its People and a Corporation, 1880–1950" (PhD diss., University of California, Los Angeles, 1954), 237.

13. Ibid., 235; Malone, *Battle for Butte,* 214, 236; *Chicago Tribune,* January 16, 1923; *Spokesman-Review* (Spokane, Wash.), November 2, 1915.

14. *New York Times,* May 13, 1957.

15. Bradley Dean Snow, "From the Sixth Floor to the Copper Dome: 'The Company's' Political Influence in Montana, 1920–1959" (master's thesis, Montana State University, 2003), 175. For more on Anaconda and its influence, see Isaac F. Marcosson, *Anaconda,* New York (Dodd, Mead & Company, 1957); Dennis L. Swibold, *Copper Chorus: Mining, Politics, and the Montana Press, 1889–1959* (Helena: Montana Historical Society Press, 2006), 25–53. See also Richard T. Ruetten, "Burton K. Wheeler, 1905–1925: An Independent Liberal under Fire" (master's thesis, University of Oregon, 1957), 4. There is still debate about the extent of Anaconda hegemony over Montana in the period when Wheeler was battling the company. For a discussion of the various interpretations, see Snow, "From the Sixth Floor to the Copper Dome," 11–15. My own analysis finds me generally agreeing with the comment of former Montana legislator John M. Schlitz, who is quoted in Snow's study. "The plain fact," Schlitz said in 1956, "is that Montana people *think* Anaconda runs the state, whether or not it does." In his 1947 book *Inside USA,* journalist John Gunther wrote, "Anaconda, a company aptly named, certainly has a constrictor-like grip on much that goes on, and Montana is the nearest thing to a 'colony' of any American state."

16. Burton K. Wheeler, interview by Paul Hopper, May 1, 1968, part 3, 10, Columbia Center for Oral History, Columbia University Libraries, New York City, hereafter CCOH; Wheeler and

Healy, *Yankee from the West*, 79–80; Jules Alexander Karlin, "Progressive Politics in Montana,"in *A History of Montana*, vol. 1, ed. Merrill G. Burlingame and K. Ross Toole (New York: Lewis Historical Publishing, 1957), 264.

17. Wheeler and Healy, *Yankee from the West*, 83.

18. Karlin, "Progressive Politics in Montana," 264; Ruetten, "Burton K. Wheeler, 1905–1925," 9–10; Wheeler and Healy, *Yankee from the West*, 85.

19. Thomas J. Walsh letter to William Jennings Bryan, November 26, 1910, Thomas J. Walsh and John Edward Erickson Papers, Library of Congress, Washington, D.C., hereafter Walsh Papers; J. Leonard Bates, *Senator Thomas J. Walsh of Montana: Law and Public Affairs from TR to FDR* (Urbana: University of Illinois Press), 52–61.

20. Ruetten, "Burton K. Wheeler, 1905–1925," 12–13.

21. Walsh to Wheeler, May 22, 1912, Walsh Papers; *Butte Miner*, August 27, 1912.

22. Ruetten, "Burton K. Wheeler, 1905–1925," 13–15; Walsh letter to James C. McReynolds, July 21, 1913, Walsh Papers.

23. Karlin, "Progressive Politics in Montana," 256; Ellis Waldron and Paul B. Wilson, *Atlas of Montana Elections, 1889–1976* (Missoula: University of Montana Publications in History, 1978), 44. See also Jules A. Karlin, *Joseph M. Dixon of Montana*, pt. 1, *Senator and Bull Moose Campaign Manager, 1867–1917* (Missoula: University of Montana Publications in History, 1974).

24. Ruetten, "Burton K. Wheeler, 1905–1925," 15–17; Karlin, "Progressive Politics in Montana," 257; *Billings Gazette* and *Anaconda Standard*, October 19, 1913.

25. Wheeler and Healy, *Yankee from the West*, 104; Walsh to Wheeler, October 23, 1913, Walsh Papers.

26. Ruetten, "Burton K. Wheeler, 1905–1925," 17–19.

27. *Helena Independent*, January 26, 1917; Wheeler and Healy, *Yankee for the West*, 110–11.

28. Quoted in Ruetten, "Burton K. Wheeler, 1905–1925," 19.

29. Ibid., 20–21.

30. Ibid., 21–23. Wheeler's long memory caused problems years later for Albert Galen. When President Herbert Hoover prepared to nominate Galen to a seat on the Interstate Commerce Commission in 1929, Wheeler made it known that he would oppose the nomination on the grounds that Galen had once been convicted of jury tampering in Montana. Hoover quickly thought better of the nomination and appointed William E. Lee of Idaho instead.

31. Gutfeld, *Montana's Agony*, 3.

32. The best and most complete account of the North Butte Mine Disaster is Punke, *Fire and Brimstone*. See also K. Ross Toole, *Twentieth-Century Montana: A State of Extremes* (Norman: University of Oklahoma Press, 1972), 144–48.

33. Punke, *Fire and Brimstone*, 203; Gutfeld, *Montana's Agony*, 24–25. Two particularly good accounts of U.S. entry and involvement in World War I are Justus D. Doenecke, *Nothing Less Than War: A New History of America's Entry into World War I* (Lexington: The University Press of Kentucky, 2011) and David M. Kennedy, *Over There: The First World War and American Society* (New York: Oxford University Press, 1980).

34. Michael P. Malone, Richard B. Roeder, and William L. Lang, *Montana: A History of Two Centuries* (Seattle: University of Washington Press, 1991), 274.

35. Botkin, *Frank Little and the IWW*, 296–97. Since 1956, Montana Highway Patrol officers have featured "3-7-77" on the shoulder patch of their uniforms.

36. Dubofsky, *We Shall Be All*, 392–93.

37. Burton K. Wheeler interview by John Paxon, February 7, 1972, transcript in Burton K. Wheeler Papers, Montana Historical Society, Helena, hereafter Wheeler Papers, MHS. See also Wheeler and Healy, *Yankee from the West*, 141–42; *Anaconda Standard*, August 2, 1917.

38. *Butte Miner*, July 21, 1917; Punke, *Fire and Brimstone*, 209; *Helena Independent*, August 2, 1917; *Butte Miner*, August 2, 1917. Will Campbell's role as editor of the *Helena Independent* is covered in Charles Sackett Johnson, "An Editor and a War: Will A. Campbell and the *Helena Independent*, 1914–1921" (master's thesis, University of Montana, 1970).

39. Wheeler and Healy, *Yankee for the West*, 139–140.

40. Ruetten, "Burton K. Wheeler, 1905–1925," 24–25; Punke, *Fire and Brimstone*, 189–90, Gutfeld, *Montana's Agony*, 49. Ironically, as Dennis Swibold points out in *Copper Chorus*, his study of Anaconda's long control of the Montana press, Wheeler was for short time in 1913 a shareholder in the *Helena Independent*, the paper that most consistently questioned his performance and patriotism as U.S. attorney.

41. Wheeler to Walsh, November 26, 1917, Walsh Papers; Stewart quote is from Dave Walter, *Montana Magazine*, "Past Times," September/October 2001. Anticipating his 1918 reelection campaign, Walsh took several steps to protect his threatened political flank, not all of which in hindsight seem entirely principled. For example, Walsh was the Senate sponsor of the federal sedition law, modeled directly on the state sedition law passed by the Montana legislature. The controversial federal law, repealed in 1921, seems out of character for a man who distinguished himself as a fine constitutional lawyer before he entered politics.

42. Arnon Gutfeld, "The Ves Hall Case, Judge Bourquin, and the Sedition Act of 1918," *Pacific Historical Review* 37, no. 2 (May 1968): 163–78.

43. Punke, *Fire and Brimstone*, 224. See also Geoffrey R. Stone, *Perilous Times: Free Speech in Wartime, from the Sedition Act of 1798 to the War on Terrorism* (New York: W. W. Norton, 2004), 160–62; Clement P. Work, *Darkest before Dawn: Sedition and Free Speech in the American West* (Albuquerque: University of New Mexico Press, 2005), 114–18. The Hall case also precipitated a tragic end for a Montana judge who was caught up in the growing political hysteria. During the course of his trial, Hall called as a character witness Judge Charles L. Crum of Forsyth, Montana. Crum, a Republican and former county attorney, had twice been elected judge and held strong opinions about the war and free speech. The judge's support for Hall's free speech rights and his own reportedly pro-German sympathy—not to mention his German-sounding name—immediately became a statewide issue. After defending Hall's free speech rights the judge was vilified in the press, a Rosebud County committee called for his resignation, and the legislature, with the enthusiastic support of Governor Stewart, began impeachment proceedings. After several weeks under mounting pressure—the judge's sixteen-year-old son was dying of cancer at the same time—and desiring to put the controversy to rest, Crum agreed to resign and forwarded his resignation letter to the governor. But rather than accept the resignation and put an end to the impeachment proceeding, Stewart forwarded Crum's letter to the legislature, which then for three days debated the impeachment of a judge who had already resigned.

44. Punke, *Fire and Brimstone*, 225.

45. Nancy Rice Fritz, "The Montana Council of Defense" (master's thesis, University of Montana, 1976), 90–106; *Roundup (Mont.) Record*, March 29, 1918, quoted in Dave Walter,

"Patriots Gone Berserk: The Montana Council of Defense, 1917–1918," *Montana Magazine,* September/October 2001, 78–85; Gutfeld, *Montana's Agony,* 61. Wheeler's former associate in the U.S. attorney's office, Republican Sam Ford, Montana attorney general in 1918, was among the few officials during this period who insisted on due process, resisted the hysteria, and counseled tolerance. Ford publicly pleaded with the Council of Defense not to infringe on free speech by banning all public meetings, and he pushed for charges to be brought against assailants who manhandled a Nonpartisan League organizer into the basement of the Elks Lodge in Miles City. The Council ignored Ford's request.

In 2006 then-governor Brian Schweitzer signed a "proclamation of clemency" posthumously granting unconditional pardons to seventy-eight Montana citizens convicted under Montana's 1918 state sedition act.

46. Ruetten, "Burton K. Wheeler, 1905–1925," 34.

47. Wheeler to Walsh, April 1, 1918, Walsh Papers.

48. Bates, *Senator Thomas J. Walsh,* 158; *Helena Independent,* April 15, 1918.

49. Bates, *Senator Thomas J. Walsh,* 158. Wheeler allowed his frustration with the press to get the better of him when he joined with a number of other Butte attorneys to help arrange financing—a sizeable $12,500 loan—to launch a pro-labor newspaper that could provide another, perhaps more objective perspective on issues in Butte. It was, as Michael Punke correctly notes (*Fire and Brimstone,* 190), "a highly questionable action for an officer of the federal judiciary," and Wheeler "quickly backed away from the venture, perhaps after having given more serious thought to the conflict of interest it represented."

50. Testimony at hearings of the Montana Council of Defense, cited in Ruetten, "Burton K. Wheeler, 1905–1925," 39–40.

51. Ibid.

52. Toole, "History of the Anaconda Copper Mining Company," 190.

53. Ibid.

54. Ruetten, "Burton K. Wheeler, 1905–1925," 43; K. Ross Toole, *Montana: An Uncommon Land* (Norman: University of Oklahoma Press, 1959), 218–19.

55. Wheeler to Walsh, July 9, 1918, Walsh Papers; Walsh to Hugh R. Wells, July 26, 1918, Walsh Papers.

56. Bates, *Senator Thomas J. Walsh,* 160–61; James J. Lopach and Jean A. Luckowski, *Jeannette Rankin: A Political Woman* (Boulder: University of Colorado Press, 2005), 109–23; Wellington Rankin's biography is part of the Wellington Rankin Papers at the Montana Historical Society, Helena.

57. Wheeler to Walsh, August 23, 1918, Walsh Papers; Walsh to Wheeler, August 29, 1918, Walsh Papers.

58. Jerry W. Calvert, *The Gibraltar: Socialism and Labor in Butte, Montana, 1895–1920* (Helena: Montana Historical Society Press, 1988), 116.

59. Wheeler's report to the U.S. attorney general, Department of Justice file, National Archives and Records Administration, Washington, D.C.

60. Wheeler and Healy, *Yankee from the West,* 162–63; *Butte Miner* and *Butte Bulletin,* September 28, 1918; Toole, "History of the Anaconda Copper Mining Company," 186.

61. Wheeler to Walsh, October 2, 1918, Walsh Papers.

62. *Helena Independent,* October 3, 1918.

63. Bates, *Senator Thomas J. Walsh*, 164.

64. Wheeler and Healy, *Yankee from the West*, 162–63; *Butte Miner*, October 10, 1918.

65. Waldron and Wilson, *Atlas of Montana Elections*, 70.

66. Bates, *Senator Thomas J. Walsh*, 168.

67. C. B. Nolan to Walsh, November 17, 1918, Walsh Papers.

68. Wheeler to Walsh, December 12, 1918, Walsh Papers.

69. Toole, *Montana*, 218.

CHAPTER 2

1. Wheeler and Healy, *Yankee from the West*, 174–82.

2. Mary Lou Collins Koessler, "The 1920 Gubernatorial Election in Montana" (master's thesis, University of Montana, 1971), 121–31; Ruetten, "Burton K. Wheeler, 1905–1925," 54; Wheeler and Healy, *Yankee from the West*, 165.

3. Jeffrey A. Johnson, *They Are All Red Out Here: Socialist Politics in the Pacific Northwest, 1895–1925* (Norman: University of Oklahoma Press, 2008), 157; Robert K. Murray, *Red Scare: A Study in National Hysteria, 1919–1920* (Minneapolis: University of Minnesota Press, 1955), 9.

4. Malone, Roeder, and Lang, *Montana*, 280–81, 317–20; Toole, *Twentieth-Century Montana*, 70–71, 80–81; Waldron and Wilson, *Atlas of Montana Elections*, 7–9. See also A. G. Mezerik, *The Revolt of the South and West* (New York: Duell, Sloan and Pearce, 1946), 53.

5. Malone, Roeder, and Lang, *Montana*, 242–43, 314–18; Toole, *Montana*, 237–40.

6. Robert L. Morlan, *Political Prairie Fire: The Nonpartisan League, 1915–1922* (Minneapolis: University of Minnesota Press, 1955), 22–31; Geoffrey Perret, *America in the Twenties: A History* (New York: Simon and Shuster, 1982), 117, 119. Michael J. Lansing's *Insurgent Democracy: The Nonpartisan League in North American Politics* (Chicago: University of Chicago Press, 2015) offers a broad discussion of the tactics of the league and attempts to connect its legacy to current politics.

7. Morlan, *Political Prairie Fire*, 30–31; *Grand Forks Herald*, April 6, 1916. See also Nels Erickson, *The Gentleman from North Dakota: Lynn J. Frazier* (Bismarck: State Historical Society of North Dakota, 1986). Charges of political corruption directed against North Dakota Nonpartisan League candidates surfaced in 1921, and a recall election was mounted against NPL-supported Governor Lynn Frazier and several other officials. By a narrow margin Frazier became the first governor recalled in the United States. Frazier engineered a remarkable political turnaround a year later and was elected to the U.S. Senate, where he served as a reliable vote in the progressive bloc and a committed noninterventionist until 1940.

8. See Verlaine Stoner McDonald, *The Red Corner: The Rise and Fall of Communism in Northeastern Montana* (Helena: Montana Historical Society Press, 2010); Verlaine Stoner McDonald, "The Producers News and the Farmers' Movement in Northeastern Montana, 1918–1937," in *Montana Legacy, Essays on History, People, and Place*, ed. Harry W. Fritz, Mary Murphy, Robert R. Swartout Jr. (Helena: Montana Historical Society Press, 2002), 152–76; *Producers News*, May 3, 1918.

9. Toole, *Twentieth-Century Montana*, 191–92; Work, *Darkest before Dawn*, 144–46.

10. Gutfeld, *Montana's Agony*, 102–15; William MacDonald, "The New United States," *Nation* 109 (May 3, 1919), 691–92; *New York Times*, December 7, 1919. See also Howard, *Montana*, 243–44; Arnon Gutfeld, "The Levine Affair, A Case Study in Academic Freedom," *Pacific Historical Review* 39, no. 1 (February 1970): 19–38.

11. Koessler, "1920 Gubernatorial Election in Montana," 42–43.

12. Wheeler and Healy, *Yankee from the West,* 171; Ruetten, "Burton K. Wheeler, 1905–1925," 50–51.

13. Theodore Saloutos, "The Expansion and Decline of the Nonpartisan League in the Western Middle States, 1917–1921," *Agricultural History* 20 (October 1946): 235–52.

14. *Helena Independent,* April 18, 1918.

15. Ruetten, "Burton K. Wheeler, 1905–1925," 53.

16. Swibold, *Copper Chorus,* 200; *Butte Miner,* June 23, 1920.

17. Wheeler's account of the Dillon boxcar incident is from Wheeler and Healy, *Yankee from the West,* 173–75. See also Koessler, "1920 Gubernatorial Election in Montana," 52–4.

18. *Anaconda Standard,* July 1, 1920; *Butte Bulletin,* July 1, 1920. See also the Missoula weekly, *New Northwest,* July 2, 1920; and Richard T. Ruetten, "Togetherness: A Look into Montana Journalism," in *The Montana Past: An Anthology,* ed. Michael P. Malone and Richard B. Roeder (Missoula: University of Montana Press, 1969).

19. Wheeler and Healy, *Yankee from the West,* 176–77; Bates, *Senator Thomas J. Walsh,* 18; Koessler, "1920 Gubernatorial Election in Montana," 54–55.

20. Waldron and Wilson, *Atlas of Montana Elections,* 76; Snow, "From the Sixth Floor to the Copper Dome," 39.

21. Wheeler and Healy, *Yankee from the West,* 177–78.

22. Ibid., 179; Ruetten, "Burton K. Wheeler, 1905–1925," 60; Koessler, "1920 Gubernatorial Election in Montana," 69–70.

23. *Great Falls Tribune,* August 21, 1920.

24. *Helena Independent,* October 26, 1920.

25. Koessler, "1920 Gubernatorial Election in Montana," 44; Howard, *Montana,* 246.

26. Toole, *Twentieth-Century Montana,* 233–34; Ruetten, "Burton K. Wheeler, 1905–1925," 56; Koessler, "1920 Gubernatorial Election in Montana," 44–45.

27. Jules A. Karlin, *Joseph M. Dixon of Montana,* pt. 2, *Governor versus the Anaconda, 1917–1934* (Missoula: University of Montana Publications in History, 1974), 50, 57.

28. Swibold, *Copper Chorus,* 202; Karlin, *Joseph M. Dixon,* pt. 2, 46; Ruetten, "Burton K. Wheeler, 1905–1925," 56.

29. Wheeler and Healy, *Yankee from the West,* 180–81. The Minnesota candidate tagged with supporting "free love" was Henrik Shipstead. Both he and Wheeler were elected to the U.S. Senate in 1922. See Barbara Stuhler, *Ten Men of Minnesota and American Foreign Policy, 1898–1968* (St. Paul: Minnesota Historical Society Press, 1973), 77.

30. Wheeler and Healy, *Yankee From the West,* 180–81; Lee Rostad, *The House of Bair: Sheep, Cadillacs and Chippendale* (Helena, Mont.: Sweetgrass Books, 2010), 104–106.

31. Ibid., 105; Ruetten, "Burton K. Wheeler, 1905–1925," 58; *Helena Independent,* October 28, 1920.

32. C. B. Nolan letter to Walsh, October 8, 1920, Walsh Papers; Waldron and Wilson, *Atlas of Montana Elections,* 76–84; C. R. Johnson, "The Nonpartisan League Defeated," *Nation* 111 (December 1, 1920), 614.

33. *Anaconda Standard,* November 3, 1920.

34. Ruetten, "Burton K. Wheeler, 1905–1925," 61; Koessler, "1920 Gubernatorial Election in Montana," 139–42.

35. *Great Falls Tribune*, November 7, 1920; Wheeler and Healy, *Yankee from the West*, 183–84.

36. Howard, *Montana*, 247–49; Nolan to Walsh, February 20, 1922, Walsh Papers. Dixon's battles with the 1921 Montana legislature are covered in Karlin, *Joseph M. Dixon of Montana*, pt. 2, 62–83; and Snow, "From the Sixth Floor to the Copper Dome," 48–99.

37. Wheeler and Healy, *Yankee from the West*, 185–86.

38. Wheeler to Walsh, April 20, 1922, Walsh Papers; Wheeler to Walsh, May 10, 1922, Walsh Papers.

39. Waldron and Wilson, *Atlas of Montana Elections*, 90.

40. Wheeler and Healy, *Yankee from the West*, 191.

41. Ibid., 194–95; Ruetten, "Burton K. Wheeler, 1905–1925," 70–71.

42. Waldron and Wilson, *Montana Atlas of Elections*, 90–93. Evidence of the extent Wheeler's turnaround is contained in the election results from two Montana counties. Running for governor in 1920, Wheeler won 29 percent of the vote in Deer Lodge County (Anaconda), but running for the Senate in 1922 he won the same county with more than 69 percent. Wheeler had barely squeezed out 50 percent of the vote in Silver Bow County (Butte) in 1920, but in the 1922 Senate race he came close to capturing 70 percent.

43. Wheeler and Healy, *Yankee from the West*, 196; Ruetten, "Burton K. Wheeler, 1905–1925," 28–32; John Thomas Anderson, "Senator Burton K. Wheeler and United States Foreign Policy" (PhD diss., University of Virginia, 1982), 37.

CHAPTER 3

1. Colman, *Mrs. Wheeler Goes to Washington*, 56–58.

2. Ibid., 59–61. Wheeler also wrote at length about his 1923 Russian trip in *Yankee from the West*, 199–203.

3. *New York Times*, June 8, 1923.

4. *New York Times*, November 23, 1923.

5. Clarence C. Dill, *Where Water Falls* (Spokane: Clarence D. Dill, 1970), 103; *New York Times*, November 4, 1923; Ruetten, "Burton K. Wheeler, 1905–1925," 33. Wheeler told Ruetten in a 1956 interview that Virginia Democratic senator Claude Swanson hurried to his desk after his objection was voiced and asked, "Why don't you follow your leaders?" Wheeler's reply: "Who in the hell is leading around here?"

6. David Burner, *The Politics of Provincialism: The Democratic Party in Transition, 1918–1932* (New York: Alfred A. Knopf, 1968), 45.

7. "Majority Elects Minority Chairman, January 9, 1924," U.S. Senate, http://www.senate.gov/artandhistory/history/minute/Majority_Elects_Minority_Chairman.htm.

8. Wheeler and Healy, *Yankee from the West*, 208.

9. Ruetten, "Burton K. Wheeler, 1905–1925," 77–82; Richard Drake, *The Education of an Anti-Imperialist: Robert La Follette and U.S. Expansion* (Madison: University of Wisconsin Press, 2013), 450.

10. Michael A. Genovese and Victoria A. Farrar-Myers, eds., *Corruption and American Politics* (Amherst, Mass.: Cambria Press, 2010), 143.

11. Robert K. Murray, *The Harding Era: Warren Harding and His Administration* (Minneapolis: University of Minnesota Press, 1969), 18–20; James N. Giglio, *H. M. Daugherty and the Politics of Expediency* (Kent, Ohio: Kent State University Press, 1978), ix.

12. *New York Times*, February 21, 1920; Robert K. Murray, *The Politics of Normalcy: Government Theory and Practice in the Harding-Coolidge Era* (New York: W. W. Norton, 1973), 8–9. See also John W. Dean, *Warren G. Harding* (New York: Henry Holt, 2004), 51–60; Eugene H. Roseboom and Alfred E. Eckes Jr., *A History of Presidential Elections, from George Washington to Jimmy Carter*, 4th ed. (New York: Collier Books, 1979), 150–51; Murray, *Harding Era*, 69–70.

13. Ruetten, "Burton K. Wheeler, 1905–1925," 83–85; *New York Times*, December 16, 1922; Perret, *America in the Twenties*, 133; Murray, *Harding Era*, 298–99; Keller: Giglio, *H. M. Daugherty and the Politics of Expediency*, 152–53.

14. *New York Times*, June 8, 1922.

15. Murray, *Harding Era*, 18; Giglio, *H. M. Daugherty and the Politics of Expediency*, 154–55; Robert Sobel, *Coolidge: An American Enigma* (Washington, D.C.: Regnery, 1998), 243.

16. Quoted in Sobel, *Coolidge*, 263–64.

17. Ruetten, "Burton K. Wheeler, 1905–1925," 87–88; Murray, *Harding Era*, 474. Robert Murray says Wheeler was wrong about a link between Daugherty and Albert Fall. "Fall did not consult with Daugherty on the legality of the oil leases or ask his opinion on any leasing matter," but since the two men were both friends of Harding they were "linked together in the public mind."

18. Congressional Record, 68th Cong., 1st Sess., 2769; also quoted in Giglio, *H. M. Daugherty and the Politics of Expediency*, 168–69.

19. *New York Times*, February 29, 1924.

20. Ibid. See also Harry M. Daugherty and Thomas Dixon, *The Inside Story of the Harding Tragedy* (New York: Churchill, 1932), 214. Daugherty's book is an unabashed defense of his and Harding's conduct in office and, as such, should be taken with a grain of salt. Still, the book does offer insights into Daugherty's thinking about Wheeler and the Senate investigation.

21. Congressional Record, 68th Cong., 1st Sess., 3301.

22. Marian C. McKenna, *Borah* (Ann Arbor: University of Michigan Press, 1961), 201–204; David Greenberg, *Calvin Coolidge*, American Presidents Series (New York: Henry Holt, 2006), 52; Giglio, *H. M. Daugherty and the Politics of Expediency*, 69.

23. Ruetten, "Burton K. Wheeler, 1905–1925," 89–90.

24. Giglio, *H. M. Daugherty and the Politics of Expediency*, 168.

25. *New York Times*, March 11, 1924. For more on Edward Doheny, see Margaret Leslie Davis, *Dark Side of Fortune: Triumph and Scandal in the Life of Oil Tycoon Edward L. Doheny* (Berkeley: University of California Press, 1998).

26. Wheeler and Healy, *Yankee from the West*, 220.

27. Giglio, *H. M. Daugherty and the Politics of Expediency*, 159; Murray, *Harding Era*, 434–36.

28. Murray, *Harding Era*, 436.

29. Wheeler and Healy, *Yankee from the West*, 219–20.

30. Murray, *Harding Era*, 476; Ruetten, "Burton K. Wheeler, 1905–1925," 92–93; Wheeler and Healy, *Yankee from the West*, 223.

31. Giglio, *H. M. Daugherty and the Politics of Expediency*, 171–72. See also Ruetten, "Burton K. Wheeler, 1905–1925," 95. A good example of the newspaper coverage of Roxy Stinson's testimony is *New York Times*, March 28, 1924.

32. Arthur Ruhl, "At the Capitol's Vaudeville: The Daugherty Investigation," *Collier's*, April 19, 1924, 7; Bruce Bliven, "Wheeler's Way and Walsh's," *New Republic*, April 2, 1924, 148–50.

33. "Who Then Are the Traitors," *New Republic*, April 9, 1924, 9. The *New Republic* quoted several Republican National Committee news releases.

34. *Los Angeles Times*, April 12, 1924. The *National Republican*, an official publication of the Republican Party, contended that Wheeler's sensational investigation was "inspired by Bolshevik Russia."

35. Bliven, "Wheeler's Way and Walsh's"; Ruhl, "At the Capitol's Vaudeville." See also Gaston B. Means, *The Strange Death of President Harding* (1930; repr., Honolulu: University Press of the Pacific, 2001); and Robert Ferrell, *The Strange Deaths of President Harding* (Columbia: University of Missouri Press, 1996).

36. Ruetten, "Burton K. Wheeler, 1905–1925," 94; Bliven, "Wheeler's Way and Walsh's; *Collier's*, April 19, 1924; Wheeler and Healy, *Yankee from the West*, 227.

37. Ruetten, "Burton K. Wheeler, 1905–1925," 93; Bliven, "Wheeler's Way and Walsh's."

38. Quoted in Ruetten, "Burton K. Wheeler, 1905–1925," 97.

39. Giglio, *H. M. Daugherty and the Politics of Expediency*, 173. The events leading up to Daugherty's resignation are also detailed in Donald R. McCoy, *Calvin Coolidge: The Quiet President* (Lawrence: University of Kansas Press, 1988), 212–17.

40. *New York Times*, April 24, 1924. Daugherty claimed that Wheeler and Brookhart wanted access to Justice Department files because the files contained "abundant proof of the plans, purposes, and hellish designs of the Communist International" and that the senators, enthralled by their experiences in Russia, represented "the enemy at the gate." Giglio, *H. M. Daugherty and the Politics of Expediency*, 174–75. See also Daugherty, *Inside Story of the Harding Tragedy*, 203–14; and George William McDaniel, *Smith Wildman Brookhart: Iowa's Renegade Republican* (Ames: Iowa State University Press, 1995), 285.

41. *New York Times*, March 29, 1924. The *Cleveland Press* reaction is quoted in "Why Daugherty Is Out," *Literary Digest* 81 (April 12, 1924): 5–8.

42. Sobel, *Coolidge*, 266–68. For an excellent overview of the Teapot Dome investigation and Walsh's methods, see Hasia Diner, "Teapot Dome: 1924," in *Congress Investigates: 1792–1974*, vol. 4, edited by Arthur M. Schlesinger Jr. and Roger Bruns (New York: Chelsea House, 1975), 199–15; Samuel Hopkins Adams, *Incredible Era: The Life and Times of Warren Gamaliel Harding* (Boston: Houghton Mifflin, 1939), 414; Murray, *Harding Era*, 478.

43. Wheeler and Healy, *Yankee from the West*, 234.

44. Ruetten, "Burton K. Wheeler, 1905–1925," 106; Giglio, *H. M. Daugherty and the Politics of Expediency*, 175–76.

45. Giglio, *H. M. Daugherty and the Politics of Expediency*, 172; Ruetten, "Burton K. Wheeler, 1905–1925," 94–95; Wheeler and Healy: *Yankee from the West*, 227.

46. William Allen White, *The Autobiography of William Allen White* (New York: Macmillan, 1946), 620.

47. Alpheus Thomas Mason, *Harlan Fiske Stone: Pillar of the Law* (New York: Viking, 1956), 188–89; Wheeler and Healy, *Yankee from the West*, 325–26.

48. Ruetten, "Burton K. Wheeler, 1905–1925," 101.

49. Ibid., 113.

50. "An Investigator Investigated," *Literary Digest* 81 (April 26, 1924), 8–9; *New York Times*, April 16, 1924.

51. Congressional Record, 68th Cong., 1st Sess., 5948, 5946. See also *New York Times*, April 9, 1924; and the Associated Press report on Wheeler's indictment, carried in such papers as the *Lewiston (Maine) Evening Journal*, April 9, 1924

52. Ruetten, "Burton K. Wheeler, 1905–1925," 114–16.

53. Wheeler and Healy, *Yankee from the West*, 235–36.

54. McKenna, *Borah*, 202–203; Ruetten, "Burton K. Wheeler, 1905–1925," 112–13. Borah's long career has been the subject of considerable scholarly analysis. See Leroy Ashby, *The Spearless Leader: Senator Borah and the Progressive Movement in the 1920's* (Urbana: University of Illinois Press, 1972); and Claudius O. Johnson, *Borah of Idaho* (Seattle: University of Washington Press, 1967). McKenna's book is the standard biography.

55. Ruetten, "Burton K. Wheeler, 1905–1925," 119.

56. Congressional Record, 68th Cong., 1st Sess., 8524.

57. Ruetten, "Burton K. Wheeler, 1905–1925," 121.

58. U.S. Congress, Senate, Select Committee on Investigation of Charges against Burton K. Wheeler, *Hearings before the Select Committee on Investigation of Charges against Senator Burton K. Wheeler* (Washington, D.C.: Government Printing Office, 1924).

59. Ibid.

60. Ibid.

61. Ruetten, "Burton K. Wheeler, 1905–1925," 132–33.

62. The press reaction was quoted in "An Investigator Investigated," *Literary Digest*, 81 (April 26, 1924): 8–9, and "First Blood for Wheeler," *Literary Digest* 81 (May 31, 1924): 15.

63. Congressional Record, 68th Cong., 1st Sess., 9277–80. For more on Blair Coán, see Richard Gid Powers, "Tangled in Red Webs," chap. 4 in *Not without Honor: The History of American Anti-Communism* (New York: Free Press, 1995). Coán later published a polemic that purported to uncover a vast communist conspiracy in the United States, *The Red Web: An Underground Political History of the United States from 1918 to the Present Time, Showing How Close the Government Is to Collapse, and Told in an Understandable Way* (Chicago: Northwest Publishing, 1925). Wheeler figures in the book as "the candidate of the reds for governor of Montana in 1920." In his effort to generate something that might be damaging to Wheeler, Coán interviewed Wheeler's former law partner, A. A. Grorud, a Republican who testified in the later stages of the Daugherty investigation. Coán reportedly told Grorud that he did not care about convicting Wheeler and said, "We just want to smear him." William J. Burns, head of the Bureau of Investigation, also confirmed the existence of a broad-based effort to find something that could be pinned on Wheeler and told Borah's Senate committee that Daugherty worked with the Republican National Committee to obtain information leading to the Wheeler indictment. Ruetten, "Burton K. Wheeler, 1905–1925," 127–28; *Hearings before the Select Committee on the Investigation of the Attorney General*, vol. 2, 68th Cong., 1st Sess. (Washington, D.C.: Government Printing Office, 1924) 1235.

64. Harlan Fiske Stone to John Pratt, May 28, 1924, copy in Burton K. Wheeler Papers, Montana State University, Special Collections and Archives, Bozeman, hereafter Wheeler Papers, MSU; Ruetten, "Burton K. Wheeler, 1905–1925," 178–79; Slattery's letter to Stone, May 28, 1924, is quoted in the *New York Times*, May 29, 1924.

65. Ruetten, "Burton K. Wheeler, 1905–1925," 180; *New York Times*, January 25, 1925.

66. *New York Times,* January 29, 1925. Donovan would go from his position in the Justice Department in the 1920s to great fame during World War II as General "Wild Bill" Donovan, head of the Office of Strategic Services, the forerunner of the Central Intelligence Agency. Wheeler never forgot (and apparently never forgave) Donovan's role in his second indictment. In his memoirs, Wheeler alleged that Donovan, knowing that the Wheelers were expecting a child, connived to schedule Wheeler's Montana trial to coincide with the baby's due date. In early 1929, when Donovan was reportedly under consideration by President-Elect Hoover to serve as attorney general, Wheeler and Walsh were prepared to oppose his nomination. Borah reportedly went to the Hoover and advised him that Donovan would not be a suitable choice to run the Justice Department, and Wheeler claimed that Stone weighed in to oppose Donovan too. Wheeler would revisit his dislike for Donovan years later when the two clashed over foreign policy.

67. *New York Times,* January 25, 1925; Mason, *Harlan Fiske Stone,* 194–95.

68. *New York Times,* January 29, 1925; Mason, *Harlan Fiske Stone,* 195–98.

69. *New York Times,* January 29, 1925.

70. Congressional Record, 68th Cong., 2nd Sess., 3042–51, 3054; Mason, *Harlan Fiske Stone,* 199. Harlan Fiske Stone spent twenty-one years on the nation's highest court, often voting with the liberal bloc. Franklin D. Roosevelt appointed the Republican Stone chief justice in 1941. Wheeler later spoke well of Stone, calling him an "honest, honorable, able man." Wheeler told Stone's biographer, "I believe that the only way you can account for the handling of the case against me after he became Attorney General was that he was lied to by the people in the Department."

71. *New York Times,* March 28, 1925.

72. Undated press statement in Wheeler Papers, MHS.

73. *New York Times,* April 22, 1925. See also Ruetten, "Burton K. Wheeler, 1905–1925," 176.

74. William Borah to Wheeler, August 25, 1924, William E. Borah Papers, Library of Congress, Washington, D.C.; *New York Times,* April 15, 1925; Wheeler and Healy, *Yankee from the West,* 239.

75. Ruetten, "Burton K. Wheeler, 1905–1925," 185–86; *New York Times,* April 12, 15, 17, 1925.

76. *New York Times,* April 19, 1925.

77. Ruetten, "Burton K. Wheeler, 1905–1925," 187–88.

78. Ibid., 188.

79. *Great Falls Tribune,* April 23, 1925.

80. Ruetten, "Burton K. Wheeler, 1905–1925," 189–90.

81. Wheeler and Healy; *Yankee from the West,* 240–41; Ruetten, "Burton K. Wheeler, 1905–1925," 191.

82. Wheeler and Healy, *Yankee from the West,* 241.

83. *New York Times,* April 25, 1925; *Baltimore Evening News,* June 8, 1925; *New York Times,* July 1, 1925.

84. Ruetten, "Burton K. Wheeler, 1905–1925," 193.

85. *Spokesman-Review* (Spokane, Wash.), November 5, 1926; *Pittsburgh Press,* October 15, 1927.

86. Fredrick Lewis Allen, *Only Yesterday* (New York: Harper & Row, 1964), 126; Giglio, *H. M. Daugherty and the Politics of Expediency,* 181–93.

87. Harry M. Daugherty's written reply to a federal grand jury request for information, New York, March 31, 1926, quoted in Allen, *Only Yesterday,* 102.

88. Giglio, *H. M. Daugherty and the Politics of Expediency*, 193; Mark Grossman, *Political Corruption in America: An Encyclopedia of Scandals, Power, and Greed* (Santa Barbara, Calif.: ABC-CLIO, 2003), 93. Daugherty's checkered career was reintroduced to a new generation of Americans when the popular HBO television series *Boardwalk Empire* featured the ethically challenged attorney general and Gaston Means as recurring characters.

89. Mason, *Harlan Fiske Stone*, 188. Emphasis in original.

90. Tim Weiner, *Enemies: A History of the FBI* (New York: Random House, 2012), 59.

91. Wheeler FBI file, Wheeler Papers, MSU; Weiner, *Enemies*, xvi, 55–59.

92. Weiner, *Enemies*, xvi, 55–59.

93. Wheeler and Healy, *Yankee from the West*, 243.

94. Ibid., 232.

95. *McGrain v. Daugherty*, 273 U.S. 135 (1927). See also Diner, "Teapot Dome: 1924," 214.

CHAPTER 4

1. William Hard, "Wheeler and Bryan and Dawes," *Nation*, July 30, 1924, 111–12; Mansfield interview with the author, May 4, 2001, Washington, D.C.

2. Donald R. McCoy, *Calvin Coolidge: The Quiet President* (New York: Macmillan, 1967), 242–44; Bascom N. Timmons, *Portrait of an American: Charles G. Dawes* (New York: Henry Holt, 1953).

3. Robert K. Murray, *The 103rd Ballot: Democrats and the Disaster in Madison Square Garden* (New York: Harper & Row, 1976), 227.

4. *New York Times*, June 22, 1924; *New York Evening Journal*, June 24, 1924.

5. Burner, *Politics of Provincialism*, 84; Arthur Krock, "The Damn Fool Democrats," *American Mercury*, March 1925, 257–62; William E. Leuchtenburg, *The Perils of Prosperity, 1914–1932* (Chicago: University of Chicago Press, 1958), 133; *New York Evening Journal*, June 26, 1924.

6. Kenneth Campbell MacKay, *The Progressive Movement of 1924* (New York: Octagon Books, 1972), 104; William H. Harbaugh, *Lawyer's Lawyer: The Life of John W. Davis* (New York: Oxford University Press, 1973), 216; *St. Louis Post-Dispatch*, October 25, 1924. For more on how the Klan issue affected Smith and the Democrats, see Christopher M. Finan, *Alfred E. Smith: The Happy Warrior* (New York: Hill and Wang, 2002), 181–66; and Linda Gordon, *The Second Coming of the KKK: The Ku Klux Klan of the 1920s and the American Political Tradition* (New York: Liveright, 2017), 166–70.

7. Bates, *Senator Thomas J. Walsh*, 235, 238–39; Ruetten, "Burton K. Wheeler, 1905–1925," 136–37; *New York Evening Journal*, June 26, 1924; Murray, *103rd Ballot*, 208.

8. Wheeler and Healy, *Yankee from the West*, 248.

9. Ashby, *Spearless Leader*, viii.

10. Murray, *103rd Ballot*, 232–34; Herbert Croly, "Why I Shall Vote for La Follette," in *Politics of the Nineteen Twenties*, ed. John L. Shover (Waltham, Mass.: Ginn-Blaisdell, 1970), 65.

11. MacKay, *Progressive Movement of 1924*, 143–61; David P. Thelen, *Robert M. La Follette and the Insurgent Spirit* (Madison: University of Wisconsin Press, 1976), 180–92; Patrick J. Maney, *"Young Bob" La Follette: A Biography of Robert M. La Follette, Jr., 1895–1953* (Madison: Wisconsin Historical Society Press, 2003), 34–36; Belle La Follette and Fola La Follette, *Robert M. La Follette*, vol. 2 (New York: Macmillan, 1953), 1095–97, 1110–16; Murray, *103rd Ballot*, 235–37.

12. Drake, *Education of an Anti-Imperialist*, 184–85.

13. MacKay, *Progressive Movement of 1924*, 124. For other perspectives on La Follette and the 1924 campaign, see David L. Waterhouse, *The Progressive Movement of 1924 and the Development of Interest Group Liberalism* (New York: Garland, 1991); John Milton Cooper Jr., "Robert M. La Follette: Political Prophet," *Wisconsin Magazine of History* 69, no. 2 (Winter 1985–86): 90–105; and James H. Shideler, "The La Follette Progressive Party Campaign of 1924," *Wisconsin Magazine of History* 33, no. 4 (June 1950): 444–57.

14. MacKay, *Progressive Movement of 1924*, 268.

15. Ibid., 272–3. See also Drake, *Education of an Anti-Imperialist*, 427–51; "The Progressive Party Platform of 1924," American Presidency Project, www.presidency.ucsb.edu/ws/index.php?pid=29618.

16. I use "Progressive" when referring to the political movement and the party that nominated La Follette and Wheeler in 1924 and "progressive" when referring generally to progressivism.

17. *Oregonian* (Portland), July 19, 1924; *New York Times*, July 20, 1924.

18. *Missoulian*, July 20, 1924.

19. Wheeler and Healy, *Yankee from the West*, 250–51. Wheeler used almost exactly the same language in explaining his change of heart to Richard Ruetten five years before his memoir was published. See Ruetten, "Burton K. Wheeler, 1905–1925," 141.

20. La Follette and La Follette, *Robert M. La Follette*, vol. 2, 1116.

21. Henrik Shipstead to La Follette, July 22, 1924, Robert Marion La Follette Papers, Library of Congress, Washington, D.C., hereafter RML Papers; *New York Times*, July 21, 1924. Walsh, needing to tend to his Democratic base in Montana, remained loyal to the Davis-Bryan ticket.

22. *Nation*, July 30, 1924.

23. Wheeler and Healy, *Yankee from the West*, 252–53; Colman, *Mrs. Wheeler Goes to Washington*, 91–92; Wheeler to La Follette, August 13, 1924, RML Papers.

24. MacKay, *Progressive Movement of 1924*, 180–82.

25. Ibid., 189, 184. There were few laws at the time governing campaign spending, and La Follette proposed the Senate resolution that would create a committee, chaired by William Borah, to investigate the extent of political spending.

26. Villard to Harold Ickes, undated note in Harold Ickes Papers, Library of Congress, Washington, D.C.; Ickes to Hiram Johnson, July 15, 1924, Hiram Johnson Papers, University of California Library.

27. MacKay, *Progressive Movement of 1924*, 195; Jane Addams to Harold Ickes, undated letter, in Harold Ickes Papers, Library of Congress, Washington, D.C.

28. Du Bois's editorial is quoted in David Levering Lewis, *W. E. B. Du Bois: The Fight for Equality and the American Century, 1919–1963* (New York: Henry Holt, 2000), 241–42; La Follette and La Follette, *Robert Marion La Follette*, vol. 2, 1117; W. A. Swanberg, *Norman Thomas: The Last Idealist* (New York: Charles Scribner's Sons, 1976), 92; Robert David Johnson, *Ernest Gruening and the American Dissenting Tradition* (Cambridge: Harvard University Press, 1998), 54–56; Oswald Garrison Villard, *Fighting Years* (New York: Harcourt, Brace, 1939), 503. See also Michael Wreszin, *Oswald Garrison Villard: Pacifist at War* (Bloomington: Indiana University Press, 1965), 164–68. Known as "the father of Alaska statehood," Gruening was one of only two senators voting against the Gulf of Tonkin resolution in 1964, which authorized Lyndon Johnson to expand U.S. involvement in Vietnam.

29. McKenna, *Borah*, 208–209; Ashby, *Spearless Leader*, 160–80; Richard Lowitt, *George W. Norris: The Persistence of a Progressive, 1913–1933* (Urbana: University of Illinois Press, 1971), 234–43.

30. Bates, *Senator Thomas J. Walsh*, 243; La Follette to Robert P. Scripps, August 5, 1924, RML Papers; Wheeler to La Follette, August 13, 1924, RML Papers; *New York Times*, September 2, 1924. For insights into the Klan in Montana in this period, see Christine K. Erickson, "Come Join the K.K.K. in the Old Town Tonight: The Ku Klux Klan in Harlowton, Montana during the 1920's," *Montana: The Magazine of Western History* 64, no. 3 (Autumn 2014): 49–64.

31. *New York Times*, September 2, 1924.

32. Donald J. Cameron, "Burton K. Wheeler as Public Campaigner, 1922–1942" (PhD diss., Northwestern University, 1966), 56–57.

33. *New York Times*, September 2, 1924.

34. Wheeler's Boston Common speech, September 1, 1924, RML Papers.

35. *New York Times*, September 7, 1924.

36. Villard to La Follette, September 13, 1924, RML Papers.

37. Cameron, "Burton K. Wheeler as Public Campaigner," 70.

38. Gilson Gardner, "Our Next President: La Follette or Wheeler," *Nation*, September 17, 1924, 279–80.

39. *Cleveland Plain Dealer*, September 18, 1924, quoted in Ruetten, "Burton K. Wheeler, 1905–1925," 150–51; A. B. Melzner to La Follette, September 19, 1924, RML Papers.

40. Cameron, *Burton K. Wheeler as Public Campaigner*, 76; Oswald Garrison Villard, "Wheeler Invades New York," *Nation*, September 24, 1924, 303–304.

41. *New York Times*, September 26, 1924; Sobel, *Coolidge*, 300–303; Amity Shlaes, *Coolidge* (New York: HarperCollins, 2013), 318; Ruetten, "Burton K. Wheeler, 1905–1925," 149.

42. *New York Times*, September 14, 1924; La Follette and La Follette, *Robert M. La Follette*, vol. 2, 1056–57, 1128.

43. Nancy C. Unger, *Fighting Bob La Follette: The Righteous Reformer* (Chapel Hill: University of North Carolina Press, 2000), 295–96; *Chicago Tribune*, October 19, 1924; Sobel, *Coolidge*, 303. For analysis of the criticism leveled at the Progressives on the Supreme Court issue, see William G. Ross, *A Muted Fury: Populists, Progressives, and Labor Unions Confront the Courts, 1890–1937* (Princeton: Princeton University Press, 1994), 278–81.

44. *New York Times*, October 2, 1924. See also Cameron, "Burton K. Wheeler as Public Campaigner," 78–79.

45. *New York Times*, October 2, 1924.

46. Ruetten, "Burton K. Wheeler, 1905–1925," 156–57; *New York Times*, October 2, 1924; Walsh to Daniel O'Hern, July 29, 1924, Walsh Papers. There is no evidence that Walsh seriously considered supporting La Follette and Wheeler. Walsh was too much a party loyalist to break ranks, and an endorsement would have imperiled his own reelection chances. But a favorable word about the Progressive ticket from Walsh would have helped La Follette and Wheeler in Montana, perhaps enough to allow them to carry the state. Walsh won reelection to the Senate in 1924, amassing nearly 56,000 more votes than the national Democratic ticket in Montana and nearly 30,000 more votes than the Progressives. Walsh garnered over 15,000 more votes than Coolidge in the state.

Wheeler entirely avoided the other major Montana race in 1924, the reelection contest between Governor Dixon and his conservative Democratic challenger "Honest John" Erickson. Dixon was continuing his running battle with the Anaconda Company over mine taxation, while Erickson enjoyed the quiet but effective support of the company. Wheeler supported Dixon's battles against Anaconda, but open support was unthinkable, as it would have been seen as Wheeler abandoning his party yet again.

47. *Butte Miner*, October 3, 1924; Mansfield interview with the author.

48. *Spokesman-Review* (Spokane, Wash.), October 5, 1924; *New York Times*, October 5, 1924.

49. *New York Times*, October 6, 1924.

50. Cameron, "Burton K. Wheeler as Public Campaigner," 85; *Los Angeles Examiner*, October 14, 1924; *Los Angeles Times*, October 14, 1924.

51. La Follette to Wheeler, October 17, 1924, telegram quoted in Cameron, "Burton K. Wheeler as Public Campaigner," 87; Wheeler and Healy, *Yankee from the West*, 262; La Follette and La Follette, *Robert M. La Follette*, vol. 2, 1139.

52. Cameron, "Burton K. Wheeler as Public Campaigner," 87–88. Cameron notes Michelson's views, citing the October 22, 1924, *St. Louis Post-Dispatch*. See also Wheeler and Healy, *Yankee from the West*, 262. Wheeler believed that La Follette's decision to cancel his western swing was "a serious mistake in strategy" and that the Wisconsin senator should have concentrated on "the states from Iowa west where he could have been assured of 120 Electoral votes."

53. *New York Times*, October 21, 1924. See also MacKay, *Progressive Movement of 1924*, 187–88. MacKay writes that Republicans "did not have to go out to find the funds" to finance Coolidge's campaign since "industrialists, bankers and business men, perturbed by LaFollette's attacks upon the Supreme Court, unregulated private ownership and malpractices of business elements, collected the money and brought it to the Republican headquarters."

54. Cameron, "Burton K. Wheeler as Public Campaigner," 84, 88–89.

55. *New York Times*, October 28, 1924.

56. Ibid., November 4, 1924; Wheeler and Healy, *Yankee from the West*, 263–64; William A. Degregorio, *The Complete Book of U.S. Presidents* (Fort Lee, N.J.: Barricade Books, 2001), 455. See also MacKay, *Progressive Movement of 1924*, 274–57; Burner, *Politics of Provincialism*, 136–41; *New York Times*, November 5, 1992. Theodore Roosevelt's 1912 Bull Moose campaign remains the most successful third-party effort in U.S. history. Roosevelt's eighty-eight electoral votes came from just over four million popular votes. The La Follette–Wheeler popular vote totals were larger, in part, because women were voting for president in 1924 and had not in 1912. In 1924 the Progressive ticket ran second to Coolidge and ahead of Davis in California, Idaho, Iowa, Minnesota, Montana, Nevada, North Dakota, South Dakota, Oregon, Washington, and Wyoming.

57. "Can the Election Be Bought?," *Nation* 119, October 29, 1924, 458–59.

58. MacKay, *Progressive Movement of 1924*, 136–37; Russell B. Nye, *Midwestern Progressive Politics: A Historical Study of Its origins and Development, 1870–1950* (East Lansing: Michigan State College Press, 1951), 347; Mark Sullivan, "Looking Back at La Follette," *World's Work*, January 1925, 331.

59. *New York Times*, November 6, 1924. La Follette biographer Nancy Unger writes that few supporters of La Follette and Wheeler thought the Progressive ticket could prevail in 1924, and she quotes the presidential candidate's son Phil La Follette as saying, "None of us for a minute thought we had a chance to win." Unger, *Fighting Bob La Follette*, 296.

60. MacKay, *Progressive Movement of 1924*, 258, 242. Watson is quoted in Unger, *Fighting Bob La Follette*, 307. See also Michael McGerr, *A Fierce Discontent: The Rise and Fall of the Progressive Movement in America, 1870–1920* (New York: Free Press, 2003), 315.

61. *New York Times*, February 20, 1925; *New York Times*, March 8, 1925; Unger, *Fighting Bob La Follette*, 303; Robert C. Byrd, *The Senate, 1789–1989: Addresses on the History of the United States Senate* (Washington: U.S. Government Printing Office, 1991) 246; Wheeler interview, CCOH, pt. 1, 15. In 1959 a select committee of the U.S. Senate, including John F. Kennedy and Mike Mansfield, named Robert M. La Follette Sr. one of the five greatest senators in Senate history. The others selected were Henry Clay, Daniel Webster, John C. Calhoun, and Robert A. Taft. When La Follette's statue was placed in the Capitol's Statuary Hall on April 25, 1929, Wheeler's youngest daughter, Marion, participated in the unveiling.

62. Wheeler and Healy, *Yankee from the West*, 266.

63. Roger T. Johnson, *Robert M. La Follette, Jr. and the Decline of the Progressive Party* (Madison: State Historical Society of Wisconsin, 1964), 14; McDaniel, *Smith Wildman Brookhart*, 188; Cameron, "Burton K. Wheeler as Public Campaigner," 144.

CHAPTER 5

1. Leuchtenburg, *Perils of Prosperity*, 137; Richard T. Ruetten, "Burton K. Wheeler of Montana: A Progressive between the Wars" (PhD diss., University of Oregon, 1961), 36–41; Congressional Record, 71st Cong., 1st Sess., 944

2. Ray Tucker and Frederick R. Barkley, *Sons of the Wild Jackass* (Boston: L. C. Page, 1932), 270; Ashby, *Spearless Leader*, 288. An extensive account of the Senate debate over Moses's remark appeared in the *New York Times*, November 8, 1929. The "sons of the wild jackass" comment sparked a heated debate on the Senate floor and continued in the press for months. Some Senate Republicans tried to force Moses's resignation as president pro tempore, and others demanded that he step down as chair of the Senate Republican Campaign Committee. But Moses steadfastly defended the comment, suggesting at one point that he was inspired by a biblical reference. In 1932 popular journalist Ray Tucker produced a book, *Sons of the Wild Jackass*, in which he sought to identify the "sons." The book included chapter-length profiles of Senators Wheeler, Walsh, Borah, Brookhart, Norris, Shipstead, Dill, and Nye, as well as senators "Young Bob" La Follette of Wisconsin, Hiram Johnson of California, Bronson Cutting of New Mexico, James Couzens of Michigan, and Edward Costigan of Colorado, and U.S. representative Fiorello La Guardia of New York. Known ever after as "Mule Skinner Moses," the New Hampshire senator became a victim of his famous quip, and lost a bid for reelection in 1932, and failed to regain his seat in the Democratic landslide of 1936.

3. Johnson, *Peace Progressives*, 272, 345–46; Drake, *Education of an Anti-Imperialist*, 457; Selig Adler, *The Uncertain Giant* (New York: Macmillan, 1968), 42, 69–92; Ashby, *Spearless Leader*, 95–116. See also Adler's *The Isolationist Impulse: Its Twentieth Century Reaction* (New York: Free Press, 1957). For more on the progressives and World War I and later noninterventionism, see George W. Norris, *Fighting Liberal: The Autobiography of George W. Norris* (Lincoln: University of Nebraska Press, 1945), 190–92; La Follette and La Follette, *Robert M. La Follette*, vol. 2, 657–67; Norma Smith, *Jeannette Rankin: America's Conscience* (Helena: Montana Historical Society Press, 2002), 111–14; Richard Coke Lower, *A Bloc of One: The Political Career of Hiram W. Johnson* (Stanford: Stanford University Press, 1993), 115; Bates, *Senator Thomas J. Walsh*, 147; McDaniel, *Smith Wildman Brookhart*, 44–46.

4. Anderson, "Senator Burton K. Wheeler," 59–60; *New York Times*, May 26, 1927; *Helena Independent*, November 4, 1928; Congressional Record, 70th Cong., 2nd Sess., 3841.

5. Anderson, "Senator Burton K. Wheeler," 61; *New York Times*, June 30, 1927. Wheeler wrote a series of articles on his Asia trip for the North American Newspaper Alliance. While in Tokyo, the Wheelers reunited with a nineteen-year-old Filipino servant whom they had met while visiting a family in the Philippines. Simeon Arboleda, wicker suitcase in hand, announced to the family that he wanted to go with them to the United States. As Elizabeth Wheeler Colman has written, her mother had complimented the slight young man on the way he served dinner, and the next thing she knew he had packed his bags for the United States. "Mother was thunderstruck," she said. After the compliment from Mrs. Wheeler, Simeon's father approached the senator, offering to sell his son into service. "Father, surprised and shocked, explained that Americans do not buy and sell people. He did say, however, that Simmy would be welcome to come to the United States of his own free will and work for a salary." That way he would have money to send home to his family, and if the arrangement did not work out the young man could always return to the Philippines whenever he chose. An agreement was apparently struck on the spot, and Arboleda reconnected with the Wheeler family in Japan in time for the ocean voyage back to the United States. Simeon became a much-loved virtual member of the family and remained employed by the Wheeler family until his death in 1998. The three oldest Wheeler children, John (eighteen), Elizabeth (fifteen), and Edward (thirteen) accompanied their parents on the Far East tour in 1927.

6. Leuchtenburg, *Perils of Prosperity*, 107–108; *New York Times*, December 30, 1926. On January 8, 1927, Wheeler engaged in spirited Senate debate with Republican Walter Edge of New Jersey. The exchange below, from Anderson, "Senator Burton K. Wheeler," 53–54, helps illustrate how Wheeler's noninterventionist views developed during the 1920s. Edge asked Wheeler to imagine that no U.S. marines had been sent to Nicaragua and that American lives had been lost and property destroyed as a result.

> *Mr. Wheeler:* In anticipation, then, of a bad government in England, should we land marines in Liverpool or in Belfast or in London to protect American lives? Should we have landed American marines in Italy when Mussolini overthrew the government and set up a dictatorship? Should we have landed marines or did we ever dare to land marines in Russia to protect American property and lives in Russia? Mr. President, I submit that we are simply bullying the Nicaraguan people because Nicaragua is a small nation, and we are doing it to protect men who obtained concessions from the Diaz government, which was in effect set up there at the point of a bayonet in violation of the constitution of Nicaragua.
>
> *Mr. Edge:* The Senator certainly agrees that there is a war in Nicaragua at the present time, does he not?
>
> *Mr. Wheeler:* Of course; and there was war in America at the time that the South rebelled against the North; but would we have tolerated for one moment England coming into America and putting marines in here and declaring the North a neutral zone in order to protect her interest?
>
> *Mr. Edge:* Apparently, Mr. President, if I recall the history of Nicaragua correctly, the occupation of Nicaragua by American marines over quite a long period of time at least contributed to practically the only real peace the country has ever known.

Mr. Wheeler: Then I only have to say to the Senator from New Jersey that he is sadly ignorant of the history of Nicaragua.

7. Congressional Record, 69th Cong., Sess. 2, 969–70, 2291.

8. *New York Times,* January 15, 1928; Johnson, *Peace Progressives,* 336–37. For more on U.S. policy in the region in the 1920s, see, Byrd, *Senate, 1789–1989,* 484–85; McCoy, *Calvin Coolidge,* 351–54.

9. Ruetten, "Burton K. Wheeler of Montana," 57–59; Johnson, *Peace Progressives,* 340–41. One western progressive who did not oppose naval expansion was California's Hiram Johnson. See Lower, *Bloc of One,* 197–98.

10. Richard Lowitt, *Bronson M. Cutting: Progressive Politician* (Albuquerque: University of New Mexico Press, 1992), 75–176; Alben W. Barkley, *That Reminds Me: The Autobiography of the Veep* (Garden City, N.Y.: Doubleday, 1954), 72.

11. *New York Times,* September 4, 1930; *Washington Herald* articles reprinted in Congressional Record, 71st Cong., 3rd Sess., 4671–74; Burton K. Wheeler, "Russia's Trend toward Individualism," *Nation's Business,* December 1930, 27–29, 100–102. See also Wheeler and Healy, *Yankee from the West,* 202.

12. Johnson, *Peace Progressives,* 346; Lowitt, *George W. Norris: The Persistence of a Progressive,* 244–59.

13. Darwin N. Kelley, "The McNary-Haugen Bills, 1924–1928: An Attempt to Make the Tariff Effective for Farm Products," *Agricultural History* 14, no. 4 (October 1940): 170–80; Ruetten, "Burton K. Wheeler of Montana," 63–65.

14. *New York Times,* April 30, 1929; *New York Times,* May 12, 1930.

15. *New York Times,* December 12, 1929.

16. Kerry E. Irish, *Clarence C. Dill: The Life of a Western Politician* (Pullman: Washington State University Press), 67–82. Edmund B. Craney founded five Montana radio stations and two television stations, as well as radio and television networks and the Montana Broadcasters Association. By virtue of his long friendship with Wheeler and his own knack for broadcast innovation, Craney became a major national voice on communications issues from the 1930s until his death in 1991. He also founded the Greater Montana Foundation and was instrumental in creating the Burton K. Wheeler Center at Montana State University in Bozeman.

17. *New York Times,* September 11, 1930.

18. *New York Times,* February 2, 1930; Johnson, *Peace Progressives,* 197.

19. *Anaconda (Mont.) Standard,* July 1, 1928. See also John E. Wiltz, *From Isolation to War, 1931–1941* (New York: Thomas Y. Crowell, 1968), 11–17.

20. Mansfield interview with the author; Don Oberdorfer, *Senator Mansfield: The Extraordinary Life of a Great American Statesman* (Washington, D.C.: Smithsonian Books, 2003), 34–38; Bates, *Senator Thomas J. Walsh,* 279; *New York Times,* May 12 and 14, 1928. Beyond endorsing Smith, Wheeler did little to help the national ticket in 1928, believing that Smith could not win due to widespread anti-Catholic sentiment. - When Smith's train arrived in Billings during the campaign, local Klan members burned a cross on Rim Rock just north of downtown.

21. Ruetten, "Burton K. Wheeler of Montana," 46–48; Waldron and Wilson, *Atlas of Montana Elections,* 113.

22. Wheeler statement of candidacy, Wheeler Papers, MHS; Ruetten, "Burton K. Wheeler of Montana," 46–48, 51; Alfred Lief, *Democracy's Norris: The History of a Lonely Crusade* (New York: Stackpole Sons, 1939), 321; Karlin, *Joseph M. Dixon of Montana,* pt. 2, 231; William Green

letter to Stephen Ely quoted in Cameron, "Burton K. Wheeler as Public Campaigner," 150; *Great Falls Tribune*, September 25, 1928. In 1928 Wheeler and Norris each endorsed Farmer-Labor senator Henrik Shipstead in Minnesota, Republicans Lynn Frazier in North Dakota, Hiram Johnson in California, and Robert La Follette in Wisconsin, and Democrat Clarence Dill in Washington.

23. Ruetten, "Burton K. Wheeler of Montana," 53; *Miles City (Mont.) Star*, October 19, 1928; *Producers News* (Plentywood, Mont.), October 5, 1928; *Great Falls Tribune*, July 14, 1928; *Great Falls Tribune*, June 29, 1928.

24. Interview with Lee Metcalf, December 12, 1959, quoted in Cameron, "Burton K. Wheeler as Public Campaigner," 151.

25. Waldron and Wilson, *Atlas of Montana Elections*, 113–18.

26. Karlin, *Joseph M. Dixon of Montana*, pt. 2, 234–35.

27. Maury Klein, *Rainbow's End: The Crash of 1929* (New York: Oxford University Press, 2001), 70–71; Colman, *Mrs. Wheeler Goes to Washington*, 74, 132–33.

28. Lowitt, *George W. Norris: The Persistence of a Progressive*, 429; *New York Times*, April 21, 1930.

29. Douglas A. Irwin, *Peddling Protectionism: Smoot-Hawley and The Great Depression* (Princeton: Princeton University Press, 2011), 3–4, 94

30. *New York Times*, January 9, 1930; Johnson, *Peace Progressives*, 349–53.

31. *New York Times*, April 21, 1930; Paul H. Douglas, *In the Fullness of Time: The Memoirs of Paul H. Douglas* (New York: Harcourt Brace Jovanovich, 1971), 71.

32. Milton R. Merrill, *Reed Smoot: Apostle in Politics* (Logan: Utah State University Press, 1990), 153, 145. See also Matthew C. Godfrey, *Religion, Politics, and Sugar: The Mormon Church, the Federal Government, and the Utah-Idaho Sugar Company, 1907–1921* (Logan: Utah State University Press, 2007).

33. Congressional Record, 71st Cong., 2nd Sess., 5414, 5494; Ruetten, "Burton K. Wheeler of Montana," 70–71; Lowitt, *Bronson M. Cutting*, 169–70; Wheeler and Healy, *Yankee from the West*, 278. Cutting's leadership on the censorship issue caught the attention of poet Ezra Pound, who began an extensive correspondence with the New Mexico senator, who had been a newspaper publisher before entering politics. The two men exchanged nearly three dozen letters from 1930 to 1935, and Pound contributed seventeen articles to Cutting's *Santa Fe New Mexican* newspaper. In one letter, written in December 1930, Cutting suggested that Wheeler, among several others, was a senator he admired. Pound and Wheeler, from 1936 to 1940, exchanged several rather perfunctory letters. The poet, who sparked great controversy during World War II with pro-fascist radio broadcasts, also corresponded frequently with William Borah. Pound's favorite senators, Wheeler included, are mentioned in several of the poet's works, including his Cantos 86, 98, and 102. The Pound-Cutting correspondence and the poet's relationship with other politicians is analyzed in detail in E. P. Walkiewicz and Hugh Witemeyer, *Ezra Pound and Senator Bronson Cutting* (Albuquerque: University of New Mexico Press, 1985).

34. Congressional Record, 71st Cong., 3rd Sess., 6618; CBS Radio speech, November 14, 1931, copy in Wheeler Papers, MHS. For a wide-ranging review of economics and foreign policy in this period, see Joan Hoff Wilson, *American Business and Foreign Policy, 1920–1933* (Lexington: University of Kentucky Press, 1971).

35. Congressional Record, 71st Cong., 2nd Sess., 5886; Horowitz, *Beyond Left and Right*, 62, 121–22.

36. George F. Sparks, ed. *A Many Colored Toga: The Diary of Henry Fountain Ashurst* (Tucson: University of Arizona Press, 1962), 287–88.

37. Congressional Record, 71st Cong., 2nd Sess., 3516–17. Wheeler's floor speech opposing Hughes's confirmation took place on February 12, 1930. Hoover makes only passing reference in his own memoir to the fight over the Hughes nomination. See Herbert Hoover, *The Memoirs of Herbert Hoover: The Cabinet and the Presidency, 1920–1933* (New York: Macmillan, 1951), 268.

38. Details of the Parker confirmation battle are taken from Richard L. Watson Jr., "The Defeat of Judge Parker: A Study in Pressure Groups and Politics," *Mississippi Valley Historical Review* 50, no. 2 (September 1963): 213–34. See also William C. Burris, *The Senate Rejects a Judge: A Study of the John J. Parker Case* (Chapel Hill: North Carolina University Press, 1962).

39. *New York Times*, April 17, 1930; Peter Graham Fish, "Red Jacket Revisited: The Case That Unraveled John J. Parker's Supreme Court Appointment," *Law and History Review* 5, no. 1 (Spring 1987): 51–104.

40. *New York Times*, May 1, 1930.

41. Hoover, *Memoirs of Herbert Hoover*, 269; *Southeast Missourian* (Cape Girardeau), May 7, 1930; Karlin, *Joseph M. Dixon of Montana*, pt. 2, 243; Watson, "Defeat of Judge Parker," 214; Kenneth W. Goings, *The NAACP Comes of Age: The Defeat of Judge John J. Parker* (Bloomington: Indiana University Press, 1990). See also Kermit L. Hall, ed., *Oxford Companion to the Supreme Court of the United States* (New York: Oxford University Press, 2005), 620, 308–309, 368.

42. Wheeler and Healy, *Yankee from the West*, 294.

CHAPTER 6

1. Donald A. Ritchie has written an excellent general history of the 1932 election. *Electing FDR: The New Deal Campaign of 1932* (Lawrence: University Press of Kansas, 2007).

2. Robert A. Slayton, *Empire Statesman: The Rise and Redemption of Al Smith* (New York: Free Press, 2001), 335–37. Raskob's support for Smith is detailed in many Roosevelt biographies, including Arthur Schlesinger Jr., *The Crisis of the Old Order*, Age of Roosevelt, vol. 1 (Boston: Houghton Mifflin, 1957), 282–83; Frank Freidel, *Franklin D. Roosevelt: The Triumph* (Boston: Little, Brown, 1956), 237–40; and Jean Edward Smith, *FDR* (New York: Random House, 2007), 251–53.

3. *New York Times*, April 27–28, 1930; Ruetten, "Burton K. Wheeler of Montana," 78–80.

4. Roosevelt to Wheeler, June 3, 1930, and Wheeler to Roosevelt, June 10, 1933, Franklin D. Roosevelt Papers, Franklin D. Roosevelt Presidential Library, Hyde Park, New York, hereafter Roosevelt Papers. See also Kenneth S. Davis, *FDR: The New York Years, 1928–1933* (New York: Random House, 1974), 9–10, 50–51; and Lela Stiles, *The Man behind Roosevelt: The Story of Louis McHenry Howe* (Cleveland: World Publishing, 1954), 77.

5. Wheeler interview, CCOH, pt. 1, 26; Wheeler and Healy, *Yankee from the West*, 295–96; Burner, *Politics of Provincialism*, 247–48. For the 1930 Montana Senate election results, see Waldron and Wilson, *Atlas of Montana Elections*, 120–22. Walsh's victory margin over Republican Albert J. Galen was nearly forty thousand votes.

6. James MacGregor Burns, *Roosevelt: The Lion and the Fox* (New York: Harcourt, Brace & World, 1956), 129. For more on Smith's break with Roosevelt, see Slayton, *Empire Statesman*, 358–62. Slayton writes that "when a reporter asked why he had split with the man who would become president, Al replied, 'Frank Roosevelt just threw me out the window.'" Irving Stone offers a sympathetic profile of Smith in *They Also Ran: The Story of the Men Who Were Defeated for the Presidency* (Garden City, N.Y.: Doubleday, Doran, 1943), 285–305.

392   NOTES TO CHAPTER 6

7. Ruetten, "Burton K. Wheeler of Montana," 81–82; J. Smith, *FDR*, 221–22.

8. Quoted in Frank Freidel, *Franklin D. Roosevelt: The Ordeal* (Boston: Little, Brown, 1954), 216; Ruetten, "Burton K. Wheeler of Montana," 81. Ruetten says, "Wheeler and Roosevelt had never been intimates, but they had struck and easy acquaintance in 1920 when Roosevelt toured Montana as the vice-presidential candidate."

9. Freidel, *Triumph*, 248; Ronald Steel, *Walter Lippmann and the American Century* (New York: Little Brown, 1980), 291.

10. Wheeler and Healy, *Yankee from the West*, 294; Bryan B. Sterling and Frances N. Sterling, *Will Rogers' World: America's Foremost Political Humorist Comments on the Twenties and Thirties—and Eighties and Nineties* (New York: M. Evans, 1989), 78.

11. Maney, *Young Bob La Follette*, 85–87; David Kennedy, *Freedom from Fear: The American People in Depression and War, 1929–1945* (New York: Oxford University Press, 1999), 64; Schlesinger, *Crisis of the Old Order*, 278; Howard Zinn, *LaGuardia in Congress* (Ithaca, N.Y.: Cornell University Press, 1958), 242–44.

12. Lowitt, *George W. Norris: Persistence of a Progressive*, 509–10, Lowitt, *Bronson M. Cutting*, 201–202; MacKay, *Progressive Movement of 1924*, 254–55; John Dewey, *The Later Works, 1925–1953*, vol. 6, *1931–1932*, edited by Jo Ann Boydston (Carbondale: Southern Illinois University Press, 1985), 355–56.

13. *New York Times*, March 15, 1932; Wheeler to Villard, January 9, 1932, Oswald Garrison Villard Papers, Herbert Hoover Presidential Library, West Branch, Iowa, quoted in Anderson, "Senator Burton K. Wheeler," 82. For views on how other progressives came to support Roosevelt's candidacy, see Irish, *Clarence C. Dill*, 103–104; Lief, *Democracy's Norris*, 371.

14. Daniel Scroop, *Mr. Democrat: Jim Farley, the New Deal, and the Making of Modern American Politics* (Ann Arbor: University of Michigan Press, 2006), 62; James A. Farley, *Behind the Ballots: The Personal History of a Politician* (New York: Harcourt, Brace, 1938), 83–84. Farley's efforts for Roosevelt in Montana and the western states are also detailed in Burns, *The Lion and the Fox*, 126–27; Schlesinger, *Crisis of the Old Order*, 281–82; Davis, *New York Years*, 217–20; Freidel, *Triumph*, 207–208. See also Donald Spitzer, *Senator James E. Murray and the Limits of Post-War Liberalism* (New York: Garland, 1985), 17.

15. *New York Times*, September 24, 1931.

16. Ibid., November 11, 1931; Steve Neal, *Happy Days Are Here Again: The 1932 Democratic Convention, the Emergence of FDR, and How America Was Changed Forever* (New York: William Morrow, 2004), 114–20; Slayton, *Empire Statesman*, 336–37. See also Cameron, "Burton K. Wheeler as Public Campaigner," 153–54. Wheeler told Cameron in a 1959 interview that he "had the Montana delegation in the bag for Roosevelt long before the convention." In July, Raskob wrote to Shouse, "When I think of the Democratic party being headed by such radical as Roosevelt, Huey Long, Hearst, McAdoo, and Senators Wheeler and Dill, as against the fine conservative talent in the party as represented by you, Governor [Harry] Byrd, Governor [Al] Smith, Carter Glass, John W. Davis, Governor [James] Cox, Pierre S. DuPont, Governor [Joseph] Ely and others . . . it takes all one's courage and faith not to lose hope completely." Quoted in Burner, *Politics of Provincialism*, 246–47.

17. Keith J. Bryant Jr., *Alfalfa Bill Murray* (Norman: University of Oklahoma Press, 1968), 32, 53–56, 214, 219. See also Francis W. Schruben, "The Return of Alfalfa Bill Murray," *Chronicles of Oklahoma* 41 (1963): 38–65; and Gordon Hines, *Alfalfa Bill: An Intimate Biography* (Oklahoma City: Oklahoma Press, 1932). The Hines book is an "authorized" campaign biography.

18. Bryant, *Alfalfa Bill Murray*, 228–29; *Chicago Tribune*, March 13, 1932; J. Smith, *FDR*, 260; *New York Times*, March 4, 1932; Edward C. Blackorby, *Prairie Rebel: The Public Life of William Lemke* (Lincoln: University of Nebraska Press, 1963), 185–86; Ruetten, "Burton K. Wheeler of Montana," 94–95; Neal, *Happy Days Are Here Again*, 38–39.

19. Burns, *Lion and the Fox*, 131; *New York Times*, March 21, 1932.

20. *New York Times*, March 24, 1932.

21. Wheeler and Healy, *Yankee from the West*, 280.

22. Ruetten, "Burton K. Wheeler of Montana," 96; Wheeler and Healy, *Yankee from the West*, 282; Wheeler interview, CCOH, pt. 1, 27–31.

23. Lief, *Democracy's Norris*, 461; Alan Brinkley, *Voices of Protest: Huey Long, Father Coughlin, and the Great Depression* (New York: Alfred A. Knopf, 1982), 77–78; Unofficial Observer [John F. Carter], *American Messiahs* (New York: Simon & Schuster, 1935), 121. The author of *American Messiahs* was identified only as "Unofficial Observer" in the first edition, but it was soon disclosed that the journalist John Franklin Carter was the author. The book remains a fascinating contemporary account of many leading political actors of the 1930s. Long's quote is from Huey P. Long, *Every Man a King: The Autobiography of Huey P. Long* (New Orleans: National Book, 1933), 289.

24. Wheeler and Healy, *Yankee for the West*, 285; T. Harry William, *Huey Long* (New York: Alfred A. Knopf, 1969), 553; William Ivy Hair, *The Kingfish and His Realm* (Baton Rouge: Louisiana State University Press, 1991), 242.

25. Hair, *The Kingfish and His Realm*, 242–43; Burns, *Lion and the Fox*, 135; Neal, *Happy Days Are Here Again*, 223–35.

26. Neal, *Happy Days Are Here Again*, 176–82. Neal devotes an entire chapter in his history of the 1932 campaign to the Hyde Park meeting.

27. Freidel, *Triumph*, 293; Cameron, "Burton K. Wheeler as Public Campaigner," 155. Wheeler is quoted in Davis, *New York Years*, 303–304; Neal, *Happy Days Are Here Again*, 181

28. Ruetten, "Burton K. Wheeler of Montana," 100–101; Alfred B. Rollins, *Roosevelt and Howe* (New York: Alfred A. Knopf, 1962), 336–37; Neal, *Happy Days Are Here Again*, 182.

29. Freidel, *Triumph*, 293.

30. Schlesinger, *Crisis of the Old Order*, 295–96. Schlesinger quotes McCormick.

31. Ruetten, "Burton K. Wheeler of Montana," 101; Schlesinger, *Crisis of the Old Order*, 293–94; Neal, *Happy Days Are Here Again*, 187–89; Farley, *Behind the Ballots*, 116.

32. Neal, *Happy Days Are Here Again*, 190–91; Freidel, *Triumph*, 297–98; Farley, *Behind the Ballots*, 117.

33. Schlesinger, *Crisis of the Old Order*, 299; *New York Times*, June 25, 1932.

34. Neal, *Happy Days Are Here Again*, 197; Farley, *Behind the Ballots*, 119. Farley writes: "We had to handle the [rule change] situation carefully because it would have been fatal for us to be put in the position of repudiating those leaders [like Wheeler] who were leading the fight to change the rule." The switch didn't prevent FDR's opponents, like Jersey City mayor Frank Hague, of accusing Roosevelt of "lacking in loyalty to his friends."

35. Neal, *Happy Days Are Here Again*, 234–35; Farley, *Behind the Ballots*, 124–26.

36. Wheeler and Healy, *Yankee from the West*, 286–87.

37. Wheeler interview, December 8, 1959, quoted in Cameron, "Burton K. Wheeler as Public Campaigner," 155; Hair, *Kingfish and His Realm*, 245.

38. Wheeler interview, CCOH, pt. 1, 35–37; Neal, *Happy Days Are Here Again*, 235. Wheeler also claimed that his efforts were instrumental in Boston millionaire Joseph P. Kennedy's support for Roosevelt. In his memoir Wheeler relates a dinner conversation the two men had in Boston during the spring of 1932 during which Wheeler convinced Kennedy to support Roosevelt. Later Wheeler claimed to have connected Kennedy with former Butte resident Frank Walker, the Democratic Party finance chairman. Kennedy reportedly contributed $37,500 during the campaign and loaned the Democrat Party another $50,000. Kennedy's biographer David E. Koskoff, in his book *Joseph P. Kennedy: A Life and Times* says it is unclear when and how Kennedy decided to support Roosevelt, but he concludes that Wheeler's claim to having interested Kennedy in supporting FDR has merit.

39. Neal, *Happy Days Are Here Again*, 281–83; David Nasaw, *The Patriarch: The Remarkable Life and Turbulent Times of Joseph P. Kennedy* (New York: Penguin Press, 2010), 176–77. See also Freidel, *Triumph*, 306–11; Burns, *Lion and the Fox*, 136–38; Farley, *Behind the Ballots*, 131–32; Schlesinger, *Crisis of the Old Order*, 307–10.

40. Farley, *Behind the Ballots*, 152.

41. *New York Times*, June 27 and 28, 1932; Grace Tully, *F. D. R.: My Boss* (Chicago: Peoples Book Club, 1949), 50–51.

42. Frank Walker, *FDR's Quiet Confidant: The Autobiography of Frank C. Walker*, edited by Robert H. Ferrell (Niwot: University Press of Colorado, 1997), 77; Charles Michelson, *The Ghost Talks* (New York: G. P. Putnam's Sons, 1944), 140. See also D. B. Hardeman and Donald Bacon, *Rayburn: A Biography* (Austin: Texas Monthly Press, 1987), 138.

43. Burns, *Lion and the Fox*, 123–25; Malone, Roeder, and Lang, *Montana*, 293–95; and Michael P. Malone, "Montana Politics at the Crossroads, 1932–1933," *Pacific Northwest Quarterly* 69, no. 1 (January 1978): 20–29.

44. *New York Times*, September 20, 1932; James A. Farley, *Jim Farley's Story: The Roosevelt Years* (New York: McGraw-Hill, 1948), 28.

45. *Montana Standard* (Butte), September 20, 1932; Malone, "Montana Politics at the Crossroads," 24.

46. Schlesinger, *Crisis of the Old Order*, 420; Burns, *Lion and the Fox*, 142; Freidel, *Triumph*, 331.

47. Paul Y. Anderson, "Roosevelt Woos the Progressives," *Nation*, October 10, 1932, 331–32; Herbert Hoover, *Public Papers of the Presidents of the United States: Herbert Hoover, 1932–33* (Washington: U.S. Government Printing Office, 1977), 658, 726.

48. Coverage of Wheeler's Utah speeches is in the *Salt Lake Tribune*, November 3, 5 and 8, 1932; interview with Wheeler December 8, 1959, quoted in Cameron, "Burton K. Wheeler as Public Campaigner," 157–58.

49. Waldron and Wilson, *Atlas of Montana Elections*, 126–31; Malone, "Montana Politics at the Crossroads," 23. Democrats Joseph Monahan and Roy Ayers won the two Montana congressional seats in 1932, and Democrats swept all but one statewide office. Roosevelt carried every Montana county except Sweetgrass. As proof that Roosevelt was not radical enough for some Montana voters, Sheridan County, in the far northeastern "red corner" of the state, gave Roosevelt only a plurality of its votes. Various third-party candidates drew scattered support in Sheridan County, with the Communist Party candidate for president receiving 576 votes.

50. Wheeler and Healy, *Yankee from the West*, 298. See also Edward Keating, *The Gentleman from Colorado: A Memoir* (Denver: Sage Books, 1964), 491–93. Keating said of Wheeler, "He

had courage, was a natural leader, and never failed to vote for the interests of the people who honored him [by sending him to the Senate]."

51. Kirstin Downey, *The Woman behind the New Deal: The Life of Frances Perkins, FDR's Secretary of Labor and His Moral Conscience* (New York: Doubleday, 2009), 114–20; Cameron, "Burton K. Wheeler as Public Campaigner," 159; Wheeler and Healy, *Yankee from the West*, 298. Downey suggests that the only person Roosevelt seriously considered for the Labor Department post was Perkins, particularly after many women, including Jane Addams, and several business leaders wrote to Roosevelt encouraging her appointment. The head of Filene's Department store, for example, told Roosevelt that Perkins was "the best equipped MAN for the job that I know of." Downey, *Woman behind the New Deal*, 115.

52. Dill, *Where Water Falls*, 64. Arthur Schlesinger Jr. writes that Roosevelt "did not intend the cabinet to become a reward for past political support." When Howe, Farley, and other aides to Roosevelt "formed an informal committee to take care of the FRBC—For Roosevelt Before Chicago—Roosevelt warned them off the cabinet." Schlesinger, *Crisis of the Old Order*, 567. This statement lends credence to the belief that Wheeler was never considered for a cabinet post and that Roosevelt wanted Walsh as his attorney general, almost certainly on the basis of Walsh's personal qualities and reputation for integrity and not as a reward for Walsh's support.

53. Wheeler and Healy, *Yankee from the West*, 298; Frank Freidel, *Franklin D. Roosevelt: Launching the New Deal* (Boston: Little, Brown, 1973), 144.

54. Raymond Moley, *After Seven Years* (New York: Harpers & Brothers), 123. Moley contends that part of Walsh's hesitation in accepting the Justice Department post involved his unwillingness to acquiesce to Roosevelt's desire that Harvard Law School professor and future Supreme Court Justice Felix Frankfurter be named solicitor general. Walsh insisted, Moley writes, that he did not "want somebody in there who will lose cases in the grand manner," and finally Roosevelt yielded on the point.

55. Wheeler and Healy, *Yankee from the West*, 298–99; Cameron, "Burton K. Wheeler as Public Campaigner," 158–59; Freidel, *Triumph*, 151; Bates, *Senator Thomas Walsh*, 328–29.

56. The story of Walsh's appointment, marriage, and death is covered in detail in Bates, *Senator Thomas J. Walsh*, 325–31. See also Wheeler and Healy, *Yankee from the West*, 299–300. For reaction to Walsh's death: *Time*, March 13, 1933; *New York Times*, March 3, 1933.

57. *New York Times*, March 3, 1933. A solemn memorial service, which Roosevelt attended, was held for Walsh in the Senate Chamber on March 6, 1933, FDR's third day in office. The senator's remains came home to Helena where a requiem Mass was said at the Cathedral of Saint Helena, with an estimated two thousand people in attendance. Wheeler was not a pallbearer, but his old Republican friend Wellington Rankin, brother of once and future congresswoman Jeannette Rankin and a former Walsh law partner, was. Another of the pallbearers, Judge Lester Loble, knowing of Rankin's deep desire to serve in the U.S. Senate, reportedly told Rankin as they hoisted Walsh's casket to hold on tight, saying, "This may be as close as you ever get to the U.S. Senate." Rankin, according to his biographer, Volney Steele, was not amused. Volney Steele, *Wellington Rankin: His Family, Life and Times* (Bozeman, Mont.: Bridger Creek Historical Press, 2002), 150.

58. Wheeler and Healy, *Yankee from the West*, 301–302. Wheeler wrote in his memoirs that since he was in line to become chairman of the Senate Interstate Commerce Committee he "had much more to gain by remaining in the Senate" than by becoming attorney general. Ibid. See also *New York Times*, March 3, 1933.

59. Wheeler and Healy, *Yankee from the West*, 299; Cameron, "Burton K. Wheeler as Public Campaigner," 160.

60. Wheeler and Healy, *Yankee from the West*, 301.

61. Cameron, "Burton K. Wheeler as Public Campaigner," 160; Malone, "Montana Politics at the Crossroads," 26.

62. Mike Malone notes, "For lack of other sources, one must hesitantly take Wheeler's view of those events. Contemporary rumors seem to confirm his memory." Malone, "Montana Politics at the Crossroads," 27.

63. Comments in the *Sidney (Mont.) Herald* were typical. The paper condemned the "self appointment" and said Erickson hardly measured up to Walsh, "whose shoes he could no more fill in these trying times than could a child." Malone, "Montana Politics at the Crossroads," 27.

64. *New York Times*, March 21, 1933.

65. "The President Frowns on Politico-Lawyers," *Literary Digest*, January 27, 1934, 8. Despite losing his seat on the Democratic National Committee, Kremer found ways to stay close to many figures in the Roosevelt administration and the national party. Press reports early in 1936 identified Kremer, "the suave and handsome prince of the Washington lobby," as chairman of that year's Jackson Day fund-raising dinner in Washington. *Tuscaloosa (Ala.) News*, January 6, 1936. See also Malone, "Montana Politics at the Crossroads," 28–29. For more on J. Bruce Kremer, see Kenneth G. Crawford, *The Pressure Boys: The Inside Story of Lobbying in America*, (New York: Julian Messner, 1939) 8–9.

CHAPTER 7

1. Jonathan Alter, *The Defining Moment: FDR's Hundred Days and the Triumph of Hope* (New York: Simon & Schuster, 2006), 6; Burns, *Lion and the Fox*, 168–71; Arthur Schlesinger Jr., "The First Hundred Days of the New Deal," in *The Aspirin Age*, ed. Isabel Leighton (New York: Simon & Schuster, 1949), 275–96; Alonzo L. Hamby; *For the Survival of Democracy: Franklin Roosevelt and the World Crisis of the 1930s* (New York: Free Press, 2004), 127–29.

2. Adam Cohen, *Nothing to Fear: FDR's Inner Circle and the Hundred Days That Created Modern America* (New York: Penguin Press, 2009), 286.

3. Freidel, *Launching the New Deal*, 448; Anthony J. Badger, *FDR: The First Hundred Days* (New York: Hill and Wang, 2008), 156; Congressional Record, 73rd Cong., 1st Sess., 1971.

4. Malone, Roeder, and Lang, *Montana*, 315–17; Gilbert C. Fite, *George N. Peek and the Fight for Farm Parity* (Norman: University of Oklahoma Press, 1954), 230; John C. Culver and John Hyde, *American Dreamer: A Life of Henry Wallace* (New York: W. W. Norton, 2000), 101–102. See also William D. Rowley, *M. L. Wilson and the Campaign for the Domestic Allotment* (Lincoln: University of Nebraska Press, 1970); and Mont H. Saunderson, "M. L. Wilson: A Man to Remember," *Montana: The Magazine of Western History* 34, no. 4 (Autumn 1984): 60–63.

5. Congressional Record, 73rd Cong., 1st Sess., 1569; Michael P. Malone and Richard W. Etulain, *The American West* (Lincoln: University of Nebraska Press, 1989), 95; Hamby, *Survival of Democracy*, 153–54. See also Bernard Sternsher, *Rexford Tugwell and the New Deal* (New Brunswick, N.J.: Rutgers University Press, 1964), 46. M. L. Wilson, the Montana economist behind the domestic allotment concept, had a long history of agricultural innovation in the state and was introduced to Roosevelt by FDR's agricultural policy advisor Rexford Tugwell.

6. Cohen, *Nothing to Fear*, 281; Wheeler interview, CCOH, May 27, 1969, pt. 1, 35; Michael Hiltzik, *The New Deal: A Modern History* (New York: Free Press, 2011), 124–25; Malone and Etulain, *American West*, 99.

7. Harold L. Ickes, *The Secret Diary of Harold L. Ickes*, vol. 1, *The First Thousand Days: 1933–1936* (New York: Simon & Schuster, 1953), 20–21.

8. Wheeler and Healy, *Yankee from the West*, 306; Ruetten, "Burton K. Wheeler of Montana," 109–13; *New York Times*, September 24, 1931.

9. *Milwaukee Sentinel*, January 4, 1932.

10. Wheeler and Healy, *Yankee from the West*, 302; Margaret Leech, *In the Days of McKinley* (New York: Harper Brothers, 1959), 89–91; LeRoy Ashby, *William Jennings Bryan: Champion of Democracy* (Boston: Twayne, 1987), 32–34, 53. Wheeler's concerns about the concentration of economic power led him to support small local banks and small businesses against the growing influence in the 1920s and 1930s of national banks with local branches and huge chain retailers. Bigness, in his view, always led to unfair competition that damaged small operators.

11. *Congressional Record*, 72nd Cong., 1st Sess., 2618. Arizona senator Henry F. Ashurst illustrated the devotion of some westerners to the silver issue when he confided to Roosevelt's treasury secretary, Henry Morgenthau, that he was "brought up from my mother's knee on silver and I can't discuss that any more with you than you can discuss your religion with me." John Morton Blum, *From the Morgenthau Diaries: Years of Crisis, 1928–1938* (Boston: Houghton Mifflin, 1959), 186; Schlesinger, *Coming of the New Deal*, 248.

12. John A. Brennan, *Silver and the First New Deal* (Reno: University of Nevada Press, 1969), 55–56; Richard Lowitt, *The New Deal and the West* (Bloomington: Indiana University Press, 1984), 113; Ruetten, "Burton K. Wheeler of Montana," 119. See also Benjamin M. Anderson, *Economics and the Public Welfare: A Financial and Economic History of the United States, 1914–1946* (Indianapolis: Liberty Press, 1979), 353–56. Anderson was a top banking industry economist in the New Deal era with a decidedly negative view of many Roosevelt policies in the period.

13. *New York Times*, January 4, 1932; Ruetten, "Burton K. Wheeler of Montana," 113.

14. Wheeler statement on silver legislation, January 4, 1932, copy in Wheeler Papers, MHS. See also Burton K. Wheeler, "The Silver Lining," October 22, 1932, 14–17; *Congressional Record*, 72nd Cong., 1st Sess., 2870.

15. Ruetten, "Burton K. Wheeler of Montana," 118; Fred L. Israel, *Nevada's Key Pittman* (Lincoln: University of Nebraska Press, 1963), 88; Brennan, *Silver and the First New Deal*, 61.

16. *Congressional Record*, 73rd Cong., 1st Sess., 1830; Brennan, *Silver and the First New Deal*, 59.

17. Moley, *After Seven Years*, 157–58.

18. Freidel, *Launching the New Deal*, 331–32; Moley, *After Seven Years*, 158–59.

19. Kennedy, *Freedom from Fear*, 231; Brinkley, *Voices of Protest*, 111–12. For more on Coughlin's support and then criticism of Roosevelt and the New Deal, see Charles J. Tull, *Father Coughlin and the New Deal* (Syracuse: Syracuse University Press, 1965); and Donald Warren, *Radio Priest: Charles Coughlin, the Father of Hate Radio* (New York: Free Press, 1996); Wheeler and Healy, *Yankee from the West*, 303.

20. Wheeler and Healy, *Yankee from the West*, 303–34; Wheeler interview, CCOH, pt. 1, 19–20; Freidel, *Launching the New Deal*, 336–37. Freidel interviewed Wheeler in 1954.

21. Ruetten, "Burton K. Wheeler of Montana," 128; *New York Times*, June 25, 1933. For a concise discussion of the 1933 World Economic Conference, see Badger, *FDR*, 141–50.

22. Wheeler to Roosevelt, July 31, 1933; Roosevelt to Wheeler, August 14, 1933; Roosevelt Papers. Wheeler must also have harbored some animus toward Roosevelt for selecting Pittman instead of him as the Senate member in the U.S. delegation to the London conference. Pittman certainly qualified for the job by virtue of his long-standing position as a western spokesman for silver interests, and Roosevelt knew that the Nevadan, unlike Wheeler, would not use the platform of the London conference to push a radical silver agenda. Still, compared to Wheeler, Pittman was a relative latecomer to support for Roosevelt, and despite his generally good mind Pittman was a serious alcoholic who during the conference scandalized London with his drinking bouts, including reportedly shooting out streetlights with a revolver. When Pittman, chairman of the Senate Foreign Relations Committee, was presented at court to King George V and Queen Mary he reportedly said: "King, I'm glad to meet you. And you too, Queen." Betty Glad, *Pittman: The Tragedy of a Senate Insider* (New York: Columbia University Press, 1986), 198–99.

23. Roosevelt to senator Joe T. Robinson, January 25, 1934, Roosevelt letters, FDR Library.

24. *Pittsburgh Press*, May 2, 1934; Wheeler interview, CCOH, May 1, 1968, pt. 1, 9; Schlesinger, *Coming of the New Deal*, 251–52; Hamby, *For the Survival of Democracy*, 152.

25. Wheeler and Healy, *Yankee from the West*, 304–306; David P. Billington and Donald C. Jackson, *Big Dams in the New Deal Era* (Norman: University of Oklahoma Press, 2006), 325n21. Wheeler was cynical about Roosevelt's approach to approving the Fort Peck Dam but not blind to the political and economic benefits. "I'm sure most of these projects have been very useful to the economy of the country. Fort Peck [Dam] was useful to the people of Montana—as well as me politically," he conceded. Wheeler and Healy, *Yankee from the West*, 304–306.

26. T. H. Watkins, *Righteous Pilgrim: The Life and Times of Harold L. Ickes, 1874–1952* (New York: Henry Holt, 1990), 538; Graham D. Taylor, *The New Deal and American Indian Tribalism: The Administration of the Indian Reorganization Act, 1934–1945* (Lincoln: University of Nebraska Press, 1980), 20–21.

27. Taylor, *The New Deal and American Indian Tribalism*, 17–18.

28. Donald L. Fixico, *Bureau of Indian Affairs* (Santa Barbara, Calif.: ABC-CLIO, 2012), 111–12. See also Kenneth Philp, *John Collier's Crusade of Indian Reform, 1920–1954* (Tucson: University of Arizona Press, 1977).

29. John Collier to Wheeler, June 16, 1926, Collier Papers, Yale University Library, Sterling Memorial Library, New Haven, Conn; Congressional Record, 69th Cong., 1st Sess., 4470–71.

30. Wheeler and Healy, *Yankee from the West*, 315–18, 105–106.

31. Congressional Record, 68th Cong., 2nd Sess., 4059–60; Wheeler Speech, August 11, 1929, Wheeler Papers, MSU. See also William Morrow Stoddart, "Whose Deal? Burton K. Wheeler and the Indian Reorganization Act" (master's thesis, Montana State University, 1996); and John Leiper Freeman Jr., "The New Deal for Indians: A Study in Bureau-Committee Relations in Government" (PhD diss., Princeton University, 1952). On the particularly contentious issue of hydropower development on the Flathead Indian Reservation, in 1930 Wheeler objected to the efforts of a private developer, Walter H. Wheeler (no relation), to acquire development rights from the tribe, fearing the developer would tie up the lucrative concession while "he sees if he can find a suitable market for the power." Wheeler helped engineer an agreement between the tribe and Montana Power—Senator Walsh also participated—that provided a royalty payment to the tribe in exchange for access to the power sites for development. Then Montana Power did what Wheeler feared the private developer would do and delayed developing the

site. Wheeler's role in the high-profile issue was proof to some critics that he had sold out the tribe and made a deal beneficial to the utility company he had so often criticized in the past.

32. Watkins, *Righteous Pilgrim*, 534.

33. Wheeler and Healy, *Yankee from the West*, 318.

34. Wheeler letter to Roosevelt, March 15, 1934, Roosevelt Papers.

35. Stoddart, "Whose Deal?," 93–94.

36. Vine Deloria Jr. *The Indian Reorganization Act: Congresses and Bills* (Norman: University of Oklahoma Press, 2002), vii–viii.

37. *Hearing before the Committee on Indian Affairs United States Senate on S. 2755*, 73rd Cong., 2nd Sess. (Washington, D.C.: U.S. Government Printing Office, 1934); Roosevelt to Wheeler, April 28, 1934, Roosevelt Papers, President's Personal File; Watkins, *Righteous Pilgrim*, 538–41; Stoddart, "Whose Deal?," 94.

38. Elmer R. Rusco, *A Fateful Time: The Background and Legislative History of the Indian Reorganization Act* (Reno: University of Nevada Press, 2000), 255–81; Stoddart, "Whose Deal?," 98.

39. Taylor, *New Deal and American Indian Tribalism*, 25–26; Jeanne Nienaber Clarke, *Roosevelt's Warrior: Harold L. Ickes and the New Deal* (Baltimore: Johns Hopkins University Press, 1996), 43.

40. Watkins, *Righteous Pilgrim*, 541; Lawrence C. Kelly, "The Indian Reorganization Act: The Dream and the Reality," *Pacific Historical Review* 44, no. 3 (August 1975): 291–312.

41. Kenneth R. Philp, ed. *Indian Self-Rule: First-Hand Accounts of Indian-White Relations from Roosevelt to Reagan* (Chicago: Howe Brothers, 1986), 107; Stoddart, "Whose Deal?," 106–107; Kelly, "The Indian Reorganization Act," 301–303; Philp, *John Collier's Crusade for Indian Reform*, 162–63.

42. Taylor, *New Deal and American Indian Tribalism*, 142–43.

43. Stoddart, "Whose Deal?, "118; Wheeler and Healy, *Yankee from the West*, 314–18; Lowitt, *New Deal and the West*, 136; *New York Times*, February 24, 1937.

44. Hearings of the Senate Indian Affairs Committee, April 5, 1937, quoted in Watkins, *Righteous Pilgrim*, 546.

45. John Collier to Wheeler, April 5, 1937, quoted in Watkins, *Righteous Pilgrim*, 546. See also "A New Deal for the American Indian," *Literary Digest*, April 7, 1934, 21.

46. Lowitt, *New Deal and the West*, 136–37; Vine Deloria Jr., ed., *American Indian Policy in the Twentieth Century* (Norman: University of Oklahoma Press, 1985), 249–50. Wheeler never stopped believing that the Indian Reorganization Act had been a "bad bill" even more badly administered. In 1943 he signed on to a report prepared in support of legislation to abolish the BIA. The report severely criticized John Collier, who, it alleged, was attempting to "promote segregation" and make "the Indian a guinea pig for experimentation" and tie Native Americans "to the land in perpetuity . . . with all the limitations of a primitive life." Three years later, during a hearing on the Pine Ridge Reservation in South Dakota, Wheeler asked a Sioux tribal leader, Moses Two Bulls, if he supported the IRA. Two Bulls replied, "Yes, we are only just getting started. It's only ten years old. How long did it take the United States Government to form a perfect organization? It takes time." Wheeler responded, "We have not entirely done it yet." Stoddart, "Whose Deal?," 150.

47. Ruetten, "Burton K. Wheeler of Montana," 153–54.

48. Ibid., 154; John Morrison and Catherine Wright Morrison, *Mavericks: The Lives and Battles of Montana's Political Legends* (Moscow: University of Idaho Press, 1997), 197–226.

49. Following a joint Wheeler-Murray 1934 campaign stop in Havre, Lulu Wheeler wrote to her daughter with characteristic bluntness: "The Murrays are back in tow now and I'd hate to bet on which one is the greater liability. It's dreadful! The Ericksons might have been a load but certainly they would have been a much more intelligent load." Murray, Lulu Wheeler said, was simply "a dummy candidate." It was a mystery to her that "anyone could live so long and learn so little and in addition he is not sensitive to his audience nor has he any political judgment." By contrast Wheeler's performance on the campaign trail, as his wife saw it, was superb.

50. Spritzer, *Senator James E. Murray*, 13–15; Ruetten, "Burton K. Wheeler of Montana," 154; Waldron and Wilson, *Atlas of Montana Elections*, 132; *Montana Record-Herald* (Helena), October 6, 1934; *New York Times*, October 11, 1934.

51. *Great Falls Tribune*, September 7, 1934; *Montana Record-Herald* (Helena), October 15 and October 22, 1934.

52. Ruetten, "Burton K. Wheeler of Montana," 59–160; Lowitt, *New Deal and the West*, 86–87; Lois Lonnquist, *Fifty Cents an Hour: The Builders and Boomtowns of the Fort Peck Dam* (Helena, MtSky Press, 2006); *Washington Daily News*, September 1, 1936; Malone and Etulain, *American West*, 106; Malone, Roeder, and Lang, *Montana*, 300–302; *New York Times*, October 2, 1937. See also Marc Reisner and Sarah Bates, *Overtapped Oasis* (Washington, D.C.: Island Press, 1990), 19. Reisner and Bates write, "Some hydrologists still wonder exactly what purpose is served by Montana's Fort Peck Dam—even today the fourth largest dam on the planet, on a river not yet grown to middling size—but Congress seems to have approved without a second thought."

53. *Great Falls Tribune*, September 10, 1934; Ruetten, "Burton K. Wheeler of Montana," 158. For more on FDR and Wheeler in this period, see Richard Neuberger, "Wheeler of Montana," *Harper's*, May 1940, 608–18. "The President seemed to forget completely his obligation to Wheeler," Neuberger wrote, "how, for example, the latter had angered [Democratic Party official] Jouett Shouse by delivering a Roosevelt speech in 1930, and how Huey Long, Hiram Johnson, and [George] Norris had followed Wheeler to the stump for him. The Montana Senator was not consulted on policy, he was not brought into the White House inner circles." Roosevelt, Neuberger observed, "traveled 675 miles across Montana without murmuring a syllable about Wheeler."

54. Wheeler to Roosevelt, April 17, 1934, Roosevelt Papers.

55. *Great Falls Tribune*, October 5, 1934. It is interesting to compare Roosevelt's treatment of La Follette, a progressive Republican, with his treatment of Democrat Wheeler in 1934. During an off-the-record chat with White House reporters in June, Roosevelt said that it was his "own personal hope that they will find some way of sending Bob La Follette back here," but he stopped short of pressuring Wisconsin Democratic leaders to endorse the young senator. Then in August Roosevelt visited Wisconsin and publicly embraced Wheeler's friend, telling the state's voters, "Your two senators, Bob La Follette and Ryan Duffy, both good friends of mine, they and many others have worked with me in maintaining excellent cooperation between the executive and legislative branches of government. I take this opportunity of expressing my gratitude to them." Days before, while in Montana, Roosevelt had not publicly spoken Wheeler's name.

56. Lulu Wheeler, undated letter to Elizabeth Wheeler Colman, in possession of author.

57. Waldron and Wilson, *Atlas of Montana Elections*, 132–35; Ruetten, "Burton K. Wheeler of Montana," 169.

CHAPTER 8

1. For more on Couzens's Senate career, see Harry Barnard, *Independent Man: The Life of Senator James Couzens* (New York: Charles Scribner's Sons, 1958). Minton's career is covered in Linda C. Gugin and James E. St. Clair's, *Sherman Minton: New Deal Senator, Cold War Justice* (Indianapolis: Indiana Historical Society, 1997). Information on Lowenthal is from "Biographical Sketch of Max Lowenthal," Max Lowenthal Papers, Elmer L. Andersen Library, University of Minnesota, hereafter Lowenthal Papers. See also Max Lowenthal Oral History, September 20, 1967, Harry S. Truman Presidential Library; and David Halberstam, *The Powers That Be* (New York: Alfred A. Knopf, 1979), 621.

2. Katie Louchheim, ed., *The Making of the New Deal: The Insiders Speak* (Cambridge: Harvard University Press, 1983), 243; John A. Carver Jr. interview with the author, March 27, 2001; John A. Carver Jr. Oral History Project, Sturm College of Law, University of Denver.

3. Davis, *New York Years*, 88–101; Schlesinger, *Crisis of the Old Order*, 124.

4. Leuchtenburg, *Perils of Prosperity*, 190–91; Wheeler and Healy, *Yankee from the West*, 307; Ruetten, "Burton K. Wheeler of Montana," 171–72; Steve Isser, *Electricity Restructuring in the United States: Markets and Policy from the 1978 Energy Act to the Present* (New York: Cambridge University Press, 2015), 23–25. Utah Power & Light Company is an example of the type of consolidation that took place in the electricity utility industry in the first decades of the twentieth century. "[The company] was organized on September 6, 1912, as a subsidiary of a large holding company, Electric Bond and Share Company (EBASCO) of New York, to consolidate dozens of large and small electric power companies in Utah and surrounding states.... Following its formation, Utah Power set out to acquire other electric companies and unify them into one large integrated 'super power system' rather than operate them as separate, independent entities. Within four years it had purchased twenty-seven utility companies and eventually absorbed more than 130. By 1922, on its tenth anniversary, Utah Power had made considerable progress towards its goal. It served 205 communities in four states, had 83,000 customers, and operated forty generating plants with an installed capacity of 224,000 kilowatts." "Utah Power & Light Company," Lehman Brothers Collection—Contemporary Business Archives, Harvard Business School, Baker Library, Historical Collections, http://www.library.hbs.edu/hc/lehman/company.html?company=utah_power_light_company.

5. Ruetten, "Burton K. Wheeler of Montana," 171–72; Mary Earhart Dillon, *Wendell Willkie* (Philadelphia: J. B. Lippincott, 1952), 33–34; Schlesinger, *Crisis of the Old Order*, 118–19.

6. Ruetten, "Burton K. Wheeler of Montana," 172–73; N. R. Danielian, "Power and the Public: What Should Be Done with the Holding Companies?," *Harper's*, June 1935, 36–47; *Hearings on Public Utilities Holding Company Act of 1935, Committee on Interstate Commerce*, U.S. Senate, 74th Cong., 1st Sess., 3; Robert Caro, *The Years of Lyndon Johnson: Master of the Senate* (New York: Knopf, 2002), 240.

7. Congressional Record, 71st Cong., 3rd Sess., 1600; Schlesinger, *Crisis of the Old Order*, 119–20. A sympathetic treatment of Insull is offered by Forrest McDonald, *Insull* (Chicago: University of Chicago Press, 1962).

8. Ruetten, "Burton K. Wheeler of Montana," 172–73.

9. Kenneth S. Davis, *FDR: The New Deal Years, 1933–1937* (New York: Random House, 1986), 530; Moley, *After Seven Years*, 303. For a concise summary of the Roosevelt administration's

402 NOTES TO CHAPTER 8

response to the regulation of the holding companies and the subsequent congressional action, see Hiltzik, *New Deal*, 205–12.

10. William Lasser, *Benjamin V. Cohen: Architect of the New Deal* (New Haven: Yale University Press, 2002), 110–13; Philip J. Funigiello, *Toward a National Power Policy: The New Deal and the Electric Utility Industry* (Pittsburgh: University of Pittsburgh Press, 1973), 42.

11. Lasser, *Benjamin V. Cohen*, 118; Arthur M. Schlesinger, *The Politics of Upheaval*, Age of Roosevelt, vol. 3 (Boston: Houghton Mifflin, 1960), 305–306; Funigiello, *Toward a National Power Policy*, 32–66. Funigiello provides an extensive, detailed discussion of the process used to draft the holding company legislation.

12. Ruetten, "Burton K. Wheeler of Montana," 175; Funigiello, *Toward a National Power Policy*, 57; *New York Times*, January 5, 1935.

13. Lilienthal's comment is quoted in Funigiello, *Toward a National Power Policy*, 60.

14. Hardeman and Bacon, *Rayburn*, 170; Wheeler and Healy, *Yankee from the West*, 308.

15. Congressional Record, 74th Cong., 1st Sess., 2199–2200.

16. Schlesinger, *Politics of Upheaval*, 308; Cohen quoted in Hardeman and Bacon, *Rayburn*, 172.

17. Crawford, *Pressure Boys*, 70; Harry S. Truman, *Memoirs*, vol. 1, *Year of Decisions* (New York: Doubleday, 1955), 151; Hardeman and Bacon, *Rayburn*, 172.

18. Ruetten, "Burton K. Wheeler of Montana," 180–81; Truman, *Memoirs*, vol. 1, 151; David McCullough, *Truman* (New York: Simon & Schuster, 1992), 217–19; Chester M. Morgan, *Redneck Liberal: Theodore G. Bilbo and the New Deal* (Baton Rouge: Louisiana State University Press, 1985), 74.

19. Undated letter in the files of the Senate Committee on Interstate Commerce, National Archives and Records Administration, Washington, D.C., hereafter Senate Committee files.

20. S. E. Watters to Wheeler, February 26, 1935; Thomas B. Schmidt to Wheeler, April 15, 1935; Tina Hakala to Wheeler, May 3, 1935, all in Senate Committee files.

21. *Western Progressive* (Helena, Mont.), March 22, 1935, quoted in Ruetten, "Burton K. Wheeler of Montana," 177; Swibold, *Copper Chorus*, 266.

22. Wheeler to Mr. and Mrs. Stackhouse, May 24, 1935, Senate Committee files; Wheeler undated form letter in Senate Committee files.

23. Report of the National Public Power Committee presented to Congress, March 12, 1935, copy in the Senate Committee files; *New York Times*, March 14, 1935.

24. Congressional Record, 74th Cong., 1st Sess., 4594.

25. Wheeler radio speech, April 2, 1935, copy in Wheeler Papers, MHS.

26. All quotes from Ruetten, "Burton K. Wheeler of Montana," 181–82.

27. Ibid., 183; Steve Neal, *Dark Horse: A Biography of Wendell Willkie* (Lawrence: University of Kansas Press, 1989), 25–27.

28. Ruetten, "Burton K. Wheeler of Montana," 181–83. The Wheeler-Willkie exchange is also mentioned in Dillon, *Wendell Willkie*, 70–71.

29. David H. Bennett, *Demagogues in the Depression* (New Brunswick, N.J.: Rutgers University Press, 1969), 72–73; Tull, *Father Coughlin and the New Deal*, 93, 99; *New York Times*, April 25, 1935; Schlesinger, *Politics of Upheaval*, 306–307.

30. *New York Times*, May 30, 1935; Ruetten, "Burton K. Wheeler of Montana," 183.

31. Funigiello, *Toward a National Power Policy*, 82; Hall, *Oxford Companion to the Supreme Court*, 757.

32. *New York Times*, May 30, 1935; Congressional Record, 74th Cong., 1st Sess., 8617; Funigiello, *Toward a National Power Policy*, 84.

33. *New York Times*, June 16, 1935; Richard Lowitt, *George W. Norris: The Triumph of a Progressive, 1933–1944* (Urbana: University of Illinois Press, 1978), 83; Norris, *Fighting Liberal*, 375–76.

34. Congressional Record, 74th Cong., 1st Sess., 8618; Funigiello, *Toward a National Power Policy*, 85.

35. Funigiello, *Toward a National Power Policy*, 86.

36. Frances Perkins, *The Roosevelt I Knew* (New York: Viking Press, 1946), 65–66; J. Smith, *FDR*, 333–34.

37. Marquis Childs, *I Write from Washington* (New York: Harper and Brothers, 1942), 189; Funigiello, *Toward a National Power Policy*, 86.

38. Moley, *After Seven Years*, 303; Ruetten, "Burton K. Wheeler of Montana," 171.

39. Funigiello, *Toward a National Power Policy*, 86–87.

40. Congressional Record, 74th Cong., 1st Sess., 8934; Funigiello, *Toward a National Power Policy*, 86–87; Ruetten, "Burton K. Wheeler of Montana," 186–87.

41. Funigiello, *Toward a National Power Policy*, 87.

42. Congressional Record, 74th Cong., 1st Sess., 8934.

43. Ruetten, "Burton K. Wheeler of Montana," 171.

44. Funigiello, *Toward a National Power Policy*, 87–88; Ruetten, "Progressive between the Wars," 186–87; telegram, FDR to Wheeler, June 11, 1935, Wheeler Papers, MHS.

45. Schlesinger, *Politics of Upheaval*, 317–18; David McKean, *Tommy the Cork: Washington's Ultimate Insider from Roosevelt to Reagan* (South Royalton, Vt.: Steerforth Press, 2004), 63–66; Lasser, *Benjamin Cohen*, 126–29.

46. Funigiello, *Toward a National Power Policy*, 89–90. For an excellent summary of Black's investigation of utility industry lobbying in opposition to the Wheeler-Rayburn bill, see William A. Gregory and Rennard Strickland, "Hugo Black's Congressional Investigation of Lobbying and the Public Utilities Holding Company Act: A Historical Review of the Power Trust, New Deal Politics, and Regulatory Propaganda," *University of Oklahoma Law Review* 29 (1976): 543–76.

47. Ruetten, "Burton K. Wheeler of Montana," 179; Crawford, *Pressure Boys*, 61.

48. Crawford, *Pressure Boys*, 61, 67; Funigiello, *Toward a National Power Policy*, 115.

49. Roger K. Newman, *Hugo Black: A Biography* (New York: Fordham University Press, 1997), 175–84; Gregory and Strickland, "Hugo Black's Congressional Investigation," 550, 553.

50. Newman, *Hugo Black*, 190; Gregory and Strickland, "Hugo Black's Congressional Investigation," 554.

51. Funigiello, *Toward a National Power Policy*, 115; "Complex Rabbit," *Time*, July 29, 1935, 9–10.

52. Schlesinger, *Politics of Upheaval*, 320.

53. Funigiello, *Toward a National Power Policy*, 89–91.

54. Ibid., 92–93.

55. Ibid., 93.

56. Wheeler and Healy, *Yankee from the Senate*, 313; *Spartanburg (S.C.) Herald*, September 6, 1935.

57. Schlesinger, *Politics of Upheaval*, 324.

58. *New York Times*, August 23, 1935.

59. Lowitt, *George W. Norris: The Triumph of a Progressive*, 83; Lasser, *Benjamin Cohen*, 123–24; Funigiello, *Toward a National Power Policy*, 262.

60. Ruetten, "Burton K. Wheeler of Montana," 191–92; Schlesinger, *Politics of Upheaval*, 324. Spurred by arguments that Wheeler's Depression-era legislation had outlived its usefulness, was stifling needed utility investment, and that state and federal regulators were able to protect consumer interests in ways not imagined in 1935, Congress repealed the last remnants of the Wheeler-Rayburn Act in 2005.

61. Schlesinger, *Politics of Upheaval*, 142.

62. Carter, *American Messiahs*, 119–22.

63. Ickes, *Secret Diary*, vol. 1, 358–59; Kennedy, *Freedom from Fear*, 242. Wheeler, without comment, voted in favor of Social Security legislation in 1935, but like most Montana politicians he also paid frequent lip service to the Townsend plan, the brainchild of Francis Townsend. Townsend's proposal, financed by a national sales tax, advocated creation of a $200 monthly stipend for every citizen over age sixty provided that the recipient agreed to spend the money within a month. Townsend's idea, simple to explain but impractical or impossible to implement, became an overnight national phenomenon. With the average old age pension in Montana amounting to $7.28 a month, Townsend's plan, even when shown to be economically dubious, was the kind of political fool's gold that few politicians could afford to completely dismiss. In 1935 the Montana legislature passed a resolution endorsing the scheme.

64. Kennedy, *Freedom from Fear*, 278; George Creel, "Man from Montana," *Colliers*, August 10, 1935, 12. Presidential memorandums, March 22, 1935 and April 8, 1935, Roosevelt Papers, President's Personal File. In April 1935 administration officials displayed uncommon interest in the appointment of a U.S. attorney in Montana, the job Wheeler once held. The appointee, Billings attorney John B. Tansil, it was suggested in one White House memo, might find ways "to crimp" Wheeler back home, to "back him into a corner" and "head off" any third-party effort he might be contemplating. Suggestions regarding the Tansil appointment were routed across a number of White House desks and finally to Attorney General Cummings, who may well have disappointed Roosevelt when he confirmed that Tansil had the support of both Senators Wheeler and Murray. Tansil would serve as U.S. attorney in Montana for fifteen years.

65. Congressional Record, 74th Cong., 1st Sess., 1212; Wheeler and Healy, *Yankee from the West*, 314; Carter, *American Messiahs*, 131; Lowitt, *Bronson M. Cutting*, 307–16; Maney, *Young Bob*, 152–53. See also Lowitt, *George W. Norris*, 136. Wheeler would have agreed with George Norris's assertion that Roosevelt's treatment of Cutting was pure ingratitude and "a blot upon the record of the Roosevelt administration." Cutting's death and reaction is also dealt with in Richard Neuberger, *Integrity: The Life of George W. Norris* (New York: Vanguard Press, 1937), 308–309.

66. Davis, *New Deal Years*, 510–11; Ickes, *Secret Diary*, vol. 1, 363–64.

67. See *New York Times*, July 30, 1935; and Michael P. Malone, *C. Ben Ross and the New Deal in Idaho* (Seattle: University of Washington Press, 1970), 104. See also McKenna, *Borah*, 337–38. McKenna writes that Farley told her "no special effort" was made to target Borah in 1936, but it is clear that Wheeler and other friends of Borah believed such an effort was planned and then abandoned.

68. Wheeler to O. B. Horsford, June 20, 1936, Wheeler Papers, MHS; Roosevelt to Farley and Rayburn, September 17, 1936, in Franklin D. Roosevelt, *Franklin D. Roosevelt: His Personal Letters, 1928–1945*, vol. 2 (New York: Duell, Sloan and Pearce, 1950), 616.

69. *Spokane Daily Chronicle*, October 29, 1936; Wheeler telegram to FDR, October 24, 1936, Roosevelt letter to Wheeler, October 26, 1936; Wheeler Papers, MSU; *Great Falls Tribune*, October 27, 1936.

70. Childs, *I Write from Washington*, 110; Waldron and Wilson, *Atlas of Montana Elections*, 140–48; *Helena (Mont.) Independent*, November 4, 1936.

CHAPTER 9

1. Herbert Hoover, *Addresses upon the American Road: 1933–1938* (New York: Scribner, 1938), 219.

2. Kennedy, *Freedom from Fear*, 324.

3. William Leuchtenburg, *The Supreme Court Reborn* (Chapel Hill: University of North Carolina Press, 1995), 106–107, 90–96; Rexford G. Tugwell, *The Democratic Roosevelt* (Garden City, N.Y.: Doubleday, 1957), 384–86.

4. Jeff Shesol, *Supreme Power: Franklin Roosevelt vs. the Supreme Court* (New York: W.W. Norton, 2010), 150. Another treatment of the Supreme Court crisis and its political fallout is in Robert Shogan, *Backlash: The Killing of the New Deal* (Chicago: Ivan R. Dee, 2006). See also Davis, *New Deal Years*, 518–21; and Linda Lotridge Levin, *The Making of FDR: The Story of Stephen T. Early, America's First Modern Press Secretary* (Amherst: Prometheus Books, 2008), 130. Levin says White House press secretary Steve Early gave Roosevelt the horse-and-buggy phrase.

5. Drew Pearson and Robert S. Allen, *Nine Old Men* (Garden City: Doubleday, Doran, 1936), 71–72. For the first time in U.S. history the Supreme Court had its own building in 1935, designed under the careful guidance of chief justice William Howard Taft and located hardly more than a five-iron shot from the Capitol. Before its construction, justices worked from their Washington homes and held court in a small chamber in the Capitol. After 146 years with no separate quarters of its own, beginning in 1935 the court had spacious chambers in an elegant building that, from a facilities standpoint, put it on par with the other coequal branches of the federal government. "A million dollars apiece for those nine old men," Huey Long had said, "and they used to sit in one room." Pearson and Allen, *Nine Old Men*, 14.

6. Shesol, *Supreme Power*, 1–7; Joseph Alsop and Turner Catledge; *The 168 Days* (Garden City, N.Y.: Doubleday, Doran, 1938), 63–64; Kenneth S. Davis, *FDR: Into the Storm, 1937–1940* (New York: Random House, 1993), 62. William E. Leuchtenburg analyzes the process of developing Roosevelt's court plan in "The Origins of Franklin D. Roosevelt's 'Court-Packing' Plan," *Supreme Court Review* (1966): 347–400. At the time of the court-packing controversy, Joseph Alsop was the Capitol Hill correspondent for the *New York Herald Tribune*. He was also a cousin of President Roosevelt. Catledge was the number two man in the Washington Bureau of the *New York Times*.

7. Davis, *Into the Storm*, 62–64; Alsop and Catledge, *168 Days*, 54–55.

8. Davis, *Into the Storm*, 64; Shesol, *Supreme Power*, 331–33, 504–505. Shesol shows that once the court-packing plan was discredited, Cummings (and others involved in its development) went to great lengths to deny or minimize their involvement. Cummings would contend years later, "When the history of the court fight is written and projected against the background of constitutional history . . . we shall come off well."

9. Alsop and Catledge, *168 Days*, 67; *Baltimore Sun*, February 7, 1937; *New York Herald Tribune*, February 11, 1937; "New Deal versus Old Courts," *Literary Digest*, February 13, 1937, 5–8.

10. Wheeler and Healy, *Yankee from the West*, 319–21.

11. McKean, *Tommy the Cork*, 88.

12. Alsop and Catledge, *168 Days*, 100–101; McKean, *Tommy the Cork*, 88–90; Wheeler and Healy, *Yankee from the West*, 320. The unpublished manuscript of Corcoran's memoir is with his papers in the Library of Congress. There are conflicting accounts of Wheeler's meetings with Corcoran. Corcoran claimed in his unpublished memoir that he met with Wheeler in the senator's office almost immediately after Roosevelt's plan was sent to Congress, which would have been impossible, since Wheeler was not in Washington that day. Corcoran recounts that during this meeting Wheeler seemed to suggest that Roosevelt was to blame for the murder of Huey Long. "Did you see what Roosevelt did to Huey?" Corcoran quotes Wheeler as asking. Corcoran claimed to have expressed shock that Wheeler might actually think Roosevelt had been involved in Long's murder. Corcoran then quotes Wheeler as saying, "Now, I've been watching Roosevelt for a long time. Once he was one of us. Now he means to make himself the boss of all of us. Well, he's made a mistake [with the court plan] . . . and this is our chance to cut him down to size."

The fact that Corcoran got the date and location of his meeting wrong and drew upon a fading memory years after the fact to prepare his memoir also diminishes the credibility of his story about Long. It seems more likely that, if in fact the Wheeler-Corcoran conversation actually took place, Wheeler was alluding to well-publicized rumors that Roosevelt had used the full power of the federal government, including the Internal Revenue Service, to investigate and punish Long and his Louisiana political organization. Corcoran, who had no success persuading Wheeler to withhold his opposition to the plan, chose to place the most sinister possible interpretation on the comment.

13. *Washington Post*, February 14, 1937. Conservative Democratic senators Carter Glass and Harry F. Byrd of Virgina and Josiah Bailey of North Carolina were also early opponents of the Roosevelt plan, as were several Republicans, opposition that did not surprise the White House. On the other hand, progressive stalwart George Norris's statement that he was "not in sympathy with the plan to enlarge the Supreme Court" was an early indication that Roosevelt's plan would meet credible resistance in Congress and not just from conservatives. See Davis, *Into the Storm*, 656.

14. Statement to the press, February 13, 1937, copy in the Wheeler Papers, MHS.

15. Michelson, *Ghost Talks*, 177; Wheeler and Healy, *Yankee from the West*, 320–22.

16. Alsop and Catledge, 102; Davis, *Into the Storm*, 71–72.

17. Wheeler and Healy, *Yankee from the West*, 322; Colman, *Mrs. Wheeler Goes to Washington*, 134–35; Walter Trohan, *Political Animals* (New York: Doubleday, 1975), 97.

18. For a further assessment of Wheeler's motives in the court fight, see Shesol, *Supreme Power*, 317–24. According to Gallup's polling, at no time during the battle over the Supreme Court did Roosevelt's plan command majority support in the country. When asked by the Gallup organization in May 1937 whether Congress should approve the court legislation, respondents by a 54-to-46 margin said no, and respondents by a margin of 68 to 32 rejected the idea of Roosevelt being able to appoint two new judges rather than the six his proposal envisioned. See George Gallup, *The Gallup Poll: Public Opinion, 1935–1971*, vol. 1, *1938–1948* (New York: Random House, 1972).

19. Kennedy, *Freedom from Fear*, 333.

20. Shesol, *Supreme Power*, 317; Marian C. McKenna, *Franklin Roosevelt and the Great Constitutional War* (New York: Fordham University Press, 2002), 320–23; Steve Neal, *McNary of Oregon* (Portland: Western Imprints, 1985), 82, 164–66. Neal credits McNary, not Wheeler, with being the prime strategist behind the overall Senate opposition to Roosevelt's plan. While McNary clearly contributed much to the strategy, it was Wheeler who held Democratic opponents together even as he consulted with Republicans, particularly Borah, in order to defeat Roosevelt's plan. See also Ruetten, "Burton K. Wheeler of Montana," 220–21. For analysis of the long-term political consequences of the court plan on Roosevelt's second term, see Patterson, *Congressional Conservatism and the New Deal*, 125–27; Burns, *Lion and the Fox*, 298.

21. Hiram W. Johnson to Hiram W. Johnson Jr., February 14, 1937, quoted in Lower, *Bloc of One*, 292; Alsop and Catledge, *168 Days*, 102–104; Caroline H. Keith, *For Hell and a Brown Mule: A Biography of Millard E. Tydings* (New York: Madison Books, 1991), 300–303; Vandenberg is quoted in Shesol, *Supreme Power*, 324.

22. Tom Connally and Alfred Steinberg, *My Name Is Tom Connally* (New York: Thomas T. Crowell Company, 1954), 189; Leaflet No. 4—La Follette-Wheeler Joint National Committee document, La Follette Papers, Library of Congress; Ruetten, "Burton K. Wheeler of Montana," 219–20; *New York Times*, February 19 and 26, March 2, 1937; Congressional Record, 75th Cong., 1st Sess., 1273. More than forty proposed amendments were introduced in Congress. As Arthur Schlesinger Jr. notes, no single proposal emerged that enjoyed "even a majority of the pro-amendment forces," and the idea of amending the Constitution to solve the perceived problems of the court became "increasingly academic and irrelevant." Schlesinger, *Politics of Upheaval*, 491–92.

Connally developed a dislike for Wheeler, and the feeling was mutual. Oddly, Connally professed to resent what he saw as Wheeler's closeness to the White House. He once referred to Wheeler as Roosevelt's "teacher's pet." The Connally-Wheeler personal relationship, never close or mutually respectful, came undone during a Senate floor debate when Wheeler criticized an amendment Connally had offered by characterizing the Texan's debate as a "stump speech." Connally, justifiably proud of his speech-making skills, replied by calling Wheeler a coward and hypocrite and then hurling a book across the Senate chamber in Wheeler's direction. "After that incident," Senate historian Ross K. Baker notes, "All semblance of civility disappeared. They went to great lengths to avoid each other even in the collegial environment of the senators' dining room." Baker, *Friend and Foes in the U.S. Senate* (New York: Free Press, 1980), 241.

23. Wheeler and Healy, *Yankee from the West*, 323–24; Burns, *Lion and the Fox*, 298; Shesol, *Supreme Power*, 356.

24. "The Court and Fascism," *Nation*, February 20, 1937, 200–201; Catherine C. Doherty, "The Court Plan, B. K. Wheeler and the Montana Press" (master's thesis, Montana State University, 1954), 20–22, 27–31. Typical of the reaction of Anaconda-controlled papers was the *Missoulian*, which editorialized in February 1937 that "any tampering with the Supreme Court will be looked upon as one more effort on the part of Mr. Roosevelt to create for himself an unassailable position."

25. *Dawson County (Mont.) Review*, February 25, 1937, quoted in Doherty, "Court Plan," 43.

26. *New York Times*, February 22, 1937.

27. Ibid.; Tull, *Father Coughlin and the New Deal*, 175.

28. Shesol, *Supreme Power*, 335.

29. Burns, *Lion and the Fox*, 299–300.

30. Shesol, *Supreme Power*, 375–76.

31. Franklin D. Roosevelt, "Fireside Chat on Reorganization of the Federal Judiciary," March 9, 1937, Roosevelt Papers, Master Speech File. Kenneth S. Davis says that Roosevelt's March 4, 1937, speech "was among the very best of his fighting speeches, and his delivery . . . was superb." Davis, *Into the Storm*, 73–75.

32. "First Member of the Senate to Back the President in '32," *Vital Speeches of the Day*, April 15, 1937, 408–409. See also Ruetten, "Burton K. Wheeler of Montana," 221–22. Roosevelt received support for his court proposal from an unexpected source. On March 18, the *Washington Post* quoted Wheeler's twenty-year-old daughter Frances, a college student, as saying, "There is more than one political viewpoint in the family." Frances, decidedly more radical in her political views than her father—Wheeler apparently thought his daughter had been influenced by her leftist college professors—left no doubt that she differed with him on the court plan and sided with Roosevelt. Lulu attempted to enforce Wheeler family discipline by declaring that "there is only one Senator in this family," but Frances's contrary view made a minor splash in the newspapers, not for the last time. Lulu Wheeler quoted in Colman, *Mrs. Wheeler Goes to Washington*, 165–65.

33. "First Member of the Senate to Back the President."

34. Harold L. Ickes, *The Secret Diary of Harold L. Ickes*, vol. 2, *The Inside Struggle, 1936–1939* (New York: Simon & Schuster, 1954), 100.

35. McKenna, *Franklin D. Roosevelt and the Great Constitutional War*, 363–65. See also Alsop and Catledge, *168 Days*, 177; Burns, *Lion and the Fox*, 301. Shesol (*Supreme Power*, 383) says: "For a quarter century Henry Fountain Ashurst had meandered through the Senate, gliding through hearing rooms and across the floor like a Shakespearean actor bemused that, somehow, he had found himself in summer stock. He wore a wing collar, a spade-tailed coat, and a pince-nez tethered by a flowing black ribbon. His speeches flowed, too; he had by his own admission, 'a mania . . . for talking,' something that he did, at length, in polysyllables. Henry Ashurst was never in a hurry."

36. Davis, *Into the Storm*, 75–76.

37. Wheeler and Healy, *Yankee from the West*, 337; McKenna, *Franklin D. Roosevelt and the Great Constitutional War*, 319–20; Ickes, *Secret Diary*, vol. 2, 98. Wheeler's informal steering committee included Democratic senators Peter G. Gerry of Rhode Island, Josiah Bailey of North Carolina, Bennett Clark of Missouri, Harry Byrd and Carter Glass of Virginia, and Millard Tydings of Maryland.

38. *Washington Post*, March 22, 1937.

39. Ibid.

40. Charles Evans Hughes to Burton K. Wheeler, March 21, 1937, copy in Wheeler, MSU.

41. Ickes, *Secret Diary*, vol. 2, 104.

42. Leonard Baker, *Back to Back: The Duel between FDR and the Supreme Court* (New York: Macmillan, 1967), 159; Mason, *Harlan Fiske Stone*, 452–53; Richard D. Friedman, "Chief Justice Hughes' Letter on Court-packing," *Journal of Supreme Court History* 22, no. 1 (1997): 83.

43. Melvin I. Urofsky, *Brandeis: A Life* (New York: Pantheon, 2009), 716–18; Baker, *Back to Back*, 153–55; Friedman, "Chief Justice Hughes' Letter on Court-Packing," 79–82. Elizabeth Wheeler Colman relates the story of her role in the Hughes letter in *Mrs. Wheeler Goes*

to *Washington*, 165–66. See also Ruetten, "Burton K. Wheeler of Montana," 225; Alsop and Catledge, *168 Days*, 124–25; Merlo Pusey, *Charles Evans Hughes*, vol. 2 (New York: Macmillan, 1951), 754–55. Baker interviewed Wheeler in 1966. Pusey offers a slightly different version of how Wheeler came to get the letter from the chief justice. See also James F. Simon, *FDR and Chief Justice Hughes: The President, the Supreme Court, and the Epic Battle over the New Deal* (New York: Simon & Schuster, 2012), 321–22.

44. Quoted in Baker, *Back to Back*, 155.

45. Wheeler and Healy, *Yankee from the West*, 329–30; Friedman, "Chief Justice Hughes' Letter on Court-Packing," 79.

46. McKenna, *Franklin D. Roosevelt and the Great Constitutional War*, 373–77; *New York Times*, April 13, 1937. The court's decisions upheld the Railroad Retirement Act, the reworked Frazier-Lemke Mortgage Act, a Washington state minimum wage law, and the National Labor Relations Act.

47. *Washington Post*, April 22, 1937. See also Ruetten, "Burton K. Wheeler of Montana," 229–30. Hiram Johnson was convinced that Roosevelt was using all the power at his disposal, including patronage, to secure Senate votes, while Henry Ashurst claimed he had received a warning that his reelection in Arizona in 1940 would be imperiled because the president believed Ashurst had conspired to kill the court plan.

48. Homer Cummings memo to Carl McFarland, May 1, 1937, and McFarland's reply, May 19, 1937, Homer Cummings Papers, University of Virginia Library, Special Collections, Charlottesville, hereafter Cummings Papers.

49. Cummings memo to Joseph B. Keenan, assistant to the attorney general, June 1, 1937; Keenan's reply of June 24, 1937; Hoover's reply to Cummings, June 4, 1937—all in Cummings Papers.

50. Ruetten, "Burton K. Wheeler of Montana," 230; Wheeler letters to Roosevelt and Tommy Corcoran, June 24, and August 29, 1936, and Roosevelt letter to Wheeler, May 18, 1937—all in Roosevelt Library.

51. Ickes, *Secret Diary*, vol. 2, 251; Shesol, *Supreme Power*, 358–66.

52. Shesol, *Supreme Power*, 444–48; McKenna, *Franklin Roosevelt and the Great Constitutional War*, 453–57. McKenna says Van Devanter's fellow justices were concerned that his retirement would be seen as giving in to the political pressure the court was under. He simply replied, "Borah favors it."

53. McKenna, *Franklin Roosevelt and the Great Constitutional War*, 459.

54. Ibid.; Shesol, *Supreme Power*, 448; Burns, *Lion and the Fox*, 304; Cecil Edward Weller Jr., *Joe T. Robinson: Always a Loyal Democrat* (Fayetteville: University of Arkansas Press, 1998), 163–64; McKenna, *Franklin Roosevelt and the Great Constitutional War*, 458–59.

55. *Montana Standard* (Butte), June 5, 1937.

56. *Great Falls Tribune*, April 24, 1937, quoted in Ruetten, "Burton K. Wheeler of Montana," 232–33.

57. *Helena Independent*, June 5, 1937. See also *Montana Standard* (Butte), June 5, 1937; *Great Falls Tribune*, June 5, 1937; and Doherty, "Court Plan," 84–91.

58. *Montana Labor News*, June 19, 1937, quoted in Ruetten, "Progressive between the Wars," 233–34; Doherty, "Court Plan," 88. The *Wolf Point (Mont.) Herald*, generally a progressive paper, editorialized in June 1937, "Wheeler is not hurting the president nearly so much as he is hurting

himself. The people of Montana owe the senator much and they are sorry to see him take this unfortunate and unnatural attitude. It is not just a difference of opinion, but bitter, relentless opposition to the things this state generally needs in the present, critical circumstances."

59. *Lewistown Democrat-News*, June 6, 1937, quoted in Doherty, "Court Plan," 89–90; James A. Farley to Roosevelt, June 16, 1937, Roosevelt Papers, President's Personal File.

60. McKenna, *Franklin Roosevelt and the Great Constitutional War*, 480–87; Shesol, *Supreme Power*, 467–71; William E. Leuchtenburg, "FDR's Court Packing Plan: A Second Life, a Second Death," *Duke Law Journal* 1985, no. 3/4 (June–Sept. 1985): 676.

61. Burns, *Lion and the Fox*, 307–308; Burt Solomon, *FDR v. the Constitution: The Court Packing Fight and the Triumph of Democracy* (New York: Walker, 2009), 222–23. See also Leuchtenburg, "FDR's Court Packing Plan," 673–89.

62. Alsop and Catledge, *168 Days*, 251. Alsop and Catledge say that they prepared their narrative by consulting "the living actors" in the political fight," in other words unnamed sources.

63. Ibid., 251–52; Burns, *Lion and the Fox*, 308.

64. Wheeler and Healy, *Yankee from the West*, 334–35; McKenna, *Franklin Roosevelt and the Great Constitutional War*, 496–97.

65. Alsop and Catledge, *168 Days*, 251–54; McKenna, *Franklin Roosevelt and the Great Constitutional War*, 497–98; Wheeler and Healy, *Yankee from the West*, 334–36; Ruetten, "Burton K. Wheeler of Montana," 236.

66. Solomon, *FDR v. the Constitution*, 226; Wheeler and Healy, *Yankee from the West*, 335–36; Shesol, *Supreme Power*, 481.

67. *New York Times*, July 7, 1937; Alsop and Catledge, *168 Days*, 253.

68. Shesol, *Supreme Power*, 481–82. Robinson relented and allowed the Senate to recess in time for the afternoon All-Star Game at Griffith Stadium. The American League won 8–3 on the strength of New York Yankee Lou Gehrig's four RBIs. Wheeler likely attended the game, since he was a fan. Roosevelt attended, threw out the first ball, and received a warm reception from the crowd of thirty-two thousand.

69. *New York Times*, July 7, 1937.

70. "Champions of the Senate Wage Wordy War Over President's Plan," *Newsweek*, July 17, 1937, 8–9; Congressional Record, 75th Cong., 1st Sess., 6883–84; *New York Times*, July 7, 1937.

71. Ruetten, "Burton K. Wheeler of Montana," 237–38.

72. Alsop and Catledge, *168 Days*, 259; *New York Times*, July 10, 1937; Congressional Record, 75th Cong., 1st Sess., 6976, 6981.

73. "Great Debate: Battle of the Supreme Court," *Time*, July 19, 1937, 10–11; *Newsweek*, July 17, 1937.

74. Shesol, *Supreme Power*, 485; Childs, *I Write from Washington*, 128; *Washington Post*, July 14, 1937.

75. Baker, *Back to Back*, 253. See also Weller, *Joe Robinson*, 166–67; Burns, *Lion and the Fox*, 308; *New York Times*, July 15, 1937. Eleanor Roosevelt is quoted in Baker, *Back to Back*, 254.

76. Ickes, *Secret Diary*, vol. 2, 162; Barkley, *That Reminds Me*, 154; "No U-Turn," *Newsweek*, July 24, 1937, 36.

77. *New York Times*, July 16, 1937.

78. Shesol, *Supreme Power*, 494–95; McKenna, *Franklin Roosevelt and the Great Constitutional War*, 505–16; Burns, *Lion and the Fox*, 308.

79. Sherwood, *Roosevelt and Hopkins*, 90; Cummings diary, quoted in Leuchtenburg, *Supreme Court Reborn*, 153.

80. Morgan, *Redneck Liberal*, 168–69; Alsop and Catledge, *168 Days*, 282–83.

81. McKenna, *Franklin Roosevelt and the Great Constitutional War*, 517; Shesol, *Supreme Power*, 498; Alsop and Catledge, *168 Days*, 286.

82. McKenna, *Franklin Roosevelt and the Great Constitutional War*, 520–21. See also Simon, *FDR and Chief Justice Hughes*, 341–42; *Chicago Tribune*, July 23, 1937.

83. Shesol, *Supreme Power*, 501–503; James A. Farley, *Jim Farley's Story: The Roosevelt Years* (New York: McGraw-Hill, 1948), 94; Solomon, *FDR v. the Constitution*, 248–51; Ickes, *Secret Diary*, vol. 2, 173–74. See also Bascom N. Timmons, *Garner of Texas: A Personal History* (New York: Harper & Brothers, 1948), 224. Timmons quotes Garner as saying that Roosevelt "never indicated in any way that he was dissatisfied with the way I handled the matter [with Wheeler]." Garner made this comment after Roosevelt's death and in the face of much evidence to the contrary.

84. Undated statements in Wheeler Papers, MHS. See also *New York Times*, August 13, 1937.

85. Quoted in Doherty, "Court Plan," 107; Ruetten, "Burton K. Wheeler of Montana," 251. Ruetten correctly says, "Wheeler's defeat in the Democratic primary in 1946 first took firm root in 1937."

86. Newman, *Hugo Black*, 253, 259. Newman interviewed Wheeler for his biography of Black. See also Howard Ball, *Hugo L. Black: Cold Steel Warrior* (New York: Oxford University Press, 1996), 90–106. The Black nomination and its relationship to the court-packing proposal is covered well in McKenna, *Franklin Roosevelt and the Great Constitutional War*, 537–45, and Davis, *Into the Storm*, 108–11. When Black's Klan connection resurfaced after the confirmation vote, Wheeler called upon Roosevelt or the Senate to appoint an impartial board to "investigate the charges that . . . Black holds life membership in the Ku Klux Klan." As the *Washington Post* reported on September 17, 1937, Wheeler used the occasion to recall his and La Follette's denunciation of the Klan in 1924, and he then took a swipe at the president. "This [the Black nomination] is a good illustration of what happens when an Administration acts hastily and what happens when Senators vote blindly for every suggestion that is made by the White House."

87. Hall, *Oxford Companion to the Supreme Court*, 743; Patterson, *Congressional Conservatism and the New Deal*, 126.

CHAPTER 10

1. Burns, *Lion and the Fox*, 358; Susan Dunn, *Roosevelt's Purge: How FDR Fought to Change the Democratic Party* (Cambridge, Mass.: Harvard University Press, 2010), 28–29.

2. *New York Times*, September 2, 1937.

3. Richard Neuberger, *Our Promised Land* (New York: Macmillan, 1938), 311; Ruetten, "Burton K. Wheeler of Montana," 260; Waldron and Wilson, *Atlas of Montana Elections*, 120–21, 127, 132–33, 140–41.

4. Neuberger, *Our Promised Land*, 309.

5. Ibid., 307–308.

6. *New York Times*, June 1 and August 5, 1937; Dunn, *Roosevelt's Purge*, 31.

7. *New York Times*, August 21, 1937; "The Congress: Last Words," *Time*, August 30, 1937, 13; Wheeler and Healy, *Yankee from the West*, 341–42.

8. *New York Times,* August 28, October 11, and October 13, 1937.

9. Alva Johnson, "President Tamer," *Saturday Evening Post,* November 13, 1937, 8–9.

10. Ibid.

11. Burns, *Lion and the Fox,* 317; Ruetten, "Burton K. Wheeler of Montana," 252; Murray letter to Roosevelt, September 14, 1937, Roosevelt Papers, President's Personal File; Wheeler and Healy, *Yankee from the West,* 343; Dunn, *Roosevelt's Purge,* 76–78. Wyoming senator Joseph O'Mahoney, another target of the Roosevelt purge, was also pointedly not invited to join the presidential entourage when it reached his state. O'Mahoney had to force his way onboard the rear platform of the presidential train.

12. *New York Times,* October 3, 1937: Ruetten, "Burton K. Wheeler of Montana," 252.

13. Mike Malone interview with Wheeler, June 9, 1970, transcript in the Wheeler Papers, MSU; *New York Times,* October 4, 1937. During the 1970 interview with Malone, Wheeler claimed that Jerry O'Connell's wife, Mazie, was on the presidential train with her husband during the stop in northeastern Montana. Apparently Mrs. O'Connell was well known to the crowd at Glasgow since she was said to have been a singer in some of the clubs frequented by crews constructing the huge dam. "She was greeted by the crowd with some enthusiasm," Malone recorded in his notes of the interview.

14. Ruetten, "Burton K. Wheeler of Montana," 256. Wheeler pitched into another high-profile fight with the Roosevelt administration in 1938 over a sweeping plan to reorganize the executive branch of the federal government. Consistent with his opposition to concentration of executive branch power and diminished legislative checks and balances, Wheeler feared that Roosevelt—or worse, "some professor from Dartmouth, or Yale, or Harvard, or Columbia"—would, under the cover of reorganization, abolish or redirect the mission of agencies important to farmers or ranchers in Montana. He worried that some future president, armed with the executive powers Roosevelt sought in the reorganization legislation, would do violence to the Tennessee Valley Authority or any number of other important national priorities. Coming on the heels of the court plan, the reorganization proposal spawned a new round of criticism that Roosevelt was attempting to consolidate political power in a way that was reminiscent of European dictators. The criticism became so hot that Roosevelt took the remarkable step of issuing a public statement saying that he had "no inclination to be a dictator." The curious statement prompted Republican senator Arthur Vandenberg to quip, "If the president says he doesn't want to be a dictator, it makes it unanimous as far as I am concerned." In spite of Wheeler's objections, the Senate narrowly approved Roosevelt's reorganization scheme in 1938, but the plan ultimately foundered in the House of Representatives. A scaled-back version eventually passed in 1939, and, while Wheeler was absent for the vote, he indicated that he would have supported this compromise.

15. *New York Times,* May 28, 1938. O'Connell's protests in Jersey City are recounted in John C. Cort, *Dreadful Conversions: The Making of Catholic Socialist* (New York: Fordham University Press, 2003), 102; *New York Times,* May 8, 1938; *New York Times,* May 10 and 28, July 14, and August 20, 1938; Jerry O'Connell letter to bishop Joseph P. Gilmore, February 16, 1938, copy in Edward Craney Papers, Montana Historical Society, Helena, hereafter Craney Papers. For the Catholic Church's role in supporting Franco, see Stanley G. Payne, *The Franco Regime, 1936–1975* (Madison: University of Wisconsin Press, 1987), 201–205.

16. Ruetten, "Burton K. Wheeler of Montana," 261; Congressional Record, Appendix 1938, 12455; Wheeler letter to C. W. Curtis, March 31, 1938, Wheeler Papers, MHS.

17. Richard Ruetten, "Showdown in Montana, 1938: Burton Wheeler's Role in the Defeat of Jerry O'Connell," *Pacific Northwest Quarterly* 54, no. 1 (January 1963): 19–29; *Washington Daily News*, July 19, 1938. See also Vernon L. Pedersen, "Jerry O'Connell Montana's Communist Congressman," *Montana: The Magazine of Western History* 62, no. 1 (2012): 3–22.

Barclay Craighead was a life-long Wheeler lieutenant and the type of political operative successful politicians must cultivate. Although he worked directly for Wheeler only from 1933 to 1935, Craighead was a constant publicist, organizer, campaign manager, and source of Montana political intelligence while occupying a variety of state and federal positions. When Wheeler's political career ended, Craighead joined Wheeler's close friend Ed Craney as a manager of Craney's Montana broadcasting empire.

18. *New York Times*, July 20, 1938; "Beat Wheeler," *Time*, August 1, 1938, 12.

19. Ruetten, "Burton K. Wheeler of Montana," 263; Jon Axline, "The Naked Truth about Jacob Thorkelson," in *Speaking Ill of the Dead: Jerks in Montana History*, edited by Dave Walter (Helena, Mont.: Falcon Publishing, 2000), 191–92.

20. Axline, "Naked Truth about Jacob Thorkelson," 192–95.

21. Mary Murphy, "Messenger of the New Age: Station KGIR in Butte," *Montana: The Magazine of Western History* 39, no. 3 (Autumn 1989): 52–63. See also Mary Murphy, *Mining Cultures: Men, Women and Leisure in Butte, 1914–1941* (Urbana: University of Illinois Press, 1997), 169–99; Ed Craney letter to Lulu Wheeler, October 6, 1937, Craney Papers. A short biography of Craney accompanies the extensive collection of his papers. Craney carried on an extensive correspondence with Wheeler from the mid-1920s until Wheeler's death.

The two became close friends in the 1920s when Craney put Butte's first radio station on the air. Craney was a true broadcasting innovator, developing his own network, featuring news and public affairs programming, employing a studio orchestra at his Butte station, and later bringing television to Montana. Craney solicited Wheeler's help on regulatory and legislative matters and may even have employed the senator to represent him on contract issues with the National Broadcasting Company. Such a relationship today would be considered an obvious conflict of interest, but at the time a member of Congress maintaining a legal practice on the side was not regarded as improper but an acceptable way for a senator-lawyer to supplement his salary.

By 1938, the Wheeler-Craney relationship was so close that Craney regularly sent the Wheelers shipments of Montana elk steak, for which Lulu Wheeler indicated a particular fondness. Craney peppered his letters to the Wheelers with local gossip and reports on fishing conditions in western Montana. Craney also regularly advised Wheeler on broadcasting policy matters and provided unflinching political support for Wheeler in Montana. In the days before gift bans prevented such things, Craney purchased for the Wheelers and had delivered as a Christmas gift an expensive radio set complete with tall aerial. As a result the Wheelers enjoyed first-rate radio reception at their cabin on Lake McDonald in Glacier National Park.

22. Memo from Ed Craney to Jacob Thorkelson, August 13, 1938, Craney Papers.

23. *Great Falls Tribune*, August 26 and September 5, 1938.

24. Ickes, *Secret Diary*, vol. 2, 435.

25. Dunn, *Roosevelt's Purge*, 32; Joseph Alsop and Robert Kintner, "Farley and the Future," *Life*, September 19, 1938, 24–28, 56–59.

26. A copy of O'Connell's 1938 Labor Day speech in Butte is in the Craney Papers; *Lewistown Democratic News*, September 12, 1938.

27. Ruetten, "Burton K. Wheeler of Montana," 268; George Seldes, *The Catholic Crisis* (New York: J. Messner, 1939), 145–46; *Montana Standard* (Butte), October 15 and November 1, 1938. Ruetten conducted interviews in 1957 with Wheeler and Barclay Craighead regarding their contacts with the bishop of Helena.

28. *Bozeman Daily Chronicle*, November 5, 1938; *Great Falls Tribune*, November 7, 1938; Ruetten, "Burton K. Wheeler of Montana," 268–69.

29. Ruetten, "Burton K. Wheeler of Montana," 270–71.

30. Ibid., 272; *Western News* (Hamilton, Mont.), October 31, 1938. Richard Ruetten writes that when he asked Wheeler about O'Connell's reelection defeat, Wheeler claimed to have no explanation for labor's eleventh-hour reversal of support for O'Connell. However, Kenneth G. Crawford writes in his book *The Pressure Boys* that it was Wheeler who engineered a quid pro quo with the railway brotherhoods. Wheeler would help the unions beat back a demand for wage concessions in exchange for their help defeating O'Connell. "Shortly after Wheeler testified (opposing the wage cut) . . . the Brotherhoods announced in their newspaper that they were opposed to O'Connell's re-election." Labor's excuse for abandoning O'Connell was based on the congressman's vote in 1937 against the Railroad Retirement Act. O'Connell indeed had voted no but because he considered the pension provisions in the legislation inadequate. "His reasons were, of course," Crawford wrote, "not mentioned in the issue of *Labor* . . . [nor] was the wage-reduction proposal. Neither Wheeler not the Brotherhoods would admit to a deal."

It seems less likely that Wheeler directly influenced the Townsend endorsement of Thorkelson, and in a 1957 interview with Ruetten he denied any involvement. Townsend was a Republican and by 1938 had turned against the New Deal. "I think it was the Republicans who got [Townsend] in here," Wheeler told Ruetten. However, it is also a fact that Townsend liked Wheeler and made supportive comments about the Wheeler when he was considering a presidential bid in 1940.

31. Wheeler interview with Mike Malone, Wheeler Papers, MSU.

32. Waldron and Wilson, *Atlas of Montana Elections*, 150–55. Thorkelson garnered 49,253 votes to O'Connell's 41,319. Montanans also approved a liquor-by-the-drink initiative in 1938, with nearly 90 percent of Silver Bow County voters approving.

33. John E. Kennedy, "Liberal's Defeat: A Case History of the Defeat of O'Connell," *Nation*, November 26, 1938, 564–65. The Anaconda-controlled press also attacked O'Connell, labeling him both a "red" and an enemy of labor. See Swibold, *Copper Chorus*, 273–75. In his memoir, Wheeler wrote that political success in Butte "was simplicity itself: you planted a foot on the bar rail and brought 'drinks for the house' in every saloon and casino in Silver Bow County and as often as possible. Since there was no paper money in Montana then, you tossed out a fistful of silver or, better yet, a five, ten, or twenty-dollar gold-piece. And if you expected change you could have stood there until doomsday without getting any."

34. *Miles City (Mont.) Star*, November 11, 1938; "O'Connell, Jerry Joseph," *Biographical Directory of the U.S. Congress*, http://bioguide.congress.gov/.

35. Patrick Casey to Barclay Craighead, November 12, 1938; copies of Craighead's letter to the Presidents of the Switchman's Union, the Machinists Union, and the assistant to William Green at the AFL, November 12, 1938; Edward Keating letter to Craighead, November 12, 1938—all in Craighead Papers, Montana Historical Society, Helena, hereafter Craighead Papers. See also Wheeler's interview with Mike Malone, Wheeler Papers, MSU.

36. Axline, "Naked Truth about Jacob Thorkelson," 197–203.

37. Kennedy, *Freedom from Fear*, 348; Dunn, *Roosevelt's Purge*, 177; *New York Times*, September 1, 1938.

38. Burns, *Lion and the Fox*, 363; H. W. Brands, *Traitor to His Class: The Privileged Life and Radical Presidency of Franklin Delano Roosevelt* (New York: Doubleday, 2008), 371–73.

39. Farley, *Jim Farley's Story*, 124–25.

40. Ibid.

CHAPTER 11

1. Frank Capra, *The Name above the Title* (New York: Macmillan, 1971), 281.

2. "Mr. Smith Goes to Washington (Original Trailer)," Turner Classic Movies, http://www.tcm.com/mediaroom/video/215966/Mr-Smith-Goes-To-Washington-Original-Trailer-.html.

3. Capra, *Name above the Title*, 282.

4. *Christian Science Monitor*, October 27, 1939; Marion Wheeler Scott interview with the author, August 13, 2002; McCullough, *Truman*, 242.

5. Wheeler and Healy, *Yankee from the West*, ix; *Washington Sunday Star*, April 21, 1940. The year 1939 was an all-time great one for American motion pictures. *Gone with the Wind* won the Oscar for Best Picture. In addition to *Mr. Smith*, other Best Picture nominees included *Wuthering Heights*, *Stagecoach*, and *The Wizard of Oz*.

6. *New York Times*, June 27, 1939, and November 16, 1939; "Issues and Men: Senator Wheeler May Be a Candidate," *Nation*, July 15, 1939, 72; "Eyes on Wheeler," *Newsweek*, November 13, 1939, 17; Richard L. Neuberger, "Senator Wheeler's Plight" *Current History*, August 1, 1937, 29–32. See also Richard Moe, *Roosevelt's Second Act: The Election of 1940 and the Politics of War* (New York: Oxford, 2013), 94–98.

7. Susan Dunn, *1940: FDR, Willkie, Lindbergh, Hitler: The Election amid the Storm* (New Haven: Yale University Press, 2013), 12.

8. Wheeler letter to Elizabeth Wheeler Colman, May 19, 1939, copy in author's collection; Marion Wheeler Scott interview.

9. Patterson, *Congressional Conservatism and the New Deal*, 289; Wheeler letter to Elizabeth Wheeler Colman, April 12, 1938, copy in author's collection. The relative strength and weakness of potential Roosevelt successors is discussed in Davis, *Into the Storm*, 528–32. See also Herbert S. Parmet and Marie B. Hecht, *Never Again: A President Runs for a Third Term* (New York: Macmillan, 1968), 10–13.

10. Hamby, *Man of the People*, 220.

11. Ibid., 220–21, 140; Robert H. Ferrell, *Harry S. Truman: A Life* (Columbia: University of Missouri Press, 1994), 137–39; Ralph L. Dewey, "The Transportation Act of 1940," *American Economic Review* 31, no. 1 (March 1941): 15–26.

12. Wheeler letter to Elizabeth Wheeler Coleman, April 12, 1938, copy in author's collection; Robert H. Ferrell, ed., *Dear Bess: The Letters from Harry to Bess Truman, 1910–1959* (New York: W. W. Norton, 1983), 307–308; Hamby, *Man of the People*, 225–27.

13. Patterson, *Congressional Conservatism and the New Deal*, 288–324.

14. Wheeler speech, "The Futility of War," delivered on *American Forum of the Air* on WOL Radio, Washington, D.C., and reprinted as "Foreign Policy and Neutrality," *Vital Speeches of the Day*, April 15, 1939, 406–407.

15. Franklin D. Roosevelt, *The Public Papers and Addresses of Franklin D. Roosevelt*, vol. 8 (New York: Macmillan, 1941), 512–22; Wayne S. Cole, *Roosevelt and the Isolationists, 1932–1945* (Lincoln: University of Nebraska Press, 1983), 329.

16. Wheeler letter to Richard Wheeler, November 13, 1939, Wheeler Papers, MHS.

17. *Cut Bank (Mont.) Pioneer Press*, June 9, 1939. Immediately following the court-packing fight in 1937 there was speculation in Montana newspapers about Wheeler's White House ambitions. The *Great Falls News* noted on August 6, 1937, that Wheeler's opposition to Roosevelt's plans had attracted support from "forces that were once hostile to the Montana senator and they are talking 'off the record' about his availability in the presidential race of 1940."

18. *Miami News*, December 26, 1939.

19. *Boston Post*, October 2, 1939.

20. Ruetten, "Burton K. Wheeler of Montana," 286. See also the *New London (Conn.) Evening Day*, July 3, 1939.

21. John Moses to Wheeler, November 25, 1939, Wheeler to Moses, December 2, 1939, Wheeler Papers, MHS.

22. Frank Knox to Wheeler, July 6, 1939, Wheeler Papers, MHS. The *New York Times* reported on July 2, 1939, that Colorado senator Ed Johnson, convinced Roosevelt would not violate the no-third-term tradition, offered to support a Wheeler candidacy. Wheeler was a "real liberal," Johnson said, "whose record for liberalism was made long before 1933 and who is so honest and trustworthy that he holds the respect and confidence of the most conservative Democrats in the land. The *Idaho Statesman* in Boise reported on December 28, 1939, that prominent Idaho progressive Ray McKaig, a Republican, Nonpartisan League leader, and close friend of William Borah, would support Wheeler if he ran.

23. Wheeler to Joseph Wolf, November 13, 1939, Wheeler Papers, MHS.

24. Frank Miles to Wheeler, July 12, 1939, and Wheeler to Miles, July 14, 1939, Wheeler Papers, MHS.

25. Ray Tucker column, *Pomona (Calif.) Progress-Bulletin*, December 19, 1939; Ruetten, "Burton K. Wheeler of Montana," 287; *Wall Street Journal*, December 21, 1939.

26. The *Times* article appeared on December 20, 1939, and Wheeler's telegram was sent the same day. A copy of the telegram is in Wheeler Papers, MHS.

27. *New York Times*, January 9, 1940; Wheeler letter to J. Burke Clements, January 17, 1940, Wheeler Papers, MHS.

28. Melvyn Dubofsky and Warren Van Tine, *John L. Lewis: A Biography* (New York: Quadrangle, 1977), 342–44. See also C. K. McFarland, *Roosevelt, Lewis, and the New Deal, 1933–1940* (Fort Worth: Texas Christian University Press, 1970), 103–105.

29. Dubofsky and Van Tine, *John L. Lewis*, 343; Wheeler letter to Elizabeth Wheeler Colman, February 10, 1940, copy in author's collection.

30. Ruetten, "Burton K. Wheeler of Montana," 288. See also Lowitt, *Triumph of a Progressive*, 319. In 1939, Norris asked Wheeler if he might run for vice president on a ticket with Roosevelt, and Wheeler rejected the idea. When Norris, who favored a third Roosevelt candidacy, began to believe that Roosevelt might not run, he indicated that he would support Wheeler but continued to hope Roosevelt would seek a third term.

William K. Hutchison, the Washington correspondent for International News Service, enjoyed a close relationship with William Borah, who died in January 1940. Hutchison wrote a series of articles following Borah's death, including a January 27, 1940, piece in which he said: "A month ago I asked [Borah] whether he had yet decided on his candidate for president. We had been talking often of Republican possibilities. His surprising reply was: 'If Burt Wheeler is nominated by the Democrats, I will support him.'" Such a move would have been unprecedented for Borah, who, while enjoying a friendly relationship with FDR and many Democrats (and often flirting with an open break with the GOP), had never openly supported a Democrat presidential candidate.

31. Wheeler for President Club materials are in Wheeler Papers, MHS; Ruetten, "Burton K. Wheeler of Montana," 288–89.

32. Robert Bendiner, "Men Who Would Be President: Burton K. Wheeler," *Nation*, April 27, 1940, 535: Hamilton Basso "Burton the Bronc," *New Republic*, April 22, 1940), 27–30; *Sunday Star* (Washington, D.C.), April 21, 1940; *Christian Science Monitor*, March 16, 1940.

33. "Burton Kendall Wheeler," *Time*, April 15, 1940, 21–22.

34. Richard L. Neuberger, "Wheeler of Montana," *Harper's*, May 1940, 609–18. William Allen White authored a less sympathetic profile, "Candidates in the Spring," *Yale Review* 29 (March 1940): 433–443. Neuberger's articles and essays appeared regularly in the *New York Times, Harper's, Reader's Digest*, the *Nation*, and other major publications. He wrote enduring books on the Pacific Northwest and political figures including George Norris and Francis Townsend. Elected to the U.S. Senate in 1954 as a Democrat in strongly Republican Oregon, Neuberger died of cancer in 1960. His impressive wife, Maureen, who went on to win election in her own right, replaced Neuberger in the Senate.

35. *People's Voice* (Helena, Mont.), March 6, 1940; *Montana Liberal* (Hamilton, Mont.), February 27, 1940; *Great Falls Tribune*, March 3, 1939; Lee Metcalf to James Murray, January 27, 1940, James E. Murray Papers, Maureen and Mike Mansfield Library, Archives and Special Collections, University of Montana, Missoula, hereafter Murray Papers.

36. Ruetten, "Burton K. Wheeler of Montana," 291; *Western News* (Hamilton, Mont.), July 11, 1940. O'Connell's biweekly paper typically carried a front-page article slamming Wheeler and promoting O'Connell's own efforts to recapture his House seat in Montana's First Congressional District.

37. Ruetten, "Burton K. Wheeler of Montana," 292; *Great Falls Tribune*, May 22, 1940.

38. Winston S. Churchill, *The Second World War: Their Finest Hour* (Boston: Houghton Mifflin, 1949), 118; *New York Times*, June 1, 1940.

39. Quoted in Ruetten, "Burton K. Wheeler of Montana," 295. A copy of Wheeler's undated speech is in the files of the Oregon Commonwealth Federation Papers at the University of Oregon Library.

40. Roosevelt speech at the University of Virginia, June 10, 1940, Roosevelt Papers, Master Speech File; Davis, *Into the Storm*, 554–56.

41. Wheeler and Healy, *Yankee from the West*, 18–21. Wayne S. Cole also recounts this story in *Roosevelt and the Isolationists*, 387–88. See also *New York Times*, April 7, 1955; and Lynne Olson, *Those Angry Days: Roosevelt, Lindbergh, and America's Fight over World War II, 1939–1941* (New York: Random House, 2013), 101. Wheeler never identified the army captain, but Lynne Olson speculates that Army Air Force Chief of Staff Henry H. "Hap" Arnold sent the captain to talk to Wheeler. The speculation is plausible since Arnold was engaged at the time in a bureaucratic battle to increase the size of the Army Air Corps and may well have desired publicity about the unprepared state of the nation's air force.

42. *New York Times*, June 21, 1940; Olson, *Those Angry Days*, 206. See also Davis, *Into the Storm*, 572–75; Elting E. Morrison, *Turmoil and Tradition: A Study of the Life and Times of Henry L. Stimson* (Boston: Houghton Mifflin, 1960), 481–83; David Kaiser, *No End Save Victory: How FDR Led the Nation into War* (New York: Basic Books, 2014), 80–81. Kaiser writes that Stimson "received at least 100 telegrams, most intensely hostile" to his accepting the appointment. Another called Stimson a "Republican Party Benedict Arnold riding a Trojan horse and leading a fifth column." Stimson was confirmed by a vote of 66–16, with Wheeler joining three Democrats and twelve Republicans in voting no.

43. Wheeler and Healy, *Yankee from the West*, 362.

44. Harold Ickes, *Secret Diary*, vol. 2, 699; Farley, *Jim Farley's Story*, 224; Dunn, *1940*, 142–43. See also Roosevelt's letter of July 21, 1940, to George Norris, Roosevelt, *Franklin D. Roosevelt: His Personal Letters*, vol. 2, 1046–47. Roosevelt told Norris that Wheeler had joined "the Haters Club," FDR's term for his most vocal critics.

45. *New York Times*, July 1, 1940. Charles Peters offers a lively account of the 1940 Republican convention and the subsequent campaign in *Five Days in Philadelphia: The Amazing "We Want Willkie" Convention of 1940 and How It Freed FDR to Save the Western World* (New York: Public Affairs, 2005). Other book-length accounts of the 1940 campaign are Moe, *Roosevelt's Second Act*; Neal, *Dark Horse*; and Dunn, *1940*.

46. *New York Times*, July 2, 1940. Interior Secretary Ickes, who speculated often during 1939 and 1940 concerning Wheeler's presidential aspirations and always seemed confident that Roosevelt would never accept Wheeler as his replacement, confided to his diary in February 1940 that labor leader Lewis had "in the bank more than a million dollars, representing an assessment of the members of the miners' union, to be put on Wheeler."

47. Lee Metcalf, letter to "Fellow Democrats," July 3, 1940, Wheeler Papers, MHS. Metcalf also sent a telegram to Wheeler the same day, saying in part: "Your announcement of candidacy for President regardless of whether Roosevelt is a candidate for re-election unbelievable in view of your promise" at the state convention. The original Western Union message is in the Wheeler Papers, MHS. See also *Great Falls Tribune*, July 3, 1940.

48. *New York Times*, July 9, 10, and 11, 1940; Wheeler to Metcalf, July 8, 1940, Wheeler Papers, MHS.

49. Childs, *I Write from Washington*, 197; Parmet and Hecht, *Never Again*, 181; Farley, *Jim Farley's Story*, 265.

50. Waldron and Wilson, *Atlas of Montana Elections*, 157; Ruetten, "Burton K. Wheeler of Montana," 300.

51. Burns, *Lion and the Fox*, 426–27; Dunn, *1940*, 142; J. Smith, *FDR*, 460; Moe, *Roosevelt's Second Act*, 223–24; *New York Times*, July 15, 1940.

52. William L. Langer and S. Everett Gleason, *The Challenge to Isolation:1937–1940* (New York: Harper & Brothers, 1952), 672; *Great Falls Tribune*, July 18, 1940. See also Davis, *Into the Storm*, 597–98; and James F. Byrnes, *Speaking Frankly* (New York: Harpers, 1947), 10. Byrnes chaired the Democratic Platform Committee during the 1940 convention.

53. Childs, *I Write from Washington*, 197. For more on the story of Roosevelt's convention "draft," see Burns, *Lion and the Fox*, 426–29.

54. Harold L. Ickes, *The Secret Diary of Harold L. Ickes*, vol. 3, *The Lowering Clouds, 1939–1941* (New York: Simon and Schuster, 1954), 254.

55. *New York Times*, July 24, 1940.

56. Marion Wheeler Scott interview.

57. *New York Times*, August 11–12, 1940. See also Anderson, "Senator Burton K. Wheeler," 135–36.

58. Congressional Record, 76th Cong., 3rd Sess., 10233.

59. Kaiser, *No End Save Victory*, 88–90.

60. Roy Ayers to Wheeler, August 25, 1940; Tom Stout to Wheeler, August 27, 1940; Lewis Penwell to Wheeler, August 29, 1940; Wheeler to Ayers, August 27, 1940—all in Wheeler Papers, MSU.

61. Wheeler letter to Harry Burns, August 30, 1940, copy in Murray Papers; Congressional Record, 76th Cong., 3rd Sess., 11785. Most noninterventionists opposed the destroyers-for-bases deal for the same reason Prime Minister Churchill supported it. Churchill wrote in his postwar memoirs that the deal "brought the United States definitely nearer to us and to the war . . . it marked the passage of the United States from being neutral to being non-belligerent." As historian Wayne S. Cole has pointed out, noninterventionists saw the deal in the same light and opposed it for the same reason the British were so eager to see it happen.

62. Brands, *Traitor to His Class*, 426–28; Langer and Gleason, *Challenge to Isolation*, 681–83; Cole, *Roosevelt and the Isolationists*, 378–79; Justus D. Doenecke, *Storm on the Horizon: The Challenge to American Intervention, 1939–1941* (Lanham, Md.: Rowman & Littlefield, 2000), 114; Wheeler to Henry Elmer Barnes, September 19, 1940, quoted in Anderson, "Senator Burton K. Wheeler," 141. See also J. Garry Clifford and Samuel R. Spencer Jr., *The First Peacetime Draft* (Lawrence: University Press of Kansas, 1986), an exhaustive history of the conscription debate.

63. Dallek, *Franklin D. Roosevelt and American Foreign Policy*, 241–42; Wheeler and Healy, *Yankee from the West*, 25; Anderson, "Senator Burton K. Wheeler, "145.

64. Burns, *Lion and the Fox*, 448–50; Dallek, *Franklin D. Roosevelt and American Foreign Policy*, 250; Willkie quoted in J. Smith, *FDR*, 477.

65. Dallek, *Franklin D. Roosevelt and American Foreign Policy*, 251.

66. Ruetten, "Burton K. Wheeler of Montana," 304–307; *Great Falls Tribune*, October 29, 1940; Waldron and Wilson, *Atlas of Montana Elections*, 158; Wheeler to Alben Barkley, November 7, 1940, Wheeler Papers, MHS.

67. Bailey Stortz to Joseph Kinsey Howard, October 29, 1941, Howard Papers, MHS; Ruetten, "Burton K. Wheeler of Montana," 308. Wheeler received post-election congratulations from Norman Thomas, who polled 1,443 votes in Montana running on the Socialist Party ticket. "I know two votes you got in Montana," Wheeler wrote, apparently referring to his own vote and that of Lulu.

68. Wheeler to Elizabeth Colman, undated letter written prior to Christmas 1940. The letter is on the stationary of the Royal Hawaiian Hotel in Honolulu and was supplied to the author by Elizabeth's daughter Carol Timmis.

CHAPTER 12

1. Robert Woito, "Between the Wars," *Wilson Quarterly* 11, no. 1 (New Year's 1987): 108–21; Gallup, *Gallup Poll*, 259, 262; Dallek, *Franklin Roosevelt and American Foreign Policy*, 253. See also Ross Gregory, *America 1941: A Nation at the Crossroads* (New York: Free Press, 1989).

2. Thomas Fleming, *The New Dealers' War: FDR and the War within World War II* (New York: Basic Books, 2001), 80–81; Wheeler and Healy, *Yankee from the West*, 31. See also Charles A. Beard, *President Roosevelt and the Coming of the War 1941: A Study in Appearances and Realities*

(New Haven: Yale University Press, 1948); Manfred Jonas, *Isolation in America 1935–1941* (Ithaca, N.Y.: Cornell University Press, 1966); James P. Philben, "Charles Austin Beard: Liberal Foe of American Internationalism," *Humanitas* 13, no. 2, (2000), 90–107.

3. Gallup, *Gallup Poll*, 189. A rival group, the Committee to Defend America by Aiding the Allies, was launched in May 1940 and chaired by newspaper editor William Allen White, a Republican. During Roosevelt's 1936 reelection campaign, White, a strong voice for the internationalist wing of the Republican Party, charged Roosevelt with using logic that was "slick as goose grease and false as hell." But by 1940 he was defending Roosevelt's foreign policy at the head of what was sometimes called the White Committee. The committee served a variety of useful functions for Roosevelt, including providing a counterpoint to America First and serving as the source of occasional trial balloons, allowing Roosevelt to measure public or political reaction to ideas while keeping his own head down.

4. Eric Sevareid, *Not So Wild a Dream* (New York: Atheneum, 1979), 62–63.

5. Ruth Sarles, *The Story of America First: The Men and Women Who Opposed U.S. Intervention in World War II* (Westport: Praeger, 2003), 207. Ruth Sarles was a full-time organizer of America First and often represented the organization in Washington, D.C. See also Olson, *Those Angry Days*, 220–27; and Mark Lincoln Chadwin, *The Hawks of World War II* (Chapel Hill: University of North Carolina Press, 1968), 9.

6. Justus D. Doenecke, ed., *In Danger Undaunted: The Anti-Interventionist Movement of 1940–1941 as Revealed in the Papers of the America First Committee* (Stanford, Calif.: Hoover Institution Press, 1990), 87.

7. Wayne S. Cole, *America First: The Battle against Intervention, 1940–1941* (Madison: University of Wisconsin Press, 1953), 12; Sarles, *Story of America First*, 12, 22. See also Justus D. Doenecke, "General Robert E. Wood: The Evolution of a Conservative," *Journal of the Illinois State Historical Society* 71, no. 3 (August 1978): 162–75. Doenecke chronicles Wood's many connections to Roosevelt and his administration, including Woods's service on a number of advisory boards, and notes that he was considered for appointment to the Securities and Exchange Commission or as head of the National Recovery Administration.

8. Quoted in Colman, *Mrs. Wheeler Goes to Washington*, 194–95; *Great Falls Tribune*, November 15, 1940.

9. Cole, *America First*, 30–31; Richard Norton Smith, *The Colonel: The Life and Legend of Robert R. McCormick* (Boston: Houghton Mifflin, 1997), 346, 407.

10. Charles A. Lindbergh, *The Wartime Journals of Charles A. Lindbergh* (New York: Harcourt Brace Jovanovich, 1970), 37. A. Scott Berg's biography, *Lindbergh* (New York: G. P. Putnam's Sons, 1998) is the standard work on the famous flier and covers Lindbergh's political activity in the prewar period in considerable detail. For another view of Lindbergh's political activities in Europe, see Kenneth S. Davis, *The Hero: Charles A. Lindbergh and the American Dream* (Garden City: Doubleday, 1959), 373–79.

11. Wheeler letter to Governor Roy Ayers, August 27, 1940, Wheeler Papers, MSU.

12. Arthur M. Schlesinger, Jr., *A Life in the Twentieth Century: Innocent Beginnings, 1917–1950* (Boston: Houghton Mifflin, 2000), 241.

13. Wheeler to Norman Thomas, January 7, 1941, Norman Thomas Papers, New York Public Library, Manuscripts and Archives Division, Stephen A. Schwarzman Building, New York City, hereafter Thomas Papers; *New York Times*, December 26, 1940; Anderson, "Senator Burton K. Wheeler," 149–52.

14. *New York Times*, December 27–28, 1940.

15. Wheeler NBC radio address, December 30, 1940, Congressional Record, 76th Cong., 3rd Sess., Appendix, 7030–32. See also Anderson, "Senator Burton K. Wheeler, 153–55.

16. William L. Langer and S. Everett Gleason, *The Undeclared War: 1940–1941* (New York: Harper & Brothers, 1953), 238–39.

17. *Peace and War: United States Foreign Policy, 1931–1941* (Washington, D.C.: U.S. Government Printing Office, 1943), 598–607; *New York Times*, December 30, 1940.

18. James MacGregor Burns, *Roosevelt: The Solider of Freedom* (New York: Harcourt Brace Jovanovich, 1970), 27–29; Dallek, *Franklin D. Roosevelt and American Foreign Policy*, 256–57.

19. *New York Times*, December 30, 1940; Wheeler speech on the NBC radio network program *National Radio Forum*, December 30, 1940, printed in the Congressional Record, 76th Cong., 3rd Sess., Appendix, 7030–32.

20. Dallek, *Franklin D. Roosevelt and American Foreign Policy*, 257.

21. *New York Times*, January 4, 1941.

22. Warren F. Kimball, *The Most Unsordid Act: Lend-Lease, 1939–1941* (Baltimore: Johns Hopkins Press, 1969), 9, 151–52, 244; Lower, *Bloc of One*, 330–32; James T. Patterson, *Mr. Republican: A Biography of Robert A. Taft* (Boston: Houghton Mifflin, 1972), 243–44. See also Kimball, "1776: Lend-Lease Gets a Number," *New England Quarterly* 42, no. 2 (June 1969): 260–67; *New York Times*, January 11, 13, and 14, 1941. For more on Ingersoll and his newspaper, see Roy Hoopes, *Ralph Ingersoll: A Biography* (New York: Atheneum, 1985).

23. Calvin Callaghan, "The Lend-Lease Debate, December 1940–March 1941: The Role of Persuasion in a Momentous Public Discussion" (PhD diss., University of Wisconsin, 1950), 317–22; Anderson, "Senator Burton K. Wheeler," 156–57.

24. Wheeler's prepared statement for the *American Forum of the Air* was printed in the Congressional Record, 77th Cong., 1st Sess., Appendix, A178–79. The popular radio program was broadcast from the Willard Hotel.

25. *New York Times*, January 15, 1941.

26. Wheeler and Healy, *Yankee from the West*, 27; Joseph P. Kennedy, *Hostage to Fortune: The Letters of Joseph P. Kennedy*, edited by Amanda Smith (New York: Viking, 2001), 527–28. See also David Nasaw, *The Patriarch: The Remarkable Life and Turbulent Times of Joseph P. Kennedy* (New York: Penguin Press, 2010), 516–17. Kennedy, recently returned to the United States after serving as ambassador to Great Britain, delivered his own nationally broadcast speech on Lend-Lease in which he straddled the highly polarized positions on the legislation. Wheeler met with Kennedy prior to his speech and later praised the former ambassador, saying he was "in entire accord with Kennedy's remarks concerning the vital necessity of keeping out of war." South Carolina Democratic senator James Brynes, who favored Lend-Lease, also praised Kennedy for his "very strong statement" that Brynes felt supported aid to Britain. Not surprisingly the staunchly isolationist *Chicago Tribune*, which had begun calling Lend-Lease "the dictator bill," headlined its report on the Kennedy speech with bold type: "DON'T ENTER WAR—Kennedy."

Folk singer Pete Seeger and the Almanac Singers released an album—*Songs for John Doe*—in June 1941. The album included a song called "Plow Under." The first verse was: "Remember when the AAA, Killed a million hogs a day, Instead of hogs it's men today, Plow the fourth one under." The chorus continued: "Plow under, Plow under, Plow under every fourth American boy." In an editorial titled "The Poison in Our System," the *Atlantic* (June 1941) called the songs "strictly subversive and illegal" and speculated that the recording venture had to have been be "Communist or Nazi financed."

27. *New York Times*, January 14, 1941; Anderson, "Senator Burton K. Wheeler," 160; Hays's letter to FDR, including a copy of Wheeler's letter, FDR's response, and Hays's follow-up, dated January 17, January 22 and February 14, 1941, Roosevelt Papers.

28. Anderson, "Senator Burton K. Wheeler," 172.

29. Ibid., 173–47; *New York Times*, February 21, 1941.

30. Wheeler's lengthy speech in opposition to HR 1776 is in the Congressional Record, 77th Cong., 1st Sess., 1513–35, 1584–1609. The speech spanned two days, February 28 and March 1, 1941.

31. *New York Times*, March 2, 1941; Murray's comments were reported in the *New York Times*, March 3, 1941. See also Anderson, "Senator Burton K. Wheeler," 183–85. Wheeler's testiest exchanges during the Lend-Lease debate were with an old adversary, Texas senator Tom Connally, who at one point accused Wheeler of ignoring a question. "If there is an agile evader on the floor of the Senate," Connally said, "I must give the palm to the eminent senator from Montana." Wheeler responded that he intended to answer all questions but in a manner of his choosing.

32. Spritzer, *Senator James E. Murray*, 31. See also Mary Murphy, *Hope in Hard Times: New Deal Photographs of Montana, 1936–1942* (Helena: Montana Historical Society Press, 2003), 56–57.

33. Spritzer, *Senator James E. Murray*, 36.

34. *Montana Standard* (Butte), November 10, 1937; Spritzer, *Senator James E. Murray*, 36; Mansfield interview with the author. In his book *Master of the Senate*, Lyndon Johnson's biographer Robert Caro calls Murray a "liberal hero, and deservedly so." Caro quotes a 1955 profile of Murray in the *New York Times* that termed the Montana senator "a classic prototype of the New Deal . . . as nearly pro-labor on all questions as it is possible to be. . . . To hear Senator Murray's response when his name is reached on a roll-call is to know at once what the New Deal–Fair Deal position on an issue is." Caro says that Lyndon Johnson, as the Senate majority leader, was acutely aware of Murray's preference "to dwell in the past," and when Johnson talked with the aging Murray—Murray was eighty-four when he retired in 1960—Johnson would often turn the conversation to the New Deal years, and Murray would respond by relaxing and becoming "his old charming self." Murray died in March 1961 after serving nearly twenty-seven years in the Senate.

35. Murray to J. C. Hallack, October 20, 1941, Murray Papers.

36. Wheeler Interview, CCOH, pt. 4, 16–17; Spritzer, *Senator James E. Murray*, 62. For more on Murray's evolution from isolationist to internationalist, see William B. Evans, "Senator James E. Murray: A Voice of the People in Foreign Affairs," *Montana: The Magazine of Western History* 32, no. 3 (Winter 1982): 24–35. For an overview of Murray's career, see George Bousliman, "The 1954 Campaign of Senator James E. Murray" (master's thesis, University of Montana, 1964).

37. Wheeler speech "The Road to War," Wheeler Papers, MSU.

38. Langer and Gleason, *Undeclared War*, 275–84; Kaiser, *No End Save Victory*, 164–72. See also Cole, *Roosevelt and the Isolationists*, 422; Martin Gilbert, *Winston S. Churchill: Finest Hour, 1939–1941* (Boston: Houghton Mifflin, 1983), 1040; George W. Herring, *From Colony to Superpower: U.S. Foreign Relations Since 1776* (New York: Oxford, 2008), 525; Kimball, *Most Unsordid Act*, 232; Robert J. McMahon and Thomas W. Zeiler, eds., *Guide to U.S. Foreign Policy: A Diplomatic History* (Thousand Oaks, Calif.: CQ Press, 2012), 185. Most of the debt accumulated

by Britain as a result of Lend-Lease was written off by the United States when new postwar loans were negotiated in 1945. Britain made its last loan payment to the United States in 2006.

39. Sherwood, *Roosevelt and Hopkins*, 265–66; James MacGregor Burns and Susan Dunn, *The Three Roosevelts: Patrician Leaders Who Transformed America* (New York: Grove Press, 2001), 438.

40. Cole, *America First*, 51; Doenecke, *In Danger Undaunted*, 25; Geoffrey Kabaservice, *The Guardians: Kingman Brewster, His Circle, and the Rise of the Liberal Establishment* (New York: Henry Holt, 2004), 38.

41. Quoted in Anderson, "Senator Burton K. Wheeler," 193. See also *New York Times*, April 4, 1941. Evidence of the America First Committee's financial support for Wheeler is contained in a telegram that aide Bailey Stortz sent to America First staffer Page Hufty in October 1941. Stortz told Hufty that he and Wheeler would soon be in Chicago, adding, "Could you be sure and have a five hundred dollar check for me when we get there." America First Committee Papers, Hoover Institution, Stanford University, Stanford, Calif., hereafter AFC Papers.

42. *Detroit Times*, April 8, 1941.

43. Anthony Cave Brown, *The Last Hero: Wild Bill Donovan* (New York: Times Books, 1982), 94–95. Brown writes that "an important Democratic cabal" formed around Wheeler and Tom Walsh during the time of Wheeler's Justice Department investigation in 1924 and that the group blocked Donovan's efforts to become attorney general. Wheeler, Brown says, "never ceased to attack Donovan when he became Roosevelt's intelligence master in July 1941," and Brown writes that Wheeler was Donovan's "first important enemy in Washington."

44. All speeches quoted in Anderson, "Senator Burton K. Wheeler," 194–96, and *New York Times*, April 16, 17, and 19, 1941.

45. Dallek, *Franklin Roosevelt and American Foreign Policy*, 265; Gallup, *Gallup Poll*, 279.

46. George Rothwell Brown, "Political Parade" column, April 28, 1941, copy in AFC Papers; General Robert Wood letter to Wheeler, May 8, 1941, AFC Papers.

47. Anderson, "Senator Burton K. Wheeler," 199–200; Wayne S. Cole, *Charles A. Lindbergh and the Battle against American Intervention in World War II* (New York: Harcourt Brace Jovanovich, 1974), 148; *New York Times*, May 24, 1941.

48. Wheeler speech at the America First Committee rally at Madison Square Garden, May 23, 1941. The New York Chapter of AFC reprinted Wheeler's speech as a pamphlet, including a response card that could be used by those wishing to become a member of the committee and make a financial contribution. Pamphlet in the author's collection.

49. Lindbergh, *Wartime Journals*, 494, *New York Times*, May 24, 1941. Newbold Morris, who served as president of the New York City Council from 1938 to 1945, was later a two-time Republican candidate for mayor of New York and in 1960 was appointed by Mayor Robert F. Wagner to replace Robert Moses as New York parks commissioner.

50. Anne Morrow Lindbergh, *War Within and Without: Diaries and Letters, 1939–1944* (New York: Harcourt Brace Jovanovich, 1980), 187.

51. Curt Gentry, *J. Edgar Hoover: The Man and the Secrets* (New York: Penguin, 1992), 225–27; Sullivan iquoted in Olson, *Those Angry Days*, 326–27. For more on the FBI in this period, see Athan G. Theoharis and John Stuart Cox, *The Boss: J. Edgar Hoover and the Great American Inquisition* (Philadelphia: Temple University Press, 1988), 157–98.

52. J. Edgar Hoover memorandum to General Edwin M. Watson, February 26, 1941, Roosevelt Papers.

53. Hoover memorandum to Watson, March 19, 1941, Roosevelt Papers; Cole, *Roosevelt and the Isolationists*, 485–87; Doenecke, *Storm on the Horizon*, 275; John E. Moser, *Right Turn: John T. Flynn and the Transformation of American Liberalism* (New York: New York University Press, 2005), 115–16, 148–49.

54. Douglas M. Charles, *J. Edgar Hoover and the Anti-interventionists: FBI Political Surveillance and the Rise of the Domestic Security State, 1939–1945* (Columbus: Ohio State University Press, 2007), 172–77; Cole, *Roosevelt and the Isolationists*, 484. Douglas Charles documented the growth of the FBI during the Roosevelt administration from 391 agents and an annual appropriation of $2.5 million in 1934 to 1,596 agents and a nearly $25 million budget in 1941. By the end of World War II, the bureau had grown to 4,370 agents and an annual budget of more than $44 million.

55. Presidential press conference transcript January 31, 1941, Roosevelt Library.

56. *Chicago Tribune*, February 1, 1941; *New York Times*, February 1, 1941.

57. *New York Times*, February 1, 1941; *Chicago Tribune*, February 2, 1941. See also Robert Dallek, *Democrat and Diplomat: The Life of William E. Dodd* (New York: Oxford University Press, 1968), 253–54; and Schlesinger, *The Age of Roosevelt*, 141–42. Dodd's tenure as U.S. ambassador to Germany is recounted in Erik Larson, *In the Garden of the Beasts* (New York: Crown, 2011). See also Fred Arthur Bailey, "A Virginia Scholar in Chancellor Hitler's Court: The Tragic Ambassadorship of William Edward Dodd," *Virginia Magazine of History and Biography*, July 1992, 323–42.

58. Cole, *Roosevelt and the Isolationists*, 484. See also Richard W. Steele, "Franklin D. Roosevelt and His Foreign Policy Critics," *Political Science Quarterly* 94, no. 1 (Spring 1979): 15–32; and Richard W. Steele, "The Great Debate: Roosevelt, the Media, and the Coming of the War, 1940–1941," *Journal of American History* 71, no. 1 (June 1984), 69–92. Winchell's hugely popular fifteen-minute Sunday-night news and commentary radio show, *Jergens Journal*, was sponsored by Jergens Lotion. An announcer introduced the show by saying that Jergens guaranteed "soft, beautiful, romantic hands," and then Winchell, employing his trademark high-pitched staccato delivery, would begin the broadcast by saying, "Good evening, Mr. and Mrs. America, from border to border and coast to coast and all the ships at sea. Let's go to press." In 1941 the comedian Bob Hope and Winchell were deemed to have the most popular radio shows in the country.

59. St. Clair McKelway, "Profiles: Gossip Writer," *New Yorker*, June 15, 1940, 26–41; Harold Brodkey, "The Last Word on Walter Winchell," *New Yorker*, January 30, 1995, 71–79. See also Michiko Kakutani, "Of Winchell and the Power of Gossip," *New York Times*, October 18, 1994.

60. Walter Kirn, "The Man Who Invented Celebrity," *New York Magazine*, October 24, 1994, 64–70; Neal Gabler, *Winchell: Gossip, Power and the Culture of Celebrity* (New York: Alfred A. Knopf, 1994), 289–90.

61. Gabler, *Winchell*, 289–90; *New York Times*, March 5, 1988; Nicholas John Cull, *Selling War: The British Propaganda Campaign against American "Neutrality" in World War II* (New York: Oxford University Press, 1995), 132. See also Thomas E. Mahl, *Desperate Deception: British Covert Operations in the United States, 1939–1944* (Washington, D.C.: Brassey's, 1995), which offers a detailed account of British efforts to influence U.S. politics and policy prior to and during World War II. Montana congressman Jacob Thorkelson, the isolationist and anti-Semitic Republican whom Wheeler helped to defeat Congressman Jerry O'Connell in 1938, was another favorite Winchell foil. In the weeks before Thorkelson lost the 1940 Montana Republican primary to Jeannette Rankin, Winchell attacked him repeatedly as "the mouthpiece of the Nazi movement in Congress."

62. Gabler, *Winchell*, 293–94; Ruetten, "Burton K. Wheeler of Montana," 263.

63. Margaret Case Harriman, "The It Girl," pt. 1, *New Yorker*, April 20, 1940, 24–30, and pt. 2, *New Yorker*, April 27, 1940, 23–29; "Cartwheel Girl," *Time*, June 12, 1939, 47–51; *Ottawa (Ontario) Citizen*, July 28, 1941.

64. Peter Kurth, *American Cassandra: The Life of Dorothy Thompson* (Boston: Little, Brown, 1990), 318, 337.

65. Cull, *Selling War*, 13.

66. Ibid., 4, 132; Steele, *Franklin D. Roosevelt and His Foreign Policy Critics*, 15–32.

67. *New York Post*, May 16, 1941; *Delta Democrat-Times* (Greenville, Miss.), February 7, 1941; Raymond A. Schroth, *The American Journey of Eric Sevareid* (South Royalton, Vt.: Steerforth Press, 1995), 193–94.

68. Cole, *America First*, 112–13.

69. *San Diego Union*, September 17, 1941.

70. Sarles, *Story of America First*, 44–45.

71. *Chicago Tribune*, April 22 and April 28, 1941.

72. Dallek, *Franklin Roosevelt and American Foreign Policy*, 261; Anderson, "Senator Burton K. Wheeler," 205–7. Arthur Schlesinger Jr., who would later provide one of the most enduring histories of the New Deal period, was in the crowd for the Washington rally. He wrote in his memoirs that "the hall was less crowded than I expected and the audience was less hysterical—which I attributed to Washington's lack of the proletarian Coughlinite elements found in industrial cities. But the audience went wild every time the name Charles Lindbergh was mentioned, as it was time and again by Wheeler, by [John T.] Flynn and even by Norman Thomas. Wheeler gave the most effective speech, I thought; Thomas was too sarcastic; Flynn, who called for a negotiated peace, was a poor speaker."

73. Winston S. Churchill, *The Second World War: The Grand Alliance* (Boston: Houghton Mifflin, 1951), 308–20; Gilbert, *Winston S. Churchill: Finest Hour*, 1092–96; Gordon Corrigan, *The Second World War: A Military History* (New York: St. Martin's Press, 2011), 432; *Times of London*, May 4, 1941; Dallek, *Franklin D. Roosevelt and American Foreign Policy*, 265–67.

74. Langer and Gleason, *Undeclared War*, 441–44; Dallek, *Franklin D. Roosevelt and American Foreign Policy*, 268; Ickes, *Secret Diary*, vol. 3, p. 552. See also Kennedy, *Freedom from Fear*, 494–96.

75. Copy of Wheeler statement, June 20, 1941, Wheeler Papers, MHS. Wheeler obviously relied upon information from the America First Committee for his statement. See also Doenecke, *In Danger Undaunted*, 275, 403; Cole, *Roosevelt and Isolationists*, 442–43.

76. *New York Times*, June 23, 1941.

77. A copy of Wheeler's Hartford speech on June 25, 1941, is in Wheeler Papers, MHS. See also Anderson, "Senator Burton K. Wheeler," 209–10; Ickes, *Secret Diary*, vol. 3, 550.

78. Wheeler letter to Robert Wood, July 1, 1941, AFC Papers.

79. Wheeler press statement on Secretary Knox, July 1, 1941, Wheeler Papers, MHS; Cole, *America First*, 158, 177; undated letter (likely the summer of 1941), Lulu Wheeler to Elizabeth Wheeler Colman, copy in personal collection of the author.

80. *New York Times*, July 4, July 8, and July 9, 1941; Anderson, "Senator Burton K. Wheeler," 212–15; and Debi Unger, Irwin Unger, and Stanley Hirshson, *George Marshall: A Biography* (New York: HarperCollins, 2015), 108–11. Roosevelt ordered a U.S. Marine Corps brigade to Iceland on June 5, a move he characterized as strictly defensive. He did not inform Congress of the deployment until after the marines had arrived on July 7. The terms of the 1940 Selective Service

Act prohibited deployment of draftees outside of the Western Hemisphere, and Roosevelt had to scramble to explain that the four thousand Marines—volunteers, not draftees—were sent to Iceland to "supplement and eventually replace" British troops on the island. Churchill, not altogether pleased by the small number of Marines deployed, nonetheless called the movement of U.S. troops to Iceland "one of the most important things that has happened since the war began."

81. Olson, *Those Angry Days*, 333–34; *New York Times*, July 25, 1941. The Senate eventually passed the draft extension, limiting it to eighteen months rather than for the duration of the emergency, as the administration had wanted, with only forty-five favorable votes. Twenty-one senators did not vote, perhaps indicating the controversial nature of the issue. The House passed the extension by a single vote, 203–202. Opinion polls showed that only 51 percent of Americans supported the proposal. Wheeler said the extremely close House vote served notice that the administration "should go slowly in trying to further commit this country to war." *New York Times*, August 14, 1941.

82. Henry L. Stimson and McGeorge Bundy, *On Active Service in War and Peace* (New York: Harper & Brothers, 1947), 378; *New York Times*, July 25, 1941. Elting Morrison's biography of Stimson, *Turmoil and Tradition*, strangely makes no mention of the franking dispute.

83. *New York Times*, July 25, 1941. See also Charles, *J. Edgar Hoover and the Anti-interventionists*, 87–90. The FBI was involved in investigating Wheeler's use of his franking privilege in the incident involving Stimson and an earlier case where apparently a pro-German organization improperly used Wheeler's frank to distribute anti-intervention material in the name of a group called American Defenders. Wheeler wrote to FBI director Hoover saying that he was "extremely anxious to ascertain whether someone is using my franked envelopes illegally, and whether someone is using my name in this connection." The FBI cited lack of jurisdiction in declining to review the matter, but, as Charles notes, Wheeler was again "associated with questionable activity in official FBI reports that, in sum, reaffirmed negative administration views about him."

84. Ickes, *Secret Diary*, vol. 3, 588–89. Roosevelt further unburdened himself in a letter to Supreme Court Justice Felix Frankfurter. Roosevelt, perhaps only half jokingly, wrote, "If somebody kidnaps Wheeler and shanghais him on board an outgoing steamer for the Congo, can habeas corpus follow him thither? You need not answer, because it would never get as far as the Supreme Court. Wheeler or I would be dead, first!"

85. *New York Times*, July 26, 1941; Congressional Record, vol. 87, 6331–35.

86. Excerpts of the Congressional Record, July 28, 1941, in Wheeler Papers, MHS. Wheeler's relationship with Hiram Johnson is explored in Robert E. Burke, "A Friendship in Adversity: Burton K. Wheeler and Hiram W. Johnson," *Montana: The Magazine of Western History* 36, no. 1 (Winter 1986): 12–25.

87. *New York Times*, July 30, 1941.

88. Ibid.; Michele Flynn Stenehjem, *An American First: John T. Flynn and the America First Committee* (New Rochelle, N.Y.: Arlington House, 1976), 59; Doenecke, *In Danger Undaunted*, 70.

89. Adler, *The Uncertain Giant*, 269–70; *New York Times*, July 26, 1941; Wheeler letter to Norman Thomas, Wheeler Papers, MSU. On August 27, 1941, Wheeler wrote to Thomas that he had "it on the best information from people close to the President that our real danger is in getting into war with Japan. Of course, if we get into war with Japan that means we are in it every place."

90. Dallek, *Franklin D. Roosevelt and American Foreign Policy*, 273; Herring, *From Colony to Superpower*, 534–35; Herbert Feis, *The Road to Pearl Harbor* (Princeton: Princeton University Press, 1950), 239. See also Eri Hotta, *Japan 1941: Countdown to Infamy* (New York: Alfred A. Knopf, 2013), 166–67. Hotta writes that, at about the time the oil embargo was implemented, Japanese government planners undertook a war game exercise that assumed that "Japan was now completely isolated economically. Therefore, it would have to go farther into Southeast Asia to procure resources by force." Under this scenario, Hotta says, "Most ministers had determined even before the simulation started that such a war would be unwinnable and should not be waged."

91. Roosevelt fireside chat on "The *Greer* Incident," September 11, 1941, Roosevelt Papers. An account of the *Greer* incident is in Richard Snow, *A Measureless Peril: America in the Fight for the Atlantic, the Longest Battle of World War II* (New York: Scribner, 2010), 136–37.

92. Thomas A. Bailey and Paul B. Ryan, *Hitler and Roosevelt: The Undeclared Naval War* (New York: Free Press, 1979) offers a detailed account of the undeclared war in the Atlantic.

93. Kennedy, *Freedom from Fear*, 497; Dallek, *Franklin D. Roosevelt and American Foreign Policy*, 287.

94. Dallek, *Franklin D. Roosevelt and American Foreign Policy*, 28; Gallup, *Gallup Poll*, 299.

95. The Wheeler-Hoover exchange is quoted in Anderson, "Senator Burton K. Wheeler," 241–42. On September 14, America First chairman Wood released a statement from an "independent group" of prominent Americans condemning the shoot-on-sight policy, which, the statement said, was "supported neither by Congressional sanction nor by the popular will. It is authorized by no statute and undermines the Constitutional provision which gives the war power to Congress alone." Lulu Wheeler was one of the fifty-eight signers of the statement.

96. Dallek, *Franklin D. Roosevelt and American Foreign Policy*, 289. Arkansas senator J. William Fulbright, an early critic of U.S. policy in Southeast Asia and the chairman of the Foreign Relations Committee, asserted in 1971 that "the fact that Roosevelt and Truman were substantially right in their assessment of the national interest in no way diminishes the blamefulness of the precedents they set. FDR's deviousness in a good cause made it easier for LBJ to practice the same kind of deviousness in a bad cause."

CHAPTER 13

1. Doenecke, *Storm on the Horizon*, 88; Herbert Kay, "Boss Isolationist," *Life*, May 19, 1941, 110–12. See also "Isolationist Organ," *Time*, December 30, 1940), 34; Anderson, "Senator Burton K. Wheeler," 198–99; Alan Brinkley, *The Publisher: Henry Luce and His American Century* (New York: Alfred A. Knopf, 2010), 246. *Life*'s profile of Wheeler was remarkably balanced in fact and tone, particularly given the strongly held interventionist attitudes of publisher Henry Luce. A lengthy memo dated October 11, 1941, written by William S. Foulis, chair of the America First Committee Speakers' Bureau, said, "As you well know, 95% of the letters received by the Speakers Bureau request the presence of Senator Wheeler at rallies all over the country." AFC Papers.

2. James Rowe Jr. memorandum to FDR, September 1, 1941, Roosevelt Papers; Ickes, *Secret Diary*, vol. 3, 589; *New York Times*, July 29, 1941. The clipping Rowe sent to Roosevelt from the *Great Falls News* is undated. Wheeler wrote to Oswald Garrison Villard on September 21, 1940, that he was "amazed to find that many of the chambers of commerce, and Lions Clubs and other organizations" in Montana "are for doing everything short of war. Many of them do not realize what they are doing." Letter in Wheeler Papers, MHS.

3. Margaret Loughrin letter to Harry C. Schnibbe, July 12, 1941, AFC Papers. Schnibbe was the assistant director of administration for the America First Committee. In the late summer of 1941, Wheeler asked America First's national headquarters to pay more attention to Montana. Committee organizer Page Hufty, in a letter to Billings chapter president Willard Fraser, said, "Wheeler wants office kept going . . . opposition putting on pressure out there." AFC Papers. Fraser was the son-in-law of the poet Robert Frost and later a colorful, popular mayor of Billings.

4. Spritzer, *Senator James E. Murray*, 59–60. Mike Mansfield was a young college professor in 1941 contemplating a second campaign for Congress, and years later he vividly recalled the intensity of noninterventionist or isolationist sentiment in the Montana prior to Pearl Harbor, sentiment exemplified by Wheeler and dedicated pacifists like Congresswoman Jeannette Rankin. Mansfield also remembered what he called "brown shirt" groups sympathetic to European fascism. Wheeler was in no way associated with the state's pro-Nazi elements, Mansfield recalled in an interview, but there were Montanans—"militia groups, you would call them today," he said—who harbored fascist beliefs and also embraced the type of nonintervention Wheeler espoused.

5. Hoover memorandum to General Edwin "Pa" Watson, September 22, 1941, Roosevelt Papers.

6. Sarles, *Story of America First*, 1, 50; Cole, *America First*, 134.

7. Cole, *America First*, 135–38.

8. Swanberg, *Norman Thomas*, 248; Glen Jeansonne, *Gerald L. K. Smith: Minister of Hate* (Baton Rouge: Louisiana State University Press, 1988), 83; Wheeler letter to Charles Schwager, February 3, 1941, Marion Wheeler Scott Papers, MSU.

9. *New York Times*, May 24, 1941.

10. Wheeler and Healy, *Yankee from the West*, 29.

11. Ibid., 233.

12. *New York Times*, July 31 and November 12, 1941; York quoted in Dunn, *1940*, 296; Steele, "Great Debate," 81; Bennett, *One World, Big Screen*, 65–66; W. A. Swanberg, *Luce and His Empire* (New York: Charles Scribner's Sons, 1972), 187. For more on the propaganda uses of newsreels, including March of Time productions, see Anderson, "Senator Burton K. Wheeler," 232. David Nasaw, in his biography of newspaper titan William Randolph Hearst, notes that the first hints from Wheeler of a possible congressional investigation of the motion picture industry coincided with the release of Orson Welles's film *Citizen Kane* (a story inspired by Hearst's life and legend) and resulting controversy. At the time of Wheeler's comments, as the *New York Times* reported, RKO, the producer of Welles's film, was under tremendous pressure not to release the movie, any mention of which had been "deleted from the news columns of the Hearst papers." Hearst, meanwhile, contacted other studio executives in his quest to have the film shelved. The *Times* observed that at such a sensitive moment, "a Congressional investigation hinted at by Senator Burton K. Wheeler . . . might be disastrous." *Citizen Kane* was eventually released on May 1, 1941, and the investigation began in September.

13. M. Todd Bennett, *One World, Big Screen: Hollywood, the Allies and World War II* (Chapel Hill: University of North Carolina Press, 2012), 81. Bennett writes that "a Gallup Poll published early in 1942 found that 86.7 percent of Bostonians and New Yorkers who had viewed pro-British productions came away favorably inclined toward Britain."

14. Ibid., 60–61. See also David Nasaw, *The Chief: The Life of William Randolph Hearst* (New York: Houghton Mifflin, 2000), 568–73; *New York Times*, January 19, 1941; Richard W. Steele, "The Great Debate: Roosevelt, the Media, and the Coming of the War, 1940–1941," *Journal of American History* 71, no. 1 (June 1984): 69–92; Larry Ceplair and Steven Englund, *The Inquisition in Hollywood: Politics in the Film Community, 1900–1960* (Garden City, N.Y.: Anchor Press/Doubleday, 1980), 159–61; John E. Moser, "Gigantic Engines of Propaganda: The 1941 Senate Investigation of Hollywood," *Historian* 63, no. 4 (Summer 2001): 731–51; John Whiteclay Chambers, "The Movies and the Antiwar Debate in America, 1930–1941," *Film and History* 36, no. 1 (2006): 44–60; and Steven J. Ross, "Confessions of a Nazi Spy: Warner Bros., Anti-Fascism and the Politicization of Hollywood," in *Warners' War: Politics, Pop Culture, and Propaganda in Wartime Hollywood*, ed. Martin Kaplan and Johanna Blakley (Los Angeles: Norman Lear Center Press, 2004), 49–59, https://learcenter.org/pdf/WWRoss.pdf.

The motion picture industry's antitrust issues dated back to the 1920s. Critics of industry practices focused on the fact that the major studios controlled virtually all aspects of the industry—production, distribution, and the booking of films. As historian John E. Moser has pointed out, one independent operator called the industry's practices "the most corrupt trusts ever known." The Senate passed legislation in 1939, legislation that Wheeler supported, but a bill was not considered in the House that would have ended many of the industry's monopolistic practices. To head off an antitrust action in 1940 against so-called block booking, the industry agreed to a consent order that was engineered by the White House.

15. Quoted in Doenecke, *In Danger Undaunted*, 384.

16. Anderson, "Senator Burton K. Wheeler," 232. Nye's role in the motion picture investigation and his response to allegation of anti-Semitism are covered in Wayne S. Cole's biography of the North Dakota Republican, *Senator Gerald P. Nye and American Foreign Relations* (Minneapolis: University of Minnesota Press, 1962), 184–93. See also Dunn, *1940*, 297.

17. Biographical information about Clark is in the D. Worth Clark Papers, Boise State University Library Special Collections and Archives, Albertsons Library, Boise, Idaho. Two of Clark's uncles served as governor of Idaho, and a cousin, Bethine, married Frank Church, who served four terms in the Senate and chaired the Foreign Relations Committee in the 1970s.

18. Cole, *America First*, 187–88; *Hartford (Conn.) Courant*, August 4, 1941; *New York Herald Tribune*, August 2, 1941. For a perspective on the role Jewish-Americans have played in the American film industry, see Neal Gabler, *An Empire of Their Own: How the Jews Invented Hollywood* (New York: Crown, 1988).

19. "Movie Makers Bank on Willkie to Foil the Propaganda Inquiry," *Newsweek*, September 14, 1941, 52; Anderson, "Senator Burton K. Wheeler," 235. For more on Hays, see Stephen Vaughn, "Morality and Entertainment: The Origins of the Motion Picture Production Code," *Journal of American History* 77 (1990): 39–65. Historian John Moser says Willkie was selected to represent the industry, despite his reported fee of $100,000, because of his pro-interventionist stand after the 1940 election and because his stature in the Republican Party "kept him from being viewed as a shill for the Roosevelt administration."

20. A copy of Willkie's letter dated September 8, 1941, is contained in the Ernest W. McFarland Papers, Arizona State Library, Archives & Public Records, Phoenix.

21. James E. McMillan, "McFarland and the Movies: The 1941 Senate Motion Picture Hearings," *Journal of Arizona History* 29 (Autumn 1988): 277–302. See also McMillan's biography of the Arizona senator, *Ernest W. McFarland: Majority Leader of the United States Senate, Governor*

and Chief Justice of the State of Arizona (Prescott, Ariz.: Sharlot Hall Museum Press, 2004). *Variety*, September 10, 1941, is quoted in McMillan's book. McFarland served two terms in the Senate, including two years as majority leader. He lost reelection in 1952 to Barry Goldwater but continued his political career, serving two terms as Arizona governor. He also served on the Arizona Supreme Court, including a term as chief justice.

22. Anderson, "Senator Burton K. Wheeler," 240; "Wheeler Charges Juke Box Films 'Lewd and Lascivious,'" United Press, October 20, 1941. Senators D. Worth Clark, Gerald P. Nye, and Bennett Champ Clark, the noninterventionists most directly associated with the motion picture investigation, suffered the political fate of so many other pre-war noninterventionists. Each failed to be reelected in 1944. Worth Clark lost a Democratic primary in Idaho to Glen H. Taylor, an unabashed liberal internationalist who later ran for vice president on the Progressive Party ticket. A Democratic challenger in North Dakota defeated Nye in 1944. Clark of Missouri also lost in a primary election in 1944.

23. Wheeler's speech in Oklahoma City, August 30, 1941, Wheeler Papers, MHS.

24. The surviving audio recordings of Lindbergh's speech indicate that he was frequently interrupted by a combination of applause and catcalls. At one point Lindbergh had to pause his speech for several seconds to let the jeers die down.

25. Fredrick L. Collins, "Why Senator Wheeler and Lindberg Work Together," pt. 2, *Liberty*, August 2, 1941, 56. Collins quoted an unnamed "long-time friend and admirer" of Wheeler as saying, "What I like about Burt Wheeler is the way he hates people's guts." Collins relayed this in print, meaning it as a compliment, and Wheeler would likely have agreed, Collins wrote, "For Burt Wheeler is smart, and he knows that there is nothing like the reputation of being a good hater for keeping a politician's name in the papers."

26. Berg, *Lindbergh*, 418–19; *Chicago Tribune*, April 26, 1941; Anderson, "Senator Burton K. Wheeler," 196; *New York Times*, April 28, 1941; Lindbergh, *Wartime Journals*, 478–80. See also Kenneth S. Davis, *FDR: The War President, 1940–1943* (New York: Random House, 2000), 172.

27. Olson, *Those Angry Days*, 381–85.

28. Lindbergh, *War Within and Without*, 223; Doenecke, *In Danger Undaunted*, 37–38.

29. Berg, *Lindbergh*, 428.

30. *New York Times*, September 13, 1941; Doenecke, *In Danger Undaunted*, 38–39, 395. See also Cole, *Lindbergh*, 160–85, for additional analysis of the Des Moines speech.

31. *New York Times*, September 25, 1941.

32. John L. Wheeler letter to R. Douglas Stewart, September 16, 1941, AFC papers; Cole, *America First*, 153–54.

33. Quoted in Olson, *Those Angry Days*, 388.

34. *New York Times*, September 23 and October 11, 1941; *Chicago Tribune*, October 9, 1941; recording of Wheeler's Billings speech in the author's collection; Anderson, "Senator Burton K. Wheeler," 242; Lulu Wheeler letter to Elizabeth Wheeler Colman, September 21, 1941, copy in author's collection.

35. Dallek, *Franklin D. Roosevelt and American Foreign Policy*, 289–91.

36. Wood to Wheeler, October 9, 1941, and Wheeler to Wood, October 14, 1941, in AFC papers. For more on the America First Committee's reaction to the amendment of the Neutrality Act, see Doenecke, *In Danger Undaunted*, 42–46.

37. Dallek, *Franklin D. Roosevelt and American Foreign Policy*, 291; Gallup, *Gallup Poll*, 302.

38. *New York Times*, October 20, 1941.

39. A copy of Wheeler's speech is in the Wheeler Papers, MHS; *New York Times*, October 31, 1941See also Anderson, "Senator Burton K. Wheeler," 251.

40. *New York Times*, November 6–7, 1941; Anderson, "Senator Burton K. Wheeler," 253–55.

41. Doenecke, *In Danger Undaunted*, 44; Dallek, *Franklin D. Roosevelt and American Foreign Policy*, 291–92.

42. Wheeler letter to Thomas, November 25, 1941, Wheeler Papers, MHS.

43. Kennedy, *Freedom from Fear*, 513–14; *Washington Post*, December 4, 1941. See also Cole, *Roosevelt and the Isolationists*, 498.

44. *Chicago Tribune*, December 4, 1941. See also Fleming, *New Dealers' War*, 1–24. Wheeler devotes the first chapter of *Yankee from the West* to the story of his involvement in the "big leak." See also Albert C. Wedemeyer, *Wedemeyer Reports!* (New York: Henry Holt, 1958), 15–43.

45. Doenecke, *In Danger Undaunted*, 436–37.

46. Anderson, "Senator Burton K. Wheeler," 263–68; Joseph E. Persico, *Roosevelt's Secret War: FDR and World War II Espionage* (New York: Random House, 2001), 132–33.

47. Wedemeyer, *Wedemeyer Reports!*, 17.

48. Ibid., 42–43; *New York Times*, December 20, 1989.

49. Wheeler and Healy, *Yankee from the West*, 32–36.

50. Fleming, *New Dealers' War*, 27; Olson, *Those Angry Days*, 421.

51. Ibid., 26–28; R. Smith, *Colonel*, 417–19.

52. Olson, *Those Angry Days*, 421–23.

53. Wheeler and Healy, *Yankee from the West*, 36.

54. R. Smith, *Colonel*, 419; Gilbert, *Churchill in America*, 246; Dallek, *Franklin D. Roosevelt and American Foreign Policy*, 312.

55. Anderson, "Senator Burton K. Wheeler," 267–68.

CHAPTER 14

1. Byrd, *Senate, 1789–1989*, 495.

2. *Billings Gazette*, December 6, 1941; *Great Falls Tribune* and *Helena Independent*, December 8, 1941.

3. Wheeler to Robert Wood, December 22, 1941, AFC papers.

4. Spritzer, *Senator James E. Murray*, 61. Rankin's controversial vote against the war declaration stunned many, even though she had voted the same way in 1917, opposing the declaration of war against Germany, but unlike 1941 she was not completely alone in that vote. "Well—look at Jeannette Rankin," William Allen White, the pro-interventionist editor of the *Emporia (Kans.) Gazette*, wrote on December 10, 1941. "Probably a hundred men in Congress would have liked to do what she did. Not one of them had the courage to do it. The *Gazette* entirely disagrees with the wisdom of her position. But, Lord, it was a brave thing: and its bravery somehow discounts its folly."

5. Doenecke, *In Danger Undaunted*, 47.

6. Lulu Wheeler to Elizabeth Wheeler Colman, December 10, 1941, copy in author's collection.

7. Doenecke, *In Danger Undaunted*, 48; Cole, *Roosevelt and the Isolationists*, 505.

8. Doenecke, *In Danger Undaunted*, 50.

9. Cole, *America First*, 199.

10. Dallek, *Franklin D. Roosevelt and American Foreign Policy*, 313; Herring, *From Colony to Superpower*, 537; Warren F. Kimball, *The Juggler: Franklin Roosevelt as Wartime Statesman*, (Princeton: Princeton University Press, 1994), 7.

11. Doenecke, *In Danger Undaunted*, 51; Anderson, "Senator Burton K. Wheeler," 269–72. Robert Caro, the biographer of Lyndon Johnson, argues in his book *Master of the Senate* that both the noninterventionists and the U.S. Senate as an institution were discredited by the pre-war foreign policy debate. Caro compares Wheeler, Nye, and other noninterventionists to the Senate's "irreconcilables" who conducted a nationwide campaign in 1919 in opposition to U.S. participation in the League of Nations. "In a single flash, the flash of bombs, the [neutrality] policy of the Senate of the United States was exposed as a gigantic mistake. The failure of the world's most powerful nation to lead—or in general even to cooperate—in efforts, twenty years of efforts, to avert a second world war must be laid largely at the door of its Congress, and particularly at the door of the Senate," Caro asserts.

12. Martin Gilbert, *Churchill and America* (New York: Free Press, 2005), 248–50; *New York Times*, December 27, 1941.

13. Krys Holmes, Sue Dailey and Dave Walter, "World War II in Montana, 1939–1945," chap. 19 in *Montana: Stories of the Land* (Helena: Montana Historical Society Press, 2008); Gary Glynn, *Montana's Home Front during World War II* (Missoula: Big Elk Books, 2011), 194. Glynn says, "The most accurate listing of Montanans killed in the war was compiled by the Montana Historical Society: the list contains the names of 1,869 Montanans killed during the war, however the actual total of dead and missing from Montana is probably between 2,000 and 2,500."

14. Glynn, *Montana's Home Front during World War II*, 9–44, 106–107, 154.

15. Anderson, "Senator Burton K. Wheeler," 274–75.

16. *New York Times*, February 21, 1942; Geoffrey R. Stone, "Civil Liberties in Wartime," *Journal of Supreme Court History* 28, no. 3 (November 2003): 215–51; Wheeler and Healy, *Yankee from the West*, 150–51.

17. Wheeler and Healy, *Yankee from the West*, 150–51. See also Stone, *Perilous Times*, 272–75; Dallek, *Franklin D. Roosevelt and American Foreign Policy*, 334–35; and Greg Robinson, *By Order of the President: FDR and the Internment of Japanese Americans* (Cambridge: Harvard University Press, 2001), 257–58. Robert Patterson was serving as undersecretary of war at the time of the Japanese American internment in 1942. President Truman later appointed him secretary of war.

18. Dallek, *Franklin D. Roosevelt and American Foreign Policy*, 335–36.

19. Ibid., 336; Stone, *Perilous Times*, 273; Leo P. Ribuffo, "*United States v. McWilliams*: The Roosevelt Administration and the Far Right," in *American Political Trials*, edited by Michael R. Belknap, rev. ed. (Westport: Greenwood Press, 1994), 181.

20. Arthur Herman, *Joseph McCarthy: Reexamining the Life and Legacy of America's Most Hated Senator* (New York: Free Press, 2000), 174. The Silver Shirts, or the Silver Legion of America, was a pro-Nazi, anticommunist, Christian spiritualist group founded in 1933 by fascist sympathizer and Hitler supporter William Dudley Pelley. At the height of the movement Pelley claimed fifteen thousand followers, primarily in the South and on the West Coast. Pelley published a weekly newspaper and magazine and ran for president in 1936 on the Christian Party ticket with the campaign slogan "Christ or Chaos." Only able to gain ballot access in

Washington State, Pelley received fewer than sixteen hundred votes. He was eventually charged and convicted of insurrection and sedition and served ten years in federal prison.

21. Anderson, "Senator Burton K. Wheeler," 278.

22. The Wheeler-Biddle correspondence is quoted in Anderson, "Senator Burton K. Wheeler," 278–79, and also printed in the Congressional Record, 78th Cong., 1st Sess., 1288–89.

23. Anderson, "Senator Burton K. Wheeler," 278–79. See also O. John Rogge, *The Official German Report: Nazi Penetration, 1924–1942* (New York: Yoseloff, 1961); *New York Times,* October 26, 1946, and March 23, 1981.

24. Dale M. Harrington, *Mystery Man: William Rhodes Davis, Nazi Agent of Influence* (Washington: Brassey's, 2001), 209.

25. *Los Angeles Times,* April 18, 1999; *Washington Post,* December 20, 1942.

26. *Chicago Tribune,* January 15, 1943; Brinkley, *Publisher,* 246.

27. "Sedition," *Time,* December 11, 1944, 24; *Washington Post,* July 16, 1944.

28. Stone, *Perilous Times,* 275, emphasis in original.

29. Ickes, *Secret Diary,* vol. 3, 628; "KGIR, Butte, Requests 50 kw. on WEAF 660 Clear Channel," *Broadcasting,* September 1, 1941, 16. Wheeler's relationship with Frank Walker, as well as Walker's role in Montana politics, is discussed in Walker's autobiography. Frank Walker, *FDR's Quiet Confidant: The Autobiography of Frank C. Walker,* edited by Robert H. Ferrell (Niwot: University Press of Colorado, 1997).

30. National Register of Historic Places Registration Form, June 1998, copy in author's collection.

31. Memos from Ickes to FDR, December 8 and December 30, 1942, and Roosevelt memo to Ickes, December 19, 1942—all in Roosevelt Papers.

32. The Wheeler-Murray feud is well documented in Donald E. Spritzer's "Senators in Conflict," *Montana: The Magazine of Western History* 23 (Spring 1973): 16–33.

33. Spritzer, *Senator James E. Murray,* 76; *Great Falls Tribune,* July 11 and July 14, 1942; Murray speech, May 14, 1942, copy in Murray Papers.

34. A copy of Wheeler's July 19, 1942, speech is in Wheeler Papers, MHS.

35. Spritzer, *Senator James E. Murray,* 77.

36. Ibid.; Waldron and Wilson, *Atlas of Montana Elections,* 165.

37. Material on Rankin is taken from his biography in the Wellington D. Rankin Papers, MHS. See also Steele, *Wellington Rankin,* 109–10.

38. Spritzer, *Senator James E. Murray,* 78–79; *Great Falls Tribune,* September 6, 1942. For Murray's treatment by the Anaconda-owned newspapers, see Swibold, *Copper Chorus,* 279, 281. Swibold says that by 1942 the Anaconda press was providing "thin but reasonably balanced coverage to most candidates," with the *Helena Independent* leaning toward Murray, the *Billings Gazette* tilting toward Rankin, and the *Missoulian* waffling. For Jeannette Rankin's impact on her brother's candidacy, see Steele, *Wellington Rankin,* 139.

39. Interviews with Louise Rankin Galt and Jack Galt, April 29, 2005, Bob Brown Oral History Project, University of Montana, Mansfield Library, Archives and Special Collections.

40. Wheeler letter to Ed Craney, undated but probably September 1942, Marion Wheeler Scott Papers, MSU.

41. Wheeler letter to Barclay Craighead, October 19, 1942, Craighead Papers.

42. Waldron and Wilson, *Atlas of Montana Elections,* 165–67. Montana Republicans also captured both houses of the state legislature in 1942, the first time that had happened since

1930. One of the political casualties of the 1942 midterm election was eighty-one-year-old independent and onetime Republican senator George Norris of Nebraska, an old Wheeler friend and frequent collaborator. Norris, who served in the House and Senate for forty years, softened his noninterventionist foreign policy views during the 1930s, and foreign affairs played little part in his defeat. Norris, after 1936 officially an independent, attributed his defeat to "hate against Roosevelt" (FDR warmly endorsed Norris in 1936 and 1942).

43. Spritzer, *Senator James E. Murray*, 79; Lulu Wheeler letter to Elizabeth Wheeler Colman, November 13, 1942, copy in author's collection.

44. Spritzer, "Senators in Conflict," 29.

45. Oberdorfer, *Senator Mansfield*, 50–51.

46. Congressional Record, 77th Cong., 2nd Sess., 8792–93, and 78th Cong., 1st Sess., 1288–89; Anderson, "Senator Burton K. Wheeler," 279–81.Wheeler's radio speech was reprinted in the Congressional Record, 78th Cong., 1st Sess., Appendix, A1063–65. Always a harsh critic of government and private-sector bungling, Wheeler lambasted as inefficient and wasteful a variety of domestic policies that he said contributed to labor and food shortages, at one point suggesting that "someone has got to take these bureaucrats and knock their heads together." See also Roland Young, *Congressional Politics in the Second World War* (New York: Columbia University Press, 1956), a concise survey of issues addressed by the wartime Congress.

47. Allen Drury, *A Senate Journal: 1943–1945* (New York: McGraw-Hill, 1963), 18, 35; Potomacus, "Wheeler of Montana," *New Republic*, September 20, 1943, 390–92. See also Gerald W. Johnson, "Wheeler Rides the Storm," *Collier's*, July 8, 1944, 11, 72–73.

48. *New York Times*, June 6, 1943; Wood letter to Wheeler, October 12, 1943, and Wheeler letter to Wood, October 15, 1943, Robert Wood Papers, Herbert Hoover Presidential Library, West Branch, Iowa, hereafter Wood Papers; *Washington Times-Herald*, November 24, 1942.

49. Wheeler CBS radio speech, June 19, 1943, copy in Wheeler Papers, MHS. For the U.S. policy of "Germany first," see Dallek, *Franklin D. Roosevelt and American Foreign Policy*, 320–21; and Anderson, "Senator Burton K. Wheeler," 288–89.

50. Cole, *Roosevelt and the Isolationists*, 523–25. Wheeler detailed his objections to a Senate resolution related to postwar organization in an April 7, 1943, speech on the NBC Blue network. He titled the talk "Americanism versus Internationalism in the Post-War Picture." A copy of the speech is in the Wheeler Papers, MHS.

51. *New York Times*, June 6, 1943.

52. Ibid., September 3, 1943; *Department of State Bulletin*, January 7, 1945, 43. See also Steven Casey, *Cautious Crusade: Franklin D. Roosevelt, American Public Opinion, and the War against Nazi Germany* (New York: Oxford University Press, 2001), 200–201, 208.

53. Cole, *Roosevelt and the Isolationists*, 536–38; E. J. Kahn Jr., "Profiles: Democracy's Friend," *New Yorker*, July 26, 1947, 28–39.

54. John Roy Carlson, *Under Cover: My Four Years in the Nazi Underworld of America* (Philadelphia: Blakiston, 1943), 484–90; *Chicago Tribune*, November 4, 1943; Moser, *Right Turn*, 158–63; Anderson, "Senator Burton K. Wheeler," 292–94; Stenehjem, *American First*, 168–70.

55. Arthur Derounian wrote two other popular books as John Roy Carlson—*The Plotters* (1946) and *Cairo to Damascus* (1951)—and many newspaper and magazine pieces investigating anti-Semitism and bigotry before his death in 1991. The journal *Commentary* said of *The Plotters* that "one could hope that the only book many Americans will ever read on fascism was a better

one. For though Carlson's energy as an investigator is boundless, his sense of historical perspective on fascism, as well as his accuracy, unfortunately leave much to be desired." Derounian died at eighty-two, according to the *New York Times*, while engaged in research work at library of the American Jewish Committee in New York. Glenn Fowler, "Arthur Derounian, 82, and Author of Books on Fascists and Bigots," *New York Times*, April 25, 1991.

56. Culver and Hyde, *American Dreamer*, 348–49.

57. *Washington Times-Herald*, May 11, 1944; *New York Times*, May 10, 1944; Wheeler and Healy, *Yankee from the West*, 390–92.

58. David M. Jordan, *FDR, Dewey, and the Election of 1944* (Bloomington: Indiana University Press, 2011), 156; Wheeler and Healy, *Yankee from the West*, 368–71.

59. Oberdorfer, *Senator Mansfield*, 62–81; Charles Eugene Hood, "'China Mike' Mansfield: The Making of a Congressional Authority on the Far East" (PhD diss., Washington State University, 1980).

60. Anderson, "Senator Burton K. Wheeler," 305; Jordan, *FDR, Dewey, and the Election of 1944*, 321–22; *Chicago Sun*, August 17, 1943. See also Stanley Weintraub, *Final Victory: FDR's Extraordinary World War II Presidential Campaign* (Philadelphia: Da Capo Press, 2012).

61. Waldron and Wilson, *Atlas of Montana Elections*, 171–77.

62. Johnson, *Peace Progressives*, 311: Jordan, *FDR, Dewey, and the Election of 1944*, 323; Cole, *Senator Gerald P. Nye*, 215–66; Lawrence O. Christensen, William E. Foley, Gary Kremer, eds., *Dictionary of Missouri Biography* (Columbia: University of Missouri Press, 1999), 184; F. Ross Peterson, *Prophet without Honor: Glen H. Taylor and the Fight for American Liberalism* (Lexington: University of Kentucky Press, 1974), 25–27.

63. Drury, *Senate Journal*, 31–32; *New York Times*, February 27, 1945. An excellent summary of the legacy of the Yalta conference is contained in S. M. Plokhy's *Yalta: The Price of Peace* (New York: Penguin, 2012). Plokhy's history of the conference makes note of Wheeler's outspoken opposition to the decisions made at Yalta, particularly those that impacted Poland.

64. Wheeler letter to Robert Wood, February 7, 1945, Wood Papers.

65. *New York Times*, April 13, 1945. See also Anderson, "Senator Burton K. Wheeler," 314. John Anderson has calculated that Wheeler had meetings with President Truman nine times before he left the Senate and fifteen more times while Wheeler was practicing law as a private citizen and Truman was still in the White House.

66. Details on the Senate Interstate Commerce Committee tour of postwar Europe are contained in the Ernest W. McFarland Papers at the Arizona State Archives in Phoenix, as well as the Ed Craney Papers, MHS. Senator McFarland preserved detailed itineraries, including extensive notes on who attended various meetings. See also Wheeler and Healy, *Yankee from the West*, 393–97; and McMillan, *Ernest W. McFarland*, 123–28.

There are two accounts of Wheeler's postwar trip to Europe that suggest he did some souvenir hunting. In a May 2003 article in the *Atlantic Monthly*, "Hitler's Forgotten Library," author Timothy W. Ryback reported seeing archival film footage of "a delegation of American senators," including Wheeler, exiting Hitler's "Berghof ruins with books under their arms." Ryback quotes a local historian as saying, "I doubt if they were taking them to the Library of Congress." A contemporary *New Yorker* piece (June 5, 1945) by Philip Hamburger—who had witnessed and written about Mussolini's death in Milan just a few days earlier—also mentions the Senate delegation's visit to Hitler's retreat at Berchtesgaden. "Sen. Wheeler, who came along several weeks later to view the wreckage of an establishment where he might have been made to feel right at home in the old days, was seen by someone tearing a telephone from a wall for a souvenir."

67. Wheeler letter to Elizabeth Wheeler Colman, undated but likely June 1945, copy in the author's collection.

68. Robert H. Ferrell, ed., *Off the Record: The Private Papers of Harry S. Truman* (New York: Harper and Row, 1980), 48.

69. *Pittsburgh Press*, July 24, 1945; Louis Fisher, *Presidential War Power* (Lawrence: University Press of Kansas, 2004), 81–90.

70. McCullough, *Truman*, 402; Margaret Truman, *Harry S. Truman* (New York: William Morrow, 1973), 258. See also Joan Lee Bryniarski, "Against the Tide: Senate Opposition to the Internationalist Foreign Policy of Presidents Franklin D. Roosevelt and Harry S. Truman, 1943–1949" (PhD diss.; University of Maryland, 1972), 85–86.

71. Wheeler and Healy, *Yankee from the West*, 402–403.

72. Quoted in Anderson, "Senator Burton K. Wheeler," 321. The original, undated letter is in Joseph Kinsey Howard Papers, Montana Historical Society, Helena.

CHAPTER 15

1. Malone, Roeder, and Lang, *Montana*, 312–13. Not until Mike Mansfield's 1958 reelection did a winning Senate margin in Montana (76 percent) exceed Wheeler's win in 1940 (73 percent).

2. Wheeler speech, July 15, 1946, Wheeler Papers, MHS; Miles Romney letter to Murray, April 7, 1946, Murray Papers. For insight into Wheeler's feud with the New York newspaper *PM*, see the February 25, 1945, issue of the paper, which featured a three-page spread attacking Wheeler. See also John Gunther, *Inside USA* (New York: Harper & Brothers, 1947), 174–79.

3. Lester Loble letter to Mansfield, January 23, 1946; Mansfield to Loble, February 6, 1946; Mansfield letter to Charles McLean, January 23, 1946; McLean letter to Mansfield, January 26, 1946; telegram to Mansfield, March 4, 1946; Will E. Holbein letter to Mansfield, February 2, 1946, Lt. (junior grade) K. J. Crawford letter to Mansfield, February 8, 1946—all in Mike Mansfield Papers, University of Montana, Maureen and Mike Mansfield Library, Archives and Special Collections, Missoula, hereafter Mansfield Papers.

4. Mike Mansfield interview with the author, May 4, 2001.

5. J. Burke Clements letter to Wheeler, February 10, 1946, Wheeler Papers, MSU.

6. Wheeler letter to Desmond J. O'Neil, March 7, 1946, Wheeler Papers, MHS; *Miles City (Mont.) Star*, June 21, 1946.

7. Wheeler letter to Mearl L. Fagg, May 7, 1946, Wheeler Papers, MHS; Erickson letter to Mansfield, February 7, 1946, Mansfield Papers.

8. Joseph Kinsey Howard, "The Decline and Fall of Burton K. Wheeler," *Harper's*, March 1947, 226–36.

9. Joseph P. Kelly, "A Study of the Defeat of Senator Burton K. Wheeler in the 1946 Democratic Primary Election" (master's thesis, Montana State University, 1959), 15–17; *Missoulian*, January 5, 1999; Waldron and Wilson, *Atlas of Montana Elections*, 174.

10. Howard, "Decline and Fall of Burton K. Wheeler," 230; Craighead biography from the Barclay Craighead Papers, MHS. Clements was a remarkable political survivor, holding his state government job through four different administrations, Democratic and Republican,

dating back to 1928. Craighead was a close Wheeler associate for a quarter-century, serving on Wheeler's Senate staff, as secretary of the state Democratic Party, and head of the Montana office of the Federal Housing Administration. He helped organized the Wheeler for President Clubs in 1940. Craighead was also a financial partner with Ed Craney in several radio stations.

11. Clements letter to Wheeler, February 10, 1946, Wheeler Papers, MSU.

12. Wheeler and Healy, *Yankee from the West*, 402–403. See also Michael P. Malone's interview with Wheeler, June 9, 1970, transcript in Wheeler Papers, MSU; and Lester Loble, letter to Mike Mansfield, January 23, 1946, Mansfield Papers.

13. Spritzer, *Senator James E. Murray*, 151. For more on the politics of MVA, see Gunther, *Inside USA*, 183–89.

14. Spritzer, *Senator James E. Murray*, 144–55; Kelly, "Study of the Defeat of Senator Burton K. Wheeler," 17–18; Joseph Kinsey Howard, "Golden River: What's to Be Done about the Missouri?" *Harper's*, May 1945, 511–23; Oberdorfer, *Senator Mansfield*, 84–85.

15. Kelly, "Study of the Defeat of Senator Burton K. Wheeler," 20; Wheeler letter to Mearl Fagg, May 7, 1946, Wheeler Papers, MHS. Harry Truman was no fan of the Missouri Valley Authority, and when Murray introduced his bill in the Senate in 1944, Truman, as presiding officer, used his authority to refer the legislation to a committee that he knew was hostile to the idea. The proposal never got out of committee in the Senate.

16. *Miles City (Mont.) Star*, June 30, 1946; *Montana Standard* (Butte), July 12, 1946. See also Kelly, "Study of the Defeat of Senator Burton K. Wheeler," 34–38.

17. Kelly, "Study of the Defeat of Senator Burton K. Wheeler," 35; *Billings Gazette*, June 30, 1946.

18. "Veterans for Wheeler Committee" brochure, Wheeler Papers, MSU; Wheeler speech, undated, but apparently delivered the same day—July 7—that Wheeler spoke to the Montana Veterans of Foreign Wars convention in Helena. See also *Lewistown (Mont.) Daily News*, July 8, 1946.

19. Kelly, "Study of the Defeat of Senator Burton K. Wheeler," 36–39; "Veterans' Committee Against Wheeler" flier, Wheeler Papers, MHS. Chet Kinsey also served as secretary-treasurer of the Montana Council for Progressive Political Action, a group nearly always critical of Wheeler. Kinsey and Jerry O'Connell knew each other from their work with the council. The "Veterans for Wheeler Committee" was led by John B. Mahan, a Helena attorney who in 1958 would become national commander of the Veterans of Foreign Wars and later chair national veterans' committees for Presidents Kennedy and Johnson.

20. Philip Dray, *There Is Power in a Union* (New York: Doubleday, 2010), 472–74; Jack Barbash, "Why Unions Try to Influence Government," *Industrial and Labor Relations Review* 1, no. 1 (October 1947): 66–79; Steven Fraser, *Labor Will Rule: Sidney Hillman and the Rise of American Labor* (Ithaca, N.Y.: Cornell University Press, 1991), 432. Sidney Hillman played a pivotal role in shaping of the Democratic ticket during the party's 1944 convention when he provided a crucial endorsement of Harry Truman as Roosevelt's running mate. While potential vice presidential candidates were under consideration, Roosevelt told associates to make sure to "clear it with Sidney" before proceeding with a final selection. Hillman's influence later became an issue in the campaign, with Republican candidate Thomas Dewey alleging, "With the aid of Sidney Hillman . . . the Communists are seizing control of the New Deal . . . [in order] to control the Government of the United States."

21. Wheeler form letter on his campaign positions, May 31, 1946, copy in Craney Papers.

22. Jordan, *FDR, Dewey, and the Election of 1944*, 156–57, 203–204; McCullough, *Truman*, 310, 332; Wheeler and Healy, *Yankee from the West*, 402–403; Dray, *There Is Power in a Union*, 505; Robert H. Zieger, *The CIO: 1935–1955* (Chapel Hill: University of North Carolina Press, 1995), 253–93.

23. *Report of the Special Committee to Investigate Senatorial Campaign Contributions and Expenditures*, 80th Cong., 1st Sess. (Washington, D.C.: U.S. Government Printing Office), January 31, 1947, 5.

24. Spritzer, *Senators in Conflict*, 31–32; notes on Michael P. Malone interview with Wheeler, June 9, 1970, copy in the Wheeler Papers, MSU.

25. William Green letter to Wheeler, May 16, 1946, Wheeler Papers, MSU; quote in Kelly, "Study of the Defeat of Senator Burton K. Wheeler," 49–50. See also Spritzer, *Senators in Conflict*, 32.

26. Jeremy Brecher, *Strike!* (Oakland: PM Press, 2014), 216–17; Dray, *There Is Power in a Union*, 493–95; Malone, Roeder, and Lang, *Montana*, 329; *Chicago Tribune*, April 15, 1946.

27. McCullough, *Truman*, 498–506; *Chicago Tribune*, May 31, 1946.

28. Gordon Reid, "How They Beat Wheeler," *New Republic*, July 29, 1946, 99–100; *Kansas City Times*, July 12, 1946; *Butte Daily Post*, July 10, 1946.

29. Frank H. Jonas, "The Art of Political Dynamiting," *Western Political Science Quarterly* 10, no. 2 (June 1957): 374–91. See also Frank H. Jonas, *Political Dynamiting* (Salt Lake City: University of Utah Press, 1970), 6–15. Jonas writes that Walter Quigley, paid by the CIO, worked on Jim Murray's successful reelection campaign in 1948.

30. Wheeler letter to S. E. Most, April 24, 1946, Wheeler Papers, MHS; *The Plot against America* flier, copy in the Wheeler Papers, MHS; David George Kin, *The Plot against America: Senator Wheeler and the Forces behind Him* (Missoula: John E. Kennedy, 1946), 343, 190–91, 197. Wheeler enjoyed the company of attractive, outgoing, politically involved women. He and Lulu enjoyed enduring friendships, for example, with Alice Longworth Roosevelt and Cissy Patterson, the editor-publisher of the *Washington Times-Herald* newspaper, both of whom shared Wheeler's foreign policy views. Wheeler was, however, devoted to his wife, and there is no evidence that he was ever unfaithful to her during their fifty-five-year marriage.

31. "David Plotkin, 68, Writer and Editor," obituary, *New York Times*, April 1, 1968; David George Kin, *Women without Men: True Stories of Lesbian Love in Greenwich Village* (New York: Brookwood, 1958).

32. Wheeler letter to Estelle Hughes, May 2, 1946, and Wheeler letter to J. Edgar Hoover, April 22, 1946, Wheeler Papers, MHS.

33. *Report of the Special Committee*, 5.

34. *Butte Daily Post*, July 10, 1946; Spritzer, *Senators in Conflict*, 32.

35. *Report of the Special Committee*, 5–6.

36. Ibid., 6–8.

37. Ibid.

38. John E. Kennedy letter to CIO Political Action Committee, March 16, 1946, and Tilford E. Dudley letter to Kennedy, April 2, 1946. Both letters, as well as a telegram to Kennedy on the same subject, are in the CIO Political Action Committee Archives, Wayne State University, Walter P. Reuther Library, Detroit.

39. *Chicago Tribune*, July 13, 1946.

40. Seth Rosenfeld, *Subversives: The FBI's War on Student Radicals, and Reagan's Rise to Power* (New York: Farrar, Straus and Giroux, 2012), 120; Wheeler and Healy, *Yankee from the West*, 408.

41. Wheeler speech, July 15, 1946, copy in Wheeler Papers, MHS.

42. Kelly, "Study of the Defeat of Senator Burton K. Wheeler," 59–68; Waldron and Wilson, *Atlas of Montana Elections*, 180.

43. Oswald Garrison Villard letter to Wheeler, July 18, 1946, Wheeler Papers, MSH; Robert Wood letter to Wheeler, July 19, 1946, Wood Papers.

44. Wheeler letter to Norman Thomas, August 3, 1946, Thomas Papers.

45. Author interview with Edward Wheeler, May 4, 2001. See also Colman, *Mrs. Wheeler Goes to Washington*, 218–22.

46. Kelly, "Study of the Defeat of Senator Burton K. Wheeler," 74. For more on Zales Ecton's career, see *Bozeman Daily Chronicle*, May 22, 2011. Ecton's biography is contained in Merrill G. Burlingame and K. Ross Toole, *A History of Montana: Family and Personal History*, vol. 3 (New York: Lewis Historical Publishing, 1957), 15. Ecton's campaign against Erickson is dealt with by Timothy J. Carman in "Sen. Zales Ecton: A Product of Reaction" (master's thesis, Montana State University, 1971).

47. Cole, *Senator Gerald P. Nye*, 213–16.

48. Kelly, "Study of the Defeat of Senator Burton K. Wheeler," 54; *Daily Missoulian*, July 12, 1946.

49. Letter from J. A. O'Neill to H. J. Rahilly, July 11, 1946, Anaconda Company Correspondence, Butte-Silver Bow Archives, Butte, Montana.

EPILOGUE

1. "On the Record," *Time*, July 27, 1946, 16–17, and *Time*, April 15, 1940. See also Gordon Reid, "How They Beat Wheeler," *New Republic*, July 29, 1946, 99–101.

2. Gunther, *Inside USA*, 174–79.

3. Howard, "Decline and Fall of Burton K. Wheeler," 228.

4. Wheeler and Healy, *Yankee from the West*, 413–15; E. H. Trandum letter to Senator Murray, July 1, 1947, Murray Papers; Colman, *Mrs. Wheeler Goes to Washington*, 223–24.

5. *Washington Post*, February 21, 1955; Amanda Smith, *Newspaper Titan: The Infamous Life and Monumental Times of Cissy Patterson* (New York: Alfred A. Knopf, 2011), 503, 539; Wheeler and Healy, *Yankee from the West*, 415; "You Can't Go Home Again," *Time*, May 31, 1954, 20. The Wheeler firm's representation of the Fairmount Corporation in a 1951 radio license transfer application before the Federal Communication Commission (FCC) caught the attention of Montana native Jim Rowe, a confidant of presidents from Roosevelt to Lyndon Johnson and a close friend of Mike Mansfield. Fairmount, which sought to obtain the broadcast license for Great Falls radio station KFBB, was a wholly owned subsidiary of the Anaconda Company. Rowe told Mansfield that "our friend" [Wheeler] was providing legal advice in the case. When news of the Fairmount application surfaced in Montana it ignited a mini-firestorm of protest. One critic told the FCC that giving Anaconda a radio station "would simply be tightening its stranglehold on us" and "would be entirely contrary to the public interest in Montana." Labor and liberal farm groups were also upset that Wheeler's law firm was involved in the matter, and Wheeler must have known that his involvement could become an issue. By 1954, however, it is

likely that he no longer cared about the public reaction. Fairmount—or Anaconda—eventually withdrew the application but not before being forced to publicly disclose more than had ever been known about its interlocking directorships and ownership of Montana newspapers. Historian Dennis Swibold has written that the entire affair left Anaconda shut out of broadcast ownership and "stuck with its newspapers, with their leaking bottom lines, and their credibility groaning under decades of political baggage." Ironically, in part because of Wheeler's involvement in the case—Swibold says that from a political perspective Anaconda "could hardly have made a poorer choice" picking its legal counsel—his onetime nemesis suffered a level of negative public scrutiny that thirty years earlier would have been impossible to contemplate. Swibold, *Copper Chorus*, 290–96.

6. Wheeler letters to Wellington Rankin, April 15 and April 21, 1958, copies in author's collection; Wheeler letter to W. H. "Bill" Tulley, October 15, 1954, Murray Papers; Wheeler to Max Lowenthal, May 7, 1954, Lowenthal Papers; Wheeler to John T. Flynn, April 26, 1954, Wheeler Papers, MSU; Waldron and Wilson, *Atlas of Montana Elections*, 205. See also *Great Falls Tribune*, October 30, 1954; and *Glasgow (Mont.) Courier*, October 21, 1954.

7. Murray letter to Matthew J. Connelly, February 8, 1951; Truman letter to Murray, February 10, 1951—both in Truman Papers, Harry S. Truman Presidential Library, Independence, Missouri.

8. Francis R. Valeo, *Mike Mansfield: Majority Leader* (Armonk, N.Y.: M. E. Sharpe, 1999), 31. On another occasion LBJ told a *Newsweek* reporter that "Mike [Mansfield] is a cross between Jeannette Rankin and Burton K. Wheeler and I don't need advice from either of them." Obendorfer, *Senator Mansfield*, 225.

9. Frances Sayler letter to Max Lowenthal, January 7, 1955, Lowenthal Papers; Marion Wheeler Scott interview.

10. Wheeler letter to Max Lowenthal, June 21, 1954, Lowenthal Papers; France Wheeler letter to Lowenthal, December 4, 1954, Lowenthal Papers. "Frankly, I don't know McCarthy," Wheeler wrote to Max Lowenthal in 1953. "I have never been impressed with him. I know nothing of his honesty and integrity." But Wheeler also worried about what he believed was bipartisan naïveté about the dangers of Soviet and Chinese communism. "I was opposed to Roosevelt's foreign policy," Wheeler wrote to Lowenthal, "I was opposed to Truman's foreign policy, and I am opposed to the foreign policy of this [Eisenhower's] administration."

11. Wheeler letter to Max Lowenthal, June 1, 1951, Lowenthal Papers; *Hearings before the Committee on Un-American Activities, U.S. House of Representatives*, 81st Cong., 2nd Sess., July 12, 13, 14 and August 8, 1950 (Washington, D.C.: U.S. Government Printing Office), 2753; Walter Goodman, *The Committee: The Extraordinary Career of the House Committee on Un-American Activities* (New York: Farrar, Straus and Giroux, 1968), 373–74.

12. Frances Sayler letter to Max Lowenthal, March 11, 1955, Lowenthal Papers; transcript of Frances Sayler's testimony before the House Un-American Activities Committee, March 2, 1955, copy in Records of the House Committee on Un-American Activities, National Archives and Records Administration, Washington, D.C., 121–27, copy in author's collection; Wheeler letter to Max Lowenthal, November 3, 1958, Lowenthal Papers; Gloria Sayler, correspondence with the author, January 1, 2014. Frances's daughter, Gloria Sayler, recalled that the United Electrical, Radio and Machine Workers of America, for which her mother worked, "was … widely considered the Communist union." Both her parents had been involved in the Progressive Party

in 1948. Frances's husband, Alan Sayler, was also the Michigan chair of the 1948 Progressive Party presidential campaign of Henry Wallace. "My father's belief was that [the HUAC subpoena of Frances] was part of the right wing/capitalist retaliation against unions for the gains they made before and after World War II," Gloria Sayler wrote to me. "The timing of the hearing before HUAC was just before a major union contract vote on the East Coast that involved UE workers. His thought was that they hoped to have headlines about 'Senator's Daughter and UE organizer questioned before HUAC' to disrupt the vote."

13. Philip Roth, *The Plot against America* (Boston: Houghton Mifflin, 2004); *New York Times*, October 3, 2004.

14. Frances Sayler to Max Lowenthal, September 24, 1956, Lowenthal Papers; Wheeler and Healy, *Yankee from the West*, 430; Cabell Phillips review in *New York Times*, December 9, 1962. See also Anderson, "Senator Burton K. Wheeler," 336; and Wheeler letter to Norman Thomas, February 4, 1963—both in Thomas Papers.

15. Colman, *Mrs. Wheeler Goes to Washington*, 240; Wheeler letter to Max Lowenthal, September 20, 1962, Lowenthal Papers; Wheeler letter to Wellington Rankin, September 25, 1962, Wheeler Papers, MSU; Edward Cooper letter to Max Lowenthal, September 18, 1962, Lowenthal Papers.

16. *New York Times*, January 8, 1973; *Washington Post*, January 8, 1973. Wheeler was buried next to his wife at Washington's Rock Creek Cemetery.

17. Anderson, "Senator Burton K. Wheeler," 331, 334. Several pre-war noninterventionists did repudiate their onetime views. "I was one hundred percent wrong in believing we could stay out of the Second World War," Massachusetts Republican Henry Cabot Lodge Jr. said in a 1952 interview with the *Saturday Evening Post*. "But that was my first incarnation. I am an older and wiser man—at least I hope I am." Michigan Republican senator Arthur Vandenberg, a onetime staunch isolationist, famously embraced bipartisan internationalism in a Senate speech in 1945 declaring that the country had to stop "partisan politics at the water's edge."

18. Wheeler interview, CCOH, pt. 4, 3–4; Justus D. Doenecke, *Not to the Swift: The Old Isolationist in the Cold War Era* (Lewisburg, Pa.: Bucknell University Press, 1979), 243. At Jeannette Rankin's ninetieth birthday celebration in 1970, Wheeler reconnected with former Alaska senator Ernest Gruening, a friend from the 1924 Progressive Party campaign, who cast one of only two votes against the 1964 Gulf of Tonkin resolution that became Lyndon Johnson's ticket to escalate U.S. involvement in Southeast Asia. The two antiwar dissenters praised each other's battles against war, with Gruening calling Wheeler's peace efforts prior to Pearl Harbor a "courageous" and "gallant attempt."

19. *Milwaukee Journal*, June 29, 1971.

20. Wheeler and Healy, *Yankee from the West*, 399; Doenecke, *Not to the Swift*, 247.

21. Chalmers Johnson, *The Sorrows of Empire: Militarism, Secrecy, and the End of the Republic* (New York: Henry Holt, 2004), 1–14; Drake, *Education of an Anti-Imperialist*, 458. Wheeler authored the last op-ed piece of his life in 1973, arguing against congressional efforts to force Richard Nixon to turn over tape recordings related to the Watergate incident. Invoking Justices Hughes and Brandeis during the court-packing controversy and their refusal to testify before a congressional committee, Wheeler argued, as Nixon did, that, short of an impeachment process, "the request of Congress for the White House tapes may constitute a . . . threat to the integrity of the decisional processes of the President." Wheeler badly misjudged the import

of the Watergate crimes and Nixon's tape recordings when he predicted that a "constitutional confrontation" had been created over tapes that "in all likelihood . . . will shed little, if any, light on the Watergate controversy." The Supreme Court's unanimous decision, of course, forced Nixon to surrender the tapes, which provided conclusive proof of the president's own involvement in the Watergate coverup and led directly to his resignation.

22. Wheeler and Healy, *Yankee from the West*, 428.

23. Ibid., 429; Mansfield interview with the author.

BIBLIOGRAPHY

MANUSCRIPT COLLECTIONS

Arizona State Library, Archives & Public Records, Phoenix
    Ernest McFarland Papers
Boise State University, Albertsons Library, Special Collections and Archives
    D. Worth Clark Papers
Butte–Silver Bow Public Archives, Butte, Montana
    Anaconda Company Correspondence
Franklin D. Roosevelt Presidential Library, Hyde Park, New York
    Franklin D. Roosevelt Papers
Harry S. Truman Presidential Library, Independence, Missouri
    Harry Truman Papers
Harvard College Library, Houghton Library
    Oswald Garrison Villard Papers
Herbert Hoover Presidential Library, West Branch, Iowa
    Gerald P. Nye Papers
    Walter Trohan Papers
    Robert Wood Papers
Hoover Institution, Stanford University
    America First Committee Papers
Library of Congress
    William E. Borah Papers
    Thomas Corcoran Papers
    Harold L. Ickes Papers
    Robert M. La Follette Papers
    Thomas J. Walsh and John Edward Erickson Papers
Montana Historical Society, Helena
    Edward Craney Papers
    Sam Ford Papers
    Joseph Kinsey Howard Papers
    Jeannette Rankin Papers
    Wellington Rankin Papers
    Burton K. Wheeler Papers
Montana State University (MSU) Library, Special Collections and Archives, Bozeman
    Elizabeth Wheeler Colman Papers
    Marion Wheeler Scott Papers
    Burton K. Wheeler Papers

National Archives and Records Administration, Washington, D.C.
  Records of the House Committee on Un-American Activities
  Records of the Senate Committee on Interstate and Foreign Commerce
New York Public Library, Manuscripts and Archives Division, Stephen A. Schwarzman Build-
  ing, New York City
  Norman Thomas Papers
University of California, Berkeley, Bancroft Library
  Hiram Johnson Papers
University of Minnesota Libraries, Archives and Special Collections, Elmer L. Andersen
  Library, Minneapolis
  Max Lowenthal Papers
University of Montana, Maureen and Mike Mansfield Library, Archives and Special Collec-
  tions, Missoula
  Mike Mansfield Papers
  James E. Murray Papers
University of Oregon Libraries, Special Collections and University Archives, Eugene
  John Flynn Papers
University of Virginia Library, Special Collections, Charlottesville
  Homer Cummings Papers
Wayne State University, Walter P. Reuther Library, Detroit
  CIO Political Action Committee Archives
Yale University Library, Sterling Memorial Library, New Haven, Conn.
  John Collier Papers

GOVERNMENT DOCUMENTS

Hearing before the Committee on Indian Affairs United States Senate on S. 2755, 73rd Cong., 2nd
  Sess. Washington, D.C.: U.S. Government Printing Office, 1934.
Hearings before the Committee on Un-American Activities, United States House of Representatives,
  81st Cong., 2nd Sess. Washington, D.C.: U.S. Government Printing Office, 1950.
Hearings before the Committee on Interstate Commerce United States Senate on S.1725, 74th Cong.,
  1st Sess. Washington, D.C.: U.S. Government Printing Office, 1935.
*Hearings before the Select Committee on Investigation of Charges against Senator Burton K. Wheeler
  of Montana.* 68th Cong., 1st Sess. Washington, D.C.: Government Printing Office, 1924.
Hearings before the Select Committee on the Investigation of the Attorney General. 11 vols. 68th
  Cong., 1st Sess. Washington, D.C.: Government Printing Office, 1924.
Peace and War: United States Foreign Policy, 1931–1941. Washington, D.C.: U.S. Government
  Printing Office, 1943.
Report of the Special Committee to Investigate Senatorial Campaign Contributions and Expenditures,
  80th Congress, 1st Sess. Washington, D.C.: U.S. Government Printing Office, 1947.

BOOKS

Adams, Samuel Hopkins. *Incredible Era: The Life and Times of Warren Gamaliel Harding.* Boston:
  Houghton Mifflin, 1939.
Adler, Selig. *The Isolationist Impulse: Its Twentieth Century Reaction.* New York: Free Press, 1957.

———. *The Uncertain Giant, 1921–1941: American Foreign Policy between the Wars*. New York: Macmillan, 1965.

Allen, Frederick Lewis. *Only Yesterday; An Informal History of the Nineteen-Twenties*. New York: Harper & Row, 1964.

Alsop, Joseph, and Turner Catledge. *The 168 Days*. Garden City, N.Y.: Doubleday, Doran, 1938.

Alter, Jonathan. *The Defining Moment: FDR's Hundred Days and the Triumph of Hope*. New York: Simon & Schuster, 2006.

Anderson, Benjamin M. *Economics and the Public Welfare: A Financial and Economic History of the United States, 1914–1946*. Indianapolis: Liberty Press, 1979.

Arkes, Hadley. *The Return of George Sutherland: Restoring a Jurisprudence of Natural Rights*. Princeton: Princeton University Press, 1994.

Ashby, LeRoy. *The Spearless Leader: Senator Borah and the Progressive Movement in the 1920's*. Urbana: University of Illinois Press, 1972.

———. *William Jennings Bryan: Champion of Democracy*. Boston: Twayne, 1987.

Badger, Anthony J. *FDR: The First Hundred Days*. New York: Hill and Wang, 2008.

Bailey, Thomas A., and Paul B. Ryan. *Hitler vs. Roosevelt: The Undeclared Naval War*. New York: Free Press, 1979.

Baker, Leonard. *Back to Back: The Duel between FDR and the Supreme Court*. New York: Macmillan, 1967.

Baker, Ross K. *Friend and Foe in the U.S. Senate*. New York: Free Press, 1980.

Ball, Howard. *Hugo L. Black: Cold Steel Warrior*. New York: Oxford University Press, 1990.

Barkley, Alben W. *That Reminds Me*. Garden City, N.Y.: Doubleday, 1954.

Barnard, Harry. *Independent Man: The Life of Senator James Couzens*. New York: Scribner, 1958.

Bates, J. Leonard. *The Origin of Teapot Dome: Progressives, Parties and Petroleum, 1909–1921*. Urbana: University of Illinois Press, 1963.

———. *Senator Thomas J. Walsh of Montana: Law and Public Affairs, from TR to FDR*. Urbana: University of Illinois Press, 1999.

Beard, Charles A. *President Roosevelt and the Coming of the War, 1941: A Study in Appearances and Realities*. New Haven: Yale University Press, 1948.

Belknap, Michael R. *American Political Trials*. Rev. ed. Westport: Greenwood Press, 1994.

Bennett, David H. *Demagogues in the Depression: American Radicals and the Union Party*. New Brunswick, N.J.: Rutgers University Press, 1969.

Bennett, M. Todd. *One World, Big Screen: Hollywood, the Allies and World War II*. Chapel Hill: University of North Carolina Press, 2012.

Berg, A. Scott. *Lindbergh*. New York: G. P. Putnam's Sons, 1998.

Billington, David P., and Donald C. Jackson. *Big Dams in the New Deal Era: A Confluence of Engineering and Politics*. Norman: University of Oklahoma Press, 2006.

Blackorby, Edward C. *Prairie Rebel: The Public Life of William Lemke*. Lincoln: University of Nebraska Press, 1963.

Blum, John Morton. *From the Morgenthau Diaries*, vol. 1, *Years of Crisis, 1928–1938*. Boston: Houghton Mifflin, 1959.

Botkin, Jane Little. *Frank Little and the IWW: The Blood That Stained an American Family*. Norman: University of Oklahoma Press, 2017.

Brands, H. W. *Traitor to His Class: The Privileged Life and Radical Presidency of Franklin Delano Roosevelt*. New York: Doubleday, 2008.

Brecher, Jeremy. *Strike!* Rev. ed. Oakland: PM Press, 2014.

Brennan, John A. *Silver and the First New Deal*. Reno: University of Nevada Press, 1969.

Brinkley, Alan. *The Publisher: Henry Luce and His American Century*. New York: Alfred A. Knopf, 2010.

———. *Voices of Protest: Huey Long, Father Coughlin, and the Great Depression*. New York: Alfred A. Knopf, 1982.

Brown, Anthony Cave. *The Last Hero: Wild Bill Donovan*. New York: Times Books, 1982.

Burner, David. *Herbert Hoover: The Public Life*. New York: Alfred A. Knopf, 1979.

———. *The Politics of Provincialism: The Democratic Party in Transition, 1918–1932*. New York: Alfred A. Knopf, 1968.

Bryant, Jr., Keith J. *Alfalfa Bill Murray*. Norman: University of Oklahoma Press, 1968.

Burlingame, Merrill G., and K. Ross Toole, editors. *A History of Montana*, vol. 1. New York: Lewis Historical Publishing, 1957.

Burns, James MacGregor. *Roosevelt: The Lion and the Fox*. New York: Harcourt, Brace & World, 1956.

———. *Roosevelt: The Soldier of Freedom: 1940–1945*. New York: Harcourt Brace Jovanovich, 1970.

Burns, James MacGregor, and Susan Dunn. *The Three Roosevelts: Patrician Leaders Who Transformed America*. New York: Atlantic Monthly Press, 2001.

Burris, William C. *The Senate Rejects a Judge: A Study of the John J. Parker Case*. Chapel Hill: North Carolina University Press, 1962.

Byrd, Robert C. *The Senate, 1789–1989: Addresses on the History of the United States Senate*. Washington, D.C.: U.S. Government Printing Office, 1991.

Byrnes, James F. *Speaking Frankly*. New York: Harper & Brothers, 1947.

Calvert, Jerry W. *The Gibraltar: Socialism and Labor in Butte, Montana, 1895–1920*. Helena: Montana Historical Society Press, 1988.

Cannadine, David. *Mellon: An American Life*. New York: Alfred A. Knopf, 2007.

Capra, Frank. *The Name above the Title*. New York: Macmillan, 1971.

Carlson, John Roy. *Under Cover: My Four Years in the Nazi Underworld of America: The Amazing Revelation of How Axis Agents and Our Enemies within Are Plotting to Destroy the United States*. Philadelphia: Blakiston, 1943.

Caro, Robert. *The Years of Lyndon Johnson: Master of the Senate*. New York: Knopf, 2002.

Carter, John F. *American Messiahs*. New York: Simon & Schuster, 1935.

Casey, Steven. *Cautious Crusade: Franklin D. Roosevelt, American Public Opinion, and the War against Nazi Germany*. New York: Oxford University Press, 2001.

Ceplair, Larry, and Steven Englund. *The Inquisition in Hollywood: Politics in the Film Community, 1900–1960*. Garden City, N.Y.: Anchor Press/Doubleday, 1980.

Chadwin, Mark Lincoln. *The Hawks of World War II*. Chapel Hill: University of North Carolina Press, 1968.

Charles, Douglas M. *J. Edgar Hoover and the Anti-interventionists: FBI Political Surveillance and the Rise of the Domestic Security State, 1939–1945*. Columbus: Ohio State University Press, 2007.

Chase, A. W. *Dr. Chase's Recipes, or, Information for Everybody*. Ann Arbor: R. A. Beal, 1874.

Childs, Marquis. *I Write from Washington*. New York: Harper & Brothers, 1942.

Christensen, Lawrence O., William E. Foley, and Gary Kremer, eds. *Dictionary of Missouri Biography*. Columbia: University of Missouri Press, 1999.

Churchill, Winston S. *The Second World War: The Grand Alliance*. Boston: Houghton Mifflin, 1951.

———. *The Second World War: Their Finest Hour*. Boston: Houghton Mifflin, 1949.

Clarke, Jeanne Nienaber. *Roosevelt's Warrior: Harold L. Ickes and the New Deal*. Baltimore: Johns Hopkins University Press, 1996.

Clifford, J. Garry, and Samuel R. Spencer Jr. *The First Peacetime Draft*. Lawrence: University Press of Kansas, 1986

Coán, Blair. *The Red Web: An Underground Political History of the United States from 1918 to the Present Time, Showing How Close the Government Is to Collapse, and Told in an Understandable Way*. Chicago: Northwest Publishing, 1925.

Cohen, Adam. *Nothing to Fear: FDR's Inner Circle and the Hundred Days That Created Modern America*. New York: Penguin Press, 2009.

Cole, Wayne S. *America First: The Battle against Intervention, 1940–1941*. Madison: University of Wisconsin Press, 1953.

———. *Charles A. Lindbergh and the Battle against American Intervention in World War II*. New York: Harcourt Brace Jovanovich, 1974.

———. *Roosevelt and the Isolationists, 1932–1945*. Lincoln: University of Nebraska Press, 1983.

———. *Senator Gerald P. Nye and American Foreign Relations*. Minneapolis: University of Minnesota Press, 1962.

Colman, Elizabeth Wheeler. *Mrs. Wheeler Goes to Washington: Mrs Burton Kendall Wheeler, Wife of the Senator from Montana*. Helena, Mont.: Falcon Press, 1989.

Connally, Tom, and Alfred Steinberg. *My Name Is Tom Connally*. New York: Thomas Y. Crowell, 1954.

Corrigan, Gordon. *The Second World War: A Military History*. New York: St. Martin's Press, 2011.

Cort, John C. *Dreadful Conversions: The Making of Catholic Socialist*. New York: Fordham University Press, 2003.

Crawford, Kenneth G. *The Pressure Boys: The Inside Story of Lobbying in America*. New York: Julian Messner, 1939.

Cull, Nicholas John. *Selling War: The British Propaganda Campaign against American "Neutrality" in World War II*. New York: Oxford University Press, 1995.

Culver, John C., and John Hyde. *American Dreamer: A Life of Henry Wallace*. New York: W. W. Norton, 2000.

Dallek, Robert. *Democrat and Diplomat: The Life of William E. Dodd*. New York: Oxford University Press, 1968.

———. *Franklin D. Roosevelt and American Foreign Policy, 1932–1945*. New York: Oxford University Press, 1979.

Daugherty, Harry M., and Thomas Dixon. *The Inside Story of the Harding Tragedy*. New York: Churchill, 1932.

Davis, Kenneth S. *FDR: Into the Storm, 1937–1940*. New York: Random House, 1993.

———. *FDR: The Beckoning of Destiny, 1882–1928*. New York: G. P. Putnam's Sons, 1972.

———. *FDR: The New Deal Years, 1933–1937*. New York: Random House, 1986.

———. *FDR: The New York Years, 1928–1933*. New York: Random House, 199.

———. *FDR: The War President, 1940–1943*. New York: Random House, 2000.

———. *The Hero: Charles A. Lindbergh and the American Dream*. Garden City, N.Y.: Doubleday, 1959.

Davis, Margaret Leslie. *Dark Side of Fortune: Triumph and Scandal in the Life of Oil Tycoon Edward L. Doheny*. Berkeley: University of California Press, 1998.

Dean, John W. *Warren G. Harding*. New York: Times Books, 2004.

Degregorio, William A. *The Complete Book of U.S. Presidents*. Fort Lee, N.J.: Barricade Books, 2001.

Deloria, Vine, Jr., ed. *American Indian Policy in the Twentieth Century*. Norman: University of Oklahoma Press, 1985.

———. *The Indian Reorganization Act: Congresses and Bills*. Norman: University of Oklahoma Press, 2002,

Dennis, Lawrence, and Maximilian St. George. *A Trial on Trial*. Torrance, Calif.: Institute for Historical Review, 1984.

Dewey, John. *The Later Works, 1925–1953*, vol. 6, *1931–1932*. Edited by Jo Ann Boydston. Carbondale: Southern Illinois University Press, 1985.

Dill, Clarence C. *Where Water Falls*. Spokane: Clarence D. Dill, 1970.

Dillon, Mary Earhart. *Wendell Willkie*. Philadelphia: J. B. Lippincott, 1952.

Doenecke, Justus D., editor. *In Danger Undaunted: The Anti-Interventionist Movement of 1940–1941 as Revealed in the Papers of the America First Committee*. Stanford, Calif.: Hoover Institution Press, 1990.

———. *Nothing Less Than War: A New History of America's Entry into World War I*. Lexington: University Press of Kentucky, 2011.

———. *Not to the Swift: The Old Isolationists in the Cold War Era*. Lewisburg, Pa.: Bucknell University Press, 1979.

———. *Storm on the Horizon: The Challenge to American Intervention 1939–1941*. Lanham, Md.: Rowman & Littlefield, 2000.

Douglas, Paul H. *In the Fullness of Time: The Memoirs of Paul H. Douglas*. New York: Harcourt Brace Jovanovich, 1971.

Downey, Kirstin. *The Woman behind the New Deal: The Life of Frances Perkins, FDR's Secretary of Labor and His Moral Conscience*. New York: Doubleday, 2009.

Drake, Richard. *The Education of an Anti-Imperialist: Robert La Follette and U.S. Expansion*. Madison: University of Wisconsin Press, 2013.

Dray, Philip. *There Is Power in a Union*. New York, Doubleday, 2010.

Drury, Allen. *A Senate Journal: 1943–1945*. New York: McGraw-Hill, 1963.

Dubofsky, Melvyn. *We Shall Be All: A History of the IWW, the Industrial Workers of the World*. Chicago: Quadrangle Books, 1969.

Dubofsky, Melvyn, and Warren Van Tine. *John L. Lewis: A Biography*. New York: Quadrangle, 1977.

Dunn, Susan. *1940: FDR, Willkie, Lindbergh, Hitler: The Election amid the Storm*. New Haven: Yale University Press, 2013.

———. *Roosevelt's Purge: How FDR Fought to Change the Democratic Party*. Cambridge: Harvard University Press, 2010.

Emmons, David E. *The Butte Irish: Class and Ethnicity in an American Mining Town, 1875–1925*. Urbana: University of Illinois Press, 1990.

Erickson, Nels. *The Gentleman from North Dakota: Lynn J. Frazier.* Bismarck: State Historical Society of North Dakota, 1986.

Farley, James A. *Behind the Ballots: The Personal History of a Politician.* New York: Harcourt, Brace, 1938.

———. *Jim Farley's Story: The Roosevelt Years.* New York: McGraw-Hill, 1948.

Feis, Herbert. *The Road to Pearl Harbor.* Princeton: Princeton University Press, 1950.

Ferrell, Robert H. *Dear Bess: The Letters from Harry to Bess Truman, 1910–1959.* New York: W. W. Norton, 1983.

———. *Harry S. Truman: A Life.* Columbia: University of Missouri Press, 1994.

———, ed. *Off the Record: The Private Papers of Harry S. Truman.* New York: Harper & Row, 1980.

Finan, Christopher M. *Alfred E. Smith: The Happy Warrior.* New York: Hill and Wang, 2002.

Fisher, Louis. *Presidential War Power.* Lawrence: University Press of Kansas, 2004.

Fite, Gilbert C. *George N. Peek and the Fight for Farm Parity.* Norman: University of Oklahoma Press, 1954.

Fixico, Donald L. *Bureau of Indian Affairs.* Santa Barbara, Calif.: Greenwood, 2012.

Flake, Kathleen. *The Politics of American Religious Identity: The Seating of Senator Reed Smoot, Mormon Apostle.* Chapel Hill: University of North Carolina Press, 2004.

Fleming, Thomas. *The New Dealers' War: FDR and the War within World War II.* New York: Basic Books, 2001.

Fraser, Steven. *Labor Will Rule: Sidney Hillman and the Rise of American Labor.* Ithaca, N.Y.: Cornell University Press, 1993.

Freidel, Frank. *Franklin D. Roosevelt: Launching the New Deal.* Boston: Little, Brown, 1973.

———. *Franklin D. Roosevelt: The Ordeal.* Boston: Little, Brown, 1954.

———. *Franklin D. Roosevelt: The Triumph.* Boston: Little, Brown, 1956.

Fritz, Harry W., Mary Murphy, and Robert R. Swartout Jr., editors. *Montana Legacy: Essays on History, People, and Place.* Helena: Montana Historical Society Press, 2002.

Funigiello, Philip J. *Toward a National Power Policy: The New Deal and the Electric Utility Industry.* Pittsburgh: University of Pittsburgh Press, 1973.

Gabler, Neal. *Winchell: Gossip, Power and the Culture of Celebrity.* New York: Alfred A. Knopf, 1994.

Galbraith, John Kenneth. *The Great Crash 1929.* New York: Pelican, 1961.

Gallup, George. *The Gallup Poll: Public Opinion, 1935–1971,* vol. 1, *1938–1948.* New York: Random House, 1972.

Genovese, Michael A. *The Presidential Dilemma: Revisiting Democratic Leadership in the American System.* 3rd ed. New Brunswick, N.J.: Transaction, 2011.

Genovese, Michael A., and Victoria A. Farrar-Myers, eds. *Corruption and American Politics.* Amherst, Mass.: Cambria Press, 2010.

Gentry, Curt. *J. Edgar Hoover: The Man and the Secrets.* New York: Plume, 1992.

Giglio, James N. *H. M. Daugherty and the Politics of Expediency.* Kent, Ohio: Kent State University Press, 1978.

Gilbert, Martin. *Churchill and America.* New York: Free Press, 2005.

———. *Winston S. Churchill: Finest Hour, 1939–1941.* Boston: Houghton Mifflin, 1983.

Glad, Betty. *Pittman: The Tragedy of a Senate Insider.* New York: Columbia University Press, 1986.

Glasscock, C. B. *The War of the Copper Kings: Builders of Butte and Wolves of Wall Street.* New York: Grosset & Dunlap, 1935.

Glynn, Gary. *Montana's Home Front during World War II*. Missoula: Big Elk Books, 2011.

Godfrey, Matthew C. *Religion, Politics, and Sugar: The Mormon Church, the Federal Government, and the Utah-Idaho Sugar Company, 1907–1921*. Logan: Utah State University Press, 2007.

Goodman, Walter. *The Committee: The extraordinary Career of the House Committee on Un-American Activities*. New York: Farrar, Straus and Giroux, 1968.

Gordon, Linda. *The Second Coming of the KKK: The Ku Klux Klan of the 1920s and the American Political Tradition*. New York: Liveright, 2017.

Greenberg, David. *Calvin Coolidge: The American Presidents Series: The 30th President, 1923–1929*. New York: Times Books, 2006.

Gregory, Ross. *America 1941: A Nation at the Crossroads*. New York: Free Press, 1989.

Grossman, Mark. *Political Corruption in America: An Encyclopedia of Scandals, Power, and Greed*. Santa Barbara, Calif.: ABC-CLIO, 2003.

Gugin, Linda C., and James E. St. Clair. *Sherman Minton: New Deal Senator, Cold War Justice*. Indianapolis: Indiana Historical Society, 1997.

Gunther, John. *Inside USA*. New York: Harper & Brothers, 1947.

———. *Roosevelt in Retrospect: A Profile in History*. New York: Harper & Brothers, 1950.

Gutfeld, Arnon. *Montana's Agony: Years of War and Hysteria, 1917–1921*. Gainesville: University of Florida Press, 1979.

Hair, William Ivy. *The Kingfish and His Realm*. Baton Rouge: Louisiana State University Press, 1991.

Halberstam, David. *The Fifties*. New York: Villard Books, 1993.

———. *The Powers That Be*. New York: Alfred A. Knopf, 1979.

Hall, Kermit L., ed. *Oxford Companion to the Supreme Court of the United States*. New York: Oxford University Press, 2005.

Hamby, Alonzo L. *For the Survival of Democracy: Franklin Roosevelt and the World Crisis of the 1930s*. New York: Free Press, 2004.

———. *Man of the People: A Life of Harry S. Truman*. New York: Oxford, 1995.

Hammett, Dashiell. *The Novels of Dashiell Hammett*. New York: Alfred A. Knopf, 1965.

Hannigan, Dave. *De Valera in America: The Rebel President and the Making of Irish Independence*. New York: Palgrave Macmillan, 2010.

Harbaugh, William H. *Lawyer's Lawyer: The Life of John W. Davis*. New York: Oxford University Press, 1973.

Hardeman, D. B., and Donald C. Bacon. *Rayburn: A Biography*. Austin: Texas Monthly Press, 1987.

Harrington, Dale M. *Mystery Man: William Rhodes Davis, Nazi Agent of Influence*. Washington, D.C.: Brassey's, 2001.

Hawley, E. W. *The New Deal and the Problem of Monopoly*. Princeton: Princeton University Press, 1966.

Hendel, Samuel. *Charles Evans Hughes and the Supreme Court*. New York: Kings Crown Press, 1951.

Herman, Arthur. *Joseph McCarthy: Reexamining the Life and Legacy of America's Most Hated Senator*. New York: Free Press, 2000.

Herring, George W. *From Colony to Superpower: U.S. Foreign Relations since 1776*. New York: Oxford, 2008.

Hines, Gordon. *Alfalfa Bill: An Intimate Biography.* Oklahoma City: Oklahoma Press, 1932.

Holbo, Paul Sothe, ed. *Isolationism and Interventionism, 1932–1941.* Chicago: Rand McNally, 1967.

Holmes, Krys, Sue Dailey, and Dave Walter. *Montana: Stories of the Land.* Helena: Montana Historical Society Press, 2008.

Hoopes, Roy. *Ralph Ingersoll: A Biography.* New York: Atheneum, 1985.

Hoover, Herbert. *Addresses upon the American Road, 1933–1938.* New York: Scribner, 1938.

———. *The Memoirs of Herbert Hoover: The Cabinet and the Presidency, 1920–1933.* New York: Macmillan, 1951.

———. *Public Papers of the Presidents of the United States: Herbert Hoover, 1932–33.* Washington, D.C.: U.S. Government Printing Office, 1977.

Horne, Gerald. *The Color of Fascism: Lawrence Dennis, Racial Passing, and the Rise of Right-Wing Extremism in the United States.* New York: New York University Press, 2006.

Horowitz, David A. *Beyond Left and Right: Insurgency and the Establishment.* Urbana: University of Illinois Press, 1997.

Hotta, Eri. *Japan 1941: Countdown to Infamy.* New York, Alfred A. Knopf, 2013.

Howard, Joseph Kinsey. *Montana: High, Wide and Handsome.* New Haven: Yale University Press, 1959.

———, ed. *Montana Margins: A State Anthology.* New Haven: Yale University Press, 1946.

Hull, Cordell. *The Memoirs of Cordell Hull.* New York: Macmillan, 1948.

Ickes, Harold L. *The Secret Diary of Harold L. Ickes,* vol. 1, *The First Thousand Days: 1933–1936.* New York: Simon & Schuster, 1953.

———. *The Secret Diary of Harold L. Ickes,* vol. 2, *The Inside Struggle, 1936–1939.* New York: Simon & Schuster, 1954.

———. *The Secret Diary of Harold L. Ickes,* vol. 3, *The Lowering Clouds, 1939–1941.* New York: Simon & Schuster, 1954.

Irish, Kerry E. *Clarence C. Dill: The Life of a Western Politician.* Pullman: Washington State University Press, 2000.

Irwin, Douglas A. *Peddling Protectionism: Smoot-Hawley and the Great Depression.* Princeton: Princeton University Press, 2011.

Israel, Fred L. *Nevada's Key Pittman.* Lincoln: University of Nebraska Press, 1963.

Isser, Steve. *Electricity Restructuring in the United States: Markets and Policy from the 1978 Energy Act to the Present.* New York: Cambridge University Press, 2015.

Jeansonne, Glen. *Gerald L. K. Smith: Minister of Hate.* Baton Rouge: Louisiana State University Press, 1988.

Johnson, Chalmers. *The Sorrows of Empire: Militarism, Secrecy, and the End of the Republic.* New York: Henry Holt, 2004.

Johnson, Claudius O. *Borah of Idaho.* Seattle: University of Washington Press, 1967.

Johnson, Jeffrey A. *They Are All Red out Here: Socialist Politics in the Pacific Northwest, 1895–1925.* Norman: University of Oklahoma Press, 2008.

Johnson, Robert David. *Ernest Gruening and the American Dissenting Tradition.* Cambridge: Harvard University Press, 1998.

———. *The Peace Progressives and American Foreign Relations.* Cambridge: Harvard University Press, 1995.

Johnson, Roger T. *Robert M. La Follette, Jr. and the Decline of the Progressive Party.* Madison: State Historical Society of Wisconsin, 1964.

Jonas, Frank H. *Political Dynamiting.* Salt Lake City: University of Utah Press, 1970.

Jonas, Manfred. *Isolation in America 1935–1941.* Ithaca, N.Y.: Cornell University Press, 1966.

Jordan, David M. *FDR, Dewey, and the Election of 1944.* Bloomington: Indiana University Press, 2011.

Kabaservice, Geoffrey. *The Guardians: Kingman Brewster, His Circle, and the Rise of the Liberal Establishment.* New York: Henry Holt, 2004.

Kaiser, David. *No End Save Victory: How FDR Led the Nation into War.* New York: Basic Books, 2014.

Karlin, Jules A. *Joseph M. Dixon of Montana*, pt. 1, *Senator and Bull Moose Campaign Manager, 1867–1917.* Missoula: University of Montana Publications in History, 1974.

———. *Joseph M. Dixon of Montana*, pt. 2, *Governor versus the Anaconda, 1917–1934.* Missoula: University of Montana Publications in History, 1974.

Katznelson, Ira. *Fear Itself: The New Deal and the Origins of Our Time.* New York: Liveright, 2013.

Keating, Edward. *The Gentleman from Colorado: A Memoir.* Denver: Sage Books, 1964.

Keith, Caroline H. *For Hell and a Brown Mule: The Biography of Millard E. Tydings.* Lanham, Md.: Madison Books, 1991.

Kennedy, David. *Freedom from Fear: The American People in Depression and War, 1929–1945.* New York: Oxford University Press, 1999.

———. *Over There: The First World War and American Society.* New York: Oxford University Press, 1980.

Kennedy, Joseph P. *Hostage to Fortune: The Letters of Joseph P. Kennedy.* Edited by Amanda Smith. New York: Viking, 2001.

Kimball, Warren F. *The Juggler: Franklin Roosevelt as Wartime Statesmen.* Princeton: Princeton University Press, 1991.

———. *The Most Unsordid Act: Lend-Lease, 1939–1941.* Baltimore: Johns Hopkins Press, 1969.

Kin, David George. *The Plot against America: Senator Wheeler and the Forces behind Him.* Missoula: John E. Kennedy, 1946.

———. *Women Without Men: True Stories of Lesbian Love in Greenwich Village.* New York: Brookwood, 1958.

Kittredge, William, and Annick Smith, eds. *The Last Best Place.* Helena, Mont.: Falcon Press, 1992.

Klein, Maury. *Rainbow's End: The Crash of 1929.* New York: Oxford University Press, 2001.

Kurth, Peter. *American Cassandra: The Life of Dorothy Thompson.* Boston: Little, Brown, 1990.

La Follette, Belle Case, and Fola La Follette. *Robert M. La Follette*, vol. 2. New York: Macmillan, 1953.

Langer, William L., and S. Everett Gleason. *The Challenge to Isolation, 1937–1940.* New York: Harper & Brothers, 1952.

———. *The Undeclared War, 1940–1941.* New York: Harper & Brothers, 1953.

Lansing, Michael J. *Insurgent Democracy: The Nonpartisan League in North American Politics.* Chicago: University of Chicago Press, 2015.

Larson, Bruce L. *Lindbergh of Minnesota: A Political Biography.* New York: Harcourt Brace Jovanovich, 1973.

Larson, Erik. *In the Garden of the Beasts.* New York: Crown, 2011.

Lasser, William. *Benjamin V. Cohen: Architect of the New Deal.* New Haven: Yale University Press, 2002.

Leech, Margaret. *In the Days of McKinley*. New York: Harper & Brothers, 1959.

Leighton, Isabel, ed. *The Aspirin Age, 1919–1941*. New York: Simon & Schuster, 1949.

Leuchtenburg, William E. *The Perils of Prosperity, 1914–1932*. Chicago: University of Chicago Press, 1958.

———. *The Supreme Court Reborn: The Constitutional Revolution in the Age of Roosevelt*. Chapel Hill: University of North Carolina Press, 1995.

Levin, Linda Lotridge. *The Making of FDR: The Story of Stephen T. Early, America's First Modern Press Secretary*. Amherst, N.Y.: Prometheus Books, 2008.

Lewis, David Levering. *W. E. B. Du Bois: The Fight for Equality and the American Century, 1919–1963*. New York: Henry Holt, 2000.

Lief, Alfred. *Democracy's Norris: The Biography of a Lonely Crusade*. New York: Stackpole Sons, 1939.

Lilienthal, David. *The Journals of David Lilienthal: The TVA Years*. New York: Harper & Row, 1964.

Limerick, Patricia Nelson. *The Legacy of Conquest: The Unbroken Past of the American West*. New York: W. W. Norton, 1987.

Lindbergh, Anne Morrow. *War Within and Without: Diaries and Letters, 1939–1944*. New York: Harcourt Brace Jovanovich, 1980.

Lindbergh, Charles A. *The Wartime Journals of Charles A. Lindbergh*. New York: Harcourt Brace Jovanovich, 1970.

Long, Huey P. *Every Man a King: The Autobiography of Huey P. Long*. New Orleans: National Book Company, 1933.

Longworth, Alice Roosevelt. *Crowded Hours*. New York: Charles Scribner's Sons, 1933.

Lonnquist, Lois. *Fifty Cents an Hour: The Builders and Boomtowns of the Fort Peck Dam*. Helena, Mont.: MtSky Press, 2006.

Lopach, James J., and Jean A. Luckowski. *Jeannette Rankin: A Political Woman*. Boulder: University of Colorado Press, 2005.

Louchheim, Katie, ed. *The Making of the New Deal: The Insiders Speak*. Cambridge: Harvard University Press, 1983.

Lower, Richard Coke. *A Bloc of One: The Political Career of Hiram W. Johnson*. Stanford: Stanford University Press, 1993.

Lowitt, Richard. *Bronson M. Cutting: Progressive Politician*. Albuquerque: University of New Mexico Press, 1992.

———. *The New Deal and the West*. Bloomington: Indiana University Press, 1984.

———. *George W. Norris: The Persistence of a Progressive, 1913–1933*. Urbana: University of Illinois Press, 1971.

———. *George W. Norris: The Triumph of a Progressive, 1933–1944*. Urbana: University of Illinois Press, 1978.

MacKay, Kenneth Campbell. *The Progressive Movement of 1924*. New York: Octagon Books, 1972.

Maddox, Robert James. *William E. Borah and American Foreign Policy*. Baton Rouge: Louisiana State University Press, 1969.

Mahl, Thomas E. *Desperate Deception: British Covert Operations in the United States, 1939–1944*. Washington, D.C.: Brassey's, 1995.

Malone, Michael P. *The Battle for Butte: Mining and Politics on the Northern Frontier, 1864–1906*. Helena: Montana Historical Society Press, 1995.

————. *C. Ben Ross and the New Deal in Idaho.* Seattle: University of Washington Press, 1970.

Malone, Michael P., and Richard W. Etulain. *The American West.* Lincoln: University of Nebraska Press, 1989.

Malone, Michael P., and Richard B. Roeder, ed. *The Montana Past: An Anthology.* Missoula: University of Montana Press, 1969.

Malone, Michael P., Richard B. Roeder, and William L. Lang. *Montana: A History of Two Centuries.* Rev. ed. Seattle: University of Washington Press, 1991.

Maney, Patrick J. *Young Bob: A Biography of Robert M. La Follette, Jr., 1895–1953.* Madison: Wisconsin Historical Society Press, 2003.

Marcosson, Isaac F. *Anaconda.* New York: Dodd, Mead, 1957.

Mason, Alpheus Thomas. *Brandeis: A Free Man's Life.* New York: Viking, 1956.

————. *Harlan Fiske Stone: Pillar of the Law.* New York: Viking, 1956.

McCartney, Laton. *The Teapot Dome Scandal: How Big Oil Bought the Harding White House and Tried to Steal the Country.* New York: Random House, 2008.

McCoy, Donald R. *Calvin Coolidge: The Quiet President.* Lawrence: University Press of Kansas, 1988.

McCullough, David. *Truman.* New York: Simon & Schuster, 1992.

McDaniel, George William. *Smith Wildman Brookhart: Iowa's Renegade Republican.* Ames: Iowa State University Press, 1995.

McDonald, Forrest. *Insull.* Chicago: University of Chicago Press, 1962.

McFarland, C. K. *Roosevelt, Lewis, and the New Deal, 1933–1940.* Fort Worth: Texas Christian University Press, 1970.

McGerr, Michael. *A Fierce Discontent: The Rise and Fall of the Progressive Movement in America, 1870–1920.* New York: Free Press, 2003.

McKean, David. *Tommy the Cork: Washington's Ultimate Insider from Roosevelt to Reagan.* South Royalton, Vt.: Steerforth Press, 2004.

McKenna, Marian C. *Borah.* Ann Arbor: University of Michigan Press, 1961.

————. *Franklin Roosevelt and the Great Constitutional War: The Court-Packing Crisis of 1937.* New York: Fordham University Press, 2002.

McMahon, Robert J., and Thomas W. Zeiler, eds. *Guide to U.S. Foreign Policy: A Diplomatic History.* Thousand Oaks, Calif.: CQ Press, 2012.

McMillan, James E. *Ernest W. McFarland: Majority Leader of the United States Senate, Governor and Chief Justice of the State of Arizona.* Prescott, Ariz.: Sharlot Hall Museum Press, 2004.

Merrill, Milton R. *Reed Smoot: Apostle in Politics.* Logan: Utah State University Press, 1990.

Mezerik, A. G. *The Revolt of the South and West.* New York: Duell, Sloan and Pearce, 1946.

Michelson, Charles. *The Ghost Talks.* New York: G. P. Putnam's Sons, 1944.

Moe, Richard. *Roosevelt's Second Act: The Election of 1940 and the Politics of War.* New York: Oxford, 2013.

Moley, Raymond. *After Seven Years.* New York: Harper & Brothers, 1939.

Morgan, Chester M. *Redneck Liberal: Theodore G. Bilbo and the New Deal.* Baton Rouge: Louisiana State University Press, 1985.

Morgan, Ted. *Reds: McCarthyism in Twentieth Century America.* New York: Random House, 2003.

Morlan, Robert L. *Political Prairie Fire: The Nonpartisan League, 1915–1922*. Minneapolis: University of Minnesota Press, 1955.

Morrison, Elting E. *Turmoil and Tradition: A Study of the Life and Times of Henry L. Stimson*. Boston: Houghton Mifflin, 1960.

Morrison, John, and Catherine Wright Morrison. *Mavericks: The Lives and Battles of Montana's Political Legends*. Moscow: University of Idaho Press, 1997.

Moser, John E. *Right Turn: John T. Flynn and the Transformation of American Liberalism*. New York: New York University Press, 2005.

Murphy, Bruce Allen. *The Brandeis/Frankfurter Connection: The Secret Political Activities of Two Supreme Court Justices*. New York: Oxford University Press, 1982.

Murphy, Mary. *Hope in Hard Times: New Deal Photographs of Montana, 1936–1942*. Helena: Montana Historical Society Press, 2003.

———. *Mining Cultures: Men, Women and Leisure in Butte, 1914–1941*. Urbana: University of Illinois Press, 1997.

Murray, Robert K. *The Harding Era: Warren Harding and His Administration*. Minneapolis: University of Minnesota Press, 1969.

———. *The 103rd Ballot: Democrats and the Disaster in Madison Square Garden*. New York: Harper & Row, 1976.

———. *The Politics of Normalcy: Government Theory and Practice in the Harding-Coolidge Era*. New York: W. W. Norton, 1973.

———. *Red Scare: A Study in National Hysteria, 1919–1920*. Minneapolis: University of Minnesota Press, 1955.

Nasaw, David. *The Chief: The Life of William Randolph Hearst*. New York: Houghton Mifflin, 2000.

———. *The Patriarch: The Remarkable Life and Turbulent Times of Joseph P. Kennedy*. New York: Penguin Press, 2010.

Neal, Steve. *Dark Horse: A Biography of Wendell Willkie*. Lawrence: University Press of Kansas, 1989.

——— *Happy Days Are Here Again: The 1932 Democratic Convention, the Emergence of FDR, and How America Was Changed Forever*. New York: William Morrow, 2004.

———. *McNary of Oregon*. Portland, Ore.: Western Imprints, 1985.

Neuberger, Richard. *Our Promised Land*. New York: Macmillan, 1938.

Neuberger, Richard, and Stephen B. Kahn. *Integrity: The Life of George W. Norris*. New York: Vanguard Press, 1937.

Neuberger, Richard, and Kelley Loe. *An Army of the Aged*. Caldwell, Idaho: Caxton Printers, 1936.

Newman, Roger K. *Hugo Black: A Biography*. New York: Fordham University Press, 1997.

Norris, George W. *Fighting Liberal: The Autobiography of George W. Norris*. New York: Macmillan, 1945.

Nye, Russell B. *Midwestern Progressive Politics: A Historical Study of Its Origins and Development, 1870–1950*. East Lansing: Michigan State College Press, 1951.

Oberdorfer, Don. *Senator Mansfield: The Extraordinary Life of a Great American Statesman*. Washington, D.C.: Smithsonian Books, 2003.

Okrent, Daniel. *Last Call: The Rise and Fall of Prohibition*. New York: Scribner, 2010.

Olson, James S., and Abraham O Mendoza. *American Economic History: A Dictionary and Chronology.* Santa Barbara, Calif.: ABC-CLIO, 2015.

Olson, Lynne. *Those Angry Days: Roosevelt, Lindbergh, and America's Fight oOver World War II, 1939–1941.* New York: Random House, 2013.

Parmet, Herbert S., and Marie B. Hecht. *Never Again: A President Runs for a Third Term.* New York: Macmillan, 1968.

Parrish, Michael E. *The Hughes Court: Justices, Rulings, and Legacy.* Santa Barbara, Calif.: ABC-CLIO, 2002.

Patterson, James T. *Congressional Conservatism and the New Deal: The Growth of the Conservative Coalition in Congress, 1933–1939.* Lexington: University Press of Kentucky, 1967.

————. *Mr. Republican: A Biography of Robert A. Taft.* Boston: Houghton Mifflin, 1972.

Payne, Stanley G. *The Franco Regime, 1936–1975.* Madison: University of Wisconsin Press, 1987.

Pearson, Drew, and Robert S. Allen. *Nine Old Men.* Garden City, N.Y.: Doubleday, Doran, 1936.

Perkins, Frances. *The Roosevelt I Knew.* New York: Viking Press, 1946.

Perret, Geoffrey. *America in the Twenties: A History.* New York: Simon & Schuster, 1982.

Persico, Joseph E. *Roosevelt's Secret War: FDR and World War II Espionage.* New York: Random House, 2001.

Peters, Charles. *Five Days in Philadelphia: The Amazing "We Want Willkie" Convention of 1940 and How It Freed FDR to Save the Western World.* New York: Public Affairs, 2005.

Peterson, F. Ross. *Prophet without Honor: Glen H. Taylor and the Fight for American Liberalism.* Lexington: University Press of Kentucky, 1974.

Philp, Kenneth R. *John Collier's Crusade of Indian Reform, 1920–1954.* Tucson: University of Arizona Press, 1977.

————, ed. *Indian Self-Rule: First-Hand Accounts of Indian-White Relations from Roosevelt to Reagan.* Chicago: Howe Brothers, 1986.

Plokhy, S. M. *Yalta: The Price of Peace.* New York: Penguin, 2012.

Powers, Richard Gid. *Not without Honor: The History of American Anti-Communism.* New York: Free Press, 1995.

Punke, Michael. *Fire and Brimstone: The North Butte Mining Disaster of 1917.* New York: Hyperion, 2006.

Pusey, Merlo J. *Charles Evans Hughes,* vol. 2. New York: Macmillan, 1951.

Reisner, Marc, and Sarah Bates. *Overtapped Oasis.* Washington, D.C.: Island Press, 1990.

Ritchie, Donald A. *Electing FDR: The New Deal Campaign of 1932.* Lawrence: University Press of Kansas, 2007.

Robinson, Greg. *By Order of the President: FDR and the Internment of Japanese Americans.* Cambridge: Harvard University Press, 2001.

Rogge, O. John. *The Official German Report: Nazi Penetration, 1924–1942.* New York: Yoseloff, 1961.

Rollins, Alfred B. *Roosevelt and Howe.* New York: Alfred A. Knopf, 1962.

Roosevelt, Franklin D. *Franklin D. Roosevelt: His Personal Letters, 1928–1945,* vol. 2. Edited by Elliott Roosevelt. New York: Duell, Sloan and Pearce, 1948.

————. *The Public Papers and Addresses of Franklin D. Roosevelt,* vol. 8. New York: Macmillan, 1941.

Roseboom, Eugene H., and Alfred E. Eckes Jr. *A History of Presidential Elections, from George Washington to Jimmy Carter.* 4th ed. New York: Collier Books, 1979.

Rosenfeld, Seth. *Subversives: The FBI's War on Student Radicals and Reagan's Rise to Power.* New York: Farrar, Straus and Giroux, 2012.

Ross, William G. *The Chief Justiceship of Charles Evans Hughes, 1930–1941.* Columbia: University of South Carolina Press, 2007.

———. *A Muted Fury: Populists, Progressives, and Labor Unions Confront the Courts, 1890–1937.* Princeton: Princeton University Press, 1994.

Rostad, Lee. *The House of Bair: Sheep, Cadillacs and Chippendale.* Helena, Mont.: Sweetgrass Books, 2010.

Roth, Philip. *The Plot against America.* Boston: Houghton Mifflin, 2004.

Rowley, William D. *M. L. Wilson and the Campaign for the Domestic Allotment.* Lincoln: University of Nebraska Press, 1970.

Rusco, Elmer R. *A Fateful Time: The Background and Legislative History of the Indian Reorganization Act.* Reno: University of Nevada Press, 2000.

Russell, Francis. *In the Shadow of Blooming Grove: Warren G. Harding in His Times.* New York: McGraw-Hill, 1968.

Sarles, Ruth. *A Story of America First: The Men and Women Who Opposed U.S. Intervention in World War II.* Westport, Conn: Praeger, 2003.

Schlesinger, Arthur M. *The Crisis of the Old Order.* Age of Roosevelt, vol. 1. Boston: Houghton Mifflin, 1957.

———. *A Life in the Twentieth Century: Innocent Beginnings, 1917–1950.* Boston: Houghton Mifflin, 2000.

———. *The Politics of Upheaval.* Age of Roosevelt, vol. 3. Boston: Houghton Mifflin, 1960.

Schroth, Raymond A. *The American Journey of Eric Sevareid.* South Royalton, Vt.: Steerforth Press, 1995.

Scroop, Daniel. *Mr. Democrat: Jim Farley, the New Deal, and the Making of Modern American Politics.* Ann Arbor: University of Michigan Press, 2006.

Seldes, George. *The Catholic Crisis.* New York: J. Messner, 1939.

Sevareid, Eric. *Not So Wild a Dream.* New York: Atheneum, 1979.

Sherwood, Robert E. *Roosevelt and Hopkins: An Intimate History.* New York: Harper & Brothers, 1948.

Shesol, Jeff. *Supreme Power: Franklin Roosevelt vs. The Supreme Court.* New York: W. W. Norton, 2010.

Shlaes, Amity. *Coolidge.* New York: HarperCollins, 2013.

———. *The Forgotten Man.* New York: HarperCollins, 2007.

Shogan, Robert. *Backlash: The Killing of the New Deal.* Chicago: Ivan R. Dee, 2006.

Simon, James F. *FDR and Chief Justice Hughes: The President, the Supreme Court, and the Epic Battle over the New Deal.* New York: Simon & Schuster, 2012.

Slayton, Robert A. *Empire Statesman: The Rise and Redemption of Al Smith.* New York: Free Press, 2001.

———. *Newspaper Titan: The Infamous Life and Monumental Times of Cissy Patterson.* New York: Alfred A. Knopf, 2011.

Smith, Jean Edward. *FDR.* New York: Random House, 2007.

Smith, Norma. *Jeannette Rankin: America's Conscience.* Helena: Montana Historical Society Press, 2002.

Smith, Richard Norton. *The Colonel: The Life and Legend of Robert R. McCormick.* Boston: Houghton Mifflin, 1997.

Snow, Richard. *A Measureless Peril: America in the Fight for the Atlantic, the Longest Battle of World War II.* New York: Scribner, 2010.

Sobel, Robert. *Coolidge: An American Enigma.* Washington, D.C.: Regnery, 1998.

Solomon, Burt. *FDR v. the Constitution: The Court Packing Fight and the Triumph of Democracy.* New York: Walker, 2009.

Sparks, George F., ed. *A Many-Colored Toga: The Diary of Henry Fountain Ashurst.* Tucson: University of Arizona Press, 1962.

Spritzer, Donald. *Senator James E. Murray and the Limits of Post-War Liberalism.* New York: Garland, 1985.

Steel, Ronald. *Walter Lippmann and the American Century.* New York: Little, Brown, 1980.

Steele, Volney. *Wellington Rankin: His Family, Life and Times.* Bozeman, Mont.: Bridger Creek Historical Press, 2002.

Steinberg, Alfred. *Sam Rayburn: A Biography.* New York: Hawthorn Books, 1975.

Stenehjem, Michele Flynn. *An American First: John T. Flynn and the America First Committee.* New Rochelle, N.Y.: Arlington House, 1976.

Sterling, Bryan B., and Frances N. Sterling. *Will Rogers' World: America's Foremost Political Humorist Comments on the Twenties and Thirties—and Eighties and Nineties.* New York: M. Evans, 1989.

Sternsher, Bernard. *Rexford Tugwell and the New Deal.* New Brunswick, N.J.: Rutgers University Press, 1964.

Stimson, Henry L., and McGeorge Bundy. *On Active Service in War and Peace.* New York: Harper & Brothers, 1947.

Stiles, Lela. *The Man behind Roosevelt: The Story of Louis McHenry Howe.* Cleveland: World Publishing, 1954.

Stone, Geoffrey R. *Perilous Times: Free Speech in Wartime, from the Sedition Act of 1798 to the War on Terrorism.* New York: W. W. Norton, 2004.

Stone, Irving. *They Also Ran: The Story of the Men Who Were Defeated for the Presidency.* Garden City, N.Y.: Doubleday, Doran, 1943.

Stratton, David H. *Tempest over Teapot Dome: The Story of Albert B. Fall.* Norman: University of Oklahoma Press, 1998.

Strum, Philippa. *Louis D. Brandeis: Justice for the People.* Cambridge: Harvard University Press, 1984.

Stuhler, Barbara. *Ten Men of Minnesota and American Foreign Policy, 1898–1968.* St. Paul: Minnesota Historical Society Press, 1973.

Swain, Martha H. *Pat Harrison: The New Deal Years.* Jackson: University Press of Mississippi, 1978.

Swanberg, W. A. *Luce and His Empire.* New York: Charles Scribner's Sons, 1972.

———. *Norman Thomas: The Last Idealist.* New York: Charles Scribner's Sons, 1976.

Swibold, Dennis. *The Copper Chorus: Mining, Politics and the Montana Press, 1889–1959.* Helena: Montana Historical Society Press, 2006.

Taylor, Graham D. *The New Deal and American Indian Tribalism: The Administration of the Indian Reorganization Act, 1934–1945.* Lincoln: University of Nebraska Press, 1980.

Thelen, David P. *Robert M. La Follette and the Insurgent Spirit.* Madison: University of Wisconsin Press, 1976.

Theoharis, Athan G., and John Stuart Cox. *The Boss: J. Edgar Hoover and the Great American Inquisition.* Philadelphia: Temple University Press, 1988.

Timmons, Bascom N. *Garner of Texas: A Personal History.* New York: Harper & Brothers, 1948.

Toole, K. Ross. *Montana: An Uncommon Land.* Norman: University of Oklahoma Press, 1959.

———. *Twentieth-Century Montana: A State of Extremes.* Norman: University of Oklahoma Press, 1972.

Trohan, Walter. *Political Animals.* New York: Doubleday, 1975.

Truman, Harry S. *Memoirs,* vol. 1, *Year of Decisions.* New York: Doubleday, 1955.

Truman, Margaret. *Harry S. Truman.* New York: William Morrow, 1973.

Tucker, Garland. *High Tide of American Conservatism: Davis, Coolidge, and the 1924 Election.* Austin, Tex.: Emerald Book Company, 2010.

Tucker, Ray, and Frederick R. Barkley. *Sons of the Wild Jackass.* Boston: L. C. Page, 1932.

Tugwell, Rexford G. *The Democratic Roosevelt.* Garden City, N.Y.: Doubleday, 1957.

Tull, Charles J. *Father Coughlin and the New Deal.* Syracuse: Syracuse University Press, 1965.

Tully, Grace. *F. D. R.: My Boss.* Chicago: Peoples Book Club, 1949.

Tytell, John. *Ezra Pound: The Solitary Volcano.* New York: Doubleday, 1987.

Unger, Debi, Irwin Unger, and Stanly Hirshson. *George Marshall: A Biography.* New York: HarperCollins, 2015.

Unger, Nancy C. *Fighting Bob La Follette: The Righteous Reformer.* Chapel Hill: University of North Carolina Press, 2000.

Urofsky, Melvin I. *Louis D. Brandeis: A Life.* New York: Pantheon, 2009.

Valeo, Francis R. *Mike Mansfield: Majority Leader.* Armonk, N.Y.: M. E. Sharpe, 1999.

Villard, Oswald Garrison. *Fighting Years: Memoirs of a Liberal Editor.* New York: Harcourt, Brace, 1939.

Waldron, Ellis, and Paul B. Wilson. *Atlas of Montana Elections: 1889–1976.* Missoula: University of Montana Publications in History, 1978.

Walker, Frank. *FDR's Quiet Confidant: The Autobiography of Frank C. Walker.* Edited by Robert H. Ferrell. Niwot: University Press of Colorado, 1997.

Walkiewicz, E. P., and Hugh Witemeyer, eds. *Ezra Pound and Senator Bronson Cutting: A Political Correspondence, 1930–1935.* Albuquerque: University of New Mexico Press, 1995.

Walter, Dave, ed. *Speaking Ill of the Dead: Jerks in Montana History.* Helena, Mont.: Falcon Publishing, 2000.

Ward, Geoffrey C. *Before the Trumpet: Young Franklin Roosevelt, 1882–1905.* New York: Harper & Row, 1985.

———. *A First Class Temperament: The Emergence of Franklin D. Roosevelt.* New York: Harper & Row, 1989.

Warren, Donald *Radio Priest: Charles Coughlin, the Father of Hate Radio.* New York: Free Press, 1996.

Waterhouse, David L. *The Progressive Movement of 1924 and the Development of Interest Group Liberalism.* New York: Garland, 1991.

Watkins, T. H. *Righteous Pilgrim: The Life and Times of Harold L. Ickes, 1874–1952.* New York: Henry Holt, 1990.

Wedemeyer, Albert C. *Wedemeyer Reports!* New York: Henry Holt, 1958.

Weiner, Tim. *Enemies: A History of the FBI.* New York: Random House, 2012.

Weintraub, Stanley. *Final Victory: FDR's Extraordinary World War II Presidential Campaign.* Philadelphia: Da Capo Press, 2012.

Weller, Cecil Edward, Jr. *Joe T. Robinson: Always a Loyal Democrat.* Fayetteville: University of Arkansas Press, 1998.

Wheeler, Burton K., and Paul Healy. *Yankee from the West.* Garden City, N.Y.: Doubleday, 1962.

White, William Allen. *The Autobiography of William Allen White.* New York: Macmillan, 1946.

———. *Puritan in Babylon.* New York: Macmillan, 1938.

Wicker, Tom. *Dwight D. Eisenhower.* American Presidents Series. New York: Henry Holt, 2002.

William, T. Harry. *Huey Long.* New York: Alfred A. Knopf, 1969.

Wilson, Joan Hoff. *American Business and Foreign Policy, 1920–1933.* Lexington: University Press of Kentucky, 1971.

Wiltz, John E. *From Isolation to War, 1931–1941.* New York: Thomas Y. Crowell, 1968.

———. *In Search of Peace: The Senate Munitions Inquiry, 1934–1936.* Baton Rouge: Louisiana State University Press, 1963.

Wittes, Benjamin. *Confirmation Wars: Preserving Independent Courts in Angry Times.* Lanham, Md.: Rowman & Littlefield, 2006.

Wittner, Lawrence S. *Rebels against War: The American Peace Movement, 1941–1960.* New York: Columbia University Press, 1969.

Wolfskill, George. *The Revolt of the Conservatives: A History of the American Liberty League, 1934–1940.* New York: Houghton Mifflin, 1962.

Work, Clement P. *Darkest before Dawn: Sedition and Free Speech in the American West.* Albuquerque: University of New Mexico Press, 2005.

Writers' Project of Montana. *Copper Camp: Stories of the World' Greatest Mining Town, Butte, Montana.* Helena: Riverbend Publishing, 2002.

Wreszin, Michael. *Oswald Garrison Villard: Pacifist at War.* Bloomington: Indiana University Press, 1965.

Young, Roland. *Congressional Politics in the Second World War.* New York: Columbia University Press, 1956.

Zelizer, Julian E. *Arsenal of Democracy: The Politics of National Security, from World War II to the War on Terrorism.* New York: Basic Books, 2010.

Zieger, Robert H. *The CIO: 1935–1955.* Chapel Hill: University of North Carolina Press, 1995.

Zinn, Howard. *LaGuardia in Congress.* Ithaca, N.Y.: Cornell University Press, 1958.

ARTICLES AND BOOK CHAPTERS

Alsop, Joseph, and Robert Kintner. "Farley and the Future." *Life,* September 19, 1938.

Anderson, Paul Y. "Roosevelt Woes the Progressives." *Nation,* October 12, 1932.

Astorino, Samuel J. "The Contested Senate Election of William Scott Vare." *Pennsylvania History* 28, no. 2 (April 1961).

Bailey, Fred Arthur. "A Virginia Scholar in Chancellor Hitler's Court: The Tragic Ambassadorship of William Edward Dodd." *Virginia Magazine of History and Biography* 100, no. 3 (July 1992).

Barbash, Jack. "Why Unions Try to Influence Government." *Industrial and Labor Relations Review* 1, no. 1 (October 1947).

Basso, Hamilton. "Burton the Bronc." *New Republic,* April 22, 1940.

Bendiner, Robert. "Men Who Would Be President: Burton K. Wheeler." *Nation,* April 27, 1940.

Bliven, Bruce. "Wheeler's Way and Walsh's." *New Republic,* April 2, 1924.

Brodkey, Harold "The Last Word on Walter Winchell." *New Yorker,* January 30, 1995.

Burke, Robert E. "A Friendship in Adversity: Burton K. Wheeler and Hiram W. Johnson." *Montana: The Magazine of Western History* 36, no. 1 (Winter 1986).

Chambers, John Whiteclay. "The Movies and the Antiwar Debate in America, 1930–1941." *Film and History* 36, no. 1 (2006).

Collins, Fredrick L. "Why Senator Wheeler and Lindberg Work Together." *Liberty,* July 26, 1941, August 2, August 9, August 16, 1941.

Cooper, John Milton, Jr. "Robert M. La Follette: Political Prophet." *Wisconsin Magazine of History* 69, no. 2 (Winter 1985–86).

Creel, George. "Man from Montana." *Collier's,* August 10, 1935.

Danielian, N. R. "Power and the Public: What Should Be Done with the Holding Companies?" *Harper's,* June 1935.

Dewey, Ralph L. "The Transportation Act of 1940." *American Economic Review* 31, no. 1 (March 1941).

Diggins, John Patrick. "Power and Authority in American History: The Case of Charles A. Beard and His Critics." *American Historical Review* 86, no. 4 (October 1981).

Diner, Hasia. "Teapot Dome: 1924." In *Congress Investigates: 1792–1974,* vol. 4, edited by Arthur M. Schlesinger Jr. and Roger Bruns, 2385–89. New York: Chelsea House, 1975.

Doenecke, Justus D. "American Isolationism, 1939–1941." *Journal of Libertarian Studies* 6, nos. 3–4 (Summer–Fall 1982).

———. "General Robert E. Wood: The Evolution of a Conservative." *Journal of the Illinois State Historical Society* 71, no. 3 (August 1978).

———. "The Isolationist as Collectivist: Lawrence Dennis and the Coming of World War II." *Journal of Libertarian Studies* 3, no. 2 (Summer 1979).

Erickson, Christine K. "Come Join the K.K.K. in the Old Town Tonight: The Ku Klux Klan in Harlowtown, Montana during the 1920's." *Montana: The Magazine of Western History* 64, no. 3 (Autumn 2014.)

Evans, William B. "Senator James E. Murray: A Voice of the People in Foreign Affairs." *Montana: The Magazine of Western History* 32, no. 3 (Winter 1982).

Fish, Peter Graham. "Red Jacket Revisited: The Case That Unraveled John J. Parker's Supreme Court Appointment." *Law and History Review* 5, no. 1 (Spring 1987).

Friedman, Richard D. "Chief Justice Hughes' Letter on Court-Packing." *Journal of Supreme Court History* 22, no. 1 (1997).

Gardner, Gilson. "Our Next President: La Follette or Wheeler." *Nation,* September 17, 1924.

Gregory, William A., and Rennard Strickland. "Hugo Black's Congressional Investigation of Lobbying and the Public Utilities Holding Company Act: A Historical Review of the Power Trust, New Deal Politics, and Regulatory Propaganda." *University of Oklahoma Law Review* 29 (1976).

Gutfeld, Arnon. "The Levine Affair: A Case Study in Academic Freedom." *Pacific Historical Review* 39, no. 1 (February 1970).

———. "The Ves Hall Case: Judge Bourquin and the Sedition Act of 1918." *Pacific Historical Review* 37, no. 2 (May 1968).

Hard, William. "Wheeler, Bryan and Dawes." *Nation,* July 30, 1924.

Harriman, Margaret Case. "The It Girl." *New Yorker,* April 20, April 27, 1940.

Haste, R. A. "What Is Wheeler." *Nation,* October 29, 1924.

Howard, Joseph Kinsey. "The Decline and Fall of Burton K. Wheeler." *Harper's,* March 1947.

———. "Golden River: What's to Be Done About the Missouri?" *Harper's,* May 1945.

Johnson, Alva. "President Tamer." *Saturday Evening Post,* November 13, 1937.

Johnson, C. R. "The Nonpartisan League Defeated." *Nation,* December 1, 1920.

Johnson, Gerald W. "Wheeler Rides the Storm." *Collier's,* July 8, 1944.

Jonas, Frank H. "The Art of Political Dynamiting." *Western Political Science Quarterly* 10, no. 2 (June 1957).

Karmel, Roberta S. "Breaking Up the Banks." *Hastings Law Journal* 62, no. 4 (March 2011).

Kay, Herbert. "Boss Isolationist." *Life,* May 19, 1941.

Keenleyside, Hugh L. "The American Political Revolution of 1924." *Current History* 21 (March 1925).

Kelley, Darwin N. "The McNary-Haugen Bills, 1924–1928: An Attempt to Make the Tariff Effective for Farm Products." *Agricultural History* 14, no. 4 (October 1940).

Kelly, Lawrence C. "The Indian Reorganization Act: The Dream and the Reality." *Pacific Historical Review* 44, no. 3 (August 1975).

Kennedy, John E. "Liberal's Defeat: A Case History." *Nation,* November 26, 1938.

Kimball, Warren. "1776: Lend-Lease Gets a Number." *New England Quarterly* 42, no. 2 (June 1969).

Kirn, Walter. "The Man Who Invented Celebrity." *New York Magazine,* October 24, 1994.

Krock, Arthur. "The Damn Fool Democrats." *American Mercury,* March 1925.

Ledeboer, Suzanne G. "The Man Who Would Be Hitler: William Dudley Pelley and the Silver Legion." *California History* 65, no. 2 (June 1986).

Leuchtenburg, William E. "FDR's Court Packing Plan: A Second Life, a Second Death." *Duke Law Journal* 1985, nos. 3–4 (June–September 1985).

———. "The Origins of Franklin D. Roosevelt's 'Court-Packing' Plan." *Supreme Court Review,* 1966.

Malone, Michael P. "Montana Politics at the Crossroads, 1932–1933." *Pacific Northwest Quarterly* 69, no. 1 (January 1978).

McKelway, St. Clair. "Profiles: Gossip Writer." *New Yorker,* June 15, 1940.

McMillan, James E. "McFarland and the Movies: The 1941 Senate Motion Picture Hearings." *Journal of Arizona History* 29 (Autumn 1988).

Moser, John E. "Gigantic Engines of Propaganda: The 1941 Senate Investigation of Hollywood." *Historian* 63, no. 4 (Summer 2001).

Murphy, Mary. "Messenger of the New Age: Station KGIR in Butte." *Montana: The Magazine of Western History,* 39, no. 3 (Autumn 1989).

Neuberger, Richard L. "Senator Wheeler's Plight." *Current History* 46, no. 5 (August 1, 1937).

———. "Wheeler of Montana." *Harper's* 180, May 1940.

"O'Connell, Jerry Joseph." *Biographical Directory of the U.S. Congress.* http://bioguide.congress.gov/.

Pedersen, Vernon L. "Jerry O'Connell: Montana's Communist Congressman." *Montana: The Magazine of Western History* 62, no. 1 (2012).

Philben, James P. "Charles Austin Beard: Liberal Foe of American Internationalism." *Humanitas* 12, no. 2 (2000).

Polk, J. G. "Wheelhorse of Defense." *Scribner's Commentator*, March 1941.

Potomacus. "Wheeler of Montana." *New Republic*, September 20, 1943.

Punke, Michael. "The Extraordinary Session of 1918." *Montana Quarterly*, Fall 2007.

Reid, Gordon. "How They Beat Wheeler." *New Republic*, July 29, 1946.

Ross, Steven J. "Confessions of a Nazi Spy: Warner Bros., Anti-Fascism and the Politicization of Hollywood." In *Warners' War: Politics, Pop Culture, and Propaganda in Wartime Hollywood*, edited by Martin Kaplan and Johanna Blakley, 49–59. Los Angeles: Norman Lear Center Press, 2004. https://learcenter.org/pdf/WWRoss.pdf.

Ruetten, Richard. "Showdown in Montana, 1938: Burton Wheeler's Role in the Defeat of Jerry O'Connell." *Pacific Northwest Quarterly* 54, no. 1 (January 1963).

Ruhl, Arthur. "At the Capitol's Vaudeville: The Daugherty Investigation." *Collier's*, April 19, 1924.

Saloutos, Theodore. "The Expansion and Decline of the Nonpartisan League in the Western Middle States, 1917–1921." *Agricultural History* 20 (October 1946).

Saunderson, Mont H. "M. L. Wilson: A Man to Remember." *Montana: The Magazine of Western History* 34, no. 4 (Autumn 1984).

Schruben, Francis W. "The Return of Alfalfa Bill Murray." *Chronicles of Oklahoma* 41 (1963).

Shideler, James H. "The La Follette Progressive Party Campaign of 1924." *Wisconsin Magazine of History* 33, no. 4 (June 1950).

Smith, J. W. Brabner. "Subversive Propaganda, the Past and the Present." *Georgetown Law Journal* 29, no. 7 (April 1941).

Spritzer, Donald E. "Senators in Conflict." *Montana: The Magazine of Western History* 23, no. 1 (Spring 1973).

Steele, Richard W. "Franklin D. Roosevelt and His Foreign Policy Critics." *Political Science Quarterly* 94, no. 1 (Spring 1979).

———. "The Great Debate: Roosevelt, the Media, and the Coming of the War, 1940–1941." *Journal of American History* 71, no. 1 (June 1984).

Stone, Geoffrey R. "Civil Liberties in Wartime." *Journal of Supreme Court History* 28 (November 2003).

Sullivan, Mark. "Looking Back at La Follette." *World's Work*, January 1925.

Thakar, Nidhi. "The Urge to Merge: A Look at the Repeal of the Public Utility Holding Company Act of 1935." *Lewis and Clark Law Review* 12, no. 3 (Fall 2008).

"Utah Power & Light Company." Lehman Brothers Collection—Contemporary Business Archives, Harvard Business School, Baker Library, Historical Collections. http://www .library.hbs.edu/hc/lehman/company.html?company=utah_power_light_company.

Vaughn, Stephen. "Morality and Entertainment: The Origins of the Motion Picture Production Code." *Journal of American History* 77 (1990).

Villard, Oswald Garrison. "Wheeler Invades New York." *Nation*, September 24, 1924.

Walter, Dave. "Patriots Gone Berserk: The Montana Council of Defense, 1917–1918." *Montana Magazine*, September/October 2001.

Watson, Richard L. Jr. "The Defeat of Judge Parker: A Study in Pressure Groups and Politics." *Mississippi Valley Historical Review* 50, no. 2 (September 1963).

Wheeler, Burton K. "Russia's Trend toward Individualism." *Nation's Business*, December 1930.

————. "The Silver Lining." *Liberty*, October 22, 1932.

White, William Allen. "Candidates in the Spring." *Yale Review* 29 (March 1940).

Woito, Robert. "Between the Wars." *Wilson Quarterly* 11, no. 1 (New Year's 1987).

THESES AND DISSERTATIONS

Anderson, John Thomas. "Senator Burton K. Wheeler and United States Foreign Policy." PhD diss., University of Virginia, 1982.

Bousliman, George. "The 1954 Campaign of Senator James E. Murray." Master's thesis, University of Montana, 1964.

Bryniarski, Joan Lee. "Against the Tide: Senate Opposition to the Internationalist Foreign Policy of Presidents Franklin D. Roosevelt and Harry S. Truman, 1943–1949." PhD diss., University of Maryland, 1972.

Callaghan, Calvin. "The Lend-Lease Debate, December 1940–March 1941: The Role of Persuasion in a Momentous Public Discussion." PhD. diss., University of Wisconsin, 1950.

Cameron, Donald J. "Burton K. Wheeler as Public Campaigner, 1922–1942." PhD diss., Northwestern University, 1966.

Carman, Timothy J. "Sen. Zales Ecton: A Product of Reaction." Master's thesis, Montana State University, 1971.

Doherty, Catherine C. "The Court Plan, B. K. Wheeler and the Montana Press." Master's thesis, Montana State University, 1954.

Freeman, John Leiper Jr. "The New Deal for Indians: A Study in Bureau-Committee Relations in Government." PhD diss., Princeton University, 1952.

Fritz, Nancy Rice. "The Montana Council of Defense." Master's thesis, University of Montana, 1976.

Hood, Charles Eugene. "'China Mike' Mansfield: The Making of a Congressional Authority on the Far East." PhD diss., Washington State University, 1980.

Johnson, Charles Sackett. "An Editor and a War: Will A. Campbell and the *Helena Independent*, 1914–1921." Master's thesis, University of Montana, 1970.

Kelly, Joseph P. "A Study of the Defeat of Senator Burton K. Wheeler in the 1946 Democratic Primary Election." Master's thesis, Montana State University, 1959.

Koessler, Mary Lou Collins. "The 1920 Gubernatorial Election in Montana." Master's thesis, University of Montana, 1971.

Ruetten, Richard T. "Burton K. Wheeler, 1905–1925: An Independent Liberal under Fire." Master's thesis, University of Oregon, 1957.

————. "Burton K. Wheeler of Montana: A Progressive between the Wars." PhD diss., University of Oregon, 1961.

Snow, Bradley Dean. "From the Sixth Floor to the Copper Dome: 'The Company's' Political Influence in Montana, 1920–1959." Master's thesis, Montana State University, 2003.

Stoddart, William Morrow. "Whose Deal? Burton K. Wheeler and the Indian Reorganization Act." Master's thesis, Montana State University, 1996.

Toole, K. Ross. "A History of the Anaconda Copper Mining Company: A Study in the Relationships between a State and Its People and a Corporation, 1880–1950." PhD thesis, University of California, Los Angeles, 1954.

ACKNOWLEDGMENTS

One reason to study history is to live, at least in the mind, with vastly interesting and entertaining people. And researching and writing history necessarily and happily involves meaningful encounters with countless people who guide, encourage, explain, and often keep the researcher-writer from errors both large and small. While researching and writing about Burton K. Wheeler I have accumulated innumerable debts to the wonderful, smart, and engaging people I encountered.

My search to understand Wheeler's story began at Montana State University in Bozeman with Dr. Gordon "Corky" Brittan, then director of the Wheeler Center for Public Policy. His friendship and encouragement inspired me as I plodded on and on with this project. Corky connected me with Edward Wheeler, who kindly and patiently explained to this complete stranger his view of his father's story. The same kindness and patience, as well as enthusiasm for this book, has been repeatedly extended to me by Bradley Snow, a great-grandson of Senator Wheeler who is also an accomplished historian and sharp student of politics. Brad provided steady encouragement and stimulated much discussion about Wheeler's life and times. Brad also helped facilitate my interview with Marion Wheeler Scott, the delightfully outspoken youngest Wheeler daughter. Elizabeth Wheeler Colman's daughter, Carol Timmis, kindly provided me access to many of her mother's and grandmother's letters, which provided rich insight into Lulu Wheeler's full political partnership with B. K. as well as Elizabeth's role in many political events. Frances Wheeler Sayler's daughter, Gloria, was kind enough to meet with me and correspond about her own remarkable mother.

I am deeply indebted to the board and staff of the Wheeler Center for their encouragement and support of this book on the life and times of the center's namesake.

My longtime friend and onetime business partner Chris Carlson served as an enthusiastic and politically savvy sounding board and early reader. Rick Ardinger, the supremely talented and passionate former director of the Idaho Humanities Council, a lover of all things historic and literary, provided calm and reassuring encouragement. My dear friend Pam Parks served as a wise and kind editor, an astute reader, and a remarkable advocate and supporter. I regret every day that another dear friend and former colleague, Clareene Wharry, is not alive to see this book. Clareene read most of the early manuscript, often more than once, and her careful obsession with the written word made everything she touched better. Carroll College historian Bob Swartout read several early chapters and gave freely of his expertise. The esteemed Franklin Roosevelt biographer Arthur Schlesinger Jr. kindly answered my letters and generously steered me to sources. My onetime boss and longtime mentor, former Idaho governor Cecil D. Andrus, also did not live to see this work completed. Cece Andrus was a guy who lived in the present politically, and I am not at all sure he understood my fascination with the past, but he was a superb sounding board and the best practitioner of the political arts I have ever seen up close. To have such friends is truly a great blessing.

Too many librarians to name helped me track down obscure books, articles, and documents. My particular thanks go to Kim Allen Scott who runs the special collections department at the terrific library at Montana State University. Kim early on pointed me in all the right directions, as did another MSU Library star, Jan Zauha. Countless helpful, patient, and thoroughly professional librarians helped me at libraries in Boise, Idaho; Manzanita, Oregon; Tucson, Arizona; the University of Montana; Boise State University; the University of Arizona, the Arizona Historical Society, and the Hoover Institution Library at Stanford University, home to the remarkable collection of the papers of the America First Committee. I owe a huge debt of gratitude to the superb staff of the Montana Historical Society in Helena. The society maintains a broad and deep collection of papers related to Montana's fascinating political history, and it is no overstatement to say that the Montana Historical Society is among the best state archives, if not the very best state-level archive in the nation. The wonderful Butte–Silver Bow Public Archives, led by the incomparable Ellen Crain, provides a historical feast for a researcher hoping to understand Butte, America, and its priceless characters.

The presidential libraries, operated by the National Archives, are treasures, and my heartfelt thanks goes out to the staff at the Franklin D. Roosevelt Presidential Library at Hyde Park, New York, the Herbert Hoover Presidential Library in West Branch, Iowa, and the Harry S. Truman Presidential Library in Independence, Missouri, for their unfailing courtesy and helpfulness in researching Wheeler's interaction with each of these presidents. The incredible Roosevelt Library provided an extremely valuable fellowship that facilitated a visit to the home of the thirty-second president and access to the vast archives of the Roosevelt presidency.

I am compelled for reasons of gratitude and admiration to mention three individuals who unfortunately I never had the pleasure of meeting but upon whose shoulders I gladly stand. The impact of each is felt throughout this volume. Richard Ruetten, a Montana native, devoted a good deal of his scholarly life to understanding B. K. Wheeler. Ruetten's superb research and fine writing was of immense help to me. The same can be said for historian John Anderson, whose dissertation on Wheeler's foreign policy views was indispensible to my work. The late Montana historian and Montana State University president Michael Malone once contemplated writing a biography of Wheeler, and I know it would have been an outstanding work had he lived to undertake such a project. Malone's notes from his interviews with Wheeler, and his extensive writing on Montana history, made my work much easier.

I also relied extensively on Wayne S. Cole's various works on Wheeler and the noninterventionists prior to World War II, as well as on Justus D. Doenecke's scholarly and insightful research and writing on the America First Committee. I only hope this book adds in some small way to the understanding of that critical and fascinating period that these two outstanding historians have explored so well.

I owe an unknown *New York Times* headline writer a thank you for inspiring the title of this book. When the *Times* reviewed Wheeler's memoir in 1962 the headline read: "Life and Times of a Political Hell-Raiser from Montana." That sums it up pretty well.

The superb staff of the University of Oklahoma Press nurtured and educated me, always kindly, about the world of publishing. I am particularly indebted to Chuck Rankin, who knows Montana well and whose encouragement and enthusiasm for this project never flagged. Press managing editor Steven Baker was patient with my inquiries and generous with his assistance. Also, the sensitive and skilled editorial assistance of freelancer Patricia Heinicke vastly improved the manuscript, while Chris Dodge polished every page with his masterful copyediting and unfailingly helpful suggestions.

To the members of my family, particularly sons Nathan and Rob, and to all the friends whom I have burdened with the stories of B. K. Wheeler, Franklin Roosevelt, Charles Lindbergh, the America First Committee, Montana, and U.S. Senate history, I can only once more beg your indulgence and thank you for your patience and good humor.

Finally, without my chief researcher, eternally positive cheerleader, best critic, critical first (and second and third) reader, and most supportive advocate, Dr. Patricia Johnson, I would never have finished this project. I dedicate it to her as a small and inadequate gesture of the love and admiration I hold for a truly remarkable person.

Any errors of judgment or interpretation and any factual mistakes are mine alone.

INDEX